PSYCHOLOGY, RELIGION AND HEALING

Psychology

Religion and Healing

A critical study of all the non-physical methods of healing, with an examination of the principles underlying them and the techniques employed to express them, together with some conclusions regarding further investigation and action in this field

LESLIE D. WEATHERHEAD

M.A.(Manch.), Ph.D.(Lond.), Hon.D.D.(Edin.)
Minister of the City Temple, London
Honorary Chaplain to Her Majesty's Forces

Revised Edition

ABINGDON PRESS
Nashville • *New York*

PSYCHOLOGY, RELIGION AND HEALING

ISBN 0-687-34885-4

Library of Congress Catalog Card Number: 54-6986

PRINTED, AND BOUND AT NASHVILLE,
TENNESSEE, UNITED STATES OF AMERICA

PREFACE

IN THE FIRST WORLD WAR a young doctor, working in the desert amongst troops stationed north of Baghdad, talked about his dreams to two young chaplains far into the night. I was one of the chaplains.

That doctor was a remarkable man. He practised psychological treatment of an impressive kind when what was then called "The New Psychology" was very new indeed. He practised hypnotism, both as a means of investigating the deep mind of the patient and also of giving him suggestions of courage, confidence and recovery. Further, he had as great a spiritual faith and power as I have ever seen. He would go out into the desert, and for hours he would concentrate his mind on one patient with a kind of spiritual intention. On returning he would sometimes find remarkable results. The patient, previously sleepless, would be asleep; or, discontented, would have found peace of mind; or, in despair, had begun to believe in his own recovery. In one case, a man apparently unable to walk was walking about the ward. The doctor claimed that when he had done all he could for a patient by all the arts of medicine, the turning point in the illness was sometimes determined by adding this form of prayerful concentration.

I was a very young chaplain at the time, and only recently set free for chaplaincy duty by the Indian Army, in which I had enlisted as a combatant officer. I had wanted to be a medical missionary, but neither my family nor I could afford the cost of medical training. The combination of healing and religion had always fascinated me. When this doctor turned to us two chaplains and said, "You padres ought to be doing most of this," I felt he was right. I remembered that Jesus said, "Heal the sick," and I had always had an uneasy feeling that to relegate *all* healing to the material methods of the doctors, splendid though that work is, did not really answer the challenge of our Lord's words. Nor could I believe that His challenge was met by the psychologists, especially those who had no place for religion in their thought or practice.

I therefore determined to learn all I could about non-physical ways

7

of healing. When the doctor and my fellow-chaplain were both killed, I felt an even greater urgency to try to understand the ways in which psychology, religion and healing were related.

On returning to Madras in 1919 I was lucky in being allowed to join a small study group of doctors and ministers. Considering we all lived busy lives, it was a strenuous training, for we took it in turns to introduce a new book each week and read a paper on it which was the basis of discussion.

My ministry in England since I returned in 1922 has only deepened in me the conviction that many people are suffering, even from supposedly physical illnesses, who need not suffer (*a*) if we knew how to release and direct to them the resources of the spiritual world, and (*b*) if both ministers and doctors were alert and trained to see and to understand the early signs of psychological disturbance and to secure immediate treatment, ideally in some environment where physically, psychologically and spiritually the patient could be investigated and the whole personality integrated. We are only at the very beginning of such work, but a vast area of useful service opens up, and I can only hope that this book may be of some small service in this field, and perhaps provide a stimulus to others to devote their lives to a piece of work which so badly needs doing.

. . . . .

In May 1949 I was privileged to give the Lyman-Beecher Lectures at Yale University. I had arranged with the Dean to entitle them "The Place of Healing in the Life of the Modern Church," but rather late in the day I was asked by the Yale authorities to change the subject. I called the new series "The Responsibilities of the Minister to His People," and spoke from notes, not having found time to write out a new set of lectures. My themes were:

The Minister's Responsibility:
1. In Conducting Public Worship.
2. In Private Counselling.
3. In Public Intercession.
4. In Offering the Divine Forgiveness.
5. In Offering the Divine Love.
6. In Healing Certain Types of Illness.

Nearly all the material of my Yale Lectures is included in this book, and I hope the Lyman-Beecher Foundation authorities will forgive me for reprinting the material in rather a different form and within the scope of a larger work. I have never enjoyed any professional experience as I enjoyed going to Yale, and I should like here to express my gratitude to Dean Weigle, the staff and the students who gave to my elder son—who accompanied me—and to myself such heart-warming cordiality.

• • • • •

The substance of my thesis for the degree of Doctor of Philosophy in the University of London is also included in this book.

Many friends have given me advice. My first words of thanks must go to the Rev. Professor Eric S. Waterhouse, Principal of Richmond College, London University, where I myself was trained as a student. He has guided my study, read through the book in manuscript form, and continually given me advice and counsel based on his immense learning and experience in this field.

Another friend, Dr. Geoffrey Evans, has kindly read through the proofs. I have benefitted from his advice also.

My friend, the Rev. John Crowlesmith, read the first draft of the book and put at my disposal his wide knowledge of every form of non-physical healing. I can never repay the debt I owe to him, when, over-pressed by his many other duties in connection with the Marriage Guidance Council and his church at Cambridge, he painstakingly went through my manuscript, making notes which I always considered most carefully.

My friend, the Rev. Fred Roberts, M.A., who lectures on Psychology to the students of Handsworth Methodist College, Birmingham, has allowed me to read a most informative and valuable essay which he wrote on "The Psychology of C. G. Jung in Relation to Religious Thought and Experience."

I have also had the help of a theologian and New Testament scholar, the Rev. Prof. Philip S. Watson, M.A., of Handsworth College, Birmingham, who has been kind enough to read the proofs.

Yet in mentioning these friends I must make it clear that I am not evading responsibility. I alone am responsible for the views put forward. My friends do not always accept my conclusions.

• • • • •

As to books consulted, I have printed particulars of most of them in footnotes and in the Bibliography at the end. I have not wittingly derived help from any unacknowledged source.

Finally, I must express the very deepest gratitude to my secretary, Miss Winifred Haddon, for her painstaking work in typing and re-typing this book, checking references and lifting from my shoulders much of the laborious drudgery of preparing a long book for the Press, and to Miss Eleanor Allison my gratitude for her help in preparing the Index. My wife and my daughter, Margaret, have given me invaluable help in correcting the proofs and indexing.

9

LESLIE D. WEATHERHEAD

"This is the great error of our day in the treatment of the human body that physicians separate the soul from the body."—PLATO.

"Perhaps at the moment the prevailing view is that which declines to separate body and mind in the way to which we have become accustomed since the days of Descartes. Man is something more than a carcass loosely coupled with a ghost."—PROFESSOR SIR CYRIL BURT, D.Sc.

"One of the most striking results of the modern developments of our knowledge concerning the influence of mental factors in disease is that they are bringing back medicine in some measure to that co-operation with religion which existed in the early stages of human progress."—DR. W. H. R. RIVERS.

"Sometimes it is more important to know what kind of a fellah has a germ than what kind of a germ has a fellah."—SHATTUCK.

" 'Tis not the body but the man is ill."—DR. WEIR MITCHELL.

"From the cowardice that shrinks from new truth,
From the laziness that is content with half-truths,
From the arrogance that thinks it knows all truth,
O God of Truth, deliver us."
ANCIENT PRAYER.

"Without God, we cannot. Without us, God will not."
ST. AUGUSTINE.

CONTENTS

CONTENTS

SECTION VI

DO MODERN RELIGIOUS METHODS OF HEALING
NEED PSYCHOLOGY?

SECTION VII

THE MODERN SEARCH FOR HEALING THROUGH
PSYCHOLOGY AND RELIGION

APPENDICES

15

CONTENTS

MAN'S EARLIEST SEARCH FOR HEALING

MAN'S EARLIEST SEARCH FOR HEALING

DISEASE WAS RIFE on this planet before man came into existence, and it has continued ever since. Students of the remains of prehistoric animals tell us quite definitely that those remains bear indubitable evidence of the early existence of painful disease. It is quite false to suppose that disease only appeared with man and is wholly attributable, as some suppose, to man's sin.[1]

As soon as man appeared, he began to deal with pain and illness, and it is important for our study to realise that from the earliest times, long before the Christian Era and long before anything that could be called medical science was born, men were healed of their diseases by nonphysical methods directed towards their minds rather than their bodies. They sought integration or wholeness of personality, and found it through processes of the mind and spirit. It was religion which first attacked the misery of disease and tackled the problem of suffering.

Further, we must realise that humble origins do not vitiate the value of the thought and practice which grow from them. The science of medicine has some of its roots in magic and superstition. Religion has some of its roots in instinctive emotions and tendencies.[2]

[1] G. G. Dawson, in *Healing: Pagan and Christian* (Macmillan, 1935), says that the earliest example of vertebrate disease due to infection known to scientists is that of a reptile which broke one of its dorsal spines. "This became infected so that an incurable inflammatory condition arose, known today as osteomyelitis." The age of these fossilised remains is uncertain because the scientists differ. The physicists, basing their calculations on radio-active phenomena, say the reptile died about one hundred and thirty million years ago. The zoologists say much later—about eight million years ago. Both agree that disease is much older than man. Fossilised remains exist of a dinosaur with a bone tumour, while some remains show signs of bacterial infection. Bacteria of the micrococcus and diplococcus orders have been found in coal, in the fossilised fæces of fish and in other remains of the Carboniferous Era going back, according to the physicists, one hundred and sixty million years. Relics from the Pleiocene, Palæolithic and Neolithic Ages show signs of spine curvature, tuberculosis of the spine, arthritic malformations and rheumatoid affections among men who lived three hundred and fifty thousand years ago.

[2] See Waterhouse, *The Dawn of Religion*, especially pp. 24 ff. (Epworth Press, 1948).

We have insufficient data by which to trace back to its earliest beginnings the history of healing through the mind. We can safely say, however, that Palæolithic man wore charms and amulets. The fact of illness burdened man even in those far-off days, and he sought every possible means to prevent and combat it. The discussion of how primitive man, amid magic and superstition, sought to prevent and heal disease does not come within our present survey. But it is interesting, from such sources as Frazer's *The Golden Bough*, to realise that even primitive man suspected that the ills of the body were related to the mind and the soul.[3] Modern man is turning again to the condition of his mind and spirit in order to account for many of the illnesses of the flesh. He suspects that the latter may have their origin in states of mind and may find their most useful therapy in the creation of healthy mental attitudes. The *British Medical Journal* of August 24, 1946, points to worry as the suspected cause of such apparently physical illnesses as the gastric and duodenal ulcer. Five thousand years ago health and disease were believed to depend on states of mind, though men then believed that a mental state of reverence for, and fear of, a god brought health, while indifference or hostility to the deity brought disease.

We should go back to Æsculapius to trace, in the rudiments of a scientific curiosity, the origin of anything worthy to be called scientific psychotherapy, and then, of course, not scientific at all in our sense. His is the familiar name of the originator of the art of healing, and both scientific and religious methods of healing—as far as the present state of our knowledge goes—may be said to begin with him. The Greeks knew him earlier as Asklepios, the Greek god of medicine, said to be the son of Apollo and the nymph Coronis. But the Egyptians claim that Asklepios was apotheosised from the human magician Imhotep, which means "he who comes in peace"—a good title for the father of mental and spiritual healing—who was magician and architect to King Zoser of the third Egyptian dynasty in 2900 B.C. He seems to have become a demi-god and then entirely to have lost his human character. He was invoked as a god and was believed to visit suffering people during their sleep and heal their pain and disease—another interesting function of the father of both religious healing and psychotherapy, for both have underlined the importance of processes that happen during sleep.

Imhotep's name, cult and fame passed from Egypt into Persia and Greece, where temples were erected to him under the name Asklepios the god of healing, regarded as the son of Apollo. Hygeia the daughter of Asklepios was the Greek goddess of health and was worshipped in

[3] Dr. C. J. S. Thompson has written a fascinating book on this point, called *Magic and Healing* (Rider & Co., 1946).

the temples. The practice of sleeping (incubation) in these sanctuaries was very common, it being supposed that the god or goddess effected cures or prescribed remedies to the sick in dreams. Actually, patients stayed all night and slept in the precincts of the temple, while priest-physicians, having prepared the minds of patients by lectures and talks, whispered suggestions in the name of the god into their ears. Reading of this in modern days, we can realise the effectiveness of this method. The patient may have been asleep or awake or between the two states. The priest was, in any case, *acting for the god*, and the patient was in a highly suggestible state. We must admit that the temples of Æsculapius were the first hospitals, though this has been claimed for the Christian hospitals of later days. The symbol of the god was a snake, and this, rather than the story of Moses lifting up the serpent in the wilderness, accounts for the badge worn on the cap and tunic of a British army doctor today. Harmless yellow snakes glided about the temple area and were trained to lick the sores of patients and thus—it was believed—to heal them. Since the snake incarnated the god, it was the god himself who healed. *Here we have the earliest known form of religious suggestion for the cure of illness.* Most of the diseases treated were of the "incurable" variety, and the literature about "incubation" shows that blindness was most successfully treated by the use of "divine ointment." [4] Paralysis and lameness figure in the list, as also do abscesses and internal troubles. It was a costly treatment. Phalysios of Naupaktos gave two thousand gold *staters* to the temple as a thank-offering for the restoration of his eyesight. There was preparatory instruction by the priest, followed by rites and sacrifices which made the patient expectant and suggestible. "All who were healed offered sacrifice (especially a cock), and hung up votive tablets, recording their names, diseases and the manner in which they had been healed. Many of these tablets have been discovered at Epidaurus, the god's most famous shrine. . . . The cult of Asklepios was introduced into Rome by order of the Sibylline books (293 B.C.) to avert a pestilence. The god was fetched from Epidaurus in the form of a snake and a temple assigned to him on an island in the Tiber." [5]

It is important to realise, however, that while this deification almost obliterated the historical character, Æsculapius was, in fact, a historical character and a famous physician.

Greek culture gradually began to be felt in Rome, but at this time,

[4] See Mary Hamilton, *Incubation* (1906), and William Brown, *Personality and Religion*, p. 73 (Univ. of London, 1946).

[5] *Encyclopaedia Britannica*, Vol. I, p. 263.

no Latin scientific literature about healing developed, and Rome never had the theoretical interest in knowledge for its own sake which Greece possessed. But as Rome became master in the eastern Mediterranean and captured what had been the Empire of Alexander the Great, the influence of Greek thought grew, and after the battle of Pydna (168 B.C.) Greek hostages in Rome, who had brought with them a whole library of medical books, disseminated the Greek ideas and methods of treatment. The Greeks always revered the doctor. He is described in the Iliad as "a man worth many others," and the world owes much to the Greeks for their enthusiasm in spreading their principles and methods of healing.

Astrologers, sorcerers, magicians, in Egypt, Babylonia, Judea, Chaldea, Arabia, Greece and Rome, believed in the efficacy of charms and incantations, of strange concoctions and in religious rites, and at this stage it is impossible to separate spiritual and physical healing. Indeed, it is not wholly possible even now. Here, in this strange medley of superstition and magic, were the origins both of religious healing and psychotherapy. Material remedies did something, but the religious element—if the word can be used at such an early stage—played a part also, and the influence of gods was vital.

It is strange, as one contemplates Jung's use of the word-association test, to think of the Babylonian priest reciting long lists of devils until he came to the one that visibly affected the patient, and was thus held to be the cause of the disease. It is strange, as one contemplates Coué's instructions to a patient to repeat the words "Ca passe" and to count the number of times he says those words by fingering knots in a cord, to compare so modern a direction with the practices of antiquity, in which the magician untied a knot in a cord as he recited each new spell. It is strange to recall the Bible story of the wise men coming from a land where it was believed that the stars affected men's health, and then to realise that even today cheap newspapers give a space to horoscopes, and our language, in words like "lunatic," "mercurial" or "saturnine," reveals earlier beliefs concerning the part played by the moon and the planets in the drama of healing.

Healing methods truly deserving the description "scientific" began with Hippocrates, born in the island of Cos, off the coast of Asia Minor, about 460 or 470 B.C. He came to a world full of shrines to Asklepios, full of superstition and the ascription of disease to distant planets and to supernatural causes, and seems to have been the first to deny the supernatural origin of disease. Writing of epilepsy, then called "the sacred disease," he said one thing to which we shall have occasion to refer again, and which is far from being recognised by our own contemporaries: "It seems to me that the disease [epilepsy] is no more divine than any other. It has a natural cause just as other diseases have. *Men think it is divine only because they do not understand it.*" [6] He it was, says Celsus, writing in the first century A.D., "who first separated medicine from philosophy."

A mass of legend surrounded Hippocrates, but he has held the veneration of scientific healers throughout the ages, and fortunately escaped apotheosis. Plato and Aristotle both refer to him with respect. He made observations and recorded them. He made inferences without being deterred by current superstition or preconceived ideas. His directions to young surgeons might well be read to the medical and surgical graduates of today,[7] and the Hippocratic Oath is still taken by doctors on qualification at some universities. Modern psychotherapists and religious healers should especially heed its conclusion. "Whatsoever things I see or hear concerning the life of men, in my attendance on the sick or even apart therefrom, which ought not to be noised abroad, I will keep silence thereon, counting such things to be as sacred secrets."

The Jews did not make anything like the progress of the Greeks, and Harnack tells us in his great work, *The Expansion of Christianity,*[8] that it was well into the third century A.D. before the scientific methods of Greece began to percolate into Jewish practice, producing a strange effect which we must notice.

In Old Testament times little was done to alleviate pain and suffering, for the Jews believed that Jehovah controlled every part of life and ordained both sickness and health. Sickness was the result of His disfavour and was a punishment for "sin." Health was a sign of His favour and a reward for "righteousness."

For the Jews the cure of disease, then, was a sign of the divine forgiveness and an assurance that the patient was at peace with God. Prayer for health, however, had a place in the practices of the Rabbis. One Rabbi used to pray over the sick and declare, "Such a one will live; such a one will die." When asked how he knew, he said, "If any prayer is fluent in my mouth, I know that it will be well received." There seems no evidence that the ancient Rabbis, though they held that

[6] Italics mine.

[7] Under the title, *Concerning Things in the Surgery,* he wrote, "The nails of the operator are neither to exceed or come short of the finger-ends. Practise all operations with each hand and with both together, your object being to attain ability, grace, speed, painlessness, elegance and readiness. Let those who look after the patient present the part for operation as you want it, and hold fast the rest of the body so as to be all steady, keeping silence and obeying their superior."

[8] Translated by Moffatt (Williams and Norgate, 1904).

suffering was sent by God, refused on principle to use any drugs of whose efficacy they were aware.[9] Material remedies were apparently not excluded—Isaiah himself directed that a plaster of figs should be used to treat Hezekiah's boil.[10] I am told that the Essenes had a high standard of physical hygiene and preached the care of the body as well as of the soul.

It is of importance to note—in view of conclusions reached in the later portions of this book—that as early as Isaiah's day (*circa* 700 B.C.) health was believed to result from harmony with God, bringing with it divine favour, and the cure of disease could be brought about only if the patient were restored to that favour. The dominating factor in health or disease was the condition of the patient's mind and soul. And it will be remembered that Job's so-called comforters repeatedly hinted that he would not be suffering so terribly unless in his past life there had been sins which he would not admit. Once more, in the light of the present understanding of conversion hysteria and psychosomatic disease, it is exceedingly interesting to find in one of the oldest dramas in the Bible the belief that repressed guilt was a fruitful cause of physical ailments.

Yet, of course, in early Jewish thought the conception of illness outlined above, of part of which modern psychotherapists would approve, is by no means as simple as that. It is clouded over by superstition. A whole philosophy of demons entered into the picture, and this we must examine later. Josephus tells us that leprosy, tabes, asthma, cardiac diseases, and especially nervous diseases, were regarded as the work of devils. Amongst the Jews in pre-Christian times it was believed that sorcerers could bewitch their victims, lay magic spells upon them, and cause them either to be victimised by, or delivered from, the demons who brought disease. Even though the punishment of sorcery was death,[11] sorcerers flourished until after the time of Christ. We read of their activities in the books of Acts and the Revelation of St. John.[12]

Clearly, the early Jews carried the practice of anything worth calling scientific psychotherapy no farther; nor until the time of Christ did they practise what we now call spiritual healing. Save for the use of a few simple remedies and the prayer that God would forgive the sufferer, and so set him free from pain and disease which were the marks

---

[9] Mishna, Berakhoth, 5:3.

[10] Isaiah 38:21. The Regius Professor of Anatomy at Glasgow University reminds us that "the Mosiac Law contains the very first code of *preventive* medicine." See *A Doctor Looks at the Bible*, D. M. Blair, M.B., D.Sc.

[11] Exodus 22:18.

[12] Acts 8:9-11, Revelation 9:21, 18:23, 21:8.

of the divine disfavour, the Jews seem rather to have accepted illness as the will of God. They knew very little of the healing art as it was practised in the civilised world of Greece and Rome, so near to them, and yet, in some ways, so far from them.

The Wisdom Literature, as seen, for example, in Ecclesiasticus 38:1-15, shows an appreciation of the work of the physician,[13] but at the same time a kind of uncomfortable feeling that the use of material remedies was an impious interference with the purposes of God, who sent suffering upon men to teach them moral lessons and to punish them for their sins. The teaching of the Rabbis just before the coming of Christ is typified in a declaration of Rabbi Jonathan. "Disease," he says, "came for seven sins, slander, shedding blood, false oaths, unchastity, arrogance, robbery and envy." We shall see later how Jesus Christ was careful not to let the sufferer believe that his suffering was necessarily due to his own sins. In many cases this was not, and is not, true. But He did regard disease as part of the kingdom of evil and broadly due to elements in the universe which should be eliminated by all who sought to do the will of God. He seems to have regarded God's ideal purpose for every man as perfect health of body, mind and spirit, and, although that ideal integration was seldom attained, Christ worked for it, and believed Himself to be doing in this way the will of God. That will might be defeated for a time, for ignorance, folly and sin could all deflect its intention, but, in Christ's view, God was always trying to replace ignorance by knowledge, folly by wisdom and sin by holiness. Therefore, nothing that was the fruit of ignorance, folly or sin could be truly regarded as the will of God, at least in the sense of being His ideal intention. Disease and illness could only be regarded as the will of God in the limited sense that, of course, God wills that causes should produce effects. If man acts contrary to God's laws, whether through ignorance, folly or sin, he has to bear the consequences in the sufferings of his body, mind and spirit, and the unity of the great human family means that just as the individual enjoys assets to which he is not entitled as an individual, so he will be called upon—because of his unity with the human family—to suffer liabilities which he does not individually merit. When in the Gospel narrative we see Christ healing disease, we have evidence that the ideal intention of God is perfect health, and the heresy which attributes illness to

[13] The physician is to be honoured "for verily the Lord hath created him and from the Most High cometh healing." The patient is to "pray unto the Lord" and "put away wrong doing," but then he is to "give place to the physician," and "let him not go from thee, for thou hast need of him. There is a time when in their very hands is the issue for good."

personal or family sin, a heresy which retarded the healing methods of the Jews before Christ's day, making them more backward than neighbouring nations in the matter of medical and surgical science and skill, is exploded by His touch.

The modern Church has underlined this point of view. The 1920 Lambeth Report on the Healing Ministry of the Christian Church contained the following words:

"Health is God's primary will for all His children, and disease is not only to be combatted, but to be combatted in God's name as a way of carrying out His will. . . . However (disease) may be brought about, and in whatever way it may be overruled for good, it is in itself an evil."

In the methods of Jesus faith played a vital part in cure, and later in this book we shall ask just what is meant by faith, what part it plays in cure, how it can be evoked, and to what extent the responsibility for producing it lies with the patient and to what extent it lies with the healer. But we may say, in passing, that the faith required for healing is not, and never has been, theological in its character. That is to say it has not been a faith in the truth of creedal statements. It has rather been expectant trust in a person. Such faith is necessary in all treatments, and Jesus seems to have evoked it again and again and to have been unable to work without it.

We have surveyed the history of non-physical healing from earliest days to the time of Christ only in a very superficial manner because a detailed survey would take us too far afield. But our survey prepares us to turn next to the healing work of Christ, in order to see whether, and to what extent, His work throws an important light on the whole question of spiritual healing and on the relation between psychology and religion in contemporary techniques. We shall ask whether Christ's work was a natural development from the cures which preceded it, whether psychological theories can account for it, whether modern methods of healing have anything to learn from it, and whether it was wholly supernatural and unlikely to be repeated. To that task we now turn.

EARLIER METHODS OF HEALING
THROUGH RELIGION

1

CHRIST'S HEALING MIRACLES

IN THIS CHAPTER certain assumptions will be made. The first is that in the first three gospels, at any rate, we have reliable records of the real acts of a historical Person. As Professor H. G. Wood says,[1] "The broad fact of the ministry of healing and many of the particular incidents are guaranteed by evidence which cannot reasonably be disputed." I shall not enter into the discussion whether the stories of the healing miracles of Jesus had reached a stage of legend. I shall not consider them as allegories or parables. I am aware that the story of the cure of a blind man, for example, is considered by some to be the story of the illumination of one who was blind in soul; that when we read that Jesus cleansed lepers, we are only to understand that He was friendly with sinners, and so on. The evidence that in the first three gospels we have authentic stories of real cures is to me convincing.

Further, I shall not assume that the stories of the healing miracles are records of the cures of purely psychogenic disorders, though, if they were, I should not have dismissed them, for as Janet said, "Nothing is more difficult to cure than a neuropath." [2] For one thing, as we shall see, it is exceedingly difficult, even now, to draw a hard-and-fast line between the psychogenic and the physiogenic, and I can find no evidence in the synoptic gospels that the cure of physically caused illness is excluded by the evidence. As Bishop Ryle says, "An examination of the gospel records quickly disabuses us of this easy way of explaining the miracles of Christ; and the 'neurotic theory' is quite insufficient to account for them." [3]

[1] Peake's *Commentary on the Bible* (Nelson, 1920).

[2] Janet, *Psychological Healing*, Vol. I (Macmillan, 1925).

[3] Ryle, "The Neurotic Theory of the Miracles of Healing," *Hibbert Journal*, April 1907.

I shall also assume the divinity of Christ. I have summarised the evidence which convinces my own mind about this in an earlier book,[4] and I shall not repeat it here. I believe in the true humanity of Jesus Christ, but I cannot confine His personality within the meaning of that word. However little we understand the meaning of words like "divinity" or "deity," we need them unless we disregard entirely some of the most impressive evidence about Him within the pages of the New Testament.

Nor must we forget that although no modern theologian uses the healing miracles as evidence of divinity, to the early Christian they formed part of His credentials. "The view that the early Christians first recognised Christ as Lord by a divine intuition, and then came to interpret His miracles as 'signs' of the Rule of God cannot be sustained." [5]

With these assumptions in mind, we turn to study the healing miracles of Christ, only to find that they at once present us with an important problem. Are we to regard them from the human standpoint as falling within psychotherapeutic categories; the work of a great psychotherapist, or even a religious genius born before His time, whose therapeutic methods show a great advance on any healing work accomplished before Him, but methods which we are able to study from a purely scientific point of view and follow in modern psychological practice? Or are we, on the other hand, to regard Him as a supernatural person, revealing by His amazing healing power, forces and energies which belong to another plane of activity normally above our reach, but penetrated to some extent by His followers, who subsequently wrought similar miracles of healing in His name?

I think the answer is the latter, but this need not preclude us from learning many valuable lessons, even in the realm of scientific healing, by the study of Christ's work. After studying the question for many years, however, I cannot completely fit the healing miracles of Christ into the categories of modern psychotherapeutic practice. The latter is illumined by the former, but the former are not explained by the latter.

Perhaps an illustration will make the point clear. Let us imagine two ignorant savages discussing together the injuries which one of them has received. We can imagine that the wounded one is asking the advice of the other. The advice would probably be that the patient should bind up his wounds, lie up for a day or two and let Nature do her healing work. Unless sepsis set in, the patient would probably recover. But supposing, at the request of the injured man, a highly trained mod-

[4] *His Life and Ours* (Abingdon-Cokesbury, 1933).

[5] Harold Roberts, *The Sanctions of Christian Healing*, p. 10 (Epworth, 1950).

ern surgeon broke into the situation from his superior level of understanding, and with his modern scientific equipment and his up-to-date
knowledge of remedies. Supposing, without necessarily understanding
how his treatment worked, he used modern aids to recovery chosen
with care based on insight into the nature of the injuries. Then the
patient would recover in a very short time, and, from the savages' point
of view, the result would be a miracle, the breaking through of law-
abiding energies, familiar on the higher plane of the surgeon's culture,
but quite inexplicable on the lower plane of the savages' intelligence.

It seems to me that all healing methods known to modern science,
including psychological methods, are on one plane. Many are efficacious and we wisely continue to use them and to seek others in the
same category. But Christ functioned on a higher plane and used
methods in a different category altogether. His unique relationship to
God made Him at home in the spiritual world, and when He broke
into a situation of human pain and distress, of body or mind, He
brought with Him the energies of the plane on which He Himself
lived. To put the matter in another way, the energies of the Kingdom
broke through. He came to lift humanity onto that level, to make
men see the Kingdom of Heaven and enter it. The healing miracles
were the "signs" of the new age, to be expected in the new order
which Christ initiated. They were in a different category from the
miracles recorded in the Old Testament. And when He was asked
the famous question by the messengers from John the Baptist, "Art
Thou He that cometh, or look we for another?" [6] He pointed to the
cures as evidence that the Kingdom had already come where He was
at work, and that His followers would continue His healing work *on
that plane*.[7] "Our limitations are not His bounds, nor even ultimately
our bounds." [8]

While it is of immense value to do everything in our power to release the energies of the universe for the healing of men on the physical
and mental planes, we shall not be able to release the energies referred
to by Christ, and which we might call the energies of the Kingdom,
by purely scientific research. Rather are we likely to find them when
the quality of spiritual apprehension releases them as normally as
energies of a physical and psychological nature are released on the
lower plane. Science has a necessary and most valuable part to play in
healing, as we shall see, but it may well be that humanity follows a false

[6] Matthew 11:3.
[7] Matthew 11:11; cf. Luke 7:22 and especially 28.
[8] W. R. Maltby, *The Significance of Jesus* (Harper, 1929).

track if men imagine that there are no other powers in the universe relevant to healing save those which yield to scientific research. It may indeed be that man has taken a false turn because he was not willing to pay the price demanded in terms of moral effort and spiritual insight before the energies of the spiritual realm could be released. Man prefers to remain content with research, discovery and invention on the lower plane, leaving the immense resources of the spiritual world untapped. On such a spiritual plane law undoubtedly reigns, but it may be law of a different order, to be discovered less by intellectual effort than by spiritual discipline and insight.

It seems important to add further that success in healing is not expected from the solitary individual, however saintly, but rather that the powers of the Kingdom are manifested through the fellowship of the whole Church (κοινωνία). It is the *Church,* not the individual, that is the extension of the Incarnation. Individuals will no doubt possess healing power, but not normally of themselves.[9] They will rather be fingers of the whole body of Christ. The Holy Spirit was poured out at Pentecost on a group of men and women who had passed through a discipline. It was a discipline that was gruelling in the extreme. Physically it wore them out. We find, again and again, that they fell asleep if they had opportunity—at the Transfiguration, for instance, and during our Lord's agony in the Garden. But just as metals which will not unite at a low temperature can be fused at a high one—made, indeed, into a subsequently inseparable alloy, stronger than any of its separate constituents—so we find that the personalities of the disciples were fused into a unity by the furnace of the fellowship with Christ, which became their school and ultimately their glory. In such a school, Matthew the tax-gatherer is safe from the knife of Simon the Zealot, who, by his vows, is pledged to stab anyone taking money from his own countrymen and handing it over to the hated Roman. It is amazing, as we look back on it, to watch Jesus welding these disciples into a unity. Such a group became ready to receive the gift and power of the Holy Spirit, who, through them, released His energies into the lives of those with whom the members of the group came into contact. It may well be that the whole fellowship of the Church needs to be raised to a higher spiritual level today before individual healers in it can repeat the healing activities of the Son of God, and that until groups within the Church today are willing to pass through the same kind of discipline, the healing ministry of the Church will be restricted. No medical or psychological research can produce anything but a coun-

[9] The abnormal people with a "gift" of healing are discussed later. See p. 138.

terfeit of the power of the Kingdom which broke through whenever Christ was at work, a power which He promised to His disciples if they kept the conditions by which alone this type of healing is accomplished.

I wish now to make three points which clear a way to the understanding of Christ's healing miracles.

1. It will be observed that no argument is being brought forward in these pages that the healing miracles of Christ were a breach of the laws of the universe. In my opinion, the healing miracles represent the normal activities of a Person living on that high plane of experience and of communion with God. So far from being a breach of law—as they have so often been supposed to be—they illustrate the scope and wealth of law, and point to the fact that even on this higher plane, to which I have referred, there is cosmos and law, and never chaos and confusion. "We say," said St. Augustine, "that all portents [= miracles] are contrary to nature, but they are not so. For how is that contrary to nature which happens by the will of God, since the will of so mighty a Creator is certainly the nature of each created thing?" [10]

Perhaps an illustration may make the matter clearer. The laws of God, to which we refer as the laws of Nature, seem to me comparable with the daily habits of a man who tries to regulate his life in the best way. For instance, every day he takes the same route between his home and his work. He has thought things out, and that route, let us suppose, is the quickest way. Let us imagine that he is so punctual and dependable and regular that people could set their watches by his passing their homes. But on a few mornings in the year his wife is ill and, at her request, he varies his usual route to call at the doctor's house and ask the latter to visit his wife. There is no chaos or caprice in this variation, but he is a person reacting to a person in need. He is the master, not the slave, of his routine, which now is varied in response not to speed, but to need. He is a loving person serving a needy person who is the object of his love and who trusts him, loves him and believes in him.

So it would seem to me absurd to suppose that God is the victim of His own laws. He is able to use them and modify them so as to accomplish His loving purposes. Laws are His habits, but they are not independent of Him. *His activity is that which makes them laws.* He is a Person who loves persons, and in response to the need of those who believe in Him, He can at any point vary His activity. Such variation is no more a sign of chaos in the universe than, in the illustration above, the man's deviation of route on his way to work was a sign of chaos or caprice. In miracle God may act in a way surprising to us, for we

[10] Augustine, *The City of God*, Book 21, chapter 8.

know so little of the possibilities open to Him. He will not break the dependability of the universe, or make it impossible for us to learn its laws, but He may surprise us by revelations of the richness and complexity of law. Further, conditions of need and of faith on our part may enable Him to use the powers of a higher plane of being in a variation which more perfectly expresses His will. As Browning said, "All's love, yet all's law."

We must part, in my view, with the old-fashioned theory that the divinity of Christ implies that He could and would *suspend* the working of the laws of the universe. To do that would have implied a criticism of His Father's foresight and wisdom when those laws were first laid down. It is recorded that Jesus said: "My Father worketh even until now, and I work." [11] "The Father abiding in Me doeth His works." [12] "The Son can do nothing of Himself but what He seeth the Father doing: for what things soever He doeth, these the Son also doeth in like manner." [13] Here we are listening to One who, so far from interrupting the reign of law, delights in its power to assist Him in His healing work. He honours God's law-abiding cosmos and identifies His own purposes with those of God. He alone, of all the sons of men, seems at home in His Father's world and able to tap the energies available under conditions of faith and love. Indeed, He is reported to have blamed His disciples when their daring was not great enough to achieve results,[14] and on another occasion He is reported to have said that still greater works than His own should be done.[15]

It is open to the scientist, of course, dogmatically to assert that this or that is impossible, but unless he is referring to something inherently self-contradictory, it would seem presumptuous to decide what is and what is not possible. Presumably the laws of the universe are not likely to defeat its highest ends, and if man's truest blessedness is the highest good in the universe, that which contributes to it is not impossible because of some iron reign of law, but because man's blessedness would not be served by the so-called impossible event. In other words, many things that untutored minds think ought to happen, and think God ought to make happen, do not happen, not because limited power makes them impossible, but because unlimited love makes them ultimately immoral. It is incredible that God is hindered in the doing of His loving will by the laws which He Himself has made. It is incredible that He is imprisoned in His own system. When one studies the acts of Christ, one feels that what we call a miracle is the act of One

[11] John 5:17.   [12] John 14:10.   [13] John 5:19.
[14] Mark 9:19, Matthew 17:20.   [15] John 14:12.

34

who lived on a higher spiritual plane than any which we normally penetrate, and that spiritual energies of immense power were at His disposal.

It is not necessary to suppose that He understood the laws of the spiritual plane in any scientific sense such as that in which Einstein understands the laws of gravity and relativity. Jesus was truly human, and probably in many ways a child of His age. In His day "science" was unknown and a "scientist," in our sense, would have been an anachronistic monstrosity. But Christ was as much at home on the plane in which these immense spiritual energies were at work as we are at home in a world where gravity and relativity operate. We know of their operation and use the energies involved, even though we do not technically understand their action. Christ could call into operation the laws of the spiritual world, and it was the stricture imposed upon Him by man's well-being or by man's refusal to co-operate, not some fixity of law, that limited His activities. The phrase, "He did not many mighty works there because of their unbelief" (ἀπιστία),[16] refers not to any lack of theological belief in Himself as divine, but to a sneering attitude of contempt which made impossible the atmosphere of trustful expectancy in which alone He could work. As we shall see, He seems to have needed a kind of mental co-operation from others in order to heal some patients.

2. Again, we may dismiss the thought that He performed His healing miracles in order to draw attention to His own nature. Some writers still seem to cling to the thought that He worked miracles to prove that He was divine or to impress the bystanders. His own temptations, which He Himself must have revealed to His disciples, prove that that was as far as possible from His thoughts. Indeed, He condemned the Scribes and Pharisees for demanding signs,[17] and His reverence for the normal workings of the human mind was so great that He would never disable them by an exhibition of overwhelming power. Even amidst the working of miracles one finds a restraint lest what might almost be called a divine exuberance thrust men into decisions which did not carry the consent of every part of their personalities—mind, feeling and will.

The temptation to win men's allegiance by conjuring tricks or to overcome their hesitancy by dazzling displays of magic, He put from Him. On the other hand, just as a good man would rescue a child in

[16] Matthew 13:58.
[17] Matthew 12:39, 16:4 "an evil and adulterous (=idolatrous) generation seeketh after a sign"; cf. Mark 8:12, 13:22, Luke 11:16, 29.

danger because his good nature prompted him to the deed, so, when man's highest welfare was at stake, Christ did not hesitate to use the powers of the spiritual world in order that He might achieve His divine end, even though they were strikingly unusual on the plane on which most of us live, and were, therefore, bound to cause amazement in the minds of the onlookers. As Dr. Vincent Taylor says, "Miracles are primarily works of compassion and of power." [18] It must be underlined that His healing acts were *natural to Him* and an expression of His Father's law, though for those looking on the wonder element was the predominating impression they made. We call them miracles because neither knowledge nor experience furnishes any precedent for them and because they are a break-through into the human plane of the operation of laws belonging to a higher plane. It seems important to emphasise this so that we may realise that the *motive* of Christ's miracles was in harmony with all His other motives, and one with His love for God and love for men, His trust in God and His desire for man's well-being. The critics of miracles should not concentrate on what appears to them to be the incongruity of the miracles with that tiny part of the universe with which they have become familiar. They should concentrate on the congruity of the miracles with the whole of the ministry of Christ—His life and death and resurrection and post-resurrection ministry in the Spirit.

At the same time, we *may* find that some of the miracles are on the normal plane of activity even for people like ourselves. Indeed, the early Church found that this was so, and in a subsequent section we shall study the healing work of that era, and here we may, indeed, find that it is useful to identify some of the psychological mechanisms that operated.

An older theology used to claim that the miracles proved Christ's divinity, but apart from the fact that many things called miraculous in the first century are commonplace today, it is hard to follow the argument that divinity is proved by something so wonderful that the mind of the beholder cannot understand it. During the First World War the writer lived for a time with Arabs who could not believe that a message could be sent from Basra to Baghdad faster than an Arab horse could run. The electric telegraph was a "miracle," but I do not remember anyone imputing divinity to the telegraphist. We should be nearer the truth if we said that the *desire* to heal another, rather than the power to do so, pointed towards divinity. In this study we cannot

---

[18] *The Formation of the Gospel Tradition*, p. 133 (Macmillan, 1933).

pursue the point, save to note that divinity is in the same category as goodness, and not in the same category as marvellous acts.

It does not now seem to me sufficient to define a miracle, as Dr. Fosdick does,[19] as "God's use of His own law-abiding powers to work out, in ways surprising to us, His will for our lives and for the world." By such a definition the element of wonder alone makes a happening "miraculous." This seems to me unsound. Subsequent understanding of the event robs it of this miraculous element. We need a definition that makes the miraculous element a break-through of *spiritual* energies. Man is too prone to "the superstitious habit of attributing to a special act of divine volition any event which is not easily explained by reference to some human will, or by the scientific knowledge available at the time." [20] In the area of healing we must especially be on our guard against this superstition.

The phrase, "Nothing but a miracle will save him," usually implies that those who will not call on God in the area of the known and curable, expect God to act in some supernatural way just because they are in the realm of the unknown and incurable. It should, however, be remembered that God's activity is evidenced just as definitely in a treatment which relies on a drug as in one which depends on "spiritual healing." God is assumed to work in the latter more than in the former only because in cases of "spiritual healing" man is in the dark concerning the laws at work and the manner of their operation.

I would define miracle as follows: A miracle is a law-abiding event by which God accomplishes His redemptive purposes through the release of energies which belong to a plane of being higher than any with which we are normally familiar.

Miracles have always happened because God is ceaselessly at work, and at work with needy persons. Because of our ignorance, they are often surprising, but miracles are not to be confused with the merely marvellous, nor are healing miracles to be identified or confused with psychological treatments, however wonderful the latter may be. Let us, in this essay, keep the word "miracle" to describe events which show a break-through from the spiritual plane of being in which Jesus was so perfectly at home and to which most of us are such strangers.

By the "spiritual plane of being" I mean what the New Testament means by God's "reign" (βασιλεία): "The coming of God's βασιλεία in the person and work of Jesus Christ is the theme of the Gospel

---

[19] *The Modern Use of the Bible* (Macmillan, 1924).

[20] *Christus Veritas*, W. Temple, p. 192 (Macmillan, 1930); cf. the description of epilepsy as the "sacred disease" (p. 30).

teaching: it is, for those who witness it, 'a tasting . . . of the powers (δυνάμεις) of the Age to come.' " [21]

Though, no doubt, in some accounts of miracles the "wonder element" is enhanced, yet for the New Testament writers the spiritual forces at work in the situation and the spiritual meaning and implication of the acts themselves were the main interest. The powers of a new age were manifested in Christ, and His activities were an earnest of what would happen when His Kingdom came. Had not the prophets told them that the "Day of the Lord" would be signified by the fact that illness was cured? "Then the eyes of the blind shall be opened, and the ears of the deaf shall be unstopped. Then shall the lame man leap as an hart, and the tongue of the dumb shall sing." [22] Many passages seem to show that our Lord Himself took this view— e.g., to the twelve, "As ye go, preach, saying, 'The kingdom of heaven is at hand. Heal the sick,' " [23] and again to the seventy, "Heal the sick . . . and say unto them, 'The kingdom of God is come nigh unto you.' " [24] "If I, by the finger of God, cast out demons, then the kingdom of God has come upon you." [25]

The miracles of healing, then, herald a new age of spiritual power: something very different from the development in a largely pagan society of psychological theory and practice. And, since all disease was regarded as due to sin, the miracles of healing would have a double significance in the eyes of Christ's contemporaries. They would not only be regarded as the healing of the body, but also the forgiveness of sin. They would be symbolic demonstrations of God's forgiveness.

From the standpoint of the modern European, it is hard for us to realise what an opening of the windows of heaven Christ's healing miracles were. First, until He came, the orthodox Rabbinical teaching—with some variations which we have noted—was that since disease is God's will, to heal is an act of impiety. Medical science was disapproved of by Jewish leaders. Jesus's healing was a scandal on a weekday, let alone on the Sabbath.[26] When Jesus called the hampering of a woman's powers through illness the work of Satan,[27] we can only imagine the faces of His hearers. When He denied that suffering was the will of God,[28] or a direct and personal punishment for sin,[29] His hearers must have been startled indeed.

[21] Hebrews 6:5; cf. Alan Richardson, *The Miracle-Stories of the Gospels* (Harper, 1942).

[22] Isaiah 35:5; cf. Ezekiel 24:27.

[23] Matthew 10:7.   [24] Luke 10:9.   [25] Luke 11:20; Matthew 12:28.
[26] Matthew 12:1ff.   [27] Luke 13:16.   [28] Luke 13:1-5.
[29] Luke 13:4.

Second, in the surrounding pagan world, as Harnack has shown,[30] the gods were interested only in the healthy. This met human need so inadequately that it is not surprising that Æsculapius, the god of healing, amongst all the ancient pagan gods, held out longest against Christianity, and Celsus complained that the latter attracts "the sick, the fools and the sinners." No wonder. For here was a Healer and a Pardoner; a Friend of fools and a Saviour of sinners.

We do not understand the significance of the miracles while we concentrate on their wonder or think of them as only in the same category as modern therapeutic achievements. They may throw light on the latter, and the latter on them, but running through the miracle stories is a divine light but infrequently seen in a purely therapeutic treatment today. The miracles of Jesus are no more in the same category as modern treatments than the parables of Jesus are in the same category as other stories, and for the same reason. The miracles compel amazement and admiration, but properly regarded they evoke faith and worship, and it was mainly for this reason they were handed down.

I would therefore argue that even if by psychological means we learnt to do the things that Jesus did, there would be an essential difference between our activities and His. And while I hope to show that it is useful for us psychologically to identify some of the laws which operated, we are still separated from Him, in that He achieved the same end by a different route, partly because of what He was Himself and partly because of the response He could win from the patient by the outpouring of a divine love which may be of the same essence as our love for men—for love is of God—but which is as different as Niagara is different from the dripping of a tap.

This comes home to us very vividly when we compare the long laborious methods of psychoanalysis with the speedy way in which His patients were restored to health. Nor can we suppose that the commission to His disciples was a commission to study medicine or surgery or psychology, or any other science, though I have no doubt in my mind of the immense value for religion and for men's welfare of these studies. It was a commission calling upon them, through faith and prayer and character, to enter His world, which He called the Kingdom of Heaven, and use the energies available therein.

It makes nonsense of Christ's healing ministry to say that religion and health are never connected, and at this early stage of our argument I want to suggest that there must be spiritual energies which have greater sway over the body and the mind than anything that science has brought within her tabulations and formulæ. Indeed, our quest may

[30] *Expansion of Christianity*, Vol. 1, pp. 121 *et seq.*

well lead us to the view that the most powerful curative factor in the world is spiritual, and, indeed, that many diseases now called organic are, as it were, *spiritual*, and not merely psychological, disharmonies translated into terms of organic disability. Just as many illnesses—some forms of paralysis, for example—formerly treated only by the use of physical remedies are now found to yield to psychological treatment, even though we know so little about the power of the mind over the body; so, when we have truly progressed farther into the realm of the spirit, we may find that the energies of the latter are of a potency we cannot yet estimate, and that when *they* are released, troubles of mind and body which now baffle us may be overcome. The *British Medical Journal* actually printed these words: "No tissue of the human body is wholly removed from the influence of spirit," and, as I hope to show later, brilliant specialists in their own field are willing to admit that the primal cause of such troubles as gastric and duodenal ulcers, some forms of skin affections, of asthma and paralysis, and much of what is called functional disease may be not only psychological in origin, but spiritual: that is to say, not merely an inharmonious relationship between the mind and what might be called its secular environment, the world of true ideas, but between the soul and God.

Jesus appears to teach that there is a spiritual kingdom which men may enter through the Christian fellowship and in which healing energies are at work more powerfully than men have ever dreamed. The keys of this kingdom seem to be "faith" on the part of the patient and "love" on the part of the healer. We must interpret these two words later, for it is most important not to put an onus on the unhealed patient by saying that he had insufficient faith. There can be healing without faith, and there can be faith without healing, and immense issues turn on what is meant by "faith." This we shall study later.

Christ's healing work is misunderstood if it is supposed that He laid His hands on every patient and put the onus on the latter to have "faith" to be healed. That is often what the modern "healer" does, and the argument in this book will be hostile to many of his methods. Jesus Christ had more in common with a modern surgeon than with a modern faith-healer, for Christ always knew the nature of the patient's trouble and why it had befallen him, and He varied His technique accordingly. This is not to deny that He did lay His hands on people to heal them.[31]

We shall turn now to those healing incidents which illustrate this difference in technique—a technique which, I claim, used psychological mechanisms, but through which flowed a power derived from

[31] Cf. Mark 1:41, 5:23, 6:5, 8:23; Luke 4:40, 13:13. His followers did this also—Acts 9:17, 28:8.

spiritual realities. The mere healing of the physical body never circumscribed our Lord's intention.

I am attempting in this essay a classification of the healing miracles which I think has never been attempted before. It is a classification based on the psychological mechanisms which operated. This does not mean that we can dismiss a miracle as merely an illustration of suggestion, for example. I have tried to make it clear already that in my opinion the healing works of Christ cannot be marshalled into psychological categories, as though the latter completely accounted for them.

At the same time, if, as the New Testament says, "all things were made through Him" [32] and "in Him all things hold together," [33] then it would seem natural for the Master of law to use the laws of human nature, including the human mind, and we may base our classification on that understanding without denying that there enters in an element from a supernormal plane.

In the following scheme I have included every known healing miracle of Christ. I have described one in each classification fully and, for the sake of brevity, offered notes on all the others.

CLASSIFICATION I

Cures which Involve the Mechanism of Suggestion

1a. *The Cleansing of a Leper:*
   Mark 1:40-45, Matthew 8:1-4, Luke 5:12-14.
1b. *The Cleansing of Ten Lepers:*
   Luke 17:11-19.
2. *The Woman with Haemorrhage:*
   Mark 5:25-34, Matthew 9:20-22, Luke 8:43-48.
3. *The Man by Bethesda's Pool:*
   John 5:1-18.
4. *The Blind Man at Bethsaida:*
   Mark 8:22-26.
5. *Blind Bartimaeus:*
   Mark 10:46-52, Luke 18:35-43 (patient's name not given).
   Matthew 20:29-34 (probably the same incident, though Matthew characteristically mentions two men).
6. *The Man Born Blind:*
   John 9:1-41 (Matthew 9:27 relating to two blind men in house may be the same incident).

[32] John 1:3. (R .V. Marg.)
[33] Colossians 1:17. (R. V. Marg.) Moffatt has, "all coheres in Him."

7. *The Woman whom Satan had Bound:*
   Luke 13:10-17.
8. *The Man With Dropsy:*
   Luke 14:1-6.
9. *Peter's Mother-in-Law:*
   Mark 1:29-31, Matthew 8:14-15, Luke 4:38-39.
10. *The Man with a Withered Hand:*
    Mark 3:1-6, Matthew 12:9-14, Luke 6:6-11.

CLASSIFICATION II

Cures which Involve a more Complicated Technique

11. *The Gerasene Demoniac:*
    Mark 5:1-20, Matthew 8:28-34, Luke 8:26-39.
12. *The "Possessed" Man at Capernaum:*
    Mark 1:23-28, Luke 4:33-37.
13. *The Dumb and Blind Demoniac:*
    Matthew 9:32-33, 12:22, Luke 11:14 (the same incident).
14. *The Deaf Stammerer:*
    Mark 7:32-37.

CLASSIFICATION III

Cures which Involve the Influence of a Psychic
"Atmosphere" or the "Faith" of People other than the Patient

15. *The Paralytic at Capernaum:*
    Matthew 9:1-8, Mark 2:1-12, Luke 5:18-26.
16. *Jairus' Daughter:*
    Matthew 9:18-26, Mark 5:21-43, Luke 8:40-56.
17. *The Daughter of the Syro-Phoenician Woman:*
    Mark 7:24-30, Matthew 15:21-28.
18. *The Centurion's Servant* } (perhaps two accounts of the same
    The Nobleman's Son } incident):
    Matthew 8:5-13, Luke 7:1-10, John 4:46-54.
19. *The Epileptic Boy:*
    Mark 9:14-29, Matthew 17:14-21, Luke 9:37-43.

All the healing miracles of Jesus are included above, except the alleged healing of the ear of Malchus, servant of the high priest.[84]

[84] Luke 22:49-51, but note Mark 14:47, Matthew 26:51, John 18:10.

It is strange that all four evangelists narrate the scuffle in the garden and the *wounding* of Malchus, but only Luke, a doctor at that, states that a healing took place (22:51). This healing is quite unlike any other recorded healing of Jesus, and it has been suggested that "in the original tradition some ambiguous word was used in Christ's command to Peter, 'Restore it [the sword] to its place,' [35] and that Luke interpreted the restoration as applying to the ear." [36] This is conjecture, but as this is the only surgical case in all the records of healing in the gospels, and is recorded by only one evangelist, even though all four report the incident, it is not well enough authenticated to rank as one of the healing miracles of the gospels from which deductions may be made. Jesus probably compassionately intervened—"Suffer ye thus far," or "Let Me at least bless this man" —and when the ear healed, those from whom Luke drew his material gave the story a miraculous twist. The story is not to be rejected as impossible, but it is surrounded with greater difficulties. Even St. Augustine symbolised it as though he doubted its exact historicity.

The stories of raising from the dead are outside the scope of our present study, and are not dealt with here. They, of course, present still greater difficulties. I include a note about the daughter of Jairus inasmuch as in the face of Christ's definite statement, "The child is not dead," [37] it seems a little odd to insist that she was. Bishop Gore says, "There is nothing in Mark's story to show that the girl was dead." Hastings' *Dictionary of the Bible*, in the article on "Miracle," says, "It is noteworthy that the statement that the child was really dead was not made by Christ Himself" (Vol. III, p. 390). See also Hugh Martin commenting on the parallel passage in *Luke's Portrait of Jesus*, p. 61 (S.C.M.).

CLASSIFICATION I

Cures which Involve the Mechanism of Suggestion

1*a*. The Cleansing of a Leper:
   Mark 1:40-45, Matthew 8:1-4, Luke 5:12-14.
   "And there cometh to Him a leper, beseeching Him, and kneeling down to Him, and saying unto Him, If Thou wilt, Thou canst

---

[35] Matthew 26:52, John 18:11.

[36] Abbott, *Classical Review*, 1893, Ex Shafto, *Wonders of the Kingdom* (Doran, 1924).

[37] Mark 5:39, where Καθεύδει means normal sleep and never means death. When Jesus speaks of Lazarus being asleep (=dead) another word is used, κοιμαω, which can mean either to sleep or to die. Cf. Matthew 9:24, Luke 8:52, with John 11:11.

make me clean. And being moved with compassion, He stretched forth His hand and touched him, and saith unto him, I will; be thou made clean. And straightway the leprosy departed from him, and he was made clean. And He strictly charged him, and straightway sent him out, and saith unto him, See thou say nothing to any man: but go thy way, show thyself to the priest, and offer for thy cleansing the things which Moses commanded, for a testimony unto them. But he went out, and began to publish it much, and to spread abroad the matter, insomuch that Jesus could no more openly enter into a city, but was without in desert places: and they came to Him from every quarter."

To understand the story we must see the setting clearly. Both Mark and Luke show that Jesus was eager to concentrate on His preaching ministry rather than on that of healing. But this leper, breaking all the rules of the Mosaic Law, followed Him. Indeed, the sentence in Mark 1:43, "He strictly charged him and straightway sent him out," could be translated, "He sternly rebuked him and bundled him out at once." The words "strictly" and "sternly charged" carry the implication of anger, and in classical Greek the same word is used of the snorting of horses.[38] The words used suggest that the leper had come right into the synagogue in which Jesus was preaching.[39] The word translated "moved with compassion" ($\sigma\pi\lambda\alpha\gamma\chi\nu\iota\sigma\theta\epsilon\grave{\iota}\varsigma$) is translated in one ancient manuscript as "being angered." We can only guess at the mixture of emotions which the word indicates: compassion for the man, mixed with anger, in that his importunity thrust on Jesus the appearance of sanctioning the breaking of the Mosaic Law—a thing He was anxious to avoid whenever possible. The emotions of Jesus are, of course, beyond us. Miss Lily Dougall [40] says of His reporters that they "had little power of analysis and no precise nomenclature for emotions shading into one another." She adds, "When in a passion of grief at the insane blunders and self-destructive course of His opponents, He told them truths that His profound insight revealed of character. . . . How liable would His disciples be to call His emotions anger, themselves feeling angry on His behalf!"

We note in this context the vivid imperatives that follow in Mark's

[38] It is used in Mark 14:4, where the disciples "snorted" at the waste of ointment. Cf. John 11:33 (R. V. margin).

[39] Mark 1:39, Luke 4:44.

[40] *The Practice of Christianity*, p. 92 (Macmillan).

narrative. "Tell no one! Go away! Show thyself to the priest, and offer for thy cleansing the things which Moses commanded!" [41]

It is impossible accurately to say what the disease was in the case we are examining. Some Greek doctors use the word "λέπρα" for skin diseases other than leprosy. On the other hand, the Septuagint always uses "λέπρα" for leprosy as distinct from other skin diseases. True leprosy was known in Asia as early as 200 B.C.

It is important to notice that in Leviticus 13 and 14 the priest seems to have been given directions for distinguishing leprosy from other skin diseases and for declaring whether the patient need be isolated or not. But the word is obviously used in the cases of patients who were *expected to recover*. The patient is to show himself to the priest every seven days. This would be a waste of time in what we call leprosy, for the progress of the disease is so slow that no changes would be noticeable in that period. Further, the priest had power to declare the patient cured, and presumably often did so, yet until the recent use of chaulmoogra oil derivatives no people suffering from what *we* call leprosy ever recovered. The latter form of the disease, which sometimes lasted as long as twenty or thirty years and was marked by the rotting away of the nose, toes, fingers, etc., and by unsightly ulcers and terrible deformities, was completely incurable until comparatively recent times.

The view is now generally accepted that in the New Testament the word "leprosy" was used to cover a variety of skin diseases, like psoriasis and eczema, marked by white, scaly scabs on the skin, and that it was not regarded as a terrible disease in itself nor as highly contagious, but was *dreaded because it made its victims ceremonially unclean*. From that point of view it loomed ominously large in the minds of the Jews of our Lord's day, for it meant social ostracism and the deprivation of the consolations of religion. Above all, it represented the curse of God.

This point seems emphasized in the New Testament by a curious and interesting differentiation between lepers and other patients. Jesus sent out His disciples to "*heal* the sick," and to "*cleanse* the lepers." [42] I do not wish to exaggerate the importance of such a point. It may be that the two words "heal" and "cleanse" are interchangeable, but I can find no case in which the word "healed" is used of leprosy, and in the case we are discussing the patient never seems to have doubted Jesus' *ability* to heal his disease. What ap-

[41] Mark 1:44.
[42] Matthew 10:8, 11:5, Luke 7:22, etc.

parently amazed him was Christ's willingness to touch him and to declare him clean. Aretæus, writing of lepers in the first century says, "Such being their condition who can avoid flying from them, were it even his father or son or own brother? There is also the fear of infection." [43]

The healing of a skin disease by a word may tax our Western credulity to the utmost. Yet when we come to discuss the relationship between the emotional condition of the deep mind and skin disease, we shall find many interesting parallels.[44]

1*b*. *The Cleansing of Ten Lepers:*
  Luke 17:11-19. The above note on leprosy applies here.

2. *The Woman with Hæmorrhage:*
  Mark 5:25-34, Matthew 9:20-22, Luke 8:43-48.

In this case, though the cure is ascribed to Jesus, the woman was healed before He knew anything about it. Note that this woman had expectancy, but not "faith" in any developed Christian sense at all. It is important to remember that many unhealed Christian people have had a far greater faith in Christ than this woman had, illustrating again the fact that one can have faith without healing and healing without anything worth calling faith. The case before us illustrates the mechanism of suggestion more than it illustrates any great religious experience. The disease is thought to have been menorrhagia (excessive loss) or dysmenorrhoea (painful menstruation). Marr says "a uterine fibroid." [45] There is nothing to indicate discomfort or pain in the wording of Matthew and Luke. Dysmenorrhoea is due to a spasm of uterine muscle over which there is no voluntary control, and here psychotherapy is of the greatest value. Menorrhagia is not primarily of spasmodic origin and has an organic cause, such as an unhealthy lining of the uterus, or a fibroid tumour as suggested by Marr. Suggestion therapy would not normally be of such value in menorrhagia. Any discomfort and pain were probably less troublesome to the woman than the ceremonial uncleanness. Note that in the opinion of the onlookers she passed on the latter to Jesus by touching His clothes. Her uncleanness deprived her of all the consolations of religion.

[43] Quoted from Weymouth, *Through the Leper Squint*. I owe the reference to Dr. Joan Frayn.

[44] See p. 371.

[45] George S. Marr, M.A., M.B., Ch.B., D.Litt., *Christianity and the Cure of Disease*, p. 29 (Allenson).

It is not really surprising that He knew someone had touched Him, even though crowds surrounded Him, for she probably tugged at the tassel—called the *zizith*—affixed to the border of His robe.[46]

Matthew omits the idea that Jesus perceived that virtue had gone out of Him. Luke omits the statement in Mark that the patient "grew rather worse." Luke's "could not" be healed by any (doctors) means, "was unable to benefit from the treatment."

Note Jesus' tender word, "daughter," from a Jewish Rabbi to an "unclean" woman. Note also that suggestion is still used, and is frequently successful, in cases of menstrual difficulties.[47]

3. The Man by Bethesda's Pool:
John 5:1-18.

Jesus' question might well be translated, "Do you really want to be well?" Disease is often—if unconsciously—an escape mechanism. It is incredible that for thirty-eight years the patient was incapable of getting himself into the moving waters if he had seriously wanted to try this treatment. Note also that the patient did not even know until later who had cured him (verse 13). Faith in Christ, therefore, as the word is usually understood now, could not have been the operative factor. It is possible that the patient found it more interesting and more profitable to remain in the spotlight of publicity and in the receipt of sympathy and alms, and to maintain his illness for these reasons, than to be cured and thus to be uninteresting and compelled to earn a living or starve. Many neurotics—quite unconscious of the fact and therefore not in any sense blameworthy—cling to their illnesses because the latter attract sympathy and love. By means of illness patients are excused facing the hard world without losing "face" among their friends or seeing themselves as cowards. They truthfully say that they want to be well, but there is an unconscious and much more powerful motive which makes them want illness. It is easier to face the handicap and even pain of illness than the demands which would be made upon them if they were well.

The writer was recently told, by a famous surgeon, of a woman whose case had been diagnosed as inoperable cancer, and who was then informed that a mistake had been made and that there was no discoverable disease at all. She refused, however, to leave the hospital,

[46] Matthew 9:20, Luke 8:44; cf. Numbers 15:38.
[47] Cf. examples in Ford's *Hypnotism*, p. 110, and in Delius, *The Treatment of Disturbances of Menstruation by Hypnotic Suggestion*.

and was more upset at being told she was well than that she was dying. "I cannot bear the thought of facing life again," she said.

Janet quotes an interesting case from *L'automatisme psychologique*, as follows: "A woman, thirty years of age, was suffering from complete paralysis of the lower limbs after being bedridden for years. While she was seated in a chair, and while Dr. Piasecki of Havre, who had taken me to see her, was standing in front of her talking to her on indifferent matters and apparently engaging her whole attention, I told her in a low tone to get up and walk. To her own amazement, she did as she was told and was cured from that time." [48] After some years there was no relapse. [49]

The words of Jesus in the case we are studying, "*Sin* no more, lest a worse thing befall thee," definitely suggest that the patient had produced his illness to escape facing life, and that Jesus, exposing this, was guarding him against a more painful illness. A neurotic illness must carry some disability or it will not deceive even the patient, and if the earlier bluff had been exposed and the patient had refused to face life, his unconscious mind would have found it necessary to produce a worse illness in order to conceal the true motive of the latter from the patient himself.

This must not be interpreted to mean that all neurotic patients are hypocrites. Far from it. Most neurotic illness begins in unconscious mechanisms, and no one can be blamed for processes which are wholly unconscious. At the same time, many neuroses develop from a cowardly attitude to life which begins consciously—as in the case cited above—and then, through habit, becomes unconscious by a trick of the deep mind which aims at concealing the cowardice of a patient from his own scrutiny. Even forgiveness for sin—because it seems irrelevant—is then insufficient to conquer the disease, for the guilt is repressed into the unconscious to such an extent that the patient does not feel guilty at all. He must be helped to discard the faulty way of reacting to his difficulties. There *is* sin in consciously running away from life, even if afterwards an unconsciously induced illness covers the shameful tracks. This is what I conceive to have happened in the case cited above, and accounts for our Lord's stern words, "Sin no more!"

4. *The Blind Man at Bethsaida:*
    Mark 8:22-26.

Note that Christ both touched the patient and used saliva. It is interesting to remember that for many years it was believed that there was healing power in the touch of a great person. In our own

---

[48] Janet, *Psychological Healing*, Vol. I (Macmillan, 1925).   [49] *Ibid.*

country "touching" by the King dates back to Edward the Confessor, and was in vogue from Henry VII to Anne. Charles II "touched" nearly one hundred thousand people. Thousands more watched the ceremony. Boswell says [50] that Johnson's little son was "touched" by Queen Anne in 1712, but without avail.

Similarly, it was believed for centuries that the saliva of a saintly or exalted person had a powerful therapeutic effect. Tacitus [51] records that the Emperor Vespasian restored a blind man by the same means. Here is the passage: "A certain man of the people of Alexandria, well known for his loss of sight, kneeled down and begged of Vespasian to cure his blindness. He desired that the Emperor would be pleased to put some of his spittle on his cheeks and eyes. Vespasian at first began to laugh: then he ordered his physicians to give their opinion. They said that the power of sight had not been completely eaten away. If the cure succeeded, Cæsar would have the glory: if not, the poor miserable object would only be laughed at. Vespasian did what was desired and the blind man saw immediately. The tale is told by eye-witnesses, even now when falsehood brings no reward." [52]

Jung writes of an African Negro mountain tribe, the Elgonyi, and, describing one of their ceremonies, adds, "If they have spittle on their hands, this is the substance which, according to primitive belief, contains the personal mana, the force that cures, conjures and sustains life." [53]

The way Jesus laid His hands on the man's eyes may have been motivated by concern lest the sudden glare of the Eastern day should harm the unused eyes. If so, there was prevention as well as healing in His touch.

Note that here we have an illustration of Christ using a popular *medical* measure and one recommended by Galen, the physician of Marcus Aurelius. Jesus reinforced the power of suggestion by the use of a physical measure in which everybody in those days believed. Ancient Egyptians believed in the efficacy of saliva as a cure for blindness, and also that to curse a man and at the same time to spit in his eyes would cause blindness. Pliny in *Historia Naturalis* (28:7, Bohn's trans.) says, "We may well believe that opthalmia may be cured by anointing, as it were, the eyes every morning with fasting spittle."

[50] *Life of Johnson,* Vol. I, p. 42.

[51] *Historia,* Vol. IV, p. 81.

[52] I owe the translation to Bishop Barnes, *The Rise of Christianity,* p. 120 (Longmans, 1947).

[53] *Modern Man in Search of a Soul* (Harcourt, 1933).

Quoting thus, Dr. Joan Frayn says, "It is likely that [Christ's] exceptional δύναμις would provide stimulus sufficient to make some homely expedient effective." [54]

The question has sometimes been asked as to whether Jesus gave authority to a mere superstition. It is possible that He was the child of His day to the extent of actually believing that saliva was efficacious, a belief probably based on the practice of animals in licking their sores. It seems to me more likely that He reinforced the power of suggestion and expectancy in the most powerful way He knew, thus influencing the patient regardless of whether saliva was actually of therapeutic value or not.

5. *Blind Bartimæus:*
    Mark 10:46-52, Luke 18:35-43, Matthew 20:29-34.
    There are discrepancies here. Luke places the incident at Christ's entry to Jericho, Mark and Matthew at the exit from Jericho. Bartimæus had not always been blind. He asks that he may *regain* his sight.

The touch of Jesus is important again. Note the respect the patient pays to Jesus—putting on his coat first. Shafto notes that the Sinaitic–Syriac version requires ἀπολαβών (put on) in place of ἀποβαλών (take off), and that Mrs. Smith-Lewis noted in Syria that a labouring man would put on his cloak as a mark of respect. Bartimæus, sitting in the sun without his *abbas*, would put it on to meet Jesus. Many soldiers who had an exciting experience subsequent to blindness caused by shell-shock recovered their sight. The excitement and presence of the crowd would greatly increase the power of suggestion. Hadfield describes the value of having groups of people for this reason when seeking to induce hypnosis. Few, he says, can resist the suggestion that they are falling asleep when those around them show signs of doing so. Suggestion is always more potent when numbers of people are present.

6. *The Man Born Blind:*
    John 9:1-41.
    Again saliva is used (see above). The man is told to wash in Siloam. His expectancy is thereby increased, and the shadowed arches round the pool would protect the newly-found sight from too great a strain. See notes on blindness in 4 and 5 above.

[54] *London Quarterly Review,* January, 1950, pp. 32-33.

7. *The Woman whom Satan had Bound:*
   Luke 13:10-17.

Luke, the doctor, alone recounts this story, but has no other diagnosis than "a spirit of infirmity"—to him, and apparently to Jesus, she was one whom "Satan hath bound." The fact that she was "immediately made straight" (v. 13) suggests a hysterical paraplegia rather than an osteitis, as Hastings' *Dictionary* suggests (Vol. III, p. 328), and the idea of a *spirit* of infirmity suggests a nervous origin. Luke, the doctor, is fond of ascribing disease to demons. In 4:39 he says, "Jesus *rebuked* the fever." This is the same word used by Mark for casting out a demon (1:13). The attractive part of the story is the evidence it provides that to the mind of Jesus illness and disease were part of the kingdom of evil, which it was His mission to overthrow. Here is the answer to those who think of their illness as "the will of God." This is an instance of the "laying on of hands." Professor J. A. Findlay says, "She was bent double, but not demon-possessed. Jesus never laid His hands on demoniacs."

8. *The Man with Dropsy:*
   Luke 14:1-6.

Whether "dropsy" as described in Luke 14:2 is what we now call dropsy is uncertain. Both the incidents numbered 7 and 8 seem to be told with more emphasis on Christ's readiness to heal on the Sabbath than on any "miracle." Micklem[55] comments, "There is a disease known as Angio Neurotic Œdema which I understand to be a functional complaint." It is possible that a man suffering from this would be termed ἰδρωπικός (afflicted with dropsy). This is the only use of this Greek word in the N.T. "A solitary instance of this disease among the healing acts of Jesus." [56]

9. *Peter's Mother-in-Law:*
   Mark 1:29-31, Matthew 8:14-15, Luke 4:38-39.

Students of hypnotic phenomena—and hypnotic treatment is suggestive treatment—will recall that the temperature of a hypnotised person can be lowered or raised at the will of the operator. I have described my own experiments in this field in *Psychology and Life* [57] and in *Psychology in Service of the Soul* [58] and later in this book [59]

[55] *Op. cit.*
[56] *Expositor's Greek Testament,* Vol. I (Doran).
[57] Abingdon-Cokesbury, 1935.
[58] Macmillan.
[59] P. 109.

Hadfield reports a variation of twenty degrees in twenty minutes under such conditions. The report that Jesus *"rebuked"* the fever (Luke 4:39) sounds like suggestion used to lower the temperature to normal. The fever may have been malaria.

10. *The Man with a Withered Hand:*
    Mark 3:1-6, Matthew 12:9-14, Luke 6:6-11.

Mark suggests a dramatic setting. The Sabbath controversy was a burning issue, and its discussion alone would have made the situation tense. Increased suggestion was effected by the order (as in Luke), "Stand forth in the midst," and "He looked round about on them all." The presence of the "all" increased the power of suggestion. As we have seen, "Suggestibility is largely a phenomenon of the group." [60] Note the complete absence of any doubt on the part of Jesus that the man would respond. Jesus is saying, "You can do *it.*" The man believed it when the suggestion came with the certainty in Jesus' voice, and the love that streamed from our Lord's personality into that of the patient. The details do not allow us to make any diagnosis with confidence. Dr. R. J. Ryle regarded it as a case of "infantile paralysis" (? anterior poliomyelitis), and adds, "It does not belong to that class of nervous disease which admits of treatment by moral impression or emotional shock." While this may be true, I am informed by a Harley Street psychiatrist that hysterical contracture would account equally for the condition described. Very soon the lack of adequate circulation would produce the result described as "withered."

CLASSIFICATION II

Cures which Involve a more Complicated Technique

11. *The Gerasene Demoniac:*
    Mark 5:1-20, Matthew 8:23-34, Luke 8:26-39.

"And they came to the other side of the sea, into the country of the Gerasenes. And when He was come out of the boat, straightway there met Him out of the tombs a man with an unclean spirit, who had his dwelling in the tombs; and no man could any more bind him, no, not with a chain; because that he had been often bound with fetters and chains, and the chains had been rent asunder by him, and the fetters broken in pieces: and no man had strength

[60] See Grensted, *Psychology and God,* Bampton Lectures for 1930, p. 92 (Longmans); William Brown, *Science and Personality,* pp. 86 ff.; William Brown, *Mind and Personality* (Putnam).

to tame him. And always, night and day, in the tombs and in the mountains, he was crying out, and cutting himself with stones. And when he saw Jesus from afar, he ran and worshipped Him; and crying out with a loud voice, he said, What have I to do with Thee, Jesus, Thou Son of the most High God? I adjure Thee by God, torment me not. For He said unto him, Come forth, thou unclean spirit, out of the man. And He asked him, What is thy name? And he saith unto Him, My name is Legion; for we are many. And he besought Him much that He would not send them away out of the country. Now there was there on the mountain side a great herd of swine feeding. And they besought Him, saying, Send us into the swine, that we may enter into them. And He gave them leave. And the unclean spirits came out, and entered into the swine: and the herd rushed down the steep into the sea, in number about two thousand; and they were choked in the sea. And they that fed them fled, and told it in the city, and in the country. And they came to see what it was that had come to pass. And they come to Jesus, and behold him that was possessed with devils sitting, clothed and in his right mind, even him that had the legion: and they were afraid. And they that saw it declared unto them how it befell him that was possessed with devils, and concerning the swine. And they began to beseech Him to depart from their borders. And as He was entering into the boat, he that had been possessed with devils besought Him that he might be with Him. And He suffered him not, but saith unto him, Go to thy house unto thy friends, and tell them how great things the Lord hath done for thee, and how He had mercy on thee. And he went his way, and began to publish in Decapolis how great things Jesus had done for him: and all men did marvel." [61]

I have chosen the incident quoted above for the fuller note in this classification because it illustrates better than any of the other healing miracles the way in which Christ altered His treatment to suit His patient, was not content to demand a "faith" which put all the onus on the patient, and took great pains to understand the case. I said earlier that Christ had much more in common with the modern doctor than with the modern faith-healer. Here is the perfect illustration of that fact. The modern faith-healer lays his hands upon the patient and demands "faith," and the onus of getting better is on the patient. Christ is not content to lay His hands upon this man. He spends the greater part of the night in the most careful diagnosis and treatment.

[61] Mark 5:1-20; cf. Matthew 8:28-34, Luke 8:26-39.

Let us look at the incident closely, for it is one of the most important for our purpose in the whole of the gospel records.[62]

Jesus is very tired, and has fallen asleep on the cushion in the stern of the boat as His disciples row Him across the lake from west to east. Then, as frequently happens nowadays on the lake, a great storm suddenly arises. The hot air rises from the lake; the cold air sweeps through the gorges between the mountains that surround it, and in a very short time the water is lashed into fury. Jesus is still asleep, but the disciples are terrified. It is important to notice this strain upon their nerves, in view of what happens later. "Lord, carest Thou not that we perish?" they cry. Jesus awakens, and, very characteristically, the storm dies down suddenly, while Jesus is saying—as I think to the panic-stricken hearts of the disciples rather than to the storm-demon—"Peace, be still!"

They reach the eastern shore of the lake at eventide. At this point a gully or *wadi*, which I have myself explored, runs down to the shore, and we can imagine Jesus and His men walking up it in the dusk. This is Gentile territory. At the top of the *wadi* is a place of tombs, which to the Jew is a devil-haunted region. Furthermore, pigs are feeding in a great herd on the bluff at the top of the *wadi*, and to the Jew they are unclean animals. On a blazing June morning in 1934 I found this place strangely uncanny, weirdly desolate. If it made that impression on a Western mind on a sunny June morning, after a peaceful voyage in a motor-boat, we can imagine the effect produced on the minds of the superstitious disciples, who thought pigs were unclean and graveyards full of devils, in the dusk of the late evening as they landed on what to them was a foreign shore, after a terrifying voyage during which they had been almost drowned.

It is important to note that, although this incident is still called the story of the Gadarene demoniac, Gadara is twenty-five miles from the lake, and cannot have been the scene of this incident. We can hardly imagine two thousand pigs travelling twenty-five miles, crossing a wide and deep river called the Yarmuk, and throwing themselves into the sea! Mark speaks of "the country of the Gerasenes," but Gerasa is still farther away. It is the modern Jerash, which is thirty miles from the lake.

The late Mr. T. R. Maltby suggests that Peter, speaking Aramaic with a Galilean accent, used to talk about Ger'sa, and that Mark,

[62] I have repeated here some ideas printed in an earlier book, *It Happened in Palestine* (Abingdon, 1936), but it seems important to do so.

spelling it out in Greek letters, called the people Gerasenes, and was supposed by critics to have made a mistake, when he was only reporting with his usual accuracy. The village called Khersa, just behind the bluff to which I have referred, is undoubtedly the place indicated, for here we have the only spot on the whole shore of the lake where steep ground falls into deep water.

The strain on the nerves of the disciples is far from over, for as they mount the bluff at the head of the ravine they hear the hideous laughter of a lunatic and the terrifying clanking of his chains. Crying out and cutting himself with stones, the patient rushes up to Jesus, falls down before Him, shouting, with a loud voice, "What have I to do with Thee, Jesus, Thou Son of the most High God?" In the chapter on Demonology which follows I shall comment on the way in which people possessed by devils could recognise Jesus easily. We can imagine that Jesus, at any rate, was quite calm. Though He had come across the lake to find rest, and chosen that place because there He was unlikely to be disturbed, He gives Himself to this poor, wild patient driven into exile, and spends most of the night with him.

I wish to concentrate the reader's attention most on the treatment Jesus uses. First of all He tries suggestion. The Greek present imperative could be interpreted thus: "Jesus kept on saying to him, 'Come forth, thou unclean spirit, out of the man.' " But the treatment fails. We may hazard the opinion that the patient had gone too far into his psychosis to be fully aware of what was happening.[63] He was not sufficiently *en rapport* with the Healer for suggestion to be the requisite treatment. So Jesus uses another method, which to the modern psychologist is full of significance. He says to him, "What is thy name?" Mark adds the comment, "He saith unto Him, 'My name is Legion; for we are many,' " and it may, indeed, be that that is the correct explanation. But, in passing, we may be awake to another solution which modern psychology helps us to understand.

It is to be remembered that the word "name" and the word "power" are synonymous in the New Testament. When the disciples went out in the *name* of Jesus, they went out in the *power* of Jesus, The text, "Whatsoever ye ask of the Father in My *name*, He will give it," may be translated, "Whatsoever ye ask of the Father, if it is in

[63] The late Professor James Hope Moulton tells us that in Luke 8:29 the true meaning of the Greek word translated "oftentimes" implies "it had long ago obtained and now kept complete mastery of him" (*Grammar of New Testament Greek*, Vol. I, Prolegomena, 2nd ed., 1906).

My *power* to give it to you, I will." [64] The very fact that Jesus asked the patient his name would be understood by the patient to mean that Jesus was seeking power over him by trying to understand the power that was controlling him. In the East to this day to surrender one's name to a person is to give that person power over one. So a number of my own men in an Indian regiment—a company of which I commanded during the First World War—would not disclose their true name. They kept it written on paper contained in a little cylinder tied upon their person, and gave another name, for they believed that if they disclosed their true name, they would give me an uncanny power over them. Similarly, an Indian bride frequently will not give up her name to her bridegroom until after their marriage, when alone he has any rights or power over her. We remember that in the old Genesis story (32) the angel asks Jacob his name, and Jacob gives it. But when Jacob says to the angel, "Tell me *thy* name," no name is given. The angel had power over Jacob. Jacob had no power over the angel. Savages will rarely disclose their true names, for similar reasons.

In asking the patient's name, then, Jesus is really saying, "Trust Me, Confide in Me. Tell Me what *power* it is that has dominion over you." And when the patient answers at last with the word "Legion!" it may indeed be that he felt possessed by many devils. But it may also be that the word "Legion" was a key to the origin of the shock which had brought on the illness.

In the First World War a man was found in no-man's land, wandering about between our trenches and those of the enemy, and the only word he could say was "Arras." This was the town in which he had been tortured to make him impart information, and the torture had driven him mad. Similarly, I remember the case of a man in a mental hospital during the First World War who had been tortured by the Germans, and the only word he would utter was the word "Boche." Here, in St. Mark's story, we have a man muttering the word "Legion," and it is not fanciful to suppose that he had suffered some shock at the hands of the Roman legion. We know from the story of the massacre of the innocents the kind of thing the Roman legion could do, and, indeed, it is possible that this patient had witnessed this dreadful affair. If he had seen tiny children slaughtered, and had rushed in from the sunny street terrified of the approaching soldiers whose swords were dripping red with blood, and had cried, "Mummy, Mummy, legion!" (if we may modernise

---

[64] I have worked this out more fully in *When the Lamp Flickers* (Abingdon-Cokesbury, 1948).

his language), then it would be no flight of imagination to suppose that the childhood's shock—especially if the patient had a hereditary emotional unbalance—would be quite sufficient to drive him into psychosis. And now the community had exiled the patient right out of the security of their own fellowship into a wild graveyard in a foreign land, where he is left to live amongst the pigs, terrified by spasms of fear which leap up from his repressed memories into consciousness, and express themselves in maniacal frenzies and in loud cries.

The destruction of the herd of swine is simple to understand. It is a well-known fact that pigs easily panic. I have on my files a Press cutting describing an incident in which fifty-six prize pigs stampeded when the smoke of a fire enveloped the piggery.[65] If the word "Legion" induced an emotional abreaction or storm by which the patient recovered the early memory of a shock caused by Roman soldiers, or possibly Herod's police, there is not the slightest doubt that the repressed emotion would find vent in shrieks and cries. It may well be that the swineherds had been attracted to the scene by the unusual presence of a body of men (Jesus and His disciples) late at night where they were watching their pigs. The diversion of having something to do in the night, during the monotonous hours, would draw them near to the patient, and, untended, the pigs may easily have stampeded when the patient shrieked, and, as the herdsmen left Jesus and rushed towards them to seek to allay their fears, the pigs may easily have rushed over the edge of the cliff and fallen into the deep water. Nothing could have been more opportune from the patient's point of view, for he believed that a devil must have some kind of incarnation, and if not that of a man, then that of an animal. Furthermore, the patient and all his contemporaries believed that deep water is the only finally satisfactory way of getting rid of devils. We remember the words of Jesus about those who were cruel to little children, that it would be better for them to have a millstone round their neck and that they should be drowned in the *depths* of the sea. The deep sea would finally dispose of a devil, and a person cruel to a child was thought of as possessed. We remember again the reference to a devil wandering through the *waterless* places, and our own saying about being "between the devil and the deep sea." A sailor who had to repair a ship which had been damaged just below the water-line was said to be in this predicament. He was exposed to the devil while above the water-line and to death by drowning below it, even

[65] *News Chronicle,* September 6, 1933.

though no devil could pursue him into deep water. Everybody in Jesus' day believed that devils hated water, and that if the body in which they were incarnate were drowned, then, and then only, were the devils finally disposed of.

No doubt the demoniac interpretation was useful to the swineherds when they had to account for the loss of apparently the whole herd. We can imagine their expostulations and excuses. "Guarding pigs from human thieves is one thing," we can hear them say, "but we can't be expected to guard them against devils sent into them by the magic of a powerful master of the black arts."

It is not derogatory to the divine power and character of Jesus to imagine that, with greater power than we have, He yet did follow a now familiar psychological technique, recovered the buried memory of cruelty which had disturbed the patient's mind, brought it to the surface, accompanied by a fierce emotional abreaction which had terrified the pigs and their keepers, and that at daybreak those who came to see what had happened found the patient in his right mind. The patient asks that he may become one of Jesus' followers, and we need not hesitate to use the word "transference." Who would not transfer his affections to One who could set him free from so terrible a malady? But Jesus, of course, was perfectly right in not allowing this. The man would become a prize exhibit. He would be pointed at and singled out, and that would be bad for him and unhelpful to Jesus, so he is instructed to go home and tell his friends the great things that the Lord had done for him. But it is a very human and characteristic touch which adds, in all three gospels, that the people asked Jesus to depart from them. "They were holden with great fear," says St. Luke,[66] and we are not surprised. The whole dramatic scene must have been terrifying in those early days. Indeed, it is quite alarming nowadays to witness the powerful abreaction of long-repressed emotion. Besides, here is a Healer who does not seem to mind if two thousand pigs perish in one night, if only one soul is set free from bondage.

I wish to make it very clear that the above description is not an attempt to explain away a miracle by using familiar psychological mechanisms. So far as I know, there is no parallel case in modern psychology. By no methods known to us can a patient as far advanced in psychosis as was the man from Khersa be brought back to sanity and to a desire to serve the Kingdom of God. The incident seems to me to illustrate the point already made, that the power of Christ

[66] 8:37.

broke through from that higher plane on which He habitually lived, and seems miraculous to us because we are unfamiliar with that plane and with what may happen on it.

At the same time, the incident seems to me also to illustrate a technique which Christ used and with which we are becoming more familiar. Miracle is very different from magic, and Christ had nothing to do with the latter. If miracle be understood to mean an abrogation of law, He had nothing to do with the former. The incident is a miracle in the sense defined earlier. But it illustrates the fact that though the energies released belonged to a supernormal plane, Christ took pains to suit His method to His patient, and here we find Him employing a far more complicated technique than that of the mere laying on of hands. He seems here to have used a technique with which analytical investigation has made us familiar.

12. *The "Possessed" Man at Capernaum:*
    Mark 1:23-28, Luke 4:33-37.

Literally (v. 23) "There was a man *in* an unclean spirit. Jesus rebuked him and said, 'Hold thy peace,' " or literally, "Be muzzled." The same word is used in Mark 4:39, where, *in the narrative*, the storm is addressed as a *demon*. J. A. Findlay says the word was technically used in the language of Greek magic to express "binding" a person by the use of a powerful spell to render him impotent to harm.

Here we seem in a different atmosphere from that of Classification I. "What is there in common to us and Thee, Jesus of Nazareth? Thou hast come to destroy *us*." Is this multiple personality in ancient guise? "I know Thee who Thou art, the One who belongs entirely to God"—as I, or we, do not—suggests an acute state of mental conflict. A convulsive seizure sounds like the modern violent abreaction, or discharge of emotion repressed for a long time in the unconscious mind.

How did the "demons" recognise Jesus? The patient "possessed by a demon" is certainly in an abnormal psychological state. May he not have been able to "read" the subconscious mind of Jesus, and thus recognise Him? I myself attended a séance and listened to a medium, purporting to bring a message from a relative I had lost, giving an account of the nature of the life after death which had been for a long time my own idea of that life—an idea I had committed to writing shortly before the séance. It struck me that the medium—obviously psychically abnormal—might be reading my own deep mind. Might not a "possessed" patient find that he had access to our Lord's deep mind? "Belief in possession," said Janet, "is only a popular conception of a psychological truth."

It is a good rule not to resort to a complicated explanation of an incident if a simpler one will do equally well, but here neither the multiple-personality theory nor that of demons is simple. We have not enough material to be dogmatic.

13. *The Dumb and Blind Demoniac:*
    Matthew 9:32-33, 12:22, Luke 11:14.

All three accounts may refer to the same case. Hysterical blindness and dumbness common in psychotherapeutic cases offer interesting parallels. A psychiatrist I know recently had a case of a man who was blind only because the muscles of his eyelids failed to hold them up. He went about holding up his eyelids with his fingers. Immediate cure followed his self-discovery that he was afraid to face the future—a situation dramatised by his "blindness." Note that if once the idea that blindness is indeed a fact is received and accepted by the mind, then *the patient stops looking,* and real blindness through atrophy begins; cf. Acts. 13:11. "Thou shalt be blind, not seeing the sun for a season." The curse would easily be effective for this reason if guilt made it seem just and authority made it seem certain.

14. *The Deaf Stammerer:*
    Mark 7:32-37.

This interview took place in private (v. 33). Jesus took the patient out of the reach of the contra-suggestion of scoffers. Touching the ears and the use of spittle would strongly increase suggestion. Note Jesus looking up to heaven, which the deaf man would interpret as prayer to God. The man's feeling of isolation is ended. The "sighing" may have been *felt* as breath on the patient's cheek. Note how Jesus, unable to reach the man through the sound of words, uses the man's other senses to "get through" to him. The Aramaic word *ephphatha* seems retained to emphasise the first word the man heard. It would be unforgettable, and would reinforce the patient's hold on his restored health if any recurrence of his malady seemed imminent. Note Mark 7:37: they were "beyond measure astonished." Nine times Mark uses this word suggesting violent astonishment mixed with fear. The "bound tongue" was thought to be the binding spell of a special "demon." [67] Notice how Christ gives the man confidence and increases expectation. Saliva is used again. Fingers are put into the patient's ears and his tongue is touched. The word "stammerer," so often used of this case, disguises the true situation.

[67] Deissmann, *Light from the Ancient East,* p. 306, Ex Micklem, *op. cit.*

The patient had not even heard his own voice for a long time, and so speaks in a muttering way hard to follow.

Deafness and speech difficulties are often hysterical, and obviously deafness and mutism are closely associated; hearing often returning when speech is restored. MacDougall cites an interesting case of dumbness which he treated. I have discussed it in *Psychology and Life*.[68] All psychiatrists with experience of men in the Forces have had cases of hysterical deafness and aphonia, often occurring simultaneously in the same patient.

CLASSIFICATION III

Cures which Involve the Influence of a Psychic "Atmosphere" or the "Faith" of People other than the Patient

15. *The Paralytic at Capernaum:*
    Matthew 9:1-8, Mark 2:1-12, Luke 5:18-26.
"And when He entered again into Capernaum after some days, it was noised that He was in the house. And many were gathered together, so that there was no longer room for them, no, not even about the door: and He spake the word unto them. And they come, bringing unto Him a man sick of the palsy, borne of four. And when they could not come nigh unto Him for the crowd, they uncovered the roof where He was: and when they had broken it up, they let down the bed whereon the sick of the palsy lay. And Jesus seeing their faith saith unto the sick of the palsy, Son, thy sins are forgiven. But there were certain of the scribes sitting there, and reasoning in their hearts, Why doth this Man thus speak? He blasphemeth: who can forgive sins but One, even God? And straightway Jesus, perceiving in His spirit that they so reasoned within themselves, saith unto them, Why reason ye these things in your hearts? Whether is easier, to say to the sick of the palsy, Thy sins are forgiven; or to say, Arise, and take up thy bed, and walk? But that ye may know that the Son of man hath power on earth to forgive sins (He saith to the sick of the palsy), I say unto thee, Arise, take up thy bed, and go into thy house. And he arose, and straightway took up the bed, and went forth before them all; insomuch that they were all amazed, and glorified God, saying, We never saw it on this fashion." [69]

[68] P. 278.
[69] Mark 2:1-12; cf. Matthew 9:1-8, Luke 5:18-26.

Here is a miracle which it is not easy to classify. I believe that its main purpose was to show forth the right Jesus had to forgive sins, and the miracle is written down that readers might believe in that authority.

It might conceivably be used as an illustration of the power of a suggestion with that authority behind it, evidently powerful enough to break the guilt complex from which the patient was suffering. Here is an eloquent illustration of a physical disability being entirely cured by a new spiritual relationship. Nothing is said to the paralysed patient about his legs. The curative factor is the forgiveness of sins.[70]

I include it here as an illustration of my third classification—that is, the miracles in which the attitude of the bystanders seems the most important factor—because I am so impressed by the fact that in all three gospels we find the phrase, "Jesus seeing *their* faith"—that is to say, the faith of the friends of the patient.

Look briefly at the setting of the incident. Jesus is staying with Peter, and we imagine a little house (such as I have often visited myself in the East) built round four sides of a tiny courtyard, and of one storey only. There is a flat roof, which can be reached by an outside stairway from the street. Anyone who was entertaining Jesus would know that he must expect crowds. I imagine, therefore, that Peter did what a man would do in such circumstances today. He turned the centre courtyard into an extra and large room by putting a temporary roofing above it. Today one sees a few light planks covered with a tarpaulin. In those days no doubt straw matting would be used, or even a light bamboo framework covered with loosely locked tiles.[71] It is not a strong roof. It is only for a temporary purpose and rests on the four sides of the hollow square. But it shelters those beneath from the blazing sun and from the rain.

Four men are carrying the stricken patient, and probably the latter was only a youth in his teens, for the Greek word *teknon* might truly be translated by the word "child." It was probably a term of endearment, perhaps not very different from our "laddie." St. Paul used the same word of Timothy.[72] It might well be that the men carrying the paralysed boy are relatives. When they arrive, they find the whole house and the courtyard crowded with people to whom Jesus is speaking, and they cannot get near. So, using the

[70] Matthew 9:2, Mark 2:5, Luke 5:20.

[71] Luke definitely speaks of "tiles," but it is uncertain what the word means (Luke 5:19). Mark seems to be thinking of a tiled roof when he speaks of the roof being "*broken up*" ('εξορυξαντες).

[72] 2 Timothy 1:2; cf. Philemon 10.

stairway from the street on to the flatroof, they carry the sufferer up and proceed to remove the temporary roofing until there is an aperture large enough to let down the stretcher.

We can imagine the feelings of the boy as he is let down with ropes near where Jesus is standing. Everybody in the audience would suppose that the boy had sinned, or he would not be sick. This was the current belief of the day, and it occurs again and again.[73] I cannot answer the question as to how Jesus knew that it was in fact sin that was troubling the boy. The details given are not sufficient. It may be that Jesus knew him or those who had brought him, or that there was a common story about him. It may be that a mind like that of Jesus had telepathic powers above the normal. We shall look at the subject of telepathy later (p. 239). In face of the evidence for telepathy recently assembled, I find it hard to believe that Jesus did not know instantly what was passing in the mind of another. The phrase, "He, knowing their thoughts . . ." [74] must often have described the situation.

It is not unusual in psychological work to find that a sense of guilt causes paralysis. In the famous composite volume called *The Spirit*, edited by Canon Streeter,[75] Dr. Hadfield, the well-known psychiatrist of Harley Street, tells of a soldier completely paralysed because the desire to run away from the enemy was in acute conflict with the desire to do his duty. The paralysis—of course produced unconsciously—solved the problem, though at the expense of the patient's health. As a paralysed man, he could not be expected to go into battle, but at the same time the guilt of being a coward was assuaged by the fact that his reason was such a good one. He was paralysed. The paralysis thus ended the fear and relieved the guilt of duty undone. It is possible that, in the Biblical story we are studying, the boy's legs were paralysed and it is not fanciful to say that he could not "walk away" from his sins. They were with him day and night. All psychologists would recognise that it is possible that the unconscious part of his mind produced the paralysis so that he might win sympathy if his guilt were discovered. Everyone knows the kind of defence which runs, "You cannot punish me, I am ill already." Indeed, again and again repressed guilt produces a trauma as a satisfaction to the unconscious mind of the patient that he is being punished as he knows he really deserves to be.

[73] Cf. John 9:1 ff. "Rabbi, who did *sin*, this man or his parents, that he should be born blind?"

[74] Matthew 9:4, 12:25, Luke 5:22, 6:8, 9:47, 11:17, etc.

[75] Macmillan, 1919.

At any rate, when Jesus, with that authority of His, uttered the words of forgiveness, the boy rose, picked up his mat and departed. Thereafter the narrative concerns itself with the question of our Lord's authority to forgive sins, and this is beyond our subject at the moment.

We can imagine, however, that wrong had been committed, and fear—always produced by guilt—followed. It may be that the boy's mind was in a state of immense conflict which had drained him of energy. It is well known that if the mind can hand over its anguish to the body, and thus ease the strain upon itself, it will do so. It seems a simple matter for the unconscious mind, as it were, to say to the body, "I cannot bear this strain which the terror of guilt has brought upon me. You must take over. By producing a paralysis you can get the patient out of his immediate fear for his safety. You can win for him feelings of sympathy from others and you can maintain for him that sense of being punished which he deserves, and you can do all this at the same time." Here we have a characteristic picture of what has been called conversion hysteria. That is to say, the conversion into physical terms of a mental state that has become intolerable. No Rabbi had spoken to the boy of forgiveness. He may have deemed the illness as the will of God and representing the curse of God, and thereby made the boy's state worse than ever. But Jesus broke up the complex by that authoritative assertion of forgiveness which seems to have seeped right through the conscious and reached the unconscious and determining part of the boy's mind.

But I return to what, for our purpose, seems to me the most important part of the story, and that is the thrice-reiterated phrase, "Seeing *their* faith." In all the miracle stories in this section it would appear that a kind of psychological atmosphere, built up by His own love on the one hand, but dependent also on the trustful expectancy of at least a few "believers" on the other hand, made our Lord's healing power much higher in its potential than it otherwise would have been. In a later portion of this book I shall discuss the subject of healing through prayer, and here I think is part of the argument in favour of that practice. I can imagine Jesus, with the boy before Him, looking up to the hole in the temporary roof through which the patient has been let down, and seeing the faces of the four men who had brought him, eloquent with an intensity of longing, and shining with expectancy and trust. If it is true to say that Jesus could do in one place no mighty work because of the people's unbelief,[76] it is surely true to say that His power to heal was immensely increased by an attitude such as the four men showed. The presence of the crowd, given that atmosphere, would increase suggestibility, would increase the power of Christ's words to the paralysed boy.

If the foregoing description of what happened be accepted, then what is in some quarters called "absent treatment" is provided with some reasonable explanation, and one wonders whether the daughter of the Syro-Phœnician woman and the servant of the Centurion were influenced at deep mental levels by the expectancy kindled in the hearts of those dear to them when the latter besought Jesus for healing on their behalf.

When we come to discuss intercession for the sick, it will be necessary to take into account the phenomenon of telepathy, especially in relation to the theory that at very deep levels possibly all human minds are united. It may be that on such a level the mind of Christ actually made contact with the mind of absent patients, and that He was enabled to do so the more easily by reason of the faith of the friends of the patients. This does not mean that any miracles are "only telephathy," but it may be that the mechanism of telepathy played a part in conveying the energies of the mind of Jesus to the deep minds of absent patients. This does not explain away such energy, any more than the discovery of wires carrying an electric current, say from a battery to a lamp, explains away the necessity for the battery. In the stories in this category the divine power which Christ initiated seems to have been the therapeutic factor, but apparently it depended on some kind of psychic conditions or atmosphere created by the mental attitude of at least a few of those looking on. Prof. C. H. Dodd, of Cambridge writes, "It appears that the authority of Jesus penetrated to the subconscious depths of personality where so many of the more mysterious disorders of mind and body have their source." [77]

16. Jairus's Daughter:
Matthew 9:18-26, Mark 5:21-43, Luke 8:40-56.
This case is commonly regarded as a miracle of resurrection from the dead. It is strange that this should be so, since, although some held the view that the girl was dead, Jesus clearly did not.[78] He does, however, seem to have depended on the psychic atmosphere produced by the faith of others. He turns all doubters and wailers out of the

[77] *Man and His Nature*, p. 82.
[78] Matthew 9:18, cf. 9:24; Mark 5:35, cf. 5:39.

room.[79] He calls to the bedside His three most intimate friends, on whose faith He could count: Peter, James and John. He assures them that the girl is not dead, but asleep. He then energetically calls to her, using a pet name by which she may have been called by her mother— literally, "Get up, my little gazelle!" He then hands her to her mother with the simple words, "Give her something to eat," thus bringing matters down to humdrum, simple doing, so valuable to the nerves of both mother and patient, and keeping the latter from the curious eyes of the crowd outside.

17. *The Daughter of the Syro-Phœnician Woman:*
    Mark 7:24-30, Matthew 15:21-28.

In this third group the patient is not in co-operative contact with the healer. In this incident she is not even present. I have discussed this story in *It Happened in Palestine.* We may note the woman's faith and Christ's willingness to respond, the kind of co-operation seen in 15. A spiritual atmosphere of therapeutic potency is a common factor.

18. *The Centurion's Servant; The Nobleman's Son:*
    Matthew 8:5-13, Luke 7:1-10, John 4:46-54.

See 17 above. Probably three accounts of the same story, but in none are we told what was really wrong. Luke describes the patient as at the point of death. Matthew speaks of paralysis, and says the patient was in great pain. John says he was at the point of death and had had fever. Absent treatment in which prayer seems the potent factor is described later in this book (see p. 232 ff.). Absent treatment by hypnotic suggestion is vouched for by the Society for Psychical Research. In its *Proceedings,* Vol. III, p. 100, it is recorded that in 1885 a certain Dr. Biggs of Lima caused a cross to appear on a previously hypnotised subject every Friday for four months, though for the first three he was two thousand miles away from the patient. But in the case before us there is no evidence that Jesus had seen His patient at all. Yet, if the prayers of a thousand people can be proved to have availed for a patient in a London hospital—as I hold to be the case—it need occasion no great impediment to credulity to be told that our Lord could heal by believing in the patient's recovery, using, as He did so, the expectant trust of those who made the request and asserting the result forthwith.

Here again it may be that at an unconscious level of the mind our Lord's mind actually made contact with that of the patient. It is

[79] Mark 5:40.

attractive to think that in a sense Jesus did go to the patient as He promised to do (Matthew 8:7), and that the therapeutic forces in His mind flowed into the deep mind of the patient, achieving his recovery.

19. The Epileptic Boy:
Mark 9:14-29, Matthew 17:14-21, Luke 9:37-43.

This is a most fascinating case to the student both of the gospels and of psychology. I quote it under this category because the determinant therapeutic factor seems to have been the faith of the patient's father. The patient himself was not in what could be called co-operative contact. Jesus seemed to imply that it would be enough if the father believed that cure was possible; that if the father would only believe, the necessary "atmosphere" would be provided for Jesus to cure his son. The disciples were blamed for having insufficient faith to create this "atmosphere."

Much of the interest of the story turns on the sentence in Mark 9:29, "This kind can come out by nothing, save by prayer." (The best authorities and all modern translators omit the words "and fasting.")[80] Dr. C. C. Torrey, Professor of Semitic Languages in Yale University, translates the verse as follows: "Such as this cannot by any means be cast out, *not even by prayer.*" With Professor Craig, the New Testament scholar of Yale, I had a long interview with Professor Torrey about this verse when I was in America. If this translation is correct, it is very significant. Some scholars (Dr. Matthew Black, for instance) think that the illness may have been psychotic rather than merely epileptic, or a form of psychosis superimposed upon epilepsy. We may note that St. Matthew described the patient as "moonstruck," which the Revised Version translates by "epileptic." Dr. Black says,[81] "I would be inclined to agree with you that something more than epilepsy was involved here so far as the mind of Jesus is concerned."

If the illness were mainly psychotic, Dr. Torrey's translation of Mark 9:29 is significant, in that psychotic patients seem less frequently helped by intercession or so-called faith-healing. Prayer offered in their own presence or resorted to by themselves makes some mental patients much worse, increasing their sense of guilt, and sometimes pushing their trouble deeper into their minds. I am told that no cases

[80] "Certain codices add 'and fasting' but there is no doubt that this is one of those later additions to the text that stresses the value of asceticism." Major, Manson and Wright, *The Mission and Message of Jesus* (Dutton, 1938).

[81] In a letter to me from the University, Leeds, dated December 26, 1948.

of mental cure have been claimed at Lourdes, but I find this opinion of no value since mental cases are not welcomed as "official" patients. In the light of Dr. Torrey's translation, it may be that prayer is not the relevant way of co-operating with God for the healing of psychotic patients, but this does not mean that prayer for the mentally ill should be regarded as useless. The very thought that he is being prayed for, apart from clinically observable results, can give a mentally disturbed patient just the sense of security which he needs. Did our Lord's words mean that the cure of such a patient imposed some extraordinary strain upon Himself which the disciples, at their lower level of spiritual development, had not been able to meet?

I set forth the above as a possibility, but have consulted half a dozen scholars, asking them whether Dr. Torrey's translation, which he claims is based on the Aramaic, is sound. It is necessary to add that not one of them supports Dr. Torrey's translation, and some feel that though Dr. Torrey has sought to interpret the Aramaic text behind the gospels in an ingenious way which is often brilliant, his translation cannot be entirely satisfactory. Prof. the Rev. J. Alex. Findlay writes: "There is no subject on which experts differ more repeatedly and seriously than they do in this business of retranslation into Aramaic." [82]

Dr. T. W. Manson, of the University of Manchester, writes me,[83] "I have a note of Torrey's conjecture—it is nothing more—in my copy of the gospels, with the comment made when I first saw it, 'very improbable.' I should not modify that opinion except to add the words, 'quite arbitrary.' " My friend Dr. Norman Snaith agrees. Obviously, where the scholars differ one must not make too important a deduction from Dr. Torrey's translation. Dr. Matthew Black, who has published a work on the Aramaic behind the gospels, expresses doubt as to whether Mark 9:29 is really an original saying belonging to that story at all.

The case before us is usually regarded as one of epilepsy, but the latter is notoriously hard to diagnose. Various views on it are quoted in the chapter on Demon Possession.[84]

It is possible, as H. P. Newsholme has pointed out,[85] that the case before us was not epilepsy at all, but a repressed fear seeking relief in consciousness. The personality tries to keep it repressed, and to do so calls all the psychic energies of the body away from the tasks

[82] *British Weekly*, June 22, 1950.
[83] December 22, 1948.
[84] P. 89.
[85] *Health, Disease and Integration*, p. 131 (Allen and Unwin, 1929).

they normally perform. Thus there is no energy left to maintain thought, so the patient loses consciousness; there is none to maintain supervision of the visceral and muscular systems, then none to control the sphincters, then none to maintain respiration. It is only when death is at hand that the instinct of self-preservation calls the mind back to run the body, instead of repressing fear. With a loud yell the fears are sent back to the cellar, if one may put it thus, or called out altogether by an authority over life such as Christ possessed.

Note, in conclusion, in regard to this case, how carefully Jesus makes enquiry from the patient's father and learns as many details as possible of the case. This is what a modern doctor would do, but what a modern faith-healer seldom does.

. . . . .

My own conclusion, from a study of our Lord's miracles in the light of modern psychology, is that while the mental mechanisms which He used can sometimes be identified through our modern psychological knowledge, the miracles certainly cannot be regarded merely as psychotherapeutic treatments. We can learn much that is valuable for psychological techniques by watching Christ at work, but we shall not be able to do the things He did by becoming cleverer psychologists. It seems to me clear that something else is demanded: that we must live our lives on a higher plane and love men with a disciplined devotion akin to His own. Could not Christ's word to the disciples in the last-mentioned case be summarised thus: "Your prayer-life was not strong enough to cure this patient"?

The cures of Jesus—to answer dogmatically the questions which I asked earlier—are not a progressive development of the healing art as men knew it before Him. In the miracle stories we are in a different world. Psychological theories can illumine, but cannot explain, Christ's healing work. Much of it, I think, we must call unique if we call Him—as I do—unique. Ideally, however, He desired His Church to carry on His work. He commissioned His disciples to heal, and He worked through them and with them in His post-Resurrection life in the Spirit. If His Church will pay the price, and will both use the insights which modern psychology can give and the spiritual powers available through Christ, then immense energies can be released for the healing of men. We turn now, therefore, to estimate how far the early Church carried out her Lord's methods as well as His commands.

2

HEALING IN THE EARLY CHURCH

IN THIS CHAPTER we propose to discuss healing in the early Church from Christ's Ascension until the point at which healing became a negligible part of the Church's practice.

In the early years of the Christian era the healing of the body played an enormous part in Christian practice. It is not generally recognised that, in the pagan world at this time, getting treated for an illness was by no means easy. Doctors were scarce and lived in cities, where alone they could get enough patients to make a living. They usually charged huge fees. Consulting the deity, by incubation or as an oracle, involved heavy fees to the priests of the temple of the god. Indeed, it was just in this matter of healing that Christianity showed itself different from, and superior to, all other contemporary religions. In the latter the deity clearly preferred the healthy and the fit to be his worshippers. The sick were the prey of the powers of darkness and, until they were well again, could not please the gods. Celsus, the Platonist opponent of Christianity (born about A.D. 178), sneered at Christianity, as did some of his contemporaries, just because the Christian sick and sinful people were acceptable to their God, who would not cast them off, and who, indeed, had sent His Son to save them. Julian the Apostate as late as the fourth century charged the Christians with seeking to obtain followers by bribing the sick. "These impious Galileans," he said, "give themselves to this kind of humanity; as men allure children with a cake, so they . . . bring converts to their impiety. . . . Now we can see what it is that makes these Christians such powerful enemies of our gods. It is the brotherly love which they manifest towards strangers and towards the sick and the poor."

There was no doubt whatever about Christ's original mission to the sick and the sinful. "And He called unto Him the twelve, and began to send them forth by two and two; and He gave them authority over the unclean spirits. . . . And they went out, and preached that men should repent. And they cast out many devils and anointed with oil many that were sick and healed them." [1] St. Luke, the doctor, is very explicit: "Jesus gave them power and authority over all devils and to cure diseases. And He sent them forth to preach the kingdom of God, and to heal the sick. . . . And they departed, and went through the villages, preaching the gospel, and healing everywhere." [2] Later we have the appointment of the seventy others. "He sent them two and two before His face into every city and place whither He Himself was about to come. And He said unto them, 'Heal the sick that are therein and say unto them, The Kingdom of God is come nigh unto you.' . . . And the seventy returned with joy, saying, 'Lord even the devils are subject unto us in Thy name.' " [3]

When we reach the records called the Acts of the Apostles, we find that some of these acts are definitely cures of disease. "Many wonders and signs were done by the apostles." [4] "By the hands of the apostles were many signs and wonders wrought among the people." [5] "Stephen, full of grace and power, wrought great wonders and signs." [6] There is a more definite reference about Philip in Samaria, where we read, "Many with unclean spirits and many that were palsied and lame were healed." [7] And in Acts 8:13 we read that Simon "continued with Philip, and beholding signs and great miracles wrought, he was amazed." Paul and Barnabas speak of the signs and wonders God had wrought among the Gentiles by them,[8] and in 28:9, concerning the healing activities of Paul on the island of Malta, we read, "The rest also who had diseases in the island came and were cured." [9] The famous text

---

[1] Mark 6:7, 12-13, 9:18, 38 and Matthew 7:22 support the same conclusion.

[2] Luke 9:1-3.

[3] Luke 10:1, 9, 17.

[4] Acts 2:43.

[5] Acts 5:12.

[6] Acts 6:8.

[7] Acts 8:7.

[8] Acts 15:12.

[9] Hugh Frame, in *Wonderful Counsellor* (Harper, 1935), notes the two different Greek words used in this passage and translates as follows: "It came to pass that the father of Publius lay sick of a fever and of a bloody flux; to whom Paul entered in and prayed and laid his hands upon him and *healed* him. So when this was done, others also, which had diseases in the island, came and were *treated*."

71

in St. James's Epistle (5:14): "Is any among you sick? Let him call for the elders of the Church," is as clear a proof as words can supply that *all* cases of sickness were at this time the concern of the Church. The following, however, are more specific healing miracles. As in the case of those recorded in the gospels, I shall give brief notes on each. Every healing miracle recorded in the New Testament will then be included in our survey, even though space precludes a full discussion of them all.

1. *Peter and John Heal a Lame Man at the Gate Beautiful:*
   Acts 3:2-10.

Here the evidence is very unsatisfactory. The patient is described as a professional beggar. His begging is emphasised, his "faith" minimised. When Peter and John said, "Look at us," he "attended, expecting to get something from them" (Moffatt). Yet he seemed pleased at his cure (v. 8), and his cure brought such prestige to the Apostles that they were treated as gods. The forcefulness of Peter's method cleansed him of the neurotic desire to go on being ill in order to make a living by begging (cf. No. 3, p. 47). Note the treatment. Peter "fastened his eyes" on him, commanded the patient to look at him,

---

Frame claims that θεραπεύω used by Mark and Luke is a technical word, "which, used strictly, never meant to cure but to treat, to tend as a doctor tends his patients. Luke, who was a doctor, certainly used the word in its technical sense— 'Jesus laid His hands on every one of them and treated them.' "

The present writer felt unconvinced by Mr. Frame's comment and consulted Dr. Ryder Smith, a well-known authority. Dr. Smith tells me that "θεραπεύω" in secular Greek often means "cure," and that in the New Testament there seems to be no case where it cannot mean "cure," but there *are* some cases where it cannot mean "treat," and other examples again where the context implies that the treatment succeeded. Dr. Smith does not think one can deduce that the word was used for "treat" without implying either a cure or a failure. In a personal letter to the writer, he says, "What would be the point in mentioning such instances? If Jesus treated without healing, what a weapon for His enemies! " Dr. W. F. Howard agrees. On the other hand, Ramsay in *Luke the Physician*, and Dr. Joan Frayn in the *London Quarterly Review* (October, 1949), believe that θεραπεύω refers to treatment given, with or without healing, while 'ιάομαι is used to denote the fact of cure. The latter notes that θεραπεύω is only used when Jesus is present and performs the healing in person, while 'ιάομαι is used even if Jesus is not present. Nowhere is it claimed in the N.T. that Jesus cured all who were brought to Him, and the number of cases cannot be estimated partly through difficulties in translating these words. There is no evidence that Jesus never saw a patient more than once. J. Frayn says (*op. cit.*, p. 326), "It is more natural to suppose that except in a few cases, the sufferer was not cured upon his first encounter with Jesus." Micklem, however, says, "We have no good grounds for believing that any of the patients about whom the narratives tell us needed more than one 'treatment' to be healed" (*op. cit.*).

called on the name of Jesus, and "took him by the right hand and raised him up." Note the confidence and certainty of Peter, the man whose character had been weak and impulsive. Are the spiritual temperature of the healer, the quality of his communion with the living Christ, and the unity of spiritual strength of the fellowship to which he belongs, important factors in the power to heal in this way?

2. *Patients are Cured by the Shadow of Peter and Handkerchiefs Which Had Touched Paul:*
   Acts 5:15-16, cf. Acts 19:12.

This may have been the origin of cure by sacred relics so far as *Christian* healing is concerned. In the catacombs of Rome, where many martyrs and Christian saints were buried, Christian pilgrims came to worship at the tombs. They took oil from the lamps burning in the shrines and believed that it had therapeutic value. They touched the tombs and the bodies of the saints with handkerchiefs and carried the latter away as relics and used them to bring health to the sick. This practice was continued for seven centuries. In the eighth and ninth the bodies were moved to the basilicas in the city and the catacombs were deserted. Note that in India the shadow of Gandhi was thought to have healing power. The shadow of an outcaste, falling, say, on a Brahmin's food, is thought to be so potent for evil that the Brahmin sitting down to eat his rice will throw it away if the shadow of a pariah falls over it.[10] Note the story of the wounded soldier at Scutari kissing the shadow of Florence Nightingale as she went round the wards in the Crimean War. The story in Acts 5 suggests that the road of suggestibility was used, but an energy greater than psychological suggestion travelled along it: an energy of love and power belonging to a higher spiritual order.

3. *Ananias Restores the Sight of Saul:*
   Acts 9:17.

Paul's blindness, which followed his conversion, was, no doubt, of the hysterical type. In saying this no charge is being made against the Apostle. The word is so loosely used today that to call a person "hysterical" is to speak disparagingly of him. I am using the word "hysteria" here in its technical sense. It implies an emotional unbalance. A hysterical person makes an exaggerated emotional response to a

---

[10] This does not hold now in the great modernised cities, but it is still true in remote country villages.

stimulus, either in terms of feeling, which he often expresses un-restrainedly, or else in terms of a physical disability into which the emotion is converted. Hence we speak of "conversion hysteria." At this stage in his life Saul could not see where he was going. He could not "see ahead," as we say. As so often happens in the case of a hysterical person, the body took over part of the sense of strain, and the blindness was simply the psychosomatic symptom of his inability spiritually to see his way. As soon as he was made sure of the next step and was prepared to look, the word of Ananias was enough to make him see.

4. *Peter Heals Æneas of Palsy:*
   Acts 9:32-34.

The narrative suggests that Æneas was well known. If so, he would know the story of miraculous cures, and this would increase the power of suggestion. A man who had had what we call paralysis for eight years would normally find it impossible to rise up and make his bed, since his muscles would require time to recover tone. Conversion hysteria suggests a possible alternative. In those days it would unavoidably be classified as paralysis. At the same time, we cannot argue from the unusual to the impossible, or we make the very mistake I tried to guard against earlier. Hysterically caused contractures continued over a long period have, however, been known to clear up in a very short time, as suggested by the following case taken from "An American friend in whom we have entire confidence": "One of my neighbours, after lying on her back for *thirty years,* under the care of my own medical attendant, from unceasing nausea, called in a new physician. He gave her some homeopathic powders and assured her that she would be sick no longer. She *at once arose and resumed her active out-door occupations* after this long interval." [11]

5. *Paul Heals a Cripple at Lystra:*
   Acts 14:8-10.

Paul, "fastening his eyes upon him, and seeing that he had *faith to be made whole,* said with a loud voice, 'Stand upright on thy feet.' " Note the similarity to the confident treatment used by Peter at the Gate Beautiful. We need not ignore the fact that some cases of paralysis clear up, but the patient does not realise that the organic

[11] Italics mine. Quoted by F. W. H. Myers and A. T. Myers, M.D., F.R.C.P., in a paper on Mind Cure, etc., in the *Proceedings of the Society for Psychical Research,* June 1893.

situation is different and does not try to walk. He continues the habit of being lame to which he has become accustomed. Strong suggestion persuades the patient to make the effort, and he finds that the organic cause of lameness has cleared up and he can walk at once. In our cases at the City Temple Psychological Clinic this has happened. Recently one patient who came on crutches, walked out without them.

6. *Paul Exorcises a Maid with a Spirit of Divination:*
   Acts 16:16-18.

The girl seems not to have been in any sense a "patient," so I do not regard this as a case of "healing." She does not appear to have done anything but irritate St. Paul. After all, what she said was surely true: "These men are servants of the Most High God, which proclaim unto you the way of salvation." What finer testimony did St. Paul want? Perhaps he did not approve of fortune-tellers and soothsayers. Anyway, "casting out" the spirit which was alleged to possess her cost him dearly. Paul and Silas were thrown into prison, beaten with rods and put in the stocks, because her masters "saw that the hope of their gain was gone."

7. *Paul Heals Publius' Father of Fever and Dysentery:*
   Acts 28:7-8.

An interesting case of the "laying on of hands" which was successful, followed by attempts to cure others which were not successful. (See footnote on p. 71.) We have not enough evidence to make any useful comment.

Here, I think, are all the cases of which we have any record in the New Testament, where the immediate followers of Jesus exercised a healing ministry, and my task now is to ask whether they can be classified, as we classified the healing miracles of Jesus Himself (see p. 41). I repeat the classifications:

> *Classification I*, in which the psychological mechanism at work is suggestion—ability to make it powerfully on the part of the healer and ability to respond to it with "faith," or, as I would prefer to call it, *expectant trust*, on the part of the patient.
>
> *Classification II*, in which we note more than the mechanism of suggestion, viz. a more technical method *in which less faith*

75

is demanded of the patient and more skill required from the healer.

Classification III, absent treatment in which little—perhaps nothing at all—is demanded from the patient, but in which an "atmosphere" is required from his relatives, friends or the onlookers.

When we examine the facts we find that all the healing miracles of the Acts fall in Category I. That is to say, they are all instances of cures in which the mechanism of suggestion is the one that is used to bring about cure. There are no careful and lengthy treatments, such as we have noted in the case of the man amongst the tombs— a treatment which took even Christ some time—and there are no cures in the absence of the patient. There seems to be a simple challenge made by the healer to the "faith," or rather trustful expectancy, of the patient and the mention of the name and power of Jesus.

In my opinion, we now begin to glimpse a most important fact for our study: that, as we get further from the experience at Pentecost, there seems:

(i) a less powerful energy at work;
(ii) a uniform method of treatment[12] and one which made a much smaller demand on the healer;
(iii) a treatment becoming more and more similar to those practised by contemporary non-Christian exorcists.

When we pass on in the history of the early Church and leave behind us the Gospels and the Acts of the Apostles, we find these three factors are more and more obvious. If this conclusion be established in what follows—as I believe it is—it is a conclusion of the gravest significance for our understanding of healing through religion. Here is the evidence:

St. Justin Martyr (A.D. 100-165) speaks, in his dialogue with Trypho, of the gift of healing, and comments on the power of the name of Christ in exorcising demons, but extracts from his writings seem to

---

[12] The practice of incubation persisted, but I am not including it here because it was not a treatment by a healer. The patient carried out, in reference to a Christian Church, the same kind of practices as I described earlier in regard to Greek temples (see pp. 20-21). He prayed in the church and then slept there. Praying and fasting and disciplined devotion often brought him to a state of mind in which he dreamed or saw a vision of the saint after whom the church was named. Following this experience, not far removed from a self-hypnosis or trance, he often declared himself cured.

indicate that the Church was letting go the ministry of healing. St. Irenæus (A.D. 120-202) remarks that certain "heretics" "can neither confer sight on the blind, nor hearing on the deaf, nor chase away all sorts of demons. . . . Nor can they cure the weak or the lame or the paralytic, or those who are distressed in any other part of the body as has often been done in regard to bodily infirmity." [13] The quotation would seem to show that the early Christian Church was more successful than this, but there is little evidence of a ministry of healing of the quality described in the Acts.

Origen of Alexandria (A.D. 185-253) also speaks of the expulsion of evil spirits and the performance of many cures, and adds, "Some of them more remarkable than any that have existed amongst the Jews and these we ourselves have witnessed." But he notes also the cures that were occurring in the civilisations around him, and adds this most illuminating comment: "Such curative power is of itself neither good nor bad, but within the reach of godless as well as of honest folk. . . . The power of healing diseases is no evidence of anything specially divine," [14] though he asserts that the healing power of Christ was greater than that of Æsculapius.

In Tertullian (A.D. 155-230) we find a good deal of evidence that the healing work of the Church was carried on in his day, and he even speaks of the dead being brought back to life. After a study of the relevant passages, Miss Frost writes: "It can be seen that in his day there were very many attested cases of healing to be found, both amongst rich and poor, that they covered a wide range of physical and mental disease, including the raising of the dead, and that the methods used were holy anointing and prayer." [15]

St. Ambrose (A.D. 340-397), Bishop of Milan, records the incident of a blind man being healed through touching the border of the garments in which the bodies of two martyrs were discovered beneath the pavement of the church, and says, "Is not this like what we read in the gospel?" [16] as if it were unusual to find such a close similarity.

St. Chrysostom (A.D. 357-407), though he constantly speaks of miracles having ceased, refers to healing as being a matter of common occurrence,[17] and reports that commonly patients "put away their

[13] I owe this quotation to Percy Dearmer, *Body and Soul* (Dutton, 1923).

[14] *Contra Celsus*, Book 3, chapter 25. I owe this quotation to Harnack, *Expansion of Christianity*, Vol. I, p. 131 (Williams and Norgate, 1904).

[15] Evelyn Frost, *Christian Healing* (Morehouse, 1940).

[16] *The Letters of St. Ambrose*, No. 22, pp. 17-18.

[17] Percy Dearmer, *op. cit.*

diseases by anointing themselves with oil in faith," the oil being taken from the sanctuary lamps hanging before the altars of the churches.

St. Augustine (A.D. 354-430) records the fact that miracles were happening in his time, though he regarded them as very unusual and apparently becoming more and more rare. He writes as follows: "And for miracles there are some wrought *as yet*, partly by the sacraments, partly by the commemorations and prayers of the saints, but they are not so famous nor so glorious as the other; for the scriptures which were to be divulged in all places, have given lustre to the first in the knowledge of all nations, whereas the latter are only known unto the cities where they are done or some parts about them. And, generally, there are few that know them there, and many that do not, if the city be great; and when they relate them to others they are not believed so fully and so absolutely as the other, although they be declared by one Christian to another." [18]

St. Jerome (A.D. 340-420) as late as 390 reports the use of oil which had been blessed as being an "infallible cure" in cases of snake-bite.

St. Cuthbert (A.D. 635-687) used water and oil, both having been blessed, to cure disorders.

Officially the Church still practised healing. Harnack says that some bishops were trained physicians, and G. G. Dawson says that the seventeenth Canon of Hippolytus, dating from the fourth century, contains a prayer ordered to be said at the ordination of all bishops, "Grant him, O Lord, to loose all bonds of the iniquity of demons, the power to heal all diseases and quickly to beat down Satan under his feet." [19]

But even as early as the end of the third century a change had come over the Church. There was no longer a united solidarity in the fact of a pagan world. Division had weakened the Church's power. Slackness in discipline and lack of faith had lowered her spiritual potential. Controversy, heresy and apostasy had lowered the spiritual temperature. Individual Christians seemed able, here and there, to bring back health to the sick, but the power of the united fellowship had departed. Miss Frost writes: "From the time of Cyprian (200-258) onwards, the Church is involved in controversy. The problems of discipline and order and theological definition land the Church in a battle-field; the first freshness of the spirit-filled life of the previous centuries has passed away. No longer has the Church all things in common. No longer is it of one heart and mind. No longer is there the same degree of power in prayer. No longer is there a rich harvest

[18] St. Augustine, *The City of God*, Book 18, chapter 8. (Italics mine.)
[19] G. G. Dawson, *Healing; Pagan and Christian* (Macmillan, 1935).

of testimony to healing, although never has the power of healing the sick by prayer and sacrament been completely lost. However weak the Church, there are those who know the power of prevailing prayer and the joyful experience of the restoration of physical health by the power of the risen Christ." [20]

This evidence of the condition of the art of spiritual healing in the early Church has been discussed by many authorities, such as those already quoted, and especially by Harnack, and it is not necessary to linger in detail upon it, but from it we may draw some important conclusions. The fact is that in the first three centuries of our era the Church increasingly lost the gift of spiritual healing, and the following paragraphs summarise the situation.

1. The power of Jesus, due to His relationship with God, His trust in God, His communion with God and His love for men, availed mightily to heal others when He dwelt among men in the flesh. Love at a higher potential than the world has ever known, streamed from His personality in healing power, and He could convey to His disciples His power to heal in a way that surprised them, for He had welded them into a united fellowship which was, in a true sense, an extension of His own incarnation. The disciples were astonished at the power that was thus released. It spelt the integration of their own personalities and healing for others. "Even the devils are subject unto us in Thy Name," [21] they said. When Christ's physical presence was removed, the Holy Spirit continued the same work among the Apostles, but even for them the strain on faith was probably greater than when Christ was visibly present. When those who had known Jesus in the flesh passed away, faith diminished, love weakened and the potential of healing power was lowered.[22]

2. As Pentecost faded into past history, the fellowship began slowly to disintegrate; the faith of the Church in the power of the Holy Spirit, and that love for men which is derived only from love to God, or rather a sense of God's love for men, diminished to such an extent that we note an insidious difference in the nature of the healing

[20] Evelyn Frost, *op. cit.*

[21] Luke 10:17.

[22] No doubt some remained faithful and maintained the devotional discipline necessary to keeping their communion rich and strong. But the strain was there, and Christ recognised it in His words of praise for those who "have not seen and yet have believed."

technique. Less is demanded from the healer. More is demanded from the patient. The onus is more and more put on the patient to have "faith," but the power to call forth faith is sadly lowered.

Of course, it may be said that there can never be another Jesus, and it is too much to ask that the same success in healing should be demanded from Christ's followers as He Himself achieved. But while there is something in this, the modern Church cannot so easily escape the challenge. During the physical lifetime of our Lord the disciples were astonished at their own success, as we have seen. Further, Jesus not only healed, but commissioned *them* to heal, and even if *we* dare not point the finger, *He* blamed them when they failed.[23] Then, again, as we saw in regard to Peter and John at the Gate Beautiful, in the very earliest days after Pentecost they *had* the assets they needed for healing: an immense confidence, and a power which was sufficient to call out the necessary response from the patient.

The change in technique is sinister. Whereas Jesus always learnt the nature of the patient's trouble and, as we have seen, altered His methods accordingly, His followers became increasingly content to lay all the onus for recovery on the patient, and the formula "in the name of Jesus" became a charm instead of the means of conveying a power possessed by the healer through his communion with the living Christ and the strength of the undivided fellowship of the Church.

3. No doubt the followers of Christ put their preaching first, and in doing so they followed His own example. This fact may account for a lesser importance being given to healing, but it cannot be responsible for the great diminution in healing work as the years passed. If success had been maintained by healers, the prominence of healing would have been maintained by patients. One reluctantly writes down the sentence—Christ's followers found that their power to heal had gone. As St. Cyprian once wrote, "The sins of Christians have weakened the power of the Church," and though the early Church rationalised and pretended that God had "withdrawn the gift given to the Apostles," or that He no longer "willed to heal" and that Christians had "to bear their sufferings as Christ His Cross," and that illness was "a punishment for sin and must not be interfered with," yet the grim truth was as stated.

4. Methods of healing by material means were quickly coming in from Greek culture. This materialistic medicine made very little

[23] Mark 9:19, Matthew 17:17, Luke 9:41, "How long shall I bear with you?" etc.

demand, if any, on the faith of the patient and required no qualifications of a moral character from the healer. Further, though its
results were not so startling and apparently miraculous, they were
definite and could be relied on, and a method so reliable and which
demanded so little from either healer or patient was bound to have
an immediate and immense success. It is not surprising that non-physical
methods of healing were left behind when drugs were first used, and
their immediate, noticeable, predictable and unfailing results were
discovered by an excited community. Tatian made a protest against
this invasion of science. He regarded it as "not becoming to ascribe
to matter the relief of the sick," and he asserted, truly enough, that
confidence in drugs and material remedies detracted from "the pious
acknowledgment of God." Men did not behold God working *through*
the new methods. God was left out. The drugs acted whether or not
the patient believed in God. The insidious disease of materialistic
humanism set in. Man has discovered drugs! He can do without God.
"Glory to man in the highest; for man is the master of things."

5. Quack exorcists and healers who made no reference to the power
of Christ in the apostolic sense were getting results by the mere mention of His name.[24] Even Origen asserted, "The force of the exorcism
lies in the name of Jesus," and sometimes he seems to have taken a
pagan view of the matter and encouraged superstition. The power
of this superstition gradually displaced the power of faith and love.
The sale of holy relics abounded, though it was hotly opposed by the
authorities of the Church,[25] and even the devout followers of Jesus,
whose spiritual loyalties were unimpaired, must have been disturbed
to find that pagan exorcists could obtain similar results to themselves.

6. The conversion of the Roman Emperor, Constantine, to Christianity in *c.* A.D. 325, was a very doubtful gain to the cause of Christ.
It made it easy to be a "Christian." Christianity became the done
thing, the conventional profession of the ordinary citizen, the "State

[24] Deissmann quotes a long exorcism of Jewish origin into which a pagan
exorcist had introduced the name of Jesus in order to strengthen the prescription!
See *Light from the Ancient East,* p. 192 *et seq.* (1909).

[25] Optatus (Bishop of Milevi, *c.* 370) says that in Carthage a woman called
Lucilla formed the habit of carrying a relic and kissing it before she partook of the
Eucharist, and that both the Archdeacon and the Bishop reproved her for this
practice. The opposition to relics was overwhelmed by the popular demand for
them, but revived in the Middle Ages chiefly by St. Thomas Aquinas. He was very
cautious in the matter, and points out that the only justification for the veneration
of relics is that of reverence for the person to whom they belonged. He apparently
did not believe that the relics in themselves had healing power. See *Summa, III,*
25, art. 6.

religion." All the Court "darlings" were Christians now. The spineless sycophants who giggled out their fatuous days in the luxury of a Roman Court, the sleek, shrewd parasites who battened on her energy and power were "converted" overnight. After all, the Emperor had been worshipped as a god until yesterday. When Rome changed her emperors, men changed their gods. If the Emperor changed his god—well, what of it? The Court was accommodating. It was no new or hard demand to change one's god. If Christianity were the new fad, so be it. If to profess the new religion were the done thing, why complain? After all, what does one's religion matter? It makes no difference one way or the other. So men argued, and with as little concern as a modern bridge party of lazy, selfish women learns, in the midst of a hot afternoon, that hearts, not spades, are to be trumps for the next game, the supine world around the Emperor learned that Christianity, the religion Nero persecuted, was to be officially adopted. Rome yawned and accepted the fact that it was now a Christian State. There were no martyrdoms, no persecution, no risk of disfavour now. Rather the reverse. Self-seeking politicians wore the Name that was once hated, despised and feared. Loose women, miscalled Noblewomen, claimed a description, to earn which their nobler sisters had been thrown naked to the lions. The Name above every name had been written on the pale foreheads of the young knights of Christ who had died for Him by hundreds and ridden forth to declare to a sneering and indifferent world the good news of the Gospel. But that was over now. But it was a disaster that Constantine was "converted." He may have seen a cross in the sky, surrounded by the words, "*In hoc signo vinces*," but he produced a Christianity that left out the Cross, and might well have made a cushion its symbol. Christianity became, in fact, a polite veneer without power or beauty. Paganism remained, but now it was labelled Christianity as it is today. The religion of Christ has never recovered either, except for brief periods of revival, and without a nucleus of real saints—growing rarer in this country but increasing overseas—it could not have survived.

7. Both science, popularly understood, and faith, popularly understood, began to be misunderstood. Science is even now reckoned by many as an understanding of what are thought of as secular laws, and faith is often regarded as belief without evidence. Therefore, secular science always makes that kind of faith more difficult. And by the end of the third century science was becoming established and faith driven out. We shall comment on this important point later. Suffice it to say that if the laws of prayer, for example, had become explored and were as well known as the laws of science, as popularly understood,

faith would not be more difficult in the religious field than it is in astronomy.

When we add these reasons together, we see why the importance of religion in the field of healing diminished. It continued only in a few monasteries where real saints and united Christian communities maintained communion with the living Christ and therefore His power to heal.

We turn now to ask, "What were, in fact, the main healing *methods* of the early Church in the post-apostolic years?" The answer is prayer, anointing with oil and the laying on of hands. There is a famous passage in St. James's Epistle which, though it must have been responsible for much good, was also responsible for making all three methods into a magical rite instead of a sacrament. The passage is important enough to be quoted in full.

"Is any among you suffering? Let him pray. Is any cheerful? Let him sing praise. Is any among you sick? Let him call for the elders of the Church; and let them pray over him, anointing him with oil in the name of the Lord: and the prayer of faith shall save him that is sick, and the Lord shall raise him up; and if he have committed sins, it shall be forgiven him. Confess therefore your sins one to another, and pray one for another, that ye may be healed. The supplication of a righteous man availeth much in its working." [26]

Prayer for the sick has been carried on continuously in the Christian Church from our Lord's day to this, and we shall discuss it later. We know that the earliest disciples used oil. Mark says, "They cast out many devils and *anointed with oil* many that were sick, and healed them." [27] Jesus probably initiated or, at least, approved this method, and His brother James advised it. The use of oil was carried on by the early Church until the eighth century, but the expectation of recovered health by this means dwindled, as we shall see. Our evidence that it persisted is taken from the writings of the following saints, who refer to it approximately at the date which follows their names: Tertullian (200), Origen (249), Jerome (354), Partheneus (355), Martin (395), Ambrose (397), Chrysostom (407), Augustine (430), Bede (700). As for the laying on of hands, Jesus practised it, as we have seen, and the early Church carried on the practice. Ananias used it in the case of Saul,[28] and St. Paul in the case of Publius.[29] It is still practised, and will therefore be discussed in the section entitled, "Modern Methods of Healing Through Religion." [30]

[26] James 5:13-16.   [27] Mark 6:13.   [28] Acts 9:17.   [29] Acts 28:8.
[30] P. 129.

In the early post-apostolic years, the common practice would be for the patient, if he were well enough, to go to church. There the bishop would lay hands upon him and he would be anointed with oil. Sometimes the oil was taken from the lamp hanging before the altar in church; sometimes it was touched with some sacred relic and then applied; sometimes people brought their own oil, had it "blessed" by a bishop and applied by him, or sometimes by themselves. Many who attended church were carried there on beds or litters, and besides the laying on of hands and the anointing, they received the Holy Communion. Often, however, there were so many that the bishop could not lay hands on all of them or anoint them. He then extended his hands above them and blessed them. If the patient could not go to church, he called for the elders, who visited his home. No doubt their number increased the suggestibility of the patient at home, just as the large congregation would so increase it at church. Then, *in the quietness of his own home*, the patient made a confession of sin. In spite of the teaching of Jesus [31] and Paul,[32] the patient probably believed, and was allowed to believe, that his illness was a punishment for sin. The elders then authoritatively declared the forgiveness of God, and the patient no longer felt cut off from divine grace. After he had been anointed and prayer offered for him, he would often express the sense of feeling recovered, and, if so, he was encouraged to attribute his cure to God.

If the elders were men of God who regarded the use of oil sacramentally—that is, as the outward sign of the inward grace and power of God—if they had the love of God in their hearts and could convey it to the patient, and if their quality of life could call forth expectant trust from the patient, no doubt good often followed, though even then the criticism could be offered that the patient had to submit to the same treatment *whatever the nature of his malady*, and this, as we have seen, was not the way of Jesus. But the "ifs" above were rarely fulfilled, and a process that brought no cure could not last indefinitely as a mere ceremonial.

The student of healing cannot but be deeply interested by what, in fact, actually happened. Finding that, for the reasons given, treatments with oil—and sometimes with holy water [33]—had fewer and fewer successes so far as the recovery of health was concerned, the very meaning of the service of anointing with oil insidiously altered. The Council of Trent in 1549 taught that unction "blots out sins, if any remain to be expiated," and that it strengthens the soul of the patient

[31] See Luke 13:16—"bound by *Satan*."

[32] See II Corinthians 12:7—"a messenger of *Satan*."

[33] The holy water was to be drunk, not applied.

to bear more easily "the troubles and sufferings of disease, and more easily to resist the temptation of the demon lying in wait for his heel, and sometimes *when it is expedient for the soul's salvation, recovers bodily health.*" [34]

This is a very different emphasis, and shows the diminished expectation which reflects the lost confidence of the Church and the faith of her ministers. No doubt the importance of sin was emphasised in early days, and no doubt a patient worried by guilt and unabsolved could have little faith in healing. But in early days the emphasis of unction was on healing, not on forgiveness. The word "save" in the passage from St. James quoted above meant "to make whole." It is the same Greek word used in the story of the woman with a hæmorrhage, "Thy faith hath *made thee whole.*" [35] And the word "raise up," in the famous passage from St. James already quoted ("the Lord shall raise him up"), is the same as that used in the miracle described in Matt. 9:5, where our Lord said, "Arise and walk." There is no doubt at all that the early Scriptural value of unction and its main intention in the early Church was the healing of the body. When this became difficult because the faith of the Church was at a lower ebb, the meaning of unction slowly changed, and was relevant almost entirely to the forgiveness of sins.

We find that nowadays it is a rite for the final absolution of the dying, and it has been this since about A.D. 800, when Bishop Theodulph of Orleans issued a pastoral instruction "which reads like a manifesto issued with the object of introducing a new observance," in which unction is ordered to be administered as a preparation for death.[36] By 1151 unction had become one of the seven sacraments with only secondary reference to health, since it was used only for "one who seems to be in danger of death." In medieval times, indeed, a person who had received extreme unction was expected to die. If he recovered he had to live as one dead. He was not allowed to marry, nor was he allowed to alter his will. So far from its original intention had the practice of anointing with oil departed.

In 1718 an attempt was made to restore the practice of anointing with oil for recovery. This intention is expressed thus:

"The Anointing with Oil in the Office for the Sick is not only supported by Primitive Practice, but commanded by the Apostle Saint

[34] Italics mine.
[35] Mark 5:34.
[36] Father Puller, *The Anointing of the Sick in Scripture and Tradition,* pp. 193-194 (S.P.C.K., 1904).

James. It is not here administered by way of Extreme Unction, but in order to Recovery.

"Then the Priest shall take some sweet Oil of Olives; and putting it in a decent Vessel, he shall stand and consecrate it according to the form following: 'O Almighty Lord God, who hast taught us by thy Holy Apostle Saint James to anoint the sick with oil, that they may attain their bodily health, and render thanks unto thee, for the same; look down, we beseech thee, and bless and sanctify this thy creature of oil, the juice of the olive: grant that those who shall be anointed therewith may be delivered from all pains, troubles, and diseases both of body and mind, and from all the snares, temptations, and assaults of the powers of darkness, through our Lord Jesus Christ thy Son; who, with thee and the Holy Ghost, liveth and reigneth ever one God, world without end. Amen.' "

But this intention is sadly watered down in the Prayer Book used today, where we have, "Grant that he may take his sickness patiently and recover his bodily health, if it be Thy gracious will"!

It is little wonder that, as far as healing went, the process of unction dropped out. Men preferred to resort to some wonder-worker, or saint, or to use relics, or to trust themselves into the hands of a person with an alleged gift of healing, or to resort to drugs and medicine, finding that medicines have exactly the same result on the just as on the unjust; on the evil as on the good. And faith is hardly necessary.

There is no doubt that with the passing of the healing ministry of the Church, a factor of immense importance was lost. The Church no longer carried out a direct and indubitable command of her Lord. It is true that individuals carried it on in a sequence unbroken to the present day. Saints like St. Bernard of Clairvaux (1091-1153), St. Francis of Assisi (1182-1226), St. Catherine of Siena (1347-1380), Martin Luther (1483-1546), St. Francis Xavier (1506-1552), George Fox (1624-1691), John Wesley (1703-1791), Father Matthew (1790-1856), Pastor Blumhardt (1805-1880) and Father John of Cronstadt (1829-1908) were all healers who, with no psychological technique, but through their communion with Christ by His power, healed the sick. They bring the ancient tradition of the Church up to the reach of modern memory. It is true also that many hospitals were founded by the saints,[37] yet they soon lost their distinctively Christian function. The

[37] Though the fact is rarely recognised, hospitals were *not* first created by the Church. They were known in much earlier days in the older civilisations. In Ireland there was one opened in 300 B.C. and in India one in 252 B.C. In Mexico one is known to have flourished before Columbus. We have referred already to the

Kingdom of Heaven receded. Groups which lived on the high level of spiritual life attained by the apostolic band disintegrated. The energies of the Kingdom were untapped, and the Church more and more tended to leave the art of healing minds and bodies to the scientists, whose discoveries thrilled the popular imagination, and, who with little or no demand or faith, were able to bring about such amazing cures. The pressure of secular society was too much for the Church. If the Church had associated herself at this point with science and given it her support, at the same time maintaining her own spiritual temperature and opening the Kingdom of Heaven to all believers, who knows what miseries of disease and illness might have been warded off from subsequent generations? But although the Church officially associated herself with the healing of the sick, she disapproved of the method of the scientist. For some time the Church continued to work with cases of mental illness, and, though her methods were primitive, the gospel of love, the sense of sympathy and fellowship, and a good deal of what we should now call "occupational therapy," together with exorcism, which—whatever our views on demons—taught that derangement and nervous illness are not God's will and must be fought and overcome, helped enormously to cast out the morbid fear and the desolating feeling of being unloved which are at the root of so much neurotic and psychotic illness.

But, even in this realm, the healing ministry of the Church seemed sinking towards its collapse. The hour of the doctor had arrived. Recognising it, the doctor rightly refused to be hampered by an ecclesiastical obscurantism that tried to insist on a false theological explanation of the origin of disease, and which regarded medicine as an invasion of religion's sacred province and scientific treatments as an intolerable impiety.

Indeed, the doctor was dismissed without ceremony. Under ecclesiastical influence the Emperor Justinian (A.D. 527-567) closed the medical schools of Athens and Alexandria in 529. The disapproval of medicine on the part of the Church continued through the centuries, though here and there in monasteries medical manuscripts were copied. But the end came in 1215, when Pope Innocent the Third condemned

Temples of Æsculapius. Of course, these earlier hospitals depended on the pity of men. The upkeep of hospitals was first taught as a duty when the implications of Christianity were perceived. The word "hospital" first referred to the institutions where *hospitality* was given to pilgrims on the way to the Holy Land. Many were so ill through the rigours of the journey that they had to stay for long periods. Some were so infirm that they remained until their pilgrim friends called for them on the way back. These older, infirm folk stayed at annexes to the hospitals called "infirmaries."

surgery and all priests who practised it. In 1248 the dissection of the body was pronounced sacrilegious and the study of anatomy condemned. Progress in medicine required dissociation from the Church, and the two healing streams—both of God—divided, never to come together again seriously until today.

3

THE PROBLEM OF DEMON POSSESSION[1]

THE IDEA THAT the human personality can be possessed by demons is widely rejected today by the educated westerner as an outworn superstition. Evidences and symptoms which to the easterner of olden days pointed to demon possession are either dismissed as unfactual, or explained in terms of nervous or hysterical illness. The modern man has no place for demons, and when he reads, in a passage in St. Mark's Gospel to which I shall return, that a demon "dasheth him down: and he foameth and grindeth his teeth, and pineth away," [2] the modern man murmurs, "Epilepsy," with a superiority which, he assumes, leaves no questions unanswered. Even so careful a writer as Prof. C. H. Dodd seems to identify "demon possession" with "split personality or schizophrenia if you like the technical term." [3]

After certain observations in the East, wide enquiry from scholars, and such study as I have been able myself to pursue during the last thirty years, I am at least certain of one thing: that the matter cannot be treated in this light-hearted way. The problem is not solved nearly so easily as that.

In the first place, our Lord clearly spoke about demons, cast them out, commanded His followers to cast them out and appeared to believe that their power over men was the cause of certain illnesses.

I am aware, of course, of the way in which the modern man seeks to meet the difficulties. He alleges three possibilities:

1. That Jesus was the child of His age in such matters; that His real

---

[1] This chapter in shorter form appeared as an article in the *London Quarterly Review*, April, 1949, and is reproduced by permission of the Editor.

[2] Mark 9:18.

[3] *Man and His Nature*, p. 82 (Broadcast Talks—S.C.M.).

humanity involved the sharing of the contemporary ignorance of the true cause of symptoms commonly described as showing demon possession.

2. That although He knew better, He made a concession to the ignorance of those around Him, and it may be conceded forthwith that "He could not have spoken so effectively to His time if He had not spoken in its terms." [4]

3. That, like a wise mind-healer of today, He was unwilling to act or speak in a way which might make His patient suppose that He thought the patient's malady "mere imagination." The patient, then, as now, would lose that confidence and rapport which are so essential, unless the healer, for the time being at any rate, accepted the patient's own story of his troubles. If a healer of the mind, then or now, gave the patient the idea that in his—the healer's—opinion demons were the result merely of a disordered imagination, the patient would be driven farther into the dark recesses of his illness and be more difficult to heal. In the early stages of mental treatment, at least, the physician must not contradict unnecessarily the patient's interpretation of his symptoms.

Of these three points, the last has a compelling cogency, but it ceases to have much relevance when we remember that in some instances—that of the "epileptic" boy, for instance, in Mark 9:14:29—Jesus was not talking to the patient, but to his relatives and friends. There was little reason to assume the demonic origin of symptoms when talking to anyone other than the patient himself.

Let us now examine the other two points: that Jesus was Himself ignorant of the cause of certain diseases, or that He made a concession to the ignorance of His hearers.

Here two important points must be made.

The first is this most remarkable fact. If Jesus had been the child of His age in the matter of what we are pleased to call superstition, He would have shown the fact in other matters. In opposition, to this, He went out of His way to show His own *disbelief* in the popular demonology of His day, save in so far as *disease* caused by alleged demon possession was concerned. As Dr. William Menzies Alexander, a doctor of medicine as well as a student of divinity, showed some years ago,[5] "He commanded His disciples to gather up the fragments; thus

---

[4] C. H. Dodd, *The Authority of the Bible* (Harper, 1929).

[5] William Menzies Alexander, M.A., B.Sc., B.D., C.M., M.D., *Demonic Possession in the New Testament: Its Relations, Historical, Medical and Theological* (T. & T. Clark, 1902).

discouraging the idea that demons lurk in crumbs. He had no faith in the ceremonial washing of hands; so repelling the notion that spirits may rest on unwashed hands. He asked a draught of water from the woman of Samaria and thereafter entered the city; proving that He had no fear of drinking borrowed water and no belief in local shedim. He retired repeatedly to desert places and fasted in the wilderness; therein rejecting the popular conception that the waste is the special haunt of evil spirits. ... The association of demons with animals is in conflict with Christ's assertion of God's special care over them." In a word, apart from the context of disease and the possible exception of the storm on the lake,[6] Jesus makes no reference to devils, *though the conversations around Him were full of references to them.* He makes an exception when He talks about certain types of illness. Then He does seem to accept the view of demon possession. There is a significance in such a marked exception.

The second is that although the language used in Mark 7:32 ff. about the deaf stammerer implies a demon, and that in Luke 11:14 ff. expressly states that the patient was the victim of demon possession, Jesus does not speak as though He attributed *all* disease to demon possession. Matthew even differentiates between being possessed by a devil and being insane (4:24 and 17:15). σεληνιάζεσθαι is to be a lunatic. δαιμονίζεσαι is to be possessed of a devil.[7] In the stories of Jairus' daughter, the woman with the hæmorrhage in Mark 5:21 ff., the leper in Mark 1:40 and the paralytic in Mark 2, the man with the withered hand in Mark 3, and centurion's servant in Matthew 8:5, the blind man in Mark 8:22 and 10:46, there is no suggestion of demon possession.[8]

These two points seem to me to indicate that whatever Jesus thought about disease, He did not share the beliefs of His day in regard to

---

[6] Mark 4:39, "Be muzzled" is the same word used by Jesus in casting a "devil" out of a man (cf. Mark 1:25). The use of the word may be accounted for by (*a*) the possibility that Jesus believed in a storm demon, (*b*) that Jesus made a concession to the disciples who thus believed, (*c*) that Peter thought Jesus was exorcising the storm demon, and used this word when telling Mark the story, (*d*) that Mark introduced it himself, or (*e*)—the interpretation I favour—that Jesus addressed the words "Peace, be still," to the men in the boat, who spread panic and uselessness in a storm by giving expression to the "demon" of fear. See my *When the Lamp Flickers* (Abingdon-Cokesbury).

[7] See Hastings' *Dictionary of the Bible*, Vol. I.

[8] My authority here is Professor J. Alexander Findlay, of Didsbury College, Bristol.

demons. *Only in the context certain diseases, not all,* does He mention them.

Is it possible that our Lord believed in demon possession in certain cases and that He was right in so doing?

Turning to the case of the so-called epileptic boy in Mark 9:14 ff., it seems to me very arbitrary to declare that what is there called "demon possession" is epilepsy and nothing more. I have already quoted (pp. 66-68) a significant opinion on this point.

If anyone really understood what epilepsy was, my argument might break down, but no one appears to do so. Jung claims that it is a form of hysteria and, quoting Steffens, writes,[9] "We are forced to the conclusion that in essence hysteria and epilepsy are not fundamentally different, that the course of the disease is the same, but is manifest in a diverse form in different intensity and permanence."

Savill counters this view strongly[10]—and indicates differences between epilepsy and hysteria. Charcot coined the phrase "hystero-epilepsy," but Walshe—one of the greatest authorities on the matter—says [11] that such a label "has no place in clinical neurology and its use *betrays uncertainty in the mind of the observer as to what he is looking at,* together with a natural desire to be right whatever the nature of the attack."

H. P. Newsholme, Medical Officer of Health for Birmingham, believes that epilepsy is psychogenic, and quotes Rows and Bond (*Epilepsy,* p. 170, 1926) to the effect that it is caused by repressed fear.[12]

Beaumont defines epilepsy as "a chronic disorder in which there are recurrent attacks of unconsciousness, with or without convulsions, *due to no known cause.*" [13] Walshe defines it as "the expression of a sudden and transient disturbance of cerebral functions." [14] "Epilepsy," he adds, "has no morbid anatomy that has yet been discovered with the resources at our disposal." [15]

Post-mortem examinations do not reveal any satisfactory cause. The

---

[9] *Analytical Psychology.*

[10] *System of Clinical Medicine,* Ed. Warner (Williams & Wilkins, 1944).

[11] F. M. R. Walshe, *Diseases of the Nervous System* (Williams & Wilkins, 1947). (Italics mine.)

[12] *Health, Disease and Integration,* p. 131 (Allen and Unwin, 1929).

[13] *Medicine,* p. 329 (J. & A. Churchill, 1945). (Italics mine.)

[14] *Op. cit.,* p. 114.

[15] *Op. cit.,* p. 115.

appearance of the brain is "in general either entirely negative or of such indefinite character as cerebral congestion. . . . In chronic cases of epilepsy such lesions as atrophy and degeneration of brain substance or vascular disease are frequently met with, but are, as is well known, common to many other forms of nervous disease and are much more probably the consequences rather than the cause of epileptic attacks. . . . Practically all that can be said about the direct cause is that . . . uncontrolled discharges of energy, *devoid of any purposive action*, take place from time to time in an unusual manner." [16] It is known that hereditary disposition, inter-marriage of relatives, intemperance, sudden fright, prolonged mental anxiety, overwork and alcoholism are predisposing conditions, but they are not causes, and they are also predisposing conditions of other diseases.

Unless, then, one has decided *a priori* that demons do not exist and that devil possession is impossible, I would point out that, in spite of all our Western and modern superiority of scientific nomenclature, we are no farther on in our understanding of epilepsy by calling it "epilepsy," than by ascribing it to possession, since no one knows what epilepsy is, what causes it, what happens when an attack takes place, or what cures it.[17] The guess that this mysterious brainstorm is due to some form of possession cannot, at our present level of knowledge, be dislodged by modern science. My own "hunch" is that light will be thrown on epilepsy from research into psychic phenomena rather than from the physical or psychological fields.

The modern man says, "But there are no such things as demons." How does he know? As far as I know, educated members of all branches of the Christian Church believe in angels, whom the New Testament describes as "ministering spirits, sent forth to do service for the sake of them that shall inherit salvation" (Hebrews 1:14). Why should there not be in the universe personalities, other than man, opposed to God and working harm in man? What about the "world-rulers of this darkness" and "the spiritual hosts of wickedness in the heavenly places"? (Ephesians 6:12). Paul wrote of them, and Westcott thinks that the emphasis on "*our* wrestling is not against flesh and blood" implies a call to Christians to do battle with demons. In other words,

[16] Black's *Medical Dictionary*, p. 325. (Italics mine.)

[17] Pliny claimed that in his day it was cured by "the lights of a hare, salted, taken in white wine for thirty days, and the heart of a black he-ass to be eaten in the open air with bread on the first or second day of the moon." (*Historia Naturalis*, 28, sec. 63; I owe the quotation to Dr. Joan Frayn.) If anyone ever was thus cured the relevance of suggestion and hypnosis in healing epilepsy receives an interesting emphasis.

everyone has his own private battle with evil, bodily tendencies, but *we* are committed to warfare against demons. Archbishop Temple believed in them and in his Gifford Lectures wrote of Satan, "Personally I believe he exists and that a large share of that responsibility [for human evil] belongs to him and to subordinate evil spirits." [18] The Report of the Commission on Christian Doctrine says (p. 46), "To believe positively in the existence of spiritual beings other than human, is in no way irrational," and Stohr, in his *Handbook of Pastoral Medicine*, writes, "The possibilities of maladies caused by demoniacal influences must be accepted by every Catholic believer as a fact beyond doubt." See p. 426 (quoted from Oesterreich, p. 200). The only theory put forward as to how they came into existence seems to be that somehow in the creative process, freewill and evil-will have produced them. There is an old legend that intercourse took place between fallen angels and the daughters of men. We shrink from this ancient way of accounting for their existence, but I should like to put forward three pieces of evidence, which seem to me to make belief in that existence credible.[19] I will not claim more than that.

1. *Evidence from the Mission-field.*

In India, where I lived from 1916 to 1922 (save for two years on active service in Mesopotamia), I have talked with missionaries, who, in spite of a Western medical education, ascribed the symptoms of some patients to possession by some evil force—if not some evil intelligence, or, to use the phrase of one, a discarnate evil spirit. Miss Mildred Cable, whom I have met in England, is a quite impeccable witness, though, of course, like any other observer, her *interpretation* of her evidence may be faulty. In her book, *The Fulfilment of a Dream* [20] she writes as follows: "Our first woman patient in Hwochow Opium Refuge became interested in the Gospel, and on her return home destroyed her idols, reserving, however, the beautifully carved idol shrines which she placed in her son's room. Her daughter-in-law who occupied this room . . . desired to become a Christian and gave us a warm welcome whenever we could go to the house. About six months later we were fetched by special messenger from a village where we were staying, to see this girl who was said to be demon-possessed. We found crowds of men and women gathered to see and to hear. The girl was chanting the weird minor chant of the possessed, the

[18] William Temple, *Nature, Man and God,* p. 503 (Macmillan, 1934).

[19] An immense amount of evidence is put forward by Oesterreich in *Possession, Demoniacal and Other* (Kegan Paul, 1930).

[20] Pp. 118 f.

voice, as in every case I have seen, clearly distinguishing it from madness. This can perhaps best be described as a voice distinct from the personality of the one under possession. It seems as though the demon used the organs of speech of the victim for the conveyance of its own voice.[21] She refused to wear clothes or to take food, and by her violence terrorised the community. Immediately upon our entering the room with the Chinese woman evangelist, she ceased her chanting, and slowly pointed the finger at us, remaining in this posture for some time. As we knelt upon the 'kang' to pray, she trembled and said, 'The room is full of gwei; [22] as soon as one goes another comes." We endeavoured to calm her, and to make her join us in repeating the sentence, 'Lord Jesus, save me.' After considerable effort she succeeded in pronouncing these words, and when she had done so we commanded the demon to leave her, whereupon her body trembled and she sneezed some fifty or sixty times, then suddenly came to herself, asked for her clothes and some food, and seemingly perfectly well, resumed her work. So persistently did she reiterate the statement that the demons were using the idol shrines for a refuge, that during the proceedings just mentioned, her parents willingly handed over to the Christians present these valuable carvings, and joined with them in their destruction. From this time onwards she was perfectly well, a normal, healthy young woman." In the same book, Miss Cable gives another interesting piece of evidence: "A spirit may take temporary possession of a human body in order to find a means of expression for some important communication, and after delivering its message leave the person unconscious of that which has taken place. An instance of this occurred in a family with which I am intimate. The eldest daughter was married into a home where she received ill-treatment from her mother-in-law. For several years she was systematically underfed and overworked, and when at last she gave birth to a son, we all expected she would receive more consideration. The hatred of her mother-in-law was, however, in no degree abated, and when the child was a month old, she brought her daughter a meal of hot bread in which the girl detected an unusual

[21] Cf. the phenomenon of the "direct voice" in modern Spiritualism, where it is alleged the spirit uses ectoplasm from the medium to construct a larynx which can be used by the spirit.

[22] "Gwei" (in the accounts from Nevius) is the term used by the common people to indicate the being whose influence is feared by all, and who receives from every family some measure of propitiatory sacrifice. We read in the "Uli chao chuan" or "Divine Panorama" that "every living being, no matter whether it be a man or an animal, a bird or a quadruped, a gnat or a midge, a worm or an insect, having legs or not, few or many, all are called gwei after death." Quoted from E. R. Micklem, *op. cit.*

flavour which made her suspicious. She threw the remainder to the dog, and, before many hours had passed, both the unfortunate girl and the dog were dead. Her father was away from home at the time, the young men of the family meanwhile carrying on the work of the farm. A few days later her brothers and first cousins, strong, vigorous, young farmers, being together in the fields, a male cousin, aged twenty-two, suddenly exhibited symptoms of distress. He trembled and wept violently. Those with him, becoming alarmed at so unusual a sight, went to his assistance, intending to take him home. He wept, however, the more violently, saying, 'I am Lotus-bud; I was cruelly done to death. Why is there no redress?' Others of the family were by this time at hand, and recognising the effort made by the girl's spirit to communicate with her own people, whom she had had no opportunity of seeing in the hour of her death, spoke directly to her as though present. Telling her the facts of the case, they explained that all demands must remain in abeyance until her father's return, when the guilty party would be dealt with by her family whose feeling was in no sense one of indifference. In about an hour's time the attack passed, leaving the young man exhausted and unconscious of what had taken place."

Mr. E. R. Micklem,[23] commenting on this kind of evidence, says, "It is important not to ignore the fact that sober-minded observers find it hard to avoid the conclusion that the term demon-possession is an accurate description of the malady. Also, the peoples amongst whom the phenomena occur are in no sort of doubt that demon-possession differs from other diseases, and that demon-possession is demon-possession. Amongst them the thought in this respect is exactly parallel to that which we find in the New Testament. While there may be some haziness as to whether ordinary diseases are attributable to natural causes or demonic (and, indeed, some are definitely attributed to demonic), there is no question that these differ from 'demonic-possession' proper. Thus Nevius says, 'The Chinese of the present day (i.e. c. 1897) have separate and distinct names for idiocy, insanity, epilepsy and hysteria, which they ascribe to physical derangement as their immediate cause, regarding them as quite distinct from demon possession. They not infrequently ascribe diseases of various kinds to evil spirits, as their originating causes, considering them, however, as differing from the same diseases originating without the agency of spirits only in origin and not in nature, and as quite distinct from the abnormal conditions of

[23] To whom I am here indebted. See his *Miracles and the New Psychology* (Oxford University Press, 1922).

'possession.' " [24] Poulain in *Des Graces d'Oraison* distinguishes between possession by a demon and obsession.[25]

2. *Evidence from the Phenomenon of Multiple Personality.*

The famous case of "Sally Beauchamp" is relevant here. Dr. Morton Prince reported to the International Congress of Psychology in 1900 this case of multiple personality.[26] This case is so familiar that it can be referred to very briefly. Miss Beauchamp—called for convenience B1 —seemed at times to leave her body, which became controlled by B2, or B3, or B4, each a completely different personality and one which did things which B1 hated and of which she disapproved. So one personality went out into the country and collected some snakes and spiders and put them in a box and posted them to B1, the original Miss Beauchamp. When B1 opened the box "they ran out and about the room and nearly sent her into fits."

No séance was necessary to induce one of the other personalities to take charge of Miss Beauchamp. Nor when one did so was there any doubt that Miss Beauchamp's body and mind were controlled by an entity completely different from the controls of, perhaps, only a few moments earlier. The patient's character was completely different according to the control, and her health varied also. One control gave her average health, another poor health, a third exuberant vitality and radiant health. Dr. Morton Prince investigated the knowledge which one personality had of the others. For example, he claims to have established that B1 knew nothing of B2 or B3, but that B3, "knew all about the *acts* of B1 and B2, but the thoughts of B1 only." It is important to remember that though I have used the word "possession," Dr. Prince concluded that all the phenomena could be explained on the hypothesis that parts of Miss Beauchamp's personality were dissociated or split off, and had an existence of their own, but, like the fingers of the hand, were, while separated, joined at the wrist and received their vitality from that unity.[27]

[24] Waldmeier in his Autobiography (p. 64) speaks of his ten years in Abyssinia, and gives a striking account of so-called "possession" quoted in Hastings' *Dictionary of the Bible*, Vol. I. Livingstone ascribed to demon possession phenomena which he witnessed amongst the Zulus. See his *Missionary Travels* quoted by Andrew Lang in *The Making of Religion*, p. 135 (1900).

[25] A. Poulain, *Des Graces d'Oraison, Traite de theologie mystique*, 5th ed., Paris, 1906, p. 423. Ex Oesterreich, *Possession*, p. 77.

[26] See *Proceedings of the Society for Psychical Research*, Vol. 15, pp. 466 ff. This case is summarised and commented on in F. W. H. Myers, *Human Personality*, Vol. I, pp. 341 ff. and by McDougall in *S.P.R.*, Vol. 19.

[27] Morton Prince, *The Dissociation of a Personality* (Longmans).

On the other hand, McDougall writes,[28] "In the one type (of which Sally Beauchamp remains the best example) the co-conscious activities become so highly developed and organised that we cannot refuse to recognise them as the activities of an independent synthetic centre, a numerically distinct psychic being, which, owing to insufficient energy of control of the normally dominant centre, escape from its position of subordination and repression, and, not without a prolonged struggle, actualises and develops in an abnormal degree its latent capacities."

He adds, "The feature of the Beauchamp case which most strongly supports this view is, perhaps, the occurrence of sustained and seemingly very real conflicts of will between Sally and the alternating phases of Miss Beauchamp's personality; these, if we accept the description given (and it is perhaps permissible to say here that the good faith and scientific competence of the reporter of the case are indisputable), were no mere conflicts of opposed impulses, such as anyone of us might experience, but conflicts of the volitions of two organised and very different personalities. Another fact brought out clearly in the description of this case, one very difficult to reconcile with the view that Sally was merely a fragment of the normal personality, is that Sally's memory was more comprehensive than that of the normal personality, since it included all or most of the latter's experiences as well as her own. . . . Sally seemed to become directly aware of these thoughts and emotions (of Miss Beauchamp) and yet to know them as Miss Beauchamp's and to regard them in a very objective manner."

It is clear that Myers came to the conclusion that "the fact of possession has now been firmly established," though, of course, this is not evidence of "demon possession." Yet, if discarnate evil intelligences exist, and if "the fact of possession has now been firmly established," it would seem to be against the evidence to assert that demon possession is incredible.

Janet seems to accept demoniacal possession. See his *Nevroses et idees fixes* (I, 383-84).

3. *Evidence from Spiritualism.*

Some will turn this page with impatience, supposing that I am trying to prove one absurdity by the use of another. I am not here, however, claiming that Spiritualism is correct in the deductions it draws from the phenomena. I will, however, state that my own studies and experience compel me to say that Spiritualistic research has uncovered

[28] William McDougall, *Body and Mind.* Used with the permission of the Macmillan Company.

a whole mass of phenomena which remains when all possibilities of fraud have been excluded.

I have attended many séances, with different mediums, all of them reliable and incapable of conscious fraud. In one, in a slum house in Leeds, where with a doctor friend, I witnessed a séance, an uneducated coal-miner in a trance spoke for nearly an hour in the perfect diction of a deceased Oxford scholar who "controlled" him, using words quite certainly beyond his normal vocabulary and maintaining throughout an "Oxford accent" completely beyond his normal powers of imitation. In another, a most dignified and saintly lady spoke with a foreign accent and expressed views quite outside the normal scope of her interests. In yet another, the medium was "controlled" in turn by a London news-boy, an Anglican clergyman, a middle-class lady and a street-corner flower-seller in a way which is capable of various interpretations but not, I am convinced, of fraud.

I am not here putting forward any plea for the acceptance of the Spiritualist hypothesis. I am introducing into my argument at this point evidence that human beings can apparently, in certain circumstances, be controlled by what appear to be other intelligences. It seems as credible to me to believe in "other intelligences" as to believe that the mediums were controlled only by their own unconsciouses. If the latter, why the completely different voices?

My own conclusions, then, about demon possession are as follows:

1. That from earliest times until modern times much disease has been *wrongly* attributed to demon possession. Modern psychology is becoming increasingly aware of the result, in terms of disease, of such emotions as pride, hate, fear, resentment, malice, jealousy and worry, especially when these emotions are harboured in the deep mind over a long period. These are "demons" indeed, and it may be that when we know more, all cases, ancient and modern, attributed to "demon pos-session" will be found to be within the area of psychosomatic disease.

2. That it is highly doubtful whether *all* cases attributed in the Bible and on the mission-field to demon possession can be completely ex-plained in terms of psychiatric nomenclature. The experiences on the mission-field may seem strange to our Western thought, but to me they seem close to the experiences related in the Bible. There, human nature is not an impenetrable entity. The individual is not isolated from the race, nor the entity called "humanity" isolated from the universe. Human nature is not essentially evil, but it has "fallen," in that it has been invaded by, and has yielded to, evil powers, which are not mere absences of good, but "wills" which are hostile to God's will and which are the spawn of the Devil, who has seized control of man's will and

turned him against God. In the Bible even "sin" and "death" are objective forces hostile to God. Nowhere do we find any Biblical encouragement for linking individual suffering with individual sin. In one sense there is such a thing as "the sin of the world," a "set-up" into which we are all born and which affects us all in terms of sin and of suffering. This itself is the result of evil wills. Why should their invasion of men's spirits seem incredible?

It is significant that the Anglican Church still maintains its exorcists. In the time of Origen (b. A.D. 185) the exorcist ranked third in the grade of orders of clergy. His method sounds strange today. Making the sign of the cross on the patient's head, he made the latter kneel, if able to do so, and sprinkled his brow with holy water. Then the exorcist asked the devil his name and adjured him, by the holy mysteries of the Christian religion, not to afflict the patient any further. Laying his hands on the patient's head, he said, "I exorcise thee, unclean spirit, in the name of Jesus Christ; tremble, O Satan, thou enemy of the faith, thou foe of mankind who hast brought death into the world, who hast deprived men of life and hast rebelled against justice, thou seducer of mankind, thou root of all evil, thou source of avarice, discord and envy!" "The act of Christian exorcism is twofold—it does not end with the 'rebuke' and expulsion of the demon, but is completed by the invocation of the Holy Spirit to enter the temple of God vacated by the evil spirit." [29]

3. That belief in the possibility of demon-possession is not incompatible with the tenets of the Christian religion or contradicted by any reputable scientific research.

It is interesting here to recall that John Wesley [30] often ascribed phenomena which accompanied his preaching to demon-possession. Professor Findlay [31] makes two interesting observations. The first is that Wesley mentions demon possession much more in the early days of his field-preaching than in later years. Demon-possession is also mentioned much more in the early pages of St. Mark than in the records of Christ's later ministry. It is not mentioned at all in the fourth gospel. Does the excitement of the early stages of a religious revival bring into activity these symptoms? Is it because the "demon" (the unconscious) fights against new-birth?

The second is that demon-possession seems localised; more common in some places than others. The fourth gospel deals largely with the

[29] Evelyn Frost, *Christian Healing* (Morehouse, 1940).
[30] Wesley's *Journal* for October 25, 1739, and subsequent days.
[31] In the *British Weekly*, December 23, 1948.

Judæan ministry, and demon-possession seems unknown. The Synoptists give instances which are all confined to the north of Palestine. There is one case at Tyre, which was outside Palestine altogether (Mark 7:24 and Matthew 15:21). In the Acts we hear of it in Samaria (8:7) and at Ephesus (19:12).

4. Finally, I desire to make a comparison with poltergeist phenomenon. If I hear strange noises in a room, I seek to understand their cause, and the last hypothesis to which I am driven is that they proceed from poltergeists.

Yet, having examined the evidence and listened to the most convincing accounts of two of my friends, both witnesses of the phenomena, one an English judge and the other a Scottish solicitor, I cannot deny that they occur.

Similarly, the last hypothesis to which I am driven in accounting for illness of mind and body is the hypothesis of demon-possession. Yet, in view of what is written above, I cannot rule it out as impossible, especially in regard to the far-off days of the Biblical narrative and the far-off places of the world where the power of Christ has yet had little chance of overcoming His enemies.[32]

[32] This chapter was written before the publication of *Essentials of Demonology —A Study of Jewish and Christian Doctrine, Its Origin and Developments*, by Edward Langton, D.D. (Epworth Press, 1949). Having read it, I adhere to my view as expressed above though it differs from Dr. Langton's. He says (p. 244), "Discarding as we feel we must, theories of accommodation as insufficient and invalid, we can only conclude that Jesus accepted, without serious modification, the popular belief in Satan, and the demons which was current in His time. Such an acceptance by Jesus does not prove that these popular beliefs correspond with reality."

EARLIER METHODS OF HEALING THROUGH PSYCHOLOGY

1

MESMERISM

WE SAW IN the Introduction that as far back as the Palæolithic Age pieces of human skull were used as amulets. No doubt the patient sometimes recovered, or the practice would not have been recorded. If he did, he was cured by psychology. Just as religion had its origin partly in what we shall call superstition, so psychology had its origin partly in magic.

Through the long centuries we note the development of magic. Even Paracelsus of Basle (1493-1541) was in our sense, a magician rather than a scientist, though he advocated scientific research and publicly hurled into a student's bonfire the five-volume medical canon of Avicenna, whose authority in Persia equalled that of Hippocrates in Greece. If he returned, he would have great vogue, even if he continued his old methods. He believed that nothing could be cured without a knowledge of the stars. Jupiter governed the liver, Saturn the lungs, Mars the bile and Venus the abdomen. We still use words like "jovial," "saturnine," "and martial." There are astrologers in London today, and it may be that even now we shall find a grain of truth in the old theories woven in and out of the fabric of man's integration, so often seemingly influenced by non-physical factors.

I also referred in the Introduction to the temples of Æsculapius and the incubation treatments that went on there. Galen, the famous physician (A.D. 130-200) himself a Greek, but private physician to the Roman Emperor, Marcus Aurelius, commented on the treatments thus: "We have proof that many serious illnesses can be cured solely by the shock administered to the mind." If that is true, then that is healing through psychology, and an interesting comment on electric and insulin shock therapy.

In 380 B.C., Plato, in the *Republic*, recognised the influence of the

105

mind and the emotions upon physical health. Socrates related to Plato the story of a charm which the former had obtained from a physician, who, in giving it to him, had advised him thus: "The cure of a part should not be attempted without the treatment of the whole, and also that no attempt should be made to cure the body without the soul, and therefore if the head and body are to be well, you must begin by curing the mind: that is the first thing. And he who taught me the cure of the charm added a special direction: 'Let no one persuade you to cure the head until he has given you his soul to be cured. For this,' he added, 'is the great error of our day in the treatment of the human body that physicians separate the soul from the body.' " [1] This is a pointer to a method of healing through psychology, and the astonishing thing is that, apart from religious methods, no therapeutic technique of healing the sick by non-physical means developed until we get to the earliest methods and using suggestion in the discovery of what was called "animal magnetism." [2]

Baptista Porta in (about) 1600 used a magnet which he claimed had healing properties. Probably suggestion and hypnotism more correctly described the secret of his success. His ardour was dampened by the Roman Curia, which accused him of being a magician in league with evil spirits, and stopped him from practising medicine at all. Von Helmont, Kircher (a Jesuit priest), Maxwell (a Scottish physician), James Graham, with his £50 treatment of the sick with magnetic vapours, and later (1771) Father Hell, who applied magnetised plates to the body, all used what they called magnetism, but the important name for us is that of Mesmer, 1733-1815. Mesmer was born in a little village on the shores of Lake Constance. His studies and methods form the bridge between the magical methods before him and the scientific psychological methods which followed him.

Even Mesmer believed in the action of the planets on the body, but that they did so through the instrumentality of a universal fluid which he himself described as "a kind of impalpable and invisible gas in which all bodies are immersed." This he called "the fluid of animal magnetism." Mesmer believed that this fluid could be controlled by the will, by the use of magnets and by "passes" made by Mesmer's hands, still popularly called Mesmerism. This fluid, it was believed, could be concentrated at the area of lesion or pain, and bring health.

[1] Plato, *Charmides*, 156.

[2] I do not include as a technical psychological method the advice of a medieval physician to tie a sow close to the patient's bed, and the similar remedies described by Janet! See *Psychological Healing*, Vol. I (Macmillan, 1925).

We must not linger here too long, for our main purpose is not historical, and the story of Mesmer has been told by others,[3] but in view of our subsequent critical consideration of suggestion, I cannot refrain from a brief description of Mesmer's main method.

We are to imagine a large, luxurious *salon* hung with mirrors, furnished with beautiful curtains, filled with exotic flowers, illumined by stained-glass windows, perfumed with incense burning in beautiful antique bowls. "Æolian harps sighed melodious music from distant chambers, while sometimes a sweet, female voice, from above or below, stole softly upon the mysterious silence." In the centre of a room is a circular oak tub, the bottom filled with powdered glass and iron filings. On this lay bottles immersed in water, some with necks to the centre of the tub and others pointing to its circumference. Covering the tub was a lid pierced by many holes through which had been passed iron rods, bent so as to be able to be grasped by patients grouped about the tub. In absolute silence the patients sat in several rows. They held one another's hands if the latter were not engaged by holding one of the iron rods. If a rod could be applied to the ailing spot, so much the better.

Then, with appropriate music, Mesmer appeared in a lilac robe of finest silk. In his hand was a long, iron wand, powerfully magnetised. He passed slowly among the patients, fixing them with his staring eyes, making passes with his hands and touching them with his wand. Many, we are told, recovered. Many passed into convulsive states or delirium, and these symptoms were welcomed and called "the crisis."

But instead of scientific research which might have led somewhere, Mesmer propounded a cast-iron theory and tried to push all the facts into it—the opposite of the scientific method. He magnetised water and sold it to patients. He magnetised their clothes. They ate from magnetised plates and breathed a magnetised atmosphere. A patient had only to carry some magnetised charm and he could not fall ill. In a word, Mesmer, instead of taking the forward path of science, took a retrogressive path back towards magic, incantation and spell. Money flowed in, and his name was honoured for a time, but when challenged by scientific authority he prepared a paper full of false assumptions and unproved claims. The Academy of Medicine and the Academy of

[3] See Janet, *Psychological Healing*, Vol. I.
    Marcus Gregory, *op. cit.*
    G. G. Dawson, *op. cit.*
    Mackay, *Extraordinary Popular Delusions*, Vol. I, pp. 278 ff.
    Binet and Fere, *Animal Magnetism.*

Sciences appointed commissions of enquiry.[4] Both rejected his claims, asserted that the phenomena included nothing incapable of an alternative explanation and dismissed Mesmer as a charlatan. Yet his judges did not omit to profit intellectully by his work. They held the view that his cures were due to the mental suggestion which he exerted over his patients. "It is impossible not to admit," they wrote, "that some great force acts upon and masters the patients and that this force appears to reside in the magnetiser."

This was a most important discovery, and if Mesmer had gone on from that point and reconsidered the possible nature of the force he had found, the cause of healing through psychology would have been advanced. But he did not do so. "Monsieur Court de Gébelin," wrote one paper, "has just died, cured by animal magnetism." A play made fun of his theories. Comic songs ridiculed his methods. Public opinion turned against him. Finally, in a rage of anger, frustration and mortification, Mesmer "shook the dust of France off his feet." [5] Later, he wanted to return, but his place had been filled. His reign was over, his cause discredited, his power gone.

Yet enquiries persisted. The Marquis de Puységur on his Buzancy estate "magnetised" his patients and produced in some—especially in a young shepherd called Victor—a state of somnambulism and acute suggestibility, familiar now to all students of hypnotic phenomena.

Dr. Petetin of Lyons and Deleuze, a French naturalist, continued to experiment. "The magnetic fluid," said the latter is his *Histoire critique de magnetisme animal*,[6] "is an emanation from ourselves guided by the will. . . . He who magnetises for curative purposes is aiding with his own life the failing life of the sufferer."

At this point a new form of treatment began. A somnambulist, in the state described above, was brought into contact with a patient and invited to suggest what should be done. Whereupon he would prescribe astounding remedies. A certain Dr. Clapier reported that in two months he had effected sixty perfect cures, thanks to the advice of his somnambulist.

Enthusiasm returned, and by 1840 reached the height and intensity of a religious revival. From Portugal, from India, from Germany, and especially from France, came reports of healings which are relevant to our study because they describe the power of the mind over the body. The story of healing through Psychology moves forward.

[4] Lavoisier was a member of the latter.
[5] I owe these facts to Janet, *op. cit.*, Vol. I.
[6] Two-volume work published in 1813.

2

HYPNOTISM

AT THIS POINT the significant name is James Braid. Braid was a Manchester doctor of sceptical temperament and really scientific outlook. Braid found in 1841 that by fixing his eyes on those of a relaxed patient, or getting the patient to gaze at some bright object until the eye-muscles tired, he could induce a condition that looked like sleep. It is to Braid we owe the word "hypnotism" (ὕπνος = sleep). He further discovered that in this state of induced sleep the patient exhibited characteristics that made his sleep different from the natural type. He was still *en rapport* with the hypnotist, was extremely suggestible to anything the hypnotist said, but oblivious of all else. Ideas suggested to the patient by the hypnotist, if reasonable, were carried out. Ideas suggested by another person were apparently unheard, unless the hypnotist told the patient to hear and heed them. If paralysis of a certain limb were suggested to the patient, then he appeared paralysed in that limb, but, more usefully, symptoms of diseases from which he was suffering when he came to Braid were diminished and often removed during the hypnotic state.

Braid, of course, was delighted. "Animal magnetism" was not necessary. The elaborate apparatus of Mesmer could now be consigned to the lumber room. Braid, with the bright end of his lancet case, could bring a patient into the necessary condition. Braid read a paper at the British Medical Association's Annual Congress in 1841 in which he claimed to have cured, under hypnosis, many diseases like rheumatism, paralysis, torticollis, migraine and even epilepsy. The British Medical Association refused to be impressed. Yet Braid, a true scientist, went on with his experiments. He did not understand the hypnotic condition. It is not really understood now. But he had exploded the theory of "animal magnetism." He asserted that the hypnotic state was not due to personal powers of his own or some emanation from his own personality.

Janet, in his monumental work, is reluctant to give due credit to Braid. He magnifies Braid's debt to Lafontaine and says that "Braid wandered off into phrenology and cranioscopy and believed that he was able to stimulate this or that moral faculty by rubbing this or that bump in the patient's head." [1]

Truly, for a time hypnotism was under a cloud, and was recalled to scientific interest by Charcôt and Bernheim. It is not within the scope of this book to tell fully the story of these two scientists, or of the quarrel that arose between them and which raged for many years.

Charcôt, at the Salpêtrière (originally an asylum for prostitutes and insane women), had the most astounding success with hypnotism. His reputation as a neurologist made hypnotism a reputable field for investigation. With his fascinating personality—an important factor—he impressed even the Academy of Medicine, and on February 13, 1882, hypnotic treatment became a legitimate medical method of therapy in France. This is a most notable milestone as we trace early psychological methods of healing.

Much that Charcôt claimed is now thought unsound. His three stages of lethargy, catalepsy and somnambulism were successfully criticised by Bernheim, who, in 1884, started the Nancy School in opposition to Charcôt's at the Salpêtrière. Bernheim was associated with Liébault, who opened a clinic at Nancy in 1864 and practised for more than twenty years.

By about the year 1890 hypnotic treatment had a wide vogue all over the civilised world. We read of Braid and Lloyd Tuckey in England, Esdaile in India, Sturgis, Warren, Flower, Osgood Mason, Boris Sidis and Morton Prince in America, Charcôt, Bernheim, Liébault in France, Forel and Du Bois [2] in Switzerland, Moll, Grossmann and Schultz in Germany, Delboeuf in Belgium, De Jong and Van Renterghem in Holland, Wetterstrand in Sweden, Bianchi and Fianzi in Italy, Carophilis in Greece, Strogentzy, Tokarsky and Bechterew in Russia, and the mere list of names and countries shows how widespread the knowledge and use of hypnotism had become.

Since our argument has developed to the point where we show that hypnotic suggestion was, in 1890, the main method of psychological

[1] *Op. cit.*, Vol. I.

[2] Du Bois deserves a footnote in this list because, as far as I can discover, he was the first to institute what I call "therapeutic conversations" with patients. He called them "moral orthopedics." He used hypnotism, but would seek, in heart to heart talks with patients, to help them orientate their lives better, discover the psychological origin of their symptoms and discuss with them their pattern of life. I think of Du Bois as the father of up-to-date pastoral practice.

healing, it would seem appropriate to describe it more fully. What is suggestion? What is hypnosis? How is hypnosis induced? What are its uses and dangers? What is our critical appreciation of it?

Behind all the discoveries of psychologists since Mesmer, behind the healing miracles in Classification I (p. 41), lies one of the great truths about the mind. It may be expressed as follows: If the mind really accepts an idea as true, and if the idea is reasonable, it tends by means of unconscious processes, to actualise itself or come true. To bring about the entry of an integrating idea into a mind, so that the idea may "come true" and bring health, is called treatment by suggestion. "I will define suggestion," said Bernheim, "as the action by which an idea is introduced into the brain and accepted by it." The definition is good as far as it goes, but to me it seems to lack one important factor. I should like to add the words, "without regard to evidence or proof, or even reasonable grounds." If I am trying to get a person to accept an idea and I proceed to give him ten reasons for believing it is true, I may arouse those very critical and reasoning qualities in the mind which are likely to defeat the potency of the suggestion and which, therefore, I want to remain quiescent. Janet's definition is too complicated to be a useful one: "Suggestion is a peculiar reaction to certain perceptions; the reaction consists in the activation, more or less complete, of the tendency aroused by the suggestion, in the absence of a completion of the activation by the collaboration of the remainder of the personality." [3] Here may be added another great truth about the mind. The power of the mind over the body is so immense that it is hard to say where the line of limitation runs, or what cannot be achieved in the body so long as the necessary organic apparatus is there, and not materially damaged to such an extent that the mind has no machinery, as it were, to use. Therefore, if the mind really accepts, and believes through its whole depths, an idea suggested to it that pain is passing, that disease is being overcome, that health is returning, and the ideas are *reasonable*, then, in ways that seem miraculous to those who are not students of the phenomena, the mind gets its orders carried out in the body, and health is restored.

I use the word "reasonable" because I am not supposing that suggestion could grow another leg in an hour when a bomb or shell had blown off the limb, or make a man see whose optic nerve had been destroyed. Even the mind cannot work without apparatus, though it can wonderfully use impaired apparatus, and even utilise apparatus constructed for other purposes.

[3] *Psychological Healing*, Vol. I.

I emphasise the word "if" above, because the mind does not normally receive and fully accept without question any idea presented to it. We all have a critical apparatus which in an earlier book [4] I have likened to a policeman on traffic duty. Some traffic he halts and turns back. Some he allows to pass only with reluctance. Some he unhesitatingly signals to come through. So, when ideas are presented to the mind, the critical apparatus, or policeman, rejects some, lets others through with only half-hearted approval and welcomes some. I can imagine that a cyclist approaching a town might more easily elude the vigilance of a policeman if the attempt to do so were made in the half-light of early dawn or the dusk of evening. Here also the parable illumines a truth. The early morning, when we waken, and the evening, just as we drop off to sleep, are the best times for suggestions to be made to the mind. I can imagine that a policeman on duty who refuses, say, a cyclist, the first time, might ultimately let him into the town if he presented himself again and again. So, if an idea is repeated again and again, the critical policeman is more likely eventually to allow it into the mind. Hence the value of repeating suggestions over and over again. Hence the value of the advertisement repeated on hoarding, in 'bus, tube and train. The body will carry out the behests of the mind if the ideas of the latter are both accepted and reasonable. Suggestion, then, is the art of conveying an idea to the mind of another person in such a way as to make him entirely accept it, apart altogether from the *evidence* of his reason.

Many writers distinguish between hetero-suggestion and auto-suggestion, and the distinction has value. The first is suggestion offered by another, and the second is suggestion offered by oneself. I have not laboured the distinction because, however valuable the suggestion offered to one's mind by another, yet the suggestion must be accepted by the self before it can be effective. In other words, hetero-suggestion, to be of value, must become auto-suggestion.

Hypnosis is a condition of increased suggestibility. It can be described as a dissociation, though suggestion and dissociation are not identifiable. "Suggestibility can be increased in all sorts of ways independently of dissociation." [5] To this point of view we shall return.

[4] *Psychology in Service of the Soul* (Macmillan, 1930).

[5] See William Brown, D.M., D.Sc., *Psychological Methods of Healing*, p. 112 (University of London Press, 1938). Compare also Lloyd Tuckey, *Treatment by Hypnotism and Suggestion* (Putnam, 1910). He defines hypnosis as "a condition of increased suggestibility obtained by artifice." Wingfield, *An Introduction to Hypnotism*, p. 3 (Baillière, Tindall and Cox, 1920) agrees. Cf. Janet, "Hypnotism may be defined as the momentary transformation of the mental state of an indi-

Bernheim used to say, "There is no hypnotism, there is only suggestion." Baudouin calls hypnotism "induced suggestion." To keep to the parable, we may say that in hypnosis the critical policeman is off duty. Ideas presented to the patient's mind by the hypnotist enter the mind and tend, if reasonable, to actualise or come true. Some people, to change the figure, have a high critical threshold. They are difficult to hypnotise. Others are suggestible and are easy to hypnotise. The critical threshold is so low that ideas easily wash over it and seep into the mind.

My own method of inducing hypnosis and my own observance of the phenomena associated with it seem relevant here.

The patient is invited, in a quiet room with subdued lights, to lie on a couch and relax his body completely. Any clothing tight enough to prevent relaxation, or to make the patient conscious of his body, or to prevent the hypnotist from testing rigidity should be removed. The limbs, abdomen, neck, etc., are tested to ensure that none is being held rigidly. If the weather is cold, the patient is covered with rugs. It is essential that he should be warm and that coldness or discomfort should not draw his attention to any part of his body. Then he is invited to allow his mind to become as relaxed as his body. Since most people cannot make their minds a "blank," I suggest, in a soothing, quiet voice, that he imagines himself lying on the heather of a moor on a warm, sunny day, that he can smell the thyme and the bracken and hear the drowsy hum of bees, and, in the distance, a sheep-bell; that he is watching small white clouds float slowly across the blue sky; that he feels a wonderful sense of peace and contentment already flooding his mind, and that already he is getting sleepy—can hardly keep his eyes open, in fact—and that a delicious tiredness is weighing down his limbs, and that in a minute he will be asleep.

Then, about eight inches above his head, and a little behind the line of his eyes, so as to make it a trifle hard to see without strain, I hold a metal ring, asking him if he can see the "light-spot" on it (the reflection in the ring of whatever light is in the room). On being assured that he can see it, I tell him to fix his gaze on it, blinking as much as he likes until his eyelids are tired, and that as they grow tired he is to allow them to close and simply fall asleep.

With the finger-tips of my other hand I gently stroke his forehead, gradually bringing my hand lower so that I touch his flickering or closed eyelids. As I do so, I say, very quietly and slowly, such words

---

vidual, artificially induced by a second person, and sufficing to bring about dissociations of personal memory."—*Op. cit.*, Vol. I. And cf. Milne Bramwell in *Hypnotism* (Lippincott, 1903).

as these: "You are getting sleepy. Your eyelids are getting heavier and heavier. Soon you will be asleep. Sleep! Sleep! Sleep! . . . Now you cannot raise your eyelids. They are too heavy. You cannot raise your arm. Try! You cannot! Now you are dropping into a delicious, restful sleep. Sleep deeply! More deeply! More deeply! Sleep! Sleep! Sleep! Next time I want you to go to sleep you will drop off much more quickly."

A high percentage of people are then in a hypnotic sleep. It is not normal sleep, for they are still *en rapport* with the hypnotist, and will usually answer his questions and carry out his suggestions.

The patient is readily awakened by saying, "When I count ten you will awaken with a sense of contentment, happiness and well-being in body, mind and soul. You will be rested and refreshed and feel confident and entirely capable of facing up to life." Then I count very slowly from one to ten, pausing longest at the word "nine." As the word "ten" leaves one's lips, the patient opens his eyes, sits up, and usually smiles and says how much better he already feels.[6] It is important that he should not be suddenly awakened.

Liébault describes seven stages of hypnosis which, in my view, shade one into another and are not capable of accurate division. That is to say, the hypnotist cannot be certain at any one moment that a patient is not passing into a deeper or lighter stage. Liébault classifies as follows. First a state in which the eyelids become heavy. There is a sense of drowsiness, but there is also complete consciousness, and commonly in this state the patient refuses to believe that he is hypnotised at all. As this stage passes into the next, voluntary movements, commonly carried out by reflex action, can be inhibited. In the second stage there is a certain degree of catalepsy. The patient is unable to open his eyes when told that he cannot do so, or is unable or able to raise a limb according to the suggestion made. It will be seen how valuable this knowledge is to distinguish between a paralysis psychologically caused and a paralysis caused by a lesion. The third is a very drowsy stage, with a subsequent partial forgetting of what happened during the trance. Fourth, a stage in which the patient ceases to be in relation with the outer world and hears only what is said by the operator. In this stage it is possible to suggest anæsthesia, and in my own experiments, in order to discover which stage the patient has reached, I have found that one

[6] "When I came to you," said a hypnotised patient to Dr. Hadfield, "I thought I was going to be doped; that you were going to put something in me, perhaps something I did not like. Now I know that I have lived for years in a cellar; you have lifted me out and liberated what was in me."—*The Spirit* (Macmillan, 1919). This is a typical reaction.

may drive a needle into the flesh, even to the point of drawing blood, and no sensation of pain will be felt by the patient.

Obviously the possibilities of hypnosis in cases of childbirth suggest a field which one day may be opened up by the obstetrician. Esdaile had immense success in this field in Calcutta. Baudouin recounts a case of childbirth when the whole process not only was timed by hypnotic suggestion, but the mother was not aware of her child being born until all was over. This method may come to be regarded as superior to that which involves the use of drugs and anæsthetics which is some-times followed by unpleasant symptoms. The fifth stage we might call somnambulistic, because during this stage, if the right suggestions are made, the patient will walk about the room. Moreover, in this stage illusions can be suggested. One writer tells of a lady brought into this stage of hypnosis who was told that her favourite cat had had its tail chopped off. Even when she recovered from the trance, she was found fondling the animal, and bemoaning that it had been so cruelly treated, when all the time the tail was there as usual.[7] The sixth stage is one in which suggestions made will readily be carried out after the patient awakens. In the seventh stage the patient may be so deeply asleep that he makes no response. In fact, the lighter, rather than the deeper stages, are the more valuable from the therapeutic point of view.

The case of an intelligent young woman whom I will call Ethel [8] illustrates the phenomena of hypnosis in ways I shall find useful as I develop the argument of this book. Ethel was a young girl of eighteen who had fallen a prey to what was diagnosed as pernicious anæmia. These were days before even the liver treatment had been found success-ful. When all else failed, she was brought to me at Leeds, and after repeated hypnotic treatments, during which suggestion was made that her body was manufacturing red blood corpuscles in the normal manner and that the cause of the anæmia had disappeared, she recovered. She is now happily married and has two children. I am quite prepared to be told that the diagnosis must have been wrong and that, in fact, she never really had pernicious anæmia at all. All I am trying to show is that Ethel's parents believed, rightly or wrongly—probably wrongly —that I had saved her life, and they, with her full consent, gave me permission to experiment with her.

She was very suggestible, and went quickly into a deep hypnotic

[7] I have taken some paragraphs here from my earlier book, *Psychology in Service of the Soul* (Macmillan, 1930).

[8] This was not her name, of course. It is useful because it has two "e's" as the sequel will show.

sleep. Practically all the phenomena of hypnosis could be demonstrated on Ethel, and some strange things happened. For example, on being told to come and sit at my desk without waking up, she would prepare to write at my dictation. First she wrote her name—Ethel. "But," said I, in mock horror, "didn't you know that the letter 'e' had been deleted from the English language? Write your name again." She hesitated a long time. Then she wrote "THL," hesitated again and put down her pen. Her mind accepted the idea presented to it and her hand obeyed. The received idea "came true."

But, of course, the power of the mind over the body goes much farther than this. Ethel could lie with her heels on one chair and her neck on another, without intermediate support, and on being told her body was firm and unyielding, an adult could sit on her abdomen without her body yielding.

In giving a demonstration to some Leeds doctors I proved that Ethel's temperature could be put up as high as 104° and brought down to 96° by being told, under hypnosis, that these figures represented her temperature; that her temperature was rising or falling, as the case might be. The figures were checked with clinical thermometers by medical men present. Her heart-beat could be accelerated or retarded and tested with the stethoscope, though it is possible that respiratory changes conditioned the tempo of the heart-beat as powerfully as suggestion. Any part of her body could be made completely anæsthetic at a word, and needles, if driven into her in any area declared anæsthetic, produced no reaction at all.[9] If her arm were raised and she was told it had "stuck," it could not even be pushed down. Catalepsy was complete. On being told that she had developed nettlerash on her right knee, the area was soon covered with the familiar rash of urticaria, and, most dramatic of all, when I touched her left knee with a pencil, telling her it was a red-hot iron, and bound the part with a bandage and sealed it in the presence of medical witnesses, within twenty hours she developed a blister quite painless, but puffed out with fluid. It was not a matter of a marking on the skin like the stigmata. It was a blister, and since parting with Ethel years ago I have repeated the experiment, in the presence of medical men and women, with other patients willing to be thus used.

---

[9] Major operations have been performed by means of hypnotic anæsthesia. I, myself, have helped a dentist extract teeth from a patient who, for various reasons, was unable to take an anæsthetic. Not only were the extractions painless, but hæmorrhage was restricted by suggestion. There were no nauseating reactions afterwards, and one cannot help feeling that we have, in hypnosis, nature's own anæsthetic which possibly already operates in the animal world between cat and mouse, snake and bird, etc.

One wonders what may yet be done through the power of the mind in regard to such maladies as cancer, when those powers, glimpsed in hypnotic treatment, are more fully understood and can be unleashed with enough certainty to make their use the best chance of the patient's recovery. At present this is not so. Results are too haphazard and uncertain. One never knows whether a patient is capable of being hypnotised. The nature of hypnosis is insufficiently understood. Clinical practice cannot usefully proceed far ahead of theoretical understanding in such matters as these. Yet the text-books on hypnotism record permanent cures of almost every type of illness.

Under hypnosis, Ethel, like other hypnotised patients, could remember, with ease, events that occurred so early in her life that I had to get her mother to confirm them. I could then assure myself that she was remembering the events themselves, and not merely remembering being told about them. Apparently without effort she could remember events that happened in the first few months of her life, such as when her pram overturned—an event she "lived through" again under hypnosis with a most marked abreaction.

Ethel would also carry out post-hypnotic acts. Once I told her, during the state of hypnosis, that on waking she would take the flowers from my table and put them on the mantelpiece. On waking, she blinked, and then slowly carried out the act. When I asked her why, she said, "They look better there." She was quite unconscious of any influence. On another occasion I told her, while hypnotised, that in exactly a week's time, at 5 p.m., she would sit down and write me a postcard. Her mother said at the very moment she carried out the injunction. The unconscious mind, to which the hypnotist has access, has an extraordinary way of registering time, and if a hypnotised patient is told he will wake up, say, eleven and a half minutes after his ear is pinched, he will do so punctually.

Ethel could also be induced to have hallucinations. When told that a lovely black cat was asleep on the couch near her knees, she sat up, described it and went through the movements of stroking it. On being given a blank postcard and told it was a photograph of the Prince of Wales (now Duke of Windsor), she admired it and described it, going into details about his uniform and staring all the time at a blank card. She could also be made to dream. I once told her she was dreaming she was in a small boat on a lake in a park near her home. When safely embarked (!) I told her someone was jerking the boat and it would capsize. When I said, "The boat has turned over," Ethel, who had been tightly gripping the sides of the couch (= boat), shrieked with alarm and fell off the couch on to the floor. When I took her hand to lift her, she said, "Whatever shall I do? I'm wet through!" When she was wakened she laughed heartily and said, "I had a most vivid dream," and then recounted the imagined events with complete and faultless accuracy.

Her senses could all be controlled. If, when she was hypnotised, I told her she would hear nothing, she could not detect a loud noise even close to her ears. If I told her sugar was bitter, she would spit it out, and she could smell several perfumes successively on being told that her handkerchief was drenched with them. Ethel was so suggestible that I could hypnotise her over the telephone.

Ethel on some occasions appeared when hypnotised to have the power of telling me what other people were doing. But it was not easy to get a scientifically controlled experiment. She would say that some relative was at that moment playing with a dog, and we would be unable to prove it. If we arranged it, Ethel was often unable to say what was happening.

The phenomenon of Dermographia is more striking still. Rhine says that "there appears on the skin of the patient the outline of a design or script of which he (the hypnotist) is thinking." A certain Madame Kahl of Paris could reproduce on her arm or breast in clear, red outline, a figure or letter of which the experimenter was thinking. "The experimenters agreed on telepathic skin writing as the only reasonable explanation." [10]

Many think this power is highly dangerous from a moral point of view, but two reassurances may be made.

The first is that it is inaccurate to suppose that a hypnotised patient will disclose a closely guarded secret and answer any question. If the secret is of sufficient importance, and a moral principle (e.g. loyalty to a friend) would be broken by its betrayal, the patient will not disclose it. I tried to help by hypnotism one man who would answer any question I asked him except one. Though I tried many times on many occasions, every time I asked this question he awakened at once. Of course, his awakening was a sign of the relevance of the question which caused it.

The second is that it is inaccurate to suppose that an indecent act could be perpetrated on a hypnotised subject if it offended his moral scruples, or that he could be induced to commit a crime.[11] Maudsley wrote: "It is interesting to note that the hypnotised subject will not

[10] J. B. Rhine, *The Reach of the Mind* (Sloane, 1947).

[11] See my *Psychology in Service of the Soul* (Macmillan, 1930), *Psychological Healing,* by Janet, Vol. I.

commonly do an indecent or criminal act; the command to do it is too great a shock to the sensibilities of his brain, and accordingly arouses its suspended functions." [12]

A book was published as early as 1887 by Gilles de la Tourette, called *L'hypnotisme et les états analogues au point de vue médico-legal*, in which the following illuminating story is told: "A number of persons of importance, magistrates and professors, had assembled in the main hall of the Salpêtrière Museum to witness a great séance of criminal suggestions. Witt, the principal subject, thrust into the somnambulist state, had, under the influence of suggestion, displayed the most sanguinary instincts. At a word or a sign, she had stabbed, shot and poisoned. The room was littered with corpses, and Liégeois would have been in high glee. The notables had withdrawn, greatly impressed, leaving only a few students with the subject, who was still in the somnambulist state. The students, having a fancy to bring the séance to a close by a less blood-curdling experiment, made a very simple suggestion to Witt. They told her that she was now quite alone in the hall. She was to strip and take a bath. Witt, who had murdered all the magistrates without turning a hair, was seized with shame at the thought of undressing. Rather than accede to the suggestion, she had a violent fit of hysterics." [13]

The difficulty here, obviously, in many cases is to determine what the "moral scruples" of the person are. It is easy to say that a person under hypnosis would not transgress his moral scruples, and then, if he does in fact behave immorally, to say, "Oh well, he cannot have any moral scruples." Janet says he had notes of five cases of rape and one of theft carried out on hypnotised patients, but adds that "psychological considerations make us realise that suggestion could not have been the sole factor. Disorder of the will must certainly have been a contributory cause of the crime." So! but it leaves the matter unsatisfactory. I cannot help feeling that where a patient wholly trusts the hypnotist, immoral acts could take place, especially if plausible reasons for the immoral conduct were given by the hypnotist to the patient, such as, for example, the necessity for medical examination. It is better during hypnosis to have a colleague or friend present. It has been known for a hypnotised patient to make subsequent charges against a hypnotist which had no basis at all in fact. It is well for the patient to have a witness also if such procedure would allay his fears.

A danger unsuspected by the public is that a patient hypnotised

[12] *The Pathology of Mind*, p. 52 (1879).
[13] *Op. cit.*, Vol. I.

some hundreds of times by the same method might fall asleep if that method were accidentally applied. For example, it is on record that a young woman, hypnotised some hundreds of times by looking at the bright end of a hatpin, while traveling in a tramcar, sat behind a woman in whose hat was a similar pin. The patient went to sleep, and could not be wakened by the conductor. It is not a very likely occurrence, and a hypnotised patient, unless re-hypnotised at intervals, will waken naturally if left alone, though he *may* remain asleep for several days and have to be fed before he wakens. The record—as far as I know—is ninety days. He can always be easily awakened by the person who induced the hypnotic sleep, but this should never be done suddenly.

The greatest danger, in my view, is that if hypnotic treatments are carried on many times over long periods, hypnosis seems to induce an emotional dependence of the patient on the hypnotist. If the treatments are prematurely broken off, the patient relapses. This dependence or transference can be wisely handled by both hypnotist and patient if they are people of good sense.

I think it important to state the danger, but, of course, the stories in novels of people wholly "in the power" of a hypnotist, or, without re-hypnotisation, remaining in the trance state for six months or a year, are nonsense. Few technical scientific methods have so morbidly attracted the public imagination, or been so grossly exploited by quacks, or distorted by fools, as hypnosis. Of course, nothing potent for good is incapable, by distortion, of being used for evil if it gets into the wrong hands.

Hypnosis is not very generally used among the medical psychologists whose work is known to me. This, I think, is accounted for by several facts in addition to that of the dependence just described. 1. The results are frequently temporary. 2. Analytic treatment, on lines to be described later, is more thorough and permanent. 3. The exact state of a patient when in a hypnotic trance is not clearly understood, and scientists are, for this reason, chary of using it. 4. The hypnotist naturally fears using a method which has been so stupidly and sensationally exploited by the cheap Press. Most good doctors hate to see their names and methods publicised in the Press.

From what has been gathered from the single case of Ethel, it will be seen to what extent hypnosis stimulated the young science of psychotherapy. The mind could be explored for past and "forgotten" impressions, which, though normally buried in the unconscious, yet, because never properly reacted to and allowed for, could throw up to the surface of consciousness the most disquieting and apparently irrational fears, and produce in the body the most baffling symptoms which those who could only interpret them in terms of material impairment found it difficult to understand, let alone to heal. Once remembered and brought to *normal* consciousness and dealt with by the personality in the light of a better understanding of their cause, they disappeared, sometimes in a dramatically short time.

It is important to note that to get a hypnotised patient to remember *only during the hypnosis*, the initial traumatic experience which started his illness, is insufficient. He must *remember* consciously, and not just be told. I have found it useful to suggest during hypnosis, "You will tell me about this later," and then, as the patient wakens, to say to him, "You were telling me about your life on the farm when you fell off the pony or something. Go on from there." It is better not to appear *too* keenly interested. The patient may produce a resistance, wondering "what you are up to." A dramatic, tense sort of atmosphere is all right for the novel or film. In practice a kind of casualness—as if the treatment were the most ordinary everyday affair in the world —is better.

The practice of hypnotism, then, may be said to be a definite advance in the story of healing through psychology. Normally a person has no direct access to his own unconscious. In the hypnotic state he may reveal this to the hypnotist in a way which gives the latter a clue as to the origin and nature of many of the conflicts which so disable him. What some writers have called hypno-analysis has often been found useful. Further, strong suggestions of confidence and recovery, of hope and trust may be given to the mind and more readily absorbed. By positive suggestion under hypnosis, a distressed person may be given enough temporary—and sometimes permanent—help to enable him to overcome his difficulties and achieve the integration of personality.

SUGGESTION

THE CONSIDERATION OF hypnotic suggestion—which the story of psychotherapy has reached—leads us now to consider the Coué movement, which swept across Europe like a prairie fire. Inasmuch as it was suggestion given by Coué *in the conscious state of the patient's mind*, it has a fascinating link with the mechanism of some of the healing miracles we have studied. And since it brought healing by psychological means before the attention of the whole country, it prepared the way for Freud, Adler and Jung, whose work we must consider later.

Emile Coué (1857-1926) was born in Nancy. He was an apothecary, not a doctor, not a highly educated, but a very charming man, interested in psychology, and especially in the work of Bernheim and Liébault. For a score of years he studied and experimented, and then the light shone. The patient did not need the suggestive therapy applied by another, as in hypnosis. Within himself was the power. He did not need a trance state so that direct access to the unconscious could be obtained. Ideas, if repeated again and again in a confident voice, eluding as much as possible the attentions of the "critical policeman" (see p. 112), and especially if repeated at those times when the mind was most receptive—namely, on awakening and on falling asleep— would sink into the subconscious and unconscious parts of the mind and work the expected wonder.

So, said Coué to his patients, "Say every morning and evening, 'Tous les jours, à tous points de vue, je vais mieux et mieux.' " (Every day in every way I am getting better and better.) "And," he added, with unconscious humour, "don't think what you are saying. *Say it as you say the litany at church!*" (Italics mine.)

Astounding success followed. At the height of his fame a hundred people a day thronged his garden at Nancy and filled the little parlour, where, with no ostentation and none of the paraphernalia of Mesmer, Coué saw his patients. He was no showman. He did not even explain his theories to his patients. He got them practising the formula, modifying it to suit individual requirements. There must be no negatives. There must be no naming of the illness. The unconscious would snatch at the name, and no good would be done. There must be no future tenses. Even "I shall," let alone the negative "I shall not," is putting in the future a cure that could begin now. So to the lumbago patient, for example, Coué would say, "Say this over and over again, 'My back is easier. I am able with greater and greater ease to bend it,' " and so on.

Coué did not teach patients to use will-power. He worked on the important psychological truth that if will and imagination are in conflict, the imagination wins. To say, if smitten with lumbago, "I will stretch upright without pain," but imaginatively to add under one's breath, "but I can't and I know I can't," was to bring certain failure. "I can," not "I will," are the releasing words. Coué spoke much of "the law of reversed effort," and in his own way expressed his meaning by saying, "The force of the imagination is in direct ratio to the square of the will."

It is the imagination—Coué taught—that procures for an idea its acceptance into the unconscious, and the unconscious has almost complete power over the body. We have already seen that an idea received into the unconscious can even produce a blister or a rash on the skin. No effort is required to believe that if Coué's method really does get ideas into the unconscious, bodily benefit is certain.

Of course, the factor on which everything depends is the suggestibility of the patient—that is, the facility with which he accepts ideas into his mind without critical examination. This suggestibility depends on many factors, and is taught by some to be a temporary regression to a childish level at which ideas are accepted at their face value. In my experience, education is not a deciding factor. It is commonly believed that a "simple soul" is suggestible and that an educated person is not. There is no principle here, however. The most suggestible person I ever knew was a brilliant girl who took an honours degree at Girton. Although, of course, fully conscious, she could not lift her hand off the tea-table during afternoon tea if, in a confident voice, I asserted that she could not move it. Though I was exerting no physical pressure on her hand, she would say, "Don't be silly; let me drink my tea." The least suggestible person I ever knew was an uneducated farm labourer. A child is usually more suggestible than an adult, a woman more so than a man. Abnormal states of the brain can determine suggestibility, and "temperamental" people, hardly to be classed as abnormal, are more suggestible than the phlegmatic type.[1]

The condition depends partly on the person offering the suggestion. Any lack of confidence he has in himself, or doubt as to whether or not his suggestions will be carried out, conveys itself to the patient and decreases the suggestibility of the latter. The fame, prestige and impressive character of the operator are also important factors, as every child knows. Nervous and neurotic patients are more suggestible than normal people, introverts more than extroverts, sick or tired people more than those who have "rude health." Baudouin devised an experiment for increasing suggestibility based on Chevreul's pendulum, but I have never heard of it being used in this country.

The condition depends partly on what the patient "thinks of the whole business." If he is scornful or critical to a great degree; if he thinks the operator is a fool; if he is afraid or resistant, if he is a student of hypnosis and is watching his own reactions, his suggestibility is lowered. The rapport between the person suggesting and the person receiving the suggestions is of the utmost importance.

Strangely enough, a suggestion is often more powerful when it is in the nature of an aside, rather than a statement made in a bombastic or loud voice. "Of course, you'll be all right in the morning," assuming the recovery of the child and taking it as a matter of course, is more likely to get past the critical defences than a solemn pronouncement from the foot of the bed, "In the morning you will be quite well."

I have not discussed at length the whole question of suggestion. We are examining it merely to note it as one of the most important of the earlier psychological means of healing and to pass judgment on it. Baudouin wrote a classical treatise on it, *Suggestion and Auto-suggestion*.[2] He divides his subject under three heads—Spontaneous Suggestion, Reflective Suggestion and Induced Suggestion. The first two are forms of auto-suggestion. The last, hetero-suggestion, includes hypnosis. If the patient is conscious, all hetero-suggestion (suggestion given by others) must become auto-suggestion (suggestion accepted by the self).

The tremendous success of Coué proved that there was a great deal of truth in his claim and of value in his technique. People *did* get better by his methods. Incidentally it seems to me, as I read the literature, that he had a real love for people, and that must have been a most potent factor. Thousands, however, who never met him followed his technique.

[1] McDougall, *Social Psychology*, p. 98 (Methuen, 1919).
[2] Dodd, 1921.

Night and morning, quiescent and relaxed, mumbling the words and counting, with the help of knots in a piece of string, the times they recited the incantation, people all over Europe informed their unconsciousnesses that every day in every way they were getting better and better. To the minds of ordinary people Coué brought home a most important truth: the power of the mind over the body.

Some of Coué's cases made the world wake up to this fact with almost the shock of alarm. He once noted a case of a nun confined to her bed by illness during the winter. She heard the doctor murmur—during the time when he supposed she was unconscious—"She won't outlive April." This idea became fixed in her mind. Nevertheless, for the time being she got better, left her bed, and seemed quite strong again. But to every visitor she said that she felt sure she would die in April. On April 1 her appetite disappeared as if by magic. A few days later she took to her bed once more, and died shortly before the end of the month.

Many of his disciples caused amusement by their adventures. One of them, by name Gillet, was suffering from asthma, and on a holiday journey was awakened in his hotel by a violent paroxysm of the disease. Greatly distressed through lack of breath, the patient got out of bed in the night, but could find neither matches nor the window. He felt if only he could get some air he would be better. Moving about the dark room, his hand came upon a pane of glass. Thinking it was the window, he felt in vain for the window-bolt, and as another choking paroxysm came on he lost patience, took his slipper, and broke the pane of glass. Again and again he drew deep breaths of what he thought was the fresh air. The throbbing at his temples passed, and he climbed back to bed and slept quietly till the next morning. On waking in the morning, he found that the glass case enclosing a clock was broken, and an item on his bill ("broken clock-case 5 fr.") confirmed the fact that his struggle for air had ended in his breaking the case of the clock, but since his mind accepted the idea that he had broken the window and was letting in fresh air, his body found relief.[3]

But criticism cannot be excluded altogether, and it applies *mutatis mutandis* to hypnotic suggestion.

The *symptom* of disharmony, whether of body or mind, is a signpost. It is trying to indicate the source of trouble. A raised temperature is such a signpost. Merely to remove the symptom by auto-suggestion and then to proceed to expose oneself to bitter weather might be a quick route to death. If by suggestion the energies dealing with the infection

[3] Baudouin, *Suggestion and Auto-suggestion* (Dodd, 1921).

can be reinforced, that would seem an excellent thing to do. Merely to remove a symptom of the infection might surely be to do harm.

Does not that simple illustration go far? For if our "illness" be psychological, the curing of *symptom* by suggestion seems equally dangerous. Many symptoms, physical or psychological, reveal attempts by nature to get right something that is wrong. A boil undoubtedly produces pain, but the pain immobilises the area in which it is situated, or tries to, and thus prevents the poison spreading. I remember my friend, Professor Grensted of Oxford, telling a story of a doctor who, by repeated suggestion, cured a patient of the conviction that he was a dog. The cure was reported triumphantly with the appended note, "Unfortunately he now believes that he is a water rat." The story is not quoted to amuse. It illustrates an important truth. If a symptom only is removed, the uncured disharmony may provide itself with another which may be more distressing and make a cure more difficult.

I applaud Monsieur Coué's technique and work in many cases. It takes the patient's mind away from dwelling on his illness. It turns his mind to health and gives him hope. It has an enormous value in religion, though in Coué's hands it is a faith that only goes part way. It has been called "unspiritual faith." After all, our church architecture, ritual, robes and music all aim to make men suggestible, so that ideas can more readily find access to the deep mind, and, as I hope to show later in these pages, suggestion treatment should have a far more important place in pastoral practice than it has. When the minister visits the homes of the sick, he ought not merely to *tell* the patient, worried over some earlier sin, that he is forgiven, or *tell* the timid, fretful one that God can empower him: he should *use* his psychology and get these truths into the very fabric of the mind, using deep suggestion if necessary, just as crutches may be used until a patient can walk without them.

But where physical or psychological illness is concerned, Coué's technique is to be criticised, unless it is used *after* the doctor or qualified psychotherapist has diagnosed the situation and treated it along lines which will not merely silence the symptom which tells them what is wrong, but which will deal radically with the disharmony which first caused the symptom.

Frequently it may be of value to deal with a symptom only. If the symptom is insomnia, it is good to treat the symptom and give the patient a night's sleep. If the symptom is anorexia, it is good to remove the symptom and let the patient have a good meal. Such treatment will help the condition, and some conditions will clear up altogether if the patient believes he is well. Let suggestion be used, by all means, but let the physician be awake to the fact that a symptom is a signpost pointing to something beyond itself which must often be understood if the patient is to be healed. A falling temperature in a case of malaria indicates that the natural resistance of the body is overcoming the invading organisms. If it be possible to lower the temperature by hypnosis, it would be a highly dubious undertaking, and rather like pulling down a signpost in a bewildering and strange country. The physician thereafter does not know where he is in the matter of malaria.

Even in pastoral work it is doubtful whether the priest should hush the patient with soothing words that his sin is forgiven, that God is kind, that he need not trouble about his soul any more. Such pastoral technique makes religion itself neurotic. It, too, is treating the symptom —conscience distress. It, too, makes of prayer an ointment to rub on a sore soul, and of trust in God the mere hope of being let off the consequences of evil. Such pastoral practice is disintegrating, and earns for religion the label "dope" or "the opiate of the people." Given enough suggestion at the wrong time, and the sinner only becomes a hypocrite, and his last state is worse than his first. The minister is never to condemn, never to be shocked, never to upbraid. He is to let the patient confess his sin, recall its detail, and realise the abreaction of true penitence. Let him realise that this universe allows no one to escape consequences, and that forgiveness never annuls them. It does change the retribution of an affronted moral order into the discipline of a friendly Father. But all this must be made clear. *Then* the balm of God's love may be poured in and His mercy offered.

I hope this is not unfairly critical. Coué did a great work. In many ways he was a great man and a truly Christian man. In the story of his own work which he himself authorised we find this sentence: "Monsieur Coué himself, though keeping his religious views very much in the background, lived a life in which the practical virtues of Christianity were clearly manifest." [4] All who knew Coué speak of his modesty and of his desire and readiness to help anyone in need. Every doctor and minister has benefited by his emphases. Yet symptomatology, both in medicine and in religion, has its place in helping towards an understanding of what is wrong. In order to assess the value of Coué's practices one would need—what is not available—the subsequent health record of a thousand patients whom Coué treated. Note, for example, the case of Louis Schmidt, aged forty-four, who, after an attack of indigestion, became affected with "almost complete paralysis of the arms and legs. He was sent to the departmental infirmary, and remained there for a while without improvement. When he came to consult

[4] C. H. Brooks and E. Charles, *Christianity and Autosuggestion* (Dodd, 1923).

Coué, he could hardly walk; his legs, he said, were 'like cotton wool.' After the first sitting he could walk and could even run. *He had a relapse a few months later*, but was restored to health once more by suggestive treatment." [5] We do not know whether he had a further relapse a few months later, and whether by that time the condition which caused the "paralysis" had worsened, making treatment and cure more difficult. One wonders whether diagnosis by a capable physician was confounded by his gymnastics, and whether he has permanently recovered.

The question of prayer and suggestion I have discussed in an earlier book.[6] More recently it has been most admirably dealt with by Alexander Hodge.[7] We may say briefly that it is quite inaccurate to suppose that "prayer is only auto-suggestion." It is nearer to truth to say that some forms of auto-suggestion are powerful methods of prayer. Psychology here is ideally wedded to religion. In this section, however, we have been discussing psychological, as distinct from religious, methods of healing.

Now we have reached the early nineteen hundreds. Nothing now can be called an *early* method of integration through psychology. The way has been prepared for Freud, Adler and Jung. In accordance with our plan, for the next section we turn back to discuss and to examine modern methods of healing through religion.

[5] Baudouin, *op. cit.* (Italics mine.) By permission of Dodd, Mead & Company.

[6] *Psychology in Service of the Soul* (Macmillan, 1930).

[7] Alexander Hodge, B.A., Ph.D., *Prayer and its Psychology* (Macmillan, 1931).

MODERN METHODS OF HEALING
THROUGH RELIGION

THE LAYING ON OF HANDS

THOUGH ANCIENT IN origin, this method of healing through religion is still practised, and so can be discussed here. The practice of anointing with oil is in rather a different category. The Roman Catholic usage has associated the practice of anointing with oil with what is called Extreme Unction. Amongst some Protestant groups, such as the Guild of St. Raphael (see p. 219), oil is used sacramentally as a therapeutic aid, but amongst Roman Catholics the sacrament of Extreme Unction is a preparation for death, and it is usually administered to patients who are not expected to recover.

It is important to discuss the practice of the laying on of hands. If it is sound, it ought to be practised far more widely. If it is unsound, it ought to be relegated to the dustbin of outworn magic and effete superstition. The question before us in this section is: Is the practice of the laying on of hands to be commended?

It was used by Christ repeatedly, as we have seen (p. 40). The promise was given that those who believed on Him should "lay hands on the sick and they shall recover," [1] though the authenticity of this passage is in doubt. However, the early Church continued the practice, and it would be presumptuous to say that a practice carried out by Christ, probably enjoined by Him on the disciples and practised by many branches of the Christian Church ever since, should, in the light of modern knowledge, be discontinued. There came a time when the practice was dropped by the bishops for the simple reason that it was a physical impossibility to touch everybody in the church who desired the laying on of hands. The outstretched arms often accompanying the pronouncement of the blessing at the end of a religious service are meant to symbolise the laying on of hands.

[1] Mark 16:8.

The Committee on the Ministry of Healing, a Sub-Committee of the Lambeth Conference of 1908, advised as follows: "The Committee is of the opinion that the prayers for the restoration of health which it recommends, may be fitly accompanied by the apostolic act of the laying on of hands."

The Rev. John Maillard, whose work in this field created an almost world-wide interest, provides an illustration of this practice in his book, *Healing in the Name of Jesus*.[2]

"Another remarkable instance of healing was that of a woman who had not been visited by Mr. Hickson. She lived in my district of the parish, and I discovered her on one of our periodical house-to-house visitations. I knocked at the door, but there was no response. I turned the handle and found that the door was unlocked, so I went into the passage and asked if anyone was in. A voice came from the back room, and I entered it. I discovered a poor sufferer in bed. She quickly told me her story. She had been in three of our big London hospitals and had had operations for cancer, but had not been cured by them. The last of the hospitals offered her the choice of remaining as an in-patient or of returning to her home. She had been a nurse in an East London district, and knew everything about sickness. I prayed with her and laid my hands upon her head whilst doing so. This had now become my normal practice in all home visits to the sick and suffering. Soon afterwards I took her the Holy Communion. Two days after this I visited her again, and discovered a marked improvement in her condition. She told me that when she received the Holy Communion she felt a glowing warmth in her body, and this had continued. The improvement was maintained, although the progress was slow. Bit by bit she recovered, and one of her first outings was a visit to the hospital from which she had taken her discharge. She went straight to the ward where she had been a patient, and the first person she met on entering it was the ward-sister. The sister stared at her in amazement, and at last said, 'Why, you are a resurrection!' The house-surgeon was told, and he came up to see her. He was surprised and delighted. He asked her to come back again on the students' day, so that he might tell them in the lecture-room how she had been healed, as she had been one of their interesting cases and had allowed them to subject her to experimental and drastic treatments. This sufferer became one of my dearest friends, and is today after a space of twenty-three years.

"The surgeon had not suggested that there had been a wrong

[2] Harper, 1936.

diagnosis in the first instance. It was a straightforward case of cancer, attested and treated by eminent doctors and by surgical operations, examinations, remedies and the like."

In the same book he gives other instances of a similar kind.

Alderman the Rev. Jim Wilson of the Guild of Health, in his book, *Healing through the Power of Christ*,[3] describes his method as follows:

"My own method is usually to begin with a short time of silent meditation after giving the person a constructive thought to hold in his mind about the love and good purpose of God to heal. A short, simple prayer is then said, asking God to heal. After this, I stand in front of the person who is kneeling and lay my right hand on the forepart of the head and my left on the back of the head. After a few moments, in which I try to realise that I am only the instrument by which our Lord is Himself laying on his hands, I say, 'Our Lord Jesus Christ who gave authority to His disciples that they should lay hands upon the sick that they might recover, have mercy upon you and strengthen you in spirit, soul and body, and give you faith in His power to heal. And by His authority committed unto me, I lay my hands upon you that you may recover your full health and strength, in the name of the Father and of the Son and of the Holy Ghost.' After this, I give a blessing and then remain for some time in silent thanksgiving.

"I always tell the person that, though sometimes a person is healed almost at once, in most cases the healing comes gradually and not very quickly. I also warn him not to be continually thinking of his symptoms and not to be disappointed if he is better one day and not so well the next; but to be confident that God is at work and that in time he will see what great things God will do.

"If a sick person is in bed the ministration will be given in the same way, but after the blessing and a time of quiet, I leave the sick person in that quietness, without speaking to him, so that he may sleep, as very often a really ill person will do after the ministration.

"I have purposely said little about results. These are many, and they are often quite in keeping with the results of our Lord's ministry as described in the Gospels. There are also some so-called failures. It is these that we should be most concerned about. We do not yet know enough about this ministry to be able to have as certain a touch as our Lord. This impels us to deeper search for wisdom and for power from Him."

In my opinion the practice is to be supported as a valuable means

[3] Pp. 63-64 (James Clarke, 1946).

of healing. Nor do I think it should be confined to professional clergy and ministers, so long as certain important points are safeguarded.

1. The laying on of hands, in my opinion, should be a practice limited to the private interview, not a practice followed in a public meeting open to all.[4] If others are present, care should be taken that they are entirely in sympathy with what is being done.

2. The practice of the laying on of hands must never appear to make superfluous careful medical diagnosis, to be followed by the most useful treatment which science can devise, whether medical, surgical or psychological. Within those three words are to be included such things as careful nursing, massage, electrical therapy and any material method which real scientists have discovered and sanctioned as relevant and sound. This safeguard should not be regarded as a prop to weak faith. Rather I would suggest that to deny a patient the proved abilities of the doctor and surgeon, or other adequate scientist through whom health is so often restored, could be a definitely unChristian act. When we consider the alternative, we can imagine the extreme case of a patient suffering from a suppurating appendix. If the priest excluded the doctor, practised the laying on of hands and put the onus of recovery on the patient, telling him, in his extremely serious condition, "to have faith," there is little doubt in my mind but that the patient would die. If so, his death would lie at the priest's door. Probably no priest today would act in such a manner, but the fanaticism of some people is such that the laying on of hands is a substitute for scientific treatment, when the former should be a complement to the latter. No patient should be subjected to such fanaticism, for, if he is, he is not being offered the maximum help available in the modern world.

Frequently the practice of the laying on of hands is only resorted to when all else has failed. In such cases this practice also often fails. Nor is this surprising. If disease is understood and the remedy is obvious, no other treatment is resorted to, certainly not the laying on of hands. In other areas of men's lives Heaven does not make up for man's ignorance by working miracles. Why should Heaven do so here? Divine energies are not conditioned only by man's ignorance, nor are they to be resorted to merely because—though our practice reveals we should prefer to be healed through them—medicine and surgery have, in fact, failed to help us.

3. A third condition seems to me to lie in the self-dedication of the officiating priest or minister. Ideally there should be behind him a

4 See the Section on Healing Missions, p. 197.

dedicated and disciplined group. The minister or clergyman should be the spearhead of the whole Church in this act. Ideally the whole praying community should be engaged in the sacramental act which the minister carries out in their name as well as in the name of Christ. This seems to have been practised in the early Church. I feel more and more sure that there are conditions for the priest or minister as important as the stern conditions imposed on a physician by the long, expensive years of his training and the examinations at the end of his course. One cannot help coming to the conclusion that spiritual power and insight obtained by spiritual discipline avail in this particular matter of the laying on of hands far more powerfully than any kind of psychological training.

4. The fourth condition which I would lay down concerning the practice of the laying on of hands is that if the patient is well enough, it should be made clear to him that the aim of the practice is the patient's unity with God, and that this has priority even over the aim of his recovery to health. If this is not made clear to him, and if he remains unhealed, he may fall into depression, even though the real cause of failure to recover is that his disease, the nature of which is imperfectly understood by the physician, is really in the category of purely physiogenic illness.

Let us imagine that a patient has a bone stuck in his throat. A service for the laying on of hands would surely not be followed by a marked improvement in the condition of the patient. I do not deny that even then there might be a spiritual gain, but clearly the obvious treatment is the removal of the obstruction. An obstruction in the appendix or in the bowel is in the same category as a bone in the throat, and an obscure condition which the doctor may imperfectly understand *may* be in this same category and account for the failure to recover. It seems clear to me that if a man had come to Christ, having a bone in his throat, Christ would not have laid His hands upon him, but would have referred him to some skilled physician, or possibly removed the obstruction Himself. One of the great misunderstandings about healing by non-physical means is based on the idea that resort to God is supposed to have special potency merely because man does not understand or cannot deal with the trouble that is causing his illness. If the malady has the mysterious romance of the unknown about it, it is *for that reason* considered to be a matter for prayer and the laying on of hands, and it is thought that God should immediately act. The failure of the patient to recover may be through no lack of faith on the patient's part and no lack of willingness on the divine side, but may be a pointer to the need for fuller understanding and the use of resources already within human grasp, though not yet attained.

A study of the gospels seems to demonstrate that our Lord Himself insisted on finding out what was the nature of the patient's illness. In the case of the epileptic boy,[5] we have noted the time He spent in questioning the patient's father so as to get the details, or, as a doctor would say, a history of the case. In the case of the man amongst the tombs,[6] He seems to have spent a large part of the night investigating the case and getting the history. I am impressed with the way in which this practice fell away in the early Church. The Apostles seem to have demanded faith and ordered the lame to rise, and so on, using the same technique in all cases. If they succeeded, the patient had had faith. If they failed, the patient had had insufficient faith. But their failure to cure must often have been due to the fact that they did not understand what was the matter with the patient and they did not vary their treatment. So often did they fail, even where pagan healers succeeded, that they are largely responsible for the speed with which healing in the Church fell into disuse.

An ideal situation would arise if in any given locality a Christian doctor and a vicar, or minister, with insight, acted together. One can imagine this working in a village in which both were regarded as playing a part in the recovery of a sick person. The doctor would do everything that could be done on the physical and psychological levels, but the minister or clergyman would discuss at least some of his cases with the doctor, and co-operate by instructing the patient, by prayer and the laying on of hands. He would secure the spiritual co-operation of the Christian community in the village, and his practice of laying on of hands would focus and symbolise the loving care of God. The patient's acceptance of the rite would mean his recognition of those purposes, and the effect would be to turn the patient's mind away from his illness to God. The patient should not think of the rite as in the same category as the treatment by the doctor. He would be taught to think of the laying on of hands as an act of worship. In that act God comes near to the patient, and the patient responds to God. The touching by the priest or minister is the symbol of the divine love making *contact* with the human soul. The patient is enabled to make a better response to God because of the sacramental act of the touching. Here we have the two essential things in worship—God's

[5] Mark 9:14 ff.
[6] Mark 5:1 ff.

love and man's response—and, I repeat, the patient would be taught to think of the rite as aiming at his unity with God. Thus into the patient's personality there would be discharged that spiritual energy that comes from God. Actually the act of touching has no magical significance, but it has a sacramental significance, and in cases where illness was a by-product of disunity of the soul with God—and, as we shall see, there are many such illnesses—the rite of the laying on of hands would play an even more important part than the ministrations of the doctor. To use the analogy of the motor car, to which I shall return, the doctor puts the mechanism of the car right, but the minister or clergyman makes sure that the driver knows how to drive, and is not driving so badly as to throw the mechanism out of gear.

It may be said that Christ laid His hands on people to cure them, and not just to bring them into unity with God. Yet one feels that the latter would loom the larger with Him. The opposite alternative is incredible. Further, nowhere are we told that Christ could, or did, heal everyone brought to Him, whatever the trouble may have been. He healed *many* that were sick, but not all.[7] It is impossible for the modern man to believe, for example, that Christ could restore in a moment the health of a man whose head had been severed from the neck and had rolled down a steep place into the sea, or that Christ could instantly restore the gift of sight to a man whose eyes, let us imagine, had been gouged out. It is not derogatory to suppose that even *His* immense power would need the machinery of sight to restore its function, a machinery which His Father ordained.

No one, therefore, must be distressed if the laying on of hands, for example, fails to bring him help. The failure does not necessarily point to his lack of faith. It may only point to the obscurity of the type of illness from which he is suffering, and though his handicap remains, he may be comforted by believing that his disability can be used by God and woven into God's plans. Surely there is immense comfort in the thought that St. Paul, who healed others, was not himself free from illness. He writes of his thorn or stake in the flesh.[8] He asks repeatedly that this suffering, which some think was epilepsy[9] and some

---

[7] Mark 6:5.

[8] II Corinthians 12:7-9.

[9] Galatians 4:14. "That which was a trial to you in my flesh ye despised not nor rejected; but ye received me." The word translated "rejected" could be translated, as in the Revised Version margin, "spat out," indicating the ancient custom of spitting as a means of averting from the spectator of an epileptic fit the evil spirit thought to cause epilepsy.
See Oman, *Paradox of the World*, p. 254 (Macmillan, 1921).

blindness[10] and some malaria, might be removed. The illness appears to me to have been some form of psychosomatic disorder. It was certainly accompanied by fear, depression, fatigue and insomnia. He writes: "It was in weakness and fear and with great trembling that I visited you." [11] And again: "I was crushed [?depressed], crushed far more than I could stand, so much so that I despaired even of life." [12] And again: "I got no relief from the strain of things, even when I reached Macedonia; it was trouble at every turn, wrangling all round me, fears in my own mind." [13] Later, writing to the same community, he refers to his insomnia and tells them he passed many a sleepless night.[14] Yet his prayer was not answered in the way he wanted, and within him God's voice said, "My strength is made perfect in weakness." So Paul heroically determined to transmute incurable illness into spiritual health. "Therefore will I rather glory in my weaknesses that the strength of Christ may rest upon me." [15]

Perhaps the ideal mental condition for the patient who is to receive the rite of the laying on of hands is that of entire surrender to the will of God in the circumstances. If that can be health, he will praise God. If, for various human reasons, health cannot be restored, he must try to see that while God's intention is health, that intention may be temporarily defeated by human ignorance, folly or sin at some point or another, not necessarily in the patient's own life, but in that of the whole human race of which he is a member. But the patient must try to understand that there is always a secondary or interim will of God, and that God is never finally defeated, but, as in the case of St. Paul, can weave even continued suffering into His plan, so that ultimately the patient is brought to the same point as that to which he would have been brought if health had been restored.

A problem is raised by the appearance, from time to time, of people who are often cranks and eccentrics, but who claim to have a gift of healing, and who annoy the minister and clergyman with requests to be allowed to lay their hands on the sick. The tempta-

[10] Galatians 4:15. "If possible ye would have plucked out your eyes and given them to me." Probably a reference to attacks of temporary blindness of a hysterical type. The "large letters" (Galatians 6:11) are thought by some to indicate Paul's poor sight.
[11] I Corinthians 2:3 (Moffatt).
[12] II Corinthians 1:8 (Moffatt).
[13] II Corinthians 7:5 (Moffatt).
[14] II Corinthians 11:27 (Moffatt).
[15] II Corinthians 12:9.

tion is, of course, to dismiss all such people as rather dangerous cranks and fanatics, and only too often the popular Press gives them much publicity and increases the poignancy of the problem they raise.

After much consideration, it is my view that there are certain people with strange psychic gifts who, without doubt, have brought healing to some. As far as I know, there is no satisfactory explanation of this gift. The power of suggestion plays a part in such cures, but does not wholly explain them. The gift is often quite separated from any profession of Christianity, or from any adequate knowledge or understanding of medicine or psychology. Yet, to be quite fair, this so-called gift of healing is not always a concomitant of eccentricity. A Methodist minister whom I know personally has this gift. The evidence of it is beyond cavil. He himself discovered it by accident. He was visiting the home of some of his people who were almost distracted by grief because their only child was supposedly dying. The minister went up with the parents into the child's room, and they prayed together. Then the minister, with deep feelings of pity and love, put his hands on the child's head without any thought of healing. Nothing was farther from this minister's thoughts than the laying on of hands. To his amazement, as soon as he laid them on the child's forehead, his hands trembled and shook as if with a clonus. Medically and surgically, all hope of recovery had been given up. The child stirred, opened his eyes, and then, with a sigh, went to sleep. He slept naturally and peacefully for some hours, and then, with the speed at which little children so frequently recover, he sat up, wanted food and toys and appeared to have recovered. In a few days he was well.

If this were an isolated case one could not, of course, connect my friend's action with the patient's recovery, but the same kind of thing has occurred again and again. My friend is most reluctant to use this gift. His reluctance and general demeanour recall that passage in Sabatier's life of St. Francis of Assisi[16] in which he tells how St. Francis was entertained at Toscanella by a knight whose infant son was helpless in his cradle, though long past the age of walking. "The boy's father, seeing the man of God to be endued with such holiness, humbly fell at his feet and besought him to heal his son. Francis, seeming himself to be unprofitable and unworthy of such power and grace, for a long time refused to do it. At last, conquered by the urgency of the knight's entreaties, after offering up prayer he laid his hand on the boy, blessed him and lifted him up. In the sight of all, the boy straightway arose

[16] *Life of St. Francis of Assisi* (1182-1226), translated by L. S. Houghton, p. 192 (1894).

whole in the name of the Lord Jesus Christ, and began to walk hither and thither about the house."

My friend similarly dreads limelight and publicity and the vulgarity of cheap journalism, with its blatant headlines, but, on being pressed, he has used this gift again and again with success. He would be the first to wish me to add, however, that when I was with him while he laid his hands on another patient, no physical benefit whatever followed, though when my friend touched him, the patient claimed that he felt a "current like electricity" pass through his head. It was afterwards found that this patient's trouble was a psychosomatic disorder due to a deep unconscious conflict, and the physical symptoms disappeared when the conflict was resolved. Here we have another instance showing that the laying on of hands is certainly no cure-all, but that in certain cases it is successful in restoring health.

Where a person with such a gift is a convinced Christian, I think his services should be used, so long as the safeguards and conditions referred to above are observed. Even if such a healer is not a religious person, I do not think this strange power should be unused. He could be accompanied to the sick room by the priest or minister, and invited to co-operate, as long as the patient fully understood the situation. One remembers the passage in the New Testament: " 'Master, we saw one casting out devils and we rebuked him because he followed not us.' But Jesus said, 'Forbid him not . . . for he that is not against us is for us.' " [17]

Granted that these strange gifts of healing are not understood, yet if good can be done by their use it seems a serious thing to deprive patients of any possible benefit they might receive. Tennyson possessed this gift, but never linked it with religion, although he was a deeply religious man. Yet he laid his hands on the sick and a number recovered. If people are ill and can be made better, even by a method that is not understood, it is a very serious thing to dismiss the so-called healer as a crank or a fanatic, and to allow such a label to stand between a sick man and recovery.

At the same time, such a gift should, I think, be distinguished from the one which the Church sanctioned. It does not seem to me to be in the same category as the gift possessed by apostles and saints, who attributed it to Christ, and regarded their own powers as the power of Christ working through them. St. Peter, for example, tried to cure his mother-in-law, without success; but power came to him later after Pentecost, and, with great confidence, he healed many. But he re-

[17] Mark 9:39.

garded it as a divine gift received from fellowship with Christ and with the Church, and received only after much discipline. St. Peter's healing power was not in the category of what might be called a freak endowment, with no Godward reference or rational explanation. Healing gifts without any religious reference must be scrutinized, for there are charlatans who, with half-understood psychic gifts, exploit poor people for commercial gain.

THE PHENOMENA OF LOURDES

FOR THE PURPOSE of writing this chapter from first-hand knowledge, I made the journey to Lourdes in May, 1949, accompanied by my son, who is a qualified doctor, in order to study the healings alleged to have taken place there. Instead of travelling as ordinary tourists, we enrolled as pilgrims, and travelled on one of the pilgrim trains with a hundred patients, about two dozen of whom were stretcher cases. The English pilgrimage consisted of nearly eight hundred people. The Roman Catholic authorities gave us every opportunity to witness the processions and other activities and to ask any questions we wished.

The leaders in charge of the pilgrimages to Lourdes, so far from desiring to advertise cures and attract the sensational reports of the Press, seem almost reluctant to admit cures. They repeatedly declared that the purpose of the pilgrimage is to deepen the spiritual life of the pilgrim and strengthen his faith in Christ and His Church, and that miraculous cures are of minor importance.

This is borne out by the strict regulations which attach to the publication of a miraculous cure. Let us imagine that John Smith, who is ill in London, makes the pilgrimage to Lourdes to seek recovery. In the first place, he is not allowed to be a registered patient at all if his illness is of "nervous" origin. People have gone to Lourdes with "nervous breakdowns" and have alleged that they were cured there, but the authorities take no notice of such a statement. One priest said to me, "Such people would get better anyway. We must have the cure of a definite organic illness." A medical man (Dr. de Grandmaison), in *Twenty Cures at Lourdes Medically Discussed*, lists cases of pulmonary tuberculosis, cancer of the tongue and of the breast, tuberculosis disease of the spine, ulcer of the leg of twelve years duration, compound fracture of the leg of eight years standing, and fracture of the femur of three months standing. Percy Dearmer[1] gives a longer list, including organic cases, and G. G. Dawson[2] gives a list including cases of children of thirty months cured of club-foot and bow legs.

Nor is a cure registered if an apparent organic illness is thought to have a psychological origin. Our imaginary patient, John Smith, would have to go to Lourdes armed with a dossier signed by his own doctor at home, indicating the onset of his illness, with dates, all the treatments he had tried, with dates, the opinions of any specialists consulted, with names and dates, a list of all his symptoms, a medical estimate of the severity of his illness, and so on. This dossier being in order, he is provided with a large label indicating that he is an official patient. If he is a stretcher case, he is given the utmost care by a number of young Roman Catholic men who volunteer for service to help the invalids on these pilgrimages.

Let us imagine that after bathing, or taking part in a procession, John Smith says that he feels better. First of all, he is examined by the resident doctor on the spot, with whom I had several conversations. I have never met a doctor more reluctant to admit a cure. Indeed, sometimes he appeared almost brusque with a patient, saying, "Oh, you will be just as bad tomorrow," or, "Don't make a fuss about it yet. Wait and see." This almost seemed hard on the patient, but, on reflection, I am sure the doctor was merely excluding hysterical hopes based on the flimsiest evidence of pathological change.

However, suppose John Smith the next day shows obvious signs of improvement, then at least three doctors examine him, one of whom is a specialist in his area of case. For instance, if he came with a skin infection, one of the doctors would be a dermatologist. No doubt the examinations are thorough. Modern apparatus, however, did not seem adequate. The X-ray equipment, for instance, was out of order, and other diagnostic aids, which one would have expected to find were missing altogether. Hadfield and Browne make the same comment.[3] Supposing even after such an examination John Smith still shows signs of improvement, he will be sent back to England and told to return in twelve months. After this period has elapsed he will have to bring with him another dossier showing the opinion of his home doctor and any specialist called in, with names and dates, particulars of any further treatment he has had, and then on returning to Lourdes he will be

[1] *Op. cit.*
[2] *Op. cit.*
[3] See *Psychology and the Church*, p. 238 (Macmillan, 1925).

re-examined by at least three more doctors, some of whom are also priests. If they all confirm that during the brief period of the stay in Lourdes a cure of organic disease has taken place, the Archbishop holds a commission, and can call in any medical authorities he likes, and if the cure is confirmed, then it becomes a registered cure and it is declared that Christ, through the intercession of our Lady at Lourdes, has worked a miracle on the patient, and cured him of this or that disease in a manner unknown to medical authority.

In my opinion, there can be no possible doubt that the cures of physical illnesses take place in a remarkable way. For example, a four-year-old boy went to Lourdes in August, 1938, suffering from meningitis, with paralysis of both legs and arms and with total blindness. Dr. D. made the first diagnosis, and it was confirmed by one of the pilgrimage doctors, Dr. R. After his first visit to the baths, the patient's condition remained the same, but from the second visit he came out completely cured. The case was submitted to the Medical Bureau in Lourdes, and eleven doctors signed the following statement: "No medical explanation is possible for the instantaneous disappearance of the illness and its symptoms." A year later the boy was again taken to Lourdes and re-examined by fifteen doctors, including four professors, and the earlier conclusions were confirmed. The Archbishop of the Province of Aix, Arles and Embrun was present himself when twenty doctors examined the patient and signed a statement saying, "This cure is inexplicable by human knowledge." Finally, the Archbishop set up an ecclesiastical commission which declared: "We have found an abundance of testimony proving the existence of a very grave illness and of a certain cure humanly inexplicable. In these circumstances, it has become our duty to declare the miraculous nature of the cure of —— ——."

By permission of the resident doctor at Lourdes, we were allowed to examine the records of cures which took place in earlier years, and we spent many hours translating these case-particulars from the French originals. I have added, as an Appendix, the details of two cases concerning which we made notes at the time, the first the case of a boy who was totally blind, and the second a woman who, over a period of years, had had advanced tuberculosis and had been given up as incurable. Not only were full notes of both these cases available to us, but we were allowed to see the X-ray photographs as well. I repeat my own firm conclusion that there cannot be any doubt that real cures of organic diseases have taken place.

Those who have read the beautifully written novel by Dr. Franz

Werfel, called *The Song of Bernadette*,[4] and who have seen the film of the same name, will be familiar with the origin of the healings at Lourdes. Lourdes is a little town in South France, nestling under the shadow of the mighty Pyrenees and extending into the foothills of those mountains. It would have slept in obscurity until now, one imagines, save that a young Roman Catholic girl had some remarkable religious experiences there.

At 12:30 on February 11, 1858—the Thursday before Lent—this young girl, Bernadette Soubirous, aged fourteen, very religiously inclined, who was probably in a state of religious exaltation because she was eagerly looking forward to her first Communion, for which she had been carefully prepared, was sent with her younger sister and a friend called Jeanne Abadie, to get firewood for their parents, who were poor peasants living in the village.

When they got nearly opposite a grotto, or cave, called Massabieille, they could not proceed farther along the path they were following because a stream of water which worked a water-mill was running across it. Jeanne Abadie and Bernadette's sister took off their shoes and stockings and paddled across, but Bernadette was nervous of doing so because a sudden chill of that description brought on attacks of asthma to which she was prone. She was never a robust child. However, when Bernadette saw her companions going on without her, she decided to follow their example, and began to remove her stockings. By this time the others were out of sight.

She then heard a noise which she described as the sound of a rising storm. She says that as she looked about her, frightened at the sudden sound of a violent wind blowing, out of the interior of the grotto came a golden-coloured cloud, and then a beautiful lady, more beautiful than any she had ever seen, came and stood at the entrance to an opening in the grotto, above a small bush. This lady smiled at her and beckoned to her. Bernadette knelt in rapture and began to finger the rosary which she carried. The beautiful lady then took up a rosary which had been hanging on her own right arm, and, at the end of the prayers, joined audibly in the Gloria with Bernadette. When the recitation of the rosary was over, the lady and the cloud disappeared.

By this time the other two girls had missed Bernadette, and, coming to look for her, found her on her knees by the grotto in a state of ecstasy. They saw nothing of the lady. Bernadette, however, returned

---

[4] Dr. Werfel fled to Lourdes from Occupied France, and vowed that if he escaped the Germans, he would write the story of Bernadette (Viking, 1942).

with them, braving, without any dismay, the water of the stream of whose chilliness she had previously been afraid, and even saying that she thought it warm. She confided the experience to her sister and pledged her to secrecy, but that night at family prayers Bernadette suddenly began to cry, and, in explanation, her sister told the mother the strange story. Bernadette confirmed it and gave the most minute description of the lady, and of the robe, ribbons and veil in which she appeared.

Again and again Bernadette visited the grotto, both with others—who never saw or heard anything unusual—and alone. Bernadette claimed that when she asked the lady her name, she got the reply, "I am the Immaculate Conception," a sentence which obviously does not make sense. At her ninth visit Bernadette was observed to move about, as if being directed by some person invisible to her companions, and then suddenly to bend down and scratch at the earth. As she made a hole in the ground, it filled with water, though at that time no water was known to flow underground at that point. She washed in it, drank some of it and returned to her friends and family, who thought she was quite mad. But a stream has flowed there ever since, and healing properties have been claimed for it.

There is set up at Lourdes a great tablet in the rock, bearing the following inscription in French: "In the hollow of the rock where her statue is now seen, the Holy Virgin appeared to Bernadette Soubirous eighteen times. [Dates follow.] The Holy Virgin told the child, 'Will you do me the kindness [*me faire la grâce*] to come here daily for fifteen days? I do not promise to make you happy in this world, but I will do so in the other. I wish the whole world to come here. [*Qu'il vienne du monde.*] The Virgin said to her during the fortnight, 'You must pray for sinners and be penitent on their behalf. Penitence! penitence! penitence! Tell the priests to build here a chapel, to arrange processions and to drink and bathe in the stream. Go and eat of that grass which is there [*de cette herbe qui est là*]. I am the Immaculate Conception.' "

These instructions have certainly been carried out. To the right of the mouth of the cave in which the vision was seen by Bernadette is a life-size statue of Mary, and in the centre there is a large altar. Above and behind the altar, across the face of the rock, are hanging crutches and abdominal belts which patients have discarded who have claimed to have been cured at Lourdes. On top of the cliff a most beautiful church has been built, with its doors facing at right-angles to the entrance of the cave where the statue stands. To the right and left of these doors large ramps rise up from the plain, so that invalid carriages may be wheeled up the cliff and into the church. Between these two ramps is the great open space capable of accommodating many thousands of people. At night the church is outlined with thousands of electric lights, and bright floodlights play upon the doors and upon the vast open space. By the help of loudspeakers the priest chanting in the church can be clearly heard by thousands of people in the great open space, and to see them in procession, or kneeling for the Bishop's blessing, is a most moving sight.

A pilgrim might spend a day at Lourdes as follows. First of all he would attend Mass, which is held at five, six, seven, eight and nine o'clock every morning. Then at eleven there is a service with a sermon in the church. In the afternoon the various nationalities take it in turn to lead processions from the grotto, or cave, by a wide detour back to the great open space. In the latter the sick are re-assembled, the invalid carriages in front, the sitting cases behind and the standing cases behind them. The Host is carried out of the church in a golden monstrance, and the Bishop bearing it blesses each sufferer by including the Host towards him, and prayers are said. There is an injunction to have faith in the Blessed Virgin, and one is almost wearied by the endless chanting of "Ave, Ave Maria."

Both in the morning and afternoon there are bathing facilities. The stream which Bernadette uncarthed is now conducted along pipes in which there are taps, so that water may be drawn off for drinking or carrying away, and then the pipes enter the bathing-chambers—six for women and three for men. The patient enters through heavy curtains, and is there completely stripped of all his clothes. A towel, wrung out in the water, is placed round his loins, and, if able, he descends three steps into a bath of cold water about three or four feet deep. If he is incapacitated, priests, doctors or other attendants help him into the bath until he is entirely submerged in the water. Women are helped by women assistants, nurses and women doctors. Prayers are recited while the patient is being bathed. He is not allowed to rub down with any dry towel. His clothes are replaced on him hurriedly, and he is bustled out because of the tremendous number of people who desire to take the baths.

It was this bathing that made me feel uneasy. The water flows in slowly at the top of the bath and flows out at the same level, so that the water in which John Smith bathes is practically the same water as his immediate predecessors have used. Since there are people who have come a long way, people who are far from clean, people who are too ill to be continent, and people with discharging ulcers, skin diseases, running sores and inflamed eyes, it must take a great deal of faith to be plunged beneath water which bears only too obvious signs of its filthiness, hoping to be cured. When I visited the baths I asked the priest in charge whether he was not afraid of having an epidemic on his hands. But, to my surprise, both the doctors in charge of the English pilgrims took daily baths themselves. They were, of course, Roman Catholics. One of them has since written me that he regards the freedom from infection as in itself a miracle, and that he himself bathed as an act of penance on behalf of the sick who could not go to Lourdes. The priest in charge told me that to prove his faith, he cupped his hands and drank the water every time he bathed in it. For my own part, the evidence of the state of the baths would be enough to preclude me from advising any patient I cared about in this country to make the long, tiring journey of twenty-seven hours to bathe in the sacred stream at Lourdes, though, in fact, there were no reports of any patient having been harmed by bathing, or of any epidemic breaking out. Framed in the Bureau des Constatations Médicales is a statement that when action was threatened to close the baths on hygienic grounds, three thousand doctors sent in protests.

As the dusk falls, further processions take place. Each pilgrim purchases a candle, and usually a candle-shade, which is shaped like an open tulip, with the wider aperture at the top. On the parchment of which the shade is composed the creed is printed, and one of the most impressive sights in Lourdes is to see the great square full of thousands of pilgrims, all bearing lighted candles and repeating the creed together, led by the priest, whose voice is electrically magnified. No one who has seen the vast multitude kneeling in the square, their voices like the sound of many waters, the church above them brilliantly illuminated with electric lights, and above that the outline of the Pyrenean foothills, and above all the dark blue, velvety sky of southern France, pierced by the bright stars, can ever forget the scene. Protestants though we were, and more so after Lourdes than before, we were deeply moved by this beautiful act of worship.

Yet, though there were ten thousand pilgrims in Lourdes while I was there, no one even claimed to have been cured. It is said that six hundred thousand pilgrims go to Lourdes every year. In 1948 more than two million pilgrims visited the shrine. Fifteen thousand were patients, but only one is expected to be an official "cure," although eighty-three dossiers were retained for further examination.[5]

Thus the experiences of a peasant girl began a world-famous cult, authorised finally by the Pope as the cult of Our Lady of Lourdes.

[5] *Rapport Annuel sur le Bureau Médical de Lourdes et les Pèlerinages.*

It seems important, at this point in our discussion, to analyse the experiences of Bernadette which made Lourdes a familiar name throughout the civilised world.

In my opinion, we must call her original experience an hallucination. I use the word in its technical sense, and to do so is not to disparage such an experience or the person who has it and subsequently narrates it. It is not to belittle her integrity or mental equipment. It is far from a denial of her veracity or mental competence. This must be stated inasmuch as many people, reading the word "hallucination," make unfair deductions about the mental health or emotional balance of the person who has it. An hallucination, in a very true sense, is real. It is real to the person who sees it, and we are to judge the experience as a fact, and not dismiss it because it is beyond the circle of normal experience. It may truly be called the fruit of the imagination, but the imagination is one of the most real qualities man possesses.

By an hallucination I mean that Bernadette's subjective mental state became so intense that it was projected in a way which had the same effect upon her senses as if it had happened in the objective world. Even if we accept Bernadette's account—and the vision was seen only by her—it is not difficult to see how this was built up. Here was a girl at the stage of puberty, with all the emotional instability of that stage in feminine development. All girls at the age of fourteen tend to be more religious than at other times. Bernadette was exceptionally so. She was longing for the time when she could take her first Communion. When she saw the vision, the Feast of Corpus Christi was imminent and Easter was only six weeks away.

The records make one most significant point. They state that the garments in which—according to Bernadette—the lady appeared were alleged by a young friend of Bernadette, Antoinette Peyret, to be similar to those worn at their religious ceremonies by members of a Guild of Girls called Les Enfants de Marie. What is even more important, Bernadette, who belonged to the Guild, and herself wore such clothes and had within recent months taken part in the funeral of the Guild's President, Mademoiselle Elisa Latapie, who had been a second mother to all the girls in the Guild. It is significant that when Antoinette Peyret heard about the visions, she identified the lady not as the Virgin Mary, but as Mademoiselle Latapie, who, she supposed, had returned to ask for their prayers.

The words used by the lady seen in the vision—"Immaculate Conception"—would seem to be explicable by the fact that the Pope, Pius IX, had, four years earlier (1854), proclaimed the dogma of the Immaculate Conception as an Article of Faith. The village priest, Monsieur Peyramale, had more recently preached on this subject, and all Catholic France had discussed it. This young girl Bernadette, approaching puberty and becoming slowly aware of the facts of sex, had, no doubt, pondered the meaning of the words "Immaculate Conception," and brooded over the strange facts of normal human birth, with their ancient association with "sin," and the vision brought the words behind her mind to her lips—or did the ideas in her mind produce the vision? Perhaps both. At any rate, each seems to have depended on the other.

As for the stream, it is a matter of scientic knowledge—though not understanding—that some psychically abnormal people, called water-diviners, have the gift of detecting water, even if it is hidden under the ground. A friend of mine, armed with the familiar twig, can be taken to a completely strange spot and can indicate, with a high proportion of successes, where water is likely to be found below the surface. In military operations in the desert during the Second World War, such people were employed with most useful results. Bernadette was psychically an unusual type of girl, and the gift had apparently lain dormant until stimulated by the vision.

Marcus Gregory reminds us that "in 1879 Abbé Richard, a famous hydrographist, who spent a week at Lourdes examining the springs of the district, said that if he had seen the Massabieille rock and the little hill above it, he would have expected to have found water there; and even if he had never heard of the 'Appearances' or of the spring, and had come by the railway which passes the grotto a few hundred metres away, he would have said that there was a spring of water there. The spring was a typical phenomenon of the district." [6] Dawson says that a water diviner, De Montlieu, spent eight days in the grotto, and came to the conclusion that water had always been there, and was ultimately bound to burst from the ground.[7]

It is interesting that the water has never failed since Bernadette uncovered the spring, and twenty-six thousand gallons a day now pass through the pipes. The water has been analysed, and it has been found that there is no quality in it which could medically account for the cures. The temperature is between twelve and sixteen degrees Centigrade. No scientist has ever claimed that it has any therapeutic value. In his volume entitled, *Lourdes* (p. 99), Dr. Boissarie says that a quarryman called Bourriette first conceived the idea that the water of the spring might benefit his eyes, which had been injured in

[6] *Op. cit.*
[7] *Op. cit.*

an explosion, and that it was he who was responsible for the long series of cures claimed subsequently. Nothing was said to Bernadette by the Virgin which could be construed as a promise of the cure of disease. The words, "I do not promise to make you happy in this world, but in the other" seems rather to exclude the cure of bodily disease. Bernadette was herself a lifelong asthma patient and this disease was the cause of her death. Further, it must be remembered that cures take place during the religious processions, and particularly during Mass, without any reference whatever to the water. Some cures take place even before the patient reaches Lourdes, and some even after he has left it and returned home. The water cannot count for much.

An interesting British comparison is seen in the cures reported from Holywell in Flintshire, Wales. Around the chapel and shrine of St. Winefride—a seventeenth-century virgin who, it is said, died defending her chastity and was miraculously restored to life—are stacked crutches and surgical appliances discarded by cripples who claimed to have been cured by immersion in the holy water. The maimed and deformed—I am told—are still carried there. Many make the pilgrimage to immerse themselves in the holy water which is believed to spring from the ground at the place where the martyr's head touched it.

But it appears that in 1917 (if the Press is to be believed)[8] the spring ceased and that since then the water has been laid on through a pipe from a nearby reservoir used to supply water for a textile mill. Pilgrims are, however, sometimes cured even now, though it is alleged that the water is supplied by the Urban District Council.

I wish now to attempt a critical opinion of Lourdes considered as a healing factor. We need not reiterate the immense effect on the body of the mind-soul (not distinguishing the two latter for the moment). The trouble is that there are so many factors which must be a harmonised whole before the immense non-physical energy is linked up with the patient's body. Some of the factors are known. One of them, for instance, is called, in the New Testament, "faith." It was not a theologically developed faith, but rather an attitude of trustful expectancy. Yet, unfortunately, faith is not the only condition required, and many of the conditions required before the power, as it were, will flow are unknown. Our Lord seems in many cases to have got all these factors working harmoniously, and cures resulted. Yet even He did not cure everybody. Clearly one can have faith without healing and one can have healing without faith. One of the interesting things about Lourdes is the number of sick people in the town itself who never

[8] Sunday Press, September 11, 1949.

go near the grotto. Another is that many people who have been cured are not believers in any form of Christianity at all, let alone pious Roman Catholics. As Canon Anson, a most sympathetic writer, says, they "are people who could be cured in exactly the same way by Coué, or by any other psychotherapist, without any profession of religion." [9] A Glasgow professor of surgery, Mr. Charles Buchanan, wrote in the *Lancet* of June 20, 1885, of the mistake of being over impressed when people throw away crutches and claim they can walk. He illustrates by examples the simulation of disease and the immediate power of a change in the mind, and after quoting many cases adds, "Such cases are familiar to all medical men and are the most intractable they have to deal with, *the disorder being in the imagination and not in the part.*" Mr. Buchanan made this statement immediately after a visit to Lourdes. After many months in bed with a "painful affection of the spine" a patient rose and walked without pain at a word of command from Buchanan who was forthwith regarded as a miracle worker.

The percentage of cures at Lourdes is very low. At least ninety-eight out of every hundred sick persons who visit Lourdes come back uncured. The pathos of this situation is really most depressing, and, indeed, terrible to behold. On the train on which I made my pilgrimage were just over a hundred sick people. At last money had been raised or found for them, and they were going to Lourdes. On the way down through France they were sure they were going to be better. In spite of all their doctors may have said, the great chance had come at last. And then the six days passed, and as the time ran out, their faith began to waver and their hope began to die. By walking up the train sometimes and chatting with the sick, and by visiting them in hospital while they were at Lourdes, I became acquainted with some of the patients. On the journey back not one of them complained. I never heard one grumble from start to finish. Indeed, I am told that many accept "the will of God" and go on undismayed. But the pathos of the eyes was terrible to behold and the depression hard indeed to overcome. Many patients not only went back home with the last hope gone, but it must have been a severe shock to their Christian faith.

To my mind great restraint should be exercised before advising patients to go to Lourdes. Religious faith is clearly not enough. The pious are often unhealed; the unbeliever healed. It may be that in a small percentage of cases the factors necessary to cure are all present and a cure may result. But many of these factors remain unknown, and the presence of all can only be a matter of chance. If they *are*

[9] Anson, *Spiritual Healing* (Doran, 1923).

all present, amazing cures do take place, vast forces are unleashed, but, as I have shown, the proportion of failures is so high that disappointment and depression are likely to ensue. Some patients manifest a temporary improvement in the mental atmosphere of Lourdes, where suggestibility is heightened by mass devotion, the processions and the general excitement. Back in the little home town there can be devastating relapses. In fact, patients under the guise of an emotional religion have had an inadequate psychological treatment, accompanied by just that publicity which Christ deprecated.[10]

Lourdes can, no doubt, provide a great spiritual experience. As a healing agency its proportion of failures makes it negligible. Few of its cures brought to our notice could possibly be regarded as "miracles" in the sense defined earlier in this book, and those few did not depend on the paraphernalia of Lourdes. Obviously some cures, like those quoted in the Appendix, are not understood. But there is probably no stream in Britain which could not boast as high a proportion of cures as the stream at Lourdes if patients came in the same numbers and in the same psychological state of expectant excitement. I entirely concur with the *Proceedings of the Society for Psychical Research,* which I quote,[11] "There is no real evidence, either that the apparition of the Virgin was itself more than a subjective hallucination, or that it has any more than a merely subjective connection with the cures."

Roman Catholic teaching about Lourdes is to me incomprehensible. Father Vernon Johnson's addresses to the pilgrims who attended Lourdes show how hopelessly confused is his logic.[12] No Roman Catholic writer is allowed to express in print his own private views if they are out of harmony with the official teachings of his Church, and these addresses are published by the Catholic Truth Society. We can only assume that Roman Catholic teaching about Lourdes is confused.

Father Johnson's first message includes the sentence, "Most of you will return home without being cured just because it is your business to be ill. It is a most precious business which has come to you straight from Heaven. . . . It is the most beautiful thing in the world—ordained for you from all eternity. . . . There is no other way to Heaven except suffering" (pp. 9-10).

But on p. 43 we read, "First of all, what is the cause of all this pain?

[10] See Matthew 8:4, 9:30, 16:20; Mark 5:43, 7:24, 36, 8:30, 9:9; Luke 5:14.

[11] *Op. cit.,* p. 204.

[12] Father Vernon Johnson, *Suffering and Lourdes* (Catholic Truth Society, 46th Thousand Impression, 1950).

Where is it? Did God mean it? No." But Father Johnson cannot have it both ways. He tells us that suffering is a beautiful thing ordained from all eternity, and then tells us that God did not mean it, and on p. 44 that suffering is due to the fall of man, forgetting that both suffering and death were facts of the animal creation before man appeared on the earth. Having assured us on p. 44 that suffering is the result of the fall of man, he doubles back on p. 50 and writes this: "The pain, the suffering, the death which lies before you is simply the chalice which your Heavenly Father giveth you." Having said that suffering was due to sin, he says on p. 54, "Our Lord Jesus wants our suffering for the completion of His work for souls." It is impossible to make sense of such confused statements. I cannot advise a pilgrimage to Lourdes either for the instruction of the mind or the healing of the body.

3

CHRISTIAN SCIENCE

WE COME NOW to the study of the best-known and most strongly supported of all the modern movements of healing through religion: the movement called Christian Science. We shall first of all set out the historical facts which led to the beginning of this movement. This involves giving, so far as they can be determined, the main facts of the life of its founder, Mrs. Eddy, for the facts of her life form an important factor in our estimate of the movement she initiated. Then we shall review the main text-book of Christian Science, passages from which are read at every service. The book is called *Science and Health with a Key to the Scriptures*. Then we shall examine the theories on which Christian Science is based, survey its practices, and finally make a critical examination of the movement and seek to assess its value.

A. THE FOUNDER

It is difficult even to state the facts which led to the founding of the movement now called Christian Science, because our sources of information seem to be surrounded either with an atmosphere of an almost malicious criticism, or else of uncritical and sometimes obsequious adulation. Peabody, a Boston lawyer, begins his book on Christian Science with the sentence, "Christian Science is the most shallow and sordid and wicked imposture of the ages"; [1] whereas one of Mrs. Eddy's followers declared that if she saw Mrs. Eddy commit a crime, she would blame her own eyesight, but not her heroine. The most dispassionate view, in my opinion, is that of Edwin Frankden Dakin, published by Charles Scribner and Sons in 1929. In spite of what ap-

[1] Frederick W. Peabody, *The Religio-Medical Masquerade*, p. 5 (Fleming H. Revell Co., 1910 and 1915).

155

pears to be a genuine desire to arrive at the facts, Dakin's book aroused a storm of criticism amongst Christian Scientists which was fierce enough to bring about the withdrawal of the book in America. Sibyl Wilbur's book it is hard to take seriously. The heroine is alleged to be perfect, and at times the style of the book is so flowery as to be nauseating. For example, speaking of the privilege a child of twelve, Susie Felt, had in being with Mrs. Eddy, the author says, "Such hours were hers in the twilight alone with Mary Baker (Eddy) when the divine overflow suffused sweet dew that could not harm the tender violets of a child's unfolding thoughts." Or again (p. 206), "Her balconies were filled with calla lilies of which she was particularly fond, and when she stood among them, tending and caring for them with the sunlight sifting through the leaves of the elm, making splashes of green and gold upon her cool, white gown, she made a picture of composure and purity."

The facts appear to be as follows.[2]

Mary Baker (afterwards Mrs. Eddy) was born on July 16, 1821. Her father, a farmer, was a strict Calvinist. Mary seldom went to school, because she was constantly ill, especially, it is said, from nervous disorders, including convulsive seizures and hysteria, which troubled her from childhood till the end of her long life. Even when she was writing her text-book and denying the reality of suffering, she was herself a sufferer. All her biographers testify to this, including Sibyl Wilbur, who is the author of what is described as the official life of Mrs. Eddy.[3] Dr. Ladd, the family physician, is said to have described her as hysterical and bad-tempered.

At the age of twenty-two, Mary Baker, as she was then, married George Washington Glover, a builder, and went to live in South Carolina. Glover died of yellow fever. A son was born posthumously. Mrs. Glover then lived with one of her sisters. Nervous troubles again set in. She would be in bed one moment, and the next moment would have to be sought all over the countryside. During

[2] I have quoted some material here from my former book, *Psychology in Service of the Soul* (Macmillan, 1930). That material was gathered from various sources, mainly Janet's great work, *Psychological Healing*, Vol. I. Janet draws many of his facts, as Dakin does, from *The Life of Mary Baker G. Eddy and the History of Christian Science*, by Georgine Milmine, published in New York and London in 1909. Since these facts have not been conclusively contradicted by Christian Scientists, although my own book was published twenty years ago, I assume that the facts set down in the text above may be accepted.

[3] See *The Life of Mary Baker Eddy*, pp. 59 et seq. (the Christian Science Publishing Society, 1938), and Dakin, *op. cit.*, pp. 118, 123, 127, 212, etc.

some periods of hysteria she would demand to be rocked in a cradle like a child. Some boys in the village, says Janet, would earn a few cents by "swinging Mrs. Glover."

In 1853 she married the second time, an itinerant dentist called Patterson. This marriage was unhappy, and the wife sued for divorce. She was successful on the ground of Patterson's desertion, or perhaps adultery, and she resumed the name of Glover.

She then lived with her sister, Mrs. Tilton. Janet says, "She took a great deal of trouble with her appearance, spoke mincingly, and ransacked the dictionary for unusual and grandiloquent words. She claimed to be able to find lost articles by second sight. She disclosed the whereabouts of Captain Kidd's treasures, but they were not there!"

We are told that she got on badly with her sister, and went to live with anyone who would give her shelter, and that one host, Captain Webster, with her sister's son-in-law, at one point carried her luggage into the street and slammed the door in her face.

At forty years of age she met a "magnetiser," as he called himself, named Quimby. He had been a working-class watchmaker until he studied the work of Poyen, a French magnetiser who gave demonstrations of somnambulism. Quimby then set up for himself, using hypnotic suggestion. Some writers call him "atheist"; others say he believed that he was on the track of discovering the way in which our Lord healed the sick, and he wrote ten volumes of manuscript working out his theories, and calling his technique "the Science of Health," or "the Science of Christ." Once or twice he himself used the term "Christian Science." Quimby was not an educated man, and some of his theories were muddled nonsense, but he was not insincere. He was a pioneer in the use of suggestive therapy, and if he could have had the support of real scientists and had welcomed the help they could have given him, he would have gone further. He was extremely kind to the poor, who formed the bulk of his patients, and seems, indeed, to have been a man of character.

To his rooms came the ailing Mrs. Glover, after desperate efforts to collect enough money for her fare. From their first meeting Quimby seems to have been attracted to the handsome neurotic patient, and there is no doubt at all that she was charmed with him. Mrs. Glover, like every neurotic, was delighted to be the subject of someone's interest. She had been married twice, and neither partnership had given her what she wanted. Here was someone concerned about her and offering not only sympathy, but also treatment. In a very short time she was cured of her neurotic symptoms and developed a positive transference regarding Quimby. We are told that she composed love sonnets and sent them to him and wrote him the most extravagant letters, likening his hands, for example, to those of Christ. In time she virtually became his secretary and assistant, and said that her only aim was to spread his teachings. Photographs of her letters to him can be seen in Milmine's Life. Quimby died of an abdominal tumour in January, 1866.

Janet tells us that when Quimby died, Mrs. Glover seized his manuscript books on religion and disease, copied them out, added "interpretations" of the Bible and weird commentaries of her own. Janet says, "This unlettered woman, who was unable to pen a grammatical sentence, and did not understand the first principles of punctuation, undertook to write a book." This was the beginning of the book *Science and Health*, described as "the new revelation which was to make an end of all diseases."

Wilbur claims that Mrs. Eddy afterwards purged her book of all the Quimby material, but one doubts whether this would be possible, even if attempted. Walter M. Haushalter, minister of the Christian Temple Church in Baltimore, wrote a book claiming to prove that Mrs. Eddy owed many of the more intelligent passages in *Science and Health* to a manuscript by Francis Lieber, called *The Metaphysical Religion of Hegel*, to which Mrs. Eddy is said to have had access. Haushalter prints a photograph of this document, the cover of which has a marginal note which reads as follows: "N.B. This is Metaphysical Basis of Healing and Science of Health. Same as Christ-Power and Truth-Power. (Signed) Mary Baker." Haushalter prints many parallel passages endeavouring to prove his contention anent Mrs. Eddy's "plagiarism" from Hegel and also from Ruskin, Swedenborg, Carlyle, Amiel and others.[4] Mark Twain also accused Mrs. Eddy of plagiarism.

Those who have studied neurotic traits are familiar with the fact that a neurotic person is quite capable of using literary material from another source, and yet at the same time quite sincerely believing that she has composed it herself. This seems to have been the case with Mrs. Eddy. Though she owed an enormous amount to Quimby, and perhaps to others, at the same time she did sincerely believe that what she wrote was a revelation given to herself alone.

We shall notice that throughout her life Mrs. Eddy again and again withdrew from actual contact with patients. She did this in early years when she took into partnership a young man called Richard Kennedy, aged twenty-one. He was of enormous help to her. He was

---

[4] Walter M. Haushalter, *Mrs. Eddy Purloins from Hegel* (Beauchamp, 1936).

a man of charming disposition, and understood—if anyone can be said to understand them—the teachings of Quimby. He handled Mrs. Eddy's finances, and was a great success as a healer, but according to Dakin she grew jealous of his success and her failure, quarrelled with him repeatedly, and after an outburst in which she accused him of cheating at cards, she said that he was trying to rob her and trying to kill her by transferring to her the illness of the patients he healed. This idea was an obsession with Mrs. Eddy. Malicious animal magnetism, or, as it came to be called by her adherents, "M.A.M.," was capable of destroying not only her happiness, but also her health. And all through her life she was haunted by the fear that others were causing her to be ill and to suffer both mentally and physically by directing the evil thoughts towards her. The modern practice of Christian Science, as we shall see, has delivered many people from fear, but if her biographers are to be trusted, all her life she was a pathetic victim of morbid terror and chronic anxiety. Kennedy appears to have been nearly distracted by her tantrums, and he left her, giving her six thousand dollars as compensation.

Mrs. Glover thereupon in 1871 set up a school to train others to heal by her methods, at which the premium payable was one hundred dollars, and amongst her pupils was one called Daniel Spofford, who became a great favourite. It is said that he spent twelve months trying to reduce her incomprehensible manuscript to order, and that this was the first editing of *Science and Health*.

It was Spofford who introduced Gilbert Asa Eddy, a sewing-machine agent, to Mrs. Glover, who was then fifty-six years of age. She married Eddy in 1877. This was her third marriage. A perusal of the record of the marriage discloses that Mrs. Eddy's age was given as forty, but, adds Peabody, the Boston lawyer, the marriage was "celebrated fifty-six years from the date of her birth." [5] Unfortunately, Spofford, like Richard Kennedy before him, became too popular, and the same kind of charge was made against him. He was said to be robbing her of her health so as to pass it on to the sick. Her continual bouts of illness she attributed to his directing evil thoughts upon her. "Stop thinking of me," she wrote, "or you will cut me off *soon* from the face of the earth." [6]

In 1875 she wrote to Spofford as follows: "Thou criminal, mental marauder that would blot out the sunshine of the earth, that would

[5] Frederick Peabody, *The Religio-Medical Masquerade*, p. 40 (Fleming H. Revell Co., 1910 and 1915); cf. also Dakin, *op. cit.*, p. 124, who gives her age as fifty-seven, though we are told that the wedding certificate bore the age of forty.

[6] Letter preserved by Georgine Milmine, *op. cit.*, p. 173.

sever friends, destroy virtue, put out truth, murder in secret the innocent, befouling with thy trade the trophies of thy guilt." Her hatred of Spofford was such that she went to law in 1879, accusing him of witchcraft, and though the action failed, she expelled him from the Christian Science Association. At last, says Janet, she organised a conspiracy against him, paid a large sum to a saloon-keeper called Sargent, who was to encompass the murder of Spofford. The upshot was an enormous scandal and a trial at which, Janet tells us, Mrs. Eddy and her husband were both fined. Frankly, it seems to me that here Janet, who writes with an antagonistic pen, may well be exaggerating. Wilbur says, "The monstrous charge was dismissed without a trial," [7] and makes a good case that Mrs. Eddy and her husband, who, with Arens, was arrested for conspiring to murder, were innocent of this charge.

In 1882 Mr. Eddy died of heart disease, though it was announced that he had died of arsenical poisoning "mentally administered." Mrs. Eddy alleged that the arsenic had been *thought* into him by his enemies. She sat by him constantly, says Dakin, with her face close to his, murmuring, "Gilbert, Gilbert, do not suffer so." But he died at daybreak on June 3, 1882.[8] Dr. Rufus K. Noyes of Boston, who was actually called by Mrs. Eddy to attend her husband, performed an autopsy, and showed the diseased heart to Mrs. Eddy, but Mrs. Eddy would not allow that it was anything of the kind.

At sixty-one years of age, when most people are thinking of retiring, Mrs. Eddy, with praiseworthy energy and determination, was beginning the most important part of her work. She went to Boston, and obtained the help of yet another man called Buswell, who founded a small monthly journal of Christian Science, and who was the means of introducing her to Calvin Frye, who ultimately rose to a very high position in administering her affairs, and who, although he sat in uniform as a footman on the box of her carriage, ran her household and administered many of her finances.

About this time also *Science and Health* was under revision again by an ex-Unitarian minister called the Rev. James Henry Wiggin, who endeavoured to put the work into intelligible English, making it clear that he did not share the views and had merely been employed to

[7] *Op. cit.*, p. 240.

[8] Dakin, *op. cit.*, p. 166. Here again Wilbur makes an ingenious case that Eddy died of hatred; that the hatred of his enemies and the worry thus caused to him, set up symptoms *similar to those of arsenical poisoning*. She quotes an article from the *Washington Herald* of August 1907, in which a Professor Elmer Gates is alleged to prove that hate against another can, in fact, poison him.—Wilbur, *op. cit.*, p. 268.

transcribe Mrs. Eddy's confused text into something like an intelligible document. Peabody says that Wiggin personally told him that it was a source of much mirth to him to hear Mrs. Eddy's devotees praise, as the most divinely inspired portion of a divine volume, a sermon of his own which came to be included in *Science and Health*.[9]

The Boston school was begun in 1883, and immediately became a great source of revenue. There was a primary course, a course of "metaphysical obstetrics" and a course of theology, the fee for the whole series being eight hundred dollars. One woman—Mrs. Corner—after a course of "metaphysical obstetrics" which included no anatomy at all, undertook to officiate at her daughter's confinement. Both mother and baby died, and a charge was brought against Mrs. Corner for criminal neglect. But when Mrs. Corner referred to Mrs. Eddy, the latter gave her no sympathy, and is said to have denounced her as an incapable pupil.

There can be no doubt that Mrs. Eddy's life was filled with disturbances and upheavals. A former pupil of Quimby came to Boston and alleged that Mrs. Eddy owed her main ideas to Quimby. Even some of the love-letters from Mrs. Eddy to Quimby were published in the Press. Mrs. Eddy was furious, and ordered her disciples not to read a single line on mental treatment unless she had signed it. But in spite of her insistence, a new thought-movement began, based on the more reasonable teachings of the Quimby philosophy, and the movement was divided. Yet no one can deny the immense success from her own point of view which Mrs. Eddy achieved.

In 1879 she came to Boston to found her church called "The Church of Christ (Scientist)," with herself as President, Margaret J. Dunshee as Treasurer, and seven directors. The services consisted of prayer, a reading from *Science and Health*, a reading from the Bible and a talk by Mrs. Eddy if she were present. When this church was opened thirty thousand people sought entrance, and five services were held in succession in an attempt to accommodate all who sought entry. Her biographers give a dramatic picture of this opening ceremony. Shortly afterwards, however, Margaret Dunshee, with seven other prominent students, withdrew, having publicly charged Mrs. Eddy at a service with "ebullitions of temper, love of money and the appearance of hypocrisy," [10] and, therefore, of being unfit to lead the movement. However, church after church was built in city after city in America. In 1888 there was a "triumphal demonstration" in Chicago,

[9] Peabody, *op. cit.*, p. 68.
[10] Wilbur, *op. cit.*, p. 259.

when once more people jostled one another to get near her, and people who touched her claimed that they had been healed. In 1894, the foundation stones of her "cathedral" were laid, and it was opened in 1895.

Shortly after this Mrs. Eddy retired to her Concord estate, and appeared only very seldom. In her retirement, however, she could still wield despotic power. Fisher tells us that "at two days' notice any member, of three years' standing and upwards [of the Christian Science Church] might be ordered, on pain of excommunication, to serve in Mrs. Eddy's household for a period of more than three years. 'He that loveth father or mother more than me is not worthy of me' was the text quoted in support of this astonishing manifestation of authority." [11] In 1897, when hundreds of her disciples were making a living by teaching her doctrines, she published her book, *Miscellaneous Writings*, and, it is said, demanded not only that all her followers should buy the book, but that her disciples everywhere should stop teaching Christian Science for a whole year and devote all their time to selling, without any commission, the new book. Fifty academies had to close on a week's notice and teachers had to find another way of earning a living. To this extraordinary instruction the elderly dictator added this grim threat: "If a member of the First Church of Christ Scientist shall fail to obey this injunction, it shall render him liable to lose his membership in this church."

But alas, already an invalid, even Mrs. Eddy could not keep death at bay much longer. She was so eager in her pretence at being physically well that for some time, Dakin tells us, a woman who was very much like her—Mrs. Leonard—was induced to sit in her carriage and be driven from her house every day, muffled to the ears and, even in a closed carriage, carrying a light sunshade. A famous American paper sent reporters from New York to Boston, and they exposed the facts about this paltry deception. Having called in doctors whose names are given by Dakin, and having used drugs, though all her life she had denounced both, Mrs. Eddy died of pneumonia on December 4, 1910, aged eighty-nine.[12]

[11] H. A. L. Fisher, *Our New Religion* (Smith, 1930).

[12] John V. Dittemore, a former director of the Mother Church, told the Press in September 1928 that the diary of a member of Mrs. Eddy's household had been discovered, which proved that in later years she took drugs and sent for doctors. It is generally accepted that she had treatment from dentists, and it is agreed that she wore spectacles, though she denied the fact of any kind of disease, presumably including diseases of the eyes and teeth. Dakin says she ordered her grandchildren to be vaccinated, and paid a surgeon (Dr. H. S. Dearing of Boston) to operate on

What are we to make of the life of Mrs. Eddy? Frederick W. Peabody, the lawyer of the Boston Bar to whom reference has already been made, says he "was retained by Mrs. Eddy's two sons, George W. Glover, born to her by her first husband, and Edward J. Foster, her son by adoption, to co-operate with their other lawyers . . . in the prosecution in the courts of New Hampshire of a suit in equity for the appointment of a receiver to have charge of their mother's large estate for her benefit, upon the ground that, through old age, mental weakness and delusions, if not actual insanity, she was incompetent to have the care of it. This litigation never reached a determination in the courts, but the family controversy was ultimately ended by a family settlement in which the two sons were paid approximately three hundred thousand dollars for a relinquishment of their prospective interest in their mother's estate and an agreement not to contest her will or other instrument disposing of her property." [13]

This lawyer says that in the course of his legal enquiries he has had access to private letters of Mrs. Eddy, and he writes a most damning indictment of her, calling her "the champion fraud and imposter of the age." "She is mercenary, insincere and shameless. . . . Upon theft and falsehood she has laid the foundations of the 'religion' by the sale of which she has accumulated a fortune," [14] which he assesses at "upwards of a million and a half dollars." The whole system of Christian Science he calls a "monstrous fraud," [15] and challenges "Mrs. Eddy and the whole Christian Science combination to dare to prosecute" him for libel.[16] He quotes a letter from Mark Twain, who calls her "that shameless old swindler, Mother Eddy," [17] and altogether paints a picture of a hysterical, uneducated and pretentious opportunist, callous about her own child and first husband, guilty of deliberate deceit and lying.[18] He accuses her of hatred; saying of one she disliked, "I'd like to tear her heart out and trample it under my feet," and of so completely losing her temper in one house—that of Mr. and Mrs. Alanson Wentworth—that she "with obvious intent

her sister-in-law for cancer of the breast. Dakin, *op. cit.,* p. 367 (footnote I), and p. 368.

[13] Frederick W. Peabody, *op. cit.,* p. 15.

[14] *Op. cit.,* pp. 20, 55.

[15] *Op. cit.,* p. 26.

[16] *Op. cit.,* p. 17.

[17] *Op. cit.,* p. 28.

[18] *Op. cit.,* pp. 38-39, 104-108. Dakin also gives instances of her alleged lying about her age and about the number of her church members. *Op. cit.,* p. 324.

put live coals from her stove upon a heap of newspapers in the closet," [19] slashed up the feather bed, and even cut to pieces the carpet on the floor.

Mrs. Eddy herself is alleged to have "discovered" Christian Science as follows: She fell on an icy curbstone and was carried helpless to her home. The medical verdict was that she only had three days to live. Calling for her Bible, she opened it at the healing of the palsied man. "The life divine which healed the sick of the palsy, restored her, and she rose from the bed of pain, healed and free."

In her autobiography, *Retrospection and Introspection*, she says:

"My immediate recovery from the effects of an injury caused by an accident, an injury which neither medicine nor surgery could reach, was the falling apple that led me to the discovery how to be well myself and how to make others so.

"Even to the homœpathic physician who attended me, and rejoiced in my recovery, I could not then explain the modus of my belief. I could only assure him that the Divine Spirit had wrought the miracle, a miracle which later I found to be in perfect Scientific accord with divine law."

But about this Frederick Peabody writes:

"Unfortunately for her reputation for veracity and fortunately for the truth of history, Dr. Alvin M. Cushing, the physician who attended Mrs. Eddy, or Patterson, upon this particular occasion, is still living, and as an honoured member of the profession is now practising in Springfield, Mass. Dr. Cushing expressly, and under oath, denies that he at any time believed or said that Mrs. Patterson was in a critical condition, or that there was no hope for her, or that she had but three or any other limited number of days to live, and he, with great positiveness, says that she did not, on the third or any other day of her illness, say, or suggest, or pretend, or in any way whatever intimate that she had miraculously recovered or been healed, or that, discovering or perceiving the truth of the power employed by Christ to heal the sick, she had, by it, been restored to health, and he further says that, on the contrary, on the third day and later days of this illness, he himself gave her medicine, and again in August of the same year called upon her four or five times and gave her medicine." [20]

[19] *Op. cit.*, p. 55. See also Dakin, *op. cit.*, p. 77. Sibyl Wilbur in the "official" life of Mrs. Eddy denies this, but Horace Wentworth swore an affidavit that the facts are as above.

[20] *Op. cit.*, p. 79. Dakin confirms this account, *op. cit.*, pp. 61-62. Permission for these quotations has been granted by Fleming H. Revell Co. Miss Wilbur, of course, has a very different story to tell. *Op. cit.*, p. 123 ff.

Peabody also prints a letter dated two weeks after the accident, in which she implores a Mr. Julian Dresser to help her—"as I am slowly failing." Yet her own claim stated that she made an immediate recovery. He also publishes a letter which Mrs. Eddy wrote to a friend in March, 1896, over her own autograph, but speaking of herself in the third person. Here is the letter: [21]

"While Mrs. Eddy was in a suburban town of Boston, she brought out one apple blossom on an apple tree in January, when the ground was covered with snow; and in Lynn demonstrated in the floral line some such small things."

We cannot feel very deep respect for the claim that Christian Science is a religious revelation when, three years after the claim that the revelation was made to her, we find Mrs. Eddy, then Mrs. Glover, inserting the following advertisement in *The Banner of Light*, a spiritualist paper, under date July 4, 1869:

"Any person desiring to learn how to heal the sick can receive of the undersigned instruction that will enable them to commence healing on a principle of science with success far beyond any of the present modes. No medicine, electricity, physiology or hygiene required for unparalleled success in the most difficult cases. No pay is required unless the skill is obtained. Address Mrs. Mary B. Glover, Amesbury, Mass. Box 61." [22]

Mrs. Eddy has all but claimed equality with our Lord, but what a contrast there is! Mrs. Eddy's charges are said to have been one hundred dollars in advance, with ten per cent on the students' subsequent income from practice, and one thousand dollars if, having learned the system, he did not practise. Later it was three hundred dollars for twelve, and then for seven lessons "cash strictly in advance." [23] In her book, *Retrospection and Introspection*, Mrs. Glover tells the world how, very reluctantly, she was guided to charge three hundred dollars: "When God impelled me to set a price on Christian Science mind healing [she says], I could think of no financial equivalent for the impartation of a knowledge of that divine power which heals; but *I was led* to name three hundred dollars as the price for each pupil in one course of lessons at my college; a startling sum for tuition lasting barely three weeks. This amount *greatly troubled me*. I *shrank* from asking it, but was finally *led by a strange Providence* to *accept* this fee. God has since shown me in multitudinous ways the wisdom of this de-

[21] *Op. cit.*, p. 104.
[22] Peabody, *op. cit.*, p. 122.
[23] *Op. cit.*, p. 123.

cision." [24] During a period of seven years she had four thousand students at three hundred dollars each. "Mr. Wiggin," she is alleged to have said to the minister who tried to reduce *Science and Health* to readable English, "Christian Science is a good thing. I make ten thousand dollars a year at it." [25]

B. THE BOOK

We have already noted the claim that the book, which is the Bible of Christian Science, and which is read alternately with the Bible in all Christian Science churches, was largely derived from the manuscripts of Quimby. In fact, the main testimony of the majority of writers is that the important metaphysical ideas were probably almost entirely his: the scriptural interpolations almost entirely hers. H. A. L. Fisher says that Quimby himself was an atheist and was very embarrassed by being told by Mrs. Eddy that his methods were like those of Christ. It is hard to decide this matter, but however much was owing to Quimby, and however incapable Mrs. Eddy would have been in setting out the Quimby theories unassisted, it is equally certain that Quimby could not have written *Science and Health* by himself.[26]

The book was first published in 1875, and is said to have passed through more than a thousand editions. The Christian Scientist movement has spread widely. One figure given for the number of adherents is a quarter of a million, and every loyal Christian Scientist is expected to possess the latest edition.

Even when one tries to bring an unprejudiced mind to the study of this amazing book and to understand its message, one finds it to be the most involved hotch-potch of vague, and sometimes contradictory, metaphysics that one has ever read, without any discernible order or rational sequence of ideas.

When, in later years, Mrs. Eddy had to face a charge that she was mentally incapable of managing her own affairs, Senator Chandler found his evidence in the state of mind that was revealed in the pages of *Science and Health*. "Mrs. Eddy's book," he said, "alone is proof that she is suffering from the following systematised delusions and dementia." [27]

Peabody says that a judge, in one of the many lawsuits for the recovery of tuition fees which Mrs. Eddy promulgated, said: "I do

[24] *Retrospection and Introspection*, p. 50 (Mrs. Glover's Italics).
[25] Dakin, *op. cit.*, p. 229.
[26] H. A. L. Fisher, *Our New Religion* (Smith, 1930).
[27] Dakin, *op. cit.*, p. 434.

not find any instruction given by her nor any explanations of her science or method of healing which are intelligible to ordinary comprehension, or which could in any way be of value in fitting the defendant as a competent and successful practitioner of any intelligible art or method of healing the sick. And I am of opinion that the consideration for the agreement has wholly failed, and I so find." [28]

Janet said, "I think her work can be best described as the financial exploitation of Quimby's ideas." [29]

This may be true in part, but I think a wiser estimate would be that just as Remarque wrote *All Quiet on the Western Front*[30] as a means of "exteriorising" his own repressions caused by the First World War, so the truth may well be that Mrs. Eddy's tinkering with Quimby's manuscripts and adding her scriptural interpolations was really an attempt to "exteriorise"—in William James's sense—her own neurotic repressions. I find *Science and Health* a most interesting document from the psychological point of view, because it is a translation into a torrent of words of the frantic efforts of a neurotic to escape from her own neurosis. I believe Mrs. Eddy to have been quite sincere in claiming that she did not borrow from Quimby. A neurotic, writing and re-writing, as Mrs. Eddy did, would become quite unconscious of the extent of her indebtedness. She spent hour after hour writing and re-writing it, and in later years she spent hours in re-reading what she had written. On one occasion, as an old lady, when it was read to her by a friend, she said, "How beautiful that is! Did I really write it?" It is the unsuccessful attempt of a hysteric to escape from her hysteria. For herself it did not bring release, for, if Dakin is to be believed, she was technically a hysteric almost until the day of her death. But for many others, neurotic to some extent, but not nearly to the degree which Mrs. Eddy's symptoms revealed, the book definitely has brought deliverance, and this is *part* of the success of Christian Science, for Christian Science attempts to get rid of suffering and pain, of disease and death, and fear of these things is at the base of certain neurotic attitudes. If the Christian Scientist can bluff himself that the method is effective, he may find a welcome measure of deliverance. But in order to achieve this bluff, he will have to wade through a wilderness of words and be content to be mesmerised by them. The attempt to understand them will be beyond him, for the simple reason that many of the sentences do not mean anything at

[28] Peabody, *op. cit.*, p. 124.
[29] Janet, *op. cit.*
[30] Translated from the German by A. W. Wheen (Little-Brown, 1929).

all, and he has got seven hundred pages of matter to wade through. The Rev. Henry Wiggin, an ex-Unitarian minister, is said to have been employed to get Mrs. Eddy's manuscript into something like intelligible English, but Wiggin, though he was probably glad enough to have the job and take the fees, made it very clear that he was only a literary agent, and in no sense a collaborator with Mrs. Eddy or a sharer in her views. He wrote as follows:

"Of all the dissertations a literary helper ever inspected, I do not believe one ever saw a treatise to surpass this. The mis-spelling, capitalisation and punctuation were dreadful, but those were not things that fazed me. It was the thought and the general elementary arrangement of the work. There were passages that virtually and absolutely contradicted things that had preceded, and scattered all through were incorrect references to historical and philosophical matters. The thing that troubled me was: How could I attempt to dress up the manuscript by dealing only with the spelling and punctuation? There would be left a mass of material that would reflect on me as a professional literary aid were my name to be in any way associated with the enterprise. I was convinced that the only way in which I could undertake the requested revision would be to begin absolutely at the first page and re-write the whole thing." [31]

It must not be denied, of course, that there are many beautiful ideas scattered through the book. One of them is inscribed on the wall of Christian Science churches both in London and at Oxford, and reads: "Divine love has met and always will meet human need."

Here are some other attractive passages:

1. "Prayer, watching and working, combined with self-immolation, are God's gracious means for accomplishing whatever has been successfully done for the Christianization and health of mankind." [32]

2. "In order to pray aright, we must enter into the closet and shut the door. We must close the lips and silence the material senses. In the quiet sanctuary of earnest longings, we must deny sin and plead God's allness. We must resolve to take up the cross, and go forth with honest hearts to work and watch for Wisdom, Truth and Love. We must 'pray without ceasing.' Such prayer is answered in so far as we put our desires into practice. The Master's injunction is, that we pray in secret and let our lives attest our sincerity." [33]

3. "To the ritualistic priest and hypocritical Pharisee Jesus said,

[31] Dakin, *op. cit.*, p. 225.
[32] *Science and Health*, p. 1.
[33] *Op. cit.*, p. 15.

'The publicans and the harlots go into the kingdom of God before you.' Jesus' history made a new calendar, which we call the Christian era; but He established no ritualistic worship. He knew that men can be baptised, partake of the Eucharist, support the clergy, observe the Sabbath, make long prayers and yet be sensual and sinful." [34]

4. "The material blood of Jesus was no more efficacious to cleanse from sin when it was shed upon 'the accursed tree,' than when it was flowing in His veins as He went daily about His Father's business. His true flesh and blood were His Life; and they truly eat His flesh and drink His blood, who partake of that divine Life." [35]

5. "While we adore Jesus, and the heart overflows with gratitude for what He did for mortals,—treading alone His loving pathway up to the throne of glory, in speechless agony exploring the way for us,—yet Jesus spares us not one individual experience, if we follow His commands faithfully; and all have the cup of sorrowful effort to drink in proportion to their demonstration of His love, till all are redeemed through divine Love." [36]

6. "Stand porter at the door of thought. Admitting only such conclusions as you wish realised in bodily results, you will control yourself harmoniously. When the condition is present which you say induces disease, whether it be air, exercise, heredity, contagion, or accident, then perform your office as porter and shut out these unhealthy thoughts and fears. Exclude from mortal mind the offending errors; then the body cannot suffer from them. The issues of pain or pleasure must come through mind, and like a watchman forsaking his post, we admit the intruding belief, forgetting that through divine help we can forbid this entrance." [37]

7. "It were better to be exposed to every plague on earth than to endure the cumulative effects of a guilty conscience. The abiding consciousness of wrong-doing tends to destroy the ability to do right. If sin is not regretted and is not lessening, then it is hastening on to physical and moral doom. You are conquered by the moral penalties you incur and the ills they bring. The pains of sinful sense are less harmful than its pleasures. Belief in material suffering causes mortals to retreat from their error, to flee from body to Spirit, and to appeal to divine sources outside of themselves." [38]

[34] *Op. cit.*, p. 20.
[35] *Op. cit.*, p. 25.
[36] *Op. cit.*, p. 26.
[37] *Op. cit.*, pp. 392-393.
[38] *Op. cit.*, p. 405.

Yet even in regard to the personality of God there is vagueness and confusion. "As adherents of truth," says Mrs. Eddy, "we take the inspired word of the Bible as our sufficient guide to eternal life." But she lays violent hands even on the inspired word of the Bible. The twenty-third Psalm is altered thus: "Divine Love is my shepherd, I shall not want. Love maketh me to lie down," etc.,[39] avoiding all the personal words so precious to the Christian. The personality of God is asserted in one passage and contradicted in another. Why does Mrs. Eddy assume the right to introduce her own words into passages of the New Testament? E.g. She quotes St. Paul, but inserts the word "seeming." "Paul writes, 'For if, when we were enemies, we were reconciled to God by the (seeming) death of His Son.' " [40] The evangelists were at pains to witness to the real death of Christ, but Mrs. Eddy says of the disciples, they "did not perform many wonderful works until they saw Him after His crucifixion and learned that He had not died." [41] The *real* death of Jesus is a vital element in Christian faith.

Other passages cannot be called anything else but nonsense. The word "nonsense" is a strong one. Consider, then, this sentence from page 389, lines 5 and 6, in *Science and Health*. "The less we know or think about hygiene, the less we are predisposed to sickness." In India I remember a village in which cholera broke out. It was found that discharges from the bodies of cholera patients seeped into the common well from which the whole village took its drinking-water. Real science, finding this, took steps which checked the epidemic. Ignorance of hygiene, continuing, would have decimated the whole community. Is the word "nonsense" too strong? Is it not clear that Christian Scientists could not live in a society that practised their own beliefs? They are parasitic on a community that has developed a security which their teachings would destroy. They exist through precautions based on a philosophy which contradicts their own. As Fisher says, "A strict execution of Mrs. Eddy's doctrines throughout the world would, in a very few years, extinguish human life upon this planet." [42]

Consider also the following:

1. "Divide the name Adam into two syllables and it reads, a dam, or obstruction. This suggests the thought of something fluid, or

[39] *Op. cit.*, p. 578.
[40] *Op. cit.*, p. 45.
[41] *Op. cit.*, p. 46.
[42] *Op. cit.*, p. 163.

mortal mind in solution. . . . Here a dam is not a mere play upon words; it stands for obstruction, error." [43] The origin of the name Adam, of course, is the Hebrew word אָדָם, akin to אֲדָמָה (*adamah*), or the ground, because in Genesis 2:7 we are told that God formed Adam from the ground. "Adam" = Man, a generic term, not a proper name.[44]

2. Jesus "did not depend on food or pure air to resuscitate wasted energies." [45]

3. "The disciples' desertion of their Master in His last earthly struggle was punished; each one came to a violent death. . . ." [46] *They* did not regard it as punishment, but were proud to suffer pain—which Mrs. Eddy says is unreal—and die for His sake.

4. Quoting the fourth gospel, "He shall give you another Comforter that He may abide with you for ever," Mrs. Eddy adds, with almost incredible blasphemy, "This Comforter I understand to be Divine Science." [47]

5. "If you or I should appear to die, we should not be dead. The seeming decease, caused by a majority of human beliefs that man must die, or produced by mental assassins, does not in the least disprove Christian Science; rather does it evidence the truth of its basic proposition that moral thoughts in belief rule the materiality miscalled life in the body or in matter." [48]

6. "Give us this day our daily bread" is interpreted as follows: "Give us grace for today and feed the famished affections." [49]

One had supposed that the primary purpose of pain was to warn man that something was wrong that needed righting; that the pain of a thorn indicated the wisdom of removing it, and the pain of a decayed tooth indicated that the devastation in it be repaired or the tooth extracted. Mrs. Eddy's teaching would seem to be that pain has no real existence at all; according to her it is certainly not planned as a beneficent signal that something is wrong. It could and should be treated as non-existent, as "an illusion of mortal mind." Presumably,

[43] *Op. cit.*, p. 338.

[44] See Skinner, and Genesis 1:26, 2:7. Skinner says the derivation of the name "Adam" is uncertain.

[45] *Op. cit.*, p. 44.

[46] *Op. cit.*, p. 47.

[47] *Op. cit.*, p. 55.

[48] *Op. cit.*, p. 164.

[49] *Op. cit.*, p. 17.

then, the Christian Scientist with a thorn in his foot should deny pain, not regard it as a beneficent warning. He should not allow a tooth to be extracted when at its root is an agonising abscess, though Dakin says Mrs. Eddy had all her own teeth extracted.[50] Man's pain, so far from being a beneficent warning, is, according to Mrs. Eddy, only a sign that he is still a slave to the illusion of matter, and this he ought not to be. If he is lamed; if his dental condition poisons him by its toxins, what then? Death is also an illusion. One wonders what Mrs. Eddy's attitude was to her own mother's death. "Death," she says, "will be found at length to be a mortal dream which comes in darkness and disappears with the light." [51]

Similarly, one had thought that the painfulness of a boil was a fundamentally beneficent arrangement, immobilising it so that the poison would not spread to neighbouring tissues and could be got rid of with a minimum of tissue infection. Mrs. Eddy, however, writes, "You say a boil is painful, but that is impossible, for matter without mind is not painful. The boil simply manifests, through inflammation and swelling, a belief in pain and this belief is called a boil. Now administer mentally to your patient *a high attenuation of truth* and it will soon cure the boil." [52]

"Discard all notions about lungs, tubercle, inherited consumption, or disease arising from any circumstance," we are told.[53] "Obesity is an adipose belief of yourself as a substance." "Inflammation, tubercles, hæmorrhage and decomposition are beliefs, images of mortal thought superimposed upon the body; they are not the truth of man; they should be treated as error and put out of thought. Then these ills will disappear." [54] But what does one do with a little child who has developed tuberculosis or dislocated a limb? The latter situation is made to sound quite simple. The testimony of Mrs. M. G. of Winnipeg is included in *Science and Health* (p. 636).

"My little girl, then three years old, dislocated her shoulder. . . . I undressed her and tried to twist the arm into place, but it caused such suffering that I began to get afraid. . . . I then asked the child if I should read to her;—she said, 'Yes, mamma, read the truth book.' I began reading aloud from *Science and Health*. In about half-an-hour

[50] *Op. cit.*, p. 519. "Mrs. Sargent had had enough presence of mind to slip in Mrs. Eddy's plates. Mrs. Eddy had lost every tooth in her head before she died."
[51] *Op. cit.*, p. 42.
[52] *Op. cit.*, p. 153.
[53] *Op. cit.*, p. 425.
[54] *Op. cit.*, p. 425.

I noticed she tried to lift the arm, but screamed and became very pale. ... I kept reading aloud to her, until my sister and two boys came in, when she jumped off her bed so delighted to see her cousins that she forgot her arm. She then began to tell her aunt that she had broken her arm and that mamma had treated it with the truth book. When this happened, it was about 10:30 a.m. and by 3 p.m. she was playing out of doors as though nothing had ever happened."

We see here the uselessness of the kind of testimony in the Christian Science Bible included in the third section, called "Fruitage." Was the limb broken, as the aunt was told? Was it dislocated, as the mother said? Is it not likely that the shoulder was not seriously hurt, and that the child was able to forget the pain in the excitement of seeing her aunt and cousins, and that Chrisitan Science had nothing to do with it? Are we really asked to believe that a book which a learned judge described in the language quoted on p. 166, when read to *a child of three*, completely cured a dislocated shoulder?

How does one treat a tubercular cow; or is tubercular milk really quite without danger? Mrs. Eddy says that "human mind produces what is called organic disease" [55] and that animals are controlled by their human masters. The latter inject the animals with belief in disease. But scientific research shows that disease existed among animals before man appeared on the earth.[56] "One disease is no more real than another," she says. "All disease is the result of education and disease can carry its effects no farther than mortal mind maps out the way." [57] If so, it seems odd that an epidemic of foot-and-mouth disease should spread before man's mind is aware of its outbreak. The most amusing nonsense in all the literature must surely be that quoted by Milmine. "A four-year-old horse had overeaten itself and had a bad fit of indigestion. She (Mrs. Eddy) said to it, 'You are God's horse, perfect, like all God's work. Being God's work, you cannot eat too much; you cannot have colic.' Before the treatment the poor beast was hanging its head, and its breathing was shallow and rapid; but an hour later it was all right again."

Almost as absurd was Mrs. Eddy's idea that she could control the weather. Fisher says, "To Mrs. Sargent was specially assigned the duty of 'watching the weather and bringing it into accord with normal conditions' for the Holy Mother objected to snow and thunder. 'Make

[55] *Op. cit.*, p. 177.
[56] See p. 19.
[57] *Op. cit.*, p. 176.

a law that there should be no snow this season,' was her order to the watch on June 15, 1910." [58]

Some of the sentences, as I say, are literally without meaning. I have taken them, read them out to intelligent and educated people of university training, without telling them the source, and they have denied that the words so arranged can mean anything. One of my own friends, an ardent Christian Scientist, repeated a sentence every morning, but when I asked her what the words meant, she said she did not know, but that she had been told by a Christian Science practitioner to say them. This cannot be called "Christian." Neither can it be called "Science." We are back in the era of incantation, before Christianity and Science were born.

Yet this book is regarded as divine truth. In Christian Science churches, the services in which I have attended, there are two lecterns. The Bible is read from one, *Science and Health* from the other. There is no sermon or comment, and it is often hard to see the connection between the one reading and the other. Yet one must suppose the tributes to *Science and Health* are sincere. "I wish [writes one] I could express in words what that book has brought me. It illumined the Bible with a glorious light and I began to understand some of the Master's sayings and tried to apply them. I had had a longing to live a better Christian life for many years, and often wondered why I failed so utterly to understand the Bible. Now I know; it was lack of spiritual apprehension. I did not know at first that people were healed of disease and sin by simply reading *Science and Health*, but found after a while that such was the case. At that time I had many physical troubles, and one after another of these ills simply disappeared and I found that I had no disease—I was perfectly free." [59]

Science and Health is divided into three parts. Part I is a chain of sentences numbered like the verses of the Bible, on Prayer, Atonement and Eucharist, Marriage, Christian Science versus Spiritualism, Science, Theology and Medicine, Animal Magnetism, Physiology, Creation, the Science of Being, the Practice and Teaching of Christian Science and Recapitulation. The chapter called "Recapitulation" embodies the teachings derived from Quimby, and its perusal is the quickest way of obtaining an idea of what Mrs. Eddy is talking about. Her theories are still taught to novitiates from this chapter. It is in the form of a catechism with answers.

Part II is called "Key to the Scriptures," divided into Genesis, The Apocalypse and Glossary.

[58] Fisher, *op. cit.*
[59] *Science and Health*, p. 643.

Part III, called "Fruitage," is simply a series of testimonies to the value of Christian Science. This is the easiest portion to read. It is largely in language other than Mrs. Eddy's—namely, letters of appreciation which have been sent in.

C. THE THEORY

The theory of Christian Science is stated in *Science and Health* (p. 113, lines 9-18) in the briefest possible way. Mrs. Eddy writes:
"The fundamental propositions of divine metaphysics are summarised in the four following, to me, *self-evident* propositions.[60] Even if reversed, these propositions will be found to agree in statement and proof, showing mathematically their exact relation to Truth.

"1. God is All-in-all.
"2. God is good. Good is Mind.
"3. God, Spirit, being all, nothing is matter.
"4. Life, God, omnipotent good, deny death, evil, sin, disease. Disease, sin, evil, death deny good, omnipotent God, Life."

She proceeds:
"The divine metaphysics of Christian Science, like the method in mathematics, proves the rule by inversion. For example: There is no pain in Truth, and no Truth in pain; no nerve in Mind, and no mind in nerve; no matter in Mind, and no mind in matter; no matter in life, and no life in matter; no matter in good, and no good in matter.

"Usage classes both evil and good together as *mind;* therefore, to be understood, the author calls sick and sinful humanity *mortal mind,*—meaning by this term the flesh opposed to Spirit, the human mind and evil in contradistinction to the divine Mind, or Truth and good. The spiritually unscientific definition of mind is based on the evidence of the physical senses, which makes minds many and calls *mind* both human and divine.

"In Science, Mind is *one*, including noumenon and phenomena, God and His thoughts.

"Mortal mind is a solecism in language, and involves an improper use of the word *mind*. As Mind is immortal, the phrase *mortal mind* implies something untrue and therefore unreal; and as the phrase is used in teaching Christian Science, it is meant to designate that which has no real existence. Indeed, if a better word or phrase could be suggested, it would be used; but in expressing the new tongue we

[60] Her italics.

must sometimes recur to the old and imperfect, and the new wine of the Spirit has to be poured into the old bottles of the letter.

"Christian Science explains all cause and effect as mental, not physical. It lifts the veil of mystery from Soul and body. It shows the scientific relation of man to God, disentangles the interlaced ambiguities of being, and sets free the imprisoned thought. In divine Science, the universe, including man, is spiritual, harmonious and eternal. Science shows that what is termed *matter* is but the subjective state of what is termed by the author mortal mind." [61]

Just what a man dying of pneumonia would make of this "high attenuation of truth" [62] I do not know, but let us try, from these whirling fragments of chaff and grain, to set forth what appears to be behind Mrs. Eddy's thesis.

Let it be accepted that the universe can be divided into two entities which, it is commonly believed, are interrelated and interpenetrate one another. They are Mind and Matter, or, as I should prefer to say, Spirit and Matter. The Christian theologian and philosopher regard matter as a creation of the Mind or Spirit of God, with a "reality" of its own. And no Christian who believes in the Incarnation of our Lord can despise matter as if it were essentially evil, or deny it as *real* an existence as that of mind in the present life of the world. It may, of course, be that both are deceptive illusions; that the mental processes which are so ready to banish matter as unreal are themselves untrustworthy, and that they flow from an illusory entity which we are pleased to call mind. The Christian rejoices in matter as an expression of the creative activity of God. The ideas of God, the great Spirit, are translated, for man's benefit, into a language he can understand—the language of matter. So mountains and rivers and seas, and the bodies of animals, men and women, are translations into matter of the spiritual ideas of God. Matter is not identified with spirit, but bears the image of it. To deny it as one aspect of reality is to deny the greater part of human experience. Christian Scientists will have no funerals in their churches, because they deny the reality of death. "You must admit," wrote Mrs. Eddy,[63] "that what is termed death has been produced by a belief alone." But death on the material plane is a real thing, often a beneficent thing. The spirit of man, the Christian claims, is not annihilated by the death of the body. At death the soul enters a spiritual existence. So the Christian believes. In a reverent funeral

[61] *Science and Health*, p. 114.

[62] See p. 153.

[63] *Christian Healing*, p. 18.

service the Christian does not suppose that the dead matter before him is *identified* with his loved one, but since for many years it was his means of manifestation, it is revered and quietly committed to the ground or to the flame.

Matter to most Christians is sacramental and plays a real part in the purposes of God. Granted it is more transient than spirit, less "real" in one sense, yet to deny its reality on its own plane is to bemuse the mind and make an insoluble problem of the universe.

Some have denied that spirit exists, and a gross materialism has overtaken us because of this. Mrs. Eddy's philosophy is at least a welcome revolt from that, but her denial of any reality at all to matter and the label she affixes to all thoughts about it and its variations in disease and so on, as "mortal mind," to be thrust out of consciousness, land her in an impossible situation again and again, one of the simplest and most obvious being the fact that Mrs. Eddy habitually wore gold-rimmed spectacles, ate meals, wore clothes, used false teeth and collected dollars. Yet disease, she says, is unreal; it does not exist, it is to be disregarded, excluded from consciousness. Amongst her followers it is a shameful thing to admit that one has pneumonia or that one suffers pain, yet Dakin reports that when Mrs. Eddy herself had a raging toothache, "metaphysical treatment was abandoned and several of her students scoured Tremont Street in the middle of the night, trying to find an obliging dentist." [64] I shall write later about the valuable mental attitude to disease which the Christian would do well to follow, but let us consider Mrs. Eddy's point of view.

Presumably, if Mrs. Eddy, or her most devout followers, lived in a Russian village constantly beset by wolves which swept out of the forests in the winter and attacked the villagers, she would take steps to *prevent* their onslaught; she would try to beat off their attack; in view of her immense moral courage, one can be certain that she would use all her skill to defend, say, little children in an attacked house, perhaps even interpose her own person to save the children, and use all her energies to kill or drive back the wolves.

But the pneumococcus—the germ of pneumonia—is presumably in the same category of threatening pests as these wolves. It is smaller, and can only be seen with the microscope, but there is no difference in principle between preventive medicine which seeks to prevent the disease-causing organisms from entering the body, and preventive action to preclude the entry of wolves into a home. What is the difference in principle between attacking wolves with a rifle and germs

[64] *Op. cit.,* p. 186.

with an antitoxin? What is the difference between using all available skill and energy in the case of wolves, to minimise their ravages and deal wisely with the havoc they cause, in the one case, and the heroic, and often self-sacrificing, service of the medical profession in the other case? Both show the age-long fight against those factors in the world which man must overcome for the sake of his own physical security and well-being. To my mind, Mrs. Eddy's theory, even when disentangled from her bewildering English, is illogical. I know that the mental factor in the case of disease is of immense importance, but it *applies* in the case of the wolves. *Courage* is of immense importance, and in any case the mental factor does not make the illusion void.

But the illogicality is much deeper than this and more devastating. By right thinking—Mrs. Eddy teaches—the alleged reality of matter can be made to disappear. To continue with the illustration of pneumonia, there is no such thing. It is the fruit of "mortal mind," of bad thinking.[65] But if *all* matter is the result of bad thinking, right thinking would destroy the whole material universe. Logically, then, for God, matter does not exist, and the Incarnation is a hoax and a delusion. Right thinking cannot create matter. Wrong thinking created it, brought it into being. Right thinking destroys it, and with it, of course, the instrument with which the thinking is done—namely, the brains of men and women, including Mrs. Eddy. Mrs. Eddy may have in mind the desirability of showing the unity of the universe; but, if so, she tries to do so by denying the existence of every entity but one, spirit. This is not proving unity, for there is nothing to be united. It is like trying to prove the Unity of the Blessed Trinity by denying the existence of our Lord and of the Holy Ghost. Mrs. Eddy sees evidence of mind and evidence of matter. But in a duality that makes ten thousand problems without solving one, she calls one the creation of Mind with a capital "M," and the other the creation of "mortal mind," an error of thought born of a non-existent entity. The situation is so hopelessly confused as to be incomprehensible.

Further, as Dawson,[66] Crowlesmith [67] and others have pointed out,

---

[65] But on p. 144 Mrs. Eddy denies the existence of "mortal mind." "It is meant to designate that which has no real existence." But how can *anything* be the fruit of a non-existent entity, let alone this amazing physical universe which has called forth the tributes of all scientists, artists and poets? It is certainly hard to see how "mortal mind" which does not exist, framed the stars and governs the atom. Food does not really exist and is not necessary, but Mrs. Eddy advises her followers to eat until their stupid and false beliefs change!

[66] *Op. cit.*

[67] In a lecture at Westminster College, Cambridge, January 8, 1947.

178

she had confused contradictories with contraries. Her logic, one fears, is as absent as her knowledge of anatomy.

Mrs. Eddy implies, in her fourth fundamental, for example, that contraries cancel one another out. Contradictories do, but contraries do not. Two contradictories cannot possibly both be right. The essence of contradictories is that if one is true, the other is false, and if one is false, the other must be true. The essence of contraries is that both cannot be true. Both may be false, or one may be false and the other true. The sentences, "All cows are black" and "Some cows are not black" are contradictories. The sentences, "All cows are black" and "No cows are black" are contraries. Both cannot be true. Both are in fact false.

Mrs. Eddy cannot logically argue that because God is good and real, evil, which is the opposite of good, and therefore the opposite of God, must be unreal, or because pleasure is real, pain is unreal, or because health is real, disease is unreal. What kind of logic is this? Is night the *opposite* of day, eternity of time, black of white, east of west? And if an assertion be made of the first in each case, is it to be logically denied of the second? It is the logic of *Alice in Wonderland*.

Can God logically be said to be the *opposite* of evil, and what degree of health, as no one is physically perfect, is the *opposite* of disease?

Further, what is pain? Is it even the opposite of pleasure when a mother bears it in giving life to her babe, when a father endures poverty to educate his boy, when a Damien endures it to serve Christ and share the misfortunes of the lepers?

Pain is frequently much more desirable than escape from it—a fact which few, if any, Christian Scientists seem to have realised. Many have discovered the truth and told it, when it meant pain and suffering to do either. Many have died in agony rather than deny the truth as they saw it. As Archbishop Temple says in *Christus Veritas:* "There are some forms of good deliberately chosen in which the element of pleasure is almost non-existent, while pain is very prominent. Of such good we may say what George Eliot's Romola says of the highest happiness: 'We only know it from pain by its being what we would choose before everything else because our souls see it is good.'"

I am afraid no Christian could possibly accept Mrs. Eddy's theories. Biographers say that she claimed to be equal with Christ and regarded her mission as fulfilling His own. "The second appearing of Jesus is unquestionably the second advent of the advancing idea of God in Christian Science."

More and more one bows in awe and reverence and humility before the Cross of Christ and the wonder of man's redemption through His death. But Mrs. Eddy thinks He was foolish, and writes: "Had wisdom

179

characterised all His sayings, He would not have prophesied His own death and thereby hastened or caused it." That is as near blasphemy to the orthodox Christian as utterance can go. Suffering, she says, is not real. It is an error caused by "mortal mind." When, therefore, Jesus spoke of His sufferings, He was deluded. There are no such things. When He healed and ended suffering, He dealt with an enemy which had no existence. When Mrs. Eddy herself was ill, it was because Kennedy and others by "Malicious Animal Magnetism" mentally injected evil into her. She believed that arsenic could be mentally injected thus. But why should this make her ill? There is no such thing as illness! If, says Mrs. Eddy, the victim of arsenic did not believe it was a poison—if, indeed, he believed he was immune from poisoning— he would suffer no harm. It is his foolish belief, his "mortal mind," which, accepting the idea of evil as true, works his undoing.

But what of Mr. Appleton of Ipswich, whose enemy, unknown to him, put arsenic into his cocoa? Appleton had no false beliefs. His "mortal mind" did not function. He was an ardent Christian Scientist, innocently drinking the cocoa prepared for him. But he was overtaken by "imaginary" agony which doubled him up with a pain that does not exist, and he died an "imaginary" death for which his enemy was hanged. Did his beliefs kill him? If so, it was belief in cocoa!

One cannot but reject the theory of Christian Science as set forth in *Science and Health*. It appears to deny the personality of God, the reality of the Incarnation, the gospel of redemption symbolised by the Cross, the reality of sin and the need for a savior. The problem of evil may be insoluble, but to link evil with matter and deny the existence of both does not help us much.

In her denial of the reality of matter, Mrs. Eddy, of course, was not a forerunner of the modern true scientist who sees in matter a manifestation of energy. What she denied was that anything existed outside the world of subjective ideas. "No Christian theologian has ever accepted the view that matter is unreal in the sense in which that phrase is used by Mrs. Eddy." [68] She entirely denied the reality of the objective universe. Even the mind which registers this objective universe through the senses, she denied. It was "mortal mind" identified with error and delusion. Only Divine Mind was real. "As an individual managed to suppress all human consciousness, all human senses and needs, all con-

[68] Fisher, *op. cit.*

ception of an external reality, he would then become divine. Until then he would live in error." [69]

In her denial of the reality of pain and mental suffering, she has our Lord and all the saints against her. She is inconsistent herself, as any perusal of her life will show. She suffered both mental and physical pain repeatedly. Granted that she claims that in her case it was caused by Malicious Animal Magnetism—that is, evil thoughts directed against her by others, but we are not considering the origin of the suffering, but the fact of it.

D. THE PRACTICE

The practice of Christian Science is the use of spiritual energies to cure disease of body, mind and spirit. The procedure seems to be as follows: A patient who falls ill sends for a Christian Science healer. The healer has been trained in the metaphysics of Mrs. Eddy as set forth in *Science and Health*. He, or frequently she, is usually a person of splendid character, able to win the confidence of the patient and persuade him that his illness is unreal: able also to bring spiritual power. As Mrs. Eddy finely says: "The unchristian practitioner [of Christian Science] is not giving to mind or body the joy and strength of Truth." [70] Portions are read from the Bible and from *Science and Health*. No diagnosis is made, no drugs are administered, no physical treatment recommended. The healer calls again and again, until the mental attitude of the patient is completely altered. No longer does he mope about his symptoms or turn his mind in on his sad and sick conditions. In God is perfect health and perfect joy. Let the patient turn his mind in that direction and realise his oneness with the infinite resources of God and his own real harmony with God, and he cannot be ill. Apart from his "mortal mind" and its aberrations, his illness does not exist. Why does he entertain in his body this ghostly counterpart of his wretched bad thinking? This seems the attitude of the healer and a not unfair outline of the treatment.

From many points of view, how excellent it is! When we come to the section on "Constructive Criticism" (p. 184) we shall assess its value. Suffice it to say here that the power of the mind over the body is such that, again and again, the treatment of the Christian Science healer, in spite of the faulty philosophy which we have examined, has brought health. When fear and all other unhealthy and negative emotions are

[69] Dakin, *op. cit.*, p. 105.
[70] *Science and Health*, p. 305.

banished; when disease is minimised and the thought of the patient is turned away from himself and his sad plight, to the splendour and joy of God; when recovery is believed not merely to be possible, but imminent, psychological conditions are set up within the ego which give the healing force of Nature the maximum opportunity. It is a precious and healing truth, and the Churches must recapture and restate it.

But before one can recommend anyone to resort at once to Christian Science, much must be said from another angle.

The practitioner, as such, knows nothing about medicine, or surgery, or even the anatomy of the body, or the functions of its parts. He knows nothing of psychology either, and believes it to be irrelevant.

Therefore he cannot know with understanding what is the real nature of the patient's trouble. One who heals should know this as clearly as possible or work with one who does. The treatment of the Christian Science healer is the same whatever the illness may be. Jesus did not thus work, as we have seen.

In 1909 a mother was punished for allowing her daughter to die of pneumonia without medical aid having been sought. The criticism even then was that medical aid would have saved her life. A Christian Science healer was called in, but no doctor sent for.[71] To allude to our earlier illustration, it was like letting the wolves into the cottage where the daughter was, shutting the door on them, having someone to come and tell the daughter through the window that the wolves were unreal, pray with her and read the Bible and passage from *Science and Health* to her. To change the illustration, if fire breaks out, *religious* action—apart altogether from common sense—involves throwing water on the flames, not the recital of prayers. And to exclude God from common-sense precautions and measures, to exclude the divine activity from the useful work which surgeons, doctors, dentists, nurses and others do for men, is to disobey what Christ called the greatest commandment—namely, that we should love the Lord our God with all our *minds*. Even a broken back has been treated by Christian Science, and surgery only resorted to because of "the foolishness of men." In fairness the whole section may be quoted:

"Until the advancing age admits the efficacy and supremacy of Mind, it is better for Christian Scientists to leave surgery and the adjustment of broken bones and dislocations to the fingers of a surgeon, while the mental healer confines himself chiefly to mental reconstruction and to the prevention of inflammation. Christian Science is always the most skilful surgeon, but surgery is the branch of its healing which

[71] Janet gives other illustrations. *Op. cit.*, Vol. I.

will be last acknowledged. However, it is but just to say that the author has already in her possession well-authenticated records of the cure, by herself and her students through mental surgery alone, of broken bones, dislocated joints, and spinal vertebræ." [72]

The most disturbing element in Christian Science practice, however, is the treatment of children. Let an adult believe what he likes, and try to make his practice fit his belief. Many Christian Scientists do this with a spartan courage that compels our admiration, even though we feel that the attitude behind it is mistaken and foolish.

But when little children complain of pain and are rebuked for so doing; when disease is allowed to develop to such a point that it is difficult, or even impossible, to cure, we feel that an outcry should publicly be made. It should not be permissible in law to offer little children on the altar of one's private theories, which they cannot believe or even understand, let alone share.

Two dark mists which cling around Christian Science practice must be dispeled. One concerns the sufferings of children and young people at the hands of those in charge of them, who have accepted some of Mrs. Eddy's false teaching. The other concerns the exact scientific record of the alleged cures. I am not in any doubt whatever that cures occur. The psychological reasons for this are alone sufficient. But woefully little is told us about some cures.

It is important, not only in regard to Christian Science, but in all cases of healing by non-material methods, to get as accurate a scientific diagnosis as possible before and after treatment, and avoid even the appearance of exaggeration, or a careless use of words—"cure" is one of them—which have a scientific exactitude in other spheres.

The last part of *Science and Health*—"Fruitage"—is taken up with many stories of benefit or complete health brought by Christian Science. But instead of a letter signed "E.H.R. (Ohio)," it would have been more convincing to have had a scientific statement before and another afterwards, both by different groups of real scientists, so that no one could doubt what had really happened. It is hard to accept at its face value the truth of the following words published in the New York *Sun* for December 16, 1898, where Mrs. Eddy wrote as follows:

"After my discovery of Christian Science, I healed consumption in its last stages, that the M.D.'s by verdict of the stethoscope and the schools, declared incurable, the lungs being mostly consumed. I healed malignant tubercular diphtheria and carious bones that could be dented by the finger, saving them when the surgeon's instruments were lying on the

[72] *Science and Health*, pp. 401-402.

table ready for their amputation. I have healed at one visit a cancer that had so eaten the flesh of the neck as to expose the jugular vein so that it stood out like a cord."

As lawyer Peabody said,[73] "If Mrs. Eddy, for hire, had healed, at one sitting, a cancer that had so eaten into the neck of a stranger that the jugular vein stood out like a cord, why, I ask, why in the name of God, did she not, for her love's sake, stay the progress of the loathsome disease that for seven years ate into the breast of the sister she loved?"

Before we leave the practice of Christian Science, many other questions obtrude themselves. Why is marriage so deprecated? [74] To the question, "What do you think of marriage?" Mrs. Eddy wrote, "That it is often convenient, sometimes pleasant and occasionally a love affair. . . . It sometimes presents the most wretched condition of human existence." Mrs. Eddy was also very strict about sex. Intercourse was allowed only when a child was desired.[75] In her speeches she advocated celibacy as the only real spiritual state. Although Mrs. Eddy was married three times, she allowed no marriage to take place in a Christian Science church, and, of course, no funeral either, for death is only an illusion of "mortal mind."

Again, why is Christian Science practised so rarely amongst the poor? It is the cheapest known form of dealing with disease and it has immense funds. Mrs. Eddy left it nearly three million dollars. Why did she come to regard poverty almost as erroneous as sickness? Surely money is matter and does not exist.

Why has Christian Science made no progress in Latin countries? Is it because it is a cult banned by the Roman Catholic authorities? Why is there a by-law in the Christian Science Manual (p. 87), forbidding Christian Science practitioners to teach Christian Science to Roman Catholics without the written consent of the Roman Catholic authorities? Is that consent ever given?

E. Constructive Criticism

So far our criticism of Christian Science must have seemed destructive. Research does not make the person of the founder one to be greatly admired, though, especially in her later years, no one could deny her courage, drive and determination. Her book is a strange medley of confused metaphysics, without any thread of logical reasoning running

[73] *Op. cit.*, p. 109.
[74] *Miscellaneous Writings*, pp. 52 and 286.
[75] *Science and Health*, p. 61.

through it, with some passages of beauty, but with many incomprehensible sentences. Her theories seem to me to be unsound, and the practice of Christian Science frequently a help, but frequently a menace, to those who receive it: a menace not only to physical, but also to spiritual health; for, whatever the theories about it, Christian Science does tend to make man the end, and God the means to that end. A religion which makes the individual's health its main pre-occupation cannot bear comparison with real Christianity, in which man is a means and God the end; in which, indeed, nothing matters so long as God is glorified.

Yet this misnamed movement could make a much-needed contribution to Christian thought and to the practice of the Churches. The vogue of Christian Science shows that it can make such a contribution and that other denominations are not making it. The success of Christian Science is a challenge to the Churches. And the answer to that challenge is for other Churches to teach more effectively those truths which lie behind successful Christian Science practice, and to train "practitioners" to put them at the disposal of those who would benefit from such ministrations. Thousands would then regain health without having their minds confused by Mrs. Eddy's bewildering metaphysics and without running the risk and danger involved in putting *some* of her theories into practice.

Let us look at the undoubted good in Christian Science—the good which accounts for its success—and then ask how it could be more effectively offered.

1. Perhaps the supreme contribution which Christian Science makes is that it emphasises the reality of the spiritual. Mrs. Eddy's idea that matter, pain, disease and death are not "real" has at least this degree of truth: that their "reality" is not the same quality as the "reality," say, of love. Matter, pain, death and disease—these pass away. Spirit and mind abide, and their functions, of which love is one, remain. When she says, so strangely and confusedly, that disease is only the result of bad thinking, is she not trying to say that spirit can, by the right reaction, always rise triumphantly in victory over the disease-racked body and the brooding mind, and, indeed, that frequently the cleansed and victorious spirit, in harmony with God, can banish pain, suffering and the disease, for frequently these last-named are translations into physical terms of a maladjusted spirit? There is truth in the idea that a good deal of suffering, both of mind and body, disappears when the harmony of the spirit with God is achieved. To attain this, however, Mrs. Eddy allows no differentiation. Presumably, if one fell out of the window by being pushed through it by an enemy, one's pain and discomfort and the uselessness, say, of a broken leg would still be due

to one's own faulty mental reaction. Presumably Livingstone—that man of iron faith and supreme trust—lost his grip on God every time he suffered from fever in the tropical jungles of Africa. Presumably St. Servulus, who *all his life* was unable to lift hand to mouth, or turn himself from one side to another, and who died in 590 praising God, was the victim only of "mortal mind." Presumably Mary Slessor was a similar victim. "On one occasion when she arrived at Use racked with pain, she was asked how she could endure it. 'Oh,' she said, 'I just had to take as big a dose of laudanum as I dared, wrap myself up in a blanket, and lie in the bottom of a canoe all the time.'" Would the Christian Scientist call it wicked of her to admit pain and to take drugs? St. Cecile (1883-1906) was, in 1905, "stricken with mortal illness, but in spite of severe pain and sickness, she worked on." Would the Christian Scientist have told her that pain is an illusion? The lives of so many saints abound with references to pain which is triumphed over, but not abolished. One cannot believe that all pain is to be lumped together, and that the Christian Science label can be indiscriminately attached to it all.

No attempt is made by Christian Scientists at sensible differentiation. Every kind of physical and mental disease is to be treated in exactly the same way. It is a method that has gone mad, and only the personality of Mrs. Eddy herself, with her dynamic force of will, and the strange readiness of many neurotics to be dominated by a dogmatism they are not even asked to understand, have given it the success it has had. One can only imagine what would have happened if the epidemic of typhus which threatened the whole of Italy during the Second World War had been fought with the weapons of Christian Science!

It was a stroke of genius for Mrs. Eddy that she did not merely apply the psychological truths of Quimby, but linked them with her own particular brand of religion, which was a kind of Christian maternal autocracy. I use the words carefully. All Protestant denominations have lacked something which the Roman Catholic Church has tried to supply by the cult of Mary the Mother. Roman Catholics rarely become Christian Scientists, and the fact is significant. In Mrs. Eddy, who was often called "Mother," there is a religious "Mother" of immense and dominating power, of autocratic methods, of undoubted power to heal certain afflictions, and who does not hesitate—so her biographers claim—to identify herself with Christ. She demands recognition as the woman sent by St. John in his Revelation, clothed with the sun, and with the moon under her feet, bringing tranquillity of mind and the banishment of fear. Here we have something very like Jung's archetype, the "Mother Image," and something very like the Mary-Mother of the

Roman Church. When psychology is wedded to religion, and when at both these points something is offered that normal religion superficially appears to lack, a new cult has immense dynamic power amongst those who feel the lack most keenly.

William James has accurately discerned part of the secret of the success of Christian Science in his book, *The Varieties of Religious Experience*.[76] He shows that the kernel of the doctrine is the sentiment of optimism, trust in oneself and in the universe. He writes: "The leaders in this faith had an intuitive belief in the all-saving power of healthy-minded attitudes as such, in the conquering efficacy of courage, hope and trust, and a correlative contempt for doubt, fear, worry and all nervously precautionary states of mind. . . . This system is wholly and exclusively compacted of optimism. Pessimism leads to weakness. Optimism leads to power." "The positive side of Christian Science," says William Brown, "is good and entirely true." [77]

2. Christian Science fights the stupid heresy that suffering and disease are the will of God; that they are sent as punishment for "sin"; that they are to be borne with submission and resignation. In my book of broadcast talks called *The Will of God*,[78] I have tried to restate a sound and, as I think, orthodox position, and will not repeat it here. Nearly all human pain, suffering and disease come from human folly, ignorance and sin. The will of God is that man should replace folly with wisdom, ignorance with knowledge and sin with holiness. Nothing, therefore, that is the fruit of folly, ignorance and sin can possibly be the will of God in the sense of being His intention. In a secondary, contingent sense, of course, it can be His will. If I drop a baby out of the window, it is God's will that it should suffer, or He would have made it of other substance than bone and flesh and nerves. But the point is, it is not His will that I should drop it out of the window.

It is astonishing how many Christian people still have a lingering suspicion that if they are ill, God is punishing them and that it is His will. Instead of seeing that the clue to the spiritual meaning and value of any experience is in the *future*—i.e. through their attitude to it—they search the past to find out what they have done in the *past* to deserve such a fate, and foolishly harass and worry themselves accordingly.

Christian Science will rightly have none of this false teaching. God's will is perfect health of mind, body and spirit. God Himself is holy.

[76] See pp. 94-95 and 107.

[77] William Brown D.M. (Oxon), D.Sc. (Lond.), F.R.C.P. *Personality and Religion*, p. 75 (University of London Press, 1946).

[78] Abingdon-Cokesbury, 1945.

The words "holy," "whole" and "healthy" come from the same root—the Old English word "hal," which means complete—and the Christian Scientists link them together. God wills that man should put away from him all ideas of disease, and accept His will, which is perfect health, and goes on to add that the gift is to be taken at once.

Often the teaching is bad and the onus on the patient unbearable, but let us see the value of stressing that God's will is health. Christian Science teaches that illness ought not to be, should not be, need not be. And the Christian Scientists have Christ on their side when they fight disease, regarding it, as He did, as part of the kingdom of evil, to be overcome by the spirit of love and of good.

3. The Christian Scientist makes a useful contribution to Christian living, to the maintenance of health and the cure of disease, by the way he emphasises the power of the mind over the body. I need not repeat here what was said when the doctrines and practices of Monsieur Coué were outlined and when the power and nature of suggestion were discussed.

This most important psychological truth alone accounts for a large number of the cures which Christian Science claims. When, quite legitimately, this great psychological principle—that the power of the mind over the body is all but sovereign—is linked with religious emotion, are we surprised that immense energies are unleashed in personality? We have already seen that if the mind deeply receives an idea, it tends to actualise or come true. We have seen that a blister can be raised on the skin if the mind accepts the idea that the skin is being burned. But add to the power thus illustrated the idea that God, the wholly good and loving, is personally at work to bring back health, and it will not be easy to indicate the limit of the power released. If the idea produces the blister, is it incredible that the idea that a cancerous growth was being healed could involve the cutting off of supplies of blood and nourishment from it so that even a carcinoma would conceivably slough away and perish? [79]

4. Again, the Christian Scientist has a gospel for the body. In most Christian Churches this has been entirely neglected. The New Testament did not leave it out. In the New Testament the body is not evil because it is material. It is holy because it is the temple of the Holy Ghost.[80] The religion of the New Testament does not ignore the health of the body.

[79] Note the cases of this kind reported by Dr. Howard Somervell and quoted on p. 235 ff.
[80] I Corinthians 6:19.

188

Christ was understood to speak of the "temple of His body." [81] Paul exhorts the Romans to offer their bodies as a reasonable, holy and living sacrifice to God.[82] The redemption of *the body* is part of the Gospel, and Jesus is the Saviour of *the body*.[83]

The early Church withstood the heresy of Gnosticism with three great dogmas. God was the Creator of the flesh. God was Incarnate in the flesh. God promised the resurrection of the flesh, where "flesh" meant the whole of human nature; the spirit and its appropriate means of self-manifestation sanctified to become a vehicle of the Divine nature. Hellenistic philosophy had a sharp dichotomy between matter and spirit. Spirit, indeed, was "non-matter."

The Gnostics were a party of intellectuals in the early Church who sought to harmonise Christian teaching with a philosophy which appealed to cultivated minds. Claiming a specially revealed γνῶσις from esoteric and supernatural sources, they constructed highly speculative theories about the origin of evil, the nature of God and the interplay between the spiritual and the material. All kinds of ideas, which the early Church had to fight as unsound, appeared in the teachings of Gnosticism, derived from different Oriental religions. One of these ideas was the Hellenistic dualism which taught the utter antagonism of flesh and spirit.

The Bible knows nothing of this antagonism though in the New Testament the "old Adam" is to be mortified that the soul may more fully live. The Bible honours the body—as, indeed, it is bound to if it holds fast to the dogma of the Incarnation. Christian Science, so false in its teaching about pain, and suggesting in some passages that it is a form of Gnosticism risen from the dead, yet does, on the whole, teach that the body is God's instrument and that it is a religious duty to keep it fit.

Christian Science renders a real service in opposing an idea, still strongly held in some quarters, that sickness and saintliness go together. It is even thought by some that suffering makes saints. It is more likely to make rebellious cynics or querulous neurotics. The saints have not been made saints because of suffering, but in spite of it. It has been their reaction to suffering that made saintliness, not the suffering itself. There is nothing in pain itself *quâ* pain to make heroism. Anyone who has suffered pain will support this view. No word must be said to belittle the great saintliness of some characters, but if they could have been

[81] John 2:21.
[82] Romans 12:1.
[83] Romans 8:23, Ephesians 5:23.

as fully awakened spiritually without physical disability, then, as instruments in the hand of God, they would have been of even greater usefulness through health than through disease. The matter can be put briefly: Jesus would not have been more holy if He had been the victim of disease. God does not *need* evil before He can accomplish His maximum good.

Christian Science has never fallen into this heresy. The body and mind are vehicles of the Divine Spirit. They are to be as fit as we can make them for this high purpose. Christian Science is not necessary, of course, to this New Testament doctrine. But no branch of the Church proclaims it with the same constancy.

The soul is the centre of emphasis in other Churches, and we may well and truly say that it is of greater importance. But it is safe to say that *all but the very few advanced saints are far more interested in and concerned about their bodies.* Bad temper may be worse in the sight of God than cancer, but the realisation that we have the former affects us little. We heard of the latter with dismay. Man is preoccupied with his health. His ill temper does not stop him earning his living and maintaining his home. Cancer looms up before him as "the end of everything."

Christian Science has made immense capital out of the interest of men in physical health, and who can be surprised if a "religion" that was a half-hearted affair of going to church or chapel sometimes, a "religion" without life or loveliness in it, a formal, conventional, sham thing, gives way to a radiant religion when the latter shows that it has power to draw back a loved one from the edge of the grave or give one back one's own health and strength?

5. An important contribution of Christian Science to Christian living is that it turns the attention of the sufferer away from himself to God. "Tell the sick," says Mrs. Eddy finely, "that they can meet disease fearlessly if they only realise that divine love gives them all power over every physical action and condition. . . . Turn (the patient's) gaze from the false evidence of the senses to the harmonious facts of Soul and immortal being." [84] A sufferer, especially if the illness is prolonged, if he cannot continue with any of his earlier pursuits, if he has few inner resources such as are possessed by the well-read, highly educated person, if he is much alone, and if he has neurotic tendencies, is very liable, for any, let alone all, of these reasons, to become wrapped up in himself, to allow his illness to loom too large and fill his whole horizon, to turn

[84] *Science and Health,* p. 420.

his mind in on himself with the definite result of hampering his own recovery, and to allow unhealthy emotion to seep into his mind.

In a later section of this book (p. 343) we shall show how unhealthy emotion breeds even physical disease. Perhaps the finest contribution Christian Science has made is its emphasis on the necessity of excluding negative emotions like hatred, resentment, jealousy, rebellion and so on.

To have the visits of a Christian Science healer, generally of cheerful and sanguine temperament, is good. To appreciate that the healer believes the patient can be made better, and to hear the stories of people worse than himself who are now completely well, cheers him, and to listen to readings from the Scriptures and from *Science and Health*, while much may be incomprehensible, does turn his mind to the qualities God possesses and away from the symptoms of which he complains. This is a gain indeed, and is likely to replace fear, worry and panic with courage, optimism and buoyancy, thus accelerating enormously the return to health.

The weakness of all this, however, as we have seen, is that health is the *end* of religion and God a *means* to it, and, further, those Christian Scientists who do remain ill must have their minds filled with self-recrimination. Mrs. Eddy's teaching must make them feel that it is their own fault, their own poor faith or mental obtuseness that hinders their attainment of radiant health which Mrs. Eddy points to as the *summum bonum* of religion.

6. While we may criticise many things in Christian Science, I must pay tribute here to the characters of Christian Scientists. Those I have met have not seemed proud or intolerant. They have seemed to me humble, inwardly serene and radiant, and to be in touch with spiritual resources which are all too commonly untapped. Their conception of the reality and power of God is finer than most, and rids their minds of fear. In the main they seem healthy, loving and forgiving people, practised in the discipline of excluding from themselves "hatred, malice and all uncharitableness." Above all they appear to me really to love others in the Christian sense and I am more and more convinced of the therapeutic energies released by such loving. Where Christian Science healers succeed, they do so by loving the patient back to health, convincing him of God's love. Many are ill for lack of love, and the love of relatives is too often mingled with negative emotions like fear and pity. These infect the patient's mind and hinder recovery. We all have much to learn from them here. Christian Science will continue to prosper until the other Churches take up the challenge of its successes and give prominence to the truths on which those successes are based. As my friend Dr. Harold Roberts has said, "It is not difficult to indulge

in what may appear to be a masterly refutation of Christian Science and show that it is neither Christian nor science. When that feat has been accomplished we have still to reckon with the benefits which Christian Science has brought to a large number of people and to provide not only a more satisfying doctrine, but better results." [85]

CONCLUSION

Christian Science could make a valuable contribution both to religion and healing if Christian Scientists would do several things.

1. Leave out Mrs. Eddy altogether.[86] All the Christian medical psychologists on the staff of my City Temple Psychological Clinic accept and practice all the truths that lie behind Christian Science. Mrs. Eddy is not necessary at all. Indeed, she has in the eyes of the educated and thoughtful person, degraded her own teaching and obscures the truths on which all that is sound in it is based.

Let Christian Scientists be content to recognise that the teaching she had from Quimby contained a germinal idea which is worth working out, both in theory and practice. Christian Science at its best can be much better than its exemplification in its founder. Dakin says,[87] "Mrs. Eddy lived a slave to fear until she died." Yet she was "the strange instrument by which a new concept of God was spread abroad in which fear was utterly abolished." Mrs. Eddy would have said as much herself, for in *Science and Health*,[88] she writes "Fear is the foundation of sickness and you master fear and sin through Divine Mind. . . . Fear which is an element of all disease must be cast out to readjust the balance for God." What a pity that such great truths should be impeded by being linked with a person whose life denied them! There is nothing more pitiful in all biographical literature than Dakin's vivid picture of Mrs. Eddy, racked with pain and seriously ill, sending out Mrs. Leonard, dressed exactly as Mrs. Eddy would have dressed, carrying a little parasol to shield her face even inside a closed carriage, so that the public might think that Mrs. Eddy was still well enough to take her daily

[85] *The Sanctions of Christian Healing*, p. 6 (Epworth Press, 1950).

[86] F. W. H. Myers and his brother in early days tried to persuade Christian Scientists to relinquish the title "Christian Science" and call their system "Mind Cure." He wrote, "We have adopted the more reasonable name for this system, and advise its adherents to drop the title of "Christian Science," which has naturally incurred both Christian and scientific disapproval." *Proceedings of the Society for Psychical Research*, June 1893, p. 160.

[87] Dakin, *op. cit.*, p. 197.

[88] See pp. 391-392.

ride. If the picture be true, Mrs. Eddy must have lived in terror that people would find out that she was an invalid.

2. Let Christian Scientists use the Bible as their text-book, and discard *Science and Health* altogether, or else subject it to a drastic purge, or, better still, re-write it.

3. Let them co-operate with doctors, surgeons, nurses and all qualified people who are seeking to help and to heal sufferers. Let Christian Scientists refrain from their unreasonable and stupid hostility to a noble profession. In this way they would realise that co-operation with the medical profession would not lesson the cures of Christian Science, but it would lessen the number of disasters which happen through its unintelligent application.

It is agreed by all who have studied the matter that many illnesses, even those we call physical and organic, are primarily caused by a psychological or spiritual factor like worry or fear. When that situation is realised by the patient, analysis must be followed by synthesis. The relevant, positive, healing idea must fill the mind to the exclusion of the negative, destructive idea.

If, *by chance*, without analysis or any other means of understanding what the destructive idea is, or whether, indeed, the illness comes into the psychogenic category at all, a Christian Scientist happens to hit on the relevant, positive, healing idea, and drives it into the patient's mind, the patient is healed, and the results are often startling and apparently magical. If an asthma runs back to a particular fear, and the Christian Scientist successfully implants in the patient's mind a new trust in God and confidence in himself, the asthma may disappear in a night.

But an asthma caused in a coal-miner purely by coal-dust would not thus be cured. The successes of Christian Science are "lucky hits" in the realm of a spiritualised psychological medicine. The failures are ascribed to a lack of faith on the part of the patient. Co-operation with doctors and psychologists who share a Christian experience, together with the abandonment of Mrs. Eddy's absurb metaphysics, could win for Christian Science greater successes, avoid failure and nonsense, and enable the Christian Science movement to make a most valuable contribution to the needs of men. Instead, Christian Scientists resort to silly incantations, and treat a physiogenic injury as if it were in the same category as psychogenic illness.

The Rev. Breenes Miller, in his book, *Christian Science and the Christian Faith*,[89] gives two illustrations of remarkable cures through Christian Science: first of a woman in his own church who suffered

[89] See pp. 7, 9 and 32 (Epworth Press, 1932).

for twenty years from general paralysis, and for whom "the best medical skill had been utterly unable to work her recovery," and who lay on her back "entirely unable to use her limbs." After contact with a Christian Science healer, "in a week she was walking about, perfectly well," and lived a full and active life for twenty years. He gives another case of a man he knew in Sunderland "dying of consumption," cured by anointing with oil and by prayer. The patient was at business the next day. These two cases he followed by two others. The first was a young lady, an ardent Christian Scientist, who, obeying her teachers, refused to consult an oculist. She is now blind. Another, a saintly lady, developed a "painful internal complaint." She listened to Christian Scientists, and not only died, but died having lost her faith in God.

We see in these illustrations the result of failure to differentiate and of the refusal to co-operate. Mrs. Eddy, as long as she is recognised as the authority, has made co-operation an act of hostility to the whole movement. "The hosts of Æsculapius," she said, "are flooding the world with diseases because they are ignorant that the human mind and body are myths." And again, "The reeling ranks of materia-medica with their poisons, nostrums and knives are impotent." And again, "The ordinary practitioner, examining bodily symptoms, telling the patient that he is sick, and treating the case according to his physical diagnosis, would naturally induce the very disease he is trying to cure." [90]

Co-operation with doctors would mean accurate diagnosis and scientific aid which would guard against tragedies which so frequently happen and discredit the Christian Science case. At the same time, Christian Science would be just as able to make its undoubtedly valuable contribution. Every medical man recognises the place of fear in hindering his patients' recovery. A recent writer in the *British Medical Journal* said, "Whatever exorcises the demon of fear and brings to the sick man's bed the Angel of Hope, is a powerful aid to medical treatment. To lie in the shadow of fear deprives a man of energies that might otherwise be available for curative purposes."

Perhaps even yet Christian Science may remedy its technique at this point. Later editions of *Science and Health* do suggest medical aid in certain cases: "If from an injury or from any cause, a Christian Scientist were seized with pain so violent that he could not treat himself mentally—and the Scientists had failed to relieve him—the sufferer could call a surgeon, who would give him a hypodermic injection, then,

[90] *Science and Health*, p. 161. Note also pp. 163-164.

when the belief of pain was lulled, he could handle his own case mentally." [91]

4. Christian Scientists should realize that they have got hold of some truths which need emphasis and are very relevant to health, but that it is only part of the truth, and that other parts are equally important and necessary.

5. Christian Scientists should balance their own important teaching about health with the even more important truth that man is a sinner and needs a Saviour, and that Jesus, whom Christianity claims is the Divine Son of God, is that Saviour and the only hope of the world; that He is God incarnate, God in the *flesh*, that real thing whose reality Mrs. Eddy denies; that it is better to be sick and know the Saviour, as St. Paul was, with his "thorn in the flesh," than to be well in body and only to have found in religion a cure for some of its diseases, having missed that living contact and relationship with Christ which alone is worthy to be called the Christian religion. Who is right, Mrs. Eddy in her affirmation that sin does not exist and that salvation consists in realising it, or the Fourth Evangelist, "If we say that we have no sin, we deceive ourselves, and the truth is not in us. If we confess our sins, He is faithful and righteous to forgive us our sins and to cleanse us from all unrighteousness." [92]

The question is often asked whether Christian Science will last. There appears to be no reason why it should not. It teaches, if in a fantastic, illogical and over-emphasised way, some very important truths. The Church's answer to Christian Science should not be mere condemnation. The Church will have to include those truths and practise sensibly their implications. Even then Christian Science is likely to continue for a long time. It ministers to men's desire for physical health and mental serenity. Man is told to get the difficulties of life out of the way. He is told he need not come to terms with death, for it is an illusion. Sin is another illusion; pain yet another; the body another. God is good. Let man bask in the sunshine of that idea and exclude all the above illusions. Let him wipe out the drug, the hospital, the doctor, the dark shadows of poverty and death, and think about positive and beautiful things. The weakness here, of course, is that a neurotic woman's wishful thinking cannot evade the so-called illusions indefinitely. If the Master of life suffered sorrow and pain and death, and died for human sin, it is hardly likely that Mrs. Eddy can by-pass them worthily, and the

[91] *Science and Health*, p. 464.
[92] I John 1:8.

greatest victories of man have not been found along her road of evasion, but over steep hills almost as fraught with tragedy as Calvary itself.

Christian Science has never gone down into the slums and borne on its heart the burdens of the poor. Where it is recognisable Christianity at all, it is Christianity without tears.

Christian Science still has vast funds at its disposal, splendid accommodation and equipment, devoted and loyal workers, immense influence, and, as its greatest asset, the desire of men and women everywhere to be healthy. It is not likely to fail, but the student must say "good-bye" to reason. "What can Christian Science say [cries Fisher] to the dying pauper in the slums which he will not regard as an affront to the lessons of a lifetime? It will tell him that his pain is an error, his illness an error, his poverty an error, his impending death an error. It will tell him that he is suffering from the delusion of a mortal mind. . . . To the downcast and the outcast such a philosophy is a cruel mockery. They know instinctively that it is false." [93]

[93] Fisher, *op. cit.*

4

HEALING MISSIONS

THIS BOOK OFFERS no approval of the methods used by the Four Square Gospel Movement in the healing missions carried out by Pastor Jeffreys and others. No doubt his intentions are excellent, but the dangers attending his methods are so great that neither from the point of view of psychology nor from that of true religion can they be approved.

Such a statement needs illustration, and two are here offered.

1. The first is a statement made on oath by a patient, suffering from chronic encephalitis, who is a Bachelor of Science and a Doctor of Philosophy.[1] He decided to visit Pastor Jeffreys at Liverpool on the ground that he could not be made worse and might be made better. He says that the atmosphere of the "healings" was very emotional, that after a sermon by Pastor Jeffreys, at about 10 P.M. the latter descended from the platform and "commenced the business of laying on hands." The writer says, "I was the second person he treated. . . . I was not in the slightest degree emotionally moved. After enquiring the nature of my complaint, he laid his hand on my right temple and prayed fervently. I then felt what can only be described as a current of healing power pass from him to me. As a result, I could walk a few steps without limping and the tremor ceased. He then asked was I cured, and, on receiving my reply in the affirmative, asked me to repeat, 'Thank you, Jesus.' This, I am ashamed to say, I did. *He then proclaimed my cure to the meeting.*[2] The effect, however, soon wore off. I estimate a period of about five minutes before the limp returned. The tremor, however, was absent, and I remained free from it even at breakfast next morning. I repeat, I was quite detached and had no emotional

---

[1] His statutory declaration is in my possession.

[2] Italics mine. Note the difference between this attitude and that of Jesus Christ, who said repeatedly "Go and tell no man."

197

feelings whatever beyond curiosity. I cannot explain the temporary cure, but I have heard of similar cases, in one of which a patient suffering from diabetes was cured temporarily."

2. The second took place during my own ministry in Leeds (1925-1936). A young woman, called Miss A., suffered from a lameness which, she alleged, the doctors had declared incurable. I have no idea what the diagnosis was. She never attended my psychological clinic attached to the church, nor did she at any time have any treatment from me or from anyone known to me. Neither, as far as I remember, did I ever discuss her symptoms with her. The movement known as the Four Square Gospel Movement held some services in a hall in the city, and Miss A. attended. I am told that hymns were sung one after another, including many that contained choruses which went "with a swing." During intervals between these choruses any who wished to be healed were invited up to the platform. Using a pair of crutches, Miss A. went up, and the pastor conducting the service laid his hands upon her and told her to believe that she was healed and could walk without crutches. In a state of immense emotional excitement, she threw them away and walked off the platform without them. I am told that an "electric excitement" spread through the hall. A newspaper reporter attended at her home. Her photograph appeared in the evening Press, with sensational reports of her "cure." Then, of course, letters began to arrive addressed to her from all over the country. She was in great consternation. People wrote asking whether she would advise them to bring their friends, and gave details of many pathetic case. Letters flowed in in such a volume that Miss A. could not possibly cope with the situation. This poor, uneducated, but well-meaning, girl was greatly upset by the cries for help contained in the letters she received. At first she began to reply to these letters, stating, simply enough, that all she knew was that whereas she was lame, now she could walk. The excitement lasted about three weeks, during which Miss A. walked. Then it died down, and Miss A. began to limp, collapsed and was carried home. When I last heard of her, she was using crutches and was as bad as she had ever been; with, furthermore, some very difficult problems to think about concerning the nature of faith, the power of God and the value of healing missions.

The method of Mr. James Moore Hickson was not quite so spectacular. I met Mr. Hickson in India, and talked with him at length about his work. A quiet and reverent service marked his method, prayer was offered, and frequently Holy Communion administered. Any who wished to be healed knelt at the altar rail or steps, and hands were laid upon them. They were encouraged to have faith in the power of

Christ to fulfill His purposes in them. It might not be Christ's purpose
—Mr. Hickson explained—to heal them at all, but He would give them
peace of mind, or power to witness in spite of disability.

We are on safer ground here, and great appreciation of Mr. Hickson's
work was expressed by high clerical dignitaries in Australia, New
Zealand, the United States, India, China, Japan and South Africa.

Mr. Hickson clearly believed that his method of making sick people
well was only one amongst many. Differing from Christian Scientists,
Mr. Hickson welcomed the co-operation of doctors, and said that he
had taken a course of anatomy and physiology, that he might the
better understand what he was doing. At the same time, he realised that
"the cause of much suffering in the world today lies far deeper than the
physical part of man's being. It is hidden in the mental and moral life,
where physical remedies cannot reach and are powerless to heal." [3] Mr.
Hickson felt that he had a definite call of God to do this kind of work.
"I was always conscious of our Lord's Presence, and knew that whatever help was given came from Him." [4] He planned to have a home
where treatment could be given in which doctors co-operated, and he
appointed a matron and nurses, built an adjacent chapel and appointed a
chaplain. The whole scheme came to an end, however, because the
General Medical Council of the day threatened the doctors with being
struck off the Medical Register for "attaching themselves to an institu-
tion for what they called 'covering' purposes"; covering, that is to say,
the healing methods of a medically unqualified person. Mr. Hickson
said, "Although I could not then have resident patients, I continued
to minister to the sick, and kept to my rule not to see a doctor's
patients without his knowledge and consent." [5]

Mr. Hickson's book is overburdened with testimonies of various
people to the value of his work. One bishop, however, may be quoted
as stating Mr. Hickson's point of view. Bishop Rhinelander of Penn-
sylvania writes: "Mr. Hickson in his Healing Mission stakes everything
on two truths in combination: the living power of Christ in His
Church, and the efficacy of penitence to provide a sure entrance for
that power in human life. He insists that all healing done is spiritual
healing, the direct, immediate action of the Holy Spirit of God on us
as spiritual beings. The curing of physical disorders and diseases is
secondary, not primary; incidental, not the chief end; a sign infinitely

[3] James Moore Hickson, *Heal the Sick* (Dutton, 1925).
[4] *Op. cit.*
[5] *Op. cit.*

and eloquently expressive, as in our Lord's days on earth, of the spiritual recreation and renewal which has taken place. . . . And Mr. Hickson tells us that those who come to him are always urged to realise this." [6] That this excellent point of view is grasped by many is shown by numerous striking testimonies. I quote one. "If this cure were to fail," a patient writes, "and my disease came back as bad as ever, I would still be glad I went to the Mission, for it has changed my life." [7] An unbiased journalist said, "I have always believed in the Presence of Christ, but it was more as a truth to be believed rather than a living reality. The Mission made me feel this Presence was real, and it is going to change the whole course of my life." [8] Many who witnessed Mr. Hickson's missions were convinced that the early usages of the Church were being seen again. Professor Michell, of Toronto University, who went to a mission full of prejudice and ready-made explanations, tells how he was confounded. "It was not mental suggestion, it was not psychotherapeutics . . . it was the mighty working of the Spirit of God." [9] Clearly, Mr. Hickson is a person endowed with the "gift" referred to on p. 139, and he seeks to use it through the rite of the laying on of hands (see p. 131). No one should hinder such a person from a *private* ministry.

At the same time, though the laying on of hands seems to the present writer a sound procedure, provided always that there are the safeguards enumerated earlier, yet the publicity and dangers of healing missions preclude my recommendation of them, for the following reasons:

1. The power of suggestion is too dangerously used.

In his Bampton Lectures for 1930, Professor Grensted, Oriel Professor of the Philosophy of the Christian Religion in the University of Oxford, wrote as follows: [10]

"It is of the very first importance that in any development of spiritual healing, the Church should go far beyond the crudities of mere suggestion. The great danger of missions of healing is that by their very prestige and by their impressive setting they act with immense power along these lines. They attract and profoundly affect hysterics of all kinds. But they give little guarantee that the cures so achieved are radical. Even if the patients develop a new and an edifying piety, this

[6] *Op. cit.*
[7] *Op. cit.*
[8] *Op. cit.*
[9] *Op. cit.*
[10] *Psychology and God*, pp. 117-118. By permission of Longmans, Green & Co.

may easily be nothing more than a new phase of their hysteria, as far removed from true religion as fantasy is from fact. 'This man was a sinner and he is cured. Unfortunately he now believes that he is a saint.' The old weakness of which the sin was a symptom is but written large in the new Pharisee. And there is always the disturbing possibility of relapse.

"Those who undertake such missions should be very careful on two main points. Everything should be done that those who come for healing are not led to dwell only upon the hope of cure in some specific and direct form. They should be prepared for a new realisation of the love and power of God, and be told that they are to try for a time to forget themselves and their troubles in His presence. The whole mission should be essentially an act of worship, expression and evoking faith, and *faith not in cure, but in God*.[11] And, secondly, nothing is so important as the following up of the mission by the steady education of those who have been helped. They have to learn to make their cure real by understanding the facts of their life, and supremely the fact of God Whom they must learn not only to trust, but to love. And if they cannot at first love God, let them begin by loving and serving their fellow-men. Only in a mission conducted in such a spirit can we be sure that the devils cast out will not return with seven other devils worse than themselves."

2. All that was said about the danger of curing a symptom is relevant here, but the publicity of the mission makes the danger greater. The view has already been expressed that our Lord knew the nature of a patient's troubles and changed His technique accordingly. The missioner at a healing mission to which the uninstructed public is invited does not know this any better than a passer-by in the street. The method of the healing mission is the same for all patients. All the onus is thrust upon the patient to make a sufficiently emotional response to enable cure to take place, and there is no co-operation with the medical profession at all.

3. The very serious mistake is made of misleading the patient and the audience regarding the nature of faith. The place of faith in healing is described later (p. 423), but it cannot be denied that a *successful* healing mission is one at which, presumably, large numbers of people are healed. But already we have seen how temporary the nature of such healings often is and how intolerable it is that the onus should be placed on the patient.

Consider what that onus involves. The patient either concludes that

[11] Italics mine.

he had faith, for he is better, or that he had insufficient faith, since he is no better. But the logic is at fault because, as we have seen, there can be healing without faith and faith without healing. Many a healed patient preens himself on his faith, when it is his suggestibility that has proved the important therapeutic factor. And that is a very different matter, depending largely on a mental make-up for which the individual is neither to be congratulated nor blamed. On the other hand, many a patient is unhealed who has a virile faith in God in spite of his suffering; a loving, trustful dependence on Christ, though, for other reasons, he remains unhealed. It is a very serious thing so to mislead people about faith at a healing mission. Real faith differs vitally and fundamentally from suggestibility, as we shall see. It is something we have to fight for; it is not an accident of our make-up. Further, its character is determined by its object. The quality of a faith the object of which is God and the aim of which is harmony with Him is more desirable—even if the body is unhealed—than the hysterical suggestibility such as Miss A. manifested. For a week or two, the basic neurosis remaining, she was able to change the symptom of lameness for that of an emotional religiosity. For the time being, the prestige, the importance and popularity which the mission gave her acted as love-substitutes. They brought her admiration. It is possible that the lameness was conditioned, or even caused, by the deprivation of love. Miss A. got no insight into her condition and developed no real faith in God. When the excitement of the mission faded, the spotlight of admiration grew dim, flickered and went out. Then, to get love in terms of sympathy (an essential need of a neurotic), the unconscious probably fell back on the old device of lameness. But harm was done to Miss A. and many others, and subsequent healing made yet more difficult.

4. There is no authority in the New Testament for the healing mission. Jesus seems to have treated individuals and to have preferred personal dealing in the presence of a few close friends, whose faith was strong and who understood his aims. Again and again Christ appeared to take every possible step to avoid the kind of publicity which the healing mission is bound to foster. Further, the evidence seems to be that Christ, so far from despising the work of the physician, honoured the profession. Nowhere is He reported to have said that if only men had sufficient faith, medical aids would be unnecessary. When Christ looked upon sick folk, He did not suppose that, *whatever the illness was from which they were suffering*, "believing" would make them better. The very presence of Luke, the physician, amongst His later followers suggests that He approved the use of drugs and remedies. Mrs. Eddy has never drawn doctors to the ranks of Christian Scientists,

but Medical Missionary work is felt to be a natural expression of Christ's spirit. In the story Jesus told of the Good Samaritan, the latter did not say a prayer, or lay his hands upon the sick man. He poured in wine and oil; wine because it was believed to be cleansing, and oil because it was believed to assist healing. It is hard to believe that Christ would have given such a sanction to the use of homely remedies if He believed that they were wholly irrelevant and that faith was a cure for all ailments.

5. Unless very great care is taken and attendance confined to those who have been instructed, healing missions are thronged with people in an unhealthy emotional state who want a sensation much more than they want God. The sick who are brought only want to get better, and seek to "try" the healing mission because the other remedies they have tried have failed. This is understandable, but it is doubtful whether the Church should sanction a method which has no support in the New Testament, if that method brings religion itself into misunderstanding and ill repute.

The present writer believes that great care should be taken lest a healing mission suggests that God is being used as a means to man's end. That even Mr. Hickson's methods involve the mechanism of suggestion quite removed from any relationship with religion is shown in his work. We are told [12] of a little South African girl of four years of age, cured of blindness in the left eye. She could scarcely have shared Mr. Hickson's views. It is hard to criticise here. The value of the cure is so immense to the patient that one is tempted to suppose that the end justifies the means. Further, we are told that the whole family was converted through the child's healing. But must not the cure of the few be set in perspective of the whole problem? And is the method of the mission justified by the few sporadic permanent cures which certainly take place? The present writer believes that the little girl could have been cured by other methods, and the real danger of making God a means to our end, instead of holding that God is the end and we the means, seems to the writer most important.

6. The sixth objection is a very real one. In my experience and reading many healing missions have been attended by sick folk who have found that the mass suggestion of illness and disease, and sometimes terror, has outweighed the suggestion of recovery made by the healer.

Where there are no recorded cases of cure the mass fear and depression can be terrifying. At one healing mission in Manchester, attended

[12] *Op. cit.*

203

by thousands, and at another in Liverpool, the Press alleged that not a single case of healing was even claimed.[13]

On these grounds this book opposes, therefore, the healing mission to which the uninstructed public is admitted. In an atmosphere of unhealthy excitement the nature both of faith and religion is overclouded. No clear perception of the nature of God and of His ways with men is received by those who attend. In view of the ignorance of the healer, the method must remain a "hit-and-miss" affair, and while a few may temporarily be healed (with dangers to themselves already pointed out), many are sent home depressed and hopeless, brooding over false conclusions, believing that religion is "no good," as they would say, or that their faith is insufficient to take hold of what is offered, or that God does not hear their prayers, when all these conclusions may be wrong.

I, therefore, entirely approve of Section II in the Report issued by the Sub-Committee of the Lambeth Conference of 1920, which reads: "On account of the immense importance that we attach to the spiritual preparation of the individual, as well as for other reasons, we are not prepared to give any encouragement to public missions of healing."

Services could be commended which had as their supreme aim the unity of the worshipper with God. In such a service it would be pointed out that frequently ill-health is due to disunity in this relationship, and services with healing as their secondary aim could well be held if the following conditions were strictly maintained:

1. That the priest or minister conducting the service had had a private interview, or series of private interviews, with each person who intended to come forward to receive the laying on of hands, and that in these interviews the nature of faith and of God's ways with men had been explained to the patient, so that if healing did not follow, he would not lose his faith.

2. That the priest or minister conducting such a service should have the full consent of the patient's doctor, and that in obtaining this he should know the doctor's diagnosis and, as far as possible, understand the patient's condition.

3. That the priest or minister should himself clearly understand that there are many illnesses in which the relevant way of co-operating with God is by the physical treatments which science has discovered, and that, because of their effect on the mind and spirit of the patient, while spiritual methods are not useless, the patient should not in such

[13] *Birkenhead News,* June 10, 1939.

cases be led to regard healing as the main objective, or test the value of spiritual ministration by his cure or lack of cure.

4. That no one should be admitted to such a service except the patient, one or two close and sympathetic Christian friends and a small group of selected Christian people who have previously met for prayer and discussion on the whole theme of religion and healing.

With these safeguards, much good could be accomplished. The final act, then, of the laying on of hands would be the climax of a long process, not an act of magic carried out before an excited audience eager for a sensational sign. Such a service would signify the dedication of the patient, an act of utter surrender to God in loving trustfulness, rather than an attempt to use God in order to get well, with more than a risk that after recovery God would be forgotten.

5

PSYCHIC PHENOMENA AND HEALING

OUR PLAN TO include every known non-physical method of healing compels us to discuss the phenomena often—but not always—connected with Spiritualism. Many spiritualists are hostile to religion and to the Christian Church. Others are indifferent to both. But for some Spiritualism is a religion. There exists a Spiritualist Church with many branches at which regular services are held. It is therefore convenient to discuss psychic phenomena and healing under the heading of modern religious methods of healing.

To examine adequately the case of Spiritualism in this book would take us too far afield and make too great a demand on space. After a good deal of study, conversations with spiritualists, interviews with mediums and visits to séances, I came to certain conclusions set forth in an earlier book,[1] and have little to add on the general theme, even in the light of further reading and experience.

During the quarter of a century which has passed since that book was written, I think the case for Spiritualism has become stronger. That, through mediums, some kind of contact is sometimes made with an intelligence or intelligences on some other plane of being, seems to me the most reasonable hypothesis to account for some of the carefully tested and authenticated phenomena of Spiritualism.

But even so guarded and, for the spiritualist, so unsatisfactory a statement must be further modified. Many spiritualistic phenomena are capable of an alternative explanation in terms of telepathy, the functions of the unconscious mind, the emergence of racial and ancestral memories, and so on. Further, many sincere writers, who are far from

[1] *After Death: A Popular Statement of the Modern Christian View of Life beyond the Grave* (Abingdon-Cokesbury, 1936).

206

being hostile to Spiritualism, have shown that fraud still spoils the progress of research.[2]

On the other hand, some experiences of my own in the séance room, seemed to me to make the spiritualist hypothesis as likely as any theory based on telepathy.

The spiritualist hypothesis bristles with difficulties, the main one being the trivial nature of the messages received from those said to be "on the other side." Freud writes as follows in *The Future of an Illusion:* [3]

"Unfortunately they [the spiritualists] have not succeeded in disproving the fact that the appearances and utterances of their spirits are merely the productions of their own mental activity. They have called up the spirits of the greatest of men, of the most eminent thinkers, but all their utterances and all the information they have received from them have been so foolish and so desperately insignificant that one could find nothing else to believe in but the capacity of the spirits for adapting themselves to the circle of people that had evoked them."

Perhaps personal experiences are as good evidence here as we can get, and again and again I have been bewildered by the trivial nature of supposed communications. During the last war I went to a séance with a young widow, who had lost her husband in a "blitz," and who was in a peculiarly nervous state because of a happening just before his death which she thought could be cleared up by a visit to a medium. She was greatly comforted by much that "came through," but surprised that the control on "the other side," alleged to be instructed by her husband, seemed most eager to get over to us, through the medium, one most important message. When it came, it was to the effect that next time she had her teeth stopped it would be wise not to have gold fillings, as they showed when she laughed. It was quite true that since his death she had had teeth stopped with gold fillings. It is no doubt possible that the glories of the life beyond so far exceed our present faculties that words can no more describe them than we can describe a sunset to a man born blind, or express to a man born stone deaf the splendours of Beethoven's music. But one would think that more could be said to a loving, mourning wife than a counsel about her teeth; that *some* idea of the wonder and joy of the beyond might be hinted at.

[2] See Harry Price, *Search for Truth* (Collins, 1942), Conan Doyle, *The New Revelation* (Doran, 1918). Cf. also the evidence of Joseph McCabe in *Is Spiritualism Based on Fraud?* and many cases of fraud cited in *Modern Spiritualism*, by Frank Podmore (Methuen, 1902), e.g., Vol. I, p. 205.

[3] Trans. by Robson-Scott (Hogarth Press).

The reader may consult the volumes listed in the bibliography at the end of this book, if he is interested, but in none of them is there any conception of the life after death which—far from surpassing— comes anywhere near equalling the glory and significance implicit in the restrained words of the New Testament. The heaven of the spiritualists seems very little better than the earth we know. I wrote a sentence in 1923 which I see no reason to alter: "Spiritualism has not made a single definite, valuable or original contribution to Christian thought concerning the life after death." [4] The great names quoted in support of it, like that of Sir Oliver Lodge, for instance, are names made great in other spheres. Influence and authority cannot be transferred in that way. Spiritualistic hypotheses are strongly supported, but not proved, because a bereaved father who happens to have been a great physicist believes them. And Sir Oliver's conclusions are not very encouraging to the seeker after certainty. I quote Sir Oliver's book named after his son, who was killed in the First World War.

"It may be asked, do I recommend all bereaved persons to devote the time and attention which I have done to getting communications and recording them? Most certainly I do not. I am a student of the subject, and a student often undertakes detailed labour of a special kind. I recommend people in general to learn and realise that their loved ones are still active and useful and interested and happy—more alive than ever in one sense—and to make up their minds to live a useful life till they rejoin them." [5]

Dr. Charles Mercier, in his book, *Spiritualism and Sir Oliver Lodge*, underlines this counsel with very grim warnings, and talks of hysteria and melancholia as penalties sometimes paid by the unscientific dabbler, especially if he be emotionally unstable.

We are seeking in this book to assess non-physical ways by which man may find healing of spirit, mind and body. It is most important, therefore, to stress the dangers of disintegration which sometimes follow the practices of Spiritualism.

Sir William Barrett, F.R.S., one of the most famous workers in this field, wrote a Preface to a book by the Rev. Donald Hole, entitled *Love and Death* (1922). In this Preface Barrett wrote as follows:

"Neither in pagan nor in Christian literature do we find that Spiritualism (or its equivalent) has added to the intellectual or moral advancement of the race. On the other hand, we find a singular consensus of opinion amongst Christians, in all times, of distrust and aversion to the

[4] *Op. cit.*

[5] Sir Oliver Lodge, F.R.S., D.Sc., *Raymond, or Life and Death* (Doran, 1916).

whole subject. There must be some reason for this hostility, or prejudice, as some would call it."

After mentioning the amount of trickery connected with the subject, *and the danger of moral deterioration* not infrequently observed in those who become absorbed in it, he goes on to say, "This being the case, Spiritualism becomes a treacherous quicksand upon which to build a new religion." [6]

A method which offers some hope of healing, but which threatens the dabbler with mental or moral deterioration, cannot be recommended. Yet, in two rather differing ways, without danger to the patient, the evidence is convincing that healing has been brought about by factors within the field of psychical research.

In his book, *Perceptive Healing*,[7] Dr. R. Connell submits the theory that a physical object, such as a fountain-pen or a ring, which has been in close contact with a person over a long period, carries on it an impress of the personality of its possessor so definite that a clairvoyant or "sensitive" can, by holding it, gain insight into the mind of the possessor and even into the lives of his parents, grandparents and remote ancestors with whom he is alleged to be still psychically connected.

Dr. Connell claims that the longer the object has been in contact with the individual, "the more virile his personality and the more intense or violent the emotional crises through which he may have passed while in contact with it, the more vivid and permanent the impressions he imposes on the object and the greater the likelihood of the percipient being able to visualise, apprehend and interpret them correctly." [8] The percipient, or sensitive, then enters a mental state of intensely concentrated introspection relating to the owner of the object, and writes down the images or pictures that come to his mind, the conscious mind being almost entirely dissociated. Curiously enough, the percipient holding, say, a fountain-pen, can often obtain insight into events in the patient's life which took place long before the pen was possessed by the patient.

It is supposed by Dr. Connell that ectoplasm [9]—the half-psychic, half-physical material which exudes from the body of a medium in

---

[6] This quotation from Sir William Barrett's Preface to the Rev. Donald Hole's book, *Love and Death*, is taken from the Rev. Dr. R. J. Campbell's Foreword to Lady Barrett's book, *Personality Survives Death*, p. xiii (Longmans Green, 1937).

[7] R. Connell, M.D., F.R.C.P.I., and Geraldine Cummins, *Perceptive Healing* (Rider, 1945).

[8] *Op. cit.*, p. 9.

[9] By some writers called teleplasm or psychoplasm.

trance (which the present writer has seen thus emerging and which has been photographed)—adheres unseen to any object long in a person's possession. Ectoplastic threads connect with the owner's personality. Similar threads exuded by the percipient are alleged to make contact with these, and unite the percipient with the psyche of the patient in such a manner that the former gains insight first into the personality of the patient, and then back through time to his ancestors.

If the theory can be substantiated, it is certainly an improvement on the laborious technique of psycho-analysis! Without even the presence of the patient, the percipient is alleged to gain insight not only into the patient's deep mind, but into the emotional factors behind physical and psychological illness transmitted to the patient by emotional crises through which his distant ancestors once passed.

The modern analyst supposes that neurosis is often due to some incident, or series of incidents, which happened perhaps very early in the patient's life and which have set up conflict, and he seeks by analysis to uncover such incidents, get the patient emotionally to realise and understand them and re-orientate his life accordingly.

Those who work in the field of perceptive healing think that the causal incidents may have occurred in the life of an ancestor, and that events in a patient's life stir into activity ancestral memories which have been passed on from one generation to the next. Complexes thus inherited can, it is thought, influence a patient far more powerfully than the incidents in his own life which stir them into activity; nor can any analyses, however thorough, uncover them.

In his book Dr. Connell gives a variety of cases. In some the causative factor lay in an incident that occurred during the childhood of the patient; in another, during the patient's life while in the mother's womb; in others the causative factor is alleged to have been an incident during the life of ancestors many generations removed from the patient. The cases are presented in a convincing manner, and some of the relevant facts described by the "sensitive" were later verified as correct.

For example, E. F. cannot sign his name through some inhibition overcome only by the use of alcohol. His father suffered from the same inhibition. Insight obtained in the manner described revealed that an ancestress, *by signing her name*, had had her Jewish husband tortured by the Inquisition in Spain. She had been compelled to witness the torture while carrying her child. She was driven mad, and the child was born while she was insane. When the patient read the report written by a percipient (who had had sent her an old family document conferring the Freedom of the City of London upon an ancestor), and realised the origin of his inhibition, it disappeared.

Another example cited is one of claustrophobia, in which, a specimen of the patient's handwriting having been sent to a percipient in London, the latter reported that two hundred years earlier an ancestress, again while carrying her child, was caught in a small room when wild men set the house on fire. Her terrifying experiences in the fire became part of the collective memory of that family, and were handed down in terms of a terror of fire and of being shut up in a small space.

In yet another, the dismay experienced by a musician at a trifling injury to his hand was traced by a percipient to an incident two hundred years earlier, when an ancestor's hands had been cut off by a Russian, the victim's wife being made to witness the outrage.

Dr. Connell's thesis is that, without any danger to the patient, the origins of a proportion of neuroses and psychosomatic illnesses can be unmasked and the patient helped to understand their origin and overcome their symptoms. Whatever one's prejudices, it is difficult airily to dismiss the evidence offered in this volume by a Fellow of the Royal College of Physicians of Ireland.

I have personally been much impressed with the work of Dr. and Mrs. Laurence Bendit and with their joint books, *The Psychic Sense*[10] and *This World and That*.[11] Dr. Bendit is a practising psychiatrist of the Jungian School. Mrs. Bendit (formerly Phoebe Payne) is a clairvoyant with remarkable powers. Again and again she has proved her ability to "see" what is wrong with a patient, physically, psychologically, or even spiritually. I have personally experienced her power to do this, and must add that her diagnosis can be quite devastatingly accurate. She can now control this power by an act of will, and does not normally go about with it "switched on," if one can use such an expression. She does not need to see the patient. On being given a wallet belonging to a girl two hundred miles away, Mrs. Bendit described accurately the person and the nature of a crisis through which she was passing.

Many illustrations of her powers could be given. In his foreword, Mr. L. A. G. Strong quotes the case of a man who had injured his elbow. "It was stiff and painful. Dr. Graham Howe led him to Miss Payne, with the conjuration, 'Phoebe, do your stuff!' Unhesitatingly, at a distance of five or six feet, and without uncovering the arm, she said that the sufferer had dislocated a small bone—she did not know

[10] Dutton, 1949.
[11] Faber and Faber, 1950.

its name and was obliged to describe it—and would need to have it replaced. An X-ray examination the next morning confirmed this diagnosis." [12] Many other convincing examples are given in the book.

The second method of using psychic phenomena in healing is illustrated in the anonymous writings of a person who uses the initials "E.M.S." In a volume entitled *Dr. Beale*,[13] we have a day-to-day record of an illness, with details, including the rising and falling temperatures of the patient, which was treated partly by the patient's physician, but much more intensively by "Dr. Beale," who had been dead many years, but who controlled a medium, Miss Rose, who carried out the spirit-doctor's most minute instructions. The general practitioner, Dr. Steadall, must have been very broad-minded to allow this treatment from "the other side" to be carried out on a patient in his care who was dangerously ill, but if the record is accepted at all, we must admit that the result was a very extraordinary recovery. I accept the sincerity of the writer. Whether her interpretation of the events she records is necessarily the only one, I take the liberty of doubting.

Another book by the same author (E.M.S.), called *One Thing I Know*, contains the story of her own cure by "Dr. Beale" after she had lain on her back for fifteen years. Here again the amazing story is honestly told, but the most striking section of the whole volume is the evidence of the general practitioner, Dr. Steadall, who gives his own view of the case, which, for my part, I am inclined to accept, though it rules out altogether the spiritualist hypothesis. A tribute should be paid to the authoress, who desires to establish that her cure is a proof of that hypothesis, and yet whose honesty is such that she includes in her volume the evidence of her own doctor which contradicts the case she seeks to establish.

Spiritualist newspapers publish similar cases from time to time, and no one can reasonably suppose that all these reports are foolish nonsense, or fraudulent inventions. F. W. H. Myers and his brother give details of a case in which it was alleged that the patient was cured by a Dr. Z from the "other side" who gave advice through a medium.[14] There is a field here for further enquiry. By closing doors through which truth and healing may come merely because of our own prejudices and incredulity, we do a disservice to both science and religion, and, what is worse, we allow sufferers to remain in pain and limitation

[12] *Op. cit.*

[13] Published by John Watkins (1921).

[14] *Proceedings of the Society for Psychical Research*, Vol. 9, pp. 182 ff.

without exploring every possible means of ending both. That is a very serious matter indeed.

One is always more convinced by experiences that happen to oneself than by those one reads about, and I should like, therefore, to include, as part of the evidence we are considering, an experience which came my way with a friend in whose good faith it is impossible to disbelieve. I will call him Mr. Oliver. His wife was lying very dangerously ill. The doctor seemed puzzled, so a specialist was sent for. He appears to have given a diagnosis with some hesitation, but it was acted upon. Mrs. Oliver appears to have grown worse. Worried and miserable, Mr. Oliver happened to meet a spiritualist friend of his, who advised him to get some advice from "the other side." Oliver would have nothing to do with this, but the friend himself went to a reputable medium, who immediately went into trance, got into contact with some "North American physician" who had been dead for years, and who advised an exploration in quite a different area of the body from that in which the trouble was hitherto supposed to be located. Oliver was told all this over the telephone and put in a very awkward position. He had implicit trust in the ability of his medical adviser. He dared not tell either the latter or the specialist that he had consulted a medium, even by proxy. He did not believe in Spiritualism, and he certainly did not believe that a North American doctor, who died before abdominal surgery was practised, could know anything about it. At the same time, he could not bear the thought that his wife might die and the postmortem reveal that, had he disclosed his "information," she could have been saved.

At last he hit on a solution. He told his doctor that a medical "friend" had informed him that his wife's symptom often pointed to trouble in the region of the body the medium had indicated. To make a long story short, the information was acted upon by the doctor, the diagnosis revised, treatment altered and recovery secured.

The literature of Spiritualism abounds with similar cases which are well authenticated. Yet, on the other side of the argument, I should like to place on record another experience in which a doctor, who is a friend of mine, had a patient who was a most convinced and enthusiastic spiritualist. She complained of abdominal pain, which he and a consultant diagnosed as appendicitis. An operation was advised, but the patient was adamant that this should not be done. Instead she asked that a medium should be called in. The medium was called in and went into trance, and then announced that if she laid hands on the abdomen of the patient, the pain would pass and recovery be made. But, fortunately, the pain did not pass. It was a signal of something vitally wrong. An operation was finally performed, and a situation was revealed which the surgeon declared would have caused death if surgical treatment had been longer delayed.

Podmore[15] refers to "healing mediums" receiving messages from "spirit doctors" who want to prescribe, or being called to the bedsides of sick patients. He does not advocate much notice being taken of them.

Lady Barrett, herself a famous surgeon, in the book to which reference has already been made, makes a striking reference to healing through Spiritualism. Through the well-known medium, Mrs. Leonard, Lady Barrett got into touch, so she believes, with her late husband, Sir William F. Barrett, the famous scientist. By special permission I record part of the dialogue.

F.E.B. Have you anything to tell me about healing?

W.F.B. Yes, I'm thinking of healing all the time, but what I'm telling you now should serve as a basis in a physical sense for the operation of the healing powers.

You can, I know, produce remarkable results with that healing power on poor soil without any aid through medicine or diet, but I contend you would have a greater percentage of successes if you prepared the soil and made it ready for healing.

There are two or three *systems of healing*. I will divide them into three.

    (i) *The magnetic or physical* form of healing. I call it physical though the force that changes the patient is invisible, but as it is magnetic it belongs to the realm of what we call physical matter.

    (ii) *The mental*—the mind healing—the effect of one mind on another: one mind helping another to set its own natural process of healing, or even resistance, in operation.

That can be done from our side by spirit healers, working through a suitable instrument on your side. That is the best and most efficacious form of mental and magnetic healing.

But—mental healing can be done sometimes without any interference or help from our side—simply by the effect of one mind on another on the same plane. But the power is very much strengthened when it is directed by someone on my side through someone on yours.

    (iii) There is the third type of healing which I would call purely spiritual—a Divine healing—spiritual intercession through prayer—aspiration—or what we call consciousness of the One Mind working for the good of all.

[15] *Op. cit.*, Vol. I, p. 281.

The third type of healing may not be accessible, or, I should say, may not be easily used by the average person on earth—the two other types are used more commonly.

F.E.B. How can one use the highest?

W.F.B. I think you can use it best by realising in a definite way the power—the *complete omnipotence and omniscience of the Creator*, and the fact—the *undoubted, undeniable fact* that whatever power He has is available to you in such measure as you can receive and use it.

The greater your capacity, the greater the work you can do.

Realisation of the Divine will and love is necessary—sensing perfection clearly, definitely—always seeing the vision of perfection.

But I maintain that while you are on the earth you are intended to use all the assistance from the spiritual, the mental and the physical, because the physical does exist—the physical is the soil, the channel or vehicle of expression, and must be considered.

Sir William is alleged to have added:

"I know that miracles happen in the most unlikely quarters under the most astonishing conditions, but we don't want the occasional miracle, but a system of successful healing—not an isolated case here and there, but the perfect results of a perfect system—a combination of those powers which God gave us to use. But we must prepare the soil as far as possible. . . .

"I must explain something. The spiritual healing is always available, the operator must be available, but the patient may not be able to assimilate and use the healing power, which then stays in the aura instead of entering the physical organism and doing the work in a physical sense.

"It is according to a patient's capacity for absorbing the healing power that the success of the healing depends, *but* even if the patient is in such a condition that he or she cannot make use of the power in the desired way, and it has to remain, as I said, in the aura, it will, can I say, trickle into the patient's body in some measure—it will help, but the operator or director of the power cannot ensure a complete and entire assimilation on the part of the patient."

What conclusion can we come to regarding the use of Spiritualism for the purpose of healing or integration? None, I fear, that supports the hypothesis of Spiritualism. The energies lying latent in the mind and spirit of man are indubitable. Further, there are, I believe, immense energies in the realm of spirit; those, for example, which are sometimes tapped through prayer and meditation. It may be that Spiritualism, and other phases of psychical research, like some of the Yoga practices, more common in the East, will gradually show us how to direct those energies towards the alleviation of our ills. That is in the future. But the explanation of the phenomena of Spiritualism which suggests that, through a medium, the spirits of doctors long since dead can be called up to diagnose the pain of a person living today is difficult for the modern mind to accept, especially in view of the fact that there is an alternative view which would take us just as far. Every medium is clearly an abnormal person from the psychic point of view, and often able to read the subconscious, or unconscious, mind of another, even at a distance. If in the deep mind of the patient, interpenetrated as it may be by other minds, there are ideas of what is causing illness and of what should be done to cure it, then clearly a medium, bringing these to the consciousness of the sitter, can give a picture of the illness unattainable otherwise and preparing the way for a change of diagnosis and a complete change of treatment which could lead to the recovery of the patient.

To go back to the example of the story of Oliver above, there may have been an alternative diagnosis in the deep mind of the doctor. There may have been an idea of what was wrong in the deep mind of the patient herself, or in the mind of the latter interpenetrated by other minds. A medium in trance might read it there and produce it as a message, even though the patient lives at a distance.[16]

In the face of theories which are unconvincing, whether in terms of Spiritualism or telepathy, what is to be done about the patient? If someone is very ill, can we withhold help until all is understood? Clearly, much more scientific research is called for in this field. Clearly, also, there is still much chaff mixed with the grain, and the present writer has spent hours in the séance room, in reading, and in other types of investigation with clairvoyants, clairaudients and mediums, and found the results almost entirely fruitless. Much more research must patiently be carried out before we can confidently recommend recourse to a medium for clearer light on a diagnosis, or a direct treatment, and we must find some ways of safeguarding the seeker from the undoubted dangers of spiritualistic enquiry. It should be remembered that failure is much more common than success in this field.

Inasmuch, however, as it would seem wrong to refuse all possible help to a patient suffering from pain or disability, and inasmuch as many medical treatments are used before the theories which underlie practice are fully understood; inasmuch, further, as no harm is likely

[16] Illustrations supporting the view that distance makes no difference in psychic phenomena are given in *Life Beyond Death with Evidence*, by Charles Drayton Thomas (Collins, 1928).

to be done to a *patient* if his friends, taking all necessary safeguards, seek medical insight by recourse to a medium, or by sending some possession of the patient to a "sensitive," then, so long as medical canons are not violated and the medium is not treated as a substitute for the doctor, I see no reason why this strange and unfamiliar avenue should not be explored, and the result considered as *part* of the evidence to be reviewed where immediate action is necessary to avert death, and when those who must take *some* action are utterly bewildered as to what should be done next.

Many will think this is a surrender to superstition. Spiritualists will think it is but a niggardly recognition of the immense strides which spiritualistic enquiry has already made. It may be that the spiritualist hypothesis is entirely right. For my own part, I think much of it can be explained in terms of other categories. But when someone is suffering who might be relieved; when circumstances can be so arranged that no harm can possibly be done to the patient, it would seem to me unscientific, as well as churlish, to slam a door and decide beforehand that through that door no enlightening truth could possibly come.

6

OTHER RELIGIOUS HEALING MOVEMENTS

1. The Guild of Health.
2. The Guild of St. Raphael.
3. The Emmanuel Movement in America.
4. Milton Abbey.
5. The Guild of Pastoral Psychology.
6. The Divine Healing Mission.
7. The Friends' Spiritual Healing Fellowship.
8. The Methodist Society for Medical and Pastoral Practice.
9. The Churches' Council of Healing.

TO MAKE OUR survey complete, some account must be given here of the main contemporary movements within the framework of the Churches, which seek to heal through religion and psychology.

1. *The Guild of Health* [1] was started in 1905 by Harold Anson, Percy Dearmer and Conrad Noel. Its purpose was to arouse the whole Church—not merely the Church of England, of which all three were priests—to a fresh recognition of the place of health of mind and body in the Christian message. Christ came that men might have abundant life here and now, and the health of spirit, mind and body is the concern of the whole Church and the ideal intention of God.

The present writer has nothing but the highest praise for this organisation. It regards medical and scientific skill as gifts of God, and seeks to supplement them by prayer and by the laying on of hands and the anointing with oil. Its members include doctors, psychologists,

[1] Secretary: Alderman the Rev. Jim Wilson, 5 Regent House, 72 Eversholt Street, London, N.W.1. Information from Guild of Health Office, 83 Cambridge Street, Pimlico, S.W.1.

ministers of all the Protestant denominations and ordinary members of all the Protestant Churches.

The Guild does not demand any adherence to any set creed, or even lay down rules as to how the sick should be ministered to. Some of the Guild clergy hold healing services, but with none of the sensational accompaniments of the widely advertised healing mission. Prayer and teaching seem to be the main activities of the members of the Guild, and there are groups, the members of which are pledged to offer intercession for the sick. This Guild was the nucleus invited by Archbishop Temple to discuss wider co-operation between doctors and clergy, and after his death "The Churches' Council of Healing" was formed, but the Guild of Health still functions independently.

The stated objects are:

(i) The study of the interaction of the spiritual, mental and physical factors in well-being.

(ii) The cultivation of both individual and corporate health through spiritual means.

(iii) The exercise of healing by the readjustment of the whole personality in harmony with scientific methods.

(iv) The practice of personal and united prayer in all efforts towards the fulness of health.

The Guild has about thirty branches, and publishes a magazine.

2. *The Guild of St. Raphael* [2] was formed in 1915 "with the desire that in the revival of the use of spiritual means for the healing of the sick, there should be a society for this purpose belonging distinctively to the Anglican Church. Its object is to forward this form of ministry both by sacramental means and by intercessory prayer, until the Church, as a whole, accepts Divine Healing as part of its normal work."

The aims and methods of the Guild are set forth as follows:

"This Guild was founded in 1915, and is under the patronage of the two Archbishops and thirty of our home diocesan bishops, besides many other bishops, including twenty-five in the Church overseas. It has three purposes, namely:

"(a) To unite in a fellowship of prayer, within the Catholic Church, those who hold the faith that our Lord wills to work in and through His Church for the health of her members in spirit, mind and body.

[2] Secretary: C. L. Harley, 28 Briar Avenue, Norbury, S.W.16. Correspondence on spiritual matters should be sent to the Sub-Warden, the Rev. M. Martin, St. James' Rectory, Colchester, Essex.

"(*b*) To promote the belief that God wills the conquest of disease as well as sins, through the power of the living Christ.
"(*c*) To guide the sick, and those who care for them, to Christ as the source of healing."

Its methods are also three in number:

"(*a*) To prepare the sick for all ministries of healing by teaching the need of repentance and faith.
"(*b*) To make use of the sacrament of Holy Unction and the rite of Laying on of Hands for healing.
"(*c*) To bring to the aid of the Ministry of Healing the power of intercession, individual and corporate, and also the other spiritual forces of Meditation and Silence."

This movement, though limited by its restriction to one denomination, is in my opinion entirely praiseworthy. It emphasies, as does the Guild of Health, that the will of God about suffering is entirely revealed by Christ, who sought to end it, and who taught His followers to regard healing as part of their mission. Its Guild-priests are bidden to work wherever possible with doctors, but it realises that there is a spiritual element in personality, and that through it God can bring, in many cases, direct healing which restores both mind and body. There is room for this ministry without any interference with, or substitution for, more material means of healing.

The Guild of St. Raphael recalls that the Sacrament of Holy Unction, as differentiated from the rite of Extreme Unction, fell into disuse, and seeks to restore it to the practice of the Church of England. In the English Prayer Book the form for anointing for healing was omitted, but a Form has now been drawn up and sanctioned for the Administration of Holy Unction and the Laying on of Hands.

Holy Unction may only be administered by a priest, and then only after careful preparation of the patient, with teaching on the nature of repentance and faith.

The Laying on of Hands is not a sacrament and, therefore, can be administered by lay members of the Guild, but they must be under the direction of a priest-member with the consent of the Warden and the approval of the Bishop of the diocese.

Intercessory prayer is encouraged, and groups of people are pledged to this ministry. All members of the Guild are pledged to pray daily for the sick. "They offer themselves as humble servants in the fulfilment of His will for wholeness, and leave the result to Him, sure that some blessing will come which may bring with it bodily healing, or else that inward peace which enables a Christian boldly to face suffering or death."

The Guild publishes *The St. Raphael Book of Prayers for the Sick*[3] for the use of intercessors. It contains a form for the anointing of the sick and for the laying on of hands. Where there are ten or more members in the same district, with a priest who will be their chaplain, they may form a branch of the Guild for study and corporate intercession. There are about fifty such branches, including some overseas. Isolated members may belong to Prayer Groups linked by correspondence and the sending of intercession lists.

3. *The Emmanuel Movement in America.* There arose in Boston, Massachusetts, in the year 1905, possibly as an answer to "Christian Science," a movement the purpose of which was to obtain a collaboration between ministers and doctors. In this movement, which I am told is now dissolved, both spiritual and physical means were used, the stress in the combination of method depending on the nature of the illness. The book which described this movement was *Religion and Medicine*, the joint work of Elwood Worcester, Samuel McComb (both doctors of divinity but not of medicine) and Dr. Coriat. The book, published by Moffat, Yard and Co., Boston, was highly praised by the Surgeon-General of the United States and cited in his own book, *The Progress of Medicine During the Nineteenth Century*.

Religion and Medicine describes the work done by these three men at Emmanuel Church, Boston, and was called "The Emmanuel Movement" by the Press. When Dr. Worcester resigned from the pastorate of this church, the work went on under the title, "The Craigie Foundation."

I regard this pioneer work as of the greatest importance, for it recognised *at the same time* the value of both science and religion in the cure of body, mind and spirit, and sought to use both in the art of healing. Worcester says in his book, *Body, Mind and Spirit*,[4] that he regards psychotherapy as patchwork without "the renewal of life at its source and its regulation by spiritual principles and laws." He adds, "To the combination of these motives, the scientific and the spiritual, I ascribe what I may or may not be pardoned for regarding as the superiority of our results and the permanence of improvement

[3] S.P.C.K. An address on "Divine Healing" given to the Guild on its twenty-first birthday by Lord Lang of Lambeth, is published by the Guild and regarded as its Charter.

[4] Marshall Jones Co., 1931.

in innumerable cases which had found no relief through other modes of treatment."

Too much space must not be given to this new venture, for it certainly was new in 1905, but an indication of the attitude of these three friends is seen in that they dealt with the difficult matter of "breaking the transference" of a psychological patient by teaching him about what they called the "inward transfer." He was to depend not on the psychologist, but on God, the seat of whose power and authority was within his own breast. Religious faith and a spiritual interpretation of life were taught as essential to the permanent establishment of well-being. Great importance is laid on the subconscious mind, which is regarded as the nexus between man and God, and the value of suggestion in affecting the subconscious.

The volume, *Body, Mind and Spirit*, is to be sincerely recommended. It opened up a new world for ministerial work with medical co-operation, and pointed a finger to the kind of activity the Churches of the future must undertake.

4. *Milton Abbey*[5] was opened in 1937, following the publicity accorded to the work of the Rev. John Maillard, an Anglican clergyman. His book, *Healing in the Name of Jesus*, was first published in 1936.[6] He founded a movement called "The Prayer Healing Fellowship," and claimed at one time to have over nine thousand prayer helpers, divided into groups, each of which prayed for four or five people every day.

At Milton Abbey, of which Mr. Maillard was the first warden, an attempt is made "to revive the ministry of the Church to the sick in mind and body." It is recognised that the treatment of both is inadequate if it leaves out the soul and its relation to God. Relieving a mind of a buried fear is one thing, say the workers there, but the restoration of confidence needs a positive faith which it is the privilege of the Christian religion to offer.

Yet religion is not "forced" on anyone, though he is encouraged to find out "what real religion means." It is the background or atmosphere of the place. Milton Abbey is described as a "Home for the Spiritual Treatment of Nervous Suffering," but no psychotic cases are taken. Young nervous sufferers in the early stages of neuroses are particularly welcomed. Occupational therapy is part of the routine.

This movement seeks to co-operate with the medical profession,

[5] Warden: The Rev. John Maillard, Milton Abbey, Blandford, Dorset. Branch at 18 Dawson Place, London, W.2.

[6] Harper.

yet it leaves an important place for the more direct activity of the Holy Spirit. The then Warden wrote me as follows: [7] "There is no doctor on the resident staff, but some help is given by a doctor in the neighbouring village. Our aim is ultimately to have the spiritual and the medical side functioning fully, but this is not practical politics at the moment owing to lack of funds." The "institutional atmosphere" is reduced to a minimum. "We try," say the organisers, "to strike a happy medium between leaving the patient to be quiet by himself and encouraging him, with tact and patience, to mix with others and forget what is the matter with him."

The amenities of the place are great, for the Abbey lies in the heart of beautiful Dorset scenery, and the estate, with its farm and market garden, extends for eight hundred acres, partly wooded. The cost is between £5 and £7 a week, but it is said that no one is refused on financial grounds. No bed-patients or patients needing constant oversight can be received, owing to lack of staff. The promoters hope to make Milton Abbey a kind of research establishment where illnesses which are partly physical, partly mental and partly spiritual may be investigated, studied and treated by physical, psychological and spiritual methods in harmonious combination and in an atmosphere of healthy religion and of fellowship with others. For the purpose of writing this section I visited Milton Abbey in the spring of 1948 and talked with those in charge and with some of the patients. I found myself in the fullest sympathy with the methods adopted there at that time. The plans for the development of this work, as described to me, seemed wholly admirable.[8]

5. *The Guild of Pastoral Psychology*.[9] This Guild, markedly Jungian, exists to explore the common ground between psychology and religion, and to train in psychology "those who are required by their professional duties to deal with the development of personality, and offers practical opportunities for workers of many kinds."

The Guild seeks the co-operation of doctors for the effective dealing with cases which present spiritual, psychological and physical problems.

Valuable educational work is done by the Guild through public lectures and the dissemination of the Guild's pamphlets. Seminars,

[7] Letter dated May 10, 1947.

[8] On going to Press, I hear that Mr. Maillard is taking fuller responsibility and that the contribution which the physician and psychiatrist can make to healing is likely to be given less prominent a place.

[9] Hon. Secretary: Miss Greta Hayes, 65 Cottenham Park Road, Wimbledon, London, S.W.20.

reading courses and group discussion are an important feature of the work.

The Guild commands the part-time services of experienced psychotherapists who serve its members at reduced fees and give advice on cases presented to them.

6. *The Divine Healing Mission.*[10] This organisation is predominantly Anglican, and is closely linked with the work of James Moore Hickson. One of the objects of the funds raised is said to be "to assist, under our Lord's guidance, in the development and extension of His healing ministry in His Church, in grateful remembrance of the devoted life and service of His dear servant, James Moore Hickson," and "to enable some to whom God has entrusted the gift of healing, to give more of their time to the work . . . and to enable sufferers in special cases by supplementary grants to receive the benefit of spiritual help, rest and quiet in the proper surroundings. . . ."

"The central principle of the fellowship is the recognition of the personal though unseen presence of our Lord Jesus Christ, Who is the one and only Healer, and Who, nineteen centuries ago, convincingly manifested God's will and power to heal all manner of sickness in the spirits and minds and bodies of men, and Who is carrying on His same ministry in and through His Church in the world today.

"The objects of our fellowship are twofold:

"(i) To proclaim to all men everywhere the unchanging will and power of God to heal through His Son, Jesus, today as of old.

"(ii) To make humble and loyal use of every means of Divine Healing instituted and sanctioned by our Lord, i.e. the prayer of faith— the sacraments of Holy Communion and Holy Anointing—and the Laying on of Hands, whereby the power of God is made available for the deliverance from evil bondage and affliction of the spirits and minds and bodies of all who draw near to Him in faith and loyalty.

"By the above means we believe that our Lord is using us, as members of His Church, to hasten the establishing of His kingdom of health and holiness and peace here upon the earth.

"Our membership, though perhaps predominantly Anglican, but also including members of other branches of the Christian Church, is open to all who are moved by God to seek to share with us in carrying out the two main objects mentioned above.

"From the outset we have been guided (we believe by the Holy Spirit) to seek the closest co-operation with all who are working on mental and material levels towards the same end, namely—the com-

[10] The Director is the Rev. S. H. C. Wynne, Divine Healing Mission, St. Paul's Church House, Newton Road, London, W.2.

plete health of man's whole being; and we regard the effective working of members of the medical profession and of the psychologists as deriving all its power and efficiency from the same divine Source, God Himself."

Without doubt, this organisation does immense good, and is to be commended. It has a prayer-circle union, and all over the country from 9:50 to 10 each morning its members offer intercession for the sick. It also holds healing services, and the value of these has been commented on already.

7. *The Friends' Spiritual Healing Fellowship.*[11] Dr. Howard Collier and Mr. Sydney Hurren have written a pamphlet on *The Place of Spiritual Healing in the Society of Friends,* in which they seek to direct the interests of Quakers along the following lines:

"(i) To convince Friends (and others) that this is work that they can and ought to be doing.

"(ii) To proclaim a 'Gospel-Message' concerning Health, Disease-Prevention and Healing to individuals and groups who are in a condition to hear it.

"(iii) To prepare themselves personally (under concern) for this aspect of Quaker Ministry.

"(iv) To develop Quaker Healing Groups, to study the technique, effects and methods of Spiritual and Group Healing.

"(v) If necessity shows, as it may well do, to consider the formation of Health Centres within particular Meetings with or without Rehabilitation Homes, Hospitals, etc.

"(vi) To act as a link between existing Health and Medical Services and Religious Societies with a view to completing the work of the former.

"(vii) To remember and minister to the needs of the individual for Health and for Healing and to practise social rehabilitation."

8. *The Methodist Society for Medical and Pastoral Practice*[12] was founded in 1946 under the joint presidency of Dr. Percy Backus of Harley Street and the present writer. It emerged from the work of the Methodist Spiritual Healing Committee appointed, at my instigation, in 1937 to examine the whole field covered by the ambiguous phrase, "spiritual healing." The work done involved an examination of New Testament teaching, the work of the early Church, the reasons for the decline of the practice of healing in the Church, the medical aspect and the whole renewal of interest in non-physical methods of healing which the "new psychology" kindled.

[11] Write to Friends' House, Euston Road, London, N.W.1.
[12] Secretary: The Rev. John Crowlesmith, 224 Hills Road, Cambridge.

In response to the Committee's representations, the Methodist Conference—the highest court of that Church—approved three propositions which I had the honour to put before it.

(i) That the curriculum of students for the Methodist Ministry should in future include sufficient psychological training to enable the minister to diagnose psychological illness.

This does not mean that the minister is to be encouraged to become an amateur psycho-analyst and undertake psychological treatments. His training, however, is to be arranged to equip him to recognise neurotic and psychotic symptoms. He should learn how to be able to tell when a patient needs the services of the medically trained psychiatrist, and the minister should acquire sufficient psychological insight and understanding to enable him to use his own spiritual ministrations in the most relevant way for the help of those who seek his aid. He is never to transgress on to the territory of the medical practitioner or the psychiatrist.

(ii) That experimental clinics should be set up wherever conditions make possible a co-operation between the suitably equipped minister and the sympathetic doctor, so that the help of both could be at the disposal of patients whose troubles seem to indicate the necessity for a combination of spiritual, psychological and medical aid.

(iii) That the practice of intercession for the sick, both in church and by means of prayer groups, should be encouraged throughout the Methodist Church, and reports made to the Secretary of the Spiritual Healing Committee.

As the person who submitted these propositions to the Methodist Conference, I may be permitted here to make a brief comment. The training of Methodist ministers, compared with earlier days, seems to me to have improved immensely and in the main to cover proposition (i) above. The interest of many young Methodist ministers is great.

In regard to experimental clinics, the quality of those started has been excellent, but their number is restricted by the itinerant system by which ministers move from place to place and may be followed by men uninterested in this particular phase of their work, or men who do not feel called or qualified to do it. The number of suitable doctors with whom ministers can co-operate is growing, but it is still small. In the minds of some doctors there is a suspicion of ministers who appear to "interfere." There is also amongst many general practitioners considerable ignorance of modern psychology, and no time to learn it, practice it, or co-operate with ministers and clergy.

In regard to the practice of intercession for the sick, there is evidence that this is growing, and there is a great interest in it, but it is difficult to tabulate "results," for reasons which will be seen when we discuss the question of healing through prayer.

Conferences of ministers and doctors on the whole subject, held during the last few years at Cambridge, have deepened interest in both professions, and the Methodist Conference has approved the formation of the Society with the following aims:

(i) To group together in study and clinical practice all who are interested in the religious approach to the problems of healing.

(ii) To explore the relationship between the medical and clerical professions in this matter and to set up, if possible, methods of co-operation acceptable to both professions, drawing them close together in a more sympathetic understanding of each other's part.

(iii) To found and develop seminars for the study of Christian healing in the light of medicine, psychology and theology, and to act as a clearing house in research for such groups, which it is hoped will be working simultaneously in different parts of the Church.

(iv) To issue literature, bulletins and (in time) a journal on the subject involved.

(v) To hold at least an annual conference of members at which current developments can be noted and explored.

Membership of the Society is open to all ministers, doctors and other interested people whose names are accepted by the committee.

The latter believes that this is the time to try to co-ordinate and synthesise all known non-physical methods of making sick people well. It is believed that health of body, mind and spirit is the will of God, and that illness of any kind belongs to the kingdom of evil, and should be attacked. It is realised that human ignorance, folly and sin, especially lack of trust in God, are so strongly entrenched that many must suffer. It is also realised that God can use suffering for His glory and man's blessedness, and that by a right reaction to it men can become saints. But if suffering were a condition of saintliness, Christ would not have fought it. Indeed, its normal result is rebellion, depression and despair. It is not suffering, but a heroic reaction to it, that has made sufferers into saints. Suffering is not essential to a right reaction to life and to God. If the soul awakes without being stabbed awake by pain, and makes a full response to God, the body, mind and spirit can be offered to Him unimpaired by disease, a perfect instrument in the divine hand as the body, mind and spirit of our Lord, unimpaired by illness, were offered to God before the evil plans of men brought Him to mental agony and physical pain.

The Methodist Church has awakened to the challenge of human suffering, and believes that every resource of man, inspired by the Spirit of God, should be at the disposal of the needy. This society aims at such a co-ordination, which, if perfected, would mean that no stone would be left unturned to ensure deliverance from disability whether of body, mind or spirit.

9. *The Churches' Council of Healing*[13] was started in 1944, when Archbishop Temple set up a committee to examine the whole question of spiritual healing, to co-ordinate organisations already existing for the purpose, and to promote fuller co-operation between the medical and pastoral ministers of healing. It was first called "Archbishop Temple's Development Committee for Divine Healing," but this cumbersome title was superseded by the above. Dr. Temple will always be remembered gratefully as the initiator of this challenge to all the Churches to examine, in the light both of modern science and of New Testament teaching, their attitude to this matter. Some of the movements already noticed are represented on this Council. All denominations, save the Roman Catholic, have representatives on the Council, and the President is the present Archbishop of Canterbury, Dr. Fisher.

The functions of the Council are as follows:

(i) To provide a common basis for the healing movements which stand on Christian foundations.

(ii) To draw into closer fellowship and co-operation the movements which share this common basis.

(iii) To co-operate with these guilds and other agencies in the promotion of united prayer and witness appropriate to their common aim and basis.

(iv) To afford a recognised basis for the co-operation of doctors and clergy in the study and performance of their respective functions in the work of healing, and to promote this co-operation in thought and action throughout the country.

(v) To explore the possibilities of establishing common centres of healing under adequate medical and clerical supervision.

(vi) To act as a centre for co-ordinating and distributing experience and research; and to publish the findings of this exchange of thought.

(vii) To bring the work of healing into closer relation with the regular work of the churches.

The basis of agreement for the performance of these functions is as follows:

[13] Secretary: Miss Kathleen Deal, Swallowfield Lodge, Swallowfield, Keymer, Hassocks, Sussex.

(i) All healing proceeds from the activity of the eternal creative power of God ever seeking to restore harmony to His world. God's will for man is perfect health, but sickness and disease are facts which must be faced. Part of the victory of the Cross is the truth that suffering can be completely transformed by being offered to God and being taken up into the fellowship of Christ's redemptive sacrifice.

(ii) God's infinite power can work within His responsive creation to remake the whole human personality. Divine Healing means essentially the healing of the whole man by the power of God, through a clearer understanding of His love and purpose and in obedience to His laws.

(iii) Doctors, clergy and ministers are instruments of God's healing power in the faithful exercise of their skill and patience; and all members of the churches can be used by God for healing, through their ministries of prayer and intercession, meditation and direction; and through the sacraments and other means of grace.

As I write, the Council is in the early stages of its activities, and has been hampered by the war, but it seems to me the most hopeful organisation yet brought into existence to revive the Church's ministry of healing in the light of modern science. As the two professions, medical and clerical, get together in action, and as the ideal of the Churches' Council of Healing spreads throughout the Churches, spiritual, psychological and material benefit are certain to follow.

Already a strong Medical Committee of the Churches' Council has been formed, and has met and conferred with a Committee appointed by the British Medical Association. Further, an epoch-making contact with medical authority has been made. The Chairman of the Churches' Council of Healing, the Lord Bishop of Lincoln, has led a deputation to the Central Ethical Committee of the British Medical Association.[14] This contact is so important that I quote in full from the *Supplement to the British Medical Journal:*[15]

"The Council has considered and discussed with representatives of the Churches' Council of Healing the relationship of doctor and priest or minister in connection with their respective vocations and the ways in which their co-operation will be of service to the community. Leading a deputation to the Central Ethical Committee of the B.M.A., the Bishop of Croydon (now Bishop of Lincoln) gave a concise exposition of the principles and aims of the Churches' Council of Healing. He stated as a basic principle that the subject of healing should be

[14] The Chairman is now the Lord Bishop of Coventry.
[15] November 8, 1947.

229

approached from a threefold standpoint—body, mind and spirit. These three aspects of the human being were so interdependent that successful treatment of disease in one was not possible without consideration of the others. With this conviction in mind, the late Archbishop Temple set up a committee to correlate the activities of associations already in the field. The healing of 'the whole man' was its main concern. The Archbishop's committee has now been established permanently as the Churches' Council of Healing. In its own words the Churches' Council of Healing 'affords a recognised basis for the cooperation of doctors and clergy in the study and performance of their respective functions in the work of healing, and to promote this cooperation in thought and action throughout the country.'

"Inquiries have been received on the subject at B.M.A. Headquarters, particularly on the propriety of the association of doctors with clergy as unqualified persons who might be concerned with the treatment of patients. For this reason the Central Ethical Committee invited the Churches' Council of Healing to send a deputation to discuss the matter from every angle and to obtain information concerning its objects and methods. Subsequently the Central Ethical Committee met the Medical Advisory Committee of the Churches' Council.

"From these discussions, it has become clear that this body is doing valuable work and that there exists a field for legitimate and valuable co-operation between clergy and doctors in general and between the Churches' Council of Healing and the Association in particular. The Council of the B.M.A. is of opinion that there is no ethical reason to prevent medical practitioners from co-operating with clergy in all cases, and more especially those in which the doctor in charge of the patient thinks that religious ministrations will conduce to health and peace of mind or lead to recovery. Such co-operation is often necessary and desirable, and would help to prevent abuses which have arisen through the activities of irresponsible and unqualified persons. Among other reasons the Churches' Council of Healing exists to safeguard the interests of those people who might become the victims of so-called faith healers. Much harm has been done to individuals by unreasonable appeals to the emotions and by mass hysteria.

"A central liaison has been established by the appointment of representatives of the Association to attend meetings of the Churches' Council and ex officio to serve on its Medical Advisory Committee. It is considered that most useful work may be done by close personal contact between doctor and clergyman, with an interchange of views and active co-operation where possible. With regard to the co-operation which can be secured at a divisional or parochial level, it is considered that arrangements can best be left to the B.M.A. Divisions acting in concert with any branch organisation of the Churches' Council or similar body. Joint activities might include the appointment of and co-operation with hospital chaplains and their deputies, education of the public, and informal discussions between doctors and clergy.

"In addition to the above suggestions, which in some measure have already been the custom of doctors and clergy in different parts of the country, it would seem desirable that the whole field of medical practice in relation to the work of the Church should be explored. Moral aspects in the cause, treatment and prevention of disease cannot be overlooked, and in this field also it is desirable that there should be fuller co-operation. Medicine and the Church working together should encourage a dynamic philosophy of health which would enable every citizen to find a way of life based on moral principle and on a sound knowledge of the factors which promote health and well-being. Health is more than a physical problem, and the patient's attitude both to illness and to other problems is an important factor in his recovery and adjustment to life. Negative forces such as fear, resentment, jealousy, indulgence and carelessness play no small part in the level of both personal and national health. For these reasons we welcome opportunities for discussion and co-operation in the future between qualified medical practitioners and all who have a concern for the religious needs of their patients."

We have now reviewed all the organisations working for healing through psychology and religion by means of machinery set up by the Churches. In addition, the Church of Scotland formed in 1937 its Committee on Psychology,[16] and the Iona Community (Church of Scotland) has recently examined, and on a small scale practised, this ancient ministry. The Congregational denomination has no Committee, but its representatives met in May, 1946, to consider "pastoral psychology in relation to the Congregational ministry." In reply to an enquiry sent to the Baptist denomination the President of the Baptist Union, the Rev. Dr. F. Townley Lord,[17] wrote to me as follows: "The Baptist denomination is not doing anything officially to encourage the ancient art of healing in the Church. The matter has come up at odd moments, but there is not, as yet, any Spiritual Healing Committee." *The Baptist Times* has, from time to time, published articles on co-operation between doctors and ministers.

[16] Secretary: The Rev. J. Ramsay Thomson, The Manse, Applegarth, Lockerbie, Scotland.
[17] Letter dated May 12, 1947.

THE PRACTICE OF INTERCESSION

INTERCESSION FOR THE sick is, of course, a very ancient practice, but inasmuch as it is offered by every branch of the Christian Church today, it can usefully be included among the modern methods of healing through religion.

Though practised universally in Christendom, prayer for the recovery of the sick is frequently vague, casual and unexpectant, a fact which may partly account for its disappointing results. "Bless all who are sick and make them well!" If one imagines the scope of such a prayer—including, presumably, every country under heaven—and the unexpectancy which, in all fairness, must accompany such a petition, it is hardly worth considering as a serious means of combating illness. If intercession for the sick is a futile practice, based on superstition, it must be discarded. But if it is sound, then, in spite of many problems which surround it, it must be continued with a greater intensity of purpose and a clearer idea of the intellectual implications involved.

The New Testament authority for it is indubitable. We have quoted the relevant passage already. "Is any among you sick? Let him call for the elders of the Church; and let them pray over him . . . and the prayer of faith shall save him that is sick, and the Lord shall raise him up. . . . Pray one for another, that ye may be healed." [1]

We note the phrase, "the prayer of faith." The matter of faith is dealt with in a later section (p. 423). Here it is only necessary to say that by "faith" in this section I mean trustful expectancy. I do not mean necessarily a faith filled with, and reinforced by, the intellectual content of orthodox Christianity, or that excellent quality of spirit which believes in a loving God whether recovery from illness takes

---

[1] James 5:14-16.

232

place or not. Clearly, many who were healed by Christ, such as the woman with a hæmorrhage, for instance,[2] never thought of Him as divine, never dreamed who He really was, and believed few, if any, of the intellectual tenets now incorporated into the creeds of the Church. But, with trustful expectancy, she believed that if she could get near Him she would be healed. Similarly, the blind man already referred to (p. 48) did not even know who it was who had made him see. Clearly he had no faith at all in the sense in which the word is often used in Christian groups today. In both these illustrations the patient had a trustful expectancy, that was all. Coupled with Christ's power, which in part depended on it, it was enough.

The unexpectancy with which intercession for the sick is often offered is easy to understand. People cease praying for healing because prayer seems a hit-or-miss-in-the-dark procedure compared with the scientific, understandable ways of medicine. Let me say at once, however, that prayer also has its laws and conditions. Nothing in the universe is outside law, or it would not be a *uni*-verse. Prayer seems haphazard only because we are less familiar with the laws that operate. Yet it should not be more modern, superior, "scientific," and within the realm of law, to believe in any array of glass tubes, electrodes and other scientific apparatus than to believe in a kneeling man. Surely the latter is a far more complicated piece of apparatus for harnessing divine energies.

Some of the laws of prayer seem to be slowly emerging. One seems to be that prayer is more effective when it is made for a little child than when it is made for an adult, possibly because a child's mind, especially his unconscious mind, is more vulnerable to the invasion of the forces which flow from the minds of others. A child's mind is less walled in by prejudices, preconceived ideas, doubts, fears and inhibitions. It is less hardened by cynicism or disappointment. An adult has predetermined what he regards as possible and impossible. He has his settled mental habits, and probably a closed system concerning what he "believes," and his mind rejects ideas which do not fit in with his general scheme of thought and belief.

Another law of prayer concerns love for the patient on the part of those who pray for him. If the patient is really loved—and for that to happen he must be known—by a large congregation, prayer seems more likely to be full of healing power.

Another law of prayer seems to show that those who make intercession must really concentrate on what they are doing, and not let

[2] Mark 5:25-34.

their minds wander. They must really imaginatively see the patient being made well and believe that he is recovering because they are praying. Their mental attitude must not be that of pity or worry or fear, but of confidence, serenity and optimism.

In writing this section, it is not my intention to quote widely from the extensive literature on this subject, but to base my conclusions rather on my own work. For eleven years during my ministry at Brunswick Methodist Church, Leeds, we offered, each Sunday evening, intercession for specific and described cases of illness, physical and mental. For a longer period at the City Temple, London, we have done the same, and twenty-five years of enquiry and experience may perhaps be regarded as a sufficient basis on which to build certain conclusions, and in such a long period most of the problems connected with this practice present themselves. I feel on more certain ground in considering work of which I have firsthand knowledge than of coming to conclusions based on the work of others, though my reading would indicate that had I based my conclusions on the latter, they would have been substantially the same.

Before describing my own method, I will give some examples to illustrate the last statement—viz. that the literature of the subject points to the same conclusions as my own.

1. Examples could be almost indefinitely extended by reference to devotional literature. The lives of the saints are full of cases of healing through prayer. Modern examples could be found in the story vouched for by Rosslyn Mitchell, M.P., an eminent solicitor. A close friend of his was about to be operated on for some internal swelling after examination by two surgeons. I quote the words of the patient herself: "I prayed that the hand of the surgeon might be guided so that, if it was God's will, I might be spared to my children. Then I seemed to hear a voice saying, 'Have you a still greater faith?' And I said, 'I know that God does not need a surgeon to do this, and that if it is His will, He can take it away.' I then had a feeling of great peace and went to bed. In the morning when I awoke, the lump had gone." [3]

My friend, the Rev. Dr. Sangster, told me of a woman, well known to him, who had had one breast removed for cancer and, finding a lump in the other breast, was told she must have it removed, as it also was malignant. Walking home from a prayer-meeting one night, she clutched her breast and said to her father, "The lump has gone." And so it proved to be. She has had no return of it since.

[3] Quoted from Lord Inman's *Christ in the Modern Hospital*, p. 50 (Hodder and Stoughton, 1937).

Another friend of mine, the Rev. Tom Metcalf, wrote recently to tell me of a great friend of his, the late Andrew Caird, a surgeon at Carlisle, who operated on a woman and found cancer of the stomach too far advanced for further surgical treatment. He removed a small piece of tissue and sent it for pathological examination. Cancer was confirmed. The woman had been stitched up and sent home to die. Caird declared that she could not live more than a fortnight. Her friends, however, met together regularly to pray for her recovery. Seven years later she was married and is still completely well (1950). Caird himself said that the only explanation he could give was that she was healed in answer to prayer.

The late Rev. H. W. Workman, of the Guild of Health, gives his own experiences in the following words, quoted from a lecture given at a Retreat-Conference held under the auspices of the Churches' Council of Healing, and afterwards published as a pamphlet called, *Intercessory Prayer.*

"As a boy of ten or eleven I had an accident, when jumping at school. There was nothing to show for it, and the master assumed that I was shamming and made me go on with the full school routine. A month later, I was bent double and could not hold myself upright. The doctor was called in. He said, 'It is a toss up whether this boy dies, or lies on his back for the rest of his life, or recovers.' Of course, they did not tell me that, but a boy called to another boy outside the sickroom, 'I say, have you heard? Workman is going to die!' That was a real shock, and for some days I was completely rebellious. Then I realised that that attitude was no good, and I told myself that I had always professed to believe that Christ was the Good Shepherd, my Good Shepherd, and that now I must show that I really believed that. So quietly I fought my way down on the twenty-third Psalm to resting in God. Christ was my Good Shepherd, He was going just ahead of me, it was He who was going to decide what was going to happen to me; whether life or death. The outcome was not going to be a matter of chance or luck. I came to surrender my will unreservedly to His good and perfect will. The result during those weeks of waiting was not a sense of resignation, nor merely peace of heart and mind, but the most wonderful spiritual joy and fellowship with Christ that I have ever known. I knew nothing of Divine Healing in those days, but it was, of course, the really right attitude for healing, and healed I was, so perfectly that later I became an international athlete."

Perhaps the best example of all is found in Dr. Howard Somervell's book, *After Everest*.[4] Dr. Howard Somervell is a Fellow of the Royal College of Surgeons, and was a member of the Mount Everest Expedition (1922), one of the five to reach the 28,000-feet level. He is unlikely to offer a highly-coloured story of a magical effect of prayer. He tells the story of a schoolmaster with tubercular disease, and says:

"The disease is one which medical science reckons to be well-nigh incurable when it has reached this stage. The man was going down hill and daily getting weaker and more feverish. His legs became more and more painful; and after a few weeks we took another X-ray picture and found the disease was worse in that the whole of the bone was involved. There was only one thing to do, and that was to amputate the leg to save the patient's life."

Dr. Somervell sent copies of the radiograph he had taken to one whom he regards as the greatest authority on bone diseases in India, if not in the East. Then he writes as follows:

"His answer was just as we had expected. The disease was tubercular, and the only chance of saving the man's life was to take off his leg at the knee. So we told the poor fellow that there was nothing else to be done. His reply was unexpected: 'Will you give me three weeks? I want to try the effect of praying about it.' We agreed to give him that time, and the next day he went home. In three weeks he turned up true to his promise. He had left hospital feverish, ill, flushed in the face, and only capable of being carried about. He returned in a car, but hobbling with a stick and looking much better. The wound in the leg was not healed, but the leg itself, as revealed by the X-rays, was wonderfully improved, though not yet free from the disease.

"We were amazed. What had he done to make so great an improvement? He told us quite simply that he had been quite sure it was against the will of God for any of His servants to suffer, and that he had before him a life of service to God if only he could keep his leg and his life. So he called his family and friends together and said to them, 'Look here, will you folk unite in prayer for this leg of mine that it be completely healed?' They agreed, and for a week a continuous chain of prayer was kept up by that family. One of them would pray for a quarter of an hour. Then another would take it up, and so on for over a week. In another three weeks he came to see us again. The leg had healed. He was able to walk on it and appeared almost well. A few months later he was back at school, perfectly fit, playing games with the boys, running about on both legs with no sign of disease."

[4] Pp. 274 ff. (Hodder and Stoughton, 1936).

Dr. Somervell goes on to give us the example of a man with cancer of the cheek. He says the disease was so advanced that he declined to operate upon him. Sadly he went home to die. Then he remembered the power of God through prayer, and went to his local church and persuaded his fellow church members to have frequent and united prayer that his cancer might be cured.

"Months later [says the doctor] I went to the branch hospital near to his place of abode, and a stalwart, healthy man with a healed scar on his cheek came to see me. The cancer, incurable by any method known to medical science, except radium and X-rays, had completely disappeared. I confess that in my weakness of faith I was amazed, but of the original diagnosis there can be no doubt. If we in Neyyoor, where we see five or six hundred cases of cancer of the mouth every year, cannot diagnose a case of it, who can? Explain these cases how you like, by the power of mind over the body, or by the intervention of God—the fact remains that their faith had been exercised in a way of which in our materialistic England we have no experience."

My own method of offering intercession for the sick at the City Temple is as follows:

First of all, I find that only about three or four cases can be lifted to God in prayer. It puts a very great strain on the congregation to ask people to steady their minds and hold them in intense prayer and longing for particular cases of illness. If I have the permission of the relative, I mention the name of the patient, because where the patient is known and loved it seems to me that the faith and care of the congregation can be called out more potently. Here, perhaps, is one of the scientific conditions of availing prayer. Then I try to make an imaginative picture of what is actually happening. This is the kind of thing that was said in an actual case:

"Here is Nurse So-and-so, a member of our church, a girl of nineteen, who is studying at such-and-such a hospital. She is suffering from such-and-such a disease. Her temperature is very high. She cannot sleep without drugs. She has not taken any food for some days. In imagination (I say to the people) 'go into the ward and stand with Christ next to her bed. Do not pray that she may become better, because that is putting her cure in the future. Believe that at this very moment Christ is touching her life, and that His healing power is being made manifest in her body now. Believe that He can more powerfully work in the atmosphere of our faith and love.' "

After a few moments' silence I add: "Please do not let your mind wander. Let it be steadily concentrated there, imaginatively watching and helping Christ in His healing work."

Sometimes I use the words: "Let your prayers do what your arms would do if we lived in the days of Christ's presence on earth. We should carry the patient into His presence. Believe that your prayer is bringing the patient and Christ into living proximity and vital relationship. Hold, on the screen of your imagination, a picture of Nurse so-and-so already becoming well."

After another moment or two of silence we pass on to the next case.

The case of the nurse is an actual case, and it was afterwards noticed that, although the nurse was desperately ill and did not know that we were praying for her, at that very hour her temperature went down to normal. She slept all night without a drug, and on the Monday morning began to take grapes and light food for the first time for some days. She has made a marvellous recovery, and is still, I hear, in good health, though the incident I have described occurred more than ten years ago.

I try to make it clear to the congregation that we do not imagine we are telling God something He does not know. We do not imagine that we are persuading a reluctant God to intervene in some case of illness which particularly interests us. We rather believe that in a fuller measure we are letting through God's healing, spiritual energies, which at the moment may be blocked on the human side, just as a nurse lets through God's healing material energies in a fuller measure when she cleanses a wound, for instance, or in other ways carries out her nursing ministry.

It is clear that in a great many matters Augustine's dictum is illustrated, "Without God," he said, "we cannot: without us, God will not." It seems that God waits for man's co-operation before certain things can be accomplished. As another has said, "God wills all things at the price of labour," and while we may believe that God wills and desires the complete health of every person, man must co-operate with Him in the relevant way, and the latter is often through an understanding that is costly to attain and through a faith and love demanding in its discipline.

The mistake often made is that while man clearly sees that he must co-operate with God on the physical level, and thus sees the need for medicine, surgery, nursing and other means of co-operation, he does not understand that he must also co-operate on psychical and spiritual levels.

In *Man and the Universe*, Sir Oliver Lodge truly says, "Even in medicine, for instance, it is not really absurd to suggest that drugs and no prayer may be almost as foolish as prayer and no drugs."

It now seems important to make an attempt to understand how

intercession may conceivably bring health to a patient, and to face some of the many problems involved.

We start with the knowledge of the immense power of the mind over the body, and in the section on "Mesmerism, Hypnotism and Suggestion," this has been stated, and need not be repeated. It must be remembered that the unconscious part of the mind is even more powerful than the conscious in effecting bodily changes and mental reactions.

Remembering this, we may turn, however briefly, to the recent experiments in the field of telepathy. In his book, *The Reach of the Mind*,[5] Prof. J. B. Rhine says, "Through laboratory experiments at Duke University we who have laboured there for seventeen years know that communication from one mind to another without the aid of the senses is an established occurrence." These experiments, carried out at Duke University and elsewhere, and the discussion of the subject such as we find in Whately Carrington's book, *Telepathy —an Outline of its Facts, Theory and Implications*,[6] and G. N. M. Tyrrell's *The Personality of Man*,[7] go to underline the importance of Jung's theory of the Collective Unconscious and show that although in many ways men are separate personalities, in a true sense they possess a single mind. One might suggest the analogy of the continents. Africa, Asia, Europe, America, and Australia are separate, divided by the seas, but beneath the sea they join up in one great mass. If one can imagine something changing the chemical constitution of that mass from the centre of the earth, then, however separated by the seas the continents may be, they would be affected by the factor that operated from the centre of the globe. Similarly, human beings are separated from one another in many ways, but it may be that if one goes, as it were, deeply enough into their minds, there will be found a sub-stratum which is common to all.

This seems to me to be illustrated from our knowledge of the birds. A flock of starlings, for example, sometimes containing many thousands, will wheel at once and change their direction. It is incredible that they "tell" one another. The only explanation that makes sense is that an impulse to turn strikes the collective mind of all the birds at once. In other words, the birds have one mind, although their bodies are separate. It is to be noted that they never fly into one another, but move in a unity as marvellous as it is beautiful. Apparently when they are flying in a flock they have a single mind. Professor Price, Pro-

[5] Sloane, 1947.
[6] Methuen, 1946.
[7] Penguin Books, 1946.

fessor of Logic at Oxford, in a broadcast talk afterwards published, and called *The Philosophic Implications of Telepathy*, writes as follows: "It is nonsense to suppose that minds are spatially separate entities. Minds are not objects in space. . . . We must suppose that on the unconscious level there are no sharp boundaries between one mind and another." [8]

Accepting the modern findings in regard to telepathy, one may claim that when a thousand people in a church are praying for John Smith, then, at a deep level, their mind is united with his, and their thoughts of courage, optimism and hope, their belief in Smith's recovery, and their vision of Smith as already made well, their thoughts of health on his behalf, and so on, are capable of invading his own deep mind, which is, indeed, part of their own. A congregation transmitting love and courage, hope and optimism, while holding to itself, so to speak, the mind of a sick person, can, in my opinion, alter his mental reaction, and this in turn has a profound effect upon his health.

The point was illustrated for me when I recalled two farmers in India, both of whom sank wells on their separated land, only to find that underneath both farms was a great underground lake. If *A* had put a sack of arsenic into his well, he would have poisoned the water which *B* drank. If he had put—for the sake of illustration—some health-giving salt or vitamin into his own well, he would have improved the water for *B* also. The illustration goes a long way. To sin is to poison the public reservoir. To love is to strengthen the whole community. When *A* prays for *B* he does not as it were, make a ball of prayer, throw it up to God and ask God to throw it down to *B* with greater force. He is himself in contact with *B* and both are "in God."

In his book, *Body and Mind*,[9] Dr. William McDougall writes as follows:

"Successful therapeutic suggestions and others that effect definite tissue-changes are especially significant in the present connexion; for in all such cases we have definite evidence of control of bodily processes which, *though unconsciously affected*, must be regarded as psychical. Of the limits of this power of mental control over the organic processes of the body, we are altogether ignorant, and new evidence, much of it ill-reported, and therefore valueless, but much of it above suspicion, repeatedly warns us against setting up any arbitrary limit to what may be effected in this way."

A criticism of this point of view can be anticipated. It will be said

[8] Quoted from *The Listener*, February 13, 1947, pp. 277-278.

[9] Used with the permission of the Macmillan Company. Italics mine.

that by intercession for the sick one merely means telepathy. My reply would be that the word "telepathy" is only a description of the means by which intercession may be made effective. Similarly, our great-grandfathers were puzzled when scientists wrote and spoke so much of evolution. Yet evolution did not remove the necessity of God from the creation. The process of evolution described the method of the creation—if one may so put it, the machinery which God used. Nor is the process any less divine because man in part understands it. Similarly, in regard to telepathy, the influence of mind upon mind may, indeed, help us to understand part of the machinery which God uses when men pray for the sick. If it be agreed that modern research into "Psi" phenomena opens up for us an unsuspected faculty in man, surely we ought to press this faculty into God's service. We pray with more earnestness if we have a clue as to how prayer "works." For too long prayer has been paralysed by the idea, tenaciously held in some quarters, that it only has subjective value. But there seems to me a profound difference between a mere human willing that John Smith recover, and linking up one's mental processes with the divine love and power. In the latter case the word "telepathy" is not sufficient. Inter-cessory prayer may be a far higher function of the human personality and a more potent way of releasing divine energy than the use of the word "telepathy" suggests.

An illustration may be found, perhaps, in thinking of the use of a sermon in converting a sinner. The sermon which converted John Jones was not only words. The words were used as a means of transmitting a divine power. In intercession, what we call "telepathy" may be a part of the mental machinery used to transmit a spiritual power from God. When a thousand people pray for John Jones's recovery from illness, God may use their mind-waves to carry His healing energies to Jones's body, just as He uses the words of the sermon to carry salvation to Jones's soul.

It cannot too often be stated that all healing is of God. All man can do is to co-operate with God, but that co-operation must be on every possible level. Anyone who has visited a hospital frequently has seen respiratory cases in which what is called an oxygen-tent is em-ployed. In order to give a patient the maximum chance of recovery, his breathing apparatus is surrounded by a so-called tent into which oxygen is poured. Breathing in oxygen, he is given a better chance of recovery. It may be that intercession for a patient surrounds his mind with optimism and his will with determination, even at deep unconscious levels when he does not know he is being prayed for, so that his personality is given a maximum chance of recovery. Within

241

a fellowship such as the Christian Church, people should be taught to feel that they can count on such co-operation from their fellow Church members whenever they are passing through a time of pain, or sorrow, or mental distress. St. Paul definitely asked the Corinthian Church for this sign of their affection, and wrote, "Let me have your co-operation in prayer." [10]

I now turn to some of the questions asked when the matter of intercession for the sick is discussed.

1. People ask why, if what is written above is true, all illnesses are not curable by prayer. Why, they say, do you resort to the doctor at all?

Clearly the answer is that all illnesses are not curable by prayer. Prayer is only one way of co-operating with God to bring health to men. As I have tried to show, medicine, surgery, nursing, psychology, dentistry, are other ways, and we must find the way which is relevant to the kind of case concerned. To give a very simple illustration, if a man has a thorn in his foot which is suppurating, prayer is clearly not the relevant way of healing his foot, and Jesus certainly would not have attempted it. The thorn must be removed.[11] It should be remembered that there are many cases in this category, although they do not appear to be so to us. Again and again prayer is resorted to only because all other means have failed. But it can hardly be expected that prayer will be a substitute for painstaking research to understand the cause of illness, and God called in, as it were, to make up for the ignorance or lack of skill of the doctor or surgeon. Again and again men cry out that their prayers are not answered, when the truth is that had they understood the situation, they would never have expected healing from prayer alone. No one prays about his teeth. He goes to his dentist. He understands what is the matter, and roughly understands the technique the dentist will use. It is illogical for him to complain of his unanswered prayers if an illness is in the same category, did we only know it, and calls for the skilled physician as the most relevant way of treating the illness. Prayer certainly has a

---

[10] II Corinthians 1:11 (Moffatt).

[11] I find that men have even tried to remove a thorn by incantation. In a MS. of the eighth century, in the library of the monastery of St. Gall in Switzerland, is found the following:

> To remove a thorn, say,
> "Nothing is higher than heaven,
> Nothing is deeper than His sea;
> By the holy words Christ spoke from His Cross,
> Remove this thorn from me."

C. J. S. Thompson, *Magic and Healing*, p. 21 (Rider, 1946).

value in every case of illness, but not necessarily a curative value, and it has a value not because it is in the same category as other forms of treatment, but because it is a means of establishing harmony with God, on which the welfare of the soul, and often of the body, depends.

2. Another objection is put thus: We pray for one man and he recovers. We pray for another man and he dies. We do not understand why in either case. Therefore, it is said, prayer offers no wise way of combating disease.

If a man is prayed for and does not recover, it may be, as stated above, that his illness is in the same category as a thorn in the foot, however complicated the case may appear to us. It may be thus that our co-operation with God breaks down at some point or other. It may be on the physical side, but the breakdown may be on the psychical or spiritual side. The reason why we cannot co-operate fully enough to bring back health may be either that we do not know enough, or that we have not faith or love enough.

Much research is called for into the laws of prayer. If man by research can set free such immense physical force as atomic energy, let him by research and spiritual insight set himself to release spiritual healing force through prayer. Prayer, like everything else in God's universe, is not accidental in its way of working. It is based on laws, and men must learn what those laws are and under what conditions they operate. Some of these laws I have tried to indicate already, but so little is really known of the laws of the spiritual realm.

3. Another question is whether it is to be assumed that God's will for everybody is health under all conditions.

My own conclusion is that one may work on the assumption that God's perfect intention for everybody is perfect health of body, mind and spirit. But when the question is asked whether this is God's intention *under all conditions*, it must be made clear that in some circumstances to choose health is to choose the way of selfishness, and to choose suffering is to choose the way of self-sacrificing service. There is a famous passage in Alfred Russell Wallace's book, *Travels on the Amazon*, where he relates that the physique of the natives improved in direct ratio to their distance from civilisation. This was not so much because of the "evils of civilisation," but because the savage never shares the suffering of others. The sick are not nursed: they are isolated and left to die. The weak are not protected: they are left to perish. In civilised countries the suffering of the few is the burden and concern of all, and one feels that such suffering, in the evil circumstances man has engendered, is in harmony with the interim, though of course not the ideal, will of God. Many brave men and women have courted suffering and undergone torture, and no one could pretend that suffering is to be avoided at all costs and under all conditions. Indeed, part of the Christian message is that suffering, joyously accepted and patiently borne, can be woven into God's purposes and become as effective for man's final blessedness as perfect health. Again and again, death itself, with its power of example and its challenge to action, turns out to be a co-operation with God as effective as, in other circumstances, is a rescue from death.

4. The objection is made that prayer can never be proved to be a healing factor because in any case the patient might have got well.

Clearly no one can prove that prayer is the effective factor. In the same sense, one cannot prove that a certain drug is the effective factor. The objection could always be sustained that the patient might have got better in any case. All that can be said is that over a period now of some twenty-five years, when one has collected a large number of cases of patients, given up by doctors, who have recovered after prayer, when one has noted that a significant proportion has taken a turn for the better during the time prayer was offered, one cannot confidently say that, if any drug were discovered about which the same could be said, it would be universally used and acclaimed as the curative agent, even though, like prayer, it frequently disappointed those who resorted to it.

5. The question is asked whether many cases for whom prayer is made do not temporarily recover only to relapse into illness again.

Relapse can take place, of course, whatever means for recovery are undertaken. I should like to give two illustrations from my own experience. In 1937 prayer was asked for a paralysed woman who was expecting her first baby. The surgeon was about to operate, believing that the mother could never deliver her child. Nearly two thousand people at the City Temple service engaged in intercession. The mother walked and the baby was born in the usual way.

Here is part of a letter received from a friend about this case:

"You may like to know that Mrs. T. and her baby, who were healed through the power of prayer from your fellowship, are both enjoying wonderful health, and they have been in perfect health ever since we lifted them up to Christ *a year ago*."

The second case I summarise as follows:

Some time ago, a young girl of seventeen was brought many miles from a distant county to the City Temple to be interviewed by me. I interviewed her parents and the girl herself with great care, and came to the conclusion that she needed far more help than I was competent to give her. It was definitely a psychological trouble, but it resulted in the most queer physical symptoms that one could imagine. I had read about such cases, but had never seen one, and I felt the case was beyond me altogether.

I therefore arranged for the patient to see a Harley Street specialist —a personal friend of mine, a great Christian, a fine doctor and an excellent psychologist, who used to help me at the City Temple Psychological Clinic. He spent a great many hours with the patient without being able to make the slightest impression. Sadly enough, the young girl was sent home and told that nothing could be done for her. I had a letter from her mother thanking both the doctor and myself for all we had tried to do, and telling us how grateful and yet how disappointed the family was. I learnt afterwards that the girl sobbed herself to sleep, feeling that the last hope of recovery had gone.

Some time passed, and I had a growing uneasiness that we had too easily given up her case. One night I dreamed of her, and, waking up out of the dream, I wrote down her name on the pad at the side of my bed. As soon as I got to my study the next day, I wrote to the mother telling her to inform the girl that on the following Sunday night we would pray for her. The mother says that very message made a difference to her daughter.

On the following Sunday night I asked the congregation to pray for this girl. No names were mentioned, nor was the nature of the illness revealed in any detail. Yet from that night to this there has been no return of the illness. The girl is perfectly well. She has taken up the career she wanted to take up.

Recently a Methodist District Chairman happened to meet the mother of this girl and was told the whole story. He wrote to me, having interviewed the girl himself. His report is that she is still perfectly well and has had no recurrence of her troubles. Since it is so long now since we prayed for the girl, we are hoping that the word "cure" may be used in this case.

Enquiry shows that this cure has been maintained up to the time of writing these words—more than twelve years after the patient was first seen.

6. Another objection is made by those who say they can believe that prayer can make a difference if the illness is hysterical or functional, but not if it is organic.

It must be conceded at once that there must obviously be limits to what can be accomplished through even the most faithful prayer. Prayer may be offered in a case in which it is clearly not the best way of giving help to a patient, and though not wasted, as I have tried to show, cannot possibly be rewarded by the patient's recovery. To use an obvious illustration, if a man has lost his leg, prayer that he may grow another seems to me a waste of time, though some people can be found who would not allow even such a limitation as this. Yet, even for them, a line must be drawn somewhere between the possible and the impossible. Surely a man would be laughed at who engaged in prayer for a person whose head had been entirely severed.

At the same time, it must be recognised that it is often very difficult to draw the line between the possible and the impossible, and between the organic and the functional. A whole field of psychosomatic disease is now being opened up, and it is found that many diseases have organic symptoms, but are psychological in origin.[12] There are, further, the cases of conversion hysteria where some mental conflict has been translated into, and, to some extent, relieved by, a physical symptom. In the section on the healing miracles I tried to show that many of them were cures of physical disorders wrought by spiritual means, and we certainly should not be too ready to draw the line between cases which can be helped by prayer and cases for which prayer is useless as a curative factor. One might suggest the advice, when in doubt pray, for only good can come, and however useless prayer may be in a curative sense, if the mind of the patient is buoyed up by the prayers of others and his spirit sustained by the knowledge that he is loved and cared for, then the power of his mind over his body, even in an organic illness, may be a powerful means of contributing to the restoration of his health.

7. A seventh objection is sometimes made to the effect that intercession is a misuse of prayer, in that it degrades into a treatment something that should be a means of communion with God.

This is indeed an important objection. Prayer is not in the same category as a treatment like massage, or the use of a drug, or a surgical operation. Its prime object, of course, is to bring the patient into close communion with God and in unity with His will. At the same time, it must be conceded that much illness is due to disunity with God and disharmony with His will, and if prayer is rightly used, healing will often follow as a by-product. Yet prayer is not suitably tested by its results. For instance, it is no test of a "good" prayer that health follows, and no sign of a "poor" prayer that illness remains. For reasons already given, we can have faith and piety and love and remain unhealed, and we can have healing in case after case without faith or prayer or love at all.

In spite of the reign of science, the Church must be called back to

---

[12] They are discussed in Section V, Chapters 2-4.

the ministry of intercession for the sick. In the same sentence, we read that Christ sent His men out to "preach the Kingdom of God and to heal the sick." [13] We have done the former, but the latter we have almost entirely handed over to the medical profession. The doctors have done magnificent work, but they cannot do all the work. An illustration may be found by likening man, not to a motor-car, but to a motor-car driven by a driver, the driver being the mind-soul. (I do not differentiate for the purpose of this argument.) When the car breaks down through some mechanical fault, it can be mended at the garage, and when the body breaks down because the machine is itself faulty, then the doctor and surgeon and other physical-repair specialists have their undoubted value. But a motor-car often breaks down because it is badly driven, and then what is required is the re-education of the driver—the mind-soul—and this is the place ideally for the Christian psychotherapist and for the religious expert. Here, in the mind-soul, the effect of corporate prayer is felt. It must never be supposed that the function of healing is only in the realm of medicine. It makes nonsense of all the healing ministry of Jesus to suppose that religion and health never have anything to do with one another. This corporate prayer should be offered in our church services, not in vague sentences like, "Bless all who are sick," but, where permission has been obtained, mentioning the name of the patient and making an imaginative picture so that those who pray can imaginatively *see* the patient; taking care not to paint the picture in such grey colours that the evoked emotion of pity, or even horror, kills the emotion of optimism and expectant trust. Small local groups of people who know and love the patient should be organized to pray daily for him, even though they cannot meet in one place to do so.

The spiritual world has immense therapeutic energies which are scarcely tapped in this modern age of reliance upon pure science and organic therapy. We must be called away from a materialistic interpretation of life which is invading the Church and cheating men of that power which is their heritage in Christ.

[13] Luke 9:2.

MODERN METHODS OF HEALING THROUGH PSYCHOLOGY

1

FREUD AND PSYCHOANALYSIS

(Freud, 1856-1939)

THERE ARE SOME names which denote the beginning of a new era in man's thought about the world and himself. This is true of the name of Sigmund Freud, as it is true of Newton and Einstein. We are too near to him to assess the place of his theories in the whole perspective of man's life. But it is safe to say that, both in theory and in practice, the integration of man's personality took a new turning through the contribution of his teaching.

Obviously this chapter cannot do more than outline enough of Freud's teaching to make his contribution to that integration intelligible. Those who desire to dig more deeply must, of course, consult his own works and the many books about him.[1]

Freud, a Jew of working-class family, was born in Freiburg in 1856. He himself tells us that he had no intention of taking up medicine. It was his parents' ambition. Yet from the first he was interested in science, and particularly in human behaviour. For six years, under Brücke, he worked in the neuro-physiological laboratory in Vienna. Frustrated there for lack of medical training, he became a medical student, and immediately showed signs of great promise in cerebral anatomy. "Nervous" patients interested him from the beginning, and his work was good enough to secure for him the post of lecturer in neuro-pathology at the University of Vienna.

The young neurologist was dissatisfied, however, with the theories then held to account for "nervous" conditions and the treatments used to combat them. In 1885, therefore, he went to the Salpêtrière in Paris and studied under Charcôt, whose lectures he translated into German.

[1] Perhaps the best of the latter is Dalbiez's, *Psychoanalytical Method and the Doctrine of Freud*, 2 vols. (Longmans Green, 1941). Preface by E. B. Strauss, M.D.

In 1893 Freud and Breuer published a book, called *Studies in Hysteria*, in which they sought to show that physical symptoms of hysteria have their root cause in highly emotional experiences of early life which have been "repressed" into the unconscious mind and are normally not recoverable to conscious memory.

These forgotten, and psychologically traumatic, incidents, charged with repressed emotion, are not allowed into consciousness because they are obnoxious to the patient's peace of mind, to his self-respect, to his ideal of himself, and so forth. But they do not lie dormant in the unconscious mind as mud lies at the bottom of a pond. Although withheld from consciousness, they revenge themselves, as it were, by expressing their energies in terms of mental symptoms of anxiety, or fear, or physical symptoms. A physical symptom frequently appears to be physiogenic, such as a skin disease, an asthma, a peptic ulcer, a form of paralysis, rheumatoid pains, blindness, lameness, dumbness, and so on, yet, says Freud, it is frequently the result of mental material repressed into the unconscious part of the mind.

To keep the analogy of the pond, we may imagine that the mud at the bottom contains fermenting material which sends up bubbles to the surface. So, on the surface of the mind, symptoms like the emotion of fear or the pain of asthma may be experienced, as different from their origin as bubbles are different from mud, but also as consequent. Treatment of such a fear, or other symptoms, by physical means is as unsatisfactory as pricking a bubble in the hope of stopping bubbles forming. Its buried source in the mud must be investigated. So the exploration of the material repressed in the unconscious is Freud's way of treating neurotic symptoms, whether they are felt physically as pain, or mentally as terror, panic or vague fear.

Freud found that normally much mental material is permanently repressed and never consciously expressed, but that illness could weaken the power to maintain the repression, or the instincts attached to the repressed material might be reinforced by some experience, or the repressed matter might be awakened through the association of ideas and thereupon there was often an ebullition in consciousness of the emotion locked up in the repressed matter, even though distortion gave no clue to the exact nature of the repressed material either in the emotion expressed or the physical symptom produced.[2]

The choice of physical symptom is motivated in various ways, and concerning them discussion still goes on. But it may safely be said that sometimes the choice of symptom is determined by a constitutional

[2] Freud, *Moses and Monotheism*.

weakness. Where there is a strong tendency in a family towards some particular type of illness, then the neurotic patient may, as it were, give way at his weakest link. If there is a family history of asthma, the patient may have asthma.

As I write these words there is a patient attending the City Temple Psychological Clinic who said of her asthma, "My mother had it. It is not surprising that I have got it. It is in the family." The medical psychologist who has charge of her case, however, assures me that her asthma cannot be put down wholly to this hereditary trend, but is a psychogenic disease set up unwittingly, but nevertheless unconsciously determined, in order to get the patient out of a certain difficulty.

This leads us to the second motivating factor in the choice of symptom. It is often the most convenient way the unconscious mind can hit on for getting the patient out of a difficulty. It is most important to realise that the symptom is *unconsciously* desired. No blame attaches to the patient for producing it. Indeed, he cannot consciously produce it, and people who blame the neurotic, simply show an ignorance of how a neurosis is caused. Inasmuch as the motivating factors are all unconscious, and inasmuch as we have no direct control of our unconscious activities, no blame can possibly be attached to the neurotic for being ill. Indeed, consciously the neurotic desires to be cured, and frequently spends much on physicians and on trying innumerable treatments. But the unconscious mind continues to produce the symptom which is desired, in that it is easier to bear distress of body than distress of mind, and the production of a symptom, in that it often gets the patient out of the most difficult part of the neurotic situation, relieves that situation immensely. Furthermore, the physical distress arouses far greater sympathy in others than would any mental distress, and that sympathy is a love-substitute—the next best thing to the love the neurotic craves—the deprivation of love probably accounting largely for the original neurotic condition.

Thus a soldier—described by McDougall—who bayoneted some wounded Germans in a trench, was decorated for taking the trench, instead of punished for a breach of international law. He developed a dumbness which was entirely psychogenic. It was as if the unconscious could not bear the conflict between the desire to be thought a hero on the one hand, and the fear of giving himself away and being labelled "coward" on the other. So the body was made to bear the burden. Dumbness got him out of the conflict and won him sympathy. Being dumb, he would not give himself away either in his sleep or in his cups. His mind was relieved. He "wanted" dumbness, for it was easier to bear than mental strain; it resolved the conflict; it brought him sympathy, which is a love-substitute. The desire for praise, another love-substitute, may have been the motive that led him to commit the crime.

Frequently, again, the symptom is determined by the unconscious choice of an illness which dramatises the repressed situation. Thus, in a Psychological Clinic in Ireland, conducted by a friend of mine, the Rev. Dr. W. L. Northridge, I was told of the case of a woman who could not see. There was nothing the matter with her eyes. She was not blind, but the lids dropped over her eyes, and she walked about holding them up with her two fingers. Here we have a typical situation. She *wanted* to see. As far as conscious mechanisms go, her desire was for health. But she had "converted" a refusal to look life in the face into an inability to look ahead (conversion-hysteria). The functional paralysis of the muscles of the eyelids was determined by the repression in the unconscious mind which is powerful enough to produce almost any symptom in the body if it can thereby relieve the anguish of the mind. The woman entirely recovered when, with the help of religion, she was given courage to face whatever might befall.

When we say that a symptom is desired, it will seem incredible to some that a thing like blindness can be desired, but the reasons have already been given. The so-called blindness is not blameworthy because it is produced by the unconscious. It is unconsciously desired because it gets the patient out of a difficult situation, induces the pity of others, relieves the tension and strain on the mind by diverting the mind so that it dwells on a physical trouble and not on its mental distress, and the symptom is disabling enough to make the patient's excuses for his withdrawal from life imposing enough to convince him.

In 1893, as we can imagine, such ideas as these received scant courtesy from the medical authorities. Breuer very soon became frightened by what we now call a "positive transference," by which is meant an inordinate unloading of emotional regard by the patient on to the analyst, and indistinguishable from falling in love with him. Breuer treated a woman suffering from hysteria, and she manifested an emotional dependence on, and admiration for, him that frightened him. Indeed, she refused to leave him even when cured, saying that she could not live without him. But both Breuer and Freud found something of the degree to which sex emotion is involved in the neuroses of women patients. Breuer could not stand up against the wave of unpopularity to which his association with Freud subjected him, and therefore he gave up that association and discontinued this type of treatment.

Freud kept on, and found that sexual difficulties certainly lay behind the neuroses of a high percentage of his patients. Some of these difficulties he traced back to sexual assaults in childhood, masturbation histories and what to the polite world of Vienna in 1893 were exceedingly unsavoury biographical details. Freud recognised later that a lot of these assaults never actually happened. They were imagined by the patient and unconsciously desired. But he also realised, though not at first, that to a neurotic patient even an imaginary assault can powerfully disturb the mind, and, even if it has no factual reality, it is so real to the patient as to have as great an effect on him as if it had actually happened. It must be treated as if it were factual, since an imagined assault can have the same psychological effect as an actual one.

These sex difficulties were either *suppressed*—that is, consciously withheld, the patient being too shy or frightened or ashamed to speak of them—or else they were *repressed*—that is, unwittingly, but purposefully, pushed down into the unconscious mind and forgotten, remaining out of the reach of the conscious mind of the patient and giving him complete sincerity in his inability to recognise them as part of his own experience.

Freud made it his task to bring such incidents to consciousness, and found, to the world's incredulous astonishment, that the child could sustain a sexual shock which could have the most disabling repercussions in the adult life of a neurotic patient. If the incidents and emotions were *suppressed*, the case presented small difficulty. But if *repression* had occurred, the technique was long and arduous, lasting for two or three years, even though the patient had interviews with the psychologist twice or thrice a week. This laborious search for the content of the unconscious mind and the effort to bring it to consciousness, Freud called psychoanalysis, and the word should still be reserved for his particular method. As these buried memories and nuclear incidents were brought to consciousness, there was frequently a discharge of strong emotion, sometimes in tears, sometimes in anger, resentment, hate, bitterness and so on. This discharge Freud called the "abreaction," and he regarded it as a good sign when the "abreaction" took place, as the pent-up emotion was then released and a kind of mental catharsis took place which did much to restore the patient to health.

Freud, like Breuer, found that patients transferred these emotions to him. There was a "positive transference," or, in other words, they fell in love with him or expressed intense admiration and dependence. Or they showed a "negative transference"; they hated him and sometimes almost attacked him. But Freud, unlike Breuer, found that he could use this transference in effecting cure. It took him many years to work out the way in which the transference could be used, but now dealing with the transference is an important part of his method. As the patient recovered to consciousness his emotional attitude of love or defiance, Freud allowed him to attach these feelings to himself, but later he weaned the patient from this dependence or hostility and tried to teach him how to stand alone and find a more adult and satisfying outlet for the infantile feeling now finding its expression in transferences of one kind or the other.

The doctrine that startled the world was that sex life began so early. Freud taught that there was a very early blossoming of the sex instinct which came to an end about the age of five, then followed a quiescent period, and then puberty. Formerly the sexual life was thought to begin with puberty. Freud's theory of "infantile sexuality" was rejected at first with horrified screams of denial. Freud, however, insisted that sexual life began when life began. At first it was undifferentiated from other functions, but later developed an independent existence. Yet even in early childhood, sexual incidents, such as assault, could occur, and distort the sex life of a child while he was unconscious of sex, only to disturb his sex life even more violently when he was an adult facing nervous and emotionally demanding situations.

It was a vital part of Freud's treatment that the patient should be encouraged to express outwardly the hitherto buried emotion; to *feel* as he felt in his childhood when the vital, nuclear incidents happened, and the analyst just had to accept the loving dependence or the violent antagonism of the child (which the patient had become for the time being) in his analytical treatment. Able to do this, able to see consciously his own inner self laid bare right back, if necessary, to the days of infancy, the patient was able thereafter to adjust himself accordingly and cure himself of that faulty emotional reaction to reality, to himself and to his circumstances which had disabled his life and produced neurotic illness.

Freud was always searching for hidden motives. No event in mental life or its consequent outward behaviour could be uncaused. To forget a name probably meant the dislike of a person bearing it. To dislike a colour pointed to a buried memory of some incident associated with it. A slip of the pen indicated what the patient really intended to say, and so on.[3] Freud taught that the patient will always make a "resistance" against repressed matter emerging to the conscious mind, and, without any conscious motive of deceit or hindrance, will try to keep his experiences from the scrutiny of the analyst, since his own unconscious is trying to keep them from his own.

It is unfortunate that Freud is associated, in the minds of many people whose judgment has been warped by misrepresentation, with an undue emphasis on sex. Actually, it was a remark of his teacher, Charcôt, that made Freud investigate the question of what has come to be called "infantile sexuality." "Always," said Charcôt, "in a case of neurosis, there has been trouble in the sex life of the individual."

Charcôt left it at that. Freud investigated it further. Most people regard sex as dormant in the life of the normal individual until it is awakened at puberty. Most people do not regard sex as a factor which motivates their dreams or their general behaviour. Freud believed that sex plays a part in a child's fantasies and actions from the earliest years, that adult dreams are disguised realisations of erotic desires, and that repressed sex desires play a part in the behaviour of the most normal people, and explain peculiarities which, on the surface, have not the remotest relation to sex.

Sex being what it is—the thing not discussed or even referred to, the banned tabu, the subject avoided through both fear and disgust—it is not surprising that Freud's emphasis alarmed and disgusted the public and covered his other theories with a pall of abuse and ridicule.

At the same time, Freud's theories were eagerly accepted by those who sought an excuse for immorality. As Dr. Eric Waterhouse says in an illuminating article on Freud,[4] "War seems destined always to be accompanied by a wave of sex laxity, and this made Freud's speculations more acceptable than they could have been in the days when first they were evolved."

The two theories of repression[5] and infantile sexuality[6] are regarded by R. S. Woodworth [7] as the twin pillars on which the Freudian hypothesis rests. He writes, "If we put the two theories together, we have in a nutshell the fundamentals of Freud's psychology. . . . The

[3] I have discussed unconscious motivation in *Psychology in Service of the Soul*, p. 98 (Macmillan, 1930). See also Freud's *Psychopathology of Everyday Life* (Macmillan, 1917).

[4] Eric S. Waterhouse, M.A., D.D., D.Litt., "Sigmund Freud," in the *London Quarterly and Holborn Review*, January 1940.

[5] Fully discussed in my *Psychology and Life* (Abingdon-Cokesbury, 1935),

[6] Discussed in my *The Mastery of Sex* (Macmillan, 1932).

[7] *Contemporary Schools of Psychology* (Ronald, 1931).

importance of repression, the importance of sex desire and the importance of the infantile period are Freud's three main emphases. . . . A neurosis originates in repressed infantile sexuality—that is his main proposition." But it should be clear that repressed infantile sexuality is not the peculiarity of the neurotic or those who have a neurosis at some time or other. It is a factor in the lives of everybody.[8]

Freud's treatment is directed, then, to an exploration of the unconscious, since all repressed experience is in the unconscious. This is not normally accessible to the patient. One might imagine that hypnosis would be a suitable treatment, since in a successful hypnosis the psychologist can make direct contact with the unconscious. But Freud early discovered that unless the patient *consciously* lives through the repressed experience again, often showing immense emotion as he does so and experiencing an "abreaction," or outward expression of the inner emotion, little is achieved by his recovery of the traumatic experience while he is hypnotised.

Finding out what the repressed material is, and then telling the patient, Freud called "a shortsighted mistake." "Our knowledge of what is unconscious in him is not equivalent to his knowledge of it; when we tell him what we know, he does not assimilate it *in place* of his own unconscious thoughts, but *alongside* of them, and very little has been changed." [9]

Success is sometimes achieved by a kind of hypno-analysis, by which the patient is awakened after hypnosis (during which he has discovered and recalled some "nuclear incident") to hear the psychologist say, "You were telling me about . . ." In this way the patient frequently recalls again, but consciously, the buried memory, and living through it again imaginatively, discharges the emotion repressed in it for so long, and, recognising the incident and his original reaction to it as a determinant of his early behaviour, proceeds to adjust himself to the situation it discloses, to correct the false attitude he proceeded to take to life because of it, and thus is cured of his neurosis.

Hypnosis, however, soon ceased to be Freud's main method of treatment, for there are additional disadvantages to the main one mentioned above. Many people cannot be hypnotised. Many are terrified of it. It is a good rule that clinical practice should not far outstrip intelligible theory—and no one knows precisely what hypnotising a person does to him. Not that it is harmful, but even when described as a state of increased suggestibility or of dissociation, no one quite

[8] R. S. Woodworth, *op. cit.*

[9] Freud, *Introductory Lectures on Psycho Analysis*, p. 364 (Allen and Unwin, 1922).

realises what happens. Many writers say that the transference—or emotional dependence of the patient on the hypnotist—is increased by it. Breuer discontinued this method for this reason.

Freud's main method is that of free association. The patient lies relaxed on a couch and is encouraged to say whatever comes into his mind. The first few interviews are naturally concerned in telling his story, but after that he passes from one idea to the next, his choice of subject being governed by the law of the association of ideas. He is not questioned by the analyst, save perhaps to elucidate a point that the patient has not made clear. It is important that the analyst, sitting out of sight of the patient's direct gaze, should adopt a passive role, but watching for the expressions of emotion or any other connections between the parts of the narrative, or any slips of the tongue, symptomatic movements, etc. It is astonishing to anyone who has not experienced this method or seen it in action, that comparatively quickly the patient is associating in ways that indicate to the trained analyst the ideas and complexes, conflicts and repressions in the unconscious which are the cause of his neurosis.

An illustration will perhaps put the matter briefly and clearly. A ministerial friend of mine complained, in confidence, to me that although he was very much in love with his wife, she immediately became roused to hostility and violent feeling if he went to bed ill. His going to bed at night she viewed calmly, but if he had a touch of cold or influenza she reacted violently. He rang me up to say that he had to go into a nursing home for an operation and would then come home and be in bed for some weeks, and was very frightened because she had already struck him with an electric torch and tried to kick him out of bed. Enquiry among members of the family, who were all grown up, showed that, though the parents loved one another, the wife would do almost anything to prevent her husband taking to his bed. On the least suspicion of a cold, she would dose him with drugs, and if he went to bed for a single day she showed all the feelings of exaggerated alarm and fear. I do not practise anything that is worthy of the name of psycho-analysis, but I have found that what might be called a therapeutic conversation often has remarkable results. This one did, and the method used was free association. The wife came round to my rooms, relaxed on a couch, and, starting with her dislike of her husband being in bed, was told to say whatever came into her mind. Very quickly her mind travelled back to childhood's days, and she recalled screaming on the stairs when she was told that her younger brother had been born and that she was not the only object of her mother's affection. She thus associated the idea of her mother being in bed with the idea of the deprivation of part of her mother's love. She told a number of incidents, which need not here be quoted, of violent anger against her mother: how she tried to pull her mother out of bed to make her take notice of her, and how violently she reacted against her baby brother. Quite spontaneously, without any help from me, she said that her husband had always been her protector and taken care of her, and had been more a parental substitute than a mate. Again without much help from me, she finally reached the point where she saw clearly that the fact of her husband (= mother-substitute) going to bed unconsciously reminded her of her mother going to bed, which roused the feeling of the fear of the withdrawal of love, so that her husband going to bed spelt for her the fear of his love being withdrawn. On seeing how this situation had arisen and on facing up to it, the desire to attack him entirely faded out, and since this all happened more than five years ago, and since the minister recently told me that his wife was entirely cured, one has perhaps a good illustration of the value of this method, which Freud originated, of studying the unconscious mental processes.

Freud's auxiliary method is the interpretation of dreams. "If we wish," says Dalbiez, "to have an idea of the greatness of Freud's work, we must turn primarily to the analysis of dreams. . . . Can scientific psychology afford any other examples of a psychic condition so common, coeval with humanity itself, incomprehensible for such countless ages, and yet explained at last?" [10] In 1900 Freud published, in German, his famous book on this subject, and it is doing him scant justice to attempt to survey his dream-theories here. Yet, in general, it may be said that, for Freud, a dream is the expression of a repressed desire. He admits that a dream *may* have no sexual content—dreams of food, for instance, which the hungry have—but he is suspicious that even such a dream is distorted so that the sexual element in it may remain disguised from the dreamer. Such distortion forms part of the "resistance" against the unconscious situation being explored. We desire most, he argues, that which is most strongly forbidden and under the feared tabu of society. We repress such desires into the unconscious. Sex desire, therefore, strong but forbidden, is most repressed, and forms the greater part of the dream-content. Fear maintains the repression. We dread knowing ourselves in this regard. Much more do we dread that society, with its strong tabu on sex, should know us to be the sexually hungry people which at various times we all are.

Freud divides this dream-content into two parts: the manifest con-

[10] Dalbiez, *op. cit.*, Vol. II, p. 327.

tent and the latent content. Using the simile of the stage, the manifest content we might describe as the stage scenery of the dream, and this may be built up from events which have taken place in the recent life of the dreamer. The latent content, however, might be regarded as the plot of the play, and it is obviously much harder to disentangle this when the dream is narrated by the patient. He should be invited to write down his dream the moment he wakes from it, otherwise he is almost certain to edit it and elaborate it. It may then be used as the material for more free association.

Freud speaks of the activity of the "endo-psychic censor" in a dream. He means by this that the unconscious turns the dream into a kind of cartoon. A cartoon can "put over" an offensive idea in an innocent, or even amusing, way. The point of it is driven home, but the sting is not so poignant. One of the purposes of the dream is to keep the patient sleeping, and at the same time find for him mental expression and therefore relief for his repressed longings. So, he may relate with gusto a dream he has had, unaware of its inner significance. The endo-psychic censor has so cartoonised it—if the expression be allowed—that the dreamer does not imagine that desires which, if not distorted, would waken him with disgust have been finding vent, and yet at the same time he has been kept asleep. The endo-psychic censor is a psychic force which either represses into the unconscious or disguises the conscious form of all mental material which is distasteful to conscious thought and incompatible with a man's idea of himself. Dreams show a tempest in the depths of the mind, and the memory of dreams, and the nightmares that waken us, show that the storm has, so to say, broken surface and entered consciousness. But the censor manipulates the dream so that distasteful mental material is cartoonised.

An illustration may help. During the war a young girl of seventeen related the following dream: "I was walking down the street where our house is, when suddenly some soldiers, wearing helmets, came round the corner. They stopped me, and one of them grasped my arm and took me away, and I awoke in terror." [11] It may be that the fear of invasion is the simple solution of the dream; in which case the soldiers are soldiers, and not symbols of something else. It is much more likely that the interpretation of the dream is as follows: the soldiers are merely manifest content, due to the fact that her mind is full of the war and its images. To a girl of seventeen the latent menace of that particular age is a private and personal demand of the awakening sex instinct. Subconsciously she has become aware

[11] Quoted from Maurice Nicoll, *Dream Psychology*, Oxford Medical Publications (Oxford, 1920).

of factors in life which will sweep her out of her present orbit into a strange and new life. This is the explanation of the hand on her arm leading her away.

I cannot agree with Freud's pan-sexual emphasis in his interpretations of dreams, for his theory of the "libido" would explain it not as the thrust of psychic energy flowing out like a river to the sea of personality-goals in general, but towards sexual gratification in particular. That repressed sex desire from infancy onwards is at work in the unconscious, and does operate as factor in character behaviour far more fully than most people recognise, I am entirely convinced, but I think that it is artificial to push *all* dreaming into Freud's framework. As I have shown elsewhere,[12] any deep fear or worry of the mind, as well as a desire, even though not entirely unconscious, may find expression in our dreams. Dr. Maurice Nicoll, in his book on dreams, tells of a man who had not faced up to his fear of his employers, and who dreamed he was in a desert. Before him was a very high wall. He was cowering at its foot in terror. As the patient himself remarked, he "was up against it." The fear which he had repressed into the unconscious during the day leapt out at night in terms of this dream. It would seem to me highly artificial to declare that this dream was only interpretable in terms of "repressed infantile sexuality." Here an Adlerian interpretation seems to me more likely.

Whether, then, by hypno-analysis, free association, the interpretation of dreams, the noting of slips of tongue or pen, and so on, Freud's method aims at recovering to consciousness the repressed material in the unconscious mind. In that vast depth are stored, he teaches, all the memories of the past, right back to the hour of birth, and perhaps before that. When these memories have reached consciousness and been re-lived again so as to express their emotional content, the patient can the better adjust himself to life, for his inner emotional abscess has discharged its poison—to use a physiological figure—and he can guard against recurrence because he sees the factors that formed it in the first place. If a patient lapsed, Freud argued that his treatment had not gone back far enough into the patient's childhood. Freud regarded all psycho-neurotic illness as going back to some psychological trauma, or group of traumas, in childhood, and the fixation at that point, and for that reason, of a childish attitude which had continued into adult life and rendered the patient incapable of coping with life in an adult way. So it was necessary to go back and back to infancy to "dig out" the original experience or set of ex-

[12] The chapter on "The Interpretation of Dreams" in my *Psychology in Service of the Soul* (Macmillan, 1930).

periences; to realise that one made in early childhood a pattern of reaction which has hardened and determined the reaction even of the adult. Only by such insight can a patient be led to change his pattern of reaction for one that is more mature. Frequently in Freud's hands it is alleged that a patient remembered being born, and, in view of this, we are not surprised at the length of time which a Freudian analysis may take.

Sexual experience was to Freud, the clue to neurosis. It was at once desired, but feared. Fear and desire in conflict produced anxiety, and anxiety might express itself either as conscious emotion made up of fear of something unknown (because repressed), guilt, inferiority and depression, sleeplessness and the like. This Freud called the anxiety neurosis. Or, on the other hand, a physical symptom might be developed, like blindness or paralysis, which eased the conscious emotional distress, but was, of course, physically disabling. Here the anxiety was changed or "converted" into a hysterical symptom, and the condition called conversion hysteria or anxiety hysteria developed.

So-called "neurasthenia" Freud would have explained as the fatigue and weakness due to the fact that the patient used up so much nervous energy maintaining his repressions that he had none left with which to face life. Obsessional or compulsion neurosis Freud would have explained as a ritual which the patient felt compelled to carry out to placate the sexual desires he could not express in their recognisable sexual form. The compulsion to poke the fire, to touch the lamp-post, and so on, bore only one meaning. Both objects were phallic. To wash the hands was a parable in action on the part of a patient who sought to cleanse himself from secret sexual malpractice and so forth.

In his later work Freud taught that the super-ego of man was frequently in conflict with the id, and that this conflict brought neurosis. The super-ego might roughly be called the conscience, and the id, desire. The super-ego is the artificial self built up by morbid complexes; the self we feel we ought to be because those who dominated our child-life have taught us to fear falling below it, the "introjection of the parental vetoes," as Freud called it, plus, probably, the inherited conventions imposed upon us from the centuries of tabus and demands which lie behind us. One might call it the "pedestal-self"; by which I mean the self we try to keep on a pedestal through fear of falling below the standard imposed upon us by others, or by our position, or by our own complexes. The "id" is the primeval self underneath our conventional good manners built up through civilising influences and the standards of our set. The id is the amoral instinctive self, and its energy is that of instincts constantly demanding crude expression. The id has no principle save avoiding pain and seeking pleasure, though it concurs in a "reality principle" which recognises the situation with realism and chooses what will work well rather than an immediate pleasure that soon brings pain.

The super-ego is in conflict in every man with the id, but if the conflict rages in the unconscious, and if, for instance, the super-ego is inflated by the undeserved esteem of the public, a man is like one who inhabits a room, on the ceiling of which the super-ego in the attic knocks, demanding him to come up, and on the floor of which the id in the cellar knocks, demanding him to come down and respond to its needs, and he is distracted and torn asunder. He must first recognise both elements, and then make terms with them. He must not yield to either completely, for neither would let the other have all its own way. That which he *ought* to do and that which he *wants* to do must be co-ordinated in an "ego-ideal," and then harmony can be restored. This ego (I prefer Hadfield's term "ego-ideal") is weak at first, but can become integrated and organised to face life successfully, deriving its energies from the id and the super-ego as it learns to control them. The id remains primitive and unorganised, and the super-ego impossible of attainment. Its demands produce that sense of exaggerated and pathological guilt which is so marked a feature of so many neuroses.

Freud typically thinks that the thwarted sex desire in the child is the main cause of his developing this super-ego. In both *The Interpretation of Dreams* (1900) and in his *Introductory Lectures on Psychoanalysis* (1922) Freud made much of the love of the male child for his mother and his "hatred" of his father, the father being a competitor with the child for the possession of the mother, the beloved object of infantile sexual desire. This complex raging in the unconscious, Freud called the Œdipus complex, after Œdipus, the hero of the Greek legend, who, because he was lame, was exposed by his father, Laius, the King of Thebes, with a spike through his feet, the oracle having predicted that Œdipus would kill his father and marry Jocasta, his mother. Œdipus was rescued and adopted by a foreign king, and grew to manhood, ignorant both of this parentage and his predicted fate. In his wanderings he met his father, whom he did not recognise, quarrelled with and slew him, reached Thebes and delivered it from a pest which cursed it, and was given the widowed queen as his wife. Thus he did hate his father and marry his mother, and the story served Freud well for the title of his newly discovered complex. Even as early as the age of five, the male child is passing, in his sexual development, into the phallic phase. His attachment to his mother brings him sensual longings for her physical contact and caresses. Yet his mother apparently prefers his father. They sleep together, though the child longs for his mother to sleep with him. The father thus becomes a rival—a most powerful rival, too—who probably compels his mother to desert him. The male child begins to hate his father and to want to destroy him. He frequently supposes that his father feels the same about him, and that his father will try to destroy his sexual love for his mother by rendering its expression impossible—that is, by cutting off his penis, round which sexual enjoyment and excitement are beginning to gather. We can see the conflict clearly. The boy wants his mother, but if he gets her he will call down on himself the destructive anger of his father, who will castrate him.

Most psychologists regard as gross exaggeration Freud's insistence that this represents the emotional attitude of all male children. No doubt a baby boy's love-life (libido) runs out powerfully to his mother, especially in the weaning period. The young boy may feel frustrated by his father, who wins in the competition for the mother's love. The child cannot love as the father does, and he may wish his rival were dead. But that this thrusts him into oral, anal and auto-erotic gratification, much less hate of the father, with severe repression of sexual desire, seems to me unproved. Freud suggests that these infantile emotional reactions make the male child seek to identify himself with his father, the successful lover of his mother. At the same time he develops guilt, in that he really desires to kill his father, but knows he "ought not" to wish either to kill his father or love his mother emotionally, and out of this emotional material develops his "super-ego."

If a young boy's mind develops healthily, part of his mind will realise that his father cannot allow rivals and competitors for the love of his mother. The boy will therefore repress sexual love for his mother and love her tenderly but not sexually. Then he will release the repressed hostility to his father and sublimate it in obedience and reverence, and later, comradeship, for he will recognise the father's supreme sexual rights in the mother.

A similar complex is called the Electra complex, presumably after the legendary daughter of Agamemnon and Clytaemnestra who hated the latter, her mother, and with the help of Orestes, whom she had rescued, contrived her mother's death. This complex is brought about by the girl loving her father and hating her mother, with fear and guilt emotional reactions similar to those induced in the boy by the Œdipus complex.

It is hard to understand Freud's reasoning here, for in his later writings, at any rate, he argues that *"the first sexual object of both girls and boys is the mother,"* and obviously the Œdipus complex is emphasised out of all proportion to the Electra complex. One is almost compelled to the view that a kind of mental sense of symmetry obliged him to rake up the myth of Electra. He later abandoned his belief in the Electra complex, and even withdrew the earlier emphasis he had laid on the Œdipus complex as a source of neurosis.

While much of Freud's teaching is exaggerated, we must give him first place as the pioneer psychologist who realised the importance of unconscious motivation, who outlined a hypothesis of the unconscious mind, and who first showed that the neurosis, with all its physically and mentally distressing concomitants, is in one sense *desired* because life has become intolerable in its conflicting demands; that it must be tackled from within the patient, not by drugs and outward treatment, and that to fall into neurosis is not blameworthy. The patient is ill, as a patient with measles is ill. When the neurosis has developed, he cannot control what his unconscious does to him. The unconscious factors must be dragged up into consciousness. Until then the neurotic is a *patient.* Even then he must be helped to reintegrate his personality to reality. After analysis there must be synthesis, and, in the latter, religion—as I hope to show in a later section—can play a vital part. I feel that the fundamental weakness and condemnation of Freudian psycho-analysis is its entire lack of interest in a subsequent re-orientation of synthesis. Christ's parable of the house swept and garnished and afterwards occupied by seven other devils is a most relevant comment here.

Waterhouse thinks that even the cures of a Freudian analysis are no evidence of the value of its technique. He thinks that although Freud disbelieves in suggestion, the Freudian analyst employs it, even if unconsciously. He thinks that a Freudian analysis is like a "third-degree" police examination which would make the patient ready to agree to any theory thrust upon him. He writes, "The cures wrought by psycho-analysis may conceivably owe little to the methods and even less to the dogmas of the system." [13]

[13] *Op. cit.,* p. 8.

2

ADLER AND INDIVIDUAL PSYCHOLOGY

(Alfred Adler, 1870-1937)

IT IS NOT surprising that a man like Freud should attract to himself other scientists who were impressed by his teachings. Amongst these was Alfred Adler, a young Viennese doctor of Jewish parents, who, early in life, became a Christian. He took his degree in 1895, and at first was more interested in ophthalmology than in psychiatry. Freud's influence, however, swung Adler, who was interested in philosophy and sociology, into the new interest, and he became one of Freud's greatest admirers and worked with him in the closest intimacy. Indeed, there is little doubt that Adler contributed some of the ideas which Freud worked into his system.

But in 1912 Adler felt that his ideas diverged so seriously from those of Freud that it was farcical for the two to remain in harness. Adler, who had defended Freud in the Press against some of the many attacks made against him, withdrew and started a new school of what he called "Individual Psychology." Approving neither of Jung's "Collective Unconscious" nor of Freud's sex emphases, Adler regarded each patient as, in a special sense, a separate individual in whom memory differs profoundly. "Individuals," he wrote, "do not form their unconscious memories all around the same central motive—sexuality, for instance." [1] Each individual has a different need, an inferiority for which he seeks compensation. "The method of Individual Psychology," he said, "begins and ends with the problem of inferiority." [2] Adler felt that Freud's emphasis on sex was overdone and his doctrine of the libido false. Where Adler would have described the libido as the stream of psychic energy flowing from all the instincts and

---

[1] Alfred Adler, *The Science of Living* (Greenberg, 1929).   [2] *Op. cit.*

267

coloured by them all, for Freud the libido was the energy of the sex instinct alone. True, Freud translated the word "sex" in the widest possible way. Its aspects of paternity and maternity were included.[3] Adler recognised the importance of the sex instinct and its ramifications and power, but he felt he had a clue which was a key to open doors far more easily and readily than Freud's master key of sex, which he violently used to open up any psychological problem with which he was faced.

This clue was that neurosis—the faulty emotional adjustment of the individual to reality, to himself, to others and to life generally—was almost always due to a sense of inferiority. At first Adler thought it was due to organic inferiority alone. He himself remembered vividly being hindered through rickets from joining in the active games in which his healthier elder brother delighted. Adler claimed that if, for example, a child had one leg shorter than another, or a squint, or disabling illness, he felt inferior, and frequently compensated for this feeling by some exaggerated reaction. Later, Adler modified this, and said that, for whatever cause—other than organic inferiority being allowed—the neurotic always *felt* inferior, though he might not admit it, the inferiority going back to the first five years of life, and that his neurosis was his unconscious attempt to compensate for this feeling and achieve a sense of almost god-like power. In doing so he often became a social, or even anti-social, finding his outlet apart from the "welfare" of the community. Adler dogmatically stated that "all forms of neurosis and developmental failure are expressions of inferiority and disappointment." [4] "The science of Individual Psychology," he says, "developed out of the effort to understand that mysterious creative power of life—that power which expresses itself in the desire to develop, to strive, to achieve—and even to compensate for defeats in one direction by striving for success in another. This power is teleological—it expresses itself in the striving after a goal, and in this striving every bodily and psychic movement is made to co-operate." [5]

Everyone possesses a "will to power." He writes, "Every bodily or mental attitude indicates clearly its origin in a striving for power,

[3] In an earlier book I have attempted a new classification of the instincts, reducing them to three—Self, Sex and Social, and calling their derivatives "aspects." I have listed their related emotions. See *Psychology and Life* (Abingdon-Cokesbury, 1935).

[4] Adler, *Individual Psychology*, p. vi (Kegan Paul, 1929).

[5] *Science of Living*.

and carries within itself the ideal of a kind of perfection and infallibility." If this dominating purpose is frustrated, or the patient *feels* that it is frustrated, he will seek some kind of gratification, even if it is only in the realm of pretence or fantasy. Whatever happens, he must dominate, as a family circle often knows to its cost. He will dominate any part of the community he can. That which he cannot dominate he will refuse to co-operate with. If the feeling arises that the part with which he will not co-operate and cannot dominate does not feel, or care, about him, he will harbour the view that one day it will perish, he and the party with which he identified himself being vindicated.[6] Some of the great people of the world, in Adler's view, have become great because they have, either by choice or accident, hit on a means of compensating for their sense of inferiority in a way that has brought them the plaudits of their fellows. One thinks of the Kaiser, of Napoleon, of Roosevelt, each with a pronounced "organ inferiority." Adler himself decided to be a doctor because of his own ill-health. He wanted weapons with which to fight illness because it made him miserable and inferior. In the humbler ranks, many a schoolboy, debarred from prowess at games, has shone as a naturalist or as a scholar. This "will to power," or, as I classified it in an earlier book, the assertive aspect of the self-instinct, Adler regarded as more dominating than the sex urge which Freud had labelled the main driving force of personality. Where Freud saw a patient's mental fantasies as distorted pictures of sex gratification, Adler saw them as a style of life or pattern of behaviour which delivered the patient from the sense that he was a poor, inferior, weak sort of creature, and contributed to his picture of himself as dominating his situation, at any rate to his own satisfaction.

On the other hand, of course, many become neurotic patients because their attempt to compensate for supposed inferiority, so far from making them great, brings them a crippling sense of failure and thus of conflict. Their "life plan" just does not work.

Adler claimed that he could spot this "life plan" at his first interview with a patient, and that he then found that all the symptoms of the neurosis fell into place like parts of a machine. They served both the "life plan" and the goal of superiority which the patient sought.

To achieve this superiority is obviously impossible for the neurotic in the real world, so he twists reality into fantasy to obtain a sphere in which his superiority is never denied or overthrown. This Adler

---

[6] Cf. the feeling among the Jews that God would deliver the chosen people, and in the early Church that Christ would return and carry His own people to eternal triumph, the rest of humanity being in some sense damned.

calls "the creation of a compensatory psychic super-structure." [7] The patient will also "produce" illness motivated thus: "If I had not this illness, I could succeed as easily as anyone else, and, indeed, achieve superiority over others at any point I desired." Therefore, the patient must cling to his illness, or the bluff of his claim to superiority would be called. He would see through himself. So the illness must be convincing enough, i.e. serious, and even disabling enough, to maintain the pretence. And the pretence, it may be added, is not culpable, for the patient is the last person to realise that pretence does lie behind his neurosis. He is unconscious that his symptoms are excuses for the non-fulfilment of his life-plan; substitutes for the superiority which fulfilment would bring, and that decisions which would mean grappling with life are postponed for a most satisfying reason—namely, illness.

Such a patient is common enough. He delights to report his symptoms, claims that he wants to be well, recites the enormous difficulties he is facing, blames others for his apparent difficulties and, without realising it, lacks courage. "His chief occupation in life," says Adler,[8] "is to look for difficulties. . . . He does this more to impress himself than others, but naturally other people take his burdens into account and . . . he wins his way to a privileged life, judged by a more lenient standard than others. At the same time, he pays the costs of it with his neurosis."

Like Freud, Adler believed that the pattern of life congealed as a result of very early experiences. But where Freud, the determinist, taught that inevitably certain traumatic experiences set up certain emotional stresses, Adler wrote: "We do not suffer from the shock of our experiences—the so-called trauma—but we make out of them just what suits our purposes. *We are self-determined by the meaning we give to our own experiences.*" [9] "We are masters of our own actions. If something new must be done, or something old replaced, no-one need do it but ourselves." [10]

Organic inferiority, or being so petted as to be made to feel inferior through the loss of independence, or being hated and judged to be of no use in the world, determines a definite pattern of behaviour.[11]

---

[7] *Individual Psychology*, p. 32 (Kegan Paul, 1929).

[8] *Problems of Neurosis* (Cosmopolitan Book, 1930).

[9] Alfred Adler, *What Life Should Mean to You* (Little, Brown, 1931). Italics mine.

[10] *Op. cit.*

[11] It must be remembered that "an original organic weakness *when subsequently corrected*, may yet live on in a *permanent feeling of weakness* and make an individual unfit for life." Adler, *Individual Psychology*, p. 320.

This pattern was the reaction against handicap. The sense of handicap spelt dependence and the consequent fear common in any environment in which the individual has never learnt independence. This sense of incompletion made the patient seek compensation, and Adler's treatment was that of talking with the patient and getting the patient to talk to him.

The object of the conversation was to get the patient to make an adequate social adjustment. "Social adjustment," Adler said, "is the obverse face of the problem of inferiority. It is because the individual man is inferior and weak that we find human beings living in society. Social interest and social co-operation are, therefore, the salvation of the individual." [12]

In a sense Adler's treatment proceeded backwards. He first ascertained the superiority goal, explaining to the patient, in the light of it, the conflict he had precipitated, and only then attempting to investigate the sources of the vital psychic mechanism; "retracing all the nervous symptoms back to their lowest common denominator," [13] studying with the patient the meaning of his dreams, noting any inadvertent revelations of himself which the patient might make through his mannerisms, hesitancies, choice of words, and so on, each interview leading to Adler's oft-repeated questions, "And why do you feel like that about it? What do you think is the reason of your reacting in this way? What purpose does your illness serve?" Adler's method might be summed up in the phrase, "therapeutic conversation." Gradually the patient realised how he had got into the way of making a neurotic reaction to his problems, and he was then in a position to substitute a wise for a foolish reaction, a courageous for a cowardly one, a normal for a hysterical one. "Never promise success to a patient," Adler counselled his psychologist-disciples. "Always ascribe success to the co-operation and work of the patient, who is to be employed as a fellow-worker and treated like a friend. Remember that the patient's urge to superiority makes him secure, if he can, the discomfiture of the doctor. Prophesy an aggravation of symptoms, and never show pleasure at partial success or boast about it." [14]

Adler would not allow a patient to escape with the idea that his heredity determined his behaviour. He used to say of himself that he "chose" the mental and spiritual qualities of his father in preference to the qualities of his mother. True, a child often adopted the same kind

[12] *The Science of Living.*
[13] *Individual Psychology*, p. 17 (Kegan Paul, 1929).
[14] *Individual Psychology*, p. 43.

of unsound reaction to difficulty as his mother, but Adler held it was because he copied her, not because he inherited the same kind of attitude, though he might inherit the organic defect that led to his father's choice of symptom.[15] Phyllis Bottome, in her life of Adler,[16] tells of an amusing case which Adler handled in which the patient insisted that she inherited her hysterical rash from her mother. Unfortunately for the patient, the mother disclosed the hitherto closely guarded secret that the child was adopted, and not her own at all. The hysteria had been copied. The child saw that it "worked." It got the mother out of her difficulties. By its means the mother got her own way. What more natural than that the child's unconscious mind should try the same dodge to attain the same success?

Yet Adler noted that the child of brilliant parents frequently will not copy his parents' industry and painstaking effort, which even the genius must put forward to attain the top of the tree. More likely, such a child will develop an "illness." His reaction is—"Ill as I am I cannot be expected to do what my father has done or attain the heights he has reached." Woodworth writes: "The child of very poor parents, but of attractive appearance, may adopt a begging attitude which persists later in all sorts of situations. The spoiled child seeks to be the centre of attention. That is his goal. The hated child adopts the goal of escaping to a safe distance. The eldest child adopts the attitude of keeping what he has, a conservative attitude. The second child from the start is behind in the race and develops the attitude of seeking to surpass. This may be the attitude also of the youngest child, though he is rather likely to develop the attitude of the spoiled child. The only child, never having met competition, assumes that others will serve and he rule." [17]

These attitudes tend to be fixed as characteristic reactions which persist into later life, and in the hard school of life lead to neurosis and breakdown, or to anti-social activity, or to a kind of piety not far from neurosis which justifies the patient in withdrawing from this wicked world and living in the fantasy world of an unreal religion,[18] where the "consolations of religion" are lapped up and its inexorable challenge evaded; where the love of God is basked in, and His stern severity overlooked. Again, the only child finds that others will not

[15] *Op. cit.*, p. 18.

[16] *Alfred Adler: A Biography* (Putnam, 1939).

[17] *Op. cit.*

[18] We shall discuss later to what extent religion is itself a neurosis and a cowardly retreat from the demands of living in the real world.

allow his supremacy. His "will to power," defeated in that direction, will find other, often anti-social, ways of supremacy. He may use worse language than any other boy in the class, or engage in mischief, or even crime, to satisfy his "will to power." [19] Many criminals are certainly patients needing treatment, for whom the clumsy State method of doling out scheduled punishment only does harm. On the other hand, he may join the Oxford Group, or start a prayer meeting or tell the world that he is going to be a missionary.

Treatment, then, for Adler, is first of all enquiry into the "family constellation," the discovery of the "map" of the patient's way of life, noting how he seeks to reach his goal of supremacy, how, when one goal is frustrated, he seeks another. No detail was unworthy of the Adlerian psychologist's attention. In minute things, with Adler as with Freud, a patient's inner intention might be detected.

Adler, like Freud, believed that a patient's dreams were sign-posts of immense importance. He writes, "I found their main function to consist of simplified early trials, and of warnings and encouragements favourable to the life-plan; and to have as their object the solution of some future problem." [20] And again, "We dream in the way that we would like to behave. Dreams are an emotional rehearsal of plans and attitudes for waking behaviour—a rehearsal, however, in which the actual play may never come off." [21] But where Freud would see in them repressed sexuality, Adler would regard them as dramatised situations revolving around the patient's will to power. To him they were clues to the patient's life-plan. They showed up the patient's fears and hesitancies, the obstacles in his way to some kind of supremacy and the steps he contemplated taking to surmount or avoid them. Adler's patients also showed resistance, but it was not resistance against betraying unconscious desires. To Adler the unconscious was the "not understood" rather than the repressed. "To understand," he would have said, "is to control." And the resistance was a hostility to being made well because the illness was preferable to the disclosure of circumstances which a well and healthy patient would be expected by society to tackle bravely.

To use my own nomenclature, Adler recognised that in the instinct of "self" were the *aspects* both of self-assertion and of self-abasement

[19] This point is nowhere better demonstrated than in Sir Cyril Burt's, *The Young Delinquent* (Appleton 1925).

[20] *Individual Psychology*, p. 38.

[21] *The Science of Living*. Adler expounds his view on dreams very clearly in *What life should mean to you*.

or submission. Freud gave them both a sexual twist. Sadism and masochism developed, he thought, from each respectively. Adler gave them no sexual colour, but regarded them as expressions of the will to power. He called "submission" the feminine role of passivism. Of this self-assertion he wrote at length, and labelled it "the masculine protest," it being taken for granted that "the feminine sex is inferior and by its reaction serves as the measure of masculine strength." [22] This desire for power is, "I want to be a man." "It permeates boys and girls to such a frightful degree that we are, from the very first, forced to assume that this attitude came to the front to counterbalance the non-pleasurable sensation of not being masculine." [23] Men use it to assert their supremacy over women. Women use it as over-compensation for their apparent inferiority through the fact of their femininity. The latter is similar to Freud's theory of the castration-complex. "The psyche," Adler wrote, "partakes of both feminine and masculine traits. Both appear to strive for unity, but purposely fail in their synthesis in order to rescue the personality from colliding with reality." [24] Adler seems to mean by reality, the patient's attitude to his job in life, to his love affairs, and to his social responsibilities. Hysterical illness often marks a patient's failure to face the first, sexual neurosis the second, and crime the third.

We note in Adler's treatment a more loving and kindly relationship to the patient than Freud's cold scientific method obtained. He really did love his patients in the New Testament sense of showing them endless goodwill. He once said of clergy and ministers that they were the best to spread his ideas "because their profession is already one of goodwill." On another occasion he said: [25] "The clergy are the chief practitioners of social interest by profession, and also—which specially appeals to me—they need not take money from their patients. I have always felt this to be a real disadvantage to psychologists who practice character training. It would be far better not to have a question of money between them and their patients. . . . They could treat their patients' psychological difficulties without any question of personal interest arising between them." His system is much closer to religion than Freud's, for Adler's "cure" involved that the patient, having seen how he is reacting wrongly to life, must change his entire way of living,

[22] *Individual Psychology*, p. 35.

[23] *Individual Psychology*, p. 85.

[24] I quote here from McDougall who comments on "the masculine protest" in his *Outline of Abnormal Psychology* (Scribner, 1926).

[25] Phyllis Bottome, *op. cit.*

no longer looking for ways of establishing prestige and superiority which leave the real problems of life unsolved, but serving the community, and, in losing his life, finding it. It may be asked whether a patient, apart from a power outside himself, can successfully re-direct his life along altruistic channels. Freud used to say, "Why should I love my neighbour?" Adler goes one better. The patient *must* love his neighbour. Yet that "must" is hard to fulfil. One wonders, indeed, whether its fulfilment is possible apart from religion. In my view, only as man sees his neighbour as his brother, because both are equally loved of God, can he, relying on divine grace, show that unbreakable goodwill to his brother which the word "love" connotes. "One of the greatest difficulties in treatment," said Adler, in a sentence of unusual candour, "is the fact that the patient, although he may possess the proper insight into the nature of the neurotic mechanism, still partially maintains his symptoms." [26]

With equal candour, he writes,[27] "It is not easy to change a child, who, for ten, fifteen or twenty years, has been a weakling, pampered by everyone, into the courageous man, full of the initiative, enterprise and self-confidence demanded by our times."

Adler's system has much to commend it. Many cases of neurosis seem exactly to fit the framework of his theories. He falls sometimes into absurd exaggerations which are hard to believe, as when he says, in his paper on Syphilophobia, "I have rarely encountered a case of neurosis that did not disclose, in a marked manner, a train of thought indicating a fear of syphilis."

Further, I myself hold that if one main factor in neurosis is to be indicated more than another as supremely causal, it is not sexual repression, as Freud taught, or the hunger for superiority and power, as Adler taught—though I readily conceded Adler's statement that "everyone who has developed a capacity for reading the child's soul, must have realised that every child possesses an *extraordinary craving for power and importance*." [28]

I should have named as the most potent causal factor of neurosis the frustrated hunger to be loved, where love means more than the sentimental and erotic, namely the desire for approval, the longing to be appreciated, the basic need of being treated, by at least someone, with goodwill. If so, religion, as we shall see, has a vital part to play in any thorough curative psychological treatment.

[26] *Individual Psychology*, p. 228.
[27] *Op. cit.*, p. 319.
[28] *Op. cit.*, p. 342. (Italics mine.)

Adler appears to the present writer to exaggerate the importance and frequency of the sense of inferiority almost as much as Freud exaggerates the role of sex. Adler would ascribe almost all greatness to effort educed as compensation for some defect, mental or physical, which has produced inferiority. But it would be a strange philosophy to assert the necessity of defect to attain the highest excellence, and the facts do not, in my view, support it.

3

JUNG AND ANALYTICAL PSYCHOLOGY

(Jung, born 1875)

ONE OF THE most brilliant of the band of eager disciples which Freud gathered round him was the Swiss scholar, Carl Gustav Jung, of Zurich, born at Basle in 1875, of whom Freud thought so highly that he made him president of the International Association of Psychoanalysis.

Jung shows a sympathy with the religious attitude to life, due perhaps to the fact that he was the son of a well-known Swiss clergyman. He was less a scientist than a philosopher, and a mystic philosopher at that. He drew upon himself the criticisms of his adversaries by what some regard as the most useful part of his treatment. His critics said the job of the analyst is to lay bare the causes of faulty adjustment, but not to give advice. Jung's "psychotherapeutic conversations" went farther than this. He gave advice. Having laid bare, he bound up, and was, in a truer sense than Freud, and even than Adler, a doctor of souls. As we shall see when we discuss fully his attitude to religion, he taught that religion plays an important part in mental health.

Now, however, we must note the specific contribution he brought to our theme of healing. He was a scientist also; a trained medical psychologist, with a mystical insight that made him growingly dissatisfied with Freud's scientific and clear-cut categories, and finally made him break away in 1911 from his master, and formulate with Maeder his own system, which he called Analytical Psychology.

Jung found that Freud's "pan-sexuality" did not make sense in accounting for some of the symptoms of patients whom he tried to help, even if the word "sexual" were stretched to its widest possible connotation. To Jung the "libido" was not predominantly sexual. It was the stream of psychic energy, the *élan vital* of Bergson, which flowed in every personality and gave it its driving power. Jung's view of the libido is reminiscent of the theory of physical energy held by the physicists of his day. The current of sexuality flowed in this stream. The latter included the former, but was not to be identified with it. Also contained in it were Adler's "will to power" and the energies of the other instincts, and also—and this figures largely in Jung's theory—a stream of energy having its source in racial experiences common to all men and going back in human history earlier than the differentiation of individuality.

These racial experiences, which all men shared, existed in what Jung called the "collective unconscious," and still acted potently in determining man's character and actions, his moods and thoughts.

The idea of the collective unconscious as differentiated from the personal unconscious is unique. Jung argued that if the personal unconscious alone existed, then when successful analysis took place, during which its repressed material was brought to the surface, the unconscious would be "emptied" and rendered unable to manufacture fantasies and dreams. Yet it continues to do the latter.[1] On the other hand, the collective unconscious "seems not to be a person, but something like an unceasing stream, or perhaps an ocean of images and figures which drift into unconsciousness in our dreams or in abnormal states of mind."[2] The collective unconscious thus contains "a wisdom that is deposited and lying potential in the human brain."[3]

Jung found that in ancient customs, ceremonies and tabus, in the myths and legends, the fairy stories and folk-lore, the old sagas and fables and witchcraft, the proverbs and sayings which exist in the literature of all races, these influential ideas were still enshrined, and that, during times of strain, a patient would submit to that influence and regress to primordial ways of thinking and acting. The appeal of the myth, for example, lay in the fact that it expressed a truth or an experience which men "recognised," which—if the phrase be allowed—the collective unconscious recognised. The personal unconscious was one thing. It was formed by repression, as Freud taught. But the collective unconscious, from which both the personal conscious and unconscious are born, is something very much older than the individual himself. Here is a vast reservoir of the racial memories and experiences

---

[1] *Collected Papers on Analytical Psychology*, trans. C. E. Long (Dodd, 1916), quoted from Woodward, *op. cit.*).

[2] *Modern Man in Search of a Soul.*

[3] Jung, *Two Essays on Analytical Psychology.*

of all men, inherited as part of the mind of the individual. Within every mind, functioning unconsciously, are the impulses of the savage and the ruling and directing mental factors of man at every stage of his long evolution. These impulses have never been put into language. In a sense they are deeper than thought. Says Jung, "The soul possesses historical strata, the oldest stratum of which is unconscious." [4] This collective unconscious contains instincts, ancestral modes of behaviour and ancestral interpretations of experience to which man is liable, under strain, to revert.

Dispositions arising from the collective unconscious dominated men; some appealing to one type, others dominating another. Such a disposition, or "mythological motif," or "primordial idea," or "collective image," he called an "archetype," borrowing the term from St. Augustine.[5] The instincts "form very close analogies to the archetypers," Jung tells us, "so close, in fact, that there is reason for assuming that the archetypes are the unconscious images of the instincts themselves." [6] The archetypes, he tells us elsewhere, are "inherited potentialities of human imagination." [7] They are "systems of preparedness that are at the same time images and emotions. They are not inherited ideas, but inherited possibilities of ideas, inherited with the structure of the brain of which they represent the psychic aspect." [8] Men's dreams revealed the nature of the archetype, which, in any one patient, rose up from the memories of the race buried in the "collective unconscious," and tended to make the patient think and act in specific ways. Among the archetypes Jung named are "the shadow," a kind of darker self within the ego, the "anima," or the woman within the man, the sum of the feminine characteristics present in all men, "the wise old man, the superior master and teacher and guide." All archetypes are not personalised by Jung. Some represent typical situations, or symbols of change. The patient's dreams also gave a useful clue anent his unconscious attitude to the problem which his failure to meet had made him "break down," and Jung claimed that in a patient's dreams and drawings he could recognise the symbols and images of the forgotten civilisations of Egypt, Mexico, Greece and Rome. He encouraged his

[4] Jung, *Psychology of the Unconscious* (Dodd, 1916).

[5] Jung, *Contributions to Analytical Psychology.*

[6] Jung, "The Concept of the Collective Unconscious," in *St. Bartholomew's Hospital Journal*, December 1936, p. 47. (I owe this quotation to the Rev. Fred. Roberts, M.A.)

[7] *Collected Papers.*

[8] *Contributions to Analytical Psychology.*

patients to draw and paint their dreams, and he studied these sketches carefully. He wrote of them thus:

"A feature common to all these pictures is a primitive symbolism which is conspicuous both in the drawing and in the colouring. The colours are usually quite barbaric in their intensity; often, too, an archaic quality is present. These peculiarities point to the nature of the creative forces which have produced the pictures. They are non-rational, symbolistic currents in the evolution of man, and are so archaic that it is easy to draw parallels between them and similar manifestations in the fields of archæology and comparative religion. We may, therefore, readily assume that these pictures originate chiefly in that realm of psychic life which I have called the collective unconscious. By this term I designate an unconscious psychic activity present in all human beings which not only gives rise to symbolical pictures today, but was the source of all similar products of the past. Such pictures spring from—and satisfy—a natural need. It is as if, through these pictures, we bring to expression that part of the psyche which reaches back into the primitive past and reconcile it with present day consciousness, thus mitigating its disturbing effects upon the latter." [9]

A patient unable in childhood to resist the archetypal drive, the tendency to fall back on ways of thought typical of primitive man, would attack some difficult situation in accordance with that drive. Often this would be an ineffective way of dealing with the difficulty, and failure, or, in other words, a faulty adaptation to life, would follow. As the child grew up he would forget this, but if, in adult life, he was faced with another similar and demanding crisis, he would tend to react in the same way, and, the attempt being a faulty attitude, the patient would feel unable to cope with life and become ill. He would break down. He would develop "neurosis." He would so feel the pull of age-old racial tendencies and stresses that he would be unable to make a new adaptation to some sudden demand. He might even regress to childish ways of escaping the demands of life, and sink into a life in which fantasy became his reality.[10] Without so labelling them, he would once more be in the grip of the demons and dragons, the fairies and witches, from whose clutch the race has so comparatively recently, and with such difficulty, disengaged itself. Pushed hard enough, he thus became psychotic and entirely out of

[9] *Modern Man in Search of a Soul* (Harcourt, 1933).

[10] Primitive man probably could not clearly distinguish between what we call a happening and what we call a fantasy, cf. the phrase, "I must have dreamt it." Individuality and differentiation are only comparatively recent in the history of the human race.

touch with the real world. Insanity is a retreat from a real world which has become intolerable. We speak of being *driven* mad. Even the most balanced mind is disturbed at times by moods of depression and fear which have no conscious origin, and which, Jung says, rise like a horrid miasma from the dark and silent sea of the collective unconscious.

Neurosis, then, to Jung, might be traceable in origin to some infantile failure to meet life's demand, a failure attributable again to some archetypal stress in the collective unconscious, but its exciting and immediate cause was a present failure in adaptation, and treatment lay along the line of talking over the patient's *present situation* with him, showing him how and why he "broke down" and helping him to make an effective adaptation. "Only a still existing cause," Jung wrote in *Modern Man in Search of a Soul*, "can keep a neurosis active." Where Freud would encourage the patient to seek in the past the origin of his difficulties, Jung would make him face the present. Jung regarded Freud's tendency to go back to the patient's infancy as contributing to a kind of escapism, blaming the past as if it were deterministic, instead of facing up to his very present problem. The problem, indeed, might have a significance derived from an earlier stage that even Freud taught, but it was the present that must be tackled. Jung asked, "How can I help the patient to act *now* in an adult way, and how can I harmonise— or help him do so—the gap between intelligent thought and the apparently inconsequent action that follows, and which betrays neurotic elements at work? I simply contest the notion," he wrote, "that all neuroses . . . arise without exception from some crucial experience of childhood . . . (the patient) is forced to search in his memory— perhaps over a course of years—for a hypothetical event in his childhood, while things of immediate importance are grossly neglected." [11] "I no longer find the cause of the neurosis in the past," he wrote again,[12] "but in the present. I ask what is the necessary task which the patient will not accomplish." The answer must often be that the patient, dominated by archetypes of one kind or another, refuses, or is unable, to grow up and react in an adult manner.

Just as the child *in utero* passes through the physical stages of evolution, so the individual, Jung believes, passes mentally through the stages between primitive and civilised man. But sometimes, during the emotional recapitulation, a personality gets "stuck," and although physically adult, remains psychologically fixated at some childish emotional level.

[11] *Modern Man in Search of a Soul.*
[12] *Collected Papers on Analytical Psychology.*

Unable, at this level, to face the demands of life, he "breaks down." Treatment is aimed at revealing this to him in a way which helps him to realise it himself, and then helping him to integrate his conscious ego with the non-ego material, the latter including the so-called "collective unconscious." Integration, then, for Jung, is progression towards an adult and worthwhile goal. He is sympathetic to the idea of synthesis following analysis, for what has been separated at a deep level must be joined at a higher.

On being shown the conflict between conscious and unconscious factors operating in his attempt to face his problems, the patient could be stimulated to "put away childishness" and solve them manfully. Then his neurosis disappeared. He must admit that primeval ideas and superstitions in the unconscious still have power over him. Quietly and calmly, as he contemplates all the factors which influence thought and action, and summons all his powers, he can regain the mastery of his mental world, and thus of his life. Integration was effected.

Jung teaches, however, that integration is costly and demands a self-discipline both of character and intellect. The patient must do more than assent to the psychologist. He must mentally strip naked, hide nothing from the physician, but, more importantly, face his own naked soul, however painful and whatever the temptation mentally to run away. The neurotic is often soaked in self-deception. He must, for a successful Jungian treatment, abandon every known hiding-place, come out into the open, cling no longer to tattered excuse or hide under well-worn lies which he has treated for so long as if they were truth that he now believes them to be true. All self-deception, he must learn, ruins the efficacy of treatment and makes the neurosis incurable.

One of Jung's most important claims was that men could be divided into extroverts and introverts, and that their physical make-up determines which predominates. We must spend some time on this, for it is more complicated than the words suggest. It is not merely a division into those who are objective and those who are subjective; those who look out, away from themselves, and those who look in and endlessly contemplate themselves. If it were merely a matter of such a division, we should know into which category to put ourselves. Jung says this is extremely difficult. "It is often a difficult matter to discover to which type an individual belongs, especially when oneself is in question." [13]

Introversion, to Jung, is not merely gazing morbidly at one's own mental activity; it is to live in the unreal world of fantasy. In regard to sex, for example, finding no outward expression of sex energies,

[13] *Psychological Types* (Harcourt, 1923).

introverts meditate, even in adult life, on imaginary scenes in which the prohibited objective incidents of sex activity take place subjectively with a reality greater than the sense of reality associated with a normal person's life in the objective world.

Such introversion renders the patient more and more incapable of facing any situation in the real world. He acts like a child, is upset by trifles, cannot bear criticism, flies from the stern demands of life, escaping wherever he can. The normal adaptation to reality having failed, the patient regresses to a more primitive adaptation, and then despises himself for using it and vents his spleen on all and sundry.

Jung holds that, since every patient desires to strike a balance, "to maintain psychic equilibrium," as he calls it, it being "biologically expedient" to do so, he unconsciously tends to make a compensation for the onesidedness of his type, and thus presents the appearance of being a type far different from that which is inwardly true. We see this, for example, in a person with a sense of inferiority. The form of his "compensation" may disguise the inferiority both from himself and from the observer. He may develop a fantastic pride and boastfulness not based on factual realities. As Jung says,[14] he sets up "a fiction to balance the inferiority." Both he and other observers see the camouflage, but even if they recognise it as camouflage, they cannot easily detect what it is that is being camouflaged.

But the matter is rendered more complicated by the suggestion made by Jung, that Nature herself tries to accomplish such a balance, so that a patient who is consciously an introvert is extroverted in the unconscious and vice versa. "The unconscious," he writes, "so far as we can now see, has a compensatory function in respect to consciousness."[15]

Everyone is both an introvert and an extrovert. It is the relative predominance of the one or the other that determines the type. Jung defines as follows: [16] "The introverted standpoint is one that, under all circumstances, sets the self and the subjective psychological process above the object and the objective process, or, at any rate, holds its ground against the object. . . . The extroverted standpoint, on the contrary, sets the subject below the object, whereby the object receives the predominant value. The subject always has secondary importance; the subjective process appears at times merely as a disturbing or superfluous accessory to objective events." Normality would be seen in a

[14] Op. cit.
[15] Contributions to Analytical Psychology.
[16] Psychological Types.

balanced expression of both introversion and extroversion, but what with outer circumstances and the "pull" of unconscious subjective factors, most people chronically react one way or another. This habitual reaction makes them into "types" of either introversion or extroversion.

Jung made a further distinction according to the functions of thinking, feeling, sensation and intuition. "If one of these functions prevails, a corresponding type results. I, therefore, discriminate thinking, feeling, sensation and intuitive types. *Every one of these types can moreover be introverted or extroverted* according to his relation to the object." [17] Jung felt that this view harmonised to some extent the views of Freud and those of Adler. The extrovert was dominated by feeling and motivated by the libido in Freud's sense. The introvert was dominated by thought and reverie and was motivated by the "will to power" in the way Adler conceived. For Jung the libido was the total life energy moving in the extrovert to outward objects and in the introvert to his own subjective ideas, interests and aims.

Yet it seems highly dangerous to make such a classification, especially when it is claimed that all people can be classified into one category or the other.[18] Some people definitely fall into one class or the other, but the questionnaire method certainly goes to show that there are many "ambiverts," as Jung called them, who show both introversion and extroversion in their mental attitudes.

Jung regarded the influence of early years on the patient as a factor of immense importance. Parental influence was frequently responsible for deviation from normal reaction. Over-anxiety, fussing and tenderness took from the child his normal independence and self-confidence, and in some children bred a cowardly shrinking from life and an expectation of always being shielded and looked after. In other children a "reaction trait" was established, making them aggressive, hostile to all restraining influences and authority. If parents react to life by sulking, the child will sulk. If they get their way by imperious domination of others, the child will scream and fight to get his own way, and so on.

Frequently, however, as the patient advances in age from childhood, and circumstances of adult life differ from those of the nursery, the patient will react not as he did in the nursery, but in a manner

[17] *Psychological Types.*

[18] Jung realised this in his later work and in *Modern Man in Search of a Soul,* he wrote, "What struck me now was the undeniable fact that while people may be classed as introverts or extroverts, these distinctions do not cover all the dissimilarities between the individuals in either class."

determined by the influence of the image of his father or mother still operative in his mind; an image frequently distorted by the imagination. So Jung talks of the father-imago or the mother-imago. From puberty onwards, the child, Jung teaches, must free himself from his parents. Re-birth Jung defines as psychological independence of the mother or the mother-imago. The future health and well-being of the child depend on his accomplishing this, though, frequently, to achieve this liberty makes tremendous demands on the adolescent, and involves conflicts which drain him of energy and cause him to produce neurotic symptoms, if not actual neurosis. The youngster's motive in seeking self-expression, Jung, rather strangely, calls the self-sacrifice motive. The youngster feels caught in the conflict of desiring his freedom on the one hand and of being disloyal to the parents on the other; between the budding desires for sexual expression on the one hand, and the conventions of morality on the other. A sex conflict is sometimes dealt with by the foolish device of pretending that sex is unclean, and that a "nice" person ought not even to be aware of its clamour, much less give way to it. Such a pretence does not lessen the power of the sex urge, and, by making it seem "wicked," intensifies the conflict between it and the patient's self-respect. These conflicts express themselves in terms of irritation and antagonism, or in tears, jealousy and resentment. The condition is often quickly cured by the youngster leaving home and being allowed liberty to live his or her own life and find the way alone. The condition is exacerbated by criticism or silent or otherwise, of the family.

Other conflicts cause their maximum distress at this stage, e.g. the desire for social approval, with perhaps the consciousness that the patient is not as beautiful, or attractive, or gifted, or athletic, as she or he wishes, cannot dance or dress as well as others, or feel at ease in society. Inward disapproval of the self for this or that reason conflicts with desire for approval. Much patience, much encouragement and the granting of entire freedom on the part of parents are needed, but, unfortunately, many parents cannot accept the fact that their child is grown up, or they half-consciously resent the good time the youngster has compared with their own days, or they are jealous that another than themselves can give the youngster his greatest "treats," and so the feud goes on. Left alone, the youngster will frequently face life in a plucky, adult way. Harried by his parents or grown-up brothers and sisters, he will collapse on the adult level and regress to infantile ways of meeting his difficulties.

From what has been said above of Jung's conception of the collective unconscious, it should be clear that in that conception he differs importantly from Freud. For Jung the unconscious is not only made up of material once conscious and later repressed. It is made up also of material which never has been, and probably never will be, conscious, proceeding from below upwards, not from above downwards. Jung feels that the unconscious contains more than we have acquired. He writes, "All great art lifts us beyond our conscious scenes, but when the spell is over, we lose the vision and wonder at the depths within us." [19] There do seem to be psychical qualities within us which have nothing to do with the individual and yet have a regularity and repetitiveness which suggest that they come from a deeper stratum than that of any individual mind. Instinctive activities are themselves evidence of this. No individual develops them as part of his individual equipment, and yet no individual is without them.

So, in his *Modern Man in Search of a Soul*,[20] Jung writes: "The unconscious contents are by no means exclusively such as were once conscious, and by being repressed have later grown into unconscious complexes. Quite otherwise, the unconscious has contents peculiar to itself which, slowly growing upward from the depths, at last come into consciousness." [21] Jung, rather naively, defines the unconscious as "the totality of all psychic phenomena that lack the quality of consciousness." Sometimes he speaks of "the personal unconscious," meaning the lost memories and repressed thoughts and feelings. "We emphatically say," he says, "that the personal unconscious contains all that part of the psyche that is found under the threshold, including subliminal sense-perceptions in addition to repressed material." [22] More frequently he speaks of the collective unconscious, described above, and forming his most useful and original contribution to psychological understanding.

We must not stay here to discuss the many "types" discussed by Jung in his great work, *Psychological Types*, or refer further to his patient examination of the myths, legends, folk-lore and symbolism of all nations.

Jung made a profound contribution to our understanding of the human mind, and again and again, in practical work, one finds that

[19] *British Journal of Psychology*, Vol. IX, p. 232.

[20] Harcourt, 1933.

[21] There is a fascinating similarity between Jung's concept of the collective unconscious and Plato's theory as worked out in the Meno, that knowledge is reminiscence, an idea appropriated by Wordsworth in the "Intimations." I only realised this similarity through reading Dr. W. L. Northridge's *Modern Theories of the Unconscious* (Dutton, 1924).

[22] *Papers on Analytical Psychology*.

what would otherwise be a meaningless dream, or an irrational obsession, falls into its place through the light Jung has thrown upon the collective unconscious, and on the symbolism which, from the dawn of man's emergence from lower forms of life, has played its part in his mental expression.

Jung may be thought to make a greater contribution to the integration of personality even than Freud, for where Freud has done all he can do when he has successfully completed an analysis, Jung seeks to lift the patient to a higher plane of living. What he calls "individuation" is an experience close to spiritual conversion, though neither should be regarded as final. Spiritual conversion is an experience which marks the end of man's search for the right road, but not the end of his spiritual journey. Individuation, in Jung's sense, is the wise setting of the house of one's personality in order, but it is a task at which one is wise to work for the rest of one's life.

4

McDOUGALL AND PURPOSIVE OR HORMIC PSYCHOLOGY

UNDERSTANDING ONESELF IS clearly an important part of the problem of healing. If purposefulness in human life is denied or not acted upon, man's picture of himself is importantly altered. We must look briefly, then, at what is called "Purposive" or "Hormic" Psychology.[1] Although purposefulness is taken for granted by most people, the "behaviourists" deny it. They most *purposefully* do so! If their desire to prove their own case is not purposeful, what is it? Yet one of them—Professor Kuo, a distinguished Chinese, of Fuh Tan University—writes: "The concept of purpose is a lazy substitute for careful and detailed analysis. . . . With better understanding of the . . . elementary stimuli and stimulus pattern, with more knowledge of physiological facts, and with clearer insight into the behaviour-history, the concept of purpose of whatever form will eventually disappear. . . . The human machine behaves in a certain way because environmental stimulation has forced him to do so."[2] Because purposefulness is not an "objective concept," it is banished and made by the behaviourists to appear an illusion.

McDougall, an English psychologist (Cambridge, London and Oxford) who later taught in America (Harvard and Duke), is the spokesman of the "Purposive" school. At a time when psychology was a rather dull study of memory, imagination, sensation, habit, and so on,

---

[1] McDougall takes the word "hormic" from the Greek ὁρμή an impulse, and ὁρμαω, to urge on. His books, *The Energies of Men* (Scribner, 1933), and *Introduction to Social Psychology* (14th ed., Methuen, 1919) expound his view.

[2] Z. Y. Kuo, "The Fundamental Error of the Concept of Purpose and the Trial and the Error Fallacy," *Psychological Review*, 1928, Vol. XXXV, pp. 414-433. Ex Woodworth, *op. cit.*, to whom I owe much in this section.

he opened up the question of motivation and purpose, especially in relation to the social sciences, and made psychology fascinating and practically important. Why should men control and govern their behaviour at all, if they had no motive, no purpose? Why should they desire certain goals in their conduct and act accordingly? What were man's goals, his primary needs, the end which his impulses sought to serve? These were the questions to which he addressed himself. The working of men's minds which lay behind political movements and social reforms was a theme not only of interest, but of immense importance to students of political history and of social reform. The thought-out planning, again and again, was seen to be but the servant of great primeval drives and instinctive urges, and McDougall concentrated on the latter and pleaded that their purpose be understood. Only so, he argued, could social science be placed on a firm foundation.

McDougall emphasised especially the part which the instincts play in motivation, and showed that each instinct has a characteristic emotion which provides the energy of the purposeful activity which urges personality to the instinctive goal. For example, self-preservation is an instinct of which fear is a characteristic emotion. Fear, as it were, fires the engine of the will in purposeful flight towards the goal, which is safety, or an equally purposeful fight to conquer and by conquest to achieve safety. McDougall made an elaborate list of instincts and instinctive emotions, and showed how that, even in the most cultured and civilised communities, primeval instincts will play an important part in determining behaviour, even though instinctive behaviour was conventionally covered over, its presence denied, its manifestations disguised, and its *crude* intention modified. No student of the minds of others, no one who would help others in their difficulties or study the problem of healing through psychology, can afford to pass over the important contribution which McDougall makes.

However objectively considered, behaviour shows marks of teleological activity or "goal-seeking." Goal-seeking requires motive. The primary motives, says McDougall, are provided by the instincts. But McDougall is not blind to the *ways* in which instinctive energies are modified. The instincts build up sentiments which are also built out of rational thought and true altruism. Patriotism is a good example. Here is reasonable regard for the welfare of our own country, a readiness to serve her at cost to ourselves, but also a fear for our own safety. No one can deny that patriotism flares up at its brightest and hottest not through reason or altruistic feeling, but when our own safety is threatened. The emotion of fear fires the instinct of self-preservation, and here is the driving force of patriotism. The power of the sentiment to modify behaviour is the force of the instinct, not of the reason. This is a fundamental and most important part of McDougall's teaching.

The behaviour of the individual, the community and the nation is not crudely instinctive on the one hand, nor coldly dictated by the reason on the other. The instincts combine, reasons are added, one goal may be alleged and another really sought, but the strength of the current which drives the wheels of the machine of human personality is provided by instinctive emotions.

Our purpose in this book is not importantly concerned with Mc-Dougall's thesis. Through him social psychology became a recognised branch of the subject, but he does not, in that particular field, have anything new to say that bears on the integration of the individual. At the same time, in his effort to help a patient to attain integration, the psychotherapist is, again and again, brought up against the fact that cloaked instinctive action, rationalised to look like intellectual choice, hampers the individual's understanding of himself at all points, and the individual is, so to speak, always part of the herd, and cannot be understood apart from it. Society itself, as constituted, thwarts the instinctive needs of the individual and makes him neurotic. And the neurotic must be looked at, both from the angle of his individualism and from that of the society of which he is a part. Indeed, one often feels that to secure the integration of some sick souls one would have to reorganise society from top to bottom. The alternative is often to send them back after discussion and treatment into the very maelstrom which has wrecked their poise and destroyed their peace.

McDougall is careful to make a distinction between two kinds of purposive psychology; often confused because in both the quest for a goal is to be seen. One is psychological hedonism. This teaches that the goal of all activity is pleasure. It may be a worthy and lofty pleasure, like that of success in a worthy cause or the solving of a problem in philosophy or mathematics. Or it may be a quest for food, shelter, love and so on, which are desired not so much for themselves as for the pleasure attained by success in obtaining them.

McDougall claims that this hedonist theory is false; that what we seek is the object itself—food, shelter, victory, the good of another, and so on; not just for their pleasure-value, but because in themselves they are worthy of the outgoing of our energy in often arduous quest.

He rejects hedonism not only because his researches in animal and child psychology do not support it, but because, as he points out, many of the noblest of the human race spend their life in activity which causes them pain, but which brings benefit to others. Actually, he

290

claims, they suffer more pain than pleasure, yet the quest continues.

Why this should be, he answers in what I think is an incomplete fashion, by saying that a human being seeks a certain goal because he is constituted that way. This falls in line with McDougall's research into animal psychology, where each species is constituted to seek certain goals which satisfy its needs, but, to my mind, it enthrones man's instincts—which he prefers to call propensities—above their control and diversion by the use of free-will, inspired by social, intellectual and spiritual ideals. Man is above the animals, but, like them, is motivated by instinct-intelligence factors which have been modified to meet the situation by what McDougall calls "adaptive deviation." [3]

McDougall would object to my repetition of the word "instinct" above. His change of term and the use of the word "propensity," however, seems to me to be far-fetched, especially when he writes as follows: "In the human species, the native abilities . . . become, in the long course of youthful development, so multiplied, differentiated and enriched, and so much at the service of any propensity that we cannot confidently define the nature and extent of any one native ability, or *speak with entire propriety of the existence of any instincts*," [4] and this after a list of them in his book, *Social Psychology*. Yet, he adds, "This change does not imply any radical change of view," [5] so we may as well let the older word, more generally understood, stand; recognising that "crude instinct" is seldom the sole driving force either in man or the higher animals.

When McDougall comes to discuss neurosis, he makes a most interesting classification. Putting on one side the disorders of mental life which are due to injury or disease of the brain, he illumines his theory of functional disorder by the analogy of an army. The personality in its wholeness is likened to an army made up of many units. Normally all units are in touch with one another and co-operate to carry out the operation which is demanded by the commander. An organic disability is represented by the detachment of one or more units or their complete disorganisation.

He then likens functional illness to:

(*a*) A unit, or group of units, losing touch with the main body, while itself remaining intact. The parallel here is the functional illness of the dissociated type, more common among extroverts than introverts, such as we have in the functional paralysis of a limb. The limb *in itself*

---

[3] *Energies of Men.*

[4] *Op. cit.* (Italics mine.)

[5] *Energies of Men.*

is healthy, but will not co-operate with the whole or obey the captain's command. In this category are hysteria, depression, or, more seriously, melancholia and manic-depressive psychosis.

(b) A unit, or group of units, not detached from the main body, but insubordinately acting on its own, adopting an objective of its own and attaining it by its own methods, regardless of the strategy of the commander, and, indeed, acting in opposition to the will of the latter. The parallel here is the functional illness set up by conflict, more common amongst introverts than extroverts; a conflict which may be either conscious or, because the rebellion is smothered by the rest of the army which hates to admit it, *repressed*. A tic, or involuntary recurrent movement, or a recurrent bad dream or nightmare is an instance of this. In this category are neurasthenia, obsessions, compulsions or, more seriously, paranoia and schizophrenia.

(c) A unit expresses its activities in a form quite unintended by the commander. So we might describe the perversions.

The analogy has much to commend it, but one would warn the reader against treating an analogy as though it were a proof. In (a) above, for example, conflict also often plays an early part, and an *early* history of most neuroses shows the personality attracted by two goals which are incompatible. Even if the desire for one of them is repressed into the unconscious, the disharmony remains. A functional paralysis is sometimes nature's crude way of ending the *conflict* by making one goal unattainable in a fashion which does not injure the patient's self-respect—e.g. the soldier's shell-shock. He wants to fight—that is his duty and the desire of the self-respecting part of his mind. He does not want to fight—that is his self-preservation instinct and his fear of mutilation. Paralysis ends the conflict with honour to the patient. He cannot fight now. He is *ill*.

McDougall finds no difficulty in illustrating his main thesis of hormic psychology from his own case work. A typical case, described in his *Outline of Abnormal Psychology*,[6] is that of a highly intelligent soldier who presented the curious symptom of only being able to walk with his legs widely straddled as if his feet were on opposite sides of a wide ditch. The patient was painfully conscious of looking ridiculous, but had no control by which he could walk normally and no memory of any causal factor.

No attempt at cure by substituting a new "habit-track" was likely to succeed. Hormic psychology suggests that the patient has an unconscious "purpose" in walking thus. A hidden, repressed tendency over-

[6] Case 29 (Scribner, 1926).

came all voluntary efforts to correct his absurd symptom. That repressed factor must be brought back to consciousness, so that it may be under the control of his newly integrated personality, and not working on its own as a detached fragment of personality, rather like a wandering regiment detached from the main brigade of the forces of his being.

"Steady probing and encouragement," plus the interpretation of a dream, plus the noting by the psychologist of the patient's complaint that he could not shave himself since he was "ill," elicited the following recovered memory. He related that when standing in the doorway of his dugout, shaving himself, with his legs wide apart and his back to the open, a shell fell and buried itself between his feet. He fled frantically from the spot for more than a mile. Then he returned and carried on his work.

The present symptom, then, was produced by his repressed memory of guilt at having behaved like a coward and deserted his post. In a way, the symptom is a dramatic representation of the conflict between sticking to his job and fear of his life. He will still walk, but tribute is paid to the repressed terror in that he can walk only as if still afraid of the explosion between his feet.

On having fully recollected the incident and related it, the recurrent terrifying dreams of shells gliding between his legs but never exploding, the fear of shaving, and the straddled walking, all disappeared, and never returned.

Less dramatic cures which I have myself witnessed bear out the value of the theory which lies behind McDougall's thesis.

5

DETERMINIST PSYCHOLOGY: THE BEHAVIOURIST SCHOOL

I HAVE GIVEN above a summary of the views of Freud, Adler and Jung, and added a note on the most distinctive contribution of Mc-Dougall. My aim has been to indicate how their varying views work out the theme of healing through Psychology with which this section of this book is mainly concerned. I do not propose, therefore, to examine schools of psychology which do not issue in any treatment at all. Yet we must notice briefly the behaviourists, for they claim that integration of the psyche can be reached through the application of their theories.

"Behaviourist," a term introduced by John B. Watson (born 1878), an animal psychologist of the University of Chicago, indicated the view that conduct could be exactly determined if one knew and manipulated sufficiently the psychological factors playing upon the patient. "He not only asserted the justifiability and usefulness of the objective methods of animal psychology, but seriously questioned whether they were not the only useful methods. 'It is possible,' he said, 'to write a psychology, to define it . . . as the science of behaviour, and never go back upon the definition: never to use the terms consciousness, mental states, mind, content, will, imagery and the like;' and he went on to state that the various branches of psychology had made progress just in so far as they had freed themselves from the trammels of consciousness and introspection." [1] Factors like freedom, imagination, mind, feeling and will are ignored. Factors like stimulus, response, the drives of instinct and habit—these are the important things. Watson believed that psychology could, and should, be made an exact science, and that if,

---

[1] J. C. Flugel, *A Hundred Years of Psychology* (Macmillan, 1933).

and when, it became this, both the control of behaviour and the prediction of conduct could be established.[2] There is to be no introspection. Psychology is to be an objective science like any other.

It may be pointed out in passing that no science is as "objective" as Watson pretends. We cannot describe anything and keep "ourselves" out of it. We experience the universe as human beings, and all human beings are made of thought, feeling and will. We may seek to be objective and to some extent "keep our feelings" out of it. But when "*we*" observe anything, it is observed by "*us*." And we can no more keep our *feeling* from our description of an objective entity than we can obliterate any of the other parts of our apparatus of apprehension.

Watson said that if his plan were followed and his principles accepted, then "the educator, the physician, the jurist and the business man could utilise the data in a practical way." So Watson believes in the laboratory method, not the introspection of the consulting-room; he seeks to link psychology with biology and physiology, not with philosophy and religion.

He and his colleagues did very useful work. In the field of mental tests, accuracy of perception, the study of fatigue, the behaviour of animals and children—phenomena that could be measured and studied by observers, other than the patient, and could be detached from the latter's ideas about his own thoughts and feelings—they worked in the most valuable way.

Their work linked up with the discovery of the conditioned reflex in 1905 by the Russian scientist, Pavlov.[3] Pavlov's experiments are well known, and need only be referred to briefly. He discovered that if, over a long period, at the time he fed hungry dogs with attractive food he sounded a gong or shone a red lamp, or started a metronome ticking, then these stimuli to the senses would cause the salivary glands of the dogs to discharge their secretion even though no food was within sight or smell. The dogs had so associated the gong, or the light, or the metronome, with the idea of dinner, that the stimulus alone caused the secretion to flow, though this did not go on indefinitely, and the flow of secretion dwindled if the food were omitted.

By the *conditioned* reflex, Pavlov meant the reflex action in which the response had become attached to a substitute for the natural stimu-

[2] See J. B. Watson, *Behaviourism* (Norton, 1925) and *Behaviour: An Introduction to Comparative Psychology* (Holt, 1914).

[3] Some writers claim that Pavlov's rival, Bechterew, in what was then St. Petersburg, has the priority of discovery. The latter, a neurologist, worked with motor reflexes; the former, a physiologist, worked with glandular and secretory reflexes.

lus. Pavlov's experiments, described in his book, *Conditioned Reflexes* (1927 Eng. tr.), fascinated psychologists and physiologists all over the world. He claimed to have reached a point of differentiation in them in which a dog would secrete saliva if a gong were sounded on a certain note, say C major, but that no secretion would flow if a gong were sounded on a note less than a semitone higher or lower in the musical scale. "A suitably trained dog would salivate exactly thirty minutes after the stimulus, no reaction being obtained even at the twenty-ninth minute." [4] Pavlov's conclusion was most important; it was that the understanding of behaviour lies wholly with physiology.

Watson and other behaviourists seized on this discovery as supporting their case. The fear in the dark and the irrational phobias of the neurotic are to be regarded as conditioned reflexes. Thinking was a sub-vocal speech-reaction, and emotion was an epiphenomenon of visceral reaction—if no conditioned-reflex explanation was handy.

Watson's work was hailed in America with enthusiasm. Experimental ethics were to take the place of the ethics based on religious teaching and belief. Psycho-analysis would be done away with, for scientific studies of behaviour would lead to control of behaviour, and nervous breakdown would be a thing of the past. Watson said that if he had a healthy, well-formed child and full control of him and of his environment, he could turn the child into the perfect human being. It would be interesting to meet Watson's children.

In his *Brave New World*, Aldous Huxley satirically described rows of children being subjected to a gramophone record repeating phrases over and over again until they were accepted by the children's minds, after which it was supposed their characters would respond accordingly.

Watson opened up a new path to integration which unfortunately has not yet reached success! The goods advertised have never been delivered. How can man control that which is pre-determined by physiological factors, if, as is often the case, he cannot eliminate, or even modify, the latter? How can he overcome the result of conditioned reflexes? If Watson is right, man is the victim of his own machinery, physical and mental. He cannot say, "I am the captain of my soul," but only," "I am the victim of my secretions and reflexes and reactions to stimuli."

Further, whence the illusion of responsibility, let alone the horror of a sense of guilt? According to Watson, physical factors are responsible. If Watson is right, the State is wrong to punish a man for raping a child. It was no responsibility of his; it was his glands uncorrected

[4] Flugel, *op. cit.*

by early reflex training. If a man is caught assaulting an old woman and stealing her earnings, it is unfortunate, but due to the fact that he has not been taught in childhood to associate a social conduct with the correct emotion. He can scarcely be punished. His act was predetermined by physical factors. The human, inward sense of guilt and responsibility ("I did this thing and I am responsible for it and I was free not to do it") is inaccurate, and the State is grossly unfair in holding a man responsible. Given control of material factors in man's body and environment, the perfect man could be brought forth!

Pavlov and Watson and their colleagues have made a valuable contribution to our understanding of conditioned behaviour, but, like so many enthusiasts, they explain too much. They push into their support facts which are capable of quite a different explanation. Physical factors are not to be exalted above spiritual unless the facts demand it. Let us not ask from material factors an authority they do not possess, nor expect from them the flowering of the loveliest things in human character. The facts warrant no such conclusion, as I hope to show.

COMPOSITE METHODS IN MODERN PSYCHOTHERAPY[1]

IN THIS CHAPTER I wish to ask and answer the question—Where, then, stands the modern psychotherapist? Must he study all these schools of thought, make up his mind which carries the truest interpretation of mental phenomena, which theory shall lie behind his technique, and base his treatment on it?

It is instructive to imagine that a woman, slightly crippled, has a dream that she is reclining on a couch by the fire, and that on the other side of the fireplace her husband is seated. In her dream, he rises suddenly, picks up the poker and advances. It is not clear in the dream whether he is advancing towards her or towards the fire. She has a feeling that, in a strange way, she and the fire are one. She wakens in a fever of excitement which she cannot identify as fear or desire, but says, "I felt that something tremendous was about to happen, and then I woke up."

She takes her dream to a Freudian psychologist. The solution is easy. The poker is a phallic symbol. The dream means that she desires sexual union with her husband. It is the symbolic expression of a repressed desire. Perhaps she wants a child, and feels that the fire of life is dying down and that if she is to have a child her husband must not delay. She wants to be "stirred up" by means of the poker and know that the flame of passion can be kindled. "Poking" is a slang expression for sexual intercourse.

She takes her dream to an Adlerian psychologist. He sees in it the symbol of a present inferiority. She is only a woman, and lame at that. Her husband is the dominating male. She reveals in the dream the

---

[1] At this point, the reader unfamiliar with neurosis and psychosis might usefully study Appendix 1.

298

"masculine protest"; the frustration of one who rebels against the fact that the poker is possessed by the male. It is he who wields the sceptre (= poker) of authority. Her inferiority, caused by her life-long lameness, is seeking compensation in dominating activity, such as the male shows who can move quickly towards pokers which strike fire from rock and create light and warmth. Her "will to power" is the clue to the meaning of the dream.

She takes her dream to a Jungian psychologist. He remembers an old myth from an ancient civilisation in which the hero wields a rod of iron. He educes that only two afternoons ago the patient was much impressed by a lusty male, whom she heard singing the solo from Handel's "Messiah"—"Thou shalt break them with a rod of iron and dash them in pieces like a potter's vessel." The archetypal-nature of the dream is clear. Stimulated by the solo, it has seeped up from the "collective unconscious," and represents her present problem of being unable to smash her way through her difficulties. She is regressing to the childish reaction of lying curled up near a dying fire; curled up *in utero* in a warmth which action (= birth) would end, instead of adult action which she is content to admire in others.

The hormic psychologist would be awake to the purposive "innate propensities," no longer to be called instincts,[2] aroused in the dreamer by the approach of her husband. The dream, for the purposivist, reveals a tendency which is subconsciously at work, but which has been repressed because "repugnant in some way to the dominant tendencies of the dreamer. . . . Dreams reveal . . . the nature of the conflicts to which nervous and mental disorders are so largely due, conflicts of which the sufferer knows nothing beyond the pains and disabilities which they engender, vague distresses, chronic headaches, uncontrollable impulses, obsessive thoughts, losses of memory," [3] and so on.

When she takes her dream to the behaviourist, he seizes at once on the excitement which she had on waking. It was, no doubt, a fear which was "a conditioned reflex" due to the fact that her father rose and poked the fire when she was a baby curled up in a cot near it. He poked so excitedly that coal flew out and made the hearthrug smoulder. So, any stimulus like the memory of poking the fire induces the repeated emotion of fear.

But what is the psychologist to do in the face of these multiple ways of interpreting behaviour?

[2] See McDougall's *The Energies of Men*, preface to the 2nd ed. (Scribner, 1933).
[3] *Op. cit.*

My own answer is that any well-equipped psychotherapist must be cognisant of all these schools of thought, for they all contain part of the truth. They only lead us astray when they deny the truth of other systems in the attempt to establish their own as sufficient in itself to cover all the phenomena. Even in my own limited observation of the psychoneuroses, I could produce cases which illustrate the truth in any of the systems reviewed above. My work has brought me into close contact with a number of distinguished, medically qualified psychotherapists. In one way and another I have had opportunities for studying their techniques. At the hands of one of them I, myself, had two hundred hours of "analysis," [4] and at the hands of two others, twenty and thirty hours respectively. I can speak, therefore, at first hand of the modern method of psychotherapeutic practice which I believe is not unfairly described as follows.

A complete physical examination having been made, the patient lies on a couch as completely relaxed as possible. The psychologist sits beside and a little behind him facing the same way, so that the psychologist can easily hear, but so that the embarrassment of a *vis-à-vis* interview is avoided. It is worth while taking a little time to ensure the patient's freedom from "tenseness" in the limbs. Relaxation of body so often induces relaxation of mind, and both have therapeutic value. The first two, or even three, sessions of an hour each are well spent in simply allowing the patient to tell his story. Obviously no "treatment" can proceed if the patient has material which he wants "to get off his chest." For this reason, it is wise even to allow the patient to begin his story where he likes. No doubt, it would be easier for the psychologist if the patient began at the beginning, but many will begin with their present symptoms. These are uppermost in the mind and loom largest as the reason for seeking help.

If a "rapport" of confidence is established; if the patient realises that he will not be derided or told to "pull himself together," or that it "is all his imagination," or "just nerves"; if his fears are not called "silly" or "baseless"; if he is made to realise that he has developed a psychological illness, of which all he complains of are the normal symptoms observable in every similar case and perfectly ordinary to his psychologist; that he is not going mad; that if he will patiently submit to treatment there is every chance of his complete recovery, even

[4] I use inverted commas here to indicate that, strictly speaking, the term "psycho-analysis" should only be used in regard to a Freudian treatment.

though treatment may be a lengthy matter—then the first two or three sessions have been well spent.[5]

The psychologist will also note down the age of the patient's parents and their state of mental and physical health; and if they are dead, the cause of death. He should note similar facts about the patient's brothers and sisters, aunts and uncles. He will be wise to question the patient about all his illnesses so far as he can remember them, and on such points as his home life and its happiness or otherwise. Family upheavals, quarrels, the place of religion in the home, the interests and hobbies of all the members of the family are important. The patient's sex life and development are important, as are any fears which trouble him or dreams which recur frequently. It is astonishing how the most apparently trifling facts about a patient sometimes point a finger to the clue which will help the psychotherapist in his effort to help the patient back to health.[6]

The next step is for the psychologist to make sure that in the patient's life-story there are no considerable gaps. The psychologist may well ask, for example, "But what happened to you between the ages of twelve and sixteen? You have told me nothing about that." Let us imagine that those years were spent at boarding-school. It may be that that was a most important chapter in the patient's history, and that the very act of forgetting to speak of it is significant and unwittingly purposive; an unconsciously motivated amnesia.

Then the psychologist may continue with the process of "free association." He may, that is, let the patient say anything that comes into his mind about himself and "think aloud," passing from subject to subject, without any guidance from the psychologist, save that the latter keeps him to the subject of himself, his feelings and mental reactions, and does not let him roam away on to his views on politics, and so on. Here, however, it is important that the patient should not be "kept to the point" too strictly, for he may speak, say, of his views on education, and, if uninterrupted, he may suddenly jump to his views on some teacher who, in earlier life, profoundly affected his emotional life in a way that has determined his neurotic trend.

On having listened to the story of his life and the troubles which the patient regards as most worrying, the psychologist may take up one of the crises in the patient's life, seen to be such because of the

---

[5] I think it unwise for the psychologist to *promise* recovery and very unwise to promise it within a specified time, or to make a guess at the length of time treatment will take; a guess which can only be a matter of the vaguest conjecture.

[6] The kind of information which must be gathered early is indicated in Appendix 6, p. 519.

presence of emotion obvious when that period or incident was being recalled, and ask the patient to say all that comes into his mind as he thinks about it, to re-live it, to feel again as he felt then; not to be hampered by conventional ideas of modesty, or loyalty, say, to husband or wife or to a parent, whether dead or alive; to conceal neither his own shortcomings, on the one hand, nor assume exaggerated guilt not sincerely felt, on the other, but to be as starkly honest as possible, and let his feelings express themselves as they rise in his mind.

At one time I frequently strapped a microphone over the patient's heart. The leads from the microphone went to an amplifier. By turning a knob I could make these heart-sounds so loud that they could be heard through a room, or so soft that I could only hear them through earphones. The emotion felt by the patient altered the heart-sounds, and I could tell—and if necessary persuade him—when he was talking of a theme which distressed him; a fact he would often try to deny. By means of a brass cup under, and another over a patient's hand as he sat in his chair, and a galvanometer with a beam of light for needle, I could tell when a patient was inwardly troubled. As he came near the recital of his fears, the perspiration of his hand varied, and the galvanometer registered the difference in resistance to the electric current. But such gadgets are apt to make the patient self-conscious and are not normally necessary or even advantageous.

It is no strange thing in an analysis for a patient who has conventionally "loved" a parent to break out in a bitter resentment, repressed for years; to express hate of a father or mother who may have frustrated him, and to be shocked, far more than he shocks the psychologist, at the violence of his own emotions. This honesty and the expression of honest feeling bottled up for so long is of immense therapeutic value. It is called by Freud the "abreaction," and is cathartic and cleansing.

There will be sessions which drag. The patient is late for his appointment or forgets it altogether, manifesting thus a "resistance" to treatment, or to the psychologist, or to allowing his deep mind to be exposed. He will say he "can't think of anything to say."

Some psychologists are reluctant to discuss matters with a patient or to give him advice. They think the technique should lie in the patient doing almost all the talking. Granted that the psychologist must not make the patient's decisions for him or hand him out premature interpretations of his symptoms and dreams, yet when sessions drag I have found it valuable to try to help the patient understand himself by giving him simple explanations and informal talks on psychological mechanisms, or even advice—not too dogmatically expressed—on ethical problems.

One psychologist on the staff of the City Temple Psychological Clinic does not let the patient just carry on free association. He asks questions repeatedly. "Now why do you think you felt like that? Try to feel it again. Now why do you adopt that pattern of reaction?" In his hands the treatment is excellent. Whether the interpolation of so many questions is a sound guide for most psychotherapists it is hard to say. But it is a method which minimises the risk of a session so "dragging" that the patient feels he is wasting his time and his money.

If a session of free association drags, the psychologist may find it expedient to turn to the patient's dreams. Some patients will say that they never do dream. They mean that they do not remember their dreams on awakening. Everyone dreams. If a patient on going to sleep gives himself the suggestion that he will remember his dreams, he will usually do so. He is often stimulated into remembering them by the fact that he normally pays fees for his treatments and wants his money's worth!

The dream—as a whole—has significance for the trained psychotherapist. It could be likened to a political cartoon—meaningless to one who is ignorant of the current political set-up, but significant to one who is *au fait* with the situation. Thus a dream may be meaningless to the dreamer and to his family and friends, but the trained psychologist, who already has in his mind the seething ferment of the patient's mental conflict, may see in it a most revealing clue to hidden desires, fears and hatreds and other emotional pressures. He must not *tell* the patient the interpretation, but he may help him to find it for himself. He does this by taking the main incidents in the dream (the manifest content), and, by free association on the part of the patient, getting the latter to understand the underlying significance (latent content) of the dream. While one fleeting dream may be unimportant (though even that is not arbitrary or meaningless), a repeated or single vivid dream is of great importance, and should be told by the dreamer, complete with all its detail, however nonsensical the latter may appear to be. For this purpose, it should be written down by the patient immediately he awakens. If he waits, even a few hours, he will probably edit it to make it sound either less absurd or more amusing, less sinister or more flattering to himself.

It is not necessary here to write fully on dream interpretation. I have written on it elsewhere,[7] and much depends on whether the reader interprets according to Freud, Adler or Jung. William McDougall,

[7] *Psychology in Service of the Soul* (Macmillan, 1930).

in his great volume on abnormal psychology, has a useful chapter on the different interpretations involved.[8]

In the treatment of psychogenic illness it is, of course, usually the *unconscious* mind that is unhealthy. There is a real difference between a neurosis springing from unconscious complexes and conflicts, and an emotional problem, all the factors in which are present to consciousness. The latter can often be straightened out in a few interviews. The former may need technical treatment over a long period. It is in that dark depth of the unconscious mind that the conflicts and fears abide, sending up to the surface of consciousness the symptoms which so distress the patient—symptoms that frequently give no clearer indication of the nature of the mental factor which causes them, than a rash on the skin gives of the particular toxin which is poisoning the blood-stream.

Any method, then, which lights up for the psychotherapist the conflict raging in the deep mind, is one with which he must be familiar.

Jung devised a method of word association[9] to this end. He would prepare a list of several hundred words[10] called "stimulus words," which included key words taken from the patient's dreams, or from his own account of his troubles. Armed with a stop-watch recording fifths of a second, the psychologist then read out each word to the patient, inviting him to say, when he heard the stimulus word, the word which *immediately* came to his mind, however foolish it sounded. This was called the "reaction word." The time which elapsed between the stimulus word and the reaction word was carefully noted. The *nature* of the reaction word often gave a clue to the unconscious reaction to the idea presented to the patient by the stimulus word. If, on the other hand, the patient tried to guard himself from discovery—often unconscious guarding—then the lengthened reaction *time* showed a hesitancy significant indeed.

A patient was given a list of five hundred stimulus words, including the words "water," "sea," "boat," "ship," "voyage," "rowing," "river," which were, of course, mixed with other words, and not given consecutively as printed here. To the word "water" he gave, as his reaction word, the word "deep," to "sea," "drown," to "boat," "capsize," to "ship," "wreck," to "voyage," "missing," to "rowing" he made a

---

[8] *Outline of Abnormal Psychology* (Scribner, 1926).

[9] Described fully in *Psychology in Service of the Soul.*

[10] A list of such words can be found in Jung, *Collected Papers on Analytical Psychology* (tr. Constance Long. Dodd, 1916), and also in Pfister's *The Psychoanalytic Method* (Dodd, 1917).

very long pause and then said "sink," and to "river" he gave again the word "drown." These are not the normal reaction words to such stimuli, and it does not take profound psychological insight to deduce that at deep levels of his mind the patient was playing with the idea of drowning himself.

Frequently, an unhappy home, an unrequited love affair, a sordid sexual adventure which the patient has purposefully "forgotten" are revealed by this method. The patient has repressed the memory of them and forgotten them, but because they were never healthily reacted to at the time they are like wounds which heal over superficially with pus still remaining in them. They must be opened up again, or the poison will seep into the whole system and bring the whole personality into serious disharmony. A kind of mental septicæmia will be set up. This is the answer to the criticism that analysis is against nature and that the wounds which personality sustains are better forgotten. They can only be satisfactorily forgotten after a healthy emotional reaction to them has been made. Psychological treatment is distressing because the patient has to be persuaded to remember and re-live unhappy and distasteful emotional experiences of long ago. But surgery is also distressing. It is none the less therapeutic. Psychotherapy is a kind of mental surgery. It is not to be resorted to if the patient can live an integrated, happy and useful life without it. There is no more reason to generalise and say, "Everyone should be analysed," than to say, "Everyone should have his appendix removed." But, where there is disability and distress, both procedures may be not merely useful, but the only way to integration and health.

Those who have read what was said earlier about hypnotism, may wonder why this method is not in more general use, since it is regarded by some as the "royal" road to the unconscious. I believe it to have value in "suggestive therapy"; in putting into a mind ideas which give confidence and hope to the patient, even though the effect of hypnotic suggestion is transient. But it is not widely used in making psychological investigations, for several reasons.

The idea that by hypnotising a patient the psychologist can "get anything out of him that he wants to know" is fallacious. In the first place, only a proportion of patients are hypnotisable. The proportion of those who can be deeply hypnotised is, in my experience, very small. To attempt hypnosis and to fail to induce it sometimes gives the patient the impression either that he is difficult to cure or that the psychologist is incompetent.

In the second place, it is by no means true that a hypnotised patient will answer truthfully any question put to him. He may either remain silent or wake up. I have described such a situation in the chapter on hypnotism. Loyalty to a friend, or a vow of secrecy, or even feelings of shame can defeat the hypnotist who seeks to press a patient and probe his deep mind.

Again, it is a good rule that clinical practice should not far outrun technical understanding. It is by no means clear what actually happens when a person is hypnotised. The dangers, real and imaginary, have already been dealt with in this book, and I have never known anything but good come to a patient by it, but a clearer understanding of the psychological and perhaps physiological factors involved is desirable before the adoption of a technique is to be widely recommended, and the disapproving attitude of the general public is something of a deterrent.

But a further objection remains. Clinically it appears that the patient is more thoroughly cured of a psychoneurosis if the treatment proceeds on conscious levels; that is to say if the unconscious factors behind his neurosis are brought to the surface by the methods already described. Hypnotic suggestion may cloak or smother a symptom without its cause being unearthed. Such smothering may lead the unconscious mind to choose another and more baffling symptom. Hypno-analysis, again, while useful in cases of recent shell-shock or loss of memory, may acquaint the physician of much mental material that lies behind the neurotic trends, but that is of little use to the patient, who, on waking, forgets it. It is true that he can be wakened and immediately told, "You were just telling me about . . . now go on from there." Sometimes this works. Sometimes it fails. It is of immense importance that the patient should himself make a *conscious discovery* of the factors that have made him neurotic.[11] Telling him what those factors are, on the part of the physician who has learned them while the patient was in the hypnotic trance, is often not only useless, but can postpone recovery, for the patient may deny them vehemently and strengthen his own resistance to their conscious recognition. If he accepts them, as Freud said, he will put them in his mind *alongside* his other ideas. He will not put them *in the place of* faulty ideas. Further, too many patients want the physician to do everything for them, and the very use of hypnosis weakens them in the necessary task of changing their attitude to life, working out their own salvation,

---

[11] "Colonel Grinker and Major Spregel, in their book, *Men Under Stress,* point out that . . . aviators suffering from psychic disturbances during and after combat, could not be helped by hypnosis or prolonged rest because neither gave the flier *any new knowledge about himself and his past.*" Quoted from Liebman (Simon and Schuster, 1946). (Italics Liebman's.)

doing something about the neurotic situation. This was made clear to me lately by a young wife whose husband was serving abroad, and who had fallen in love with a young man whom she refused to stop seeing regularly, and whom I will call George. "Why," she petulantly asked me, "don't you hypnotise me and make me love my husband more than George?"

The above considerations, together with the fear of hypnotism on the part of many patients and the fear on the part of many psychotherapists of using a method which has been so exploited by quacks and is still looked at askance by many orthodox doctors, account for the fact that it is rarely resorted to in the majority of psychotherapeutic treatments used today.

I have written above of an "analysis" taking years to carry through. It should be made clear that very many neuroses clear up with a much shorter treatment. Dr. William Brown says, "In my own medical practice about fifty per cent of my patients come for a course of ten hours treatment (analysis, constructive suggestion and relaxation), thirty per cent come for anything up to one hundred hours analysis, and twenty per cent come for over one hundred hours of deep mental analysis." [12]

Much is often accomplished by half a dozen "therapeutic conversations," such as a minister with a psychological training can conduct. More will be said about this later. Any treatment longer than that, and any case accompanied by severe physical symptoms, should be undertaken only by a medically qualified psychotherapist.

For our purpose now we may summarise by saying that Freud, Adler, Jung, McDougall and the rest all recognise that far below the level of the conscious mind, and far deeper than the level on which the will operates, conflicts rage amongst the instinctive emotions of man—conflicts which can produce acute mental distress like depression, insomnia, hysterical outbursts of weeping or anger, or both; conflicts so intolerable that the mind seeks relief from its burden by inducing disabling bodily symptoms which range from the chronic headache, or asthma, to the paralysis of a limb; and that a radical cure for such a condition is to be sought not in the use of drugs or in prolonged rest, though these have their place, but in bringing the patient to the point at which he recognizes the unsound attitudes to life which have brought on his neurosis, sees where he went astray, perhaps in very early days and frequently through wrong treatment on the part of others in his infancy, treatment for which he is not in the very least to blame; and, recognising his patterns of reaction to be faulty, thereafter alters them

[12] *Psychological Methods of Healing*, p. 54 footnote (University of London Press, 1938).

and thereby integrates his divided personality and wins through to health of body, mind and soul.

It is mistakenly supposed in some quarters that psychoanalysis "cures" people. It would be truer to say that, if successful, it gives the patient insight into his faulty reactions to life. His cure, however, depends on whether he puts in the requisite work on himself, and has the courage and tenacity to replace his faulty reactions by true ones. Religion can help him there, as we shall see. But many patients expect psychological analysis, or investigation, to cure them without any rigorous hard work undertaken by themselves on their own characters. Every sick person hopes to be cured without effort of his own, but such an attitude is not the royal road to health. God is at work within him. Indeed, in a sense, the universe is on the side of the man who seeks to regain his health. But also he must work out his own salvation.

The way of healing through modern psychological techniques could be described as follows:

1. The discovery, with the skilled help of the psychologist, of those factors in the deep mind, often going back to infancy—and in the early part of the treatment usually unconscious—which led the patient to adopt a faulty pattern of reaction to difficult situations.

2. The recognition of the motives that led him to adopt that pattern and of the way in which it "congealed" and hardened; determining forthwith his subsequent way of meeting life's demands.

3. The determination to substitute a true reaction for the faulty one, using all the aids open to him, such as auto-suggestion, positive thinking, the banishment of self-pity and the use of religious insight and faith.

DO MODERN PSYCHOLOGICAL METHODS OF HEALING NEED RELIGION?

1

THE NATURE OF HEALTH

ALL THE METHODS of healing studied so far, whether ancient or modern, whether labelled religious or psychological, have one supreme aim—namely the restoration of health. As we now proceed to ask how, if at all, religion and psychology depend on one another, we ought to understand clearly what we mean by health.

I suggest the following definition:

Health is the complete and successful functioning of every part of the human being, in harmonious relationship with every other part and with the relevant environment.

Physical health, then, means the complete and successful functioning of every part of the body in harmonious relationship with every other part and with its particular and relevant environment.

The health of the lung, for example, means the complete and successful functioning of the lung in harmonious relationship with every other part of the body, and with its relevant environment, which is the air. In a state of health, the activity of the lung does not interfere with or prejudice the working, say, of the heart or other organ, nor is it hindered in its functioning of inhaling and exhaling air.

The health of the eye similarly depends on the activity of the eye *"in se,"* the circulation of blood in it, the efficiency and position of its lenses, the sensitiveness of its nervous network, and so on. But, further, the health of the eye depends on its ability to establish a harmonious relationship with light—which is its relevant environment. If any of these inward functions, or the outward relationship with light, is interrupted, the health of the eye is impaired and we speak of a state of dis-ease.

Where the relationship with the relevant environment is cut off, a state of disease ensues. For example, a perfect lung is soon rendered

311

imperfect if it is deprived of air, and though the eye may be a perfect instrument and suffers no damage to its structures, yet if it is deprived of light it soon atrophies, the optic nerve ceases to operate and the eye falls into dis-ease.

The situation is not dissimilar when we turn to the matter of mental health. "Mental health," says Dr. Geoffrey Evans, "depends in some measure on adjustment to the surroundings as well as on the co-ordination and harmony in working of the components of the mind." [1] For perfect health, every part of the mental apparatus must function in harmonious relationship with every other part, and with the relevant environment which might be called the world of true ideas.

If a man thinks he is being followed everywhere he goes, when, in truth, he is not being followed at all; or if he believes, as a friend of mine did, that every wayside stone conceals a sensitive microphone carrying every word he spoke to some sinister listener, then his mind is not in harmonious relationship with the world of true ideas and is in a state well described as dis-ease.

Further, by our definition, a mind at war within itself, not having its parts in harmonious relationship with one another, is also in a state of dis-ease. It may not be serious. The patient may be able to easily to carry on his normal occupations and interests. But if he must touch every lamp-post as he goes along the road, or must rub his teeth fifteen times each way, or must have the back of his chair always against a wall, then his will, by which he carries out these compulsive acts, is out of harmony with his cognition of real situations. He has developed obsessional neurosis, a psychological illness rather than what is usually called mental illness, but still a state of disharmony and dis-ease.

If, again, he fears when there is no fear-causing situation; if, for example, he fears to cross a road though it is completely empty of traffic, then the "feeling" part of his mind is not working in harmony with thought and will. He has developed agoraphobia. Many patients come to a psychological clinic complaining that they constantly experience acute feelings of fear, but cannot tell anyone of what it is they are frightened. They have developed an anxiety neurosis. The over-depressed neurotic characteristically cannot find any joy in beauty, though he may have revelled in it before he was ill. He no longer thrills to great truths. Goodness no longer moves him. His health is broken. He is not in harmony with the world of true ideas.

But is that the whole of the matter? Is man only body and mind?

[1] Geoffrey Evans, M.D., F.R.C.P., in his Presidential Address to the Section of Medicine of the Royal Society of Medicine, delivered October 26, 1943.

If body and mind are both working properly, both in themselves and in relation to their relevant environments, is he assured of health? I think not, because in experience I find that this is not so. To argue that he ought to be would seem to me to argue that he ought to be content with the animal level of development. Animals suffer diseases of the body and of the mind.

Man, however, cannot be explained merely by the categories of body and mind. Through all the ages it has been acknowledged that he is more—a soul. Indeed, it seems true to say, not that he is a body and has a soul, but that he *is* a soul and *has* a body and a mind. The essential man seems to be spirit, capable of correspondence or communion with God. Taken by and large, man everywhere practises this correspondence. There is hardly a race or a tribe without some sort of God or gods. It is difficult satisfactorily to define the soul, but it would serve to describe it as that non-physical part of man's nature by which he claims to make contacts with God or with the gods.

The health of the spirit or soul depends on its harmonious relationship with the other parts of man's personality and its relevant environment, and for Christians the name of that environment is the God whom Christ revealed. If that correspondence is entirely cut off, or if man's Godward relationship is in conflict with other functions of the self— say the manward attitude, which might be poisoned with hate—then the soul is in a state of disease. Its health is broken. Wholeness has vanished. As lungs need air, as the eye needs light, the spirit of man needs God. It is significant here to recall that the words "health" and "whole" and "holy" and "hale," all have the same root—namely, an old English word "hal," meaning "complete." We are not surprised to learn that in different ways all the races of mankind feel:

That in even savage bosoms
There are longings, strivings, yearnings,
For the good they comprehend not.
And the feeble hands and helpless,
Groping blindly in the darkness,
Touch God's right hand in the darkness
And are lifted up and strengthened.[2]

Nor are we surprised to find that at every point in Nature, in plants, animals and man, and in man at all levels, physical, mental and spiritual, there is an urge towards wholeness or completeness.[3]

[2] Longfellow, "Hiawatha."
[3] This is worked out in my *Psychology in Service of the Soul*, in the final chapter entitled, "The Soul's Urge to Completeness" (Macmillan, 1930).

But a much more important matter emerges. The human being is a very closely-knit unity of body, mind and spirit. In such a unity there cannot be disease at any point, at any level of being, without the whole personality being to some extent affected.

Instances readily occur. Obviously, if the physical cells of the brain—which, be it remembered, is part of the *body*, not part of the mind—are injured or poisoned or diseased, then the mind, of which the brain is the particular instrument, can be thrown out of its healthy functioning. The liver is frequently blamed for depression of mind and myopic spiritual vision. Many mental illnesses are thought to be physically caused, and great success is attending the attempt to cure them by physical means, such as electro-convulsive therapy treatment, the use of insulin, prolonged narcosis, and so on.

Again, the body's health can be destroyed by the mind. We have noted in earlier pages such diseases as psychogenic asthma, skin diseases, peptic ulcers and paralyses. Conversion-hysteria is the name given to functional disease—which can be just as disabling as organic disease—caused by that tendency of the mind in handing over to the body, in terms of disability, some strain which it can no longer bear.

Similarly, there are diseases of the soul, like jealousy, hate, malice, bad temper, resentment, worry, emotional rebellion, and so on. They may be wilful sin in the theological sense. In many cases they are moral illnesses conditioned by situations and circumstances that the patient could not control. He is frequently to be treated *as* a patient, and not as a sinner or a criminal.

But these diseases of the soul are no more bounded by the soul than diseases of the body are bounded by the body, or than diseases of the mind are bounded by the mind.

The newly opening field of psycho-somatic disease shows most significantly that illnesses long regarded as entirely physiogenic are more truly described as the effects in the body of disharmony in the mind or soul; the organic concomitants not merely of psychological disharmonies, but of spiritual ones; of broken spiritual relationships with other people, such as in cases of hate and jealousy, where there is a refusal to love, and in broken spiritual relationships with God, such as we find after a shattering bereavement in which a patient experiences, over a long period, a bitter resentment against Him. Even a hardy body cannot stand so grievous a wound in the spirit; nor the wound of bereavement, but that of resentment. Kindly visitors often have enough insight to see this. "You will make yourself ill," they say, knowing that body, mind and soul are one, and the hurt of one is the hurt of all.

To say nowadays, then, in the light of psychosomatic medicine, that religion has no relation to physical illness is more than ever absurd. For what has a greater influence over unhealthy emotion than the Christian religion in its purest, least sectarian form? To separate religion and healing as though they never had any vital relationship is to make nonsense of most of the healing acts of Jesus Christ, and of all the undoubted "cures" obtained through religious means already studied in the earlier part of this book. To say that religion has no relation to psychological illness seems to me equally unsound. To take only one group of cases, guilt, repressed or conscious, is most certainly a fruitful cause of both physical and psychological, as obviously of spiritual, illness. Unless the physician can deal with guilt, then, it would seem logical to argue that he cannot effect a radical cure. It is not usual for the physician or the psychologist as such to say, "Thy sins are forgiven thee." Has not religion, then, a vital part to play in the cure of certain kinds of illnesses such as those caused by guilt? To this point we now turn.

GUILT AS CAUSATIVE OF ILLNESS AND THE RELEVANCE THERETO OF RELIGION

A. The Origin of Guilt

IN ALL PSYCHOTHERAPEUTIC practice it is found that the sense of guilt plays a large part. Sometimes, indeed, guilt, either conscious or repressed, is a determining factor in neurosis, and in the writer's own experience a sense of guilt has frequently been responsible for the onset of serious physical symptoms. We have seen (p. 60 ff.) how the removal of the sense of guilt brought the immediate cure of physical symptoms in one of the miracles of our Lord. Guilt, then, is a subject of immense importance as we view the *rapprochement* of psychology and religion.

Why do we feel a sense of guilt?

To answer this would take us back to the origin of religion itself, and I shall deal with it when we come to examine Freud's attitude to religion, for in his works he has based part of his charge against Christianity on the supposition that man himself created the idea of a righteous God in relation with whom man feels a guilty sinner.

It may be that primitive man, frightened by natural phenomena which caused him distress and suffering, personified them in gods, reduced the gods to one in order to come into relationship with him, and then endowed him with moral qualities so as to give authority to those moral standards—an authority necessary to the life and orderliness of society. Moral evil not only did not pay—one's fellows saw to that—but wrongdoing became harder. It became an affront against God. Added to the fear of man's displeasure was the fear of God's anger. Righteousness was the only way of life by which one could escape the fear of consequences which is the very heart of guilt. We still feel guilty because, from primitive man onwards, the human mind has realised that somehow, somewhere and at some time, sin means consequence, and perhaps penalty as well. Indeed, man feels he *ought* to be punished. Jung comes forward with his theory of the collective unconscious, and tells us that the racial archetypes play an important part in the development of that fear which follows doing wrong and the joy which follows doing right. Stealing, for example, from the beginning of time, has brought punishment from the tribe if the theft were discovered. "Stealing doesn't pay." "You will get into trouble if you are caught." This sort of thought is as deep in the human mind as any idea can be, and a sense of guilt would, in many sensitive minds, follow stealing, even without the training of the parent. Some "sins" seem to be universally perceptible as "wrong" without our being told so. The universe seems built on a plan which is hostile to some forms of evil.[1]

But there is an "origin" of guilt nearer home. In childhood we found that doing or saying certain things got us into trouble, brought us disapproval, if not physical pain. We therefore associated this doing with fear—the fear of painful consequences. We had to bow to our parents' ethical standards, however arbitrary and confused those standards might prove to be when our matured adult minds examined them. Fear is the painful nub of guilt, and what with the legacy of primitive man and of our own parents and teachers, it is easy to understand the power which guilty feelings have over us.

From both parents and teachers, then, on the one hand, and from the collective unconscious, on the other, we build up a "super-ego." It is a "self" which demands a certain moral standard imposed through *fear*, not through dispassionate choice. The source of the authority remains unconscious. At its bidding I do not act because it demands an ideal which I have freely chosen and to which I desire to attain for its own sake—this is the "ego-ideal," at whose behest we say not only "I ought," but "I want to." I respond to the super-ego through fear of the consequences of doing anything else. It does not whisper, "Freely choose this path, for you can see it to be the way of self-fulfilment." It whispers, "A person who aspires to be this, pretends to be that, has been trusted with this position, is assumed by the crowd to be so and so, *must*, at least as far as public knowledge goes, attain to a certain moral standard, do this and that, play such-and-such a

---

[1] Jung would have enjoyed the story of the little boy interrupted in the act of stealing sweets by a loud clap of thunder. Turning to the sky and shaking his fist at it, he muttered, "You big bully!"

part." The "id," the fundamental, primitive savage in us all, will violently oppose the demands of the super-ego, and unless a middle-way can be found, an ego-ideal which gives us a way of life satisfying to both super-ego and id, then neurosis is probable. The conflict between the super-ego and the id, between the demands of conscience—however faultily organised on even stupid and illogical standards—and the craving of desire, has been the cause of many a "nervous breakdown," especially where the conflict is repressed and therefore unconscious. Such a middle-way, so far from being a "wicked compromise with evil" or a weak surrender, is the discovery of a positive path of life which may take years to find and follow. It will not be a path of impossible achievement, remote from, and denying the existence of, all instinctive urges, such as the inflated super-ego sometimes demands.[2] It will not, on the other hand, be a complete capitulation to the unleashed, unrestrained cravings of instinctive desire. It will be a path that pays tribute to the real needs of the id (for the id is not immoral, but amoral), and the lofty demands of a super-ego *which has been seen through* and which is no longer the lair of *unconscious* complexes.

Illustrations of this super-ego are seen through every age and phase of life; in the child who is told he must do this and that because he is "mummy's good boy" and because "mummy won't love him if he is naughty" (a wicked threat), and who has been known to stand himself in the corner not because he feels in his heart that he is a bad boy but because he has fallen below the standard imposed by his mother and he fears her reaction if he fails. It is seen in the prig who is a parson's son at school, and can't forget it, torn constantly between parsonic and schoolboy standards; in the parson himself who can never forget his profession and wears a clerical collar under all circumstances and can never "come off it." These are amusing enough. But the super-ego can be a grim tyrant, and when men act through an "oughtness" not of free choice, but because of fear—a fear often arising from unconscious complexes, or of stupid and irrational conventions or of falling below a standard imposed by others—we know them to be in its grip. Defiance of the moral compulsions of the super-ego is the main cause of pathological and exaggerated guilt, and therefore of the mental and physical symptoms which follow.

The trouble is that, whatever may be the origin of conscience, we

[2] Some will say, "Surely we cannot set our standard too high!" But in effect one can if the "height" ignores other factors in the situation. So an athlete can overtrain and break down. So a pupil can attempt the impossible examination and break down. Other elements in our make-up demand to be heard and they are not necessarily "*lower*" elements.

"introject" into our own natures, to use Freud's word, the factors by which the super-ego is built up.[3] We "take them into ourselves." From the depths of the unconscious they sway us. Many people, long after reaching adult age, react to certain situations according to the drive of the moral teaching of *their* parents, and indeed to the super-egos of their parents. In my own case, for example, however I might defend intellectually the moral value of any particular film, my strict Presbyterian upbringing so imprisons me, that to see it in a cinema on a *Sunday* evening would induce such guilt as would make is impossible for me to enjoy the film. A friend of mine regularly attends church every Sunday morning, escaping with immense relief as soon as the service is over, and never giving a thought to religion at any other time in the week. His super-ego demands this from him at sixty as powerfully as his parents demanded it from him at sixteen. His parents' demands were introjected into him, and now are built into his super-ego, where unconsciously they sway his behaviour. The fact that they are un-conscious is revealed by the rationalisations he makes if teased about his church-going. He rarely goes to church on holidays, but if he absented himself while in town, his super-ego would punish him with feelings of guilt, though the action it drives him to do, Sunday after Sunday, is only a species of moral bluff. At the same time, he extracts from this weekly farce a sense of complacent well-being, instead of guilty shame. He has appeased the gods, and so to luncheon, sleep and what he really *wants* to do. Similarly, a woman of my acquaintance defied her parents and took up a profession, although her parents wished her to stay at home. Although she did remarkably well, every new achievement was the occasion of deep depression and feelings of guilt, even after her parents were dead. The power of the super-ego was repressed into the unconscious. She did not know—until analysis revealed it—why to pass a new examination brought depression. But in talking with a psychologist, she recognised the influence of a super-ego saying in terms of depression, "You ought not to have gone along a path of which your parents disapproved."

Added to that, there is no doubt that she had repressed into the un-conscious part of her mind the "death wish" against her parents. That is, she had really desired their death with part of her mind because their death would have removed their opposition and left her free to pursue with untrammelled happiness her chosen career. Obviously the death-wish was repressed as being "an awful thing to think." Convention de-mands that dutiful and "loving" daughters do not desire the death of

[3] Freud, *The Ego and the Id,* p. 47.

their parents. But the wish lived on in the unconscious, and when the parents died the patient "broke down." The death-wish was fulfilled, but guilt raised its ugly head. The guilt also remained unconscious, but bubbles from the guilt at the bottom of the well of the mind often rise to the surface in the form of anxiety and fear which disable the mind from concentrating on the daily task and rob the patient of mental peace. She cannot stop thinking of herself, accusing herself and wondering "if she might have done more." Her unconscious accuses her of murder.

Again and again, a young woman hindered from her chosen career in order to nurse or house-keep for her parents will be found to break down when they die. It is not the strain of nursing so much as the sense of guilt arising from the illogical working of the deep mind which—as it were—mocks the patient as follows: "You really wanted them to die, and now you've achieved your object, but you shall pay for your guilty wish by fear of guilt's inescapable nemesis." So the patient pays with neurosis for an unconscious guilt whose power could have been prevented if made conscious early enough. The patient should have admitted that, though she loved her parents, she hated the fact that they stifled her ambitions, and prevented her marrying. *Recognition* would have saved her from neurosis, for it ends repression. There was no need for her to desert her parents, but only to admit to consciousness her real feelings.

We see, then, how feelings of guilt can be experienced apart from any conscious wrong-doing. The enormous and oppressive sense of guilt in regard to sex must be mentioned here. Many adult people feel it is wicked to talk about it, to feel sexually hungry, or even to know about sex. Hundreds of married people feel that sexual intercourse is "base," or "animal," or something they ought not to enjoy. Only those of us who have listened to the confidences of large numbers of people know how exaggerated can be the sense of guilt which the almost universal [4] habit of masturbation can bring to those whose super-ego has been built up and inflated by the false attitude of the Victorians and by the taboo [5] on sex, to break which can make many a sensitive modern as miserable as the breaking of a tribal taboo made the savage. For the savage, the punishment of the tribe, often in terms of physical pain,

---

[4] According to recent figures, 99 per cent in males and over 90 per cent in females, at some period between fifteen and fifty.

[5] Flugel defines "taboo" as "a prohibition that carries a supernatural or a social sanction." *Man, Morals and Society* (International Universities Press, 1945). A taboo, he comments later, "is revealed as a prohibition of a desire," and again "taboos are the socialized expression of conflicts."

made him miserable. For the modern, the punishment of the outraged super-ego in terms of neurosis has a similar effect. The super-ego, indeed, acts much as the taboo. Both produce a compulsion which the victim inwardly wishes he could resist, but to which he capitulates through fear. An "oughtness" is produced which does not win free co-operation, which, in fact, produces acute conflict, but which cannot be withstood without fear of punishment or evil consequence.

Valentine [6] tells of a young woman who suffered from a nervous breakdown in which the most marked symptom was persistent insomnia and fear of sex. She dreamed that her father was killed in a motor smash. In the dream she arrived in another car driven by a man. She witnessed the removal of the corpse from the smashed car. The patient had been made much worse by witnessing two very unfortunate incidents. "She witnessed the suicide of a man who threw himself on to the electric rails just before a train came into a station. Shortly afterwards she witnessed the attempted suicide of a man who, in the public street, tried to cut his throat." Investigation showed that she feared and hated her father because he was unfaithful to her mother. The patient developed a death-wish against her father, but repressed it into the unconscious because it was "wicked." The dream, however, revealed it. So often the dream expresses a repressed *desire*. The man in the car in which she rode was the "father substitute." The patient's fear of sex was caused by the dread that any lover of hers might treat her as her father treated her mother. We note here characteristic causes of breakdown. (1) The trauma of the discovery of her father's unfaithfulness. (2) The conflict between the super-ego demanding that a girl "ought" to love her father and her inability to give him such love sincerely. (3) The guilty longing for her father's death repressed into the unconscious. (4) The conflict between her desire to marry and the fear that her lover would behave to her as her father had behaved to her mother. In this case Valentine reports that the cure came not only through making these factors conscious, but through religious fellowship, by which "she found deliverance from her inward fears and hatreds."

I have read that the Kikuyu and the Masai tribes of East Africa are governed by sixty-eight taboos. Anyone who violates a taboo becomes "*thabu*," rapidly loses weight and often dies. He dies from a sense of guilt. What the taboo did to the savage the super-ego does to us. People in civilised Britain and America still die of taboos. The examples of the self-immolation complex on p. 352 ff. come to the mind. Many a victim of neurosis loses weight and is physically ill through a sense of guilt set up by the super-ego. In the case above, the daughter ought not

[6] Cyril H. Valentine, *Treatment of the Emotions*, pp. 103 ff. (S.C.M.).

to feel shame at wishing such a father were dead, but without psychological insight she could no more escape the taboo of the super-ego than could the savage. Both set up a sense of guilt, and guilt, especially when repressed, spells illness.

In speaking of the origin of a sense of guilt, we must note that the mechanism of the "association of ideas" often sets up intense feelings of guilt.

In one case which I studied, a boy who had been cruelly treated by a father who brought up his son in what is miscalled "a godly home," where much Church- and Sunday-School-going was demanded, grew into a self-labelled "atheist." He could not always escape religious functions. When he had to attend them he was overwhelmed with feelings of guilt. When the Lord's Prayer was said, he was physically nauseated. Obviously he had transferred to "Our Father Who Art in Heaven" the hate he dared not express—and so repressed—in regard to his father on earth. Since, in his boyhood, any hostility to such a "godly" father brought a sense of guilt and fear of punishment, so now religion, which reminded him of the father-son relationship, brought, by association, the same feelings back again. Here again a feeling of guilt can arise without any conscious sense of sin being a reasonable cause. One might call it "conditioned guilt." (See p. 332.)

Sometimes guilt derives from a "sin" committed, but repressed and forgotten. Yet, if one may put it thus, the unconscious remembers it, and if a situation or setting is repeated in real life which "reminds" the unconscious of the earlier guilty occasion, the unconscious either discharges into consciousness a disturbing sense of guilt, or creates a mental or physical symptom, which *apparently* has no relation to any guilty incident, but which psychological investigation reveals as directly attributable to guilt.

One case of obsessional neurosis I studied some years ago is a case in point. The patient could never remember a certain name, though it was a common one. It was unconsciously associated in his mind with a discreditable incident which he wished to forget, but to which a sense of guilt still adhered.

In another case I knew, repressed guilt led the guilty person to project her own guilt on to her husband. Though he was entirely innocent, she really came to believe that he was guilty of the sin she had herself committed, and she actually went so far as to accuse her husband of infidelity in the presence of her two brothers.

Dr. W. L. Northridge [7] describes a case of his own in which a man

[7] In *Health for Mind and Spirit* (Abingdon, 1938).

felt compelled to hold his hands under a tap for two hours each morning. Often he was detained so long by this ritual that he was late for business. In the First World War I once shared a tent with another officer who felt compelled to wash his hands every few minutes. Since we were in the desert, where water was scarce, this obsessional neurosis was a great nuisance. These compulsive hand-washings are frequently traceable to repressed guilt, or to the fear of feeling guilty.

Another most fascinating case I was able to remedy concerned a young married woman, who lived in the country, and who developed a rash across her chest when she went shopping in the town. The strange feature was that even a shopping expedition in the town did not *always* produce the rash. To make a very long story very short, it emerged that she only developed the rash if, while shopping in the town, she saw a certain kind of motor-car. Without the "why" of it coming into consciousness at all, to see a certain type of car reminded the unconscious—in which, of course, *all* our memories are stored—of immoral incidents which had happened with a married man in the back of a similar car while her own husband was fighting overseas. The guilt was repressed, but had its revenge in the unsightly rash, making a person who would not face up to, and accept the fact of, a stained mind, compulsorily bear the stigma of a stained body. Subsequent to interviews with me, the patient promised to give up immoral relationships. She realised the fact of the forgiveness of God, of which I shall write later. She and her husband—who was told the whole story by his wife and who readily forgave her—re-affirmed their marriage vows together in my presence, and a stubborn rash, into which many ointments had been well rubbed, disappeared, and has never returned, though I am writing over six years after the incidents described.

B. The Effect of Guilt

We have seen, then, that for all men, arising from a sense of having consciously done wrong, or arising from the tyranny of the super-ego, built up as it is from the training of parents, and teachers, from *their* super-egos and from those of *their* ancestors, from events and situations associated with others in which guilt was normally incurred, from the breaking of some taboo or other, man universally experiences a sense of guilt.

What is its effect upon him?

Its effect is of two kinds. (1) If he consciously accepts the fact of guilt, the effect is depression, and if he be spiritually sensitive and introspective, it may well bow him down in despair. "O wretched man that I am," he cries with Paul, "who shall deliver me from *this body of death?*" [8] The sense of guilt seems as intolerable as the corpse strapped to the body of a prisoner by a terrible Roman custom. Wherever he went, he could not escape the stench and disgusting burden of it all. (2) If, on the other hand, the patient successfully represses guilt, pretends it is not there, "gets over it," banishes it into the unconscious, it may, from those inaccessible depths, set up a mental distress or physical illness, hard for his physician to understand and harder still to cure. Of this type of illness I have already written.[9] When the burden of the mind, conscious or unconscious, becomes intolerable, it often pushes it on to the body (to use a convenient phrase), translating its disharmony into some physical symptom which lightens that mental burden and brings to a patient who knows (if only unconsciously) that he is a guilty man who ought to be punished and lose the love of his fellows, the love and sympathy more readily evoked if the patient is "ill." ("I'm ill, you can't be unkind to me.")

It is better if a man accepts his guilt as his due, provided it follows "sin" to which he can consciously relate it, and is not merely the torture of an inflated, and often inherited, super-ego, the result of "scruples," or the result of the association of ideas. It is better that it should depress his conscious mind than poison the unconscious, for the unconscious will, in the end, indubitably send in some kind of bill which will have to be paid.

If he does "feel" consciously a sense of guilt, we notice another effect it has upon him. *He wants to put things right.* He may try to do so by rationalising. He tells himself that his sin is no worse than others have committed, that he was provoked, that it was "justified" in business deals. He may blame others in order to escape the tension of guilt. But the fact remains, he feels there is something to be done. Even though the sin may never, can never, perhaps, be found out, yet within himself the patient feels that something must be put right. This universal fact is one to which many psychologists should pay head. Its significance and importance to the patient have often been overlooked. Its significance in the sphere of crime is noteworthy.[10] A criminal once told me that though he got clear away and was intellectually certain he could never be discovered, the burden of guilt was so intolerable that he walked into Scotland Yard and gave himself up. His arrest released the tension, and he felt happier than he had been since the crime, even though he knew that drastic and inescapable punishment would follow.

[8] Romans 7:24 (R.V. Margin.) This is only one of many suggested interpretations.

[9] See Index for references to conversion-hysteria and psycho-somatic disease.

[10] For those who deal with youth, the significant volume here is *The Young Delinquent*, by Sir Cyril Burt, M.A., D.Sc. (Appleton, 1925).

In some cases this "putting right" can be done in part. At the worst I can confess my sin to the one I have wronged.[11] Sometimes I can do better, and make restitution. If I steal from another or from the Income Tax Commissioners, I can at least pay back. But even then something remains. My friend, let us say, from whom I stole five pounds, has been paid his money, but a sense of guilt remains. I remain not quite the same person as before. I am now the kind of person capable of stealing five pounds. Character deterioration has revealed itself. I have made restitution, but I still feel guilty. A court of law appreciates the fact that confessing and paying back do not put things right. Punishment follows the most abject confession. In fact, the latter makes punishment more certain than a plea of "not guilty."

So we come to that effect of guilt which we can only call the *desire* for punishment. Hegel means this when he declares that "the sinful soul has a right to its punishment." Plato means this when he says that the soul will "run eagerly to its judge." The feeling "I ought to be punished" remains, even when as complete a restitution as I can make has been made. To ease this tension men have resorted to penance; they have flagellated themselves; they have fasted and prayed; they have tried to make atonement by this sacrifice and that. When they were little boys and stole a schoolmate's penknife, not only did they have to restore the knife, they suffered a whipping also. *Then*, and then only, did the tension of guilt disappear. Men still feel the *need* of the whipping-equivalent, which, though painful, eased the tension of guilt. Yet, now they are grown up, they cannot find a way of dispersing the sense of guilt.

Freud claims that some patients deliberately resort to wrong-doing because they know that it will bring punishment, and ease their sense of guilt which originates elsewhere, probably deep in the unconscious. Such people do not feel guilty because they have consciously sinned. They sin because, for unconscious reasons, they feel guilty, and feel a consequent need for punishment.

Here we come on a new cause of psychogenic illness. Again and again in my experience the chronic headache or neuralgic pain, or even illness which is diagnosed as organic, is the punishment which the super-ego inflicts on the ego which both *desires* punishment, even while it hates it, just as the child desires to end guilt-tension, but hates the pain of the punishment. I am not, of course, suggesting that anything like all chronic illness can thus be interpreted—that would be a gross distortion of my meaning—but I am saying that I have met it often enough to

[11] Though see notes on Confession (p. 445), for sometimes it makes matters worse.

mention it in this connection. We so associated punishment with guilt in our childhood and reacted to it with both the desire for it—or rather for the ease of mind only obtainable by suffering it—and the desire to escape it, that we repeat this reaction in adult life, and the super-ego, taking its familiar role of parent-substitute, inflicts it upon us, and though we hate it and call in the doctor to cure our pain, yet our deep mind accepts it as preferable to the unrelieved tension of guilt.

Flugel, in his provocative and, in many ways, excellent book, *Man, Morals and Society*, says that so deep in man is his need of punishment that even if things go well, he feels uneasy. Knowing that we do not deserve it, we become restive if our need for punishment is not met. "Hubris," or arrogance, is so often the prelude of disaster that we fear when we have an unbroken run of what the world calls success. "It's too good to last," we say fearfully.

Strangely enough, while I was writing this section I called upon a minister who had recently passed through a most trying experience. To my amazement, he said it was almost a relief! "Why?" I asked, incredulously. "Well," he said, "for thirty years I have visited people in their times of suffering, and I have wondered why I was exempt. I had never suffered any physical or mental pain, and I knew I did not deserve such immunity. My present suffering has eased that situation considerably."

We are right in regarding this as abnormal, but it is common. We have all heard people, after a long spell of good health, fine weather, or a run of good luck in business, say, "I shall have to pay for this." Flugel has called it the Polycrates complex. Polycrates, according to Herodotus, was a tyrant in Samos whose every enterprise was successful. His friends became alarmed, and advised him to make some offering to the gods in a form which cost him something. In response to their advice, he threw a valuable ring into the sea. But when a magnificent fish, caught off the coast, was presented to him because it was such a fine specimen, his cook found the ring inside it. This was interpreted to mean that his offering was rejected; that the gods were not going to be bought off by a ring from demanding their penalties. The incident set up such a terror that a fearful calamity was impending, that certain of his allies deserted him. He was obviously a doomed man!

Freud, in *The Ego and the Id*, describes people who show signs of discontent and actually get worse, if, during analysis, the analyst speaks hopefully to them and tells them they are getting better. He says, "There is no doubt that there is something in these people that sets itself against their recovery and dreads its approach as if it were a danger. ... In the end we come to see that we are dealing with what may be called a moral factor, a sense of guilt which is finding atonement in the illness and is refusing to give up the penalty of suffering. But, as far as the patient is concerned, this sense of guilt is dumb and it does not tell him he is guilty. He does not feel guilty, he simply feels ill." [12] I take leave to doubt this conclusion if generally applied. In some cases I feel that a patient whose neurosis is caused by the deprivation of love (see p. 343) fears recovery because, while ill, he gets love in terms of sympathy from his friends and in terms of help and counsel from the psychologist. When he recovers, sympathy and advice cease, and he cannot face life without them. He, therefore, maintains a resistance against recovery.

Any close observer of human life must have noticed, in antithesis to this, that illness of body or mind frequently happens just when a person has at last got rid of all obstacles to long-sought success and happiness and has at last within his grasp the prize he has worked for for years.

A young minister was appointed to an important pulpit, and "broke down" after six months. Was it the strain of his undoubtedly great burden, or was it partly a sense of guilt which demanded the punishment of one who inwardly knew that he was quite unfitted to stand in such spiritual pre-eminence above his far worthier fellow ministers? Did the super-ego, as it were, say, "You are guilty of this and this and that. You have never paid for these sins. But if you think that a rotter like you is going to stand up there, as if he really deserved such preferment, you will find punishment awaiting you. The 'id' is not prepared for you to pretend to worthiness of that eminence, and between us we will pull you down." Flugel points out, [13] in support of this theme, that in certain cases where neurosis is attributable to what we have called the need for punishment, a severe accident causes the neurosis to clear up. The mechanism seems to be, "I ought to suffer, and in lieu of physical pain (whipping-substitute) I must suffer mentally (neurosis). Since this accident has brought me physical pain, there is no further need for me to suffer any more mental pain." The super-ego again hands over its duties to the body.

C. The Treatment of Guilt

If all this be true, we can understand how man has wrestled, both theologically and psychologically, to find a means of ridding himself of the intolerable burden which a sense of guilt imposes upon him. Every-

[12] Pp. 70-71.

[13] *Op. cit.*, where illustrations are given by this very able writer.

one who has talked with people in trouble realises something of the immense and paralysing power which guilt can have. It frequently accounts for complete breakdown in health. It drives criminals whose crimes could not possibly be discovered to give themselves up. It has frequently driven men to suicide.

The lay psychologist seems to be helpless in such a situation. He tends to tell the patient that other people have done things just as bad, that he is making himself ill about nothing, that he must deflate his super-ego and get over his troubles as best he may. Religious treatment gets nearer to the heart of the matter, and if a real conversion takes place, the burden of guilt frequently disappears at once. But a conversion is not easily engineered. Further, a faulty theology, such as is only too common amongst us, because it is unacceptable to the intelligence of the twentieth century, fails to deal with the situation.

An attempt will be made in this section to offer a treatment of guilt which is both psychologically and theologically adequate. The importance of the matter is clearly seen here, in that if no adequate treatment of guilt is applied, the burden may increase with the years, particularly if the personality is making spiritual progress. The nearer we get to the white of God, the blacker our sins appear. The great saints have always been the most sensitive to sin. St. Paul, having preached to others, fears lest his guilt will make him a castaway. Again and again in passages in his letters we see his mind tortured by the thought of sin. He calls himself "the chief of sinners," "an abortion of an apostle," "a wretched man in torment," and so on. In later days the saintly John Wesley echoed, even on his death-bed, the same kind of language.

It seems valuable at this stage to divide guilt into three classifications:

1. *Normal Guilt*

This, of course, does not present a problem for treatment. It would be absurd to suppose that any sense of guilt in the mind of a person indicated an abnormality which ought to be removed. Normal guilt I equate with the theological "sense of sin" which ought to follow the doing of wrong. Indeed, the preacher must frequently produce a sense of sin. It is a healthy and valuable spur to our will, and is the first step towards a new life. Guilt here is like that degree of pain which tells us that something is wrong. It is a valuable warning. When it persists after it has given us warning of an unhealthy soul, it becomes morbid and something to be removed, just as pain, having given us warning that something is wrong, becomes a liability to be removed after the warning has been received.

E. R. Micklem [14] reminds us of the importance of normal guilt when he contrasts Cellini with Bunyan! Cellini was assiduous in spiritual devotion, but vain, cruel, murderous and profligate. He had no sense of guilt. He seemed at peace with God and his fellows. Bunyan, ethically sensitive, moral to the core, was tortured by doubt and driven almost mad with a sense of guilt. From the psychological point of view Cellini would be regarded by many as more healthy and normal, but Bunyan was by far the finer character. True religion would increase moral sensitiveness without increasing *morbid* guilt.

2. *Exaggerated Conscious Guilt*

By this I mean an overwhelming sense of shame and an intolerable burden following some peccadillo or incident, the guilt of which the patient has exaggerated out of all proportion.

Recently I had a letter from a lady in the North of England whose "sin" appeared to me trifling, and yet who, at the age of sixty—forty years after the event—dreaded dying and "meeting her Maker."

A good illustration of exaggerated guilt is frequently seen in that which follows the practice of masturbation. Very few men and women refrain completely from this habit at some time or another, but the guilt which follows has often been so exaggerated that the patient has even believed himself or herself unfit for marriage, or thinks that the unpardonable sin has been committed.

I was recently asked in a public service when questions were allowed whether masturbation was sin, and I still think the answer I gave is correct: that it depends whether the picture on the screen of the mind at the time could be shown to our Lord without shame. Frequently the practice is followed with no picture on the screen of the mind at all. That is to say, it is just a harmless method of getting physical relief from almost unbearable tension. Lust—which I should define as sexual desire, plus intention and minus love—is sin, but many kinds of masturbation, though admittedly a species of self-relief to be reduced as far as possible, for psychological reasons, cannot be regarded as sinful. For instance, here is a young soldier on a campaign far from the wife he loves. In imagination he has sexual intercourse with her and obtains relief by masturbation. I hold that there cannot be sin in that

[14] *Queen's Quarterly*, Vol. LVI, No. 3, 1949.

act because he is only doing imaginatively what he would do innocently if he were actually with her. Again, if the picture on the screen of the mind is that of a lover far away, or even, in the case of a celibate, an imaginary lover, I should not myself attach guilt to it, though it would be well to suggest a better way of finding relief in sublimation and to point out the dangers of fixating sex at an infantile level or of becoming obsessed or enslaved by sexuality. Even the Roman Church, stern in these matters, allows a wife who does not reach her climax with her husband during intercourse, to attain her climax or orgasm by digital manipulation or masturbation, and by the same means to prepare for intercourse beforehand. [15] Frequently masturbation indicates emotional adolescence. The patient must be helped to grow up. Sometimes masturbation is sin, for in repeated imaginative scenes with a prohibited person control is lost, making the sudden actualisation of such a scene a disaster. Habit tracks formed during imaginative scenes carry impulses into regrettable action in actual life if opportunity suddenly offers. At the same time in many situations, guilt is exaggerated and that exaggerated burden must be removed.

3. Repressed Guilt

Here we have a situation in which the feelings of guilt have been so objectionable to consciousness that they have been repressed into the unconscious. The incident that caused the guilt is "forgotten." In such a situation we nearly always find an abnormal readiness to blame another inordinately for some injury, real or imagined. So common is this that when one finds in a person the habit of continually blaming another, one can usually make the safe deduction that unconscious and repressed guilt is present in the deep mind of the complainant. We may also have anxiety seeping up into consciousness though its cause is concealed from the patient, or we may have psychosomatic illness, which means that the mind has handed over its disquiet to the body in terms of a disease. This has been described, for example, in the case of the woman who developed a guilt rash when she went shopping (see p. 323). Her cure, it may be recalled, was both psychological and theological. The act which completed the cure was the repetition of the marriage service.

[15] Vicar-General D. Craisson, *On Sexual Matters for the Guidance of Father-Confessors*, p. 172. "If the husband should withdraw after ejaculation before the wife has experienced orgasm, she may then lawfully at once continue friction with her own hand, in order to attain relief. In the same manner it is lawful for the woman to prepare herself by genital stimulation for sexual union, in order that she may have orgasm more easily." Ex Van de Velde, *Ideal Marriage*, p. 193 (Random House, 1930).

The treatment of guilt I shall now proceed to outline under six headings, the order of which I regard as important.

1. EXAMINATION

The first step is to set the guilt-causing incident or incidents in the centre of consciousness and decide whether normal or exaggerated guilt is being experienced. It may be found that if the feeling of guilt is more than normal and yet conscious, it may be traced to any of four sources:

(a) The *super-ego*, or the self imposed upon us through abnormal and often unconscious fears, can produce a sense of guilt in a manner astounding to those who have not studied it. An illustration leaps to my mind from my own family. My father, a strict Scottish Presbyterian, never attended the theatre until he was over sixty years of age. After the death of my mother, I was entertaining him at my home and suggested a visit to the theatre. I was able to overcome his reluctance, and took him to a play by J. M. Barrie. At the end of the play I caught a glimpse of his face, and the expression was as eloquent as words. When I challenged him with what he was thinking, I found that my guess was right. He had thoroughly enjoyed himself, but added, "I don't think I ought to have gone."

Here we see an illustration of guilt imposed by the super-ego. Through fear of what people would think or say; through fear of appearing to let down the codes and conventions in which he had been brought up, he had accepted the view that the theatre was wicked and that to go to it was sinful. The very thought of theatre-going would have set up guilt, and even when his reason, and perhaps my example, assured him that there was nothing in the least wicked about it, the old super-ego took its revenge by producing a sense of guilt.

(b) *Scrupulosity*. A student for the ministry had been working in the slums. His social activities were most praiseworthy, but on returning to college he suddenly announced that he would never again eat a good meal; that it was sinful to eat a good dinner while so many in the slums were hungry. It was quite difficult to break down the scrupulosity which produced in him such guilty feelings whenever he had a meal, though reason clearly showed how absurd his action was.

Dr. David Yellowlees tells of a patient of his who painted a cushion cover the design of which included a bunch of grapes. When the article was ready for sale it occurred to her that wine was made from grapes and that the purchaser might take to drink. She felt so guilty that she forthwith destroyed it.[16]

[16] *Psychology's Defence of the Faith* (Harper, 1930).

(*c*) A feeling of guilt is sometimes developed through an *association* of ideas in the unconscious. We might call it conditioned guilt. I recall the case of a man who, at forty, had the most vivid feelings of guilt whenever a door shut loudly behind him, and particularly if a key were turned in the lock. Investigation showed that when he was a small boy he went into the pantry to help himself to the good things which were there, and his mother stealthily came up behind him, slammed the pantry door and locked him in. Unfortunately, instead of having a good time with the things so near to him, he was overwhelmed with guilt, and set up a howl of terror at the prospect of the beating that would follow when the door was opened. He had forgotten the incident, but in the unconscious mind the slamming of a door made him start and recover the earlier feeling of guilt he had experienced over thirty years before.

(*d*) By *masking* I mean that activity of the mind by which the feeling of guilt is taken away from the incident which really caused it and transferred to some less heinous offence. We feel very guilty about some comparatively trifling affair but keep the more serious incident unconscious. Confession does not help because we are confessing the wrong sin and still hiding the real one. Thus a man I tried to help wept bitterly at the wrong he had done by smuggling three pairs of silk stockings but repressed the memory of an act of rape during the voyage which preceded it. "When we dare not acknowledge some great sin," said Jung, "we deplore some small sin with greater emphasis."

2. Confession

In another section of this book the question of confession is discussed (p. 445), but it must be noted here as part of the treatment of guilt. If God is real, confession can be made directly to God. If this seems a profitless performance and like "talking to nothing," it is a good thing to write out one's confession, even if one tears up the document afterwards. Writing out is a form of exteriorisation, and I cannot emphasise strongly enough the value of what William James calls "exteriorising our rottenness."

If God is not real, it is valuable to confess to a friend with spiritual insight and experience. It is to be realised that it is quite unnecessary to seek the aid of a professional priest, or minister, or psychologist. The priesthood of all believers, a doctrine emphasised by Wesley, has slipped too much into the background of our religious thought and practice. The confessor, however, should have some qualifications. The patient must be quite sure that he or she will never repeat a word of what is said, not even to wife or husband. And the confessor should be a person who will not only sympathise, but will be able to offer words of counsel and show ways in which the unfettered emotion which follows confession can be translated into some constructive, positive and socially valuable deed, and not left as mere feeling. Confession should not be regarded as a kind of atonement for sin, but a way of exteriorising it in order to examine it so as to decide what measures may now be taken to outgrow it. After confession it can be seen in its right perspective and in its right relationship to an adult sense of values. Failing this, the sense of guilt will grow up again and the "patient" remain in emotional and infantile dependence on the "father" confessor. His "conscience" will be ruled by exterior codes and prohibitions instead of by interior insight.

Perhaps it is unnecessary to say here that it is by no means always wise for a husband to confess to his wife, or vice versa, though sometimes it is the best possible course. I have known a marriage ruined by a husband confessing his infidelities to his wife. He transferred the burden of his guilt to her shoulders, and she was not equipped to carry such a burden. The wife could never forget what she had been told, and all intimate marital relationships, both physical, mental and spiritual, were ended by this unwise confession.

The Roman Catholic has a clear path marked out for him here, but members of other communions should have everything that is of value in the Roman Confessional, remembering that the value is in the confession, not in the denomination or alleged authority of the confessor.

3. REPARATION

Here the way may be very simple. Reparation may be the paying of money that has been stolen, the returning of a book, or some material reparation of that kind. Or it may be that an apology must be sent to a person whom we have wronged or with whom we have lost our temper. And even if our apology, instead of being accepted with love, is regarded by the offended person as our "climbing down"; even if the reparation makes him sneer, and boast to his companions that we have capitulated, yet, at any rate, in John Wesley's phrase, we have "put the fire out of our own bosom," and the guilt we have been feeling will be dissipated. That is the important thing.

Perhaps a word can be added as to dangerous ways of making reparation. Sometimes unwise attempts at "reparation" re-open old wounds that had well-nigh healed, or spread a moral poison unnecessarily or unwisely, or add a heavy burden to another's load which the person making the "reparation" should continue to carry in secret.

But no one can afford to evade true reparation either from the psychological or theological point of view. There was nothing that Christ made clearer than that the condition of God's forgiveness is that we should be ready to forgive another; that we can find no access to God ourselves if there is anyone in the world with whom we are unwilling to put matters right. "Forgive us our trespasses *as we forgive them that trespass against us.*" "Leave there thy gift before the altar, . . . first be reconciled to thy brother and then come and offer thy gift." "If ye forgive not men their trespasses, neither will your Father forgive yours." [17]

4. THE ACCEPTANCE OF FORGIVENESS

Here, of course, we come to the very heart of the matter. The forgiveness of God, in my opinion, is the most powerful therapeutic idea in the world. If a person really believes that God has forgiven him, then the burden of guilt and the fear at the heart of it disappear.

Scripture promises are emphatic on the fact of forgiveness. Sin "will be remembered no more"; it is "behind God's back"; it is removed from the sinner as far as the East is from the West.[18] If this great idea is really received by the mind, not only by the intellect, but by the emotion as well, then it is like the dawn breaking after a long night of black torture, and I have frequently known severe physical illness clear up speedily when it has been grasped and accepted by the whole personality. Men who hear an authoritative voice, full of loving forgiveness, say, "Thy sins are forgiven thee," very speedily take up their beds and walk.

My friend, Dr. Ernest White of Harley Street, a member of the staff of the City Temple Psychological Clinic, gives an interesting illustration of the therapeutic results of the received idea of forgiveness in his excellent little book, *The Way of Release.*[19]

"A man, aged thirty-five, whom we will call A, came to me complaining of intense fear of becoming insane. For several months he had suffered from sleeplessness, loss of appetite, abdominal pains, and feeling of panic and nameless fears. He thought at one time that he had appendicitis, he lost flesh, and at last felt so ill that he had to give up work. After a few weeks' analytical treatment, he was able to resume work, but he was still far from well. Analysis continued for several months, and he improved still further, but did not get quite well. After

[17] Matthew 6:12, 6:14, Mark 11:26, Matthew 5:23-24.
[18] Jeremiah 31:34, Isaiah 38:17, Psalm 103:12.
[19] Pp. 16-17 (Marshall, Morgan and Scott, Ltd., 1947).

careful consideration, I decided to deal with him in a certain way. At the next interview I said to him, 'I have thought well over your case, and I have come to the conclusion that what you need to do if you want to get well is to turn to the God of your youth. You made a profession in your youth, and for years you have turned your back on God. If you repent and seek forgiveness, you will be restored to full health.' He was very angry, told me that he did not come to a psychologist to be told that, flung down his fee and walked out. Two weeks later he telephoned to me in great distress, and asked me to see him again. I arranged to see him in my home in the evening. When he came in he cried like a child, and said that he could not forget what I had said, and knew that it was true. We talked on until very late, and then humbly, and in true penitence, he turned to God and found forgiveness. Within a month the alteration in him was striking. He completely lost his symptoms, put on weight, and was happy and well. Two years later, on leaving for another part of the country, he telephoned to me to say how fit he felt, and that the last two years had been the happiest and healthiest in his life. He had greatly improved with psychological analysis, but he did not find complete health until his spiritual condition was dealt with. Body, mind and spirit were now in tune, and he was a whole man."

I quote two further cases from patients attending our City Temple Psychological Clinic.

"Mr. A., aged sixty-two, a business man, married with two grown-up children, stated that for many years his Christian life had been spoiled by a sense of guilt and he had felt unable to take part in any Christian work. At last the burden had become intolerable. With considerable emotion he told the story of minor misdemeanours occurring when he was twelve, seventeen and twenty years respectively. He had never been instructed in sexual matters and had never dared to tell anyone his story, thinking that he had committed some very terrible sin. Within the past few months his anxiety had considerably increased. In this case it is probable that the practice of coitus interruptus (withdrawal by the male before the act of sexual union is completed by emission), over a period of many years, had contributed to this anxiety state, since he had marked guilt feelings concerning this. The instinctual nature of his youthful indiscretions was explained to him. He was also instructed and reassured on the true meaning of forgiveness as taught in the New Testament. The combined effect of confession after so many years and the talk about forgiveness set his mind completely at rest. He is now completely well."

"Mrs. C., aged thirty-nine, married and with a child of five, had been troubled with continual attacks of depression ever since she was nineteen, and recently had become more depressed and very irritable and unable to concentrate. Since the age of seventeen she had been obsessed with blasphemous thoughts which recurred so frequently that her life had become a misery. These were associated with a deep sense of guilt, and although she was a Christian woman and a member of the Church of England, she had been unable to attend Communion or any Church Service for several years. She had never been able to tell anyone about her obsessive thoughts, and the burden had become intolerable. After three interviews she was so relieved that she was able to attend a Communion service for the first time for twenty years. Three further interviews took place, and by the aid of dream analysis and free association the cause of her obsessive thoughts was discovered. She completely lost all sense of guilt and is perfectly happy and well."

At this point, however, it seems to me most important that the theology of forgiveness should be described. Many people cling to the infantile idea that forgiveness means being "let off." It did mean this often in our childhood, and a boy who was forgiven by his father but also thrashed would not think much of forgiveness. We must try to grow up from this infantile conception to the proper conception of God's forgiveness, which is not the cancelling of all the effects of sin, but the restoration of a relationship. Forgiveness means that our *relationship* with God is as though we had never sinned.

I find that the best ways of understanding forgiveness is to separate in my mind the effects of sin into two parts: penalty and consequences.

(1) The penalty of sin is two-fold: separation from God and progressive deterioration of character. Forgiveness means the ending of penalty. We are no longer separated from God, and the progressive deterioration of character is arrested. In that sense we are "let off."

(2) The consequences of sin, however, are not ended by forgiveness. We must remember that we live in a world of cause and effect, and though forgiveness means the restoration of a relationship between the soul and God, the consequences of sin continue. They may be in the body, or the mind, or the soul, or in all three. The point is that forgiveness changes their nature and their effect on personality.

Forgiveness changes the consequences of sin from being merely the nemesis of a seemingly blind system of cause and effect into the discipline of a loving Father, a discipline in which the soul even rejoices, for it is making the sinner what God wants him to be and what he—now that he is awakened—wants to be.

Clearly when the Prodigal Son returned from the far country and was forgiven by his father, the penalty of sin was cancelled. He was no longer estranged from his father, and the progressive character-deterioration induced by the far-country experiences ended. But we may well believe that the Prodigal was a convalescent, possibly in body, certainly in mind and spirit, long after his return. The point was, however, that he was at home with his father and in a love-relationship, not, like his elder brother, in a law-relationship, and therefore whatever happened to him in the way of consequence, severe though it may have been, was no longer regarded as bad luck or soulless retribution or resented fate, but a discipline within that love-relationship.

We may not escape the throes of consequence, but as Pompilia said:

> there *seems* not so much pain.
> It comes most like that I am just absolved
> Purged of the past; the foul in me washed fair.[20]

Unless this distinction between penalty and consequence is made, the mind is confused by all sorts of incongruities. For example, some regard syphilis as the penalty of adultery. But syphilis can be prevented and, if contracted, can be cured. Those who think of syphilis, then, as the whip in the hand of God by which He punishes adultery, would logically have to suppose that the whip could be snatched from God's hand by those who know how to commit adultery without risking disease. "You cannot punish us now," they might be imagined as saying, "because we can prevent your visiting us with the dread consequences of venereal disease."

But clearly if I make the distinction above, I see at once that though physical consequences can be modified, no one can possibly escape the *penalty* of sin, which is separation from God and deterioration of character. And, of course, if the bodily consequences are thus evaded, it may be worse in the end for the sinner, for physical consequences might have made the sinner conscious of his separation from God, whereas to escape them may leave him dead to God's challenge. To remain unconscious of the penalty of sin because one has used devices to evade consequences only postpones the terrible awakening. The saints say it is better to suffer anything in terms of physical disability than postpone suffering until the bodily life is over, for after death the mind and the soul are involved, and, say all the saints with unanimous voice, it is much harder to bear the pain of mental and spiritual suffering than any pain of body.

The central idea in forgiveness is that it brings at once the restoration of a father-son relationship which sin had broken, and whatever consequences may have to be borne, the relationship is as true as it

---

[20] Browning, *The Ring and the Book,* line 350. (Italics mine.)

was before sin broke it. It is most important to understand this theological exposition if guilt is adequately to be treated.

5. FORGIVEN SIN MUST BE WOVEN INTO FUTURE SERVICE

It is essential that guilt should be treated in such a way that the patient is not left without anything that he can *do* about the situation. My illustration here is that of a prostitute I knew who was converted to Christianity and began to live a clean life. She subsequently married, and it would have been understandable if she had wished to forget all her earlier experiences. Actually she did a far finer thing. She opened her home to prostitutes. Thus she wove her forgiven sin into the subsequent service. She used her experiences as an asset in the new life. She knew why prostitutes fell. She understood their loneliness and their hunger for love. She knew the awful vicious circle into which they came, and she knew how hard it was to break it.

I think of another case of a man who employed a boy of seventeen. The latter stole, and the situation might easily have got into the hands of the police and the boy's life have been ruined, instead of which the employer forgave the boy *and kept his secret.* The employer explained that he himself in his teens had pilfered, and that his whole life had almost been wrecked by publicity and shame. He thereupon made a vow that if ever he employed others and one such delinquent was brought before him, he would treat him in a far more Christian manner. The employer thus used his own forgiven sin as an asset in his service to others. It may be remembered that God does not waste anything. He can even use the sins of our past life as qualifications for our present and future service. If we have fallen through sex, we may be able so to teach our children that they will guard against the snares of life in this field. One of the truest thoughts in the Bible is that God uses even the wrath of man to praise Him.[21]

6. THE ATONING WORK OF CHRIST

I have said nothing yet of the atonement of Christ and, of course, all theologians would regard this as the vital doctrine relevant to the problem of guilt. Let us now turn briefly to that.

It is not surprising that all religious systems have tried to cope with the problem of guilt. The Jews—the religious geniuses of the world—hit on the ideas of the scapegoat, the sin offering and the vicarious sufferer. If man could really believe that guilt was thus dealt with, the

[21] Psalm 76:10.

problem was solved. Yet the great prophets, even within the Jewish religion, were in doubt about the efficacy of their sacrifices. Micah asks, "Will the Lord be pleased with thousands of rams, or with ten thousands of rivers of oil? Shall I give my first-born for my transgression, the fruit of my body for the sin of my soul?" Similarly Isaiah says, "To what purpose is the multitude of your sacrifices unto Me? saith the Lord; and I am full of the burnt offerings of rams, and the fat of fed beasts. I delight not in the blood of bullocks, or of lambs, or of he goats." The Psalter expresses the same idea. After perhaps the most eloquent and moving expression of the burden of guilt to be found in the whole of literature, the Psalmist says: "Thou delightest not in sacrifice, else would I give it: Thou hast no pleasure in burnt offering. The sacrifices of God are a broken spirit: a broken and a contrite heart, O God, Thou wilt not despise." [22]

It is not surprising that with this background St. Paul and other writers in the New Testament came to believe that the clue to the meaning of the Cross could be found in Old Testament ideas of sacrifice. If these theories satisfy the mind of the reader, so be it, but I am strongly of the belief that many thoughtful men and women today do not feel that this interpretation of St. Paul of the Atonement offers a place where their minds can rest, for the modern man does not believe, and cannot accept, either the scapegoat idea or the idea behind Jewish blood-offerings. Yet in modern churches, hymns based on these ideas are still sung. For example:

> I lay my sins on Jesus,
> The spotless Lamb of God.
> He bears them all and frees us
> From the accursèd load.

Or again,

> Not all the blood of beasts
> On Jewish altars slain
> Can give the guilty conscience peace,
> Or wash away the stain.
> But Christ, the heavenly Lamb,
> Takes all our sins away;
> A sacrifice of nobler name
> And richer blood than they.

I wish here to write with great reverence and with immense respect for the feelings of others. I also wish to express the truth as I see it.

[22] Micah 6:7, Isaiah 1:11, Psalm 51:16.

The relevant truth here, as I see it, can be expressed in one sentence of immense importance. It is this: Guilt cannot be transferred.

This is not the place to expound for the modern man a theory of the Atonement in harmony with modern psychology. I have tried to do that elsewhere.[23] Suffice it to say that if I have committed sin, then, if it really is sin—by which I mean the conscious choice of known evil—nothing can alter the fact that *I* have done it, and it is a fictitious juggling with words to suppose that I can lay the guilt on anyone else. No one else can carry my *guilt* and become the blameworthy person. Many theories of the Atonement seem unsatisfactory to the modern man because that great psychological fact that guilt cannot be transferred has been overlooked or denied. There *is* a true sense in which another can "bear our sins." Great loving means a kind of identification, and he who loves us bears both our sin and shame. But in no real sense can he bear our *guilt* and become blameworthy. If I have committed adultery, it is preposterous to imagine that I can transfer such guilt to Christ. Unless such transfer were unreal, it would make Him feel blameworthy.

I am convinced in my own mind that a thought very precious to the early Church was that of Christ as the Bridegroom wedded to the Church, His Bride. This idea comes repeatedly into the view of the New Testament writers, but although St. Paul teaches it, it has been jostled out of its importance by his much later interpretation.

It should be remembered that Christ not only taught parables, but acted them. The so-called triumphal entry into Jerusalem was clearly an acted parable, and no one who knew the Scriptures would miss its significance. In my view, the events just previous to Christ's death and the dread Crucifixion itself were all parts of a parable. He Himself called it "this Passover." [24] Now, amongst the Jews from earliest times the Passover was regarded as God's marriage to Israel. Indeed, the festival started with the words, "Behold, the Bridegroom cometh!"— a sentence which Jesus quoted in His parable of the wise and foolish virgins. In a Jewish wedding, the bridegroom fetches the bride to his own home, and his first act is to stoop and wash her feet. Jesus washed His disciples' feet. It was the first part of the acted parable of His wedding to the Church. In a Jewish wedding there immediately follows the feast. Jesus arranged a supper in a "large upper room richly furnished." After the feast the next stage in a Jewish wedding is the

[23] *A Plain Man Looks at the Cross* (Abingdon-Cokesbury, 1945).
[24] Luke 22:15.

declaration or words of covenant. Jesus said, "A new covenant I give you in My blood."

To my mind it is a pity that this interpretation of His death has been overlooked by the Church. It is more attractive to the modern mind, and psychologically more sound, for it is not pretended that the act of crucifixion magically removes the sin of the world. In truth, there is no such thing as "the sin of the world." In a sense there is no such thing as "sin," but only sinful persons. He who would save from sin must change the sinful person's nature. Sin is not a debt which somebody can pay or a burden which somebody else can carry. The Crucifixion should not be regarded as balancing a kind of Divine budget, so that Christ's physical and mental sufferings are set over against men's sins. No one can give more than His life, and Christ's death means that He commits Himself to humanity, as a bridegroom to the bride, for better, for worse, and for ever. The Cross is not thus a magical removal of our sins, but a pledge that Christ will stand by us and is closely committed to us until our whole nature is changed.

One can hardly forbear quoting a great passage in the letter to the Hebrews, probably not written by St. Paul at all, where we read (7:25), "He ever liveth to make intercession for us." The Greek word "to make intercession" (ἐντυγχάνειν) does not just mean "to pray for." It means "to act on behalf of another person to whom one is committed." [25] The word makes the following picture in my own mind. Jesus is man, and therefore is equal with man, and we imaginatively see Him with His hand grasping the hand of man. But Jesus is God and on an equality with God, and we imaginatively see Him and His other hand in the hand of God. To make intercession for us means bringing His hands together not so much in prayer, but so that the hand of man may be placed into the hand of God, and God and man made one. This at-one-ment is an idea which should be at the heart of every theory of the Atonement.

This interpretation seems to me to reconcile theology and psychology. We do not pretend, what all psychologists would deny, that guilt can be transferred to an innocent person. But we do see an innocent, and indeed divine, Person endlessly committed to make us one with God, and never leaving us until that task is achieved. His Cross is both the symbol and the pledge that He will go to the uttermost to redeem us. References to his "blood" involve the same idea. This is a task which no psychology can compass. This is an act of

[25] See Westcott's *Commentary on the Hebrews*, p. 191 (Macmillan, 1892), and Peake, *The Century Bible*, p. 162 (T. C. and E. C. Jack).

God on man's behalf. This is the final dealing with sin. It is unthinkable that man should transfer his guilt to Christ, but Christ will and does transfer His grace to man, so that the evil feeling in guilt, its burden, its shame and remorse, and, above all, its sense of fear, pass away, and the guilt which was a liability is transmuted into an asset, for it is a qualification for future service.

We see, then, that in the treatment of guilt psychology can do much. It can do much in bringing to consciousness those factors which have produced the guilty feeling, but psychology, as such, has nothing to say about forgiveness and nothing to say about redemption. It is just at this point that the patient frequently feels an intolerable loneliness and helplessness. At that point he is ready for the good news of the gospel, for something to be done for him and in him which no one can do but God.

> Not what these hands have done
>   Can save this guilty soul;
> Not what this toiling flesh has borne
>   Can make my spirit whole.
>
> Thy love to me, O God,
>   Not mine, O Lord, to Thee,
> Can rid me of this dark unrest,
>   *And set my spirit free.*[26]

What a "dark unrest" guilt can be, those who seek to help their fellows know. But no patient is cured, no personality integrated, until the spirit is thus set free. I have never, in thirty years, known a psychological treatment which, in this field of guilt, could by itself obtain freedom for the patient without recourse to all that the Christian religion offers.

But one other word must be added. The case of such a patient as I have described must not be abandoned until the idea of God's forgiveness is really received into the mind, there to do its liberating work. One has known cases in which the inability of the patient to receive and accept forgiveness has led to his case being given up. This is indeed a serious matter. The patient may be seized with the paralysing thought that forgiveness is not for him, that even religion has failed, that he is beyond salvation, or even that he has committed an "unpardonable sin." Unless he is taken right through to the place of release, his fears may lead him to despair; the despair of those who feel—wrongly but only too poignantly—that even God can do nothing for them and that they are beyond the circle of His grace and damned for ever.

[26] Horatius Bonar. (Italics mine.)

3

THE DEPRIVATION OF LOVE AS CAUSA-TIVE OF ILLNESS AND THE RELEVANCE THERETO OF RELIGION

THE theory that the neuroses are mainly due to the feeling of deprivation of love, especially in early childhood, is one which has been advanced and taught for many years by Dr. J. A. Hadfield as Lecturer in Psychopathology and Mental Hygiene in London University.[1]

It is a revolutionary theory, but my own observation and experience support it. It may seem a dangerous generalisation to attempt to trace the diverse psycho-neurotic symptoms to one common cause, and no doubt there are some exceptions, but the evidence of the truth of Hadfield's basic principle is, in my view, convincing.

"Love" in this connection does not mean sexual love or romantic, sentimental love alone, though both must be included and both fulfil a need. "Love" in this connection connotes that affection, goodwill and appreciation which must surround the life of every little child unless his personality is to be threatened by distortion. If love is given to him to the degree to which he has a right, then, even though he may be punished for his faults or deprived of many other advantages— for example, a good education, plenty of pocket-money and a good time generally—his mind will develop without distortion and his mental attitudes to himself and to the world generally will be free from neurotic trends.

If, however, he is denied love, in the sense defined, nothing on

---

[1] These views have now been incorporated in a book, *Psychology and Mental Health*, by J. A. Hadfield, M.A., M.B., Ch.B. (Macmillan, 1950), published since the typescript of this book was completed. Dr. Hadfield was kind enough to read this chapter in type.

earth appears to make up to him the deficiency. He may be treated to expensive presents and holidays and provided for in every possible material way, but if he has no love, it profiteth nothing.[2]

It is interesting to find support for this view in the work of an anthropologist. Abram Kardiner, in *The Psychological Frontiers of Society*, says that the Alorese—primitive inhabitants of the Dutch East Indies—systematically deprive their children of any love or care. The parents unconsciously hate their children because they themselves never received love. They take revenge for this on their children, and the vicious circle is unbroken. In contrast, the Comanche Indians—a primitive but loving society—show an unusual interest in the welfare of their children and lavish affection upon them. In consequence, the children have wonderfully integrated egos.[3]

What, then, happens to the child deprived of love? He may react in several possible ways, both in childhood and in his later life. I avoid the phrase "adult life" because the neurotic deprived of love does not usually react in an adult way until his neurosis is cured. Indeed, curing him involves teaching him how childish his reactions are and helping him to find adult reactions.

Uncured, he usually reacts in one of three ways:

1. He may pathetically seek for love from others by trying to please people. We know the "clinging type" of person who so badly wants to be liked and admired that his ethical principles, his moral scruples, his sense of truth, beauty and goodness, the conclusions of his reason, are all sacrificed on the altar of pleasing people, and of pleasing them sufficiently to win their approval. Not getting the affection from his parents—or not believing in its reality, which has the same effect on his mind as deprivation—he seeks a love-substitute from other people. The schoolboy longs for the approval of the schoolmaster whom he has put on a pedestal, the schoolgirl has a "pash" (*grande passion*) on a mistress; with varying degrees of sycophancy, the employee seeks to win the praise of the employer, and failure to win praise has a desolating effect out of all proportion to its value, reducing the "patient" —for so he must be called—to depression and exaggerated despair. The child deeply loved at home, even though teased or punished, even though poor and hungry, seems to have such a deep, emotional satisfaction that he does not need to strive so pathetically for appreciation outside, nor is he made so miserable if it be withheld.

[2] The Greek word ἀγαπή, as used in the New Testament (e.g. I Corinthians 13), almost exactly expresses the sense in which the word "love" is used in this chapter.
[3] I owe this reference to Liebman's, *Peace of Mind*, p. 66 (Simon and Schuster, 1946).

It seems clear that not only neurosis but some of the great achievements in all walks of life could be traced to the deprivation of love. The records of fame could fruitfully be searched, I believe, for cases in which children, deprived of love, have grown up and married, and even marriage has been a disappointment. Physically, mentally or spiritually they have remained starved of love. Still seeking love, men and women have thrown themselves into work, and, consciously believing themselves to be working for the work's sake, their unconscious motive has been to win fame. The applause of the crowd, the goodwill of the public, the publicity of the Press, are love-substitutes and the very wine of life to their thirsty souls. The sad thing is that they remain substitutes; *wine*, not food; intoxicating but not building up and integrating personality. Many school-prizes do not make up to a boy for the fact that his mother does not *really* love him, and when, having grown up and married a frigid woman, he lectures, preaches, sings to or acts before, audiences which clap him to the echo, his heart remains unsatisfied, though the adulation of the public is better than nothing. The delirious approval of the whole community does not give to the ego what one loving woman could give, and the love-famished celebrity goes on his way, forever seeking, but forever hungry, though his hunger has given him fame and given the community a service which it might never have had if he had had real love.

2. He may develop a reaction character-trait. Here again I use a phrase of Hadfield's. Its meaning is seen in an actual case. The patient, a woman now in the fifties, was the first-born child of Mr. and Mrs. X. There was some disappointment that she was not a boy, and this the patient clearly apprehended from an early age. With her father she was a great favourite, but from the first she had very little belief in her mother's love. When the patient was six years of age, she was sent to boarding-school and her parents went to China. Life at boarding-school was hard. In those days canings were frequent. All letters were censored. The patient remembers having to re-write her letters to China, so as to make her parents believe she was happy. The schoolmistress was neurotic and sadistic. At times—while the parents were on furlough in England, for instance—the patient was spoilt at school. But for long periods she was most harshly treated and caned unmercifully on the naked body for the most trivial faults.

By the time her parents returned to England to live, they had had a second child, a much desired son. Eagerly the patient awaited her parents coming to fetch her home to live with them. How desperately she longed for a mother! But when the great day came, the mother, who admittedly had lived without her first child for six years, said to her, "Why, I'd almost forgotten I'd got you." It was a fatal remark to make. And its implications were lived up to. It was always the son who was praised, and she who was blamed. The former was "the light of his mother's eyes," and "Mummy's good little boy."

The patient still vividly remembers how her mother used to read to the two children on Sunday evenings. The mother always had her right arm round the younger child. With her left hand she held her book. The girl felt excluded, left out of the symbolised love-relation of the embracing arm. So, in her own words, she "played up." The puzzled mother wondered why her son enjoyed Bible stories while her daughter hated them. But what the girl hated was the situation in which, rightly or wrongly, she *felt* deprived of love. Again, the younger child was invited to say his prayers at his mother's knee. The girl said hers alone. She still remembers a score of incidents in which she *felt* unloved.

The patient might have become sycophantic, or found ways of pleasing her mother, or, in other ways, pleaded for love, but she was not that kind of person. She developed a reaction character-trait which could be described thus: In her heart she said, "All right, if you won't give me love, you can keep it. I know now that I can't depend on love, but I'll show that I can do without it." So, the patient developed an exaggerated independence. No one but her father who truly loved her could ever do anything for her. She shook them off, unwilling to be put under an obligation to them. "I can look after myself, I don't need you and I don't believe in your affection," was the kind of hard, exterior attitude to all others who would sincerely have loved her and appreciated her.

Of course, the hunger for love was not thus eradicated. It was repressed into the unconscious, and showed its activity there by the aggressive, negativistic, and hysterical symptoms thrown up into consciousness by the repressed complex. She formed a pattern of reaction of "playing up," and frequently, if ever she *felt* unloved or excluded, whatever the facts were, she broke out into hysterical fits of temper and passionate storms of weeping. When she was overtired and the repressing force was thus diminished, the repressed hunger for love broke out of its restraints and made its protest in the familiar symptoms of hysteria.

One of the patient's symptoms was a fierce jealousy. Jealousy is made up of two ingredients: the desire to be loved and the fear that love will be withheld. Often the measure of the jealousy is the measure both of the desire for love and the fear of its being withheld. People who have always been loved are not usually jealous because they are not afraid of losing love. The patient whose case I have given fully, because it so clearly illustrates this part of my argument, was jealous almost until her recent death, because the fear of the return of misery, consequent on thinking that she was not really loved, had so strongly implanted itself.

Secondly, she developed not only jealousy, but what might be called the "martyr-complex." She really sought ways of being "miserable" because then, perchance, others would sympathise with, or pity her. And pity and sympathy are love-substitutes, but, of course, they have to be called out by misery. A happy, healthy person, with no hardships, calls out no pity or sympathy. Although wealthy, moderately healthy and without a need in the world, she could always recite some story of mishap, inconvenience, ill-health or grievance, which would draw pity from spectators.

Thirdly, she would develop a self-immolation to an almost unbelievable degree. She would work from morning till night, and though tired out would never rest. Rest calls forth no pity. Overwork does.[4] At all costs, she must get love or one of its many substitutes. Of course, she did not wistfully ask for love. Love had deceived her, so she would never try it or trust it again. But by fierce self-persecution, in martyrdom or immolations, she would seek its substitutes. People truly loved her. But she rarely believed them or that their love was genuine and for her own sake. She insisted that it was for some other reason! This is the genuine reaction-character-trait.

Others who have repressed their hunger for love, develop hostility, cynicism or an icy and affected indifference in regard to any friendly approach from others. They suspect that "there is a catch in it somewhere," if anyone shows them goodwill. They suspect the motives of any who show them kindness. It is not quite fair to blame them. They are sick in soul and mind. At some early crisis or series of demanding occasions, love failed them when they needed it most. Unaware that every human being needs appreciation for the health of his mind, as he needs food for the health of his body, they tell themselves that they will do without love, love having let them down. They refuse it even when it is sincerely offered, and if they are surprised into receiving it—as, for instance, if during illness someone brings them flowers or fruit— they either suspect the motive of the donor, or else their eyes fill with

---

[4] "Nervous breakdown" due to overwork should be examined. People often overwork because they are both unhappy at home and ambitious. They are driven on in their ambition by the desire for praise, and they desire praise because it is a substitute for the love which is denied them at home. But love, not leisure, would prove to be the cure.

tears as if, from afar, they were wistfully gazing into some paradise forbidden to them, however normal and natural for others.

Frequently there is a neurotic desire to hurt manifested in people deprived of love. They not only revel in their own misery, but take a delight in making other people responsible for it. "I've been sitting in an awful draught since *you* left the door open." "I couldn't get a decent bath because *you* had used all the hot water." "I had a terribly wakeful night because *you* wakened me shutting your door and I could not get off again for hours." It is the emphasis on the "you did it" that marks the neurotic desire to hurt. "I am miserable and I have the right to claim sympathy from you because you made me miserable." This attitude lies behind the morbid and petulant desire to get sympathy or pity or consideration because real love is thought to be withdrawn or refused.

In many marriages we see a woman developing this kind of querulous self-martyrdom, and we can then assume that love—the real thing—between husband and wife, is dead. It may be that they keep together for the sake of the family, or of convention, but one or both of them becomes neurotic through the deprivation of love.

Our theme in this book is relative to illness rather than crime, but it may be pointed out that many criminals are manufactured from frustrated personalities deprived of love, and, in hostile reaction to the society that cheated them, they act in anti-social ways. One twenty-three-year-old criminal was recently "analysed," and it was found that he had a sadistic father against whom his mother was too weak to protect him. The boy grew up to believe that no one wanted him, that all men were against him, and, in his hostile reaction, he believed that only at the point of a gun could he wrest anything for himself. He became a useful citizen through loving care and an adjusted view of life, reached as much through the doctor's character as his treatment. At last the patient found someone who showed goodwill and who believed in him.

Short of crime, it must often be true that the selfish, ruthless men of business and the ambitious seekers for power who will tread on anyone to mount higher are disease-spots in the social body, and, individually regarded, are patients needing treatment. They are hostile to humanity in general because their parents never loved them, or loved them only on condition that they lived up to their parents' demands; demands, probably, based on *their* parents' exaggerated super-egos. Hungry for security which love would have provided, they seek to exploit ruthlessly an unloving world in order to obtain love-substitutes in terms of wealth and power.

It is perhaps unnecessary to add that sexual immorality is often due to this deprivation of real love. A man fails to find it in his wife. Another woman is hungry for love, and although she may know that she is loved only for her physical charms, even that, plus a "good time" and some money and food, may seem better than nothing, and is some kind of substitute for the real thing. Both man and girl may get only a substitute, but if real love is denied and a substitute ready to hand, it is easy to see why such a substitute as illicit gratification is resorted to. Neither party is a monster of wickedness. Both could be made both moral and content if they were truly loved. Don Juan himself tried to disguise, by his many conquests, the fact that nowhere did he find a satisfying love. Real love would have ended his quest and his "immorality."

3. The patient deprived of love may develop illness. This may be a psychoneurosis, the symptoms of which are limited—as far as the ordinary observer can ascertain—to abnormal emotional reactions or behaviour-characteristics. But bodily illness may also develop, and we may have conversion-hysteria or forms of psychosomatic illness.[5] The "pain" in the mind is "converted" into a pain in the body, for in this form it is easier to bear.

The unconscious motivation is two-fold. First, there is the quest of love which unconsciously is expressed by an illness which the conscious mind dislikes ("I really want to be well"), but which the unconscious—the far more potent part of the mind—desires. Unconsciously the patient is saying, "Now, you *must* give me love because I am ill."

Second, the form the illness takes is determined partly (a) by any constitutional weakness, (b) by a symptom which is a kind of acted parable of the desire of the patient to escape a terrifying situation (as in a case I saw the other day in a London bus, in which a man with a tic suddenly swung his body and ducked his head as if to avoid a falling beam), or (c) by a disability which saves at once the "face" of the patient and a dreaded situation (as in another case where a patient was terrified that he would, in his sleep or in his cups, confess a crime, and who thereupon became dumb).

---

[5] The difference between conversion-hysteria and psychosomatic illness is that in the latter there may be not only pain and bodily distress, but the destruction of, and change in, tissue. In the former, while there may be severe pain, there are no tissue changes. Further, the emotional cause of psychosomatic illness may be completely conscious. In conversion-hysteria the emotional causes may be entirely, and are always partly, unconscious. "The psycho-somatic headache is due to pressure from a congested circulation, even though it is set up by emotion. The hysterical headache is devised as a means of escaping responsibility and is the result of an unconscious wish, not of pressure." See Hadfield, *op. cit.*

If one knows beforehand the constitutional weakness of a patient and also the nature and cause of the neurosis, one can almost prophesy the bodily symptom which the unconscious mind will choose. For instance, if a patient has a constitutional tendency towards dermatitis and a powerful, repressed guilt complex, we should expect him to develop some kind of skin affection. A "stained mind," which a guilty person has, seems readily to become translated into a "stained body" through skin disease. In saying this, I would add that, of course, it would be grossly unfair and inaccurate to suppose that *every* patient suffering from skin disease was, for that reason, repressing some guilty secret. The skin is that organ of the body which, more than any other, has literally to face the outer world. Those who feel that they can no longer "face the world" sometimes develop skin disease.

The deprivation of love is the main causal factor behind many apparently physical illnesses, some simple and some complex. (The classic example is the case of Elizabeth Barrett Browning.)

Here is a simple one that took place in a London office.

Miss A. frequently fell into floods of tears when taking down letters, and then one day fainted and was taken home in a car, unable to walk. She went as a voluntary patient to a mental hospital, and in a few weeks was completely cured. The analyst said that she had been jilted (= deprived of love). The thought of being unwanted and unloved made her desperate for love and sympathy. In that few knew of her affairs, few give her sympathy. Then the mechanism began to work, "If I were ill, I should get sympathy." This idea was unconscious, but the effect of the unconscious mind on the body is enormous. Quite easily symptoms can be produced which evoke sympathy. When analysis brought these unconscious mechanisms to consciousness, the situation was courageously faced and the "illness" disappeared.

John B. was the "middle child." His older brother was "wanted" by both parents. His sister, seven years younger, though "an accident," was the pet, almost a kind of mascot, and very attractive and pretty. John's father was a very busy professional man; his mother a popular society woman. John felt unwanted. He could not do anything right.

When I met him, John was twenty-three, tall and handsome, a good student at the University. When we talked (he had come to discuss joining the church), John said that whenever he got tired or overwrought, he had such a severe pain in his right arm that he could not write, and to lift his arm to brush his hair was an agony.

He lay on a couch quietly letting his mind run back to childhood. Suddenly, with great emotion, he recalled the following incident which happened when he was a little boy. He had been riding his pony when he was thrown violently to the ground. He hurt his arm, and went into the house crying bitterly. His father turned him away with a rough, "Don't be such a cry-baby! Boys don't cry! You should be ashamed of yourself." He went to his mother, but she was just going out to an afternoon Bridge party. She "couldn't be bothered just then." Poor John went about miserably for the rest of the day. He was really in very great pain as well as deprived of love, and was miserable in mind and body.

At last his mother came to put him to bed. It was then found that *his arm was broken*. His father was fetched, and was more solicitous and kind than John ever remembered before or since. The doctor made a great deal of him. His older brother, who was a god to him, praised his pluck, and even his pretty little sister was given a place back-stage, at least for one act in the drama of the home. John had all the limelight and the centre of the stage. For a few delicious days he was really loved. The sling round his neck in which his arm rested was only given up very reluctantly. It was a symbol. He wore it as proudly as a girl wears an engagement ring, and for the same reason. It was a symbol that some-one loved him. When it was discarded, John slowly relapsed to the earlier place of the unloved and unnoticed boy.

Now, six feet high and of fine physique, he does sometimes get tired and depressed, and could do with some affection and love. He is ex-ceedingly shy. Little wonder. He doesn't "get about" much, nor is he fond of the dance-hall or the tennis club. When he is tired and depressed his "unconscious" whispers to him: "When you had a pain in your arm, you got love. Try having a pain in your arm!" Pain is an easy thing for the unconscious to arrange. So he has a pain, and here and there people sympathise.

But now he has "seen through" the unconscious mechanism and faced the situation on the conscious levels of the mind. Courage has come to his aid. The underground desire for love at whatever cost of pain has given way before understanding and the facing of reality. The pain has gone. The bluff has been called.

Recently a man was sent to me from a famous London hospital. A skin affection had proved intractable. A psychological cause was sus-pected. It was there, too. A quarrel between the patient and his wife had gone unbridged for a long period. The wife had withdrawn her love. In her eyes her husband had wronged her. She was adamant, and would not forgive him.

The unconscious motivation appeared to me to be as follows: *Un-consciously* the patient's mind appeared to work thus: "I *have* done wrong. I am a moral leper." (The symptom of leprosy is a *skin* affection.) "I cannot bear longer in my mind the sense of guilt. I will turn it into a stain of body. When I show signs of illness, my wife may pity me and forgive me and give me back her love."

At any rate, in my room, after several interviews, the wife forgave her husband. Prayer together was followed by a most exuberant and joyous reconciliation. In a few days the skin affection vanished. I write this more than twelve months later, but the skin trouble has never returned.

In his book *Common Skin Diseases*, one of our greatest authorities writes: "In cases (of neurodermatitis), due to worry and strain, the effect of X-rays is naturally only temporary, and sedatives, such as phenobarbitone and bromides, with periods of rest and isolation from worries, as far as may be, will be required." [6] Having met this writer, I am sure he would agree that to remove the cause of the worry would be better treatment still. One wonders how many illnesses usually regarded as caused entirely by physical factors have, if one goes still farther back in the patient's history, or deeper into his mind, the deprivation of love as either the root cause or the precipitating cause.

Everyone is familiar with the expression, "She died of a broken heart." It is indubitable that many such cases have occurred. The deprivation of love means the loss of security, frequently the loss of self-respect, the feeling of being "no use" and unwanted. These losses can be fatal. The mind reaches such a state of despair that, although suicide is generally avoided, the unconscious mind seizes on a disease or an immolation that can bring death, if death is, indeed, desired by the deep mind. For the latter is more potent even than the instinct of self-preservation.

Kathleen G. was a healthy girl of twenty, engaged as a typist at a garage near a country village. She became engaged to the curate. The date of the wedding was fixed. Kathleen was radiantly happy. Part of her happiness was derived from the thought that she would be no longer an unimportant typist in a menial job, but a lady of the manse, and, through her marriage, the social equal of anyone in the neighbourhood. But the curate broke off the engagement. From that day Kathleen developed a curious habit. She simply could not be persuaded to eat. She would even put food into her mouth and then empty it into her handkerchief or serviette, and afterwards throw it away. She became pale, thin, hollow-eyed and showed symptoms of anæmia. Her doctor could only say, "You must make her eat." Her devoted parents did their utmost, adding tears and threats and entreaties, but all to little purpose. A visit was made to a London specialist, unfortunately not a psychotherapist, and he failed to recognise the case as one of "anorexia nervosa." The specialist said, "There is nothing the matter with her if only she will eat." At last, in desperation, hearing that I had had a similar case, they brought her to me. Her mother showed me earlier photographs of a plump and bonny girl. I could hardly believe they were of the same girl. For Kathleen, aged twenty-three, weighed five stones three pounds, and her body looked like that of an Indian famine victim. Any psychologist would have recognised the "self-immolation complex" functioning deep in the unconscious. Kathleen said quite simply, "I know I ought to eat, and I do try to, but all the time I feel there is a strong inward power which is telling me I must not eat." No words could have been more apt. The "inward power" was that of a morbid unconscious.[7]

This unconscious, like the conscious, was stricken by the deprivation of love and hit on a terrible revenge against the curate. It argued—unconsciously, it must be repeated—"Don't go back to the garage or to menial work now you have lost 'face.' Don't accept the humiliation of menial work again. Don't eat! Die of a broken heart! Offer yourself up as a sacrifice on the altar of unrequited love. Then, instead of people smiling as you resume a humble task, instead of losing face, instead of a broken pride and a humiliating situation, people will be sorry for you. By dying you can get sympathy *in maximo*, see how sorry they are for you now because you already look white and ill. And besides, see what a splendid revenge you will have on the curate, how successfully you will ruin the happiness he is finding in your successor, and, furthermore, what a revenge you will have on your doctor, who told you bluntly not to be a little fool because there was nothing the matter with you."

Cases like this of "anorexia nervosa" have been known to lead to death.[8] In the one quoted above, I am convinced that Kathleen was cured by psychological investigation and subsequent religious synthesis. *First*, admittedly, a psychological technique had to be followed and causative factors in the neurosis brought from the unconscious to the conscious level. But thereafter it was through her religious faith that she became integrated.

Her mind began to run along the following lines: "Anyway, God loves me, cares for me, and has *some* purpose in my life. If B (the curate) is like that, it's a good job I found out before I married him. I'm

[7] I have quoted this case from my earlier book, *Psychology and Life* (Abingdon-Cokesbury, 1935).

[8] *Psychology and Life.*

not going to throw my life away because a man like that jilts me. I will hold my head up. I've done nothing of which I need feel ashamed. I'll live a day at a time, and show that my faith is not just a fair-weather, flimsy thing, but that it sustains me."

She did this, and entirely recovered. It gives me joy to add that she afterwards married a Methodist minister known to me, and has proved herself during the last twelve years his most able and valued helpmeet.

Is religion necessary to the cure of cases of neurotic illness caused through the deprivation of love? The answer must be that it is not always necessary.

The first stage of treatment must be analytical. So long as factors causing neurosis function in the unconscious, religion, as generally understood, is not the greatest help that can be given. A religious conversion might avail, but a religious conversion, attended by emotional abreaction and catharsis, cannot be engineered. Of course, if a person of Christ's dynamic spiritual energy and power were operating, an entirely different conclusion might be reached. An attack on any kind spirit which believed on Him, might well be regarded as the maximum of disease, physical or mental, made by a Divine Spirit through a human help conceivable.

It certainly cannot be claimed that in religion alone is cure to be found, for if, for example, during treatment the patient fell deeply in love, it might well be that all further treatment would be speedily proved unnecessary. Further, many medical psychologists who scorn religion have cured patients suffering from neuroses caused by the deprivation of love. When a patient discovers that his illness of mind and body runs back to a deprivation of love on the part of a parent, he may well find liberty and health by arguing with himself thus: "Very good, what if I were unwanted? I am free now from my parents. Others, who bulk now much more largely in my life, will give me love in the sense of goodwill. I will no longer be held by the dead hand of the past. Now I know where the chain is that held me in bondage, I will snap it at once." Cure of symptom often follows such a decision.

When this has been said, however, I would go on to add that the Christian religion, properly applied, in the broadest sense and freed from sectarian bias, can, when analysis has been done, most powerfully aid the subsequent process of integration.

It is not enough to explain to the patient: "You are suffering because, in childhood you were not truly loved. During analysis you have become conscious that, because your mother did not really love you, you hated her. You repressed both your hatred and aggression against her and your own resentment. Now you have recognised these factors, you must find your release in the realisation that you are loved by God."

This will not do, because the love of God, *at that stage*, is an idea and not an experience. If it is an idea emotionally realised, that is better. But as yet even the love of God is only mediated through *persons*.

In an ideal church there exists a central group of people, with a warm experience of God in their own hearts and a capacity and willingness to receive a person into such a real fellowship that the love of God is mediated through loving persons to the patient.

It has become the practice of some of the medical psychotherapists who help me at the City Temple to introduce suitable patients to our Fellowship Groups. This is not done from the religious motive only, but from the psychotherapeutic motive. And again and again I have watched cases of neurosis, getting, on the one hand, sound treatment, and on the other, love through fellowship, breaking out of the prison of their morbid introspection and fears, and finding new life, new joy and new peace. Group-therapy is meeting with success under various conditions. I am sure that a group, meeting for Christian fellowship, discussion and prayer, has a very high therapeutic value.

Surely, here is a situation in which psychology needs the help of religion for complete success with many patients. "Most people," said Dr. Geoffrey Evans in his presidential address to the Medical Section of the Royal Society of Medicine, "require a constant supply of appreciation for their mental health and happiness." If they cannot get it at home, the Church should help at this point. Here is a point at which the minister of religion and the psychotherapist can co-operate. Surely, here also is the kind of thing every church should exist to do. The Church is criticised because "old maids" attend in large numbers. But is there any disgrace in this? I shall discuss later whether religion is itself a neurosis (p. 407). True Christianity, I hold, is not. But even if it were, even if the fellowship of the Church were the exchange of one neurosis for another, inasmuch as the Church's teaching is neuroticised, it is at least an improvement to make such a change. It breaks the loneliness of many lives, and it offers a love-substitute which is more satisfactory than most.

"Love," said Rauschenbusch, "is the energy of a steadfast will bent on fellowship." At its best, the Christian fellowship of loving people mediates the love of God through persons, calls for self-sacrificing service to the needy for love's sake and in co-operation with other lovers of Jesus Christ. It is better than keeping a lapdog, or developing a whining self-pity, or a hostile, cynical character-reaction-trait, or an illness designed to attract sympathy.

I have known cases in which the cause of illness was traced rather to a sense of deprivation of "social love," if the expression be allowed. One patient felt a misfit in society and dreaded going into any kind of company at all. She was cured when her instructed insight realised this and when she was introduced to a Christian fellowship where "everybody loved everybody." There is such a thing as the complete cure of neurosis, or other psychogenic illness, through the loving community. The Church should be just that.

Short of happy marriage—which itself can be ruined if love *only* runs out to the beloved—there is no more integrating factor in personality, more powerful or more socially valuable, than a sense of the love of God, flowing into human hearts, both directly from Him and through His other lovers in the fellowship of the Church, and then out to the starved lives of others whom men come to love for His sake and whom they seek to serve in His name.

4

OTHER EMOTIONAL STATES AS CAUSATIVE OF ILLNESS AND THE RELEVANCE THERETO OF RELIGION

FOR SOME STRANGE reason, even though he admits that his personality is made up of thinking, willing and feeling, man, although proud of the thinking that has led to systems of philosophy and to scientific invention, proud also of the achievements of the human will, is ashamed of his emotions. British and American people belong to a tradition that teaches that one's feelings should usually be concealed. One must not "wear one's heart upon one's sleeve." Feelings are just as authentic and valuable a part of personality as thinking and willing, but they are never recognised in the same cordial way. Traditionally we "hide our feelings." We are a little ashamed of them. Emotion is the "poor relation" of personality.

The analogy takes us a good way. To illustrate my argument, I am imagining a snobbish family, proud of some of its members, obliged to recognise the existence of the poor relation, but always relegating him to the basement kitchen, never letting him appear on important occasions, trying to pretend he is not there, never giving him his due, and sometimes sending him away altogether. What happens? In the underground kitchen he takes his revenge and makes trouble, doing damage away from the sight of others. If dismissed, he sends threatening letters and blackmailing demands, most of them anonymously, and now he cannot be reasoned with. There is no peace until his authentic relationship is admitted and he is brought back into the family circle, given his rights and kept under our eye so that we can control him.

So with our feelings. We pretend they are not there. We drive them below the surface of consciousness into the basement kitchen of the

357

mind, even banishing them into the unconscious. They make trouble, threaten and blackmail us until we are literally sick with them, without recognising the cause of the disturbance. They write, as it were, terrifying, but anonymous, letters. And in the unconscious we can no longer control them. The unconscious is not normally accessible to our scrutiny and command.

This treatment of the emotions is unhealthy in the literal sense of that word. The present popularity of music, drama and the cinema, the immense sale of volumes of poetry, the new passion to look at the pictures of great artists,[1] indicate that, starved of emotional satisfaction, men are turning to various forms of art for the chance to express, through their response to art, emotions which, when concerned only with their own hearts, they have been taught to conceal, suppress and finally repress into the unconscious. Aristotle remarked that the great tragedies of Greek drama were in this sense cathartic and gave man, by proxy, the chance to work off in tears, or glee, or horror, or revenge, the unexpressed emotions of his own personality. Aristotle held that it is a mistake to try to kill or starve the emotions, and that tragedy is a vent for such an emotion as fear. If the latter is artificially stirred in drama, it is, Aristotle held, drained off from the deep mind, which is thus freed from its disquietude. For an emotion like pity, drama provides an æsthetic satisfaction. Pity refines fear, and fear pity.[2] It is indubitable that sex feelings can be sublimated in creative work, like painting pictures or writing poetry. Some scholars think that in primitive times art began among those who, for some reason, like injury or deformity, could not express the sex urge in a biological way.

It is a healthy thing to express emotion whenever its expression will do no harm to ourselves or another. More will be said about this when we discuss confession.[3] The Hebrew poets, as the Book of Psalms demonstrates, gloried in expressing emotion, whether of joy or sorrow. The convention which, for instance, forbids the expression of sorrow, is overdone, both in adults and children.

> Give sorrow words: the grief that does not speak
> Whispers the o'er-fraught heart and bids it break.

[1] When Van Gogh's pictures were exhibited at the Tate Gallery in London in 1948, queues formed at nine o'clock in the morning and people waited for hours to be admitted, even in bad weather.

[2] *Ars Poetica*, Chapter vi, Saintsbury's translation. Cf. also *Aristotle on the Art of Poetry*, S. H. Butcher, Chapter 6 (1895).

[3] See p. 445.

[4] "Macbeth," Act IV, Sc. 3.

Even little children are able to bear grief better than deceit. I have read of a mother who, when their father died, sent her children away to save them pain and distress and hushed up the fact of his passing. The children formed the conclusion that the mother had murdered their father, and the traumatic effect of this terrible shock produced neurosis in all three.

It is essential—if the expression of emotion would harm another and we cannot express it either in appropriate actions or in words to another —to admit it readily to our own consciousness, to recognise it for what it is, even if it be hate for a relative whom convention demands we should love; to accept it and deal with it, but never to pretend to ourselves that it does not exist, or adopt a policy of turning from it until it is "forgotten." Every emotion still exists in the unconscious, and all we have done is to banish the poor relation to a place from which he can still blackmail us without our being able any longer to control him.

Here I wish to write down a sentence and mark it by special type:

If emotion is neither expressed in its appropriate action nor even admitted to consciousness, it will have its revenge by setting up some form of mental or physical distress.

Our feelings of joy and appreciation should be far more readily expressed, especially when we have recognised to what an extent our fellows need appreciation. To praise another costs so little. It does, for that other, so much. Some have supposed that to praise another will make him conceited. A glance into our own hearts dispels the illusion. We are humbled rather than made conceited by praise. But if praise is withheld, a man, in his desperate need for appreciation, will praise himself, and thus become conceited. In a word, praise is the cure of conceit rather than its cause. Praise, which is quite a different thing from flattery, should be far more freely expressed.

But the main difficulty lies with the feelings which the conventions of polite society compel us to hide. Many an adolescent really hates one or both parents—at least at intervals—and we who are parents have no right to expect, let alone demand, that our children should "love" us simply because we are their parents. After all, they did not ask to be born. We must *win* their respect and love, and take at least as much trouble to deserve it as we take in regard to others whose friendship and love we crave to have.

If the adolescent cannot confide his "hate" to a close friend, let him admit it to himself, not pretend it is not true. Many a wife hates her husband—at intervals—and vice versa. We may remember for our comfort that one can love and hate the same person almost at the same time. Love and hate are like the two sides of the same coin.[5] Emotions like jealousy, fear, hate, resentment, frustration, bitterness, remorse, anger, cruelty, aggressiveness, greed, should at least be acknowledged and recognised by full consciousness. It is untrue, foolish and unhealthy to pretend that we never feel thus, if, in fact, we do. Mental honesty is the first requisite of mental health. We simply must accept facts. We have so often been told that these emotions are wicked that we pretend we do not have them; that, like the poor relation, they do not really belong to us. But *they* are not wicked—though the action to which they may drive us may be if we do not control them—and it is just self-deception to pretend that they do not exist. A man will sneer at his wife, after he has flirted with another, and accuse her of jealousy. But the jealousy is understandable. It is the fear of being deprived of love, and the measure of jealousy may be the measure of love. If the husband wants to cure her jealousy, he must find ways of proving to his wife that she need not fear any deprivation of his love. It is instinctive to fear the deprivation of love, and in the last chapter we caught a glimpse of the reasons which justify such a fear.

The woman quoted on p. 319, who repressed her wish that her parents would die, is an illustration of our point here. She should have admitted the "death wish" to consciousness in some way as follows: "I must admit that if my parents died, I should not honestly regret it. They have always stood in my way. They have prevented my being married and even frustrated the poor alternative of my career. They have never really loved me nor I them. I have been useful to them, and that is all. But it is my duty to look after them, and I will face the task and do it cheerfully and as well as I can." Then there is no *repressed* guilt, or hate, or anger, or resentment, or malice to cause conflict in the unconscious mind between pretence and reality, between the demand of conscience and the demand of desire, between the super-ego and the id.

The emotion of sex-desire is particularly causative of illness because convention so fiercely demands that it be hidden. Modesty is a beautiful thing, but the attitude which regards sex as a murky and furtive secret is stupid, unhealthy and dangerous. I will not write fully about it because I have done so elsewhere.[6] The theory that the sex urge must, at all costs, find bodily expression if illness is to be avoided, is fictitious nonsense invented by those who seek a sanction for exculpating their

[5] Ian Suttie, *The Origins of Love and Hate* (Kegan Paul, 1935).

[6] *The Mastery of Sex through Psychology and Religion* (S.C.M., 1931).

uncontrolled desires. Repression is dangerous here, as with other emotions. But repression is confused with suppression. Repression follows *the refusal to recognise the emotion in consciousness.* Suppression—which is the conscious control of emotion and of the acts to which emotion tends to drive us—is not followed by illness of body or mind. The difference between repression and suppression is clearly seen if we consider their opposites. The opposite of suppression is expression. The opposite of repression is recognition. It is conscious recognition that is so important. If, because we have been ignorant or mistaught about sex, we pretend we never have sex desires, we banish this poor relation—sex emotion—into the unconscious. That is to say, we repress it. But the poor relation does not cease to exist. He plagues us with a particularly unpleasant kind of blackmail, and neurosis is often, and sex perversion sometimes, the result. There is nothing evil in having sex desires. Everyone has them. There is no need to find them bodily expression. Jesus Christ, perfectly human, did not so express them. But it is essential to recognise them and admit the desires to our own consciousness, saying, perhaps, "Yes, I should like to indulge my sex desires, but it is my duty to control this urge and try to turn its energies into other channels of useful power until I can express them physically in ways which do not rob me of my self-respect."

Aggression and anger, if repressed into the unconscious, can cause vague feelings of fear. When we were children, and were angry and aggressive, we were frequently punished. We *feared* punishment. Sometimes the vague fears which harass us, and which we cannot explain to ourselves, arise from the fact that we are repressing feelings of aggression or anger which we think we "ought" not to have; an "oughtness" thrust upon us by the super-ego in ways we have already studied. Down in the unconscious they light up the thoughts of fear, because fear was once associated with them. The banned aggression remains unconscious, but the unbanned fear rises to consciousness and makes us afraid, we know not why.

All pretending to ourselves is psychologically unhealthy, and integration demands that we admit these emotions to consciousness, even if we cannot express them in the action which a savage would be able to use without the condemnation of polite society. Even we who are creatures—I nearly wrote "victims"—of a highly developed social set-up, may find *some* action that eases pent-up feelings, and many have found that "a good cry," or a ten-mile walk, or the love of a dog, or a good film, or chopping firewood, or even doing household chores, has cleansed "the stuff'd bosom of that perilous stuff that weighs upon the heart." But let us turn to the effect of emotion on the body.

From earliest times man has suspected a relationship between his feelings and his physical health. "As a man thinketh in his heart, so is he," [7] is an old maxim, and its last three words refer not only to a spiritual but also to a physical condition. For centuries expectant mothers have been warned that violent feelings might affect the temperament, character, and even the physical health, of the unborn. There cannot be many mothers, who, at some time or another, have not said to a child, "You'll make yourself ill worrying like that." Even if it be only in dreams, we have been "paralysed through fear," "rooted to the spot in horror." In waking life we have seen people "red in the face through anger," "white with passion," "rigid with terror," and so on. We have felt eerie through a good ghost story until our "hair has stood up on end." We have known a fear which could make us "tremble in every limb." We have had news which brought beads of perspiration to our brow, or even "turned someone's hair grey in a night." Our eyes have "started from their sockets," our hearts raced, our "feeble knees" have knocked together and our tongue "cleaved to the roof of our mouths"; our bowels have "been as water." What Dr. Walter B. Cannon proved to be true of cats, dogs, rabbits and guinea-pigs, we have found true of ourselves. He wrote, "Very mild emotional disturbances are attended by the abolition of peristalsis." [8] Emotionally upset, we literally cannot digest our food. Many have vomited on being made to feel the emotion of disgust. Darwin tells of a young man who vomited on being told he had been left a fortune.[9] Indeed, there is not much of our body remaining that can be said to be unmoved by our emotions. When they are too much for us, they achieve the object of getting us out of a painful situation altogether, for a time at least, and we swoon away in a "dead faint."

I have used these common phrases—some of them Biblical—to show how familiar the idea is. The formula of M. Coué is, of course, based on the principle that the state of the mind influences the physical health of the body. To the extent to which the mind really accepts an idea about the body, then to that extent, if reasonable at all, the idea tends to actualise or come true.

The emotion of feeling better, induced by repeating Coué's famous phrase, literally affects the amount of the healthy secretions, and what is more significant, as we shall see, is that *emotion can change the*

[7] Proverbs 23:7.

[8] Walter B. Cannon, Professor of Physiology at Harvard University, in *Bodily Changes in Pain, Hunger, Fear and Rage* (Appleton, 1920).

[9] *The Expression of the Emotions in Man and Animals* (Appleton, 1910). Darwin noted that very different emotional states bring about very similar bodily accompaniments.

chemical composition of the bodily secretions. Wittkower gives us fascinating evidence of the effect of the emotions on the body. While a patient was under deep hypnosis, Wittkower gave him suggestions of joy, sorrow, anxiety and annoyance. The bile which flowed spontaneously from the duodenal sound was caught in test-tubes, which were changed every five minutes. In over twenty experiments Wittkower found that joy, sorrow and anxiety increased the bile secretion. Annoyance inhibited the secretion of bile either entirely or, in some patients, almost entirely. There were also qualitative changes in the bile.[10]

The odd thing, considering the widespread acceptance of the view that the attitude of the mind affects profoundly the health of the body, is that few have asked and answered the next two questions:

1. *How* does the mind come to affect the body? What are the links in the chain of causation by which that intransigent thing called matter responds to an idea or feeling in the mind, so frequently regarded popularity as only of ephemeral importance? [11]

2. Is there a relation, not only between the state of the feelings and the temporary state of the body (e.g. "I was rooted to the ground in horror"), but also between the emotional content of the deep mind over a long period and physical disease? Further, is there, perhaps, some light even on the problem of how certain diseases came to exist at all?

Some years ago (1929) Dr. H. P. Newsholme, the Medical Officer of Health for the city of Birmingham, wrote a book which impressed me greatly when I read it and the thesis of which still seems to me of immense importance. He called his book, *Health, Disease and Integration,* [12] and for the matter contained in the next few paragraphs I am deeply in his debt.

First of all, let the reader realise *the fact* that a feeling in the mind does definitely, in specific cases, release, and possibly create, a secretion. A telegram of news that a close relative is dead releases—may we not say manufactures?—something that was not there before: a quantity

---

[10] Helen Flanders Dunbar, *Emotion and Bodily Changes,* 3rd Edition, p. 287 (Columbia University Press, 1935). Heyer, quoting some experiments of Langheinrich, also says that psychic influence on bile secretion is proved.

[11] Cf. such sayings as "It's only an idea of mine," or "Don't bother about your feelings," or, most misleading of all popular sayings, "It's only your imagination!"

[12] H. P. Newsholme, M.A., M.D., F.R.C.P., B.Sc., D.P.H. (Allen and Unwin). Dr. Newsholme has kindly read this chapter and made certain suggestions which I have gladly embodied. He is not to be held responsible for my use of his research, but I am glad to have his assurance that I have not distorted or misrepresented his point of view, which his later work has supported even more strongly than when he wrote the book.

of saline liquid called tears. At the risk of being tedious, I wish to expatiate on the point. The tears were not there, save in potential, before the news was received. Crying is not like turning on a tap and running off a liquid stored in some reservoir behind the eyes. Yet in a few moments there is brought into new existence, by that process of the mind we call feeling, enough liquid to soak a small handkerchief. Feeling has *created* a fluid with a certain chemical composition which can be ascertained by chemical tests.

Just as feeling can create fluid, feeling can alter the chemical constitution of fluids created by the chemical processes of the body in other ways and for other purposes. When, for example, we tell the young mother to encourage happy and contented thoughts while she feeds her baby at the breast, we are on scientific, not sentimental ground, because her feelings, if violent enough, can change the chemical constitution of her breast-milk. And if those feelings are both violent and unhealthy, they can create in the breast-milk toxins capable of poisoning the baby.

Eric Pritchard, in his book *Infant Education*, gives a striking instance of this, as follows:

"There is a well-known instance on record of absolutely sudden death carrying off a baby which, although previously in perfect health, sank dead on its mother's bosom immediately after a meal. Previously to suckling her infant, the mother had experienced a terrible mental shock occasioned by a fight between her husband and a soldier who happened to be billeted in the house. The mother, trembling with fear and terror, threw herself furiously between the combatants, wrested a sword from the soldier's hand, broke it in pieces, and threw it away. Following on this violent excitement the mother nursed her infant, with the result recorded." [13]

Commenting on this illustration, Newsholme adds, "There is no essential difference in mechanism between the secretion of milk by the breast glands and the secretion of saliva by the salivary glands and of mucus by the mucous glands; so that emotion, if sufficiently intense, may conceivably produce a toxic change in the saliva, or in the mucus of the nasopharynx." He goes on to quote C. S. Myers [14] to the effect that "emotion alone can give rise to increase of pressure and albumen content, and even, according to some, to leucocytosis in the cerebrospinal fluid."

[13] Ex Newsholme, *op. cit.*, p. 55.

[14] In "A Final Contribution to the Study of Shell-Shock," *Lancet*, January 11, 1919.

If this argument is valid, we reach the conclusion that certain conditions of disease hitherto regarded as physiogenic can conceivably be set up [15] not by infective sources outside the body, but through the action of the emotions in being able to release or create toxins within the body, altering the chemical contents of some of the body's important fluids.

When we ask *how* these toxins are produced, the answer may be that constantly in the body there is a katabolic and an anabolic activity at work. By the first is meant the breaking down of bodily tissue, and by the second its building up. Health depends on the balance between the two. The metabolism or chemical changes that take place in the body are carried on by "enzymes of two opposed main groups, the one causing breaking down and the other the building up of the tissues." [16]

Now comes the most important stage of the argument. It is claimed that extreme nervous activity produces vast amounts of a katabolic enzyme—a home-manufactured "virus"—normally followed by somatic activity producing anabolic enzyme and building the body up again, but that *where there is emotion generated which is not allowed to express itself in action*,[17] katabolic enzymes are produced without subsequent anabolic action. Such katabolic enzymes, in the illustration given, poured into the milk of the nursing mother and poisoned the baby.

Such enzymes might as normally flow into the mucus of the nasopharynx, or the saliva, or the bowel, and so on, and produce symptoms of illness, not due to bacteria introduced from outside the body and harboured within it, but by a katabolic poison manufactured by an emotional reaction of an unhealthy nature in the deep mind.

Most people are aware that the body contains bacteria which are healthy and friendly to the body—the so-called saprophytes. But a change in the chemical composition of the fluid in which these benign bacteria live may possibly convert friendly bacteria into hostile ones, saprophytes into parasites.[18]

I quote further from Dr. Adami.

"Every pathogenic microbe has closely related forms or species differ-

[15] I am not foolishly suggesting, "are always set up," or even, "are usually set up."

[16] *Op. cit.*, p. 63.

[17] Italics mine.

[18] Note the following quotation from Dr. J. G. Adami: (Italics mine) "Diphtheria gains its simplest explanation as being due to the acquirement, within recent times, of virulent properties by *some previously harmless diphtheroid bacillus* growing in the throat and upper respiratory passages." *Op. cit.*, p. 97. This view is, of course, only a guess, and a consultant whom I questioned gave his opinion that it was "unheard of, unproved and unlikely"!

ing from it in little beyond the fact that the one is virulent, the other non-virulent. Next, it is to be noted that these allied species are found suggestively growing in the cavities or on the mucous surfaces of the body, in the same habitat as the virulent forms, or again in water and foodstuffs. . . . This state of affairs in itself leads to the conclusion that pathogenic microbes at some period, or periods, have originated from the microbes saprophytic upon the body surfaces, or existing commonly in the water and foodstuffs; that they have originated by adaptation of these forms to growth, not merely on, but within the tissues." [19]

Now, if it is sound, this is a conclusion of enormous importance. While we have been supposing that the germs of disease are incomprehensible creations of God whose ways are past finding out, it may appear that our hates and fears, our worries and angers have poisoned our own systems and brought into being hostile organisms which are outside God's original plan of creation altogether, and that to pay new attention to the emotional content of the deep mind might open up a most rewarding field of research, enquiry and action.

One's mind is kindled by the situation that is disclosed, and one must be forgiven if, for the moment, one leaps from the argument to speculation. Supposing cancer is originally caused by repressed worry! Supposing even germ-invasion diseases are given birth by our dark fears and hatreds! Supposing arthritis is, as Dr. Flanders Dunbar thinks, "a mask for a deeply buried emotional disturbance"! [20] Supposing, as Wittkower states, "situations which arouse aggressiveness or endanger the delicately poised security system of the patients often precede the onset of symptoms of T.B." [21] Supposing our Lord healed men by pouring into their minds the torrent of His own love, which drove out all other emotions which were the hot-bed of fermenting parasites of disease! Patients, then, would surely *"feel"* better at once—as, indeed, anyone would—and *be* better when the changed emotion in the deep mind, say from hate or fear or jealousy or resentment or bitterness to love, no longer provided a breeding-place in which harmful bacteria could propagate.

[19] J. G. Adami, *Medical Contributions to the Study of Evolution*, p. 23 (1918). Ex Newsholme, *op. cit.*, p. 65.

[20] Helen Flanders Dunbar, *Mind and Body*, p. 225 (Random House, 1947).

[21] Edward Wittkower, M.D., in *A Psychiatrist looks at Tuberculosis* (National Association for the Prevention of Tuberculosis, 1950). Wittkower thinks it is often safer to assess a patient's prognosis on the basis of his personality and emotional conflicts than on the basis of the shadow on the film. He says in his Preface "The best results from the treatment of tuberculosis are attained when the patient is thought of not only as possessing diseased organs but also a sick personality."

Let it be admitted that, as yet, much here is speculation. Yet I quote Dr. Newsholme again: [22]

"We can conceive, as a deduction of pure speculation, and with no knowledge at present of its bearing in practice, that an extreme change in the emotional state of an individual might give rise to the following sequence of events: (a) First a change in the secretions of the naso-pharynx or of the bowels, finding expression from one point of view in the dryness of the mouth, or the increased nasal secretion or the looseness of the bowels which often accompanies strong emotion; then (b) through the chemical alteration of these secretions, or by the enzymic action of the products of the emotion, a transformation of harmless saprophytic organisms inhabiting naso-pharynx or bowel into by no means harmless parasites, virulent to their host, and virulent to other individuals if coughed or sprayed on to them, or otherwise conveyed; finally (c) the irritation produced by the altered tissue fluids in naso-pharynx or bowel might conceivably cause multiplication of bacteria as well as their transformation in character."

Nothing I have written above should be twisted to infer that *all* disease can be explained along these lines, but let us open our minds to the possibility that acute emotion—*especially if repressed over a long period and more especially if the responsive action to which it prompts is denied*—can produce an enzyme which induces a katabolic action, which so alters the chemical constitution of certain fluids of the body, such as the mucus of the bowel or naso-pharynx, as to change benign bacteria, which work no harm on their host, into virulent bacteria which can kill their host, and if received into other bodies accomplish their destruction also.

Newsholme hypothecates that a katabolic enzyme which he calls a kind of autogenous "virus" can act like the exogenous "specific" virus of poliomyelitis and produce a condition identical with the latter.[23] His book works out this theme in regard to encephalitis lethargica, disseminated sclerosis, and even rheumatism and tuberculosis [24] and infectious diseases, not for one moment pretending that these diseases can on every occurrence be traced to a purely psychological factor, but noting carefully the emotional condition of the patient prior to the attack of disease, and suggesting the possibility that, in the final analysis, the state of the deep mind may be an adjurant, and even, on occasion, the causative factor, "the stirring to activity of a micro-organism, previously at rest in the tissue fluids, by a change in the 'neutrality' of

---

[22] *Op. cit.,* p. 65.
[23] *Op. cit.,* p. 79.
[24] *Op. cit.,* p. 114.

these fluids—a change which might be produced, among other causes, by psychical factors causing emotional disturbance." [25]

It has seemed important to me to spend time and space on the thesis of this remarkable book, for it is directly relevant to my argument that emotional states of the mind conceivably produce not only a vague sense of illness, or the so-called functional illnesses, but even organic disease.

If this conclusion can be hazarded for a moment—and the important work of Flanders Dunbar, Weiss and English in America supports it [26] —then some important deductions would seem to follow. One is that the distinction between organic and functional disease is more than ever blurred. Another is that modern medical research into such illnesses as gastric ulcer, asthma, coronary thrombosis and certain skin affections fits into such a picture as we have suggested. Another is that psychotherapy may come to have a new significance in the treatment even of so-called organic disease. The most important deduction of all, to my mind, is that religion, which has, as one of its main functions, the altering of a person's emotions from negative to positive, from fear to trust, from hate to love, and so on, may be seen to be of supreme relevance in the prevention and healing of disease, including organic disease. Let us consider these deductions.

In some quarters it is readily believed that spiritual and psychological methods of treatment are valuable for what is called functional disease, but useless in what is called organic disease; useful in cases of psychogenic disorder, but useless in what is popularly thought of as a much more serious matter, physically caused disease. This distinction has led some to suppose that all the cases cured by Christ were cases of psychogenic disorder; a suppostion impossible to substantiate.

Most modern thinkers agree that it is hard, if not impossible, to draw the line between the two. Some cases of disorder can be put into the right category without fear of contradiction. If a man breaks his leg at

[25] He quotes D. C. Muthu (*Pulmonary Tuberculosis*) as saying, "We are now beginning to see that the foundations of tuberculosis lie deeper than the presence of tubercle bacilli, and that if man is ultimately a spiritual being, the mental, moral and spiritual factors have an important bearing in the causation and the cure of disease," and records that it has been suggested that the tubercle bacillus is merely a transmutation form of a non-pathogenic, non-acid-fast bacillus normally present in the alimentary canal. On the relationship between tuberculosis and emotion see Helen Flanders Dunbar, in *Mind and Body*, pp. 223 ff. (Random House, 1947).

[26] Dr. Helen Flanders Dunbar has done some important work in this field in the department of Psychiatry at Columbia University, New York. Dr. Edward Weiss and Dr. Spurgeon English are respectively the Professors of Clinical Medicine and Psychiatry at the Temple University Medical School, Philadelphia.

football, the injury is organic. No one could call it functional or psychogenic in origin, or argue that it should be treated by psychological or religious methods, though even in such a case the mental attitude counts for something. A contented mind means a quicker cure, and worry spells delay. If a man is struck dumb by shell-shock—it being proved that there has been no injury to his vocal apparatus—no one supposes that the disability is organic or physiogenic, though even there massage of the throat-muscles may be of help. Psychological or spiritual factors thus *aid* the cure of physical or organic disorders. Physical factors similarly *aid* psychogenic disorders.

But between the two categories there is a wide border-country in which are all manner of illnesses and disabilities which our ignorance makes it impossible to classify categorically. It is interesting that Coué would not recognise a limitation of his method to any one classification of disease, and claims, for example, to have cured club-foot and tuberculosis by suggestion.[27] Some of Coué's notes are impressive—e.g. "Woman of thirty in third stage of pulmonary consumption. Increasing emaciation notwithstanding hyperalimentation. Cough, shortness of breath, expectoration; seems to have only a few months to live. Preliminary experiments indicate great sensitiveness. Suggestion, immediate improvement. From the next day a decline in morbid symptoms begins. Improvement continues from day to day; weight increases rapidly though hyperalimentation has been discontinued. After a few months cure seems complete." Eight months after this note was written by Coué, the patient wrote to him to say she was pregnant and in splendid health. A later report showed no relapse. Baudouin takes the same view and writes:

"We have to note that there is no radical difference between the action of suggestion when its results are purely functional and its action when its results are organic. If we admit that suggestion can act in the former cases (and this has long been admitted), there need be no difficulty about acknowledging the reality of its action in the latter cases. For certain persons of pseudo-scientific mind, persons who regard as 'incomprehensible' everything which disturbs their habits of thought, the organic effects of suggestion are 'inadmissible' until they have seen these effects experimentally verified—and even thereafter. Such persons are extremely illogical. They admit that suggestion acts on the circulation, on the secretions, and in a localised fashion upon the various parts of the body, doing this through the intermediation of the vasomotor nerves. Now let us suppose that the vasomotor mechanism stimu-

---

[27] *Self-Mastery through Conscious Auto-Suggestion*, p. 47. Cf. Baudouin, *op. cit.*, p. 232.

lates or restricts the circulation through the capillaries supplying some particular group of cells, and that this action is persistent. Thereupon the cells of this group will, as the case may be, enjoy an excess of nourishment, or will be insufficiently supplied. They will prosper like parasites or they will atrophy. The suggestive action which manifests itself in the case of tumours, local malformations, etc., can be very simply explained on these lines, without having recourse to any laws other than those with which we are already familiar." [28]

The remarkable case of Madame Coirin is related by Percy Dearmer. In 1716, when she was thirty-one, she fell from her horse, and paralysis and an ulcer followed. In 1719 the ulcer was in "a horrible condition." In 1720 her mother refused to allow an operation, "preferring to let her die in peace." In 1731, "after fifteen years with an open breast," she asked a friend to say a prayer for her at the tomb of the blessed François de Paris, touch the tomb with her garments and bring back some earth. This was done on August 10. On the 11th the patient wore the garment which had touched the tomb, and on the 12th touched the wound with some earth. It began to heal, and by August 31 had closed up. On September 24 the patient went out of doors. Charcôt commented on this case of so-called cancer in "La Foi qui guerit" (1897), and said, "What wonder, since we know how rapidly troubles of the circulation can appear and disappear?" Dearmer comments thus: "Troubles of the circulation! A breast built up again after fifteen years! But we are here in the very heart of the organic region! Where shall we draw this line, which is so often taken for granted, between functional and organic, between nervous and other diseases? . . . It is easy to belittle a miracle by saying that it merely cured a trouble of the circulation; but—merciful heaven! *if we can by religious influence trim the vasomotor system, where is the tissue that we cannot touch?*" [29]

"I confess," says Principal Cairns in *The Faith that Rebels*, [30] "that unless one possesses a comfortable *a priori* theory which enables one satisfactorily to decide as to what is or what is not true beforehand, it is extremely difficult to escape from the conclusion that diseases, usually called organic, sometimes yield to psychological methods as certainly as many that are called functional. Sober thoughts," he adds, "may yet revert to Luther's saying, that if we have faith enough to be healed, there is no disease from which we may not recover, and the dictum of the *Bristish Medical Journal* that 'there is no tissue of the human body

[28] *Suggestion and Auto-Suggestion*. By permission of Dodd, Mead & Company.
[29] *Op. cit.* (Italics mine.)
[30] Harper, 1929.

wholly removed from the influence of spirit,' is at least a significant step in this direction."

McDougall, again, deduces from his experiments in hypnotism that the belief is justified "that the normal processes of growth and repair are in some sense controlled by mind, or by a teleological principle of which our conscious intelligence is but one mode of manifestation among others." [31]

As long ago as 1900 Kleen cited the case of a German officer "whose diabetes and whose Iron Cross for valour both came from a stressful experience in the Franco-Prussian War," and even earlier (1898) Naunyn ascribed diabetes in a man to the feelings he experienced on discovering his wife in the act of adultery.[32]

Dr. Geoffrey Evans, consulting physician to St. Bartholomew's Hospital, London, wrote as follows in *Bart's Journal*, February 1945: "Much ill-health, including organic disease, such as coronary thrombosis and peptic ulcer, is due to emotional and nervous shock and strain." Dr. Witts, Nuffield Professor of Clinical Medicine at Oxford, alleged that many organic diseases had emotional causes. He instanced a case of fibrositis and another of rheumatism which he believed to have been caused by the emotion of sadness following bereavement.

Let us look at some diseases which might appear organic in origin and are certainly marked by distressing physical symptoms, and see what further modern medical research says about them.

1. SKIN DISEASES

A skin disease appears to the layman as an obvious example of an organic disease having a purely physical origin. The ordinary layman has no idea of the work already done in estimating the effect on the skin of emotional and nervous states. In *The Physiology of Faith and Fear*,[33] Dr. William S. Sadler, of the Post-Graduate Medical School of Chicago, wrote, "The psychic state, by its influence through the nerves and upon the circulation, is able very markedly to interfere with the normal process of elimination through the glands of the skin. Faith undoubtedly assists in skin elimination while fear unquestionably hinders and hampers the process." Dr. Sadler sets out fourteen ways in which

[31] *Body and Mind*, cf. also passage already quoted from McDougall.

[32] Kleen, *On Diabetes, Mellitus and Glycosuma* (Philadelphia, 1900), pp. 22, 37-39.

Naunyn, *Der Diabetes Mellitus* (Vienna, 1898), p. 72. Ex Cannon, *op. cit.*, p. 67.

[33] McClurg, 1925.

fear affects the skin adversely. J. H. Stokes and D. M. Pillsbury have set out to collect and collate the literature on the subject. They write: "We undertook this task with little realisation of the labour and time required for even a partial fulfilment. When our bibliography approached three hundred titles on the general aspects of the matter alone, it became evident that such a *résumé* could not be offered."

Yet it would be surprising if the skin were not frequently a pointer to emotional states. The blush, the dry skin, the moist skin, the hot or cold skin notably indicate emotional states. Why not, therefore, skin diseases, particularly when we remember that the skin is the intermediary, in a sense, between the inner and outer worlds, and almost every concern we have with the body includes a concern with the skin? Many organs can be forgotten. The skin rarely fails to obtrude its abnormalities into consciousness. Hypnotic suggestion, we recall,[34] can produce blister or urticaria or itching.

As long ago as 1904, Malcolm Morris wrote, "Herpes may be taken as the sign of a skin lesion of a nervous origin," [35] and Dr. Hellier described, in the *British Medical Journal*,[36] a patient who developed psoriasis whenever he had a sore throat, another if his skin were injured by a scratch, another whose rash recurred every time he sat for an examination. The *Medical Echo*,[37] a quarterly review of current medical literature, writes: "Many skin lesions are obstinate, or, if relieved, tend to recur because they are so often a reaction to the personality of the patient. . . . The morbid changes in the skin are the expression of a reaction to nervous strains and stresses. . . . Urticaria, eczema and psoriasis are often associated with emotional disturbances which the patients undergo. Though there are essential differences in the pathological anatomy of these disorders, an underlying psychological factor can often be traced in all of them. . . . There can be no question that a fright is often the antecedent of an attack of alopecia. . . . Rosacea is usually regarded as a vasomotor neurosis due to reflex irritation from the stomach. But the psychologists hold that an unconscious guilty conflict may be the source of the irritation. Thus there is the case of a young woman who abandoned the whole of her social life to nurse her father. Two days after he died she developed a severe rosacea, and this was attributed to the strain of nursing her father. The psychological explanation, however, was that the patient felt her father to be a great

[34] See p. 116.
[35] Malcolm Morris, *Diseases of the Skin*, p. 154.
[36] April 29, 1944.
[37] March, 1946, Vol. 22, No. 84: "The Skin as a Site of Neurosis."

burden and that she must unconsciously have desired his death. When he did die, the fulfilment of her suppressed wish produced a sense of guilt, and she, therefore, developed a guilty flush, i.e. rosacea." [38]
Dr. G. G. Robertson, in the *Lancet* (July 10, 1947), argues in the same way. He quotes the story of Job, who developed a skin disease after the shock of the loss of his worldly wealth, when he was puzzled because God had apparently deserted him. Dr. Robertson goes on to give cases in his own practice in which a sense of injustice at any rate coincided with, and perhaps caused, intractable skin disease. A girl who had worked for five years in a tobacco factory without any trouble, suddenly developed a dermatitis of the hands which would not clear up. The patient said that a forewoman had treated her unjustly and made her life unhappy. When the patient was transferred to another department of the same factory, although still handling tobacco, her skin completely recovered in a few days.

The Ministry of Labour took a man from the work he knew and where he was amongst friends, and sent him to a shipyard where he was unhappy. He resented the injustice of this treatment. Above a cut in his leg he developed a dermatitis which would not heal. On returning to his own job, it cleared up at once.

Obviously a patient could not "bring on" dermatitis of his own volition. It is as though the sense of injustice, intolerable to the mind, is handed over to the body and expressed in disease.

Dr. Millais Culpin, in *The Nervous Patient* (p. 97), says that "dermatologists are casting round for explanations of skin diseases as nervous phenomena."

Baudouin describes a case, reported in the *Bulletin École de Nancy*, 1914, of a woman of Nancy who had suffered for three years from an intractable eczema of the hands and who was cured by suggestion "in a few sittings." [39]

Dr. Bonjour in *Les Guerisons miraculeuses modernes*,[40] quotes the following case:

"Moi-même, j'ai été le témoin de guérisons instantanées de maladies organiques et microbiennes à la suite d'une émotion. Un malade atteint d'eczéma prurigineux, devenu secondairement le siège de lésions microbiennes, a guéri en 48 heures après une émotion, alors que la maladie

---

[38] I should have wished to use the word "repressed," keeping the word "suppressed" for *consciously* bottled up ideas, and the word "repressed" for ideas held down in the *unconscious* part of the mind, purposefully, but unwittingly.

[39] *Suggestion and Auto-Suggestion*, Charles Baudouin (Dodd, 1921).

[40] Ex Micklem, *ibid*.

avait résisté aux soins éclairés des professeurs Lassar, de Berlin, Fournier, de Paris, et Kaposy, de Vienne. Une malade a guéri en quelques heures d'une affection pityriasique de la peau s'étendant du cou aux pieds. Cette malade a été examinée et suivie par un specialiste auquel je l'avais adressée. Il fit d'abord le diagnostic d'eczéma, puis de pityriasis. L'affection cutanée disparut en une nuite à la suite d'une émotion que je provoquai afin que la malade se soumît aux exigences que nécessitait le traitement."

Lloyd Tuckey, in *Treatment by Hypnotism and Suggestion*,[41] claims that itching conditions of the skin have frequently been cured by hypnotic suggestion.

When we remember that warts on the skin have been frequently cured by suggestion—for no one can suppose that the quaint remedies like moistening each with saliva while the moon is full, or tying a ribbon round the affected hand, have power in themselves [42]—and that blisters on the skin can easily be raised by hypnotic suggestion,[43] we have, with the illustrations above, strong evidence that suggestion therapy can be, under certain conditions, powerful to heal skin affections. The unconscious mind can very quickly adjust blood supply, and, under suitable conditions, the condition can be healed. Micklem adds, "It is evident that certain skin diseases at least do not need to be hysterical in origin (in the sense of being caused by suggestion) in order that they may be amenable to treatment by psychotherapy." [44]

Major Miller (quoted by MacKenna in *The Lancet*, November 25, 1944) has explained how the skin of a conceited or narcissistic personality reacts when the individual is subjected to mental conflict. "In addition to his self-esteem, he usually concentrates on his personal appearance, and he presents a dignified facade to his environment. When such a person begins to fail and a sense of inadequacy overcomes him, the fear of falling from his self-raised pedestal determines a profound mental conflict. He solves this conflict and escapes from duties and responsibilities which he can no longer face, by means of a skin eruption, usually of a exudative type. This enables him to retire, without shame, from a life situation which has become insupportable."

All this has an interesting relevance to the cure of so-called "leprosy" in the gospels, already commented on (see p. 43).

[41] Putnam, 1910.

[42] Baudouin, *op. cit.*

[43] I have described my own experiments in this field in *Psychology and Life* (Abingdon-Cokesbury, 1935) and *Psychology in Service of the Soul* (Macmillan, 1930).

[44] *Op. cit.*

Stokes and Pillsbury, whom I have quoted above,[45] give the following as their conclusion. "The larger our experience and the more careful our search, the more we are inclined to believe that in the urticarias and urticarial dermatitides of middle life, in the diathetic eczemas and rosacea, and even in dermatoses which, like epidermato-phytosis, seem far removed from psychological considerations, the tension make-up, the personality defect, the conflict and anxiety, the repression and the complex have their place as causal influences, to be sought out and rectified side by side with, and sometimes even before, the correction of the more apparent physical dysfunction."

2. Gastric and Duodenal Ulcers

Again, the peptic ulcer was, until recently, supposed to be physically caused. No doubt, a nutritional deficiency as *a* cause, but all modern teachers of medicine agree that psychogenic factors are not only initiatorily causal, but are responsible for relapse and recurrence. An article called "A Study of Peptic Ulcer," by Hugh Gainsborough, M.D., of St. George's Hospital, London, and Eliot Slater, M.D., of the Maudsley Hospital, London, printed in the *British Medical Journal* for August 24, 1946, may be referred to as strongly supporting the above statement. In this article we are told, for example, of a plumber, aged fifty, who had "five large hæmorrhages, each one preceded by a period of great stress. . . . In fact, he foresaw the actual incidence of his last two hæmorrhages." Emotional upset increased the vascularity of the gastric mucous membrane and increased acid secretion. A middle-aged woman with a gastric ulcer, who had relapsed twice, and in whom a partial gastrectomy was recommended, entirely recovered while awaiting admission to hospital because in the waiting period "she had achieved both personal happiness and a freedom from financial worries which had beset her." Another patient, a young woman, "with a gastric ulcer near the cardia which did not heal after two prolonged periods of treatment, achieved rapid healing after she married—though it must be reported that her husband promptly suffered a relapse of his duodenal ulcer"!

The evidence for regarding peptic ulcer as psychogenic is im-

[45] Ex Dunbar, *Emotions and Bodily Changes*. Other authorities on skin diseases are quoted to the same effect, such as Bunnemann, Klauder, Crutchfield, Mayr, Barinbaum, Schindler, Bloch, Stern, Polland (who claims that herpes praeputialis is frequently contracted by married men after extra-marital intercourse, not after intercourse with their own wives. That is they develop it only under circumstances of unusual emotion), Jacobi, Winkler, Sack, etc.

pressive.[46] Draper (1942), for whom the ulcer patient is always a neurotic patient, says he has often observed the onset of symptoms one to ten days after severe financial loss, a business reverse, a sexual slip, a violent argument or some personal frustration. Robinson (1937) concludes that "emotional conflict in an individual with ulcer diathesis is alone essential for the production of chronic gastric ulcer." Necheles (1937) says that "most ulcer patients are persons of the worrying, highly-strung type." Davis and Wilson (1937) found that a change of work, financial difficulties, illness or misfortune were causative factors. Wilson (1939) believes that psychological treatment "offers at least as much hope of saving life as other therapeutic approaches, and, since it is probably directed to the basic disturbance, it may possibly prove more successful in the end." Morris and Titmuss (1944) found "a rise in the mortality from peptic ulcer in wartime which reached its height in the last quarter of 1940 when air raids were severe."

The authors of the article, in their conclusion, write as follows: "The results of medical treatment were disappointing, and on our figures one-third of the patients can be expected to relapse within four months. The failure was not as regards the healing of the ulcers, but in the prevention of relapses after return to work. Consequently more attention should be paid in the follow-up period to the adjustment of work conditions, the use of resettlement facilities under the Disabled Persons Act and *the careful discussion with the patient of his social and psychological problems*." [47]

American research arrives at the same conclusion. Lindemann, a well-known American consultant, found that unexpressed grief was causally linked with ulcerative colitis. Thirty-three out of forty-one of such patients had developed the disease "in close time-relationship with the loss of an important person." Moses Einhorn, who wrote a paper in the *American Journal of Medical Science* (No. 179 (1930), pp. 259-264), based on cases of gastroduodenal ulcers in eight hundred patients, writes: "Psychic influences, such as anger, shock, emotion and business reverses, play a causative role in the development and recurrent attacks of ulcer." In *Psychosomatic Medicine*, by Edward Weiss, M.D., and O. Spurgeon English, M.D.,[48] both of the Temple University Medical School, Philadelphia, we have, for example, the case [49] of a young man

[46] I owe the following facts to the article in the *British Medical Journal* referred to above.

[47] Italics mine.

[48] W. B. Saunders and Co., 1943.

[49] P. 247.

of twenty admitted to hospital with peptic ulcer, set up by worries about his engagement. He felt his girl had tried to rush him into being engaged to her. Because of his worry he could not concentrate on his work and made a serious error, which was discovered by his superior, who humiliated him by taking away certain responsibilities from him. This upset him further, and made him irritable and quarrelsome and more worried still, until, in his own phrase, "his stomach went back on him."

It was explained to the patient that his conflict over the marriage situation had to do with the precipitation of his illness, and that so long as the conflict persisted it would be impossible to bring about permanent cure. The patient grasped this, and felt he must make up his mind to marry or not to marry. He chose the latter. The patient recovered, and remained well in spite of the fact that within three years he had married another girl.

The authors say that again and again they find emotional conflict precedes gastro-intestinal hæmorrhage of ulcer origin. They add, "We, of course, do not believe that there is a direct connection between psychological disturbance and ulcer formation, but rather, as Alexander has stated, the psychological difficulties may be responsible for changes in muscle tone and secretion which assist in disturbing the ulcer area." [50]

I am surprised at this conclusion. It looks as if there is a very definite and direct connection. They themselves add that "men with functional disturbances of the stomach have a very high incidence of mental difficulties." [51]

3. ASTHMA

It has long been recognised that there is often a causal connection between an emotional state and asthma. "I think now," says Liebman.[52] "of a splendid young man who literally was choked to death by asthma, because, after his mother's death, he married a girl that his mother had not liked. His extreme sense of guilt not only prevented him from enjoying the fulness of life with a married woman, but actually caused a five-year illness and ultimate death."

A patient had an attack of asthma when a chandelier fell from the ceiling in front of him; another on receiving sad news; another on hearing a fire alarm; another when a dog jumped on him. The explanation given is that the affect is discharged upon the visceral nervous

[50] P. 249.
[51] P. 251.
[52] Liebman, *op. cit.*, pp. 34-35.

system and mobilises the well-adjusted mechanism of the asthma attack in people with the asthmatic diathesis or constitutional predisposition.

The first appearance of asthma is frequently preceded by strong emotional disturbance. Take, for example, the following:

"Case 9.—O. B., æt. fifty, municipal secretary. Since 1912 the patient has suffered from asthma which developed suddenly. The patient is the youngest of four brothers and sisters. He always felt himself slighted. Especially a sister two years older had always been given preference by the parents. As a child the patient always suffered from a lack of love and tenderness. In professional and monetary matters his brothers and sisters had always been superior to him. In 1912 the patient's mother died. When the inheritance was distributed, the patient was passed over. He could get over the monetary loss, but not the injury. At this time he developed asthma." [53]

Ferras reports the case of a young French officer who returned to Paris in 1814 after recovering from a serious wound. When he noticed foreign soldiers at the gates of the city, he was so moved that he was immediately seized with a feeling of indisposition, and the same night had a severe attack of asthma. In the nights following he had similar attacks, and they did not cease until fourteen days after the first attack. In 1815 the attacks recurred after a new grief.

Yet note that other individuals pass through the strongest emotions without asthma attack, so that a *purely* emotional origin must be ruled out. "It must be assumed that the emotion encounters a psychological or organic predisposition and sets the machinery going." [54] The French physician, Trousseau, was aware that exposure to emanations in a stable or to dust rendered him liable to some difficulty in breathing, but this was usually of a trivial character. Sometimes, however, he lost his temper with his coachman in the stable. This contingency was invariably followed by a severe paroxysm of asthma.[55] In asthma of some duration the fear of further attacks causes a vicious circle.

A further case is taken from a publication by Moos. One of his patients, a domestic servant, had to work hard during the day and to nurse the master of the house, who suffered from asthma, at night. In a state of despair because of this situation, with which she felt she could not cope, she herself was attacked by asthma one night.

Emotional excitement seems capable of making a substance allergic to a patient which in ordinary conditions is not allergic to him. Moos

[53] *Journal of Mental Science,* July, 1935, p. 542.

[54] *Ibid.*

[55] *Medical Echo,* July, 1946.

had a patient, a miller, who could not stand the mill dust in the mill of his angry father; in another mill, in spite of the dust, he was free of the disorder.

Dr. Flanders Dunbar, in her monumental and scholarly work, already referred to, *Emotions and Bodily Changes*, which she subtitles, "A Survey of Literature on Psychosomatic Interrelationships," provides evidence from a wide field to support the view here put forward, that a seemingly physical disease, like asthma, often has a non-physical cause. Here are some authorities whom she quotes.[56]

Malinowski wrote in 1913, "The psychogenesis of asthma is a very old conception. Only the method of psychoanalysis has enabled us to come nearer to the essential nature of asthma and to see the absurdity in the old clinical distinction between bronchial asthma and nervous asthma. The various successes of somatic therapy do not in any way argue against the psychogenetic concept. We are familiar with such phenomena in all neuroses. The pedagogic value of other procedures, especially breathing exercises in all their forms, can be denied as little as the sedative value of drug therapy by narcotics. But in the future we shall consider as a true causal therapy only the treatment of the basic anxiety hysteria."

Reichmann calls bronchial asthma "a curable neurosis of the respiratory tract." Williams, Biermer and Curschmann call asthma "a reflex neurosis." Weber and Störch call it a "secretory neurosis." Eichhorst calls it "a central or bulbar neurosis." Costa has come to believe "that a psychic or psychosexual cause will be found in every case of bronchial asthma," and adds that "*asthma becomes fixated only through the neglect of this etiological factor followed by an irrational polypragmatic drug therapy.*" Costa notes the value of hypnosis in stopping attacks of asthma, but points out the necessity of analysing the *causes* of the asthmatic symptoms. Mohr says that psychotherapeutic treatment for bronchial asthma was begun by Delius and himself in 1910, and that results proved that this was the only safe way. He says, "Even if the allergic theory of asthma were later to be confirmed, this could in no sense alter the fact that asthma is curable by psychotherapy." Moos writes, "The fact that the psyche is almost always the primary, most usual and most important factor (in asthma) is now recognised by most writers." He gives details of seven cases all cured by psychotherapy when all other means had failed. Lowenstein, Schultz, Naber, all write to the same effect. Pollnow, Petow and Wittkower review forty-five cases of bronchial asthma psychotherapeutically treated. Liek, a surgeon

[56] Dunbar, *op. cit.*

who used to carry out operations for bronchial asthma, came to the conclusion that "the decisive factor is not the character of the surgical procedure itself *but the personality of the surgeon.*" (Italics mine.) He writes: "It is no longer legitimate today to attack functional disturbances in the nervous system by means of operations, the least one can say concerning which is that they are superfluous. They have nothing to do with exact research as long as the psyche is left out of account."

We have only noted three types of illness which used to be regarded as physiogenic. We find them often psychologically caused, and often "set off" by emotional factors. It is probable that many more diseases arise in the same way. Even the common cold is now thought by some to be precipitated by emotional states. One writer in the *British Medical Journal* writes, "I do not wish to imply that there is no infective ætiology of the common cold but I am convinced that the primary cause can be emotional." [57]

What does emerge is that the area of illness to be deemed purely organic in origin is dwindling. The literature of the subject abounds in illustrative cases in which almost any type of illness develops either after some emotional upheaval, or as a means of evading some unpleasant situation. Such evasion, of course, is not dishonourable, since activity of the conscious will cannot produce symptoms in a manner convincing enough to satisfy the patient himself.

What I have tried to show in the cases of skin disease, peptic ulcer and asthma is that the *causes* of each are often largely psychological or spiritual. True, there must be predisposing conditions which determine that one man, through emotional stress, develops one illness and another develops another—the diathesis or constitutional tendency, as it is called —but the psychological factor is shown to be causal, inasmuch as if it were absent no disease whatever would develop. The weakness which the psychological factor increases to the point of disablement would remain an unnoticed tendency. The physical situation alone, while causal of tendency, is not causal of disease. Indeed, some writers think a tendency to asthma is as common as a tendency to sea-sickness.[58]

This statement is borne out by Rogerson,[59] who noted three cases of children who had attacks of asthma if they ate certain foods *at home,*

[57] October 21 and November 11, 1950.

[58] "The truth may well be that everyone has an asthma threshold, a certain greater or lesser inborn susceptibility to the condition, much in the same way that everyone might be said to have a sea-sickness threshold." Sanderson quoted by F. Croxon Deller, M.D. in the *Post-Graduate Medical Journal*, February, 1946.

[59] *Medical Echo*, July, 1946.

where their parents continually quarrelled. The children were alleged to be allergic to these foods. But when away from home, and therefore *out of the atmosphere of fear*, the children could eat these foods with impunity. The "allergic" response disappeared. No asthma followed. We may surely say, then, that the psychic factor, not the material factor; the fear, not the food, was the causal factor of the asthma. At the same time, there must be many cases of asthma physically caused and in which the psychological factor is secondary.

The fascinating question which we have, as yet, no means of answering is: To what extent are a multitude of other diseases frequently organic concomitants of psychological or spiritual disharmonies? [60] It may even be that all our magnificent physical research and experimental remedying on the physical plane are journeys along the wrong roads; that while we may learn much as we travel on them, we shall not reach the destination we seek until, with equal enthusiasm, we travel along psychic and spiritual roads.

Space forbids our doing more than skate over the vexed question anent the influence of the glandular secretions.[61] Materialists assert that moral qualities can be engendered by material toxins or secretions alone. If a man is brave, it is no virtue; it is because he has a certain secretion in excess of the coward, and so on.

It is a strangely illogical position. We are not made sad because the tears flow. The tears flow because we are sad. In other words, the secretion does not create the emotion; the emotion creates or liberates the secretion. If tears are injected into the eye-ducts, we are not made sad. When we are afraid, adrenalin is discharged into the blood-stream and we are keyed up and made ready for fight or flight. But if adrenalin is *injected* into the blood-stream, we are not made afraid. As Professor Cannon, formerly of Harvard wrote: "We can laugh and cry and tremble. But forced laughter does not bring happiness, nor forced sobbing sorrow, and the trembling from cold rouses neither anger nor fear." [62]

It is true that body and mind are so inextricably mingled that certain

[60] I have read, for example, of a woman of thirty-four, shut in and refusing to have any contact with anyone if she could help it, who suffered simultaneously from constipation, vaginismus and spastic retention of urine. She was shut in in more senses than one and physical remedies would be likely to do less good than an enquiry as to why her soul was in prison.

[61] The reader may care to consult, *The Glands of Destiny*, Geikie Cobb (Macmillan, 1928) and *The Glands Regulating Personality*, Louis Berman of Columbia University, New York (Macmillan, 1928).

[62] Walter B. Cannon, *op. cit.*

toxins do influence behaviour—alcohol does, for example—and man is culpable if, knowing that in excess it makes his character deteriorate, he continues to drink excessively. It may be that, for reasons beyond his control, toxins or secretions are poisoning his blood and affecting his character. In such a case he cannot be blamed, but is a patient. There is such a thing as moral illness physically conditioned. No deduction can be made from these facts which would justify us in supposing that man is the *victim* of his secretions, and that whether he does good or ill is neither to his credit nor blame. Normal people are not in doubt that their actions are, within limits, freely determined, that emotions which they can control, govern the secretions which alter character, and not vice versa.

Recently, in the *Hibbert Journal*,[63] a writer who called his article "Surgery and Sin," claimed that a man had been made morally better by surgical operation. In the issue of January 1947 Professor Clement Webb pointed out that the described operation did not raise any problem not already raised by the frequently observed cases in which an improvement in health, brought about by medical treatment, had, as its consequence, an improvement in conduct. Webb refers to an incident recorded by Roger Bacon where the use of a certain medicine was believed to have changed the character of a French prince in the thirteenth century, but Bacon did not regard this as inconsistent with current theological speculations. Webb asks, "Was Mr. North's debauched young Frenchman guilty of 'sin,' or a patient suffering from psychological illness, or a victim of moral illness?"

He points out that the operation which was alleged to improve the young Frenchman's character may have made him a greater *sinner* than before. He may have gratified his appetites just as much after, as before, the operation, *but not in a way society complained about*. If he *resisted* temptation before the operation, but after it did not resist *because the new-found way of self-indulgence did not bring him social disapproval*, he was a greater sinner after the operation than before it.

Certain forms of insanity are said to be physically caused. Here we have a material factor apparently causing a non-material factor— behaviour—to deteriorate. Many problems are at present insoluble in this field. We may hazard the speculation that the material factor does not wound the inner psyche, or true self of personality, any more than a man's power to see is affected by his being enclosed in a room with none but frosted-glass windows. He, looking out, sees a distorted world, as the mental patient does. Those who try to see him—I am imagining they cannot enter the room where he is, but many only peer

[63] October, 1946.

through the window—see a distorted personality. But all the time, he, the patient himself, may be essentially unaffected by these facts, and may go on living most of the time in another room in the house of life, a room into which we have no access. I have noticed that mental patients often have lucid intervals when they seem entirely normal, and between these intervals they seem to make spiritual progress. Just before death, mental patients are frequently sane, and it is then found that they have made amazing spiritual progress, even through years of mental illness. This I have had confirmed by medical men and women who have specialised in insanity and mental illness. At the Annual Meeting of the Lebanon Hospital for Mental Diseases a former chaplain in a mental hospital said that when refractory patients had some physical illness such as pneumonia "they became under that high temperature completely sane, telling him the whole history of their lives, which revealed plainly how the mental breakdown had arisen. He came to realise how people whose conscious minds are completely out of reach are helped by spiritual contact on the level of their unconscious mind." [64]

We can only speculate here. The distressing truth about a mental patient is that he is no longer fully *en rapport* with the real world. But there is no evidence that his soul is affected, and those who believe in an after-life—as I do—may think of such a person escaping at death from the prison of a diseased body, with no deterioration of the capacity of his soul, to revel in the life of the spirit.

From our study in this chapter it seems to me proved that not only in cases of functional disorder, but also in cases of organic disease, the emotional factor in the mind of the patient, often unconscious, is one of immense importance. Often, indeed, of such importance as to be regarded as causal, in that, without the emotional factor, while there might be a tendency to certain diseases, the diseases themselves would never develop if the emotional factor were absent.

Dr. Loring-Swain, an American doctor, makes a claim, my citing of which must not be taken to mean complete agreement. It seems too sweeping to me and very unjust to many arthritic patients of whom it is simply not true. Yet the opinion of Loring-Swain is significant. I quote from the *Proceedings of the Congress on Rheumatism* of 1938, where he is reported to have said:

"Spiritually the rheumatoid-arthritis patients studied had no vital faith and were, therefore, fearfully facing life's responsibilities alone. The correlation of these negative reactions with the joint flare-up was astonishing in the two hundred and seventy-five cases under observation. Five years of observation has convinced us that just facing these

[64] *Guild of Health Magazine*, November, 1950, p. 11.

negative attitudes is not enough to overcome them, but with the development of a faith, fear goes, improved health follows and, most important of all for the future welfare of the patient, personality changes take place. We find that unless a patient can return to his old environment improved in body, intelligently understanding his adjustment problems and with a faith which gives confidence for the future, he has no real guarantee of permanent health. All our combined medical and orthopædic skill is vitally essential for recovery, but because of the psychogenic factors found in most rheumatoid arthritics, we will fail to prevent recurring attacks unless we develop in the patient himself a power to control his negative emotional reactions.

"Much of the future progress in the art of healing the body will come along lines that recognise, and have an answer for, the healing of the soul. More people are sick because they are unhappy than unhappy because they are sick."

But it is hard for many—especially doctors who have been trained to look only for a material cause of disease, bacteria, toxins, trauma, etc.—to receive this viewpoint. The older orthodox medicine still holds that the sequence is always: cellular disease—structural alteration—physiological or functional disturbance—emotional symptoms. The newer orthodoxy is amended thus—at least in some cases: functional disturbance—cellular disease—structural alteration. In my own mind, after studying the evidence referred to, I am convinced that the order of the development of disease is often: emotional trauma—psychological or spiritual disturbance—functional impairment—cellular disease—structural alteration. Again and again, even in the limited experience and observation which my own work has afforded me during the last thirty years, I have realised that where a person represses an unhealthy emotion over a long period and cannot *express* it in words or action, or bring it to conscious recognition at all, the mind, unable longer to carry the burden, finds a kind of expression of it in bodily terms which means either functional or organic disease.

Here is a case which every practising psychologist and many ministers could parallel. In a home I know are two girls. The elder is naturally of quiet disposition, her mother's pet and her father's idol. The first child frequently is. The second child is of turbulent disposition, a born rebel. She longs to be admitted to the circle of love which consists of her father, mother and elder sister. But quietly and unremittingly she is excluded. She expresses her resentment and love-hunger by violent temper tantrums, and is then punished. Temper, therefore, does not pay. Further, it proves—to her—that she is not loved. Deprived of love and hungry for love, she manufactures a huge resentment which she must not show, for it defeats her object. She represses it into the unconscious and becomes outwardly docile and obedient in order to win love. Her dreams are violent compensations, but even if she tells them, no one understands them. She lives this lie right on to adult years, and marries a man who also starves her of love in her own right. One suspects he married her to better his prospects with her father, in whose employment he is. Rage and resentment and bitterness and frustration fill her unconscious mind, and, being repressed, find "organic language" in high blood pressure. Before psychological treatment had progressed enough to help her, she died of extreme hypertension. Her illness, deemed organic, was undoubtedly psychogenic, and could probably have been cured by bringing to consciousness the repressed resentment, and bringing her into a fellowship—such as the ideal church provides—where she would have been loved for her own sake and, through the love of others, been healed by the love of God.

One of the strange and interesting things about psychosomatic illness is that, in a sense, the race has always "known it" and has embodied its experience in its forms of language. I have known of a case of blindness caused through a refusal to "look ahead"; of abdominal disease because a patient "couldn't stomach" a certain situation; of bronchial catarrh that was cured when a patient "got something off his chest"; of anorexia nervosa due to a patient being "starved of love"; of disease of the œsophagus brought on because a patient could not "swallow" the facts of an emotional situation. A patient "itching" for revenge develops a pruritus, and a paralysed arm has been known in a patient who repressed the desire to strike another.

Further, the immense power of the association of ideas is commonly forgotten. A child who at the table witnessed throughout childhood the quarrelling of his parents, developed in manhood violent indigestion whenever his peace of mind was threatened. The man whose story is told on p. 350 had a pain in the arm whenever he felt unhappy and unloved. Illustrations of this point are legion. But we must pass on.

Is religion relevant to all this? I claim that it may turn out to be supremely relevant. I am not thinking, of course, of any narrow sectarian religion, but of the soul's relationship to God—a relationship made possible by the love of Christ and a God whose character is manifested in Christ.

May it not be that one of these days we shall know, through both science and experience, that if our relationship with God means—as it should—that the love of Christ is the permanent feeling in our deep mind, then that love will sweep out all unhealthy emotions like fear, jealousy, pride, resentment, anger, worry and the other emotions that set up illness? Such a love would act in two ways. It would give us security of soul, and thus inward serenity and peace of mind, for what greater security in an insecure world exists than that which prompts us to say and to believe: "I am loved of God and I trust myself utterly to Him." It would give us also an outgoing love for others, constraining us to serve them in Christ's name and, in so doing, *forget ourselves*. Once we can stop our endless thinking about ourselves, our neuroses are liable to wither and die. Self-willed concentration directed only to our own self-concerns, makes any neurosis flourish.

Two things must be added.

1. No case is being made out in this essay that *all* disease is caused by unhealthy feeling, or can be cured by replacing a thing like resentment by a thing like the love of God. Germ-invasion diseases flourished before man existed. Even if some organisms have been produced through the action of emotions like anger, they exist as a menace through infection, and may be carried to others. We do not know under what conditions the latter may be immune from infection. I cannot see any wisdom in trying to make the tentative hypothesis, outlined here, cover all the phenomena of illness. There remains a most definite place for the physician, the surgeon and the psychologist.

At the same time, I believe that the future will reveal a most important spiritual factor in some illnesses, and religion, in the broad sense, a most relevant factor in its prevention and cure. To this we shall return in the last chapter.

2. In any case, religion is not a kind of remedy to apply when drugs and poultices, surgery and injections have failed. Religion is primarily a harmonious relationship between God and man. A wise man will seek that relationship as soon as he discovers the reality of God and of His love. In humility and penitence, longing to be one with God because He is love and beauty—and not merely because we want to be well—we may find that our illness was due to disharmony on this, the highest plane of man's relationship with his Environment. If so— if, that is, our illness was in the category not of the physio-genic or the psycho-genic, but the spirito-genic—then, to restore the broken relationship and find the harmony of soul with God which may be the central core and essence of health, will bring us wholeness and healing because it brings us holiness.

Just in case it should appear that the argument of this chapter is modern and new-fangled, I quote two passages from John Wesley. In his *Journal*, May 12, 1759, he wrote as follows: "Reflecting today on the case of a poor woman who had continual pain in her body, I could not but remark the inexcusable negligence of most physicians in cases of this nature. They prescribe drug upon drug, without knowing a jot of the matter concerning the root of the disorder. . . . Whence came this woman's pain? (which she would never have told had she never been questioned about it). From fretting for the death of her son. And what availed medicine whilst that fretting continued? Why then do not all physicians consider how far bodily disorders are caused or influenced by the mind; and in these cases, which are utterly out of their sphere, call in a minister?"

And in his *Primitive Physick*, he wrote: "The love of God, as it is the sovereign remedy of all miseries, so in particular it effectively prevents all bodily disorders the passions introduce, by keeping the passions themselves within due bounds; and by the unspeakable joy and perfect calm serenity and tranquillity it gives the mind, it becomes the most powerful of all the means of health and long life."

AN EXAMINATION OF JUNG'S ATTITUDE TO RELIGION [1]

AS WE SAW earlier (p. 277), Jung, the son of a well-known Swiss clergyman, is much more sympathetic to religion than is Freud. He does not dismiss it as an illusion, nor regard it as a crutch which could and should be thrown away by the emotionally adult. "A religious attitude is an element in psychic life," he writes, "whose importance can hardly be overrated." [2] And again, "The concept of God is simply a necessary psychological function." [3] Religion he defines thus, in his book. *Psychology and Religion:* "Religion, as the Latin word denotes, is a careful and scrupulous observation of what Rudolf Otto aptly termed the 'numinosum,' that is a dynamic existence or effect not caused by an arbitrary act of will. On the contrary, it seizes and controls the human subject which is always rather its victim than its creator. . . . Religious teaching as well as the consensus gentium always and everywhere explains this condition as being due to a cause external to the individual."

With his immense interest in, and profound knowledge of, the mystical background of all the religions, Jung realised that in the minds of many patients religious truth, not thought out but accepted,

---

[1] I must explain that I have not written on Adler's attitude to religion, for the simple reason that he says practically nothing about it himself. He appears to have believed that man is the captain of his soul and must save himself. In his *Understanding Human Nature* he scoffs at those who fly to God to do for them what they should do for themselves. In *The Neurotic Constitution* he scoffs at those who fly to God for a security he thinks they should find elsewhere. His philosophy seems to me weakened in that he sees no place for God (cf. *Individual Psychology*). His attitude might be labelled a beneficent humanism.

[2] *Modern Man in Search of a Soul.*

[3] *Collected Papers on Analytical Psychology.*

and religious experience, not rationalised but most fervently felt, were the very foundation of character. To sneer at religion would be thus a psychological error of treatment of the very greatest magnitude. "The psychologist must remember," he says,[4] "that certain religious convictions not founded on reason are a necessity of life for many persons." He goes on to show that, for many patients, religion gives life a sense of meaning and purpose essential to his psychological stability, and adds, "The physician's recognition of the spiritual factors in their true light is vitally important."

Jung even speaks of spirituality as an "instinct." He writes,[5] "Spirituality appears in the psyche as an instinct also. . . . It is not derived from another instinct . . . it is a principle sui generis." "Individuation," [6] which is Jung's word for integration, is the goal of his treatment, and he is sure that this is impossible without religion.

Indeed, in some passages Jung sounds like an apostle of Christianity: "It is not the children of the flesh, but 'the children of God' who know freedom. . . . We moderns are faced with the necessity of rediscovering the life of the spirit; we must experience it anew for ourselves. It is the only way in which we can break the spell that binds us to the cycle of biological events." [7]

One of his paragraphs in this book strongly supports the *rapprochement* between psychology and religion. He wrote: [8] "During the past thirty years, people from all the civilised countries of the earth have consulted me. I have treated many hundreds of patients, the larger number being Protestants, a smaller number Jews, and not more than five or six believing Catholics. Among all my patients in the second half of life—that is to say, over thirty-five—there has not been one whose problem in the last resort was not that of finding a religious outlook on life. It is safe to say that every one of them fell ill because he had lost that which the living religions of every age have given to their followers, and none of them has been really healed who did not regain his religious outlook. This, of course, has nothing whatever to do with a particular creed or membership of a church."

[4] *Modern Man in Search of a Soul.*

[5] *Contributions to Analytical Psychology.*

[6] Jung in *Two Essays on Analytical Psychology* defines Individuation as becoming "a single discrete being, and, inasmuch as the concept of individuality embraces that innermost, last, and incomparable uniqueness of our being, it also includes the idea of becoming one's own real self."

[7] *Modern Man in Search of a Soul.*

[8] *Op. cit.*

"It is indeed high time," he adds, "for the clergyman and psychotherapist to join forces to meet this great spiritual task. . . . It seems to me that side by side with the decline of religious life, the neuroses grow noticeably more frequent." [9]

Such an attitude is most attractive, and the above passages have been quoted many times. Yet concerning them some comment seems necessary in estimating the soundness of Jung's attitude to religion.

In the first place, I wonder if the statement really can be substantiated that neurosis is as frequently caused by a faulty religious attitude as Jung suggests. His language is exceedingly strong. Of patients over thirty-five, he says, "It is safe to say that *every one* of them fell ill because he had lost that which the living religions of every age have given to their followers, and none of them has been really healed who did not regain his religious outlook."

Frankly, I cannot believe this. In the first place, many of the greatest saints have been neurotic. Neurosis is so frequently set up by *unconscious* factors. It is quite unfair to blame the patient for *unconscious* conflict and tell him that had he possessed what religion can give him, he would not have fallen ill. Some of the finest Christian people I have ever known have suffered from "nervous breakdowns" through factors for which they certainly could not have been blamed. In the treatment that, in my opinion, should follow analysis, I believe that religion should, and can, play a most valuable part, but Jung's claim goes far beyond this.

In the second place, to say that *none* of the psychoneurotic patients over thirty-five was really healed who did not regain a religious outlook is, to me, incredible. Patients of this age and over have suffered from psychoneurosis precipitated by bomb explosion and shell-shock, and were entirely cured without mention of religion. Many materialistic psychiatrists, reluctant to admit that religion has any place at all in the field of neurosis, would be a little surprised to hear that none of their patients was "really healed" without it. Of course, much turns on what Jung meant by "really healed." If he meant "symptom-free," then, in my view, his claim cannot be substantiated. If he meant by "healed," brought into a state of complete harmony at all levels— body, mind and spirit—with the relevant environment, then his statement could stand, for it is arguable that no one is *perfectly* whole who has no traffic of any kind with God.

In the third place, it seems that Jung regards all religions as belonging to the same category and equal in value. Indeed, he often appears to compare Christianity unfavourably with the religions of the

⁹ *Op. cit.*

East,[10] especially Protestant evangelistic Christianity. He writes, "The Protestant is left to God alone. There is no confession, no absolution. ... He has to digest his sins alone and he is not too sure of divine grace which has become unattainable through lack of a suitable ritual." [11]

In the famous quotation we are discussing, he says that the patient fell ill "because he had lost that which *the living religions of every age* have given to their followers." [12]

Jung has a very high regard for Christ. In his book *Psychological Types* he makes a spirited defence of Christ against the charge sometimes brought against Him that He was insane. "He was, therefore, no paranoiac, as indeed the result also proved. The views advanced from time to time from the psychiatric side concerning the morbidity of Christ's psychology are nothing but ludicrous rationalistic twaddle, altogether remote from any sort of comprehension of the meaning of such processes in the history of man."

A convinced Christian should pay high tribute to the truths in other religions, and, so far from seeking to destroy them, should regard them as preparations for a Christianity, cleansed from biased sectarianism. For example, in *The Psychology of the Unconscious*, he writes, had the authentic experience of communion with the living Christ can equate Christianity with other religions, as Jung does, especially in regard to the significance of the death of Christ.[13] He refers to the story of the Cross as not unique in religious mythology [14] as if it too were a myth. Sometimes his language would make one doubt whether Jung *really* accepts the historicity of Christ. The Christian religion, he says, sets up the Saviour "considered as real." [15] He speaks of its "rationalistic theology with its Jesus historically insisted upon." [16] He even speaks of the "historical and philosophical weakness of the Christian dogmatism and the *religious emptiness of an historical Jesus*." [17]

---

[10] E.g. *Two Essays on Analytical Psychology*, where he writes, "Christianity is a mystery religion now in a faded and degenerate form." And in *Modern Man in Search of a Soul*, he says that the East is turning our spiritual world upside down. He declares that a primitive religion is better suited to primitive peoples than Christianity.

[11] *Psychology and Religion.*

[12] Italics mine. Cf. *Psychological Types.*

[13] *Modern Man in Search of a Soul.*

[14] *Psychology of the Unconscious.*

[15] *Ibid.*

[16] *Ibid.*

[17] *Ibid.* (Italics mine.)

So eager is Jung to trace ideas to myths that he does not realise how different a religion Christianity is.

The fact that Jung imperfectly understands the central message and vital heart of Christianity is seen in the passages which reveal that, to him, the Christian way of life is a matter of "imitating Christ." He criticises Christianity for asking men to "imitate Christ." Consider the following passages: "We Protestants must sooner or later face this question: Are we to understand the 'imitation of Christ' in the sense that we should copy His life and, if I may use the expression, ape His stigmata; or in the deeper sense that we are to live our own proper lives as truly as He lived His in all its implications? It is no easy matter to live a life that is modelled on Christ's, but it is unspeakably harder to live one's own life as truly as Christ lived His." [18] And again: "The modern man, moreover, is not eager to know in what way he can imitate Christ, but in what way he can live his own individual life, however meagre and uninteresting it may be. It is because every form of imitation seems to him deadening and sterile that he rebels against the force of tradition that would hold him to well-trodden ways." [19]

But one wonders where Jung got the idea that the heart of Christianity was "imitating Christ." Although brought up a Protestant, he had leanings towards Roman Catholicism, and though it is important to understand him, it is also important not to regard him as an authority on personal religious experience. Jung is a psychologist. He is not entitled to write about religion with the same authority. He has never had a religious experience of his own, or so it would appear. One is tempted to turn on Jung with a quotation from one of his own works where he says that religious experience is absolute. "It is indisputable. You can only say that you have never had such an experience and your opponent will say, 'Sorry, I have.'" [20] Jung's own religious experience seems to me to be very sub-Christian. He, therefore, misunderstands what a Christian believes *as a result of an authentic experience*. In another place[21] I have tried to meet this heresy, but a few sentences may serve to show its fundamental weakness. To advise people to "imitate Christ" is no gospel at all. It puts all the strain on the Christian's will-power. The Christian Way becomes something the Christian must achieve. But the heart of the Gospel is something God

[18] *Modern Man in Search of a Soul.*
[19] *Ibid.*
[20] *Psychology and Religion.*
[21] *The Transforming Friendship* (Abingdon-Cokesbury, 1931).

does in Christ through the Holy Spirit;[22] something He has done and is doing and will do for anyone who trusts Him. The power in Christianity is not in man's effort to imitate Christ, but in Christ's love for man, forgiveness of man and power to change man. Thus it is a Gospel with wings, not an exhortation with spurs. St. Paul would not recognise Jung's brand as Christianity at all. For St. Paul even the fight was a fight of *faith;* not of effort. Man is to use his will, of course, but Paul's message was an invitation to "put on Christ," to believe in this crucified, risen and ever-living Redeemer. With the author of the letter to the Hebrews, Paul would have said, *"He* is able to save them to the uttermost that come unto God by Him." [23]

There is a further attitude of Jung's in regard to religion which seems to me unsound. To him it is a means to an end. It is a way of getting the patient better.

Some of Jung's sentences are almost objectionable in their utilitarianism. For example, *The Psychology of the Unconscious,* he writes, "The Christian religion seems to have fulfilled its great biological purpose, in so far as we are able to judge. It has led human thought to independence and has lost its significance, therefore, to a yet undetermined extent. . . . In consideration of the fact that this religion has rendered, nevertheless, inconceivable service to education, one cannot reject it, eo ipso, today. *It seems to me that we might still make use in some way of its form of thought* and especially of its great wisdom of life, which for two thousand years has been proven to be particularly efficacious. The stumbling block is the *unhappy combination of religion and morality.* That must be overcome." [24]

The Christian does not thus think of Christianity. Without repeating what was said in the chapter on "Intercession," we insist that the aim of Christianity is the reconciliation of the soul with God, through Christ's grace and man's penitence. If healing of mind and body follows, well and good. But God is an end, not a means. To use religion as a useful treatment because other treatments have failed; to "try Christianity" because our holidays, surgical operations, ointments, drugs and massage have failed, is so to misunderstand Christianity as to become incapable of "using" it. What is used, if this misconception be held is not Christianity at all, but a false, even if specious, substitute; not the real thing, but a sham.

One cannot avoid the conclusion, from his references to it, that

---

[22] Jung speaks of the Holy Spirit as "a phenomenon of the collective unconscious" (*Contributions to Analytical Psychology*).

[23] Hebrews 7:25. Cf. Philippians 4:11-13.

[24] Dodd. First italics mine; second italics Jung's.

Jung has a dangerously inaccurate conception of what Christianity is. Yet one remains thankful for his evaluation of spiritual factors and their importance, for his emphasis on integration, and for his tribute to the significance of Christian ideas. We are the victims of disintegrateing moods and fantasies which rise from the collective or absolute unconscious. But Jung shows they are to be dealt with. We are to relax and allow them to come to consciousness. Then we may recognise the archetypes or collective images, symbols which are identical with those in the men of bygone times whose civilisations have perished.

As we recognise these images which rise, we may, in calm contemplation, achieve, through consciously confronting them, the power to rule them, though not to exterminate them. So long as we do not give way to spiritual pride, we can create a "virtual point," a centre of balance between conscious and unconscious—the unconscious being "only the modern name for the realm of the gods, or the internal counterpart of the external universe." [25] a kind of reconciliation between the self and the external world. In such a reconciliation the mind, says Jung, finds its peace. Jung would answer the question at the head of this section— "Do Modern Psychological Methods of Healing Need Religion?"—in the affirmative. He lays all religions under tribute. I would venture to correct his conception of Christianity, but would pay tribute to the success with which some of my friends have brought healing to stricken men and women by the theory and practice derived from him. My study of Jung drives me to the conclusion that his research into the human mind has forced him to recognise man's helplessness to save himself completely and rise to the heights of his possibilities without the aid of religion.

[25] See Alan W. Watts on "Jung" in *Tomorrow* (December 16, 1946).

6

AN EXAMINATION OF FREUD'S ATTITUDE TO RELIGION

PROFESSOR FREUD DID not think much of religion. He would not only have answered the question at the head of this section with an emphatic "No!" but he would have labelled the Christian religion as an illusion. In his view, man must have this illusion dispelled. It may have had its uses as a temporary crutch for the emotionally lame, but it is itself a neurosis. Making an analogy between obsessional neurosis and religion, he writes, "The true believer is in a high degree protected against the danger of certain neurotic afflictions; by accepting the universal neurosis (religion), he is spared the task of forming a personal neurosis." His religious dogmas are "neurotic survivals." [1]

Freud, one of the greatest minds since Newton, is so bound up with our thesis that his point of view in regard to religion must be examined. It is most fully expounded in his two books, *Totem and Taboo* and the book already quoted, *The Future of an Illusion*. The following paragraphs summarise his view based on both these books.

Primitive man, he reminds, us, lived a life full of fears. The great forces of Nature—earthquake, whirlwind, flood, thunder, lightning and tempest—appalled him. He saw no way of becoming their master. Indeed, we have not mastered them ourselves. Wild animals and snakes moved through his jungle home, immensely more powerful than himself. He dreaded them and felt at their mercy. Within himself he knew the ravages of bodily disease. He noted, with dismay, the fact of insanity. He felt himself the helpless plaything of immense forces which he could neither understand nor subdue and which ruined his crops, killed his fellows, brought pain to himself and death to those

[1] *The Future of an Illusion*, translated by Robson-Scott (Liveright, 1928).

he loved. So he personified them in order to get into relationships with them. He invented the god of the storm, the demon of disease, and so on. Unable to sway them to his will, he sought means to appease their wrath. He created images of animals and worshipped them. He built shrines for them. The first houses were built for the gods, not for men. He prayed to the gods and made sacrificial offerings to them. Religion, says Freud, was born in fear.[2]

As primitive religion grew and developed, the immense number of gods was reduced to one, so that "man's relations to him could recover the intimacy and intensity of the child's relation to the father." [3] The moral values which men developed because society and, later civilisation were unworkable without them, were thrust upon this Deity, and notably in Christianity, though foreshadowed in Judaism,[4] He was dubbed the Father of all men.

This double development of ascribing to the Deity both morality and fatherliness, Freud greets as a triumph of man's way of making his god fulfil his own felt needs.

As to morals, man found himself with "instinctual wishes," [5] and for a time expressed them in crude satisfactions. He took what he wanted, and knew nothing of the "wrongness" of stealing. He took a woman as his lust dictated, and had no conscience-distress in regard to adultery. Even incest and cannibalism were untainted by moral scruples. All would have been well except for one fact. Every other man wanted to follow *his* "instinctual wishes," and conflict ensued.

A moral code, therefore, became the only means by which society

[2] Cf. Westermarck: "The old saying that religion was born of fear seems to hold true, in despite of recent assertions to the contrary." The best discussion of this point I have read is found in Prof. Erie S. Waterhouse, *The Philosophical Approach to Religion*, p. 16 ff. (Epworth Press, Revised Edition, 1947).

[3] *Op. cit.*, p. 34. This was, of course, a long process. Jehovah, for example, was but the tribal God of the Israelites, who in earliest days was a "storm-god" and "mountain" god combined, and dwelling in the heights of Sinai. In Egypt, Amenhotep IVth ended the existing pantheon, and, by making the rising sun the emblem of religion, made it clear that, in his view, God was one and God was good. This process is still going on. But there remain more than a million gods in the Indian pantheon.

[4] Psalm 103:13: "Like as a father. . . ." Perhaps a stronger word than "foreshadowed" is indicated. A lovely prayer in Ecclesiasticus (23:1) begins, "O Lord, Father and Master of my life," and in *The Book of Jubilee* (124-125) (trans. R. H. Charles) we find, "They shall know that I am their Father in uprightness and righteousness and that I love them." See Fosdick, *A Guide to Understanding the Bible* (Harper, 1938).

[5] *Op. cit.*

could be made to work. Conscience was built up as a mental mechanism because violations of the code were so severely punished by the tribe that men feared to do an anti-social thing. That they would still like to do them is plain to every psychologist. Incest wishes are commonly uncovered during psycho-analysis, and killing often happens, and is sometimes enjoined by the tribe or State, and called war or capital punishment. But the compulsion of the tribe became internalised in personality, and man's super-ego took the unruly elements of mankind under its jurisdiction.

Obviously, the moral code would have immense authority if it had the sanction of the Deity. So we have morality ascribed to Him and believed to be His nature.

As to fatherliness, Freud, in *Totem and Taboo*, claims that even the man who is physically adult is still emotionally a child. He still, therefore, longs for a father. He wants to be able to go to his father for protection, so he dubs his god omnipotent. He wants to go to his father for advice, so he prays. In a word, he creates a god who will give authority to the morality without which society disintegrates, and, at the same time, stifle his own fears with the concept of divine omnipotence: a god, further, who fulfils the demands of man's growing sense of values, like justice and fair-play. Since man both fears and hates death; since he both desires to live again after death and cannot —if this life be all—make sense of the pain, misery and injustice around him, he invents belief in a future life in which he himself will live in bliss, be punished for his sins, but rewarded for his morality—a world in which all the injustice and pain of this world will be compensated and justified. The strength of religious ideas Freud ascribes to the strength of the wishes which religion fulfils.[6]

It is interesting to note that Freud, without setting out to do so, gives us a clue as to why God came to be thought of as the father rather than the mother. Apart from the way in which women were despised,[7] Freud recognises that although the mother is the first love-object and source of protection, she is soon replaced by the stronger father to whom the child has an ambivalent reaction. The father was

[6] *Op. cit.*

[7] Women were despised in the East in olden days to a degree which is unrealised in the West today. Every Jewish boy every day thanked God he had not been born a girl, and was taught to do so by his own mother. To be born a girl in India today is to bear the mark of the contempt of the gods. Reincarnation in an animal is to be preferred. Girl-babies are still, in country places, viewed as marks of the ill-favour of the gods and are not infrequently thrown to the jackals in the jungle.

himself a danger, perhaps partly because both child and father wanted all the affection of the mother.[8] Thus the father was feared no less than he was longed for and admired. The person who was in charge of thunder, lightning, tempest, disease and flood, was one to get on one's side if possible. He was both feared as a rival, and often an angry, terrifying one, and yet he was desired as a patron and protector. The word "father," then, fitted him much better than the word "mother."

The only hope of influencing such a person is obviously to enter into relationships with him. Man, in earliest days, learned to do that with the persons he could not subdue or ignore in his own and in neighbouring tribes. So he tries to get into relationship with God and to deal with the catastrophes of life, such as disease, insanity, natural calamities, and so on, as something done to him by that Person whom he recognises is so great that he cannot either subdue Him or ignore Him. Sacrifices and offerings, then, an attempt to appease and propitiate, an attempt to win favour by living the moral life which it is believed the deity demands, fall into place. The shadow of these fear-stricken attitudes still falls even on the lives of so-called Christian men and women.

Now, says Freud in triumph, all this religious business belongs to the infancy of the race. Men must grow up. As for morality, it is, in Freud's eyes, homogeneous with obsession.[9] He gives a highly empiricist explanation of the appearance of the moral sentiment by the progressive interiorisation of the child's training.[10] As for their fears, men must be taught to part with the old fairy stories which they made up to quieten and subdue them. He tells a good story of one of his own children listening to fairy stories, and then asking, "Is this true?" "Having been told it was not," says Freud, the child "would turn away with an air of disdain." Then he adds, "It is to be expected that men will soon behave in like manner towards the religious fairy tales." [11] Indeed, he complains that the "feeble mentality of the average grown-up," compared with the "radiant intelligence of a healthy child," is due to a religious upbringing. Freud demands the "primacy of the intelligence" and asks, "How can we expect people who are dominated by thought-prohibitions to attain to the psychological ideal—the primacy of the intelligence?" [12]

[8] Cf. Freud's emphasis on the Œdipus Complex described on p. 264.
[9] See Dalbiez, *Psychoanalytical Method and the Doctrine of Freud*, Vol. I, p. 388 (Longmans Green, 1941).
[10] *Op. cit.*, Vol. II, p. 300.
[11] *Op. cit.*, p. 51.
[12] *Op. cit.*, p. 83.

What is our answer to Freud? My answer is threefold.

1. *To desire a father does not invalidate the fact that he may exist.*

I think our answer must begin with a frank recognition that, no doubt, much of Freud's description of the origin of religion corresponds to the facts. It is hard to see how primitive man could possibly have come to contemplate the thought of God, save along some such lowly path as Freud has indicated. But I cannot see that such an admission invalidates religion. If I assert the fact of physical hunger—a desire for food—and deduce that, in a rational universe, that fact points to the fact of food, does my concept of food mean that food is necessarily a figment of my imagination and cannot exist? Assuredly not. If, then, I assert the fact of spiritual hunger—a desire for a fatherly God—and dream that there is a Satisfaction for it, that there is One who created the world, works His purposes out in it, gave man his sense of values, and can vindicate Himself and justify all those events which seem to deny them, and is least erroneously thought of as a Father, does my dream deny the reality? As assuredly not. Of course, man had to tread a humble road to apprehend God, but his desire does not deny the possibility of its fulfilment. In a rational universe, rather the reverse. Hunger involves the existence of food. The fact that I can make a fantasy of a person outside myself does not disprove the fact of that person's existence. Rather the reverse. Every fantasy rests on *some* objective basis. Because as a child I want a father and dream there is such a being, why am I, for that reason, mistaken? May not my dream be true? Freud forgets that, apart from supernatural apparitions which would have unhinged the mind of primitive man, God's only way of revealing Himself was to allow man to discover Him through his own needs. All man's discoveries are divine revelations, and not less divine when man takes to himself all the credit of their discovery. Freud's fundamental fallacy, as I see it, is that he begins by *assuming that God does not and cannot exist.* But he gives no reason for such an assumption. "From then on," he writes in *Moses and Monotheism* (1912), "I have never doubted that religious phenomena are to be understood only on the model of the neurotic symptoms of the individual, which are so familiar to us, as a return of long-forgotten, important happenings in the primeval history of the human family, and that they owe their obsessive character to that very origin"; and again, "Psycho-analysis has proved that the idea of God in the life of the individual and of the people has its origin in the veneration and exaltation of the father." Actually, it has proved nothing of the sort.

A baby, during the terrible events of war in the Middle East, was separated from his father. He grew through the early years without knowing whether he had a father or not. Then he began to dream about his father, and then to day-dream. In both dream and day-dream his father was invested with the most wonderful characteristics. The father personified protection, tenderness, wisdom, helpfulness, comfort, challenge and strength. At last, when peace came, the family was reunited. The only way in which dream and reality did not fit was that the reality was far grander than the dream. If this is possible for an infant human, it is possible for an infant humanity. It surely is not surprising that humanity, striving to comprehend the concept of God, should use the concept of the father, especially in a land made famous by patriarchs like *Father* Abraham. Our Lord could think of no better picture of God, and it is hard to believe that there is higher authority.[13] Psycho-analytic investigation is valid in its own sphere. It cannot transfer its authority to the sphere of religion.

2. *Christianity is a historical religion, not a religion invented to fill a need.*

Freud does not deal with the Christian religion at all. He may think he has done so, but his brand is unrecognisable. St. Paul would certainly not have recognized it. Let me quote Freud's definition of religion:[14] "Religion consists of certain dogmas, assertions about facts and conditions of external (or internal) reality which tell one something one has not discovered for oneself and which claim that one should give them credence."

Let me set over against Freud's anæmic words a paragraph by Canon Barry, now Bishop of Southwell:[15]

"The Gospel as it was first proclaimed, the Gospel which converted the Roman Empire and reclaimed our fierce pagan ancestors for Christian civilisation and ordered liberty, was not extracts from the Sermon on the Mount. It was far more tragic and more realistic.

---

[13] "In the more mystical branches of Mohammedanism, the Divine Being is repeatedly referred to as the Beloved, and it would be as logical to regard religion as a manifestation of sexuality as to explain it as being the result of the persistence of childish attitudes in adult life." Kenneth Walker, *Meaning and Purpose,* p. 75 (Jonathan Cape, 1944).

[14] *Op. cit.*

[15] *What Has Christianity to Say?* (Harper, 1938).

It was the story of a Young Man, dedicated to a new age of Love and Truth, Righteousness and Freedom, murdered by a totalitarian state in uttermost agony of body and mind, broken by the hard facts of life, His claim discredited and His cause lost, Who held on through disaster and defeat, serene in His confidence in God, and in the hour of failure was victorious. . . . He was offered a religion of escape, and in the forty days in the wilderness He indignantly and decisively rejected it. He refused to live in an inner world of dreams unrelated to the facts of life and the concrete actualities of the world."

I should say that Christianity is a way of life which involves a belief that Jesus Christ was a historical person who was in a unique relationship with God, who changed men's lives, who rose from the dead, and who, through His spirit, still changes men's lives wherever He is seriously and adventurously followed.

The evidence for these statements can only briefly be set out here, [16] but they do not violate the "primacy of the intelligence" nearly so much as do some of Freud's theories. They are, in fact, believed all over the world by a larger number of people than ever before in history.

The historicity of Jesus, vouched for by the younger Pliny (c. 61-114), Tacitus (c. 55-120), Suetonius (c. 75-150) and Josephus (c. 37-100), is as well authenticated as the historicity of Plato.

Pliny, in his letter to Trajan written from Bithynia in A.D. 112, says, "They (the Christians) claimed that the extent of their crime or wrong-doing had been merely that they used to meet on a fixed day before dawn to sing in alternate verses a hymn to Christ as to a god, and to bind themselves by oath, not for any criminal purpose, but that they would not commit theft, robbery or adultery, or break their word or fail to return a deposit on request."

Tacitus, writing of the great fire of Rome in A.D. 64 which Nero blamed on to the Christians, says, "This name had originated with one Christus, who had been put to death by the Procurator, Pontius Pilate, in the reign of Tiberius."

Suetonius, private secretary to the Emperor Hadrian, in his *Lives of the Cæsars* says that Claudius in A.D. 49 banished from Rome the Jews who "at the instigation of Christus continually raised tumults." It is a mistaken reference, but evidence of the historicity of Christ.

Josephus, in his *Jewish Antiquities* (XVIII. 3. 3), writes: "About that time lived Jesus, a wise man, if man he may be called, for he did

---

[16] I have set it out more fully in *His Life and Ours* (Abingdon-Cokesbury, 1933).

wonderful works—a teacher of those who joyfully received the truth. He won to himself many Jews and many Greeks. He was the Christ and though Pilatus condemned Him to death, He was our Messiah and appeared on the third day."

Justin, a Samaritan Christian born about A.D. 110, who was martyred in about A.D. 165 in the reign of Marcus Aurelius, gives us some good evidence. In the *Second Apology*, he writes, "For I myself, while I was rejoicing in the teaching of Plato, heard the Christians abused. But I saw that they were afraid neither of death, nor of anything usually thought fearful, and I considered it was impossible that they were living in wickedness and promiscuity."

It is sad that the stoic Emperor, Marcus Aurelius (A.D. 121-180), a Romanised Spaniard, whose meditations have inspired many moderns, should have been responsible for the persecution of the Christians, especially the persecution in Lyons about the year 177. Marcus refers to the Christians, however, and comments on the readiness with which they met death, but he ascribes their courage not to their faith in Christ, but to their perverseness. "The soul should be ready when the hour of release from the body comes, to be extinguished, or to be scattered, or to survive. But such readiness should proceed from inward conviction, and not come of mere perversity, as with the Christians: it should result from a temper rational and grave, and—if it is to convince others—it should be unostentatious." [17]

The fact that monotheistic Jews worshiped Him and, in Pliny's phrase, "sang hymns to Christ as God"; the fact that He called Himself the Light of the World, the Way, the Truth, the Life; said that He was One with God, that the world were well lost if He be gained, that by their attitude to Him men would be judged; and His claim of sinlessness[18] make Him either the insane victim of "le grandiose delusion," or else, in a unique sense, the Son of God.[19]

The existence of the early Church and the changed attitude of His own followers would have been impossible unless He had survived death and proved His survival to His followers. And the extent of

[17] I owe some of these references to Bishop Barnes, *The Rise of Christianity*, pp. 314, etc. (Longmans Green, 1947).

[18] "On every page of the Gospel we encounter such imperial demands for obedience, as well as gracious promises of help and pardon, as it would have been an enormity for a sinful man to utter." (H. R. Mackintosh, *The Person of Jesus Christ.*)

[19] It is interesting that Bishop Barnes in his much-discussed book, *The Rise of Christianity* (Longmans Green, 1947), states that he himself worships Jesus as Divine (Foreword, p. vii.)

the Church and its continual progress in other lands [20] is strong, but not the only evidence that His Spirit still changes the hearts of men. Of all this Freud knows nothing. Speaking of the dogmas of religion, he writes as follows: "If we ask on what their claim to be believed is based, we receive three answers which accord remarkably ill with one another. They deserve to be believed (1) because our primal ancestors already believed them, (2) because we possess proofs which have been handed down to us from this very period of antiquity, and (3) because it is forbidden to raise the question of their authenticity at all. Formerly this presumptuous act was visited with the very strictest penalties and even today society is unwilling to see anyone renew it." [21]

To take the last first, presumably Freud had never heard of higher criticism and form criticism, and did not know what a fierce light had beaten on the records for hundreds of years. Of the first, he points out that "our fathers believed many erroneous things." Of course, and every modern Christian preacher teaches that everything in the Bible, or out of it, concerning God is to be rejected if it is out of harmony with the picture of God which we have in the life and teaching of Jesus. Theological thought and Biblical understanding do not stand still. Of the second, Freud says proofs "are deposited in writings that themselves bear every trace of being untrustworthy. They are full of contradictions, revisions, interpolations; where they speak of actual authentic proofs they are themselves of doubtful authenticity," and adds, "We should not be able to bring ourselves to accept anything of as little concern to us as the fact that whales bear young instead of laying eggs, if it were not capable of better proof than this." [22]

One wonders whether it was Freud's strict Jewish orthodox youthful upbringing, or some deep, and perhaps unconscious, complex, which lay behind the hostility, contempt and scorn which such words reveal, but it may be pointed out that the convincing "proof" of Christianity is to be found, not in the intellectual reasoning by which this or that dogma is defended, impressive though this often is, but by the lives of the people who have been changed by it. To survey this is to make oneself certain that the basis of Christianity cannot be an illusion. Through twenty centuries, on all shores, and in all languages,

[20] Note the impressive evidence gathered by Professor Henry P. Van Dusen in *They Found the Church There* (Scribner, 1945).

[21] *Op. cit.*

[22] *Op. cit.*

the message of Christianity has been preached and men's lives have been changed.

Freud says, "Of what significance is it for other people that you have won, from a state of ecstasy which has deeply moved you, an imperturbable conviction of the real truth of the doctrines of religion?" [23] He obviously expects the answer, "None." But I believe it to be an impressive part of the evidence for Christianity that men in China and Japan, in Africa and India, in the scorching tropics and the frozen Arctic would lay down their lives for the truth of Christianity. Is it the nature of an illusion, then, to spread across the world so that today more people are victims of it than ever before? Is it the nature of an illusion that the more men grow enlightened, the more widely Christianity spreads?

Granted that religious experience is in the realm of the emotions, it should be remembered that so is artistic experience. Why should religion be scorned more than the ecstasy of the artist, whose picture is based on objective reality, as the Christian's religion is ultimately based on the objective reality of the historical Christ?

3. *Christianity is too austere in its demands to be the kind of illusion men invent.*

For the truth of Christianity men willingly suffer torture, disgrace, banishment, imprisonment and death. Freud talks as though men have invented a God to calm their fears and a religion to cushion their lives. But Peter, instead of retiring, like his co-fishermen, in comfort in Capernaum, is crucified head downwards, and Paul, instead of the life of the learned scholar, follows a path of hazardous, dangerous and most wearisome travel, and is finally beheaded. The martyrs, saints and missionaries have followed their example to the present day. If this is a comforting illusion invented to make life easy, it can only be said that those who take it seriously have an odd idea of comfort. As Professor H. H. Farmer has said, "Nobody who had taken the trouble to enter at all deeply into the picture of God as Father, given us through Jesus Christ, could suppose that it was, or is, the mere phantasy product of feeble and half-defeated souls: the picture is much too austere, searching, demanding for that—it is, in fact, such that no weak soul would ever want to seek refuge in it." [24] If men

[23] *Op. cit.*

[24] *God and Men*, the Lyman-Beecher Lectures delivered at the Divinity School of Yale University, April 1946. (Abingdon-Cokesbury, 1947.) See the same author's *Towards Belief in God* (Macmillan, 1943).

could dismiss Christ as unhistorical, His sayings as unauthentic, the Gospel records as untrustworthy and the bases of Christianity as unexaminable, "because it is forbidden" to ask questions, they could make up a much more comfortable illusion than this. Man would not manufacture a religion like Christianity. Man has certainly manufactured some elements which he has tried to engraft on to Christianity, but they are not homogeneous and, when added, they form elements which the saints immediately recognise as spurious.

Let it be allowed that men thrust their ideas on to God and pretend those things true of Him which they would like to be true. Many, in war-time, pretended that He would protect their homes from bombs if they said their prayers. That man has much to learn about God is true. But men project on their wives at marriage qualities which they think their wives ought to possess. They have much to learn also, and spend the rest of their lives finding out their mistake! But in neither case does this prove that God or the wife does not exist, or that either does not possess qualities far more important for man's well-being than those he pretended were true. "Moreover," says B. G. Sanders,[25] "if it is argued against religion that belief in God arises from a wish-fulfilment on the part of the believer, it may also be suggested, by a corresponding argument, that disbelief in God arises from an unconscious desire that God should not exist."

No religion could live that put its greatest emphasis on being a way out of some hole. As T. R. Glover said, "Christianity began in friendship." What Christ *was*, apart from the doctrine of His Saviourhood; His friendship and the kind of life He lived, which revealed to all who came near what human life should be, drew men to Him. No ethical teaching, no satisfaction of man's mere wishful thinking, no new ritual, no insurance against evil in this world or another give us the secret of His power. It was in Himself and His relation to God, His utter certainty, His love for men and His belief in their value that made, and makes, the essence of Christianity the universal religion which it is more and more proving itself to be.

In his *Civilisation and its Discontents*, Freud attacks Christianity from another angle. He says, in effect, that Christianity demands too much. It demands that love should be the motive of all conduct, and leaves no room for the exercise of aggression, which cannot be eradicated or even sublimated if love must motivate it entirely. Civilisation, Freud thinks, would fail if Christianity reigned, for love would cause

[25] B. G. Sanders, *Christianity after Freud* (Macmillan, 1949).

its downfall. He thinks Christians should pitch their appeal lower, for they are asking the impossible.

Here again it seems to me that Freud does not really understand Christianity, or its Founder, or the real nature of love, which has in it a stern and severe aggression against evil. To read the Gospel story of Christ's words to the Pharisees and to those who cause little children to stumble, is to lose at once the false idea that Christianity leaves no room for aggression, though the latter is not truly to be thought of as merely subordinate to love, but *an expression of love*. Love has steel in it as well as flowers, and the measure of Christ's anger had to equal the measure of the protective devices with which the Pharisees and others attempted to shield themselves from the sharp shafts of truth and from yielding to the only love that could save them.

When one sees a dozen signposts all bearing the name of the same village and pointing towards the same area, one may assume that the village exists, even if one has never been there. It would be odd to deduce that there was no such village, or that men had erected the signposts thus because they wished there were. Freud, the Jew, brought up in a strictly Jewish orthodox home, never contemplated those signposts, let alone travelled the roads along which they point. Some very humble, but integrated, Christians live in the village. In quite a different sense from that of the theorists, they empirically *know* that their integration is based on their Christian experience. To deny Christianity, or relegate it to the category of an illusion, would be to deny the highest value to what is to many the most sacred experience and the most powerful transforming influence in life. Every real Christian would utterly repudiate such a denial and, as he has in the past, die rather than admit its validity. Further, his own changed life, and the changed lives of millions are the strongest evidence of the solid, unshakeable truth of the essentials of his religion.

7

IS RELIGIOUS EXPERIENCE ITSELF
A NEUROSIS?

THIS IS, INDEED, an important question. It is of little use examining the question whether psychological treatments need the aid of religion, if religion is itself a neurosis. If it is, then religious experience, instead of aiding the cure of the patient, merely lures him into the device of substituting one neurosis for another. It may be that such a substitution is an advance. I think it often is, but it postpones cure indefinitely. The patient is not encouraged to seek treatment and, further, his symptoms have been given a religious sanction. They—or some of them—will win the praise of men. The patient's pathological state is even farther removed from his scrutiny.

Obviously, we need two definitions. A neurosis may be defined as a faulty emotional attitude to experience, setting up a conflict in the unconscious part of the mind, and issuing in disabling symptoms of mental or physical distress, or both. The definitions of religion are legion. William James[1] defines religion as "a man's total reaction upon life." Recalling the etymology of the word "religion," I should define it as *man's conscious link with God (or the gods) and his response thereto.* Dr. A. N. Whitehead,[2] in one definition, calls religion "the reaction of human nature to its search for God," and in another, "what a man does with his solitariness." I value Dr. F. E. England's definition of religious experience:[3] "Religious experience is the response by the whole personality to the impress of that quality of reality as a whole which we call deity." There *is* an experience which, in Walter Pater's lovely phrase, "fills the common ways of life with

[1] *Varieties of Religious Experience* (Longmans Green, 1917).
[2] *Science and the Modern World* (Macmillan, 1925).
[3] *The Validity of Religious Experience* (Harper, 1938).

407

the reflection of some far-off brightness." With varying degrees of intensity, depending on many factors, like spiritual insight, poetic imagination, sensitiveness, culture and education, opportunities for letting beauty make its impact upon him, ability to respond to the shock of truth and the appeal of goodness, almost every man has had such an experience and in his heart has related it to something, or Someone, outside the merely human categories. H. G. Wells cannot be regarded as a protagonist of orthodox religious faith and practice. Yet he speaks for most men when he says, "At times, in the lonely silence of the night and in rare, lonely moments, I come upon a sort of communion of myself with something great that is not myself. It is, perhaps, poverty of mind and language which obliges me to say that this universal scheme takes on the effect of a sympathetic person— and my communion a quality of fearless worship. These moments happen, and they are the supreme fact of my religious life to me. They are the crown of my religious experiences." In their hearts most men believe that, at various points and in varying ways, God has touched their lives. Such an experience, whatever creeds or the lack of them may be involved, is a religious experience. It seems to have arisen from a desire to be in harmonious relationship with the Universe and its Lord. If so, and if our definition of health be accepted as "harmonious relationship with environment," then the quest for deeper religious experience is also a quest for health and integration.

In this chapter I mean by religion the Christian religion, and this I should define not too specifically in terms of intellectual belief. I should, for instance, call Peter, the fisherman, a Christian from the moment that he began to follow Christ, even though his intellectual apprehension of many of the great truths expressed in the creeds was vague, if not non-existent. I should define Christianity as *that form of religion, distinguished by a new way of life, which is the response of the entire individual—mind, feeling and will—to the impact which the living Christ makes upon him.* Such a definition may seem to leave much to be desired in terms of the intellectual minutiæ of belief. In terms of the latter, it only asks for the acceptance of Christ's historicity, His survival of death and His availability to those who seek Him today. But I believe that the heart of Christianity is enshrined in the definition. Doubts about other theological orthodoxies do not, in my view, invalidate or disauthenticate true Christian experience.

Is such a religion neurotic? If it is, I hold that it is not Christianity, but a distorted form of it. A person who has a neurosis may be a sincere Christian, but inevitably his neurosis will distort his religion, just as it will distort his other responses. This does not mean that the religion caused the neurosis, nor is religion to be judged by this neurotically distorted form of it. I hold that as his religious experience has its distortion corrected, it will tend to cure his neurosis. Religion, which is well-nigh universal, can hardly be a foreign or *essentially* unharmonious element in man's make-up. It is incredible that a religion like Christianity, spreading as it is through the whole world,[4] is a disintegrating factor in man's personality. Few would deny that if true Christianity were sincerely believed and practiced throughout the whole world, the world would be a much happier and healthier place than it is. Yet if Christian experience is a neurosis, it is a form of disease. It is odd if the spread of a disease through the world would make it healthier and happier. This is, indeed, a *reductio ad absurdum*. This "disease," it is agreed, makes man more brotherly, more ready to love his neighbour. It makes him act unselfishly, control his temper, forgo his private ambition, and, in many cases, for no visible reward, embark on some piece of service that involves poverty and loneliness, discomfort and even death. If this really is a "disease," it is much more attractive than most people's health. More widely disseminated, this "disease" would end wars, banish poverty and eliminate our other social evils. We have found a disease that is better than health!

Such a "reductio ad absurdum" may be answered by two first-rate psychotherapists who have always been sympathetic to the Christian Faith. In their essay on *The Psychology of Spiritual Healing*, Dr. Hadfield and Dr. Leonard Browne write as follows: "In religious conversion we frequently find that not only is the character changed, but old neurotic and hysterical diseases disappear. Could we command such a revolution of love in the soul, it would be at once the most direct and the most effective treatment for those diseases now laboriously treated by psychotherapy." [5]

Let it be granted, with Freud, that in the beginning religion was born partly of fear, yet while fear dominated it, the religion was distorted. As the mists of primeval thinking have cleared away, the fear-element in it has been lifted up to the point at which it has become awe, reverence and worship; a sense of the numinous in which man feels *at one and the same time* his utter unimportance, insignificance and sinfulness, and yet his utter importance to God, the dignity of being loved by such a God, and the heights of character which

---

[4] In some Eastern countries—e.g. India—at the time of writing, the Christian Church is embarrassed by the numbers seeking entrance into membership.

[5] *Psychology and the Church*, p. 256 (Macmillan, 1925).

God's dealings with him through Christ make possible. He feels *at the same time* humbled to the dust, but exalted above the stars.[6] If fear alone were operative, he would always fly from God. The fact is he longs for God, and flies *to* Him. He fears to offend, but, in his communion with God, feels that he is reaching his highest stature and realising his highest values.

The charge that Christian experience is essentially neurotic comes from those who have never had the experience. Religious experience is certainly hard to analyse, because it is subjective. But so is the experience of being in love. Granted that many lovers are neurotic. But love has not made them so. Neurosis has distorted their loving as it distorts everything they do, but love has not caused neurosis. It tends to cure it. As we have seen, the deprivation of love is a frequent *cause* of neurosis. An argument that the lover was *per se* neurotic would, in view of the great literature of the world alone, be hard to sustain. Yet the arguments in one case apply in the other. If the Christian experience is to be distrusted because it can be labelled subjective, then all experience can be disproved. The critic may say of religious experience, "I have never felt like that." The one thing he cannot say is, "And therefore neither have you." The reality and value of Christian experience are not destroyed by the label "illusion." This so-called illusion called Christian experience is a fact, and any *fact* must be taken into account. It cannot be conveniently dismissed. Even after the label "illusion" is affixed, the fact of this "illusion" must be explained and fitted into the framework of other facts.

Some words of Dr. W. R. Matthews, Dean of St. Paul's, are of value here. He writes:

"There is a fundamental fallacy in every argument which seeks to prove from psychological data that the object of experience is illusory. It is possible to give a psychological account of the genesis of any general and permanent belief, which account need contain no reference to any reality outside the mind, which leaves, in short, the problem of the validity of the belief entirely unaffected. Even if it were established that the idea of God is a projection of the human mind, we should have no further light than we had before on the question whether the idea of God corresponds to any real Being.

[6] It is important to notice that in the Bible the greatness of God is never set forth to indicate man's insignificance, but to make him feel that the resources of this great Being are at man's disposal and are working for his exaltation. E.g. "When I consider Thy heavens. . . What is man that Thou art mindful of Him?" Yet . . . *"Thou hast crowned him with glory and honour"* (Psalm 8:3 ff.). He Who "telleth the number of the stars" is He who "healeth the broken in heart" (Psalm 147:3 ff.).

"It can be shown that the concept of nature is, in a sense, a projection of mind, but it would never occur to anyone to argue, on this ground, that therefore there is no such thing as an objective world or an order of nature. Why, then, is it assumed that the same kind of argument is valid in the case of religious experience? . . . If a genetic psychological account of the origin of the idea of God proves that God does not exist, then a similar genetic account of the origin of the idea of nature proves that nature does not exist. . . . The object which science studies would have turned out to be illusory, and, with it, science itself. Now, psychology is a science, and dependent, like every other science, on the conception of an order of nature. Psychology would, then, be infected by the illusory character which pertains, on this hypothesis, to all sciences, and thus the very instrument by which we thought we had proved religion to be illusory, turns out itself to be an illusion." [7]

So much argument among psychologists of the Freudian and materialistic schools is fallacious, because it supposes that we have no contact with reality except through the senses, and that the nature of reality is known only to the psychologists concerned. It is always to their barren idea of what reality is that they bend their arguments.

The first assumption would dispose of, say, the force of gravity. No one has tasted it, touched it, smelt it, seen it, heard it, or felt it. Its *effects* have been recognised through the senses, but, then, so have the *effects* of religious experience. Who has not *seen* in men's lives the results of the Christian experience and *heard* them witness of what God has done in their souls?

It is fair to demand recognition of the fact that the results of the religious experience point more convincingly to the reality we call God than sense impressions alone point to reality in the external world. Are the senses really the reliable guide which "science" claims? I have seen a hypnotised patient stroke a cat which was not there, moving her hand in caressing movements, and I have heard her describing its colour. Her senses were so affected by the suggestion, made under hypnosis, that a black cat was there that she "saw" it. I have heard a hypnotised patient, into whose hand a plain postcard had been put, declaring that it was a photograph of a royal person and describing the uniform worn. I have heard a dying man say that he could hear wonderful music in a room where to me there was only the silence of death. Who was right? This man says the sofa cushion is green. That man says it is blue. Which is the true colour?

[7] *Psychology and Modern Problems,* edited by Dr. J. A. Hadfield (University of London Press).

Which is the reality? What is "blueness"? What is "greenness"? And how do I know that two men, both of whom call the cushion "blue," see the same colour? Get a dozen people in some situation to describe what they saw and heard, and we shall conclude that the senses are quite unreliable. All things have appearances which we never see and properties which our senses miss. No argument can be sustained that the senses are the final clue to the nature of anything, let alone its meaning and significance. Is not the effect of the religious experience in the lives of men as good evidence of reality as anything the senses can give us in the way of certainty?

Lastly, the psychologists of this school are certainly "begging the question" when they tell us that religion covers reality with "fantasy thinking" which is unreal and of the nature of dope. They assume that, though the rest of the world is ignorant, they *know* the nature of reality.

Art and poetry come in for the same condemnation. "Artistic or poetic inspiration is to be regarded as the manifestation of repressed desires." It has its origin in "neurotic symptoms." [8] The artist may *believe* that he is interpreting reality, but the Freudian analyst tells him he is only exposing the symptoms of the neurosis. Indeed, the greatest works of art of the greatest painters are reduced to diagrams which portray sick minds. As Lawrence Hyde says,[9] in speaking of Fra Angelico's painting of the encounter between Christ and the Magdalene, "The difference between this picture and an illustration from some pornographic work is for the psychoanalyst of practically no consequence."

We see, then, the bleak world which is this type of psychologist's idea of reality. Art, music, poetry, religion are to be banished. Philosophy and meditation must go. Reality is a cold, hard world of concrete and chromium-plate and steel; things men can see and touch and feel.

"Philosophies, like religions," says Ferenczi, "are works of art and fiction which . . . belong to another category than science, by which we mean the sum of those laws which, after thorough elimination, as far as this is possible, of the fantastic products of the pleasure-principle, we are compelled to accept as true." He says elsewhere that "the sense of reality attains its zenith in science, while the illusion of omnipotence here experiences its greatest humiliation." [10]

[8] Pfister, a thorough-going Freudian, in *Some Applications of Phycho-Analysis* (Dodd, 1923).

[9] In *The Learned Knife* (Scribner, 1931).

[10] Quoted from Lawrence Hyde, *op. cit.*

So the long search for reality ends in scientific naturalism, in "the absolutely discredited notion of nineteenth century materialism that reality is co-existent with the findings of science."

Such a conception of reality is as poverty-stricken as it is false. It finds its only real support in the very arguments which would banish the world in which the scientist lives. Both live ultimately through faith—the scientist by faith in the validity of reasoning and the dependability of his own mental processes, the saint by faith in the validity of his experience, his spiritual intuitions and insights, and of his relationship with God.

Why should the nobler faith be wrong? What a mad universe this must be if religious experience is an illusion! Man is undoubtedly the highest product of that universe; man's sense of values his supreme discovery; man's saintliness the highest development and expression of his sense of values. And we are asked to believe that that saintliness which is linked with some of the noblest and heroic names and deeds in history is no more than the symptom of a disease, in the same category as the slobbering indecencies of a sexual pervert or the black depressions of the psychotic!

The strength of the case of the critic who calls Christian experience neurotic lies in the fact that so few Christian people advertise in their experience what true Christianity is. So far from it being "dope," or "illusion," or "escapism," or "wishful thinking," it is so spartan and costly in its demands that man turns away from them to easier ways of living, retaining its comforting aspect, but refusing its challenge, and thus giving the critic the kind of evidence he seeks. The authentic Christian experience is a courageous trafficking with reality, so demanding that it may take from man all that he has, drive him out of all his human securities, separate him from his dearest friends and ask of him life itself. I have personally known, in other lands, Christians who have paid a terrible price for their faith, and who have told me how infinitely worth while it was. Their species of Christian experience one might call the real, unadulterated article. It is a sublime thing to witness, and its effect on others has been incalculable. Here, one feels, is the strongest evidence for the authenticity and validity of Christian experience.

Few, however, show forth to the world an undistorted Christian experience, and, seeing the distortion caused by our neurotic trends, the critic labels the experience itself neurotic.

It seems to me important to notice some of the more common ways in which Christian experience is distorted by neurosis.

1. *Christian experience is misused to cover a flight from reality.*

Freud would have plenty of material for his thesis that religion is a projection of the father-complex if he did the work of a Christian minister for six months. People who have been criticised by others, even justly and truly, pour out to God their hurt feelings in the spirit of a child whose attitude could be described thus: "My critics are 'horrid' to me, but I know You, my Heavenly Father, will be kind to me and comfort me.' Their time of prayer and quiet becomes a neurotic orgy of self-pity in which the "self" is projected on to God, a father substitute, who, to their neurotic imagination, must always offer them the candy and cushions of comfort. Unfortunately, the Bible can be quoted only too readily to support this distorted view. God, in the Psalms, is frequently imagined as the High Tower to which men flee. He is the Refuge and the Fortress. Under His wings men are invited to hide, for there no evil can touch them. Though a thousand fall at their side and ten thousand at their right hand, they are promised it shall not come near them.[11] Here is a definite invitation to misuse God as an escape from reality. No one could possibly believe it without self-deception. One wonders what Air Force pilots made of it when this psalm was solemnly read out to them by the chaplain before a gruelling airbattle in defence of Britain; a battle in which many lost their lives.

Even in the New Testament we have dangerous passages, like the spurious end of St. Mark's Gospel, where it is supposed there is safety for Christ's followers from serpents and poisons,[12] and like the prayer in the Benedictus that we may be "saved from our enemies and from the hand of all that hate us." [13]

It does not readily strike us that "they that hate us" may do God's work better than those who flatter us, for they may help us to that self-knowledge which is essential to mental health; that it is better to know the truth, even when it hurts, than to live in a world of pretence. It probably hurts just because it is the truth.

Many of the most popular hymns lead the singer into similarly dangerous waters:

[11] Psalm 91:7.

[12] Mark 16:18. The authentic gospel of St. Mark ends at 16:8. There is no inconsistency here with what was said (pp. 363 *et seq.*) about the power of an emotional state to produce toxins. That such toxins are produced by an emotion like hate plainly does not mean that a person can drink prussic acid without compunction as long as his emotional condition is ideal!

[13] Luke 1:68-79.

414

> Rock of Ages, cleft for me,
> Let me hide myself in Thee . . .
> Jesus, Lover of my soul,
> Let me to Thy bosom fly . . .

and so on.

There is a time for hiding, just as there is a time for a vessel to put into the harbour for repairs. But the escapism is justified only by the subsequent putting to sea. He who misuses religion so that he flees from the high seas of life altogether and cannot manfully face the storm, is distorting his Christianity with his own flight from reality and showing the world a neurotic symptom, instead of the witness of true religion.

2. *Christian experience is misused to provide a false security.*

All the way through life man searches for security.[14] The child looks for it in the love and protection of his parents, the adolescent in friends and, perhaps, the schoolmasters and school mistresses most admired, the lover in the beloved, the artist and poet and musician in beauty, and so on. For ever we search for that which "will not let us down," for an abiding reality in which the soul may rest.

All this is right and, indeed, inevitable, but the truly religious man knows that ultimately there is only one final security, and that is the love of God as it is revealed in Christ. All else can be taken from us, but this, the Christian believes, will never fail.

Yet, again and again, true Christianity is distorted by men's fears. Physical safety is still held to be the reward of the righteous. The Psalmist is once more quoted to this effect. The sentimental note sounded in many hymns is, through mere wishful thinking, accepted as if it were true, and men suppose that faith in God will deflect a bullet, that nightly prayer will save from bombs, even that church attendance will be rewarded with business success. All this is neurotic nonsense; the distortion of true religion by the patient's neurotic trends. Christ Himself promised His followers persecution and death, and after a life of flawless loveliness spent in healing and teaching, God did not send one angel, or lift one finger, to save Him from the torture and death meted out by Rome to the vilest criminals. One would have thought that such an end would have destroyed such a heresy. But the neurotic is typically swayed by emotion, not reason, and because he has predetermined what he would like religion to be—an insurance against calamity—he twists it to his purposes, and shows to the world

[14] I have worked this out fully in *This is the Victory* (Abingdon-Cokesbury, 1941).

not Christianity, but a craven and despicable fake-substitute, unrecognisable to St. Paul and to all the saints and martyrs, but serving his own neurotic ends.

3. *Christian experience is misused in a deceptive attempt to buy escape from the results of sin.*

Here again I must summarise an important position.[15] The death of Christ is said to accomplish man's salvation, and this idea is twisted by the neurotic to mean that because Jesus died on the Cross, man will be "let off" the results of his sin.

Not only is this impossible logic, but if it were true, it would be immoral. We live in a world of cause and effect, and the death of Christ, two thousand years ago, does not prevent certain effects—some of them physical—from following certain causes.

For clarity's sake I repeat here some points already made in the chapter on Guilt. It is better to separate the ideas of penalty from those of consequence. The chief *penalties* of sin are separation from God and the deterioration of the sinner's character. Real Christian experience clearly ends penalty. There is penitence for the past, a new beginning, and a new orientation and direction of life. The process of integration through religion begins.

The *consequences* of sin frequently remain, however. They may be physical. They are often mental. They are always spiritual. Spiritual insight is lessened. Spiritual sensitiveness is dulled. These consequences must be accepted, woven into personality and turned into an asset in ways already described. Then guilt disintegrates. Its "fear-element" vanishes. But this "weaving" is a process that demands from man grit and determination and endurance. And there is no easier way. If he seeks to evade it by emotionally "laying his sins on Jesus," he may for a time lose his sense of guilt, but the *consequences* of sin will not magically vanish, and because he does not understand why, he will find the "fear-element" in guilt returning, and then he will discredit the authenticity of the religious experience of forgiveness.

It cannot be too strongly emphasised that guilt cannot in any case be transferred from a guilty person to an innocent one, so that the former may conveniently escape the dreadful consequences of sin. If I have committed adultery—to quote the favourite sin—I cannot, by any juggling with words, escape a sense of guilt or "lay" my

[15] Fully worked out in my book, *A Plain Man Looks at the Cross* (Abingdon-Cokesbury, 1945).

sins on anybody else. I did it. That remains for ever a fact, and to pretend otherwise is just yielding to a neurotic trend, indulging in irrational wishful-thinking, and playing straight into the hands of Freud and his friends.

The truth is, however, wider than that. I did it, but inevitably I lay its shame on *all* who love me. Because they love, they share the shame, even though they cannot share the guilt. To the degree to which they love, they pledge themselves to win me back to goodness. The Christian believes that because the living Christ loves him supremely, He bears the shame and pledges Himself to self-forgetting service for as long as it takes to win man to worthy discipleship. In this true way, men speak of salvation through "the Cross." They mean that because He is the same now as in the days of His torture, He will give Himself to the uttermost now to stand by man and win man to Himself. When He lived on earth, that "uttermost" meant the Cross. So, even now, "the Cross" is the symbol and pledge of His endless ministry on man's behalf. There is nothing neurotic there.

What *is* neurotic is the absurdity of the idea of laying guilt on Him and expecting to be "let off" the consequences of sin, while one is in a universe where every cause has its effect. The forgiveness of God does not mean that we are let off consequences, though we do escape penalty in the sense defined. Consequences follow whether God forgives or not. What forgiveness does do is to restore a relationship, broken by sin, in such a way that consequences are no longer felt to be the impersonal retribution of a soulless universe, but the loving discipline of a Father; a discipline which can be welcomed because it helps make man what God wants him to be. Consequences *always* follow sin, but forgiveness changes their nature and their effect on personality. Instead of being mere retribution, and causing only remorse, they become creative and constructive discipline, causing penitence and the following of a new road.

Few things are more needed in the modern Church than teaching which exposes the neurotic and false interpretation of Christ's death, which sings hymns about being washed in His blood, as though His death were the expiation of the wrath of an angry God at a time when His beloved Son was perfectly doing His Father's will; as though, by an act of credulous superstition called "believing faith," a sinner could break the chain of cause and effect, lay His dirty sins on the innocent Son of God, and escape consequences which are inescapably registered in the molecules of his body and the fibres of his brain.

4. *Christian experience is further misused in the interests of the super-
ego to produce a "holiness" that is self-centred and narcissistic.*

Narcissus was the young man in Greek mythology who could not
love the beautiful nymph, Echo, because he loved only himself; he
saw his face in the water of a quiet pool and fell in love with his
own image. He lingered by the pool day and night, and fascinated
by himself, would neither eat nor drink, until he died.

A Christianity which, even in quest of holiness, makes a man think
only of his own perfection, love only himself, and "saving his own
soul," is a Christianity distorted by neurotic trends. It loses that
missionary fervour which in the first century was its most characteristic
note. "He that loveth his own soul, loseth it." Spiritual perfection is
undoubtedly the goal and crown of Christian experience, but men
add to their spiritual stature not only by introspection, meditation and
prayer, but by service so altruistic that the needs of others and the
desire to love and serve them exclude thoughts of self from consciousness.

He who reads the gospels carefully will notice one impressive fact.
They are full of comfort and consolation, full of references to a
loving Heavenly Father, in whose sight all men are inexpressibly
precious, full of promises of reward, now and hereafter. But there is
no word of comfort that does not involve a challenge. "Come unto
Me," says an inviting Voice, but just as clearly, "Go out into all the
world." The love of God is offered, but the terms are that we love
our neighbour. Forgiveness is offered—whatever we have done. But
on condition that we forgive others—whatever they have done. Reward, both here and in a further world, is offered, but here we are
invited to drink a bitter cup and tread a hard road, and as for the
life after death, those who talk of "pie in the sky when you die" did
not get that distorted view of Christian teaching from Jesus Christ.
The idea of hell—though admittedly distorted by our grandfathers—
came from His lips. It was He who spoke of the shut door, the outer
darkness and the age-long fire. No one can twist the words of Jesus
to create for himself the illusion of a heaven which everyone enters,
and where, for everybody, everything will come right in the end. No
other person in history ever spoke such hard words about the life after
death as Jesus did, or made it so clear that to enjoy it, a disciplined and
dedicated earth-life is essential.

Christianity should be studied as it was proclaimed in the open
air of Galilee by Jesus Christ Himself. We should not judge it after
it has been twisted by sectarian theologians who have sometimes prosti-

tuted it to satisfy their own preconceived opinions. The charge that Christianity is itself a neurosis could never have been levelled if men had proclaimed it and lived it as Christ did. It is not Christianity that is neurotic, but spurious imitations falsely called by its name. No great leader has proved less neurotic. No other ever made such demands on his followers, or sent out so many men and women gladly to suffer pain and to die in heroic, spiritual adventure. Many a neurotic has suffered pain, and often with a morbid satisfaction. *But the neurotic always complains.* The Christian missionaries and martyrs made no complaints. A sentence in the Book of Acts is true of so many. "They departed from the presence of the council, rejoicing that they were counted worthy to suffer shame for His name." [16] This does not sound much like neurosis. Any reaction less neurotic, or more truly Christian, it would be hard to find.

Malinowski wrote as follows: "Religious faith establishes, fixes and enhances all valuable mental attitudes, such as reverence for tradition, harmony with environment, courage and confidence in the struggle with difficulties and at the prospect of death. This belief, embodied and maintained by cult and ceremonial, has an immense biological value." It has an immense psychological value also, and an immense spiritual value. It seems to the writer one of the real needs of a fully integrated personality. Its dynamic is *unselfish* love, an emotion as far removed as is possible from emotions typical of neurosis. Its serenity, so far from being "dope," is an inward certainty that although this is not yet the best of all possible worlds, it is the world of best possibilities, and that it is in the hands of a God, who is truly a Father of all men, but who, so far from being weak and self-indulgent, has put them into a hard school and makes terrible demands upon them; demands, however, which are the expression of His purpose, and the measure of whose severity is the measure of the blessedness which can be attained by those who make the right response to them.

Life on earth is a hard school and the discipline is exacting, but the Christian claim is that the prize is worth it. Religious experience should be a progressive and patient attempt to understand with the mind God's purposes, to respond with the feelings to His love by loving others, and to fulfil with the will, as far as we can, His purposes. If religious experience is less than this; if it becomes dope, or an insurance, or an escape, or a flight from reality, or an attempt to buy favour and escape consequences, then it is not the Christian religion, and not any religion worth having. In such cases it is so poisoned by

[16] Acts 5:41.

neurotic factors as to be worse than useless. Since, in so many places, it is so poisoned, it is not surprising that many psychologists look askance at their patient's "faith" and feel that his "religion" is maintaining his neurotic condition. In such a situation a psychotherapist may feel it his duty to discourage his patient from religious practices until he can view the matter more normally, see things in a right perspective and rid his "religion" of its neurotic distortion.

DO MODERN RELIGIOUS METHODS OF HEALING NEED PSYCHOLOGY?

1

THE NATURE AND PLACE OF FAITH IN HEALING

THE PHRASE "FAITH healing" is used uncritically about many non-physical ways of combatting illness. Inasmuch as there *is* such a thing as healing through faith; inasmuch as Christ continually stressed the need of "faith"; it is important to our study to understand what "faith" really is and what part it plays in healing, especially in modern days.

No word is more misunderstood, or used with such a wide connotation, as the word "faith." Some people use the word in a manner that recalls the definition of Dean Inge's schoolboy, who said, "Faith is believing what you know to be untrue." "Rather," adds the Dean, "*it is the resolution to stand or fall by the noblest hypothesis.*" For many, "faith" really means, in practice, "believing" without evidence. Creeds and prayers are uttered without any critical examination of the truths involved, supposing that they are "believed," when, in truth, they are only assented to with almost as extensive a vagueness as that with which the layman "believes" that one star is a thousand light-years from the earth—that is to say, because he is told so, and either does not or cannot examine the evidence. That orthodox religious beliefs are accepted by others, enshrined in the traditions of the Church and endlessly repeated, seems to make unnecessary for some minds the task of directing the searchlights of reason and intellectual enquiry upon them. Their "faith" seems to dethrone reason; to make it unnecessary.

Ministers of religion sometimes appear to support this attitude. They tell people to "have faith," as if it were a matter as simple as turning on a tap or to "pray for faith," as if it were a gift bestowed by heaven independently of the seeker's intellectual wrestling and self-discipline.

423

When some of the mighty statements of religion seem hard to believe, people who examine them, and keep many of them in a pigeonhole of their mind labelled *sub judice*—an eminently sensible thing to do on the part of busy people who refuse to be bustled into spurious "belief"—are rebuked for not "having faith."

In no field of human activity is it more confusing to have a false idea of faith than in that of healing. From the outset it seems to me important to repeat emphatically that one can have healing without faith in Christ, and faith in Christ without healing. If, for example, at a "healing mission" a patient is healed or unhealed, the fact, in either case, throws no clear light at all on the quality of his faith. I have known splendid Christian people, with a magnificent faith in God, who have remained unhealed—and their faith has been undaunted by the fact. I have known suggestible hysterics "healed" through what they miscall "faith," when the healing is undoubtedly due to the fact that they happened to be suggestible, though they have been praised by the healer for their "faith" and taken to themselves great credit for possessing it. We should realise that faith is a thing one has to fight for. One can increase it or decrease it. Suggestibility is something we have or have not. We have little power over it ourselves, though various methods have been devised to alter it. To attain to Christian faith is a magnificent achievement. To be suggestible is not a matter either for congratulation or censure. However we may define faith, I hold that it is not necessarily proved through healing or denied by the continuance of disease.

It seems important also to add that not all those in the New Testament narratives alleged to have been healed through their "faith" were, in fact, healed through faith properly understood, even though that word is used in our translations. Professor John Macmurray somewhere says that "Christ's use of the term 'faith' does not allow us to take it as the equivalent of 'belief' in the ordinary sense of holding certain views." [1] It is undeniable that many New Testament patients tried "faith" because all other means had failed. It is hard to believe that the man by the Pool of Bethesda, who did not even know who had healed him, had what we should call Christian faith,[2] or that the woman with the hæmorrhage had anything worth calling "faith." She saw Someone going about who in His healing work had remarkable successes. She had tried many doctors and "was nothing bettered, but rather grew worse." [3] She wanted to get better, so she thought she would try

[1] I owe this quotation to W. L. Hannam, *Luke the Evangelist* (Abingdon, 1935).
[2] John 5:13.
[3] Mark 5:26.

Jesus. She turned out to be suggestible. Her illness was in the category readily healed by suggestion. She was healed. It would be cruel and inaccurate to deny that there are many sufferers today who have a far finer faith in Christ than that, but they are not healed. For one thing, they happen not to be suggestible. Modern scientific education tends to decrease suggestibility. For another, their illness is in a different category. They remain unhealed. But that is no real assessment that their faith is weak. One of the damning indictments of some healing missions, as we have seen, is that the onus is always on the patient. If he is healed, he is praised for his "faith." If he is unhealed, it is implied that he had no faith. The mission spreads a false conception about the nature of faith, the purpose of religion and the problem of suffering. Very great harm is done both by the successes and the failures of such a mission.

Obviously we need a definition of Christian faith, and my own is as follows: *Christian faith is the response of the whole man, thinking, feeling and willing, to the impact of God in Christ, by which man comes into a conscious, personal relationship with God.*[4]

In some people one of these factors will be stronger than the others. In scientific students, for instance, the thinking factor will be stronger than feeling. In some so-called "simple Christians" feeling will be stronger than their thinking, and sometimes thinking is beyond man and feeling is dead. Even so, man can give God his will and doggedly *do* what He commands, even though the road is uphill and the heavens are black with storm-clouds. Man is always safe in acting on the supposition that God's nature is higher and better than any human nature conceivable. If the highest human values like goodness, trustworthiness, love and mercy are not true of God, then man can think and frequently act more nobly than God. Noble doing, on man's part increases faith in *God*.

Maximum faith will be reached in a personality in whom thinking has penetrated as far as it can, feeling—particularly loving—is as great as it can be, and action is as daring and dynamic as the will can sustain.

We turn now to consider faith under these three headings, remembering that not one of them is sufficient by itself. Intellectual apprehension of religion can make a theologian, but not necessarily a man

4 "When the mind hath been imbued with the beginning of faith which worketh by love, it goes on by living well to arrive at right also, wherein is unspeakable beauty known to high and holy hearts, the full vision of which is the highest happiness," St. Augustine Encheiridion, c. 5.

of faith.[5] Feeling alone can create a sentimental emotionalism which is the the danger of some healing missions and revival services, and, as for "doing" alone, the New Testament has a biting word for the busy doers who think they can earn God's favour by piling up good works.

1. Faith as strengthened by knowing.

He who would have faith must intellectually be utterly and sincerely loyal to the trend of all the available evidence. "Blind faith" is a contradiction in terms, and he who exhorts others to faith by decrying or discounting the factor of reason, is not pleading for faith, but for credulity. Man must be utterly loyal to truth. Nothing that is true can undermine real faith in God, and to reject truth—wherever it is found and however it may contradict what we should like to believe—is finally disloyalty to the God of truth Who made our minds work in the way they do, and Who laid down as the first Commandment that we should love Him with them. "Thou shalt love the Lord thy God with all thy mind." Unbelief can only be blameworthy if it is a refusal to consider the evidence, or accept its conclusions, after their validity has been recognised. "The unbelief which Jesus rebuked was not aggressive denial nor too persistent questioning. It was the dull unperceiving mind settled in a hopeless mood, because it had ceased to see God. And the faith which He desired, did not mean the choking down of doubts . . . or being content with bad arguments because they are used on God's side. It was the awareness of a sincere mind to the presence and working of God in His own world." [6] It is doubtful whether we ought to propagate our own "faith," save in the sense of seeking to exhibit the truth in such a way that it cannot be rejected, save by those who cling to the darkness of their cherished beliefs, unwilling to expose them to the scrutiny of examination lest they turn out to be untrue after all. Many who harp most on the necessity of "having faith," do so with so loud a voice as to make the psychologist suspicious that they "protest too much" and are repressing a secret fear that much of what they believe by faith would be upset if subjected to the light of reasonable argument. Their attitude, put bluntly, boils down to this: "Have faith—for there is no evidence."

[5] "Nobody who considers the matter at all really believes that the climax of faith consists in an assent to any series of theological propositions or to the contents of the Creeds," Prof. and Canon L. W. Grensted, *Psychology and God*, p. 78 (Longmans Green, 1930).

[6] W. R. Maltby, *op. cit.*

Of course, our knowing cannot, as it were, reach God in comprehension. If it could, there would be no place for faith at all. But we must proceed as far as we can on the path of knowing, and then make the leap of faith to which the trend of knowing points. Thus we can apprehend even if we cannot comprehend. One can imagine a rocky islet standing up in the sea a yard or two from the cliff-edge. A road runs to the cliff-edge in the direction of the islet, but he who would reach the latter must jump from the point on the cliff-edge where the road stops. We are to follow the road of knowledge as far as it goes. But when the solid ground of reason ends, faith leaps in the direction of the islet and lands by faith in an otherwise inaccessible place. That this is the mental attitude of the scientist, as of the Christian, was illustrated for me recently in a conversation with a well-known medical specialist, who said, *a propos* of a medical hypothesis, "The facts do not quite bring us to that conclusion, but that is the direction in which they point, and we are working on the assumption that the conclusion is sound." Similarly, Sir Oliver Lodge said of Newton, "He had an extraordinary faculty for *guessing correctly*."

So it is with Christian faith. "Faith means," says the author of the letter to the Hebrews, "we are confident of what we hope for, convinced of what we do not see." [7] It is trusting where we cannot prove, but being loyal to the *trend* of the evidence. It is walking as far as we can along the road of knowing, and then making a leap of faith. That is far from dethroning reason, believing something *against* the trend of the evidence, indulging in credulity, or superstition, or trying to manufacture faith at a point which is not even approached by knowledge.

This "knowing," it must be said, is not a purely theological matter, nor is it knowledge attained only through spiritual insight and prayer, nor is it a knowledge of God's ways attained only through the study of the Bible and the great devotional literature of the Church, helpful as all these are. The discoveries of science are also the revelations of God. Here, too, the ways of God must be known. Christian men should welcome every discovery that prevents, lessens or combats human suffering, and should take a delight in spreading such knowledge. The Christian who believes that God's ideal will is perfect health of body, mind and spirit, is to use every device of science—medicine, surgery, psychology and every other relevant branch of knowledge—to fight his way back to health. Knowing, in this sense, is an ally of faith. I do not mean that the patient must himself study these sciences. But he can strengthen faith in God and in recovery by getting into

[7] Hebrews 11:1 (Moffatt).

427

touch with those who have made it their business to study them. They are the means by which God comes to the aid of His people. I have even met people who think that faith in God must only mean faith in His direct power to heal. So far from this being a superior form of Christian faith, it is foolish to reject the possibility of regaining health if another's knowledge could help us regain it. Faith in another's knowledge can be as potent as faith in our own, and both a species of Christian faith.

2. Faith as strengthened by feeling.

Obviously Christian faith cannot be a cold, intellectal projection from reason to probability. It is enormously strengthened when a *person* is the object of faith and when healthy emotion, like love, or trust, or admiration, is called forth. Many simple people, whose intellect plays a small part in their faith, have faith in Christ. Their love is so intense that it carries them over the gulf to which I have referred, in a way which proves that, in their case, faith requires little support from reason. I do not here mean "mere emotionalism" or sentimentality, whipped up by various devices, but a warm feeling that the object of faith is worthy of faith, and that a personal relationship has been established with Him.

Looking at Christ as He is pictured in the Gospels and revealed in the lives of His saints can evoke feelings which immensely strengthen faith in Him, and many can believe *in* the Lord Jesus Christ, who find it difficult to believe *about* Him many things which orthodoxy claims as the truth. By feelings like love and admiration, we frequently —and as we say intuitively—believe in our human friends before our intellect has grasped many facts about them, and the same is true of the Christian's faith in Christ.

But not only must there be the imaginative picture of Christ which calls forth feeling. There must be the imaginative picture of ourselves as loved by Him. As we watch Him in the Gospels, it would be a useful exercise to imagine ourselves taking the place of a patient to whom He ministered. Coué has taught us that the value of "I can" is greater than that of "I will." Some have glibly said that "faith is only suggesting to oneself what one would like to be true." It would be more accurate to say that suggestion is an ingredient of faith. Suggestion depends on faith, not faith on suggestion. Witness the personal prestige of Coué and the faith in him which reinforced the power of his suggestions. The feeling of confidence, that God *cares for us* and wills our health, even if, for reasons we shall discuss, we cannot have that health yet, is very important. In this way, too, we shall be helped to make the maximum response of our feelings. So says St. Mark, in a sentence of wonderful insight, "All things whatsoever ye pray and ask for, believe that ye have received them (= feel that they are yours already), and ye shall have them." [8]

3. Faith as strengthened by willing.

Faith is not perfect if it lacks a conative aspect. Faith without works is vain.[9] Faith is only a maximum in any personality when knowing goes as far as it can and leaps; when feeling is as rich as it can be, and the personality both loves and feels itself loved, and when the will "acts on the noblest hypothesis." Dr. W. R. Matthews, Dean of St. Paul's, described faith as "an attitude of active trustfulness." We recall, in the famous chapter on faith in the New Testament,[10] that "by faith Abraham . . . *went out.*" Action is part of faith.

Christ continually asked for such action on the part of those whom He healed. "Stretch forth thy hand." [11] "Go, wash in the pool of Siloam." [12] "Shew thyself to the priest." [13] "Thou hast *answered* right; this *do,* and thou shalt live," [14] and so on. The action both demanded that faith should rise to its maximum, and then proved its validity. Faith is not worth the name if it remains subjective. There must be a doing also; "betting your life there's a God," as Donald Hankey said, and acting on the bet.

Modern medicine offers an illustration of all three factors of faith in operation. My faith in my physician is increased if I find, for example, that he has a good academic qualification of which I was formerly ignorant, or that he was called in to see some important person, or that he has cured cases like mine before. *Knowing* his virtues and abilities increases faith. A feeling of affection and trust increases my faith also. So does the feeling that he cares about my case. A physician derives a large part of his prestige by his power to call forth from the patient feelings of trust and confidence. But the will must operate in action. I must *do* all I can to co-operate with him and carry out his instructions, or cure may evade me.

[8] Mark 11:24.
[9] James 2:14 ff.
[10] Hebrews 11:8–12:2.
[11] Matthew 12:13.
[12] John 9:7.
[13] Matthew 8:4.
[14] Luke 10:28.

Faith in Christ is not dissimilar. The more I know about Him and the more I know Him by communion with Him, the better. The more I love Him, the better. The more I dare to act as His will directs my own, the better.

It seems to me important to stress that Christian faith is faith in a Person. As my definition said, it is our maximum response to God in Christ. Whether it is made to God, or to Christ, or to the Holy Spirit, makes no difference in experience, but the response must not be directed to any lesser object. It must be to the God who was fully revealed in Christ, not to the God of the Old Testament alone.

"It is questionable whether it is not misleading to speak as some do of His continual demand for faith. For He knew that to 'demand faith' is to set a man labouring with His own mind and perhaps tampering with his intellectual integrity in the effort to believe instead of looking at the object of faith. But it is true that He was always looking for faith and recognized it for what it was when we should have called it by quite other names." [15]

Frequently, when the words "faith" and "healing" are mentioned, the patient tries to have faith *in getting better*. This is directing faith too low, and is a kind of mental gymnastic which *need* not have anything to do with religion. It is, for example, the heart of Couéism. Others who speak of faith in Jesus mean faith in the *teaching* of Jesus. This is better, but is still faith in the efficacy of ideas. But I mean a personal relationship with a living Friend by faith, *which is of a calibre uninjured if physical health is not recovered*. I can have faith in the teaching of Hippocrates and faith in some of his methods, but I cannot have faith which makes real a personal relationship. That personal relationship seems to me the very centre and essence of the Christian experience.

It is because Christian faith is faith in a Person that men need to know something about the Person: enough to make them certain that the faith is not misplaced. Otherwise to ask for faith in Jesus is in the same category as to ask for faith in Santa Claus. "Simple faith in Jesus" was all very well in Galilee between A.D. 25 and 29. Men could see Him, listen to Him and perhaps talk to Him. Faith in Jesus was not too difficult, perhaps, for the rest of the first century. Men could meet people who had known Him, and, at first, people who were alive at the Resurrection. But child-like faith in Jesus is not easy now. It is a very great achievement. For one thing, not many men are child-like. The hard stress of modern life and the "scientific atmosphere" do not help. For another, there is a time-lag

[15] W. R. Maltby, *op. cit.*

of two thousand years. Again, not many can speak of Him with authority. And very few are like Him or can exercise a hundredth part of His loving power.

Nowadays "knowing," by study and meditation, must make up for much that would have been done in a moment if we had "known" Him in Galilee. And feeling must come as we look at the Gospels, whereas it would have come so easily if we had looked into His face. So to know and so to feel must have meant a reinforcement of the will not nearly so available today. Further, there was the spectacle of others obeying His will and finding their lives quite changed. Christ understood this difficulty. "Blessed," He said, "are they that have not seen and yet have believed." [16]

We are not necessarily to wait until we can make the Christian creeds our own, but the modern's faith in Christ—to justify the phrase, "Christian faith"—will have, I think, to get to the point at which he can at least say the following creed:

1. I believe that Jesus Christ was right in believing in the existence of a God who is both Creator and Father, utterly holy, utterly just, utterly loving and ultimately all-powerful.

2. I believe that Jesus Christ stood in a unique relationship to God; that He was God made man.

3. I believe that Jesus Christ rose from the dead and proved His survival to His followers.

4. I believe that He is still alive, and that through His Spirit He still changes the lives of those who try to take Him seriously and make as full a response to Him as they possibly can, with every part of their nature, thinking, feeling and doing.

This may seem to make Christian faith a grim requirement. Fortunately, the *amount* of faith is not the condition which evaluates it. A grain of mustard, Jesus said, is the measure of a faith required to move mountains.[17] What is done for man is not done *by* his faith, but *by* Christ *through* his faith. Faith is rather the psychological frame of mind in which alone God can get near enough to man to do *His* work. The power of faith, in one sense, is nil. It is the state of personality in which God can exert *His* power. It is the only way. Man cannot "work his passage home." He cannot earn God's mercy. He cannot deserve God's love. He can only receive it as a gift. And he receives it *through* faith which I have defined as a threefold response of human personality to God in Christ. To use a phrase of Fosdick,

[16] John 20:29.
[17] Matthew 17:20.

it is not "overcoming God's reluctance," as a spoilt dog begs for scraps when we have our meal, in "faith" that we shall throw him a morsel. The threefold response I have described is man's way of laying hold on God's willingness, of receiving what God longs to give, of co-operating with God to man's fullest and most fruitful extent. So much for the nature of Christian faith. What is its place in healing? Here several things must be said.

The Christian is to have faith in Christ because He *is* Christ. And that faith means "following" whether healing is gained or not.

A young girl, known to me, was taken to Lourdes and given a silver cross which the priest had "blessed." Too ill to join in the processions, she was told by him that when the Host was elevated she was to hold the cross tightly and have "faith" that she would recover. She did her best, but came home to die. As she was dying, she gave the cross to me. I was deeply moved when she said simply, "I want you to keep it, for it taught me a great lesson. I have learnt not to hold the cross and try to believe that I shall be healed, but to yield myself utterly to the Crucified and not mind whether I am healed or not." That is faith. It reminds one of Josiah Royce's definition of faith as "the soul's insight or discovery of some Reality that enables a man to stand anything that can happen to him in the universe." [18] That attitude of believing in Christ whether healing comes or not is far more worthy the name "faith" than the attitude which assesses our own faith, or Christ's power, or both, by the phenomenon of a healed body, often effected by suggestibility rather than faith.

Thinking that healing was a sign only of faith, the early Church was bewildered by the pagan magicians who healed people by making them wear charms, or recite incantations containing the name of Jesus. Cures were wrought by heathen exorcists who cured people who had no real faith in Jesus at all. The confusion still exists. We do not have pagan exorcists, but we have healers—many conscientious and Christian—who, because they have never thought the matter through, attach Christian labels to processes which are really just as pagan as those to which I have referred.

Another point to be clearly grasped as we discuss the place of faith in healing is that the mental atmosphere has changed through the advance of science. In our Lord's day, if the figure be allowed, the mental atmosphere which men's minds breathed was that of credulity —that is, belief without evidence. A great man, and especially a good man, could call out "faith" easily. Nowadays, the mental atmosphere

[18] Quoted from Dr. Stanley Jones, *Christ and Human Suffering* (Abingdon-Cokesbury, 1933).

is that of science, and no return to that of credulity will ever again be possible. A very great personality, by increasing the power of feeling, can diminish the need of knowing, but today the paradox is true, that faith can more easily be evoked by scientific action than by demanding belief without evidence. A patient to whom an advised treatment is scientifically *explained* is more likely to respond, by faith in the healer and belief in the treatment, than a patient who is kept in the dark so completely that he cannot see any reason for supposing that the suggested treatment can possibly do him good.

To summarise, then, healing will not happen by faith alone in cases of distress which fall within what I have called the thorn-in-the-foot category: the broken leg, the shattered skull, the gouged-out eye and so on. Many germ-invasion diseases, especially where these have been caught by infection from others, must surely be in this category too. Where physical tissue is damaged, it will need time, and often human skill and careful nursing, for recovery. Faith and hope, optimism and courage, will, even here, speed up recovery. Depression, despair, pessimism and fear will retard it. If mental disease, as some think, has a physiological basis—and some undoubtedly has—then it may be that healing will be delayed until members of the human family, trained to do so, learn how to co-operate with God in the relief of other members of the family who bear the burden of the family ignorance.

Functional disease is in a different category, and at present it is impossible, in some instances, to decide where the line between functional and organic diseases can be drawn. The study of psychosomatic disease makes it hard, indeed, to draw such a line. If organic symptoms, however, as, for instance, in cases of asthma, peptic ulcers and skin affections—to take the three already described—are traceable in the first case to factors like worry, resentment, hate and fear, it is clear that Christian faith, kindled in such a patient, would go far to bring back health and harmony.

Again, if what has been written about guilt and about the deprivation of love and the deep functioning in the unconscious of unhealthy emotions, be true—as I believe it to be—obviously the kindling or strengthening of Christian faith, by dealing with guilt, offering love and driving out unhealthy emotion, by what has been called "the expulsive power of a new affection," might well restore health. One looks with a new interest at the healing miracles of Christ, so quick in their result on bodies and minds, and wonders whether the love that streamed from Him, with such dynamic energy, did not so sweep through the personalities of those who made the response of faith, as to drive out—even from the unconscious—that unhealthy emotion which lies at the root of so much illness, much of it with organic symptoms.

Again, there are diseases, with which the psychologist is familiar, in which anxiety has been "converted" into bodily illness (conversion hysteria), or in which obsessional neurosis compels a patient to refrain from taking food (anorexia nervosa). Here, as far as we know at present, scientific psychotherapy must play a part in cure, but inasmuch as the patient's attitude to life is faulty, Christian faith, in the sense defined above, can play a most potent part in cure.

Our conclusion must be that any man, sick or well, who calls himself a Christian, should see it to be his duty to make as full a response as he can to God, the God who is like Christ and whom Christ revealed. Thought, feeling and doing must all be mobilised to this end. It is the Church's duty to call out that response in all the healthy ways known to her. If this were done, we have every reason to believe that many who are sick would be healed, for their sickness, in the last analysis, is a mal-adjustment of the soul to God, rather than a mal-adjustment of the body to the physical environment, or the mind to the world of true ideas.

Even then, some would remain unhealed for reasons given. The relevant way of co-operating with God, and thus regaining health, may be in their case beyond themselves and their own faith. They may have to wait until the human family knows enough to prevent or cure their malady. We all receive the assets of that family and gain by its skill and knowledge. Some have to suffer the family liabilities of ignorance, folly and sin. Writing to such an one, Carlyle said, "For us was thy back bent, for us were thy straight limbs and fingers so deformed; thou wert our conscript on whom the lot fell, and fighting our battles wast so marred."

This may seem small comfort to such, and I cannot deal with their problem here.[19] But, of course, they are still in the hands of a loving God. Let them try to maintain their faith in Him and make the three-fold response of knowing Him, loving Him and doing His will within the circumstances that shut them in. Many such shut-in people have done more for the world than others in full health. Their *souls* need not be sick. I believe suffering to be part of the kingdom of evil. At the same time, if suffering *cannot* be cured, God can use it, as He can, and does, use every form of temporary evil, and weave it at last into the pattern of His purposes in a manner wonderful and beautiful beyond all man's dreams. This is one of the richest truths in the Bible. The Cross is its finest example. It was God's will that Jesus should

---

[19] I have tried to deal with the suffering of the innocent in my book, *Why Do Men Suffer?* (Abingdon-Cokesbury, 1936).

be followed, not murdered. But when "by the hands of wicked men" He was put to death, then His faith rose to the demand, and, in a co-operation with God the doing of which makes us catch our breath. He wove the Cross into the pattern of divine purpose and achieved that purpose in a death which is now the greatest asset in the moral account of the world. In our little way, if the evil of our suffering cannot be replaced by health, our attitude of faith can make it an asset. "With them that love Him, God co-operates in all things for good." [20]

[20] Romans 8:28 (Prof. C. H. Dodd's translation) in his commentary *The Epistle of Paul to the Romans* (Harper, 1932).

THE NATURE AND PLACE OF SCIENCE IN HEALING

WADDINGTON'S DEFINITION OF science seems to me entirely satisfactory. "Science is the organised attempt of mankind to discover how things work as causal systems."

It is very necessary to counter the false idea, held on both sides of the fence between science and religion, that healing through faith, through prayer, or even through such psychological mechanisms as suggestion, are methods not only "unscientific" (in that the factors operating and the methods of their operation are unknown), but that those who employ them are necessarily hostile to the methods of "science" and deem them unnecessary. "Why bother with science?" says one unadmirable type of faith-healer. "Christ's disciples did not do so. If men had enough faith, such things as drugs and operations could be superseded and rendered unnecessary."

This is a point of view which we must consider.

Let us state first a fact to which both sides would agree. It is desirable—indeed, the will of God—that a sick person be made well. If men had enough faith, no doubt health, in many cases, would result without any recourse to medicine, surgery, psychotherapy and so on. But—apart from the fact that in some situations science is more relevant to healing than faith is—the truth is that men have *not* enough faith and that no one nowadays can call it forth as our Lord and His immediate disciples did. It may be that Christ's modern disciples do not fulfil the necessary conditions. An important factor is the alteration in the psychic atmosphere. "Believing," now, is rarely a projection from credulity, but from knowledge, and we can call forth faith better from the approach of understanding than from the approach of credulity; i.e. by being told simply, and without reason given, that we *must believe*.

436

Whatever the cause, faith is harder to achieve. Scientific progress has made it so by altering the mental atmosphere, though no one can reasonably doubt that science has contributed immensely to men's health and could do so to a far greater degree if we used her discoveries wisely. Are we, because faith is harder, to deny the patient such alleviation of his illness as comes from science? The methods of medicine and surgery, indeed, have been so successful, reliable and trustworthy, and those of psychology are becoming so, that "faith-healing" has seemed to most of our generation a last resource, only to be resorted to when all other methods have failed.

We can be certain that medical, and other scientific therapeutic treatments lie within the will of God. Jesus probably recommended some patients to doctors. There is no evidence that the early Church scorned the work of doctors or failed to classify disease. If this were not so, we might well ask why St. Paul did not lay hands on Timothy and heal him rather than write as he did. He wrote, "By the way, I should advise you to drink wine in moderation, instead of water. It will do your stomach good and help you to get over your frequent spells of illness." [1]

Further, in answer to some faith-healers who would dispense with science, I would re-affirm the value of classifying illness, even though we cannot draw with clearness the lines which separate the classifications. If a man has a thorn in his foot, to use my favourite illustration, no amount of faith, even if called forth by our Lord Himself, would be as effective as pulling the thorn out. One feels there must still be many illnesses which fall into that category, even though many that we formerly labelled "organic" are now seen to be organic concomitants of psychological, or even spiritual disharmony.

What is so constantly forgotten is that all healing is the activity of God. All that man can do in the matter of healing is to co-operate with Him. Even prayer is not necessarily a more religious procedure than an operation. Indeed, in medical missionary work prayer is usually offered by the surgeon before the operation. What it is so important to discover is the most *relevant* way of co-operating with God. Prayer is obviously not the best way of making a man walk whose leg has been shot off by a shell. Designing and perfecting an artificial limb probably is. And to do this latter in a scientific way, for the sake of helping a sufferer, can be as "religious" an act as prayer, and much more relevant.

Prayer for a malaria patient has value. The patient's resistance is increased. But the more relevant way of co-operating with God was

[1] I Timothy 5:23 (J. B. Phillips's translation).

found by Sir Ronald Ross when he discovered the organism that carried malaria. It is useful to recall the religious way in which he regarded his scientific quest. He wrote as follows:

> I pace and pace, and think and think, and take
> The fever'd hands, and note down all I see,
> That some dim distant light may haply break.
>
> The painful faces ask, "Can we not cure?"
> We answer, "No, not yet; we seek the laws."
> O God, reveal through all this thing obscure
> The unseen, small, but million murdering cause.

On the day of discovery he wrote as follows:

> This day relenting God
> Hath placed within my hand
> A wondrous thing; and God
> Be praised. At His command
>
> Seeking His secret deeds,
> With tears and toiling breath,
> I find Thy cunning seeds,
> O million murdering Death.
>
> I know this little thing
> A myriad men will save.
> O Death, where is thy sting?
> Thy victory, O Grave? [2]

It is so important to discover the *relevant* way of co-operating with God.

God has ordained that man shall not be cured of certain illnesses without that co-operation. As Augustine said, "Without God we cannot. Without us, God will not." But God's energies are *there* waiting to be tapped. There is a *vis medicatrix naturæ* both of the mind and soul, as well as the body. We have to find the *relevant* way of co-operating, whether it be the surgery that removes an appendix, the psychotherapy that removes a phobia, or the Christian message of forgiveness that removes the fear in guilt.

What we need is not—as some faith-healers suppose—less science, but more. For one thing, medical researchers are constantly hindered for lack of adequate equipment and financial support. It is aggravat-

[2] Quoted from *Philosophies* by permission of Sir John Murray, K.C.V.O.

ing beyond words to realise that we might be able in a few years to banish cancer and tuberculosis and many other diseases that curse us, just as cholera and plague have been banished, if we spent on scientific research the money devoted, say, to a couple of battleships. It is rather futile to ponder the mystery of so much suffering with the implication that God is responsible, if it is within man's resources to banish it within a single generation. Scientific research into ways of healing disease ought to have the fullest support of all Christians, even if some proud scientists give the impression that religion is nothing to do with the work they do. We know that all therapeutic agencies are, in a true sense, expressions of God's power, but we must not exclude scientists as colleagues because they are blind to this great fact. I know how proud some scientific workers can be. They would exclude God and religion altogether, and scorn to work with a religious colleague. They mistake descriptions of *how* God works for explanations which make Him unnecessary, which is rather like finding a watch, studying its mechanism, learning "what makes it go" and how it has been put together, and then making the foolish deduction that because one understands how it works, one need not posit the existence of the watch-maker who made it in the first instance. The scientist has sometimes imagined that his methods are the only valid methods of arriving at sound conclusions, but, even so, he is the colleague of the man of faith, for he, too, is "thinking God's thoughts after Him," to use a phrase of Kepler, the astronomer. And if the scientist has been proud and exclusive, the man of religion has been narrow and intolerant. He has forgotten that if religion is true, nothing can overthrow it, and he has feared lest his faith be taken from him, forgetting that if it can be upset by science, it ought to be, for God is Truth, and no one who loves Him must hide in a demonstrable lie and try to believe it by "faith."

But the point I also want to make in suggesting that we need not less science but more, is that we need scientific research into such matters as private prayer and public intercession. Why pray in the haphazard manner most of us do and just hope for the best?

In the matter of private prayer, a man will pray for some virtue, without any real effort at self-discipline, without excluding the factors which contribute to his downfall. He would never dream of praying to recover from pneumonia, and then going out in damp clothes when a cold east wind was blowing. He knows that for physical recovery certain rules must be kept, certain laws obeyed, certain conditions observed and he is prepared to co-operate. But man imagines that prayer is "different." He wants magic. He does not recognise that the writ of law runs here also. He asks for effects without trying to learn causes. He would laugh at a student who prayed for success at an examination after no real effort at study. But "spiritual healing," he thinks, ought to take place without any conditions. The point is immensely important, especially if, as I believe, so much of our physical health depends on our spiritual health.

In the matter of public intercession for the sick, for example, I am convinced that its efficacy is governed by laws. Law runs through the whole universe, and not through the material part of it alone. If the patient is known, is loved, is named; if those who pray really care; if they clearly understood what they are doing and why; if a word-picture is painted which helps them imaginatively to enter the sick room and see the patient and enter into his needs . . . then I am certain prayer is more potent than one sentence of a long prayer which frequently runs: "Lord, bless all those who are sick and make them better." But we need to co-ordinate and correlate our findings in the field of prayer. We need to study, for instance, the bearing of telepathy and auto-suggestion upon it, and produce in people a faith in prayer which is projected from knowing, not from half-superstitious credulity. Many still cling to the heresy that illness is "handed out" to people by an offended God. To their prayer for health they add a phrase, "if it be Thy will," which might mean, "if it be Thy secondary will that I bear this illness, help me to accept it and turn it to good, although I know that Thy primary will is health." That is sound enough. But the phrase sounds as if it means, "if You really want me to get better." The old bogey that suffering is God's chastisement and that the sufferer must bow beneath the rod, still clings to men's minds.

I wish to quote here the robust words of the anonymous priest-doctor author of *Christus Integritas*:

"The idea of the divine chastisement is not found in any of the liturgies and prayers for healing before the fifth century, and such occasional references to it which occur in the Leonine (5th century) and Gregorian (6th century) Sacramentaries may well be a later interpolation. The Christians of the first centuries had a clearer conception of the power of the healing Christ than has ever been manifested by the Church of later ages, and perhaps a deeper sense of the responsibility owed by the body of Christian believers to their brethren in sickness. The sick were not, in their eyes, victims of the divine chastisement, but victims of a 'disorder' which follows the violation of God's will, not necessarily by the individual sufferer, but by the whole race of sinful mankind whose burden of ἀνομία (= iniquity) every human being must in some measure share. It is not surprising, therefore, that the conditional 'if it be Thy will'—so common a feature in modern prayers for healing—is altogether absent from these early Christian prayers. The remedy for sickness lay not in the patient submission of the sufferer under the dread hand of God, but in his joining battle in the power of Christ against the evil hosts of disease which assailed him. And it was not a battle that he was expected to fight alone. Christ had left the needful weapons to His Church, and were not his fellow Christians at his side, ready to care for him in his sad condition, by intercession and by every ministry of mercy, just as if it had been their own?" [3]

There is a curious idea in some minds that the writ of science does not run into the area of religion at all. Granted that the scientific approach is not the only way by which reality may be apprehended, yet the words of F. H. Bradley are worth quoting: "There is nothing more real than what comes in religion. To compare facts such as these with what is given to us in outward experience, would be to trifle with the subject. The man who demands a reality more solid than that of the religious consciousness, seeks he knows not what." [4]

Many scientists intrepret reality in terms of the faith of religion. A. N. Whitehead, perhaps the most scientific of all the modern philosophers, writes:

"Religion is the vision of something which stands beyond, behind and within the passing flux of immediate things; something which is real, and yet waiting to be realised; something which is a remote possibility, and yet the greatest of present facts; something that gives meaning to all that passes, and yet eludes apprehension; something whose possession is the final good, and yet is beyond all reach; something which is the ultimate ideal, and the hopeless quest.

"The immediate reaction of human nature to the religious vision is worship. Religion has emerged into human experience mixed with the crudest fancies of barbaric imagination. Gradually, slowly, steadily, the vision recurs in history under nobler form and with clearer expression. It is the one element in human experience which persistently shows an upward trend. It fades and then recurs. But when it renews its force, it recurs with an added richness and purity of content. *The fact of the religious vision, and its history of persistent expansion, is our one ground for optimism.* Apart from it, human life is a flash of

[3] Pp. 36-37.
[4] *Appearance and Reality.*

441

occasional enjoyments lighting up a mass of pain and misery, a bagatelle of transient experience." [5]

Science might be defined as the quest for and systemisation of the truth about the universe by the method of observation and inference. Much faith is necessary often to make such inferences, as I tried to show in the previous chapter, and faith lies behind the whole scientific method—faith in the reliability of the deductive processes of the human mind; faith that all scientific discovery is not subjective illusion.

The faith required, however, by the patient told to take a pill is almost negligible. To use the illustration on p. 427, the road of knowing goes as far as we want to go. We can drive to the spot we seek in a car. We haven't to get out and jump. This fact has made it harder to have faith at any point. But *this* last fact also makes it essential to have more, not less, science. We cannot go back to the time of ignorance. We must go on.

If, as I claim, faith should be understood as utter loyalty to the trend of all the available evidence and a projection from the furthest place to which the road of knowing can take us, as well as a projection from feeling and conation, then what we need is science extended into all fields of human activity, seeking ever to find ways to link up man with God in that harmony called health which is His will.

What we must *exclude*, and expose in all its naked puerility, is "faith," so called, which is not faith, but a spurious and cheap substitute; "faith" which is a bastard credulity and superstition with no dignity in it and no foundation in knowledge; "faith" which is thought pious and devotional and praiseworthy, based on what the devotee thinks God ought to do, but which never thinks things through, never asks what in effect He does do, and what are the laws by which He works; "faith" like the feeling engendered by the medicine men in the dark jungle villages in India, evoked by muttering words which have no meaning and producing emotional states out of man's proneness to fear the unknown—especially the spiritually unknown.

No one can see with indifference the young people of our generation, living as they do in the scientific atmosphere of our schools and colleges five or six days a week, and then on Sundays expected to go to church and feel at home in an atmosphere in which immense statements are made, with the backing only of hoary tradition; in which words are used which say one thing and mean another; in which belief is demanded through "faith," presumably because no reasons can be given for it; in which passages are read, without ex-

[5] *Science and the Modern World.* Copyright 1925 by The Macmillan Company. Used by permission. Italics mine.

planation, from the Old Testament, which deny both reason and morality; in which miracles are related which puzzle the youth who— without knowing it—loves God with his mind and seeks to maintain the integrity of the mental processes God has given him, and which are never violated by the University as they are by the Church. Religion has lost the leadership she once had partly because she will not abandon what is untrue and restate her findings, as her quest for truth progresses. Scientists have much to teach us here. They do not prefer tradition to truth. They give up the most dearly held hypothesis once it is shown to be untrue. They do not say one thing and mean another, or fear to follow where truth leads.

No one can watch the youth of today turn away from the Church without longing to revise our services, interpret our faith in modern terms, assure them that Christ and all that is essential to His message can stand up, without fear, to the most searching scrutiny of science, and that, in this realm of healing which we are discussing, the truest minds in the Church welcome every discovery and treatment of science, and only beg the scientists to go further and release the energies, not only of the material world, but to invade, with their careful method, as far as they possibly can, the realm of the mind and the spirit. Here religion desperately needs the science of psychology. There are energies which flow through man's mind and spirit which could carry us far in our campaign against suffering. In some sporadic cures of the faith-healers we see those energies at work. But, as yet, we do not understand them. The best qualities in our minds reject the luck of hit-and-miss methods that may, or may not, come off. We do not understand how to release the mighty energies of the non-material universe, or know by what laws their operation is governed— and so the sick go on suffering.

Truly understood, there cannot be any real hostility in the field of healing between science and religion. Both seek to know the truth and to use it to heal the sick. All relevant truths must be co-ordinated, and each worker must welcome truth and be sympathetic to those who seek it in fields and by methods other than his own. Nothing really true, discovered in one field by one method, can ever finally deny truth discovered in another field by another method, though we are often unable to see at once how two truths are, in fact, part of one greater whole. We have to recognise them and go on thinking. A mountaineer may see two peaks of a mountain, and find their bases so swathed in mist that he cannot realise that they are really one and the same mountain. Similarly, it is often hard to see how and where twin truths are reconciled. Both theologians and scientists have made dogmatic assertions and later abandoned them. What looked like a peak of truth was a phantom of the mist. But the weather will clear as we go on climbing. And all the real peaks of truth will be seen to be one mountain in the light of God who is Himself the Truth, and the Source of our urge to discover it.

3

THE PLACE OF FAITH AND SCIENCE ILLUSTRATED IN THE PRACTICE OF CONFESSION, WORSHIP AND ASCETICISM

IN THIS CHAPTER I wish to offer some brief notes showing that some methods of healing relied on by religion would be strengthened in their healing power if their various techniques were enriched by the light which the science of psychology can now throw upon them. They are modern in the sense that they are used today. They are ancient in origin.

A. THE PLACE OF FAITH AND SCIENCE ILLUSTRATED IN THE PRACTICE OF CONFESSION [1]

There can be no doubt whatever but that the practice of confession has, throughout its long history, been an important factor in healing troubles both of the body and the mind. The practice of confession goes back to the earliest history of man. As soon as man chose evil instead of good, and chose it recognising it as evil, he concealed his act from others and sought to banish it from his own consciousness. He had "a guilty secret." As soon as he did that, he started the dreary story of the poisoned unconscious. He "fell." All the initiation and mystery cults of the ancient world call on him in their ceremonies to "confess" so that he may ease his conscience and get rid of the poison before it poisons the deep mind. Jung says that the very word "catharsis" comes from the Greek rites of initiation. The secrecy of a concealed fault shuts man off from the life of the community. A shared

[1] I have discussed the practice of Confession more fully in an earlier book, *Psychology in Service of the Soul* (Macmillan, 1930).

445

secret saved primitive man from "dissolving in the unconsciousness of mere community life," [2] and men invented secrets to preserve individuality. But a wholly private secret, especially a guilty secret, was recognised as having a destructive effect, cutting off the unhappy possessor from full communion with his fellows. The value of confession is praised in all the religious systems of the world and in some of its greatest literature.

During some research into the psychological value of confession which I carried out some years ago, I was impressed by the contribution which the poets make. For example, Bacon says: "This communicating of a man's self to his friend . . . cutteth grief in halfes." [3]

Tennyson has these suggestive lines:

> Nor could I weary, heart or limb,
>   When mighty Love would cleave in twain
>   The lading of a single pain,
> And part it, giving half to him. [4]

Spenser has this line:

> He often finds present help who does his grief impart. [5]

And Shakespeare says:
> Give sorrow words: the grief that does not speak
> Whispers the o'er-fraught heart and bids it break. [6]

The poets, as I have shown in another place, [7] have a way of thinking of their poetry as a kind of confession to the world of thoughts that they cannot hold within their own breasts without a sense of danger.

Thus Wordsworth says: "A timely utterance gave that thought relief."

Byron says: "Poetry is the lava of the imagination whose eruption prevents the earthquake."

Burns says: "My passions raged like so many devils till they got vent in rhyme."

[2] Jung, *Modern Man in Search of a Soul.*
[3] Essay 27.
[4] In Memoriam," 25.
[5] "Faerie Queen," II, 1. 46.
[6] "Macbeth," Act IV, Sc. 3.
[7] *The Afterworld of the Poets* (Epworth Press, 2nd Ed. 1937).

Goethe speaks: "Of converting whatever rejoiced or worried or otherwise concerned me into a poem and so have done with it."

Cardinal Newman says: "Poetry is a means of relieving the overburdened mind; it is a channel through which emotion finds expression."

Keble says: "To innumerable persons (poetry) acts as a safety-valve tending to preserve them from mental disease."

The cumulative effect of these witnesses is impressive. Most of us could not find it in poetry, but we must find it in some expression of words made to some other person.

If, as has been claimed earlier in this book, physical illness is often caused by emotional states, especially when the emotion is semi-repressed, it should not surprise us to find that confession which relieves the sense of guilt, frustration, resentment, fear and so on, is often a turning point in a physical illness. So Dr. Hadfield writes of a man who suffered from pressure in the head, especially round the temples. Further, he could not see clearly. He had a nagging wife who would keep him awake until two or three in the morning and then sleep while he worked. He mentioned this to no one out of loyalty to her. "When he was encouraged to let out in analysis all his feelings of animosity against his wife, his symptoms completely disappeared." [8]

A friend of mine felt that he had been very badly treated by a minister. He wrote to the latter, but got no response of any kind. My friend left the church, and was full of rage and resentment. He developed a severe ulcer in his leg which would not heal. Happening to visit him while in his city, I pleaded with him to write a different kind of letter to the minister and to put away resentment and be reconciled. He did so, and writes as follows, August 13, 1948. "By the way, this will interest you. That big, sore place on my leg healed up almost immediately after I wrote to M" (the minister). "G" (his nurse) "may say that her dressings did it, but I had been dressing it for four months without much sign of improvement. It looks as though your ideas are sound, doesn't it?" Is it fanciful to say that the pus in the wound on his leg was a kind of translation into matter of the pus of resentment in his mind, and that when he was reconciled, or had done all he could towards reconciliation, he got rid of the pus in both? I am not foolishly pretending that all ulcers have such an explanation. I am suggesting that many physical conditions cannot adequately be treated solely by physical means, since a psychological or spiritual disharmony is using them for its self-expression.

[8] J. A. Hadfield, *Psychology and Mental Health*.

The Roman Catholic Church has specialised in this form of healing treatment, but members of all religious denominations ought to have at the hands of their minister all that is of value in the Roman Confessional. They ought to feel that they can pour out their troubles to one who will regard all that is said as an inviolable confidence, who, because of his training and experience, will be able to help them, and who, because of his office, will be able, with authority and confidence, to declare to people the fact of God's loving forgiveness, a fact which is, in my view, the most powerful psychotherapeutic idea in the world.

By confession is usually meant confession to another human being. Is it not sufficient for man to confess his sins to God in the secrecy of the inner room? The answer is that it would be sufficient if he *felt* forgiven by this process. But, for most, God is so unreal that man feels he has been talking when no one was listening. Nothing happens. The catharsis is not effected. But the drastic nature of telling another human being is so costly that it is far more likely to bring that *feeling* of penitence and that *feeling* of forgiveness essential to such a catharsis.

Many are quite sure intellectually that God forgives sin, but they have never *felt* forgiven. The psychological value of confession is inhibited if all that happens is intellectual assent to the proposition that God has forgiven all past sins. The penitent needs to *feel* forgiven and to respond emotionally and conatively to the truth that his *relationship* with God is now as though he had never sinned.

There are, however, some dangers in confession.

1. There is a danger of exaggerated introspection which can end in the misery of a man who looks for sin in all his actions and sees all his motives as impure. Almost all motives are actually mixed. But motive is not to be morally assessed by its origin, but by its goal. For example, the motive of a morbid sex-curiosity might make a medical student gynæcologist, but if, in harmony with the highest ideals of the medical profession, he becomes a first-rate gynæcologist, his motive is purified thereby, and is to be assessed not by its murky origin, but by its useful goal. In his early days Livingstone was accused of exploring and sight-seeing instead of teaching in a native school. His subsequent service to the world purified his motive, and it is to be assessed in terms of achievement, not origin. It is important, however, to *recognise* and confess one's source-motive, however sublime the goal to which one moves.

2. There is a danger lest a man should confess the same sin over and over again, until his religious life and devotional acts make a more

powerful auto-suggestion of the depths to which he has fallen in the past than of the heights he is determined to scale in the future.

3. There is a danger with another type of person that he should lightly regard his sins, thinking that, in any case, he will go to Confession in a few days and wipe the slate clean again. Confession thus lessens the moral effort to overcome sin.

4. There is a danger that he should exaggerate his guilt at the Confessional for neurotic reasons dealt with in the chapter on guilt.

5. There is a danger, seen, for example, amongst some of the more neurotic members of fanatical sects to confess, or "share," sins which make the sinner "interesting" to his fellows and bring him into the limelight. With what boredom do we listen to the sins of the man who confesses to bad temper, and with what excitement and interest do we turn to the sins of a real forger, wife-beater or burglar!

Modern psychology would not only emphasise the dangers of confession, but draw attention to the limited usefulness of the practice. These limitations constitute in themselves dangers. Modern techniques of psychotherapy reveal that confession, as ordinarily understood, frequently does not go deep enough.

(i) The unconscious part of the mind is not explored by confession at all, though a trained confessor often urges the patient to examine his mind more carefully and consider the significance of some signposts in consciousness (remembered dreams, for instance) which may well point to faulty reactions to life. The patient, however, normally confesses some such sin as jealousy or hate, where a psychological analysis would show him *why* he is jealous or *why* he hates, and give him ten times greater power to overcome his tendency. Thus modern psychotherapy is of enormous importance, and at least an elementary training in it should form part of the equipment of every minister and clergyman, for, as things are, the patient grows depressed by his inability to conquer something rooted in the unconscious which may have its origin in an early phase of his own childhood, when the word "sin" had little, if any, significance.

(ii) This leads on to the second danger which modern psychotherapy makes clear: that is to say, the danger of confusing moral illness with sin. Sin must always be understood as "missing the mark" ($a\mu a\rho\tau\iota\delta$) through the conscious choice of evil in the presence of the conscious recognition of good. A certain activity might be for one person sin, but for another moral disease. The latter is due to complexes repressed in the unconscious, and condemnation of their expression is most injurious and harmful. Even the bad temper of some people, and innumerable cases of masturbation, or other sex perversions, are not sin at all, but moral illness. Modern techniques of psychotherapy would make this difference abundantly clear. Psychotherapy, as such, has no relevant word to say about sin. It is not for the psychotherapist to assess morals. First of all, it is not his business, and secondly, it would be bad treatment, for he would probably silence the patient and inflame his super-ego. At the same time, a Christian, medical psychotherapist—if the phrase may be allowed— who did not regard sin lightly on the one hand, whose idea of religion was not itself neurotic on the other, could greatly help anyone who came to him to unburden his soul, and, in fact, such a person seems to me the ideal confessor. He would be able to deduce to what extent guilt was exaggerated for neurotic reasons. He would be able to detect the unconscious origin of so-called "sin." He would be able to distinguish between moral illness and sin, and he would be able to decide whether the confession of the patient was genuine and valuable, or whether it was a perverted exhibitionism. As Jung says, "One can easily understand what it means to a patient when he can confide his experiences to an understanding and sympathetic doctor. . . . No longer does he (the patient) stand alone against these elemental powers, but a trustworthy man reaches out a hand, lending him moral aid in the battle against the tyrannical oppression of uncontrolled emotion."

Modern psychotherapeutic technique has, therefore, a most important bearing on the traditional religious practice of confession.

B. The Place of Faith and Science Illustrated in Christian Worship [9]

The worship of God or the gods is the oldest traditional religious practice in the world, and there is no doubt as to the value of this practice for integrating the human personality given two things—the worthiness of the object of worship and the psychological soundness of the worshipper's approach.

No doubt, in the earliest days the motive of worship was terror: the fear of the mysterious and supernatural, and of the evil that supernatural agencies could exert over human lives. Gradually added to fear was admiration: admiration of the majestic forces which Na-

[9] No attempt is being made here to discuss adequately the many problems involved in Christian Worship. The reader is referred to Evelyn Underhill's great book called *Worship* (Harper, 1937), E. R. Micklem's, *Our Approach to God— a Study in Public Worship* (Hodder and Stoughton, 1934), C. Anderson Scott's *The Church, its Worship and Sacraments*, and a book useful for its Bibliography as well as its Contents: *Methodist Worship in Relation to Free Church Worship*, by John Bishop (Epworth Press, 1950).

ture revealed. When admiration is added to fear, we have awe. Gradually the concept of love was added as it emerged as a "value," reaching its perfect expression in Christ. When love is added to awe, we have reverence. The reverence we express in modern worship is thus the sublimation of the fear of the savage. We should still "fear the Lord" in this sublimated way. In Christian worship we have an object, utterly worthy, the worship of God in Christ. We should have a profound objective reverence which is an approach psychologically sound, and thus, scientifically healthy.

We defined health, earlier in this book, as the harmonious relationship between every part of the self and its environment. Granted that man is body, mind and spirit, his complete health necessitates a harmonious relationship between his spirit and its environment which we call God.

Worship is the approach of man as he seeks to establish a harmonious relationship with God. The word "worship" means the recognition of that which is an object of worth. The word comes from an old English form meaning worth-ship. The word "worthy" has the same root. It is by ascribing to God the virtues on which man's values are based, that man builds these virtues into his own character and establishes the values as worth-while. When we express an emotion we strengthen it. When we admire a virtue we, to some extent, build it into our characters. Thus in worship, when we express the emotion of admiration for those qualities which God personifies, we are remade in His image, and the more we can look away from ourselves to Him, the more we benefit, paradoxical though this may sound. Worship is ruined if it is conceived as toadying, or using God for our ends.

Modern techniques of psychotherapy have shown, however, that a good deal of religious worship is unsound, for, instead of inspiring man to face the nature of reality, man has made the practice of his worship a flight from reality and a form of neurotic escapism. Such worship has not, therefore, made him stronger, but has encouraged his neurosis and made him less self-reliant and more dependent on others. In fact, religion is rightly suspect amongst many psychotherapists because, so far from healing man's neurosis, it has only exchanged one neurosis for another. It is certainly better for a neurotic to exchange his neurosis for one shared by so many others and containing so many healthy ideas and—given his worship develops—the possibility of the exclusion of the purely neurotic elements. But the trouble is that spurious religion is such a good counterfeit of the real thing that the patient accepts it as true worship, and never finds the real thing. Fur-

451

ther, he puts off the healthy person, who, looking at him, only sees in religion a sickly, egotistic escapism, reeking of neurosis, in which God is a means to the patient's neurotic ends. Real religion heals, for man is a means and God the end. Man looks away from self, and his being runs out to God until man forgets himself in the contemplation and service of God.

Real Christianity is perhaps the most heroic form of religion one can hold. The unfortunate thing is that a spurious Christianity encourages the neurotic to make of God a false image based only on his own neurotic needs, such as a projection of his own father, and where the relationship of child to father was unsound, the patient's religion is equally unsound. He merits the criticism of some schools of psychology which seek to show that the worshipper runs to God to escape the unpleasantness of facing life, just as in childhood's days he ran to his father whenever he was frightened or unhappy. Psychoanalytical techniques which reveal to the adult patient the persistence of his child-to-father relationship, and which lay bare the fears engendered during that relationship, appear to deflate the patient's religion, but they do good inasmuch as they are the only hope of his turning from a spurious religion to the real thing. It must be admitted that for thousands of people, and for tens of thousands who regard themselves as very devout, their "religion" is itself a neurosis. This point has been dealt with (see p. 407).

The writer, who has had charge of a busy church in London throughout the whole of the war period, has, again and again, noted the neurotic nature of the religion of a great many people. They have supposed that God would keep them safe from bombs. They have quoted to themselves comforting Psalms, written down several hundred years before Christ, in which God is regarded as a "high tower," or a "shield" or a "fortress." All these ideas about God are utterly false, if taken literally. They have no basis whatever in the revelation of the nature of God made by Jesus Christ, and one of the tasks which psychology and religion must both carry out is that of clarifying the nature of true religion and exposing, with the help of modern psychotherapy, those false attitudes to God which betray neurosis in those who adopt them.

There is another way in which modern psychotherapy reveals the unsoundness of a good deal of devotional worship. We find the type of person who has almost a fanatical desire to observe every religious ordinance and to attend every possible religious service, turning on the wireless whenever the Religious Department of the B.B.C. is offering a talk or a service, without any advance in moral progress, without any change in spiritual understanding. Analytical technique goes to show that such people are compensating in their fanaticism for the repression of such instincts as sex and aggressiveness, which they have never faced, but which they have forced down into the unconscious, only allowing those unconscious factors a symbolic form of manifestation in adherence to worship. The value of going to many services as a compensation for repressed guilt is obvious to any psychologist.

Yet another way in which worship has become psychologically unsound is that individuals attend who never intend to join the fellowship and belong to the beloved community. They seek a private gain to their own little souls, and respond to no challenge to give to the community except during the collection. The Church can never be strong, indeed it is not in truth the Church at all, if it is only a congregation of units. True worship is never reached by gathering a miscellaneous crowd and getting them all to sing the same hymns and listen to the same words. True worship is, at its best, an offering to God on the part of a beloved community united in the love of God and the service of man. As Dr. W. R. Matthews, Dean of St. Paul's, writes, "If our Christian Churches were more truly fellowships in the spirit of Christ, we could more effectively supplement the healing work of the psychologists, for we could then give to the mind released from illness or evil, the continual support of loving and understanding companionship." [10] Such a fellowship has power, even healing power, as any minister knows who, in his ministry to individuals, feels himself to be only the spearhead of a praying and united church which is the strong arm thrusting the spear of his activities home, however privately the minister may be ministering to the needs, physical, mental and spiritual, of some lonely person.

Religious insight to which is added psychological understanding should co-operate to make the act of worshipping God the integrating force in the life of the community which it could become. Worship which frequently exaggerates in the neurotic an already over-inflated sense of guilt could involve sufficient introspection to make the extrovert look within at his own sins and thus avoid repression, and sufficient objectivity to make the introvert look without and see God and adore Him in all His glory, without coming to rash conclusions that God's chief end is to protect man—and especially the individual neurotic—from all pain and make him happy for ever. Worship could free man from guilt—a thing psychology, as such, cannot deal with, as we

[10] *Psychology and Modern Problems*, edited by J. A. Hadfield (University of London Press).

have seen—and send him out with a passion for service to others which would free his religion from neurotic elements.

Unfortunately, all the denominations of Christianity fall below the ideal, and this is not the place to diagnose and discuss the alleged failure of the Churches.[11] Gradually, by the use of beauty, including good music and great architecture and art; by preaching honest convictions and showing the relevance of Christianity to everyday living; by showing that the Church has a concern for body, mind and spirit, and, above all, by emphasising God's unfailing, unconditional love, the worship of God in His Church will take its place as one of the great integrating and healing factors in the life of the world.

C. The Place of Faith and Science Illustrated in Asceticism

Psychotherapeutic technique has an obvious bearing on the traditional religious practice of ascetism. By means of the latter, the ascetic seeks to become the master of his body and his bodily appetites, but he often does it by a method which is psychologically unhealthy. That is to say, he seeks to repress into the unconscious mind such things as sex and aggression. Modern psychotherapy would point out that that is highly dangerous, since the repressed desires and emotions live on within the deep mind, and will find some way of breaking out, and in doing so will produce conflict and neurosis.

One of the most frequent causes of so-called "nervous breakdown" is the conflict between the super-ego and the id, and here the super-ego is being built up by the pious practices of the ascetic, but the id is given no scope at all for expression.

What some of the ascetics went through as they pursued a practice which was laudable, but which we now see to have been very unhealthy, is glimpsed in the narratives of the saints themselves. Thus St. Jerome who went out into the desert to overcome his sensual desires, writes:

"How often when I was living in the desert, which affords to hermits a savage dwelling-place . . . did I fancy myself amid the pleasures of Rome! I, who from the fear of hell had consigned myself to that prison where scorpions and wild beasts were my companions, fancied myself among bevies of young girls. My face was pale and my frame chilled from fasting, yet my mind was burning with the cravings of desire, and the fires of lust flared up from my flesh."

[11] Cyril H. Valentine, in *The Treatment of Moral and Emotional Difficulties* has some valuable comments on the psychological reformation of church services which is urgently needed (Macmillan, 1938).

Modern psychological technique would show that the mastery which the ascetics sought cannot satisfactorily or healthily be reached by the attempt to repress desire into the unconscious, never wholly successful and, if partially successful, never satisfactory, but by the healthy and glad acceptance in consciousness of such elements as sex desires. They are God-given, but, like other forces in nature, they must be understood, controlled and directed to the highest ends of personality.

There is here a distinction which it is most important to make and which religionists have so often overlooked. Even such a writer as Dean Inge writes:

"Psychologists are talking of the evil of repression, and practically suggesting that the healthy life is one that gives full rein to all its instincts and impulses, and does what it likes. There Christianity, whatever form it takes, must give a firm answer. If this idea is right, then all Christian moralists and old moralists, like Plato, are wrong."

Such a confusion between psychology and religion would not arise if the religionist understood his psychology correctly. By repression we mean a refusal to recognise consciously, a purposeful, but often unwitting, refusal which thrusts the repressed matter into the unconscious part of the mind, where control over it is lost. Dean Inge confuses repression and self-control. No one is saying that all the activities of the id should find their expression in man's behaviour. Many of these must be controlled for the sake of society as well as ourselves. What is being said is that they must be recognised and dealt with by the conscious mind. The confusion would not have arisen if the difference had been noted between repression and suppression. By repression is meant the unwitting but purposeful thrusting of material into the unconscious. By suppression is meant the conscious control of the forces of the id. To clarify the matter in one sentence, the opposite of suppression is expression; the opposite of repression is recognition.[12]

Modern psychological technique would thus show the traditional religious practice of asceticism as unsound (a) if it involves the labelling of instinctive desires as *of themselves* evil, and (b) if it sanctions their subsequent repression into the unconscious.

It may be added that there is such a thing as a healthy asceticism. Western forms of religion know little of it, and the yogis, sanniyasis and the fakirs of the East are lightly regarded as cranks in the materialistic West. Yet my own view is that the East has an enormous amount to teach the West about the discipline of the devotional life, the power

[12] I have discussed repression and how it may be avoided in *Psychology and Life* (Abingdon-Cokesbury, 1935).

of the mind and of the soul, and of the reality and importance of the spiritual world. It would be a tragic and unpardonable mistake if our enthusiasm for what *we* call Christianity blinded us to the truth in other religions. God has not left Himself without witness in any of them, and no religion can be regarded as final unless it honours and includes the truth in every religion. In my opinion the truth is that the final form of Christianity has not yet emerged. Our Western interpretation of Christ is only part of it. We only see that part of Christ visible to Western eyes. The real Saviour of the world implicit in the Gospels will come into view only when all races pool their insights and all religious systems add their colour of the spectrum. Then the white light of truth will shine out as the Sun and all men wonder at its glory and power.

THE MODERN SEARCH FOR HEALING THROUGH PSYCHOLOGY AND RELIGION

THE NEEDS OF THE INTEGRATED
PERSONALITY

BEFORE WE CONSIDER what can be done in the fields of religion and psychology by co-operative methods aimed at healing, it seems important to hold in the mind the goal at which such co-operation aims. Let us look, then, briefly at the needs of the integrated personality.

(i) The maximum physical health attainable. Man should part for ever with the idea that sickness or disease is the inscrutable will of God, that He *sends* it in order to discipline man, and that resignation is the attitude of mind required of us. God created the body to be the perfect instrument of the spirit. It cannot be His will that it should function imperfectly, or that man should assent to disease without doing everything possible to attain health. God's primary will is perfect health. It may be that man cannot yet attain this. Adequate help may not be available. His own efforts may fail to restore health. All his religious efforts may not bring health, and that through no fault of his own; for, as we have seen, man can have faith without healing, and healing of the body without faith. St. Paul himself could cure others,[1] but he appears to have remained a sick man to the end of his days, though he continually prayed for health and regarded his malady as "a messenger of Satan."[2] In such a case man must endeavour so to react to illness as to win spiritual triumph from it. It is the *secondary* will of God that he should do so; by which is meant the will of God in the circumstances of evil which have overtaken him and from which he cannot immediately escape. In this sense, suffering can "discipline" man. Good comes out of evil. But it seems most important to say that the primary will of God, His ideal intention, is

[1] Acts 28:8.
[2] II Corinthians 12:7-10.

459

perfect bodily health, and that anything less—though often far from being man's fault—is a temporary victory of evil. As St. Paul said, we are to glorify God in our bodies, and present them as living sacrifices, holy (= whole, healthy) acceptable to God.[3] If suffering of mind or body is a good thing; if *only* through suffering can saintliness be reached, we have no right to try to cure it. Jesus regarded suffering as the work of evil forces in the universe, and set all His powers toward their defeat.[4] We must do the same. The Christian Scientists confuse us when they talk of pain having no reality, but they are right in denying it the same kind of reality as health. For health is something that ought to be. Disease is something that ought not to be. It cannot have the positive reality of good, for as God's will is done it will be excluded and will disappear, while health or wholeness abides for ever.

When we talk of the saints being perfected through suffering, it would show clearer thinking to say that it was by their reaction to suffering that they achieved saintliness.[5] Many of the saints were unhealthy neurotics though to say that is not to question their sincerity. Self-torture and the extremities of asceticism are not the way to sainthood. Prof. Rufus Jones wrote as follows: "I see now what a large pathological factor there has been in the lives of many mystics. . . . So far as pathological trails persisted, as they too often did, they were a liability and a handicap, not an asset. *It has been by the highway of health rather than over the bridge of disease that the largest freight of truth has come to us.*" [6] No one is free to blame another for being ill. Illness most frequently comes to us not as personal penalty, but from the ignorance, folly or sin of the great human family to which we belong. We get the family assets, and must often bear its liabilities. But God ever seeks to replace ignorance with knowledge, folly with wisdom and sin with holiness, and we must co-operate with Him by striving for these substitutions and do all we know to keep the body as fit as we can. Said a great Christian teacher to me, "It is not wicked to be ill, but it is wicked to be more ill than you need be."

I must not write here about the place of exercise, fresh air, suitable food, hobbies, a wise use of leisure, the value of sufficient sleep, or of the ministrations of the physician, the surgeon, the dental surgeon, the masseur and so on. All play their part in producing that health of body with which man can offer to God a maximum usefulness.

[3] I Corinthians 6:20; Romans 12:1; Philippians 1:20.
[4] Cf. Luke 13:16.
[5] See p. 227.
[6] Rufus Jones, *The Flowering of Mysticism,* pp. 5-6 (Macmillan, 1939).

(ii) The maximum mental health attainable. Much that has been written above applies *mutatis mutandis* to the mind. Nor should it be overlooked that, though in this book I have repeatedly stressed the power of the mind over the body, the healthy body helps the mind to attain health. Many have found, for example, that learning progressively to relax the body has helped them to relax the mind.[7] Most people have revelled in the mental peace which a long walk in the country or a swim in the sea, or the right kind of "occupational therapy" can bring. The mind seems to need also the ministry of beauty. One of my friends used to take with him on his travels, and even prop up in a hotel bedroom, a copy of some favourite picture; for, he said, the beauty composed and soothed his mind and made it ready for sleep. Great music has been proved, again and again, a balm for distressed minds. Great literature can take a harassed mind out of its troubles and bring to it the calm it needs in order to get those troubles into a truer perspective. For many, books about simple country life have a great power to soothe. They are a second-best for the town-dweller, who only imaginatively is free to live in the country. It is worth a lot of trouble to discover what can most quickly and effectively bring a measure of peace to the mind. The drama, the concert, the cinema and the dance have their place. Having some kind of fun and recreation is essential. Above all, a true friendship is a fundamental need, for the mind needs love and appreciation as the body needs food and fresh air. Some find it in marriage, but that is not essential. Friendship was necessary even to Christ. "He appointed twelve, *that they might be with Him.*" [8]

The mind seems most healthy when it feeds on truth, when it gets its due measure of affection and is believed in, and when goodwill *toward* others is practised as a constant habit, and goodwill *from* others is attracted by virtue and love. The mind then is at home in its environment, or, in other words, in harmonious correspondence with it. Dr. Dicks, a well-known psychiatrist in Leeds, used to say that mental health "consists in the protection and development at all levels of human society of secure, affectionate and satisfying human relationships, and in the reduction of hostile tensions in persons and

[7] Three valuable books may be commended here. *Release from Nervous Tension*, David Harold Fink, M.D. (Simon and Schuster, 1943), *You Must Relax*, Edmund Jacobson, M.D. (McGraw, 1942), and last, but not least, R. W. Trine's *In Tune with the Infinite* (Bobbs, 1942).

[8] Mark 3:14.

groups. It is the championship of love and the elimination of hate in human affairs." [9]

As with the body, it is our duty to keep the mind as healthy as we can, and if it is distressed by fears we cannot understand, by irrational reactions to stimuli which we know to be trivial, by obsessions which drive us where we do not want to go, by unbearable tensions and irritations which make life intolerable, by depressions which land us in a despair whose cause we cannot identify and from which nothing we do can deliver us, it is a wise thing to get the help of a psychiatrist, and just as reasonable a thing to do as to seek the help of a physician of the body concerning some malady with which we cannot cope by ourselves. It may be that the trouble is not in the conscious mind, but is bubbling up, as from the bottom of a deep pool, from the depths of the unconscious to which we have no direct access, and where, perhaps, some conflict rages, or some unhealthy emotion, quite unknown to us, suppurates, sending symptoms into consciousness, but concealing their cause from our scrutiny. In that case we need skilled psychotherapeutic treatment, just as we need a dentist for a difficult extraction. Many people are scared of psychological treatment and think there is something shameful in submitting to it. But, of course this is no more true about psychotherapy than dentistry.

Apart altogether, however, from mending a sick mind, is the vital matter of building up a sound one. Integration is a slow process, and it proceeds in the main below the levels of consciousness. It is the ideas that drop into the deep mind that determine integration or disintegration. Here we note the importance and value of the sound elements in Christian Science, the stubborn refusal to harbour negative ideas like hate, resentment, jealousy and illness, and the determination to harbour and fill the whole mind, conscious and unconscious, with thoughts of health and love and trust.

Here we see also the value and soundness of such books as Trine's *In Tune with the Infinite*, such schools of thought as Mr. Hamblin's as evidenced in his books and his monthly magazine, the Coué system, and many others to which praise is due, which guide people to eschew negative thoughts and fill the mind with positive ones. Indeed, the Greek tense suggests that we should translate St. Paul's famous words as follows: Whatever is true, or worthwhile, or just, or pure, or attractive, or high-minded, *keep on thinking* about these things.[10] And remembering how easily our last thoughts at night slip into the

[9] I owe this quotation to my friend, Alfred Torrie, M.A., M.B., Ch.B., D.P.H., D.P.M.

[10] Philippians 4:8.

462

unconscious, it is well to remember another sentence of the same great teacher, "Never let the sun set upon your exasperation." [11] It is important for integration that our last thoughts at night and first in the morning should be positive, healthy ideas of love and trust and confidence. Thus we build up an integrated personality. "By faithful reiteration," said Dr. Henry Knight Miller, "build into your mind those qualities you desire to express in your life, thoughts of love, health, happiness, success and power. These thoughts are the raw material with which Mind, the Master-Builder, the God-Power within, constructs or reconstructs your life. Give the Builder evil material and the house he builds will be of sand. It will fall. Give the Builder good material and the house not made with hands will withstand all the storms and ravages of time; firm, strong and unyielding as the Rock of Gibraltar."

(iii) The maximum spiritual health attainable. If I wrote that no one can be completely healthy without some communion with God, I should be disbelieved. Many would point to the healthy pagans who never pray or meditate or worship, and yet who look, and believe themselves to be, in perfect health. Yet I hold that the sentence is true. If my definition of health—as the harmonious correspondence of personality at all points with the relevant environment (p. 311)—be accepted, it will be seen to be true. Many who have some physical disablement are regarded as perfectly healthy in that they are not *conscious* of any hindrance. Indeed, some killing diseases leave their victim quite unconscious that anything is wrong until it is too late. Presumably a man born blind does not attach meaning to the word "sight," and only vaguely wonders why people pity him because he cannot drive a car or see a sunset. Many who attach no meaning to the word "God" are not conscious of lack or dis-ease. Yet perfect health must surely mean the perfect functioning of *all* our powers, not only of body and mind, but that function of man's non-physical nature which we call the soul and which makes man potentially capable of communion with God.

Notably many touch God in their sense of beauty, and God is touching their nature through its many forms, or through human love and friendship, even when they never consciously own His existence. Even so, I would say that *maximum* health of spirit demands some form of worship, and worship, when it is true communion with God, has again and again proved to have won, as a by-product, increased

[11] Ephesians 4:26 (Moffatt).

health for the worshipper.[12] Many who complain of their restlessness will fly to the doctor and the psychologist, when what they really hunger for is only to be found in God. Indeed, since man is a unity, it is not surprising to find that the hunger and frustration of the spirit are reflected in symptoms both of the body and the mind. And though the imperfections of the forms of worship with which they are familiar—and which may have turned them from religion—may not be able to supply that for which they seek, they must, indeed, be odd if none of the denominations can appease their longing or help them to find the true God.

By healing, then, is meant the process of restoring the broken harmony which prevents personality, at any point of body, mind or spirit, from its perfect functioning in its relevant environment; the body in the material world; the mind in the realm of true ideas and the spirit in its relationship with God.

Physical remedies and treatments are of immense value. Psychotherapy has opened up a new field through which many distressed folk have found healing. But both together cannot of themselves integrate personality, for neither can relate it to reality. One of the healthiest moments of a man's life is the moment in which, even though it be through utter despair, or through the persistence of a restlessness which can find no other satisfaction, he turns himself towards God and begins to quest for the One who all his life has been seeking him. Indeed, man's restlessness is the sign of that search. I know no wiser and no truer words in the world than the well-known words of St. Augustine: "Inquietum est cor nostrum donec requiescat in Te!" Unquiet is our heart until it rests in Thee.

It remains to be said that we must not separate man into body, mind and spirit as though he could be integrated piece-meal. One of the greatest needs of personality is to be loved. In an ideal marriage, love proves to be an integrating force which seems to do all that needs to be done, and body, mind and spirit all benefit. The whole personality flowers in a loveliness that is as beautiful as it is rare. Others, denied marriage, so love their fellows that love comes back to them and brings them a sense of harmony and power. Marriage and physical love are not essential to integration, though the latter is harder without them. We saw that the life deprived of love fell ill for that reason (p. 343), but many of the saints have found integration without marriage.

---

[12] Appendix IV to this book describes the case of a man who believed himself to be an incurable invalid and who was in constant and often severe pain. He was cured through listening to a service broadcast over the radio.

We saw also that a sense of guilt, conscious or unconscious, disintegrates the personality (p. 316). Clearly, a need of the integrated personality is a mind at peace with all men and with God. The forgiveness of man and the forgiveness of God, the surrender of those unhealthy emotions like resentment, jealousy and hate, which we saw to be causative of illness both of body and mind, as well as spirit, and their replacement by love and goodwill, are necessary to that harmony of being we call integration.

Perhaps the personality is most fully integrated in those people whose lives are devoted to one all-consuming altruistic purpose in which bodily powers, mental energies—including all the instincts and all the healthy emotions—and spiritual aspirations find their full expression. I think of some mothers of whom this seems true, but also of some rare souls cut off from what many deem the needs of the integrated personality, who have successfully sublimated instincts which could find no legitimate biological expression.

Further, modern psychology would certainly underline the words of Christ that by loving his own life, with a self-absorption which concentrates all his energies on himself, man misses the very goal he is seeking. "He that loveth his life shall lose it." It is, indeed, more than likely that a man who sets himself the very task of self integration, paying attention to his physical health, guarding his mind from every contact that might upset its serenity, seeking his soul's salvation by a devotional discipline that never drives him out to help other people, will become disintegrated in the very task of self-integration. He may appear integrated, but it will be about an insecure centre. The self as the centre means disintegration sooner or later, for the soul is cut off from its environment. The maximum integration is attainable only by those souls in whose being there is a harmony consummated by altruistic service to the world. Withdrawal from reality by the psyche at any point spells disharmony.

All branches of the Christian Church agree that conversion is the way, from the religious side, to integration of personality. Unfortunately it cannot be engineered by man in cold blood. Preaching aims at securing those conditions in which it happens. It is to be received. It cannot even be deserved or won. It is a gift of God in response to man's need and willingness by which God through Christ by His Spirit makes us one with Himself. We may note William James' definition of conversion: It is "the process, gradual or sudden, by which a self hitherto divided and consciously wrong, inferior and unhappy, becomes unified and consciously right, superior and happy, in consequence of its firmer hold on religious realities." [13]

It is obvious that few people are perfectly integrated. Perhaps Christ is the only perfect Example to which we can point. But it is obvious also that the art of healing in the future must hold this goal in view. Man must not have his body treated as though mind and spirit were separate from it and uninfluenced by it. As Dr. Cyril Burt said, "Man is not a potential corpse to which a ghost is loosely attached." He must be seen, by all who care for his health, as a unity of body-mind-spirit. The vision of doctor, psychologist and minister must extend to see him thus.

Thus—since integration is a process—may man be increasingly freed from bodily disease, mental distortion and spiritual lack of response. He may rise to the full stature of manhood in Christ, as Paul would have put it, and enter a heritage of health and power and joy which as yet he has not even glimpsed. These puny and ailing bodies, these dull and listless minds, these blind, indifferent spirits do not represent God's intention. It does not yet appear what men will be. But they will not be the slaves they are now. They will be princes and kings. We have a long way to go, but the achievement of a healthy, radiant, serene and powerful manhood and womanhood is the possibility of the future and the purpose of God.

[13] William James, *op. cit.*

2

PASTORAL AND MEDICAL CO-OPERATION

WE SAW IN Chapter I of the first section of this book that in the earliest days of the art of healing the priest was the doctor and the doctor was the priest.

We noted the cleavage between the two professions and some of the causes of it. Perhaps these causes could be summarised by saying that the priest lost faith and the doctor found science.

The question I want to ask in this chapter, and towards which I want to contribute an answer, is this: Has the time come when the two professions should seek to draw near together again at certain points and in certain ways? At any rate, the priest—using the words, for the moment, to connote the ministers of all religious denominations —has, generally speaking, acquired an interest in the science of psychology. It is now taught in all theological colleges. And the doctors— or, at least, the most far-seeing medical writers—are awake to the importance of non-physical factors in the art of healing and the importance of the state of mind of the patient. This is a path that leads directly to religion. The priest is turning with a new interest to science, and the doctor with a new respect to faith.

In America students for the ministry can take a psychological course which includes attendance at a mental hospital and, under the guidance of a consultant, actual charge of certain cases. In at least one London hospital the stated duties of the chaplain are: "To visit and make himself acquainted with the patients and with their spiritual difficulties and to collaborate with the Medical Staff under the direction of the Medical Superintendent in cases where it appears he can assist in restoring a patient's mental and spiritual health." The chaplain has a weekly meeting with the Medical Superintendent and cases are commended to his care both then and through individual doctors. The

467

chaplain has full access to case sheets in which mention may be made of religious factors. It is generally agreed by the Medical Staff that the chaplain can help most, either when the patient first comes into hospital, or after the medical treatment is concluded.

If the argument of this book is sound, then some positions are established which would have been scorned only a few years ago. For instance, it is established that a seemingly physical illness can be precipitated by an emotional condition, perhaps of worry, injustice or fear, that the same is true of *some* skin affections, *some* peptic ulcers, and, it may be, some diseases now thought to be as wholly physiogenic, as dermatitis was a hundred years ago.

It is now established that about thirty per cent of the patients in the wards of our hospitals are there through neurosis of one kind or another. Their persistent headache, insomnia, fatigue and depression, etc., are often caused by emotional conflicts functioning deep in the unconscious parts of their minds.

It is established that guilt feelings, repressed into the unconscious, or even consciously known; the deprivation of love, the long-continued harbouring in the mind, without expression or recognition, of such emotions as hate, resentment, jealousy and exaggerated fear; a heart that will not forgive and a spirit that will not receive forgiveness; a long-continued conflict between desire and conscience, which is a rough, but not inaccurate, way of speaking of the conflict between the id and the super-ego, can set up conditions that rob the mind of its peace and the body of its powers.

It is further established that even where an illness is wholly physiogenic, the attitude of mind of the patient is an important factor. His recovery will be retarded if his mind is full of resentment, bitterness, depression or despair, or the thought that God is punishing him for some past sin. It will be accelerated if he is optimistic and cheerful, and regards his illness, so far from being the will of God, as being his share of the world's burden of communal ignorance, folly or sin, which God, also, in some sense bears. The patient will not, in the long run, think his illness unfair if he grasps the thought that the world is arranged by God on a family basis, so that, using daily the assets of the family for our delight, we must all sometimes share its liabilities in terms of illness and even death, knowing that the latter is only a milestone on life's journey and cannot frustrate the divine purposes.

Now, if the above paragraphs do really represent what is established, the place of the scientist is obvious. In disease wholly physiogenic, the realm of the doctor is pre-eminent. Yet, even there, in view of the last paragraph, the right kind of minister has a place. He can minister immensely to the patient's morale, and possibly find an entry for the Spirit of God in a heart hitherto closed to Him.

In disease that has a psychogenic origin, the role of the medically trained psychotherapist is pre-eminent, but when he has brought to the surface of consciousness, say, a guilty memory, the ministry of the right kind of pastor can be of immense value, as I tried to show at the end of the section on guilt.

In view of the fact, increasingly recognised in such work as that of Weiss, English and Dunbar, that an unhealthy emotion lies behind so much disease, what might be done if a patient could be brought to open his nature to the tides of the love of God, the healthiest of all emotions, *and shown exactly just how to do that?*

I hazard the opinion, after much thought, that such streams of love poured from our Lord's personality that while many would hate Him —as some men do hate the one who incarnates love—and while many would be indifferent to Him, and produce some armour to protect them against love's assault, those who let their minds be invaded by such a love as His would find the unconscious assaulted also. Even though it is true that the unconscious is not *directly* accessible to the conscious mind, there must be a way into the unconscious through the conscious, or the whole idea of conscious auto-suggestion would be meaningless, instead of which Coué and others have shown it to be full of power. It is not incredible to me that in such a case all unhealthy emotion, all conflict that was unresolved through false choices, all guilty dread, would be swept out of even the depths of the mind by a love so powerful, desirable and cleansing.

If only we were like Him we could cure the sick—not all, but many —in the same direct way. There is no reason on His side why many of the healing miracles of the Gospels and the Acts should not be repeated. And there must be a direct way for us. The Apostles knew no science.

I have written much of psychological mechanisms, and there must be a point at which any energy from without, even the love of Christ in the days of His flesh, engaged the psychological machinery—as it were—but there is a difference in kind between the slow, limping ways of psychological treatment today and the direct and often immediate cures which He and His disciples wrought; between the energies we can release by psychology and the energies He released through love. It is as though some feeble electric current passed through a mechanism and *just* turned the wheels of some vehicle so that it reached at last its terminus, and then someone was found who, using the same machinery and apparatus, sent a current of immense energy through the mechanism and enabled the vehicle to arrive at the point we call perfect health in a few moments. As far as we know, none of Christ's cures took a long time, though I admit that an argument from Biblical silence is suspect.

It seems to me of immense importance to remember that the human personality is not just a machine, like a motor-car, but a machine controlled by a driver. Much can be done on what I shall call the garage-level. If a man breaks his leg, or, to use my favourite illustration, has a thorn in the foot, *the* most important treatment is on the garage-level, and all honour to the skilled doctors and surgeons who can deal so expertly with the machine we call the body on that garage-level.

But the human being is like a motor-car driven by a driver who is frequently inexpert. The efficiency of a car can be ruined by bad driving. A car is constructed to work well so long as the driver follows certain simples rules including the task of keeping the car on the road! How often the body is really in good order, but the psyche—the driver—either through ignorance, folly or sin, drives so badly that we are held up by the body, often in life's busiest traffic. How often the car (personality) is choked by hate or resentment, guilt or fear, though often, indeed usually, the driver (the spirit of man) does not know what is happening, and what was a smooth-running engine runs badly and sometimes breaks down. Healing, therefore, must deal not only with the car, but also with the driver. And, since the driver is an immortal spirit driving to an eternal destination, the minister of religion has a place in dealing with his success or faliure.

"Disease, as we understand it," says Dr. A. E. Clark-Kennedy, "must be due to genetic faults, adverse factors in environment, *or the way in which a man uses his mind*, or to some combination of these three factors." [1]

Consider first the part of the minister of religion in co-operative healing work.

1. From what has been said above, it may be already obvious that much depends on our standard of life. All Christian people are called upon to base their lives on Christ's. But ministers have a fearful responsibility here. One knows from the pressure and failures of one's own life how easy it is, in the multitudinous demands made upon one, to let spiritual discipline go. Again and again the minister knows that he could have helped X or Y if, when they sought his help, his own spiritual potential had been at a higher level. Clearly, if even Christ needed

---

[1] A. E. Clark-Kennedy, M.D., F.R.C.P., Dean of the Medical School of the London Hospital, in an article on "The Patient and His Disease," *Lancet*, December 2, 1950. (Italics mine.)

time for solitude and prayer and self-discipline, that He might keep that potential high, those who work in His name cannot do without it.

The task of listening hour after hour to the story of another's troubles is, perhaps, the most exacting and exhausting way of spending time. Especially is this true of the sensitive listener. It can even be alarming, for fear is infectious, and the story of depression, grief and sin can depress the listener.

To some extent the listener must put himself alongside the one who tells his woes, and a measure of sympathy must be extended. If there is no sympathy in the relationship, the story will halt and limp and then stop. It is very hard for some people to tell their story.

But the minister must not identify himself too closely in terms of emotion with the person who seeks his aid, or the latter will pull the minister down into the pit from which deliverance is being sought in the interview. There will be two depressed, or even defeated, people instead of one. The kind of interview envisaged is emotionally intimate. A story may be told which has been locked up in another personality for years. If the minister is not careful he will find his own personality emotionally invaded: a process so exhausting that he may be rendered unfit to give the maximum help. However sympathetic and sensitive he may be, the minister, so to put it, must stay on the edge of the pit, with only a rope of understanding attached to the one he seeks to help. Then, gradually, he can pull the troubled soul out of the pit of despair. Otherwise the minister's very sympathy may render him useless to help another.

But this kind of work should surely have priority over many things the minister has to do. What attendance at committees, making sermons and speeches, addressing meetings, or the routine of visiting the healthy, can be called more important than the private interview in which some burdened soul pours out his troubles and fears, his worries and anxieties, and shows to the minister's sympathetic gaze the tangle his life has become and from which he cannot see any way out?

Again and again the minister forgets that the mere act of sympathetically listening to a troubled person and avoiding giving him the impression that one is terribly busy and longing to get on with more important business, will give him vast relief.

2. The more psychology the minister knows, the better, but the present writer would suggest that it is a mistake for the minister to be in any real sense a practising psychotherapist. Half a dozen interviews, in my opinion, represent about the maximum which any one person should have allotted to him or her, when one remembers all the other claims on a minister's time and strength. If more time than this is

needed, I advise that the case be referred to a Christian medical psychiatrist whom the minister can recommend with confidence.

For one thing, any success in the matter of psychotherapy will bring so many people that the minister will soon be overwhelmed with cases whom he finds it hard, and sometimes heartless, to refuse, and those cases will so swamp his time that he will find himself in the position of giving most of his time to those who have no claim on him and a minimum to those who pay him his salary. His psychotherapy will take the whole of his time and strength.

If he wants it to do this, it would be better to take a medical degree and the Diploma of Psychological Medicine and regard that— as, indeed, it can so appropriately be regarded—as a Christian vocation.

But simple psychotherapeutic conversations can be of great value to people. So Dr. T. A. Ross, in his book, *The Common Neuroses*, writes: [2] "His case needed only free discussion for the symptoms to be dissipated." So also Dr. Maurice Nicoll writes: "Anyone who understands analytical methods, and through them has gained insight into the nature of neurotic trouble, can help neurotics without submitting them to analytical treatment. . . . Any form of treatment that gives them some adequate explanation will be of use to them. A good transference and a suitable explanation will effect great relief in many cases." [3]

All students for the ministry of the Church should, before ordination, receive sufficient psychological training to enable them to diagnose psychopathological conditions. In suitable cases the training should be extended to some work—of observation and instruction, at least—in a big mental hospital, where early psychoses could be seen. In some places, notably in America, a beginning has been made. Americans are far ahead of us in their ideas and methods for training their ministers of religion. Dr. Helen Flanders Dunbar has kindly sent me particulars of the work done by the Council for the Clinical Training of Theological Students, of which she was the Director. This Council had done five years of experimental work by 1930, and now provides students for the ministry with opportunities to obtain clinical experience "in dealing with infirmities of mankind." The Governing Board consists of physicians (representing both general medicine and psychiatry) and clergymen of various communions. In twelve training-centres, including State prisons, child-guidance clinics, mental and general hospitals, the Council Staff and its advisers supervise the clinical training of theological students irrespective of denomination. Case work, actual

[2] Longmans, 1923.

[3] *Functional Nerve Disease*. Ed. Dr. Hugh Crichton Miller (Oxford, 1920).

472

work in hospital wards, conferences with physicians and psychiatrists, social workers, etc., give the would-be minister a chance to learn about human problems not from textbooks, but from life. A course of three months in a mental hospital, two months in a prison-centre, two in a general hospital and three in a child-guidance clinic—and this is the course proposed—should equip a minister to deal with the problems he will have to meet.

Psychological training and insight help a minister, in perhaps six or seven interviews of an hour each, to straighten out some people's troubles. If the minister has been "analysed," so much the better, though I do not advise analysis for all ministers. There are behaviour-tangles, sexual morasses into which people fall, mild anxiety-states which yield to the advice of one who perceives their real nature, and so on. It is sad to think that the doctor himself often does not know what to prescribe. He prescribes bromides and barbiturates. The minister suggests prayer and faith, and the patient falls between them, for neither prescription effectively avails. Neither is the relevant way of co-operating with God for this type of patient.

Psychological training is useful, above all, in that it helps the minister to know when a person seeking his help should become a patient undergoing psychological treatment. It helps the minister in child-guidance and marriage-guidance work, which will surely fall to him.

3. In the writer's opinion, the ideal is to form a clinic working on the lines suggested in the next chapter. But this is not often possible. It may be possible, however, to discover in the neighbourhood one or more dependable psychiatrists. If not, let the minister do the best he can, even if it only amounts to getting hold of a general practitioner not hostile to psychological interpretations of illness and not hostile to religion. Discussion together on certain cases is desirable, and, if it comes to the dilemma of the patient being altogether unhelped, or the minister trying his hand, then I think that, granted medical supervision, and granted that the minister's dealing with the patient does not outrun his understanding, then the patient will benefit, and no harm will be done.

4. The minister could also do a public service and co-operate with the doctor by lecturing and preaching on some aspects of religion and psychology. The horror of psychological illness is partly due to the fact that the patient feels that no one understands. To make people realise that neurosis is a very common illness and can be treated and cured, takes the horror and loneliness away. Further, a person familiar with psychological ideas will more readily seek treatment if he needs it himself. If he has never heard of such treatment, he will take much

more persuading to undergo it. During treatment a minister can give much help to a psychologist by reassuring the patient that he is not wasting time or money, and that all is going well.

5. It is important that the minister should not ape the doctor. When the minister visits the sick, he should not discuss with the patient his medical treatment, let alone criticise his doctor, or what the doctor has suggested. Let the minister have an "interview room" or a "study," but not a "consulting room," and speak of his "people," not his "patients." Doctors are irritated by such practices.

6. It is good that marriage-guidance bureaux are being organised in numerous places. Here the minister and doctor can often co-operate. Here the point of not trespassing on the physical sphere of the doctor, or pretending to be a doctor, is important.

7. The minister has one great opportunity which he should try not to miss. He is the only professional person who has entry to a home without being summoned. If equipped with some psychological insight and a real lover of his people, he could often spot neurotic situations before they land people in neurosis. The young male lodger who is slowly getting emotionally entangled with his young landlady; the first child of a marriage being pushed into inferiority by a younger arrival; the ordinary sensitive child pushed into inferiority by a brilliant brother or sister; the "in-laws" who stay too long; the "granny" who makes bringing up a child so difficult; the daughter who, frankly, hates her mother and dare not show it; the elderly man, mentally, if not physically, unfaithful to his wife—all give scope to the minister who has enough friendship, authority, insight and tact to deal with these situations before neurosis sets in, or who, ideally supported by a co-operating doctor, dare insist on breaking up some situations even after neurosis has shown itself.

There are some cases in which psychological treatment is not indicated, but where a young daughter, for example, living at home with a hysterical and neurotic mother, should be pressed to take a situation in another town, without being allowed to feel "disloyal" or accused of "forsaking the old home." She will recover from, or escape, neurosis. Some forms of the latter are very infectious. Many a man needs, not psycho-analysis, but a week-end once a month away from a nagging wife, and many a wife would return with avidity to her household, if she could escape it and have a week with an old school or college friend once every three months. A change of residence, even temporarily, a change of work, even so simple a thing as hard exercise, a changed pattern of living, a chance for God to sweeten and strengthen life, a new way of praying, more music, keeping a dog or a cat, some artistic work for the hands to do, an occasional dance, a review of the way leisure time is spent, a friendship cultivated, the fellowship or a live church—these things do not cost much money, but they can do much to prevent neurosis. Sometimes they prevent it altogether. And neurosis can be very distressing, and treatment very long and very costly. The minister should be the preventive officer of his people's health where he can, and be able to administer first aid to a mind distressed. He should charge no fees—though it is good for people who are helped to contribute to his church funds—but he will win men's gratitude, and there is nothing more rewarding in life than to feel that at the hour of men's need they did not turn to one in vain; that one's theology was sound, and that one's psychology enabled one to say the right things and—equally importantly—not to say the wrong things.

8. The minister is not to exploit the feelings of a sick person, nor to use the latter's fear of death or disablement in an unfair way; yet, I feel, there sometimes occurs a chance to talk to the patient about God and His ways with men, which only occurs at a time of illness. For myself, I have become aware of being so afraid of "upsetting" the patient that sometimes my visits to a sick room have had no more value than that of any other of the patient's friends. They have not been really *pastoral* visits at all, and I have felt afterwards that I have failed. I have sometimes felt that the patient also was disappointed in the visit. Ministers so hate the over-pious, "holy Willie," tract-distributing attitude that they sometimes fail in the opposite direction when a sick man really longed to talk about his sins and worries and fears, to make his peace with God and be reconciled with Him.

9. Prayer for the sick and the formation of prayer circles have been discussed already.

We turn now to the part of the doctor in co-operative work.

1. If the illness is definitely and without any shadow of doubt physiogenic, the doctor is right in not wanting any help in his own sphere from the minister. But he should, gladly and not begrudgingly, realise how much the minister can do to increase the patient's morale and speed his recovery. One would like to hear of greater readiness on the part of the doctor to tell the patient's relatives to be sure to summon the minister and to show that he—the doctor—does not merely *allow* the patient as a concession to see the minister, but advocates the pastoral visit and shows that, in his opinion, it is of real importance. One wishes, too, that in the hospital and nursing-home the doctor would give instruction that the minister must be allowed to visit at any reasonable time and—in hospital—have the screens round the bed if prayer or Holy Communion are required.

2. If the illness is psychogenic, the doctor and minister should find time to discuss the case. The minister may know things about the patient's home life, business worries and private concerns, about which the doctor knows little or nothing. Just as there are things a man will only tell his doctor, there are things he will only tell his minister. Further, some ministers have greater psychological insight than some doctors.

3. There is a reluctance on the part of the doctor to co-operate with the minister which I can understand.

(a) The doctor's own training has been long, scientific and exact. He so often finds in the minister a person in whose technical ability it is impossible to have much confidence. If the doctor is psychologically trained, he finds it hard to assess the minister's psychological "training." The training in the various ministerial denominational colleges is partly to blame. Too often the minister has "read a few books on psychology," and that is all his "training" amounts to. And he has probably chosen those books himself. Such a situation does not give a doctor much confidence in the demand for co-operation. The time has come when all theological colleges should grant a Diploma in Pastoral Psychology to ordinands who successfully complete a reasonably stiff course of study. Yet, I would plead with doctors to make an attempt at co-operation. So often a patient would take from a minister some liberating word which he would resent from the doctor—a word about God's forgiveness, for instance, in a case where a guilt-complex has been unearthed; the relief of exaggerated guilt in a case where a doctor has been consulted about masturbation; some word about life after death where grief has prostrated a victim and precipitated a neurosis.

Huxley once wrote as follows: "My work in the London Hospitals taught me that the preacher often does as much good as the doctor." Percy Dearmer remembered a house-surgeon saying that his best ally was the chaplain, because every patient felt better when he had been round the ward. I once heard a specialist say that the balance between life and death was often tilted down on the side of life by the timely visit of the right kind of minister.

In the psychological field, any unbiased person would listen to Dr. J. A. Hadfield. He writes: "I am convinced that the Christian religion is one of the most valuable and potent influences that we possess for producing that harmony and peace of mind and that confidence of soul which are needed to bring health and power to a large proportion of nervous patients. In some cases I have attempted to cure nervous patients with suggestions of quietness and confidence, but without success until I have linked these suggestions on to that faith in the power of God which is the substance of the Christian's confidence and hope. Then the patient has become strong." [4] Dr. David Yellowlees writes: "It is a matter of plain historical fact that religion in its highest manifestations gives not only peace of mind, but great and increasing powers of endurance, qualities in which the neurotic is sadly lacking." [5] Dr. William Brown, Wilde Reader in Mental Philosophy at Oxford University, writes: "I have become more convinced than ever that religion is the most important thing in life and that it is essential to mental health." [6] Dr. Henry Yellowlees, in his *Clinical Lectures on Psychological Medicine*,[7] says: "Psychology is not an art; it is only the hope of an art. It is waiting for a greater than Freud—not necessarily a greater genius, but certainly a greater, because a more complete, man. When he arises, the necessities of the case will make him what we should now call something of a mystic, because his chief work will be to connect scientific truth in some unimagined way with those great realities of experience, apart from which mental life is a mechanical rattle, and mental health an impossibility. He will relate the machinery of mind, as never before, to every fact of life and of experience. It may seem a hard thing to say of him, but I expect he will believe in God. Otherwise I cannot conceive how he will succeed in reaching across the gulf between science and mysticism, between symbol and reality. One can hardly imagine that that gulf may ever be bridged and the road run clear from knowledge of mind to understanding of life and of the mysteries that lie in and around and beyond it. But should it conceivably happen, then science will have achieved her supreme triumph, and one need set no limits to its possible results.

"One cannot readily picture the lines along which this great scientist will work, nor the discoveries he will make. We can be sure, however, that he will not be false to science as we know it, though he will so enlarge its vision and scope that it will become a means of apprehending truths at which now we can only guess. When I think about this new and great scientist, I like to remember that new truths sometimes have a way of turning out to be simply old ones, expressed from a different viewpoint and in words more suited to the time. Remembering this, I sometimes wonder whether the wheel might conceivably come full circle after all, and whether science's last and greatest discovery might possibly—just possibly—prove to be a restatement of some-

[4] *The Spirit*, ed. Canon Streeter (Macmillan, 1919).
[5] *Psychology's Defense of the Faith* (Harper, 1930).
[6] Quoted from Waterhouse, *Psychology and Religion* (Harper, 1931).
[7] P. 306 (J. and A. Churchill, 1932).

thing which was said by a great mystic long ago: that 'God created man for immortality, and hath set eternity in his heart.' "

But let the doctor also remember that fears as to *his* ability often arise in the mind of the minister. A medical training does not make a psychiatrist, and the minister, with whom he fears to co-operate, may have taken, say, a good degree in psychology and know far more on the theoretical side than the average general practitioner.

(*b*) The doctor may fear that his professional status among his medical colleagues is prejudiced by co-operation with the minister, and even that he risks action from the ethical committee of the British Medical Association by working with, or "covering," an unqualified person. He need have no fear. Not only has he the guarantee quoted already on p. 229 and printed in the *British Medical Journal* and the *Lancet*, but the following verdict on this point was published: "Having taken legal advice, the Committee was satisfied that, provided a practitioner handed over a patient to a non-medical psychotherapist in good faith, had conducted a physical examination, and had satisfied himself that the non-medical 'psychotherapist' had been adequately trained, and if he was prepared to exercise general supervision of the case, he need not fear disciplinary action by the General Medical Council for 'covering,' or any civil action for malpraxis." [8]

On the point of encouraging a layman to practice medicine, some words of the late Dr. Rathbone Oliver, a distinguished American psychiatrist, are very relevant. He writes: [9] "I count among my friends one priest who is neither a physician nor a psychiatrist. . . . He describes himself very humbly as 'a young priest who is interested in mental difficulties. Often I have sent to him patients of mine who were either recovering from some mental illness or tormented by some mental difficulty, and he has been wonderfully successful with many such cases. My medical colleagues criticise me severely because I am encouraging a layman to practise medicine. I am doing nothing of the kind. I am sending certain types of unhappy, anxious or mentally ill people to a man who is a better psychologist than I am, who loves souls, and who, as a priest, has something to give distracted and tormented people that the most distinguished psychiatrist does not possess."

4. Let the Christian doctor himself show the patient that he believes in religion. Let him join, or even initiate, a discussion group, such as two

[8] British Medical Association 1941, Section IX, Report of the Committee on Mental Health, pp. 37-39.

[9] *Psychiatry and Mental Health*, John Rathbone Oliver, pp. 7-8 (Scribners, 1932).

of the doctors in my own clinic have formed, where there is co-operation between minister, doctor and patients who are well enough to attend. Let the doctor direct people to go to church and get the fellowship and love which every live church offers.

Both ministers and doctors should interest themselves in drawing up a panel of Christian, medical psychotherapists and psychiatrists. All over the country are men and women in deep trouble. Even doctors and ministers who *recognise* neurosis frequently do not know what to do with the patients. If both had a list of those who could offer treatment, it would be of enormous help. One wishes that one could write some word which would encourage young doctors to take the Diploma of Psychological Medicine and work in this field. They are badly needed, and, as long as we live in a fear-stricken world, they are likely to be needed more than ever.

THE CHURCH PSYCHOLOGICAL CLINIC

IN THIS BRIEF section the writer desires to suggest that every church, or, as a beginning, every group of churches, such as the Anglican Diocese, the Scottish Presbytery, the Methodist District or the Congregational Province, should have its psychological clinic where doctors and ministers can co-operate.

To convey my meaning I shall describe the activities of the City Temple Psychological Clinic, because it does the kind of work which I think ought to be done throughout the whole country, as we understand more about the nature of illness, the techniques of modern psychology and the nature of true, essential, unsectarian Christianity.

If the argument of this book has been accepted, it will have been established that there are many people complaining, on the one hand, of such things as "nerves," or tensions, or fears, and, on the other hand, of more definite symptoms, like pain of one sort or another, or skin eruptions, or asthmatic attacks—the list is lengthening—whose illness cannot be cured by organic or physical means. The condition can be improved by rest, by medicines and surgery. But again and again its *origin* is found to be in the mind or in the soul, and only by treating these can such sufferers be cured.

The ordinary doctor is usually of little use for such cases. He tends to interpret physical symptoms only in terms of physical origins. He works on what I have described as "the garage-level." He is skilled to repair the machine. It is no disparagement of the general practitioner to say that he has not the time—or, often, the skill—to interpret physical symptoms in terms of psychological, let alone spiritual, disharmony. If he had, in the latter case at least, he usually would not know what to do about it.

The ordinary minister is of little use in such cases also. He may counsel prayer or faith or trust in God. If the patient is living a life of communion with God on a high level; if the minister is doing so and has behind him a group of strong Christian co-operators, then it may be that energies are released in the personality of the patient that dethrone his disease and wholly eradicate it.

But in the case of ordinary people, to counsel nothing but prayer, in the case of a long-standing phobia due to factors repressed into the unconscious since childhood, is as cruel and useless as to counsel only recourse to prayer for a suppurating appendix. The patient in both cases needs skilled help.

Owing to some strange experiences through which I passed as a young staff officer at the end of the first World War, I had made a close study of the relation between the "new psychology," as it was then called (1918), and the work of the ministry. Returning to this country in 1922, I became more and more impressed with the importance of psychology, and in 1925, when I went to Leeds, I began to try to help people who were in various kinds of trouble by using what psychological insight I had acquired, and I found some medical men and women who were willing to co-operate.

When I became minister of the City Temple in 1936 I asked for the help of people who had the following qualifications: a real Christian experience of their own, a psychological qualification and a medical degree. I was fortunate in getting five or six almost at once.

The applications for assistance come, for the most part, through me. If the applicant's case can be adequately dealt with by what I call "psychotherapeutic conversations," it may not be necessary to trouble one of the doctors of the clinic staff at all. Cases are quoted in this book which only needed half a dozen interviews to set matters right. It is important to add, however, that by a "psychotherapeutic conversation" I do not mean the handing out to the patient of a piece of advice. One's own personality must not be allowed to dominate, or else the patient will do merely what the psychologist or minister tells him and only for that reason. The conversation should be designed to spread out his whole problem before the patient with all its ramifications in such a way that the patient himself will see what ought to be done and himself make the decision to do it. Such action carries the *patient's* not the adviser's authority, and gives him confidence and the sense of being the master of his soul.

Frequently, however, the case needs a more thorough-going investigation, and here I can turn the patient over to one of the doctors helping me. I do not undertake anything worth calling a "treatment." The latter, I hold, is the province of the medically qualified psychotherapist. The doctor who undertakes the case sends me a brief report as to how the patient is progressing, and at the end of the treatment I frequently see the patient again and put before him the needs of the integrated personality and discuss with him how he may meet them. With voluntary workers, it would be possible to do more in the way of following up such cases. Indeed, the ideal would be to open a centre where such cases could stay and be treated. It is often very important to have a patient away from the environment associated with his neurosis. Sometimes the home environment is the factor which has precipitated, or even caused it.

By having the clinic linked with the Church, we emphasise the place of religion in healing, and we can offer, in the fellowship of the Church, just that atmosphere of love and goodwill which a neurotic so badly needs.

I have tried to make clear, earlier in this book, that many patients need help through what might be called psychosynthesis as much as they need help through analytical investigation. The latter is not in itself curative. It reveals to the patient where he went wrong, how he came to react faultily to his life-demands, how he developed a "twist" in his character by making an unhealthy reaction to certain emotional situations. But there still remains much to do (and it seems to be not generally understood that no 'treatment' can do this for him) in the way of using the insight which the investigation has given him in order to correct these faulty reactions and to develop a more healthy character-pattern. Here true religion can play a most important part. In helping at this point the minister has a supernatural ally. It is indeed supernatural, for no natural science can explain it. It is the desire of most men and women, deep down, to be good. In might be called the "pull upward." Perhaps it is the spiritual counterpart of the *vis medicatrix naturæ* of body and mind. There is an urge to perfection, a longing for integration, a passion for completeness in personality. On this the minister can always rely.

I would close this section by expressing the hope that ministers and doctors will awaken to the fact that an immense number of people are suffering who need not suffer; that a scientific enlightenment and a spiritual insight working together could release energies of mind and spirit that could deliver them; that a vast field is thus opening up before us, thrilling in its scope and possibility, fascinating in its opportunity, and carrying, for those who dedicate themselves to its challenge, the greatest of all rewards, the gratitude of those who, after many years perhaps in the valleys of pain, depression and despair, emerge at last on to the sunny uplands of that radiant health of body, mind and spirit which God intended all His children to enjoy.

4

CONCLUSIONS AND SIGNPOSTS

WHAT, THEN, IS the upshot of our long discussion and which way do the signposts point?

Certainly everything that can be done on what I have called the garage-level to heal bodies and minds must be done. The body is a complicated machine. It is much more, for its state of health influences that of the mind, but it certainly is that. No theory of healing can be sound, or methods recommended, which overlooks that fact. At our present stage of development any attitude of mind which regards as unnecessary the doctor, surgeon, dentist, nurse, masseur or other qualified worker on the physical level stands self-condemned. Christian Science, a system that contains so much of value, stands condemned if it does not re-think its position in this regard. No amount of love, or positive-thinking, or denial of the existence of evil will take a splinter out of an eye. A thousand situations which we call disease are in that category, and many healing cults stand condemned together with Christian Science for the same reason.

At the same time, man is not mere body. His body is the instrument of the mind and the soul. The influence of the mind has been emphasised again and again in this book, and the field of the psychotherapist opens out more and more widely as we note the incidence of the neuroses, the psychoses and psycho-somatic disease. This area also is one in which highly scientific methods are necessary, and the call for a better technique is urgent.

It is probable that we are only at the beginning of the work of constructing an adequate technique for bringing to consciousness the unconscious mental material in the deep mind. Freud, Adler, Jung and many later psychiatrists have given outstanding help in acquainting us with the kind of material that becomes repressed, why it does so, and how unhealthy material repressed from consciousness revenges itself on personality, or rather, warns us of the state of affairs, by setting up physical and mental symptoms.

But no one has yet invented a technique which is adequate. Psychoanalysis, as the Freudians understand it, involves the liberation in consciousness of all the repressed material, and may take two or three years, even if the patient sees his analyst twice or thrice weekly. The burden and distress occasioned, let alone the expense, rule out such a treatment for all but the very few. Yet the need for treatment is widespread, and will become a yet greater problem when the relief obtainable through psychotherapy is realised by the general public. The use of drugs often helps the patient when his treatment seems to come to a stalemate: when he "cannot think of anything else," fails to associate, does not remember his dreams or any further incidents of childhood, but yet maintains his symptoms. It is too early yet to say whether the examination of the deep mind through the use of drugs will prove of lasting value. Valuable research is being ardently pursued. The use of hypnotism is decreasing rather than increasing: the reasons for this have been given. More and more research into speedy and thorough methods of psychological investigation is a crying need of our time. In my opinion, all methods used so far will seem to be, judged by future standards, a blundering and groping tinkering with the mind, as clumsy and intolerably tedious as the early surgical operations appear now in the eyes of the efficient modern surgeon.

It is probable that the psychologist of the future will know how to develop an extra-sensory faculty enabling him, without going into any trance-state, to preceive, possibly by some form of telepathy, the mental condition of the patient. The psychologist of the future may even develop an ability to read the unconscious, so that diagnosis will be easy and treatment direct. Some of the Eastern systems, like Yoga, may well play a part here. I believe them to be of immense importance in any elucidation of the soul-mind-body relationship. I hope and, indeed, prophesy, that religion will more and more be one of the assets of the psychotherapist of the future. After the unconscious situation has been made conscious, patients who have been made ill by repressed guilt will find health in the acceptance of forgiveness. Patients who have been made ill by unacknowledged hate will be cured by accepting the Christian doctrine of loving one's neighbour and realising it in experience. Patients who have been made ill by the deprivation of love will be taught how to obtain love through the loving community, the Church, and how to find *through persons* the unfailing love of God.

Where the psychotherapist has no religious experience of his own he will, in my opinion, be found to succeed only indifferently, compared, say, with the therapist with a spiritual insight and faith which help in synthesis as well as investigation. A religious interpretation of life on broad lines seems to me essential to a *complete* integration of personality, and thus to *complete* health.

Here an important word must be said. The ideas of Christianity, the fundamental truths and values of the teaching, life, death and resurrection of Christ, are referred to so far in this chapter as usefully playing a part in a treatment. The doctrine of forgiveness, for example, is to be brought to the aid of a person suffering from guilt, as a treatment auxiliary to that of the psychotherapist. This is a kind of scientific use of religion, and is legitimate only up to a point. It breaks down if the patient only regards religion as he regards other means of getting better. He must want forgiveness, for example, not merely because he finds guilt to have made him ill. He must want forgiveness in order that his relationship with a loving God may be restored.

Finally, I want to make an appeal to the Churches and their members to recover the lost art of healing through the direct activity of God. This is true spiritual healing. There is no need to appeal to the doctors to continue their work on the body. One only wishes that they could be set free to do it more efficiently. Every scientist, for example, at work on research which might bring, through physical means, the relief of pain and disability, ought to be able to count on the fullest support of the Government to prosecute his research, instead of being hampered, as he so often is, by lack of time, funds or material. If the fullest resources of humanity were made available, then, in one generation, many physical scourges which destroy men could be excluded, just as plague, cholera, malaria and leprosy have been already banished from the West.

Nor is there such a need to appeal to the psychotherapists, though those who are completely materialistic in their outlook might well reconsider their position. It is odd that a man equipped to treat the mind should so often interpret its disorders in a purely materialistic way. Freud himself deprecated this, and so far from demanding that only trained doctors should practice his methods, he recommended "educators and pastors" to use his technique, on the ground that they are less likely to interpret all they find wrong in terms of material defect, an interpretation to which the doctor is prone by reason of his training.[1]

Yet while there is plenty of room for improvement, psychological research is being prosecuted keenly. The recent World Congress on

[1] See Freud's Introduction to *The Psychoanalytic Method*, Oskar Pfister (Dodd, 1917).

Mental Health held in London (1948) is proof enough of that. It was attended by psychiatrists from all over the world, and its conclusions are of the greatest importance.

But what of the Church?

The truth is that she has lost a supernatural gift of healing. It is futile, in my view, to equate the healing power of Jesus with the methods of modern psychotherapy. We may usefully note—as I tried to show—that Christ's healing powers made use of certain psychological mechanisms within men's personalities. But to compare the power released in personality by the slow and doubtful methods of psychotherapy with the power released immediately by Christ, is like comparing the power of rust to eat through an iron bar with the power of an oxyacetylene flame.

Nor is this lost power to be regained by studying the sporadic cures of "healers" who, from time to time, give us a glimpse of immense recuperative powers resident in, or flowing through, personality. This is not said in disparagement of such healers. Their power can be utilised, as I have said earlier, but their power gives us no clue to the healing ministry which Christ meant His Church to carry out as one of its normal functions. It is not in exploring this avenue that the modern Church is to fiind her way.

Not Lourdes, nor Christian Science, nor Four-Square-Gospel Healing Missions, nor Spiritualism provide signposts which lead to the place of power.

The intercession of people united in love for Christ and living disciplined lives, and the laying on of hands, undertaken after prayer and self-discipline, by a priest or minister or other person who is the contact-point, so to speak, of a beloved, believing and united community standing behind him and supporting his ministration to a patient who has been taught to understand the true nature of Christian faith, are clues well worth following up. This is the true ministry of the Church as such, and, in a sense, has nothing to do with psychology at all. This is the ministry which must be recovered and which only the Church can do. For this ministry the words "spiritual healing" should be reserved.

Because of what He was, and because of His relation to, and trust in, God, Christ was able to introduce into the lives of men living on the human plane, energies which belong to the divine or supernatural plane. The effect was what we call miracle. It was as startling to men as the effect of man's intervention would be to thoughtful and reasoning dogs—if we can imagine such—whose wounds and injuries were suddenly healed by calling in resources such as penicillin, familiar and law-abiding to man, but outside the range of canine understanding. Miracles are not to be excluded. On a higher plane of being they are normal, law-abiding happenings. When they impinge on our plane, we call them miraculous and supernatural—which, indeed, they are; but they are only "above" the nature we know. They are not to be regarded as, in any true sense, a rupture of law. They are supernatural but not contranatural.

It seems equally absurd to suppose that there is a fixed and closed order, knowable by man, outside which nothing can possibly happen. So a dog might be imagined, solemnly deciding that nothing outside his understood world could possibly happen. Man is not limited to what such a dog would recognise as the limits of the possible, and God is certainly not restricted to the limited operation of the realm of law which man has found out through "science."

But if the impinging of a higher on a lower phase of life be miracle, then, while we can conceive a divine Christ working healing miracles, can man claim such a power ?

In my view, he can only claim it if that divine power works through him. And it will do so only under certain conditions. To establish those conditions, Christ established His Church. He called together men as different as possible in outlook, education and temperament, and in patience and love He welded them into a unity *which became an extension of His incarnation.* Any one of His apostles became a striking point of the whole fellowship, and the Spirit of God worked in and through the fellowship as He worked through the personality of Christ Himself. Then real "spiritual healing" became possible to the fellowship, through any one of its members. Only the point of the poker touches the coal when I poke the fire, but every molecule of the poker is involved and so is the power of my arm. The Church must feel that the whole loving community is behind the healer and so is the power of Christ, working through *all* the members to heal the patient.

But we many note the cost of producing this sense of unity, and thus of power, both to Christ and to His disciples. No one but He could ever have brought Simon, the Zealot, pledged to kill a publican at sight, into loving comradeship and unity of action with Matthew, the publican. And it took Christ Himself years to accomplish this. It was a discipline of spirit both for them and Him.

Psychology has its place as material medicine has, but neither is to be regarded as a substitute for the dynamic spiritual energy which the Church of the first century knew. We are trying to make do with both, because we are not prepared to pay the price which a healing Church costs. We pretend that the first-century healing miracles are now being repeated by psychotherapeutic treatments. We interview a patient for two hundred separate hours, and then rejoice that he does not limp quite so badly. The Apostles could say, "In the name of Jesus Christ, rise up and walk!" And it happened at once and was a permanent cure! How different was their motive! How different their faith! How different their earliest results!

Let the Church have its psychological clinics. I strongly recommend this. But Christ did not send out His Apostles to be psychologists and doctors, but to be the spearheads of fellowships made one through a discipline to prayer and corporate worship. At high temperatures even alien metals will fuse into an alloy, stronger than any constituent in it taken by itself. The love of God *can* do that for members of a fellowship who have temperamentally little in common and who, by themselves, must fail to heal, or even impress.

The way forward for the Church, then, seems clear. Let it support all that is being done to heal men through every known scientific means, but let it not be bluffed into supposing that that is the healing work it is called to do.

Many healing works carried on today, even in the name of religion, are only spasmodic and sporadic illustrations of ill-regulated and half-understood psychological phenomena. Many Christian Science cures, healing-mission cures and claims from Lourdes and other centres; many "healings" wrought often by cranks and charlatans, illustrate the power of the mind over the body, rather than the kind of thing Christ did and calls His Church to do. We know that by examining what lies behind the cures.

True spiritual healing demands another kind of preparation altogether. Let a fellowship be formed of convinced, devout and sensible people. Let them regularly pray together. It may be necessary for them to live together for periods. We forget that the disciples lived together for three years, and *lived with Jesus,* and even then were weak and undependable. When all animosities, jealousies, ambitions, prejudices, suspicions and the like have been purged away within the fellowship; when the members of the fellowship have become one, both in flaming love to Christ and an unselfish desire to help others, then they can with confidence claim to be an extension of Christ's body, a part of "*the* Church, which is His body," and an instrument which the Holy Spirit can use in the ministry of direct spiritual healing.

I have written critically of those of us who belong to and believe in the Church. And, indeed, the Church, for reasons given, has lost her power to heal.

But a paragraph here must make it clear that the patient also needs to co-operate in a way concerning which he often shows some reluctance.

Let us imagine a patient who is ill and who suspects, or, if he has been successfully analysed, knows, that his illness, physical though it may be in its obvious manifestations, is due to some psychological or spiritual factor. Let us suppose that he has formed the habit of reacting emotionally to certain situations in a way which "worked" in childhood and has hardened into a pattern of character-reaction which he cannot easily alter, even though, now, psychological analysis or investigation has brought it to consciousness and made it clear to him. Yet still he must *act*. And it is not easy to put into words what he must do. If he passionately fights for health for health's sake, and maintains resentment and aggression—even though unconsciously—because health eludes him, he may defeat his own object. He cannot help wanting to be well, of course; it is natural and right that he should, and want it with his whole heart. (Some neurotics lengthen their treatment because they cling to symptoms which bring them self-pity or sympathy or excuse. They buy sympathy by means of symptoms, and will not buy health with courage.)

But where true spiritual healing is concerned, our patient must want health as a by-product. *First* he must desire to be right in his relationship with God, with man and with life. He must work hard with himself until he has got them right. He must use whatever insights his analysis has brought him to show him where his reactions are wrong and where and how he can put them right, and he must even do so without keeping one eye on his own health.

In a sense he must accept life—even a measure of temporary illness—while he gets his relationships right. As he does this he prepares himself for what the Church ought to be able to give him through its fellowship: an inpouring of a sense of God's love and care which will for ever change his faulty emotional reaction, and exchange it for pardon, serenity, the love of which he has been deprived, and so on.

Listen to a doctor as he describes how that inward conflict, which "usually strikes the weakest link in our organism," took, in his case, the form of an obscure septic condition. He writes:

"Happily my adviser combined a sound knowledge of physical medicine with a keen insight into the non-physical problems of health. He told me that it was unlikely that physical troubles were at the bottom of my illness, and suggested that in my way of life and in my attitude towards life might be found the source of my troubles. Little by little I began to see myself as I was. Self-centred, anxious about many things, a tangle of conflicting and incompatible purposes.

"On a sunny November morning I was descending a hillside when I was aware—with deep emotion—that a clean cut must be made with the past. I must cease striving for my own ends and purposes, must cheerfully embrace whatever plans or purposes God might have for me: must be prepared to be well or ill: must subject my hitherto dominant self to the one purpose of the Lord of Life for me. As I did so, a deep Peace followed and spread out to Joy. For inward strife and chaos were given Peace and Joy. At such times we experience a lightness of heart, and adventurous abandon, which he who calculates chances in the lottery of life can never know nor comprehend. From this time on my physical health steadily improved.

"Here we find, I am persuaded, the essential living core of Spiritual Healing. It arises from the glad submission of the self as a whole, and as a personality, to the Will of God for us. To heal is to make whole: to be healed is to be made whole. It was in this manner that the Healer came to me." [2]

Those who practice the true spiritual healing—not psychological treatment, even with religious ideas as an aid to synthesis—but claiming the direct action of God, should not promise healing. The concentration must be on unity with God. When that is done, many other things will be added to the suppliant, and health is often one of them. The love and grace and power of God seep through the deep places of the personality to the control-room in the unconscious from which so many bodily functions are governed.

I would add that, if well enough, the seeker should meet in fellowship with a group of spiritually minded and loving people. The healer —always regarded as the spearpoint of the fellowship—can often do much. The fellowship itself should be able to do much more. As I have said, I have known such fellowship as the Church at its best offers, to bring health to people suffering from psychogenic disease, even when the latter has been characterised by severe physical concomitants.

I do not mean, even then, that such a fellowship would be "able to cure anything." In my view, there are situations where God has decreed that the relevant way of co-operating with Him is that of medicine, surgery, psychology or other scientific technique. What I have been describing seems to me the way forward for *the Church*. If this were not true, it would be logical to use "spiritual healing in every situation of suffering and to give it priority over every other form of treatment. Spiritual healing, in the sense of becoming one

---

[2] "Modern Theory and Practice of Healing," Dr. Howard E. Collier, printed in *The Place of Spiritual Healing in the Society of Friends* (Friends Book Centre, 1938, p. 4, 2nd ed., 1943).

with God at every possible point, is incumbent on every Christian, but spiritual healing is not the relevant way of healing everything.

If it be said that spiritual healing is made too demanding by what I have written, my reply is that nevertheless I see no easier way. The Roman Catholic Church, with its monasteries and convents, is organised already for such ends. To some extent, the Church of England is equipped with places for "Retreats." I am quite sure, in my own mind, that the Free Churches must organise some kind of community centres with the same end in view: centres for prayer and fellowship and self-discipline, and yet with all the freedom of thought and action for which our fathers suffered so much.

Man has proved himself a creature of amazing ingenuity, resource-fulness and energy. His scientific discoveries and their application to mechanical devices compel the highest admiration. If his spiritual prog-ress had kept pace with that of his sciences, we should all be living in a worldly paradise. The heart is made sick with longing and sad with frus-tration when one meditates on what life could be if every man regarded his brother as Jesus regarded His. With our modern knowledge added to unbreakable, brotherly goodwill, no one would be in want, few would be ill and all could be happy. All the resources of God's world would be at the disposal of all the members of God's world family. If man had devoted one hundredth of the energy used in scientific enquiry to the wise search for spiritual power, it is doubtful if the degree of suffering remaining would be any serious problem. Charles Steinmetz, questioned about the next great invention, said that the greatest need of the day was a laboratory for the study of religion. If only a laboratory would fill the bill!

As it is, man has released the energies of the physical world until they terrify him. He has created a Frankenstein monster that has wrecked his nerves and paralysed his brain with fear. Power has been released, but man lacks wisdom to use it. One illustration suffices. The natives of Bikini would supply it. A power released by alien scientists drove them from the island home where they and their simple ancestors had resided for centuries, but no one knows how to end the harm which that release has effected. The djinn released one summer day has poisoned the very sea, and still lurks in its depths with a horror called radio-activity, incomprehensible to them. No one knows how to drive the djinn back into its bottle, and old Father Time—on whom alone reliance is placed—is in no hurry. At the point at which man has un-leashed unrivalled power he is most hopeless. Never has he handled such power. Never has he been so frightened and uncertain.

Sincere workers in all three fields—body, mind and spirit—deserve our praise. Yet there are hardly any workers in any of these fields who act as though they realised that, grievous though man's conflicts are, he remains in a true sense one. " 'Tis not the body, but the man is ill." The whole man is the entity to which the art of healing is to be directed in the future. An illustration is to hand. I know a man who was operated on for gastric ulcer. The operation was successful, and he was discharged from hospital. But no one asked him about his worries, or talked with him about his fears, or showed him fellowship and affection, or cared for his soul. As I write, he is developing all the symptoms of another ulcer. Even the "garage work" done on him is on the level of repairing the punctured tube, but leaving the nail which caused it still in the tire. The truth is that the study of the disease itself and its local position was given first-rate attention, but the study is carried on as though that section of a patient's body existed apart from the patient's mind and spirit; almost as if it were separated from the other parts of his body. "I've got a *case* of gastric ulcer," says one doctor to another. "I've got a *case* of obsessional neurosis," says the psychologist. The word "case" is symptomatic of a tendency, in both physical and psychological medicine, to separate the local signs of disease from the whole personality of Mr. Jones, who, perhaps, is fretted to death by a nagging wife, or worried unceasingly at business, or racked with vague terror due to causes which he cannot remember—factors which have a profound influence on his physical condition. Mr. Jones's whole character-pattern is the determinant which decides what disease he develops and how it may best be handled. "There are no diseases," says a wise old adage; "there are only sick persons." It should never be forgotten that, apart from physical accidents, what we generally call disease is frequently caused by a faulty reaction of a person to the problems which his life presents. Often he starts making such a faulty reaction in very early days. The pattern of reaction becomes fixed. By the time illness sets in he is completely unconscious of any such reactions, or how they became fixated. *The whole man* must be the aim of three branches of the art of healing, and they must act in closest co-operation. Lord Horder, in an address on "Medicine and Religion," delivered at the Philosophical Institute of Edinburgh in October 1938, said, "It is clear that there is a very definite point of contact between medicine and religion. For the whole of man and not merely a part of him is concerned, or may be, in Medicine, whether this be preventive or curative, and this *whole* includes his spirituality or religious temperament." [3]

Finally, let us never forget that there is a spiritual power to heal

[3] *Fortnightly Review*, October 1938.

which has not been withheld. It has only been unappropriated. The slow development of our spiritual receptivity and insight hinder the recovery of thousands who could be healed by true spiritual healing. When the Church returns to her early devotion to Christ and creates united fellowships, even faintly like the small body of men who went out in the power of the Risen Christ and His Spirit to turn the world upside down, then a power more potent to heal than any atomic bomb to destroy will once more surge through sick souls and minds and bodies. It will be His own power and recognised as such. If disease is caused by the faulty reactions of a person—as is so often the case—then the supreme healing power will not be this or that treatment, let alone this or that drug, but *a Person healing*. Christains call that Person Christ. When He comes into His own, then the prayer will be answered which He Himself taught men to pray: "Thy kingdom come; Thy will be done on earth, as it is in heaven."

APPENDICES

1

NOTES ON THE COMMON NEUROSES AND PSYCHOSES

I APPEND HERE, for the reader to whom they may be unfamiliar, some notes on the common neuroses and psychoses. By a neurosis is meant a faulty, and sometimes disabling, emotional reaction to life at one or more points, with or without physical symptoms, the patient, however, remaining sane and *en rapport* with other people and with the real world. By a psychosis is meant the illness of a person who at some points is not *en rapport* with other people or with the real world. It is notoriously difficult sometimes to decide whether a person is suffering from a severe neurosis or whether he is becoming psychotic, but the above, in my opinion, represents the best way of making such a distinction. A neurotic patient is not insane. A psychotic patient is, even though the insanity may be slight and curable.

THE NEUROSES OR PSYCHONEUROSES

The precipitating condition of any neurosis may be some recent great emotional shock or strain, such as overwork, bereavement or worry, but the *cause* is probably a situation set up in early childhood which determined a faulty type of character-reaction, and which is now repressed into the unconscious part of the mind. Emotion linked with the situation is dissociated from the memory, but bursts through in symptoms which vary according to the type of neurosis described below.

Treatment from a medical psychologist should be obtained. A holiday may apparently cure the condition, but the patient may relapse if some further strain develops later. There is every hope of complete recovery unless the patient is too old to co-operate with the psychotherapist, or because of the nature of the illness, is unable to do so, or refuses to do so. The following are the main types of neurosis:

1. *Anxiety Neurosis*.[1] The patient feels vaguely or acutely afraid, either without being able to say what makes him so, or else ascribing his fear to a cause which to a normal adult is not a fear-causing object, such as the dark, or a closed-in space, or a wide-open space, or a sharp knife, or the company of others, etc.

He will often have one or more of the following symptoms: depression, insomnia, trembling of limbs, inability to relax, headache, undue fatigue,[2] dry mouth, cold sweat, weakness at the knees, sinking feeling in the abdomen, palpitation, loss of muscle-tone, giddiness, dilatation of pupils, etc.

2. *Conversion Hysteria*. The patient unconsciously "converts" his fear into a physical symptom. He cannot do this by an act of will, and is never to be blamed for his symptoms. Malingering does not come into the matter. His mind, as it were, hands its distress over to the body by producing a symptom which both eases its own stress—it is easier to bear pain of body than pain of mind—and gets the patient out of fear-causing situations without his losing "face." So a friend of mine, to give a trivial but revealing illustration, summoned to speak at a huge meeting, did not prepare properly. He was then full of fear that his reputation would suffer. Desire to speak was in conflict with fear of speaking badly. An hour or two before the meeting he was seized with severe vomiting and could not attend. His mind, fear-ridden, *unconsciously* developed a symptom in his body (vomiting) which served several ends.

(*a*) It took his mind off the fear of the meeting.

(*b*) It got him out of having to go and lose his reputation through being unprepared.

(*c*) It did this without the patient losing "face." The members of the audience muttered in sympathy when the chairman said that the distinguished speaker had been taken suddenly ill and could not come!

The "patient" sat up talking and smoking with me until two o'clock the next morning. All symptoms vanished by the time the meeting finished.

[1] It is interesting that the very words "anxiety" and "anxious" are used to connote both desire and fear. "I am anxious to see you" = desire. "I am anxious about you" = fear. Again and again in the anxiety neurosis it is found that the patient both desires to do a thing, but fears to do it. Desire and fear are in conflict.

[2] I have not included what is often called "neurasthenia" because I regard it as a symptom of an anxiety state. It is a form of anxiety-neurosis characterised by excessive fatigue.

Note that the power of the mind over the body is quite sufficient to produce such a symptom and to maintain symptoms for scores of years if the situation demands it. So we have people with chronic tired hearts, blood-pressures, hysterical "fits," headaches, functional paralyses and so on.

Note also that in conversion hysteria no fear is "left over." The *mind* is content. The bodily symptoms do away completely with the mental anxiety. The latter is completely "converted."

Note also that in conversion hysteria, in contrast to psychosomatic illness, no destruction of tissue takes place, though there may be severe pain and physical distress.

Treatment by a medical psychotherapist is indicated. The prognosis, given co-operation, is good.

3. *Anxiety Hysteria* is a condition midway between anxiety neurosis and conversion hysteria. There is a "partial somatisation of affect." In other words, the patient has certain conscious and irrational fears, but *some* of his fear is converted into symptoms. He tends to act in exaggerated ways as well as feeling frightened, unhappy and depressed.

4. *Compulsion or Obsessional Neurosis* is a condition in which the patient feels compelled to do, say, think or feel certain things, without his being conscious of any rational cause for such a compulsion, and being unable by reasoning to destroy it. It is unwanted and is recognised as unreasonable; yet it persists. If ignored a feeling of fear recurs.

Thus one famous patient felt compelled to touch the lamp-post outside his house whenever he entered it. If he refrained and took off his boots and sat down to supper, the compulsion was strong enough to compel him to get up again, put on his boots and carry out the ritual.

Another finds he must count up to a certain number before going to bed, or continually wash his hands, or repeat magic, or what he calls "wicked" words, or feel in all his pockets. In some cases blasphemous or obscene thoughts come continually into his mind, and cannot be driven away, even though they are loathed. Frequently he mistakenly thinks he has committed the "unpardonable sin." [8] Clearly he is not a sinner, nor is he mad or going mad. He is psychologically ill.

The compulsive act is often a disguised ritual which the unconscious mind has imposed as an alternative to a rational attitude which the patient fears for some reason unknown to himself.

Psychological treatment is definitely the course to be followed. It is often hard to find what the compulsive action is symbolising and get the patient to realise it. Yet even in cases where complete freedom is

[8] On "the unpardonable sin," see my *When the Lamp Flickers* (Abingdon-Cokesbury, 1948).

not achieved, symptoms can be lessened in intensity and much is gained by explaining to the patient the nature of his troubles.

5. *Psychosomatic Illness* is similar to conversion hysteria, save that here we find actual organic disease, often with destruction of tissue, taking place.

Modern research tends to show that *some* cases of asthma, migraine, skin troubles and gastric and duodenal ulcers, while physically distressing and often chronic, are not *caused* only by physical factors. The unconscious mind has produced the illness, taking advantage of some hereditary weakness or local organic lesion, to get the patient out of some *mentally* distressing situation, to help him to escape some ordeal or to evade some exacting experience. This is dealt with in the book.

It is the writer's conviction that a good deal of what is now thought to be organic disease, solely caused by physical factors, will be found to be ultimately caused by emotional factors deep in the mind (see Section V). This may even be true of some of the killing diseases, like coronary thrombosis, tuberculosis and cancer. They may turn out to be physical concomitants of psychological, and even spiritual, disharmony.

THE PSYCHOSES

These may be divided into two groups: (1) those in which the cause is unknown or uncertain, e.g. (*a*) the schizophrenic psychoses, and (*b*) the affective psychoses; and (2) those where the cause is known, e.g. (*a*) the toxic psychoses—bacterial, infectious, alcoholic, etc., and (*b*) the psychoses complicating some definite organic disease or injury of the brain, i.e. the epileptic psychoses, psychoses associated with syphilis, arteriosclerosis, encephalitis, senility, etc. The second group (2) are outside the scope of this book.

1 (a). *The Schizophrenic Psychoses.*

With regard to the former group (1), the schizophrenic disorders are the more frequent. Schizophrenia begins in the majority of cases between the ages of fifteen and twenty-five, affecting males and females equally. There is evidence to suggest a hereditary origin for the disease, but environmental disturbances in which there is a loss of affection (such as broken romances and bereavements), or where there is emotional stress through fear, may bring on a schizophrenic illness which otherwise might have remained dormant.

The word "schizophrenia" means a "split mind," and was adopted by Bleuler in favour of the older name "dementia praecox," because it described the splitting of the mental functions which is characteristic of the illness. This may be recognised through disorders of (i) thought, (ii) emotion and (iii) will.

(i) Thinking as expressed through the patient's speech is vague and indefinite, lacks normal continuity and strikes the observer as being in some way peculiar. The patient may describe a "blocking" of his normal thought-processes. He forgets what he was going to say next, a blank or iron curtain coming down. Often such patients will suddenly stop talking and after a few seconds resume on an entirely different topic. In answers to questions, patients are evasive or discursive, and often "talk round the point" instead of giving a definite answer.

(ii) Disorders of emotion are first apparent as an indifference towards the feelings of others and a blunting and flattening of the normal emotional responses. Thus a patient may appear listless and apathetic, or he may appear callous, and many commit crimes of violence or cruelty without experiencing any sense of fear or shame. Later there may be signs of emotional incongruity—there being a split between the thoughts expressed and the emotions accompanying them. Thus at the funeral of a dear one the schizophrenic may smile facetiously or even laugh heartily. Or, by reason of this splitting of the personality, he may show anti-social behaviour by committing brutal murders or making violent sexual assaults without experiencing any emotional accompaniments which are associated with such acts. The change in the emotional attitude of the patient is apparent from his apathetic, indifferent attitude and the difficulty of an observer to gain *rapport* with him.

(iii) The schizophrenic may show weakening of the will. This is apparent as a loss of impetus for activity, so that he becomes idle, lies late in bed, refuses to wash, dress and shave himself, and fails to turn up for work or other appointments. He sits idly doing nothing, and often thinking nothing, or else his thoughts carry him into a phantasy world of his own and fleeting grimaces cross his face as he becomes wrapped up in his day-dreams. Such a state of complete withdrawal from reality (autism) is seen only in advanced cases of schizophrenia.

Catatonic symptoms are seen as a group of motor anomalies, and may occur independently. They range from a state of stupor to a state of extreme motor over-activity. Between these extremes are found abnormalities of gait or posture, the adoption of statue-like postures, mannerisms, peculiarities of speech and so on.

In addition, hallucinations and delusions are frequent, particularly in the paranoid type of schizophrenia. This form of illness is characterised by delusions of a persecutory nature, so that normal incidents and events are misinterpreted as having a special and harmful meaning for the patient. Hallucinations are usually of hearing, and represent a "vocalisation" of the individual's abnormally vivid thoughts. They seem to him to be "more real" than reality. The patient may react violently in answer to his "voices," or may be little disturbed by them. They may be associated with various delusional systems and misinterpreted as the voice of God or the voice of the Devil.

Paraphrenia is the name given to a type of schizophrenic disorder which begins later in life and in which the personality deteriorates more slowly than in paranoid schizophrenia. Persecutory delusions and hallucinations occur, but disorders of thinking, feeling and willing are later in onset.

Paranoia. This term is now passing out of use. It was used by Kraepelin to describe a type of psychosis in which a chronic systematised delusional system occurred in an individual with an otherwise intact personality. Sooner or later other schizophrenic symptoms become apparent, however, and such cases are now usually regarded as cases of paranoid schizophrenia. The treatment of schizophrenia is a matter for the psychiatrist. Deep insulin treatment offers a high percentage of recoveries when the duration of the illness is short. Electric convulsion therapy and prefrontal leucotomy also have a place in the treatment of schizophrenia.

1 (b). *The Affective Psychoses.*

These are disorders of "affect" or feelings. If the normal "feeling state" is represented as a horizontal line, then above the line lie the manias or states of extreme elation and excitement, and below the line the depressions or states of gloom and despondency.

All individuals show some swing above and below the line in the response to the different situations and people encountered in the course of the normal daily life. Some individuals live constantly above the line and are constitutionally cheerful, and some live constantly below and are constitutionally gloomy. Some swing readily from one state to the other, according to the environmental situations to which they are subjected, and in some the swing is more apparent than in others who live closer to the line. We all know people whom we can categorise in this way, and yet they are all normal people merely representing variations of normality. They belong to the cyclothymic personality-type.

It is when people show periodic swings from one state to the other in the absence of any obvious external stimulating factors, i.e. when the change of mood arises from within the individual (or is "constitutional" or "endogenous"), or when the swing in response to external factors is extreme above the line (mania), or below it (melancholia), for considerable periods that mental illness is suspected.

(i) *The manic-depressive psychosis* is an affective psychosis characterised by periodic swings of mood either up or down, the individual's behaviour being in accordance with the direction of the mood-swings. The change of mood is the predominant feature, and in the classical manic-depressive psychosis bears no relation to the external situation; i.e. it is endogenous in origin.

This illness is commoner among the higher intellectual strata of the population, possibly because the more manic individuals are creative and energetic, and forge ahead in their work. There is a hereditary disposition to the illness. The stronger this is, the earlier the age of onset. Depressive illnesses are commoner in women, and usually begin in the thirties or at the climacteric (involutional melancholia). Mania is slightly more common in men, and generally begins in the twenties. The psychosis is rare in children. The illness may be precipitated by pregnancy, or long, exhausting illnesses.

The periodicity of the illness is variable. In women periodic depressive phases related to menstruation are common. A single depressive phase may last from three to six months. The average duration of a depressive phase in a manic-depressive psychosis is five months. Generally speaking, the manic phases are of shorter duration than the depressive phases. There is a tendency for the interval between mood-swings to become gradually shorter as age increases, while the duration of the attack becomes gradually longer. The illness is self-limited, the majority of patients recovering completely. More than half the patients have only one attack in their lives.

Modern treatment, including electric convulsive therapy, does much to relieve the depressive phases and control the manic phases. It appears to have little effect on the periodicity of the illness, however.

(ii) *Involutional melancholia* is a depressive illness of endogenous origin occurring at or about the time of the menopause. It is generally recognised as being part of the manic-depressive psychosis, but is only diagnosed when there is no previous history of mania or depressive illness. Careful questioning often reveals evidence of a "subclinical" mania or depression, however, in the patient's earlier history. This form of depression responds well to modern methods of treatment.

(iii) *Exogenous or reactive depression* is depression resulting from external circumstances; i.e. bereavement, broken love affairs, loss of security, etc., but where the degree and duration of the depression exceed the individual's normal reaction to emotional stress and adverse circumstances. Thus many reactive depressions may be classified as of psychoneurotic origin.

There is difficulty in deciding how far a depressive illness is exogenous (or environmental) and how far it is endogenous (or constitutional), as in all depressive illnesses both factors play a part. Some authorities believe that the alleged differentiation is a theoretical one and that no true differentiation can be made. Certainly the reactive depressions bear a close resemblance to the psychoneurotic depressions.

Many types of mania and depression are described. The characteristic features of mania include a feeling of elation, motor excitement, over-activity and restlessness and flight of ideas. By flight of ideas is meant a state of rapidity of thinking which is manifest in the individual's speech, so that he jumps from one thought to another and weaves into his speech any sound he hears. He jokes and makes puns incessantly, and frequently bursts into song. There is discontinuity of thought resulting from the pressure of ideas coming to consciousness.

Depressions are characterised by a sense of despondency, with a feeling of personal loss, retardation of thinking (as opposed to the flight of ideas of the manic patient) which sometimes amounts to stupor, and loss of energy and of interest in his surroundings. Physical symptoms are common, and include failure of appetite, indigestion, insomnia and constipation. In involutional melancholia the retardation of thinking is usually absent, and is replaced by a sense of apprehension, anxiety and agitation. Hypochondriacal ideas associated with the bodily functions are common, and secondary delusional ideas develop.

An attempt has been made to outline the features of the two main psychotic groups where the cause of the illness is uncertain or unknown; i.e. the schizophrenic psychoses and the affective psychoses. These notes are necessarily incomplete, but they indicate the important difference between neurosis and psychosis, though the dividing line is often hard to find. They are inserted to show the minister who would practice psychology in what difficult fields he may find himself and how important it is that he should not blunder. Much harm has been done by ministers trying to treat unrecognised psychoses by psycho-therapeutic and religious means. Much unnecessary anxiety has been caused in relatives by ministers who have made a faulty diagnosis of psychosis where only neurosis was present. It cannot be too emphatically stated that co-operation with the medical psychiatrist is essential, at least until diagnosis is established beyond doubt. I would add a reminder that the neurotic is always extremely suggestible, and that an unguarded word from either minister or doctor can wreck his happiness and do immeasurable harm.

2

CASE NOTES OF ALLEGED HEALING AT LOURDES

DURING MY VISIT to Lourdes in 1949 I was given permission to study the actual reports of patients concerning whose cure the Bureau des Constatations Medicales de Lourdes was satisfied. Omitting names, I present the following case notes:

1. The report of Dr. X., an eye specialist from Lille, on a patient A.B. who attended Lourdes from September 24 to 28, 1947. The specialist reported that improvement was contrary to all expectation, and that he felt he had witnessed a phenomenon unique in his whole experience. The medical report was supported and vouched for by the Société Medicale de Saint Luc, Saint Come and Saint Damine.

The history was that of a boy of two who had normal vision until he had an operation at this age for strangulated hernia. Following this he became practically blind and developed a squint of the left eye. He was only able to perceive the difference between light and darkness with the left eye, and in the right eye his visual acuity was impaired to the extent that he could just identify two fingers when held up at a distance not more than fifty centimetres from his eyes. He only saw shadows, and recognised people only by their voices.

The diagnosis was optic atrophy and chorio retinitis. The ophthalmic surgeon advised further opinions, and the patient was seen by two other oculists, who confirmed this diagnosis and whose certificates are in the possession of the patient's mother. The prognosis was designated "très grave." The affection was declared incurable, and until the visit to Lourdes there was no change in his condition, save a very slight amelioration of the condition of the right eye.

On September 26, 1947, when the patient visited the Stations of the Cross, he still could not see, but on the way down his mother noticed that he picked up pieces of wood from the ground and offered them to her for the fire. On September 27 he was bathed in the baths for the first time, and he commented to his mother on the beauty of the stained-glass windows of the baths. The boy was then examined by five doctors whom he had not seen before. Their report said that he could now see two fingers at one metre's distance, but could not see at two metres. The boy began to walk with greater confidence, but still walked into chairs and other obstacles which apparently he could not see, and his visual fields were very restricted.

On September 28 he was examined at hospital, and could walk without bumping into obstacles. He walked up the corridor to the lift, and asked if he could go up and down, and he recognised the colours of the buttons by which the lift was operated. Examined again by two doctors, it was found that his optic reflexes were feeble, but existent, and that at two metres he could see a dog, distinguish steps and re-marked on a chicken which crossed his path at three metres distance. On the way home in a car he could see other cars and commented on their speed. When ten miles distance from Lourdes, he could see mountains and commented on their beauty. In July 1948 the improvement was maintained, and the report gives details of this improvement.

The opinion of all the medical men consulted was that a miracle had taken place in the case of this patient, and that his sight had been restored through the Grace of our Lord mediated to him in response to prayers made on his behalf to the Blessed Virgin.

2. Here is another case, the record of which was impressive. Mademoiselle C.D. was born in 1906. In 1922, at the age of sixteen, she was diagnosed as having tuberculous peritonitis and was treated with sunlight therapy. In 1924 she developed a right-sided pleurisy. In 1928 her tuberculous peritonitis flared up again and an exploratory operation was performed. She was subsequently moved to a sanatorium for tuberculous cases. In 1931 she developed an internal tuberculous abscess, and in 1934 involvement of her kidneys was confirmed by her passing blood and tubercle bacilli in her urine. Her general condition deteriorated, and in 1935 she was operated on again for intestinal obstruction due to pressure on the intestine from enlarged tuberculous glands. Towards the end of 1935 she also developed signs of involvement of the membranes covering the brain (meningitis). In 1936 she developed severe renal pain from further involvement of the kidneys. At the end of this year she was discharged from the sanatorium, being regarded as incurable. In 1939 tuberculosis of the right lung developed and was confirmed by X-rays. In 1940 the glands in her abdomen resulted in severe intestinal colic, and she developed a high fever. There were definite

cavities now present in the right lung, and, in addition, she had septic tuberculous sinuses opening into the skin. In 1941 an attempt was made to collapse her right lung, but adhesions prevented this. She had lost a great deal of weight and had confirmed tuberculosis of the lung, kidneys, peritoneum and intestinal glands. The prognosis seemed to be hopeless.

She was taken to Lourdes on October 6, 1941. At 2 P.M. on October 7 she entered the bath, and at 7 P.M. a medical examination showed her urine to be clear of tubercle bacilli. She had no pain in the abdomen and her body seemed to have changed, in that it was supple instead of tense. She was later examined by Dr. Y., who reported that there was now no cough, that the sputum and gastric juice were negative for tubercle bacilli, and that she had no fever and no pain in the area of the kidneys.

The patient was subsequently examined by eight doctors, and the most stringent tests for tuberculosis were applied, and the conclusion reached that the patient's body was entirely free from tuberculosis.

She has been re-examined at Lourdes at yearly intervals since her cure, and the last report of her was to the effect that she was a normal healthy woman. Mademoiselle C.D. is recorded as having been cured miraculously through the offices of the Blessed Virgin.

The records contain a large number of cases of the alleged cure of tuberculosis.

A DETAILED CASE OF ALLEGED HEALING
THROUGH PRAYER

THE CASE OF DAVID HUGHES

FROM 1936 TO 1940 I kept records at the old City Temple of those for whom intercession was made in Church on Sunday evenings, but these records, with much other valuable material, were entirely destroyed by enemy bombs which fell on the Church in April 1941. Here is a record which seems to me worth noting for any who take St. James and the fathers of the early Church seriously.[1] It may be thought to point to some conclusions which I have reached along other lines: first, that one of the conditions which make intercessory prayer powerful is that those who pray should *love* the patient. The better they know him, therefore, the more they can be made to visualise the situation, and *feel* towards the patient. In the following case, night after night at Sunday evening worship the congregation was told about David, given little word-pictures of his home life, and so on. Some people got so to know and love him that they sent him presents, and some would stop me in the street and ask after him. I know they included him in their private prayers. When he recovered, he quite tearfully asked his mother whether all those people in the big London church would stop loving him now he was better!

Another conclusion I have come to is that prayers for a child seem to avail more powerfully than in the case of an adult. I hazard the view that the psyche of a child, particularly his unconscious mind, is more vulnerable—if that is the word—to invasion from God and the praying psyches of other people. It is less walled in by doubt and

[1] James 5:13-15.

fear and disappointment and cynicism, prejudices and fixed beliefs. The prayers of a thousand people to God seem sometimes to set free, through Him, energies that meet with less hindrance in the deep mind of a child than is the case with an adult.

But I anticipate. David Hughes is a little boy of four-and-a-half years of age, living in a little Welsh village near Mold. His mother, before her marriage, was a member of my church in Leeds, and I have kept in touch with her ever since. Her husband, like herself, is a trained teacher. He is the headmaster of the village school. David is their first child. He now has a little sister.

On January 25, 1948, Mrs. Hughes wired me in desperation, asking whether the congregation would pray for David, as he was very seriously ill. The diagnosis was nephritis, or inflammation of the kidneys. We did this, and maintained the practice of praying for David every Sunday evening until the middle of March. People prayed for him privately also, and some of the City Temple Prayer Groups made intercessions for him.

He himself, no prig, had a child-like religion. He told his mother that when in hospital he read a little prayer to the nurses every night, and all the other children listened. His mother says that he has a delightful little prayer book called "Look Upon a Little Child," and has been reading the prayers himself every night for some time. His mother says, "He has never been a saint; just a normal, healthy boy, full of mischief, but just now his face is absolutely beautiful."

Mrs. Hughes had to bear very depressing reports. She wrote on February 11, "All the doctors agree that permanent damage has been done to the kidneys and that David will never be the same again." Subsequently, David was sent home from hospital, presumably because nothing more could be done, and it was clearly expected that he would die. On February 19 his mother wrote, "Just a few lines from David's bedside: He is still with us, but desperately ill. The poor little chap can keep nothing down and we expect the end at any moment. The doctor says he will get sleepier and sleepier, until he sinks into a coma and then dies. He looks beautifully peaceful as I write." She adds, "I wrote a letter to you on Monday saying that by the time you received it, he would be dead. But I did not post it and tried to keep up my faith."

Then on February 24 came a most joyous letter, which runs as follows:

"A very hurried note to tell you the wonderful news that David has taken a turn for the better. A week ago there was absolutely no hope, but on Friday his kidneys began working again and the swelling began to decrease. After only passing a few ounces of urine daily for nearly six weeks, over the weekend he has passed one hundred ounces. This was the 'flood' for which the doctors waited, but which four doctors thought could not possibly happen after all these weeks. It is not anything less than a miracle and we are all convinced it is in response to prayer.

"The wonderful and amazing part is that since his life was given up, no drugs were given and the doctor who told me last Tuesday that he would soon pass into a coma cannot understand it at all. He says, 'If David can recover without drugs, it seems useless to give him any more.'"

Then came a letter on March 6 from which I will quote again:

"I was so pleased to hear from you again this week and especially to have the Service Papers. How they remind me of Brunswick days! David was really thrilled to see his name in print, and I tried to explain to him why you were all praying for him. He said to me last night, 'Mummy, write and tell that Minister of the big London Church that I am better.' And a few minutes after he said, 'Will they still go on praying for me even though I am better?'

"I am forgetting that I have not told you the wonderful news we had yesterday. A specimen of urine was taken last week to be examined for casts and also for albumen, and the doctor called yesterday with the result. I could hardly believe my ears when he said that the examination proved that no damage has been done to the kidneys at all, and that David will make a complete recovery. The doctor, who is an old man with plenty of experience, was so delighted to give me this news, as only three weeks ago he had said that David's was a terribly bad case and there was absolutely no hope of recovery, although he might last for months. He said it is absolutely incredible that this has happened.

"The Sister of David's ward said to me the day I brought him home, 'David will never do much in life, so I'm glad you'll have him for the last few months.' The House Surgeon said a few weeks ago. 'We have done all in our power, but David is not responding to treatment and we can only hope and pray now.' Then that unforgettable night when our own doctor said, looking at David asleep, 'He will get sleepier and sleepier until he passes into a coma. It's terribly bad luck for so young a child.' Then again two specialists' reports: 'Permanent damage has been done and he can never make a full recovery.' And so I could go on. We were told these things so many times that it was no wonder we gave up all hope. Yesterday's news was so amazing that I could not sleep at all last night for thinking of it. More incredible still is that, if all goes well now, David will be getting up in another week."

All this was cheering to those at the City Temple who had come to love David. But it was even more impressive to be allowed to see a letter written to a London girl by a friend of hers who is a voluntary ambulance-driver. This driver was actually the one sent with the ambulance to convey David to hospital. She afterwards told Mrs. Hughes that the day she drove David to hospital she did not think there was any chance of recovery, and that for nights she could not get his face out of her mind. Here is part of her letter:

"About six weeks ago I was sent on an ambulance call to bring a little boy, aged four-and-a-half years, from Wrexham. He was an advanced case of Bright's Disease, with no hope of recovery. I did not know the people. They live in a village about five miles away, up in the mountains.

"About a fortnight ago the District Nurse told me that he was getting better, and on Monday I went to the village to play for the Women's Institute and called at the child's home. His mother told me that after his return from hospital, David went steadily worse, hardly any urine was passed and the swellings went higher and further up his body every day. Finally, they reached the heart level and he went into a coma. Both doctors and the nurse said it was the end. It was just a question of hours—perhaps minutes.

"The mother (who is breast-feeding a little girl of eight months) went to bed, completely exhausted, while the father stayed with David to watch for any change that came. It did—in the early morning David regained consciousness and asked for his mother. When she awoke and went to him, he was sitting up to talk to her. He passed three ounces of water that morning and over fifty ounces the following day. On Monday, David was walking round the bungalow; very thin and pale, but quite strong. The doctors cannot account for it, and the Wrexham specialist told the father that prayer had succeeded where science failed. I said, 'Prayer?' and his mother said, 'Oh! yes. I wrote to Leslie Weatherhead. He has helped us all the way through.'"

Of course, it was not I who helped her, save that I wrote continually trying to help her keep up her faith in David's recovery. But the real help was the prayers of loving people.

Then comes the final letter, dated six months after the first appeal for help. We heard that David was walking and running about, and that it was a job to keep him from doing too much.

"The doctor said David was quite fit now. There is not a day passes, but we marvel at his recovery, especially when we see him running about the house just as he used to do. When he was so ill, what I most dreaded was returning here without him as I knew the place would be so full of memories."

I can confirm that Mrs. Hughes' father interviewed one of the doctors in charge of David's case. This doctor who had declared the case hopeless said, "Well, all I can say is that prayer has succeeded where medicine failed."

The above report appeared in the *Methodist Recorder* on January 27, 1949, and aroused some comments and questions as to whether full investigations had subsequently been made and whether cure was likely to be lasting.

The family doctor has now written as follows, though for obvious reasons, his name cannot be given:

"A few weeks ago a doctor who was assisting me examined the urine by the usual simple tests and found it absolutely normal."

David was then taken back to the hospital in which he lay so near to death, and was re-examined and declared perfectly clear of any sign of his old illness. Mrs. Hughes asked the doctor whether she should take David back to the specialist for re-examination, and was told that there was no need. Mrs. Hughes reports that the child is perfectly fit and well up to the time of this book going to press. She realizes that the disease may recur, but is full of hope, in that it is now over twelve months since he was declared to be dying, and since his initial recovery he has had no setback, nor can anyone find anything wrong with him.[2]

I have before me a letter from one of the medical men who examined David. He wrote as follows to Mrs. Hughes:

"I was delighted to hear from you and see from the photograph how well David appears. I have often thought about him and his dramatic recovery. You may tell Dr. Weatherhead that personally I am *quite sure* prayer played the biggest part in his cure. He was suffering from a severe sub-acute nephritis, and in the opinion of all the hospital physicians his prognosis was of the very poorest. Certainly, you may quote my opinion to Dr. Weatherhead, but you quite rightly assume that I would not wish my name to be published for

[2] My last letter from Mrs. Hughes is dated January 1, 1951. In it she reports that David is still well.

obvious professional reasons. But he is at liberty to repeat my humble opinion for any purpose he wishes.

(Sgd.) ———

M.B., Ch.B."

Here is a letter from another doctor who enclosed, for my inspection, the hospital report, and who wrote as follows:

"I am enclosing the hospital report which embodies that of a very excellent specialist, Dr. X. In this report you will observe the very serious nature of the case and the unfavorable prognosis. If you write an article on this case for any paper, I shall appreciate it that no names of doctors will be mentioned, and I shall be obliged if you will return the hospital report.

"The boy was suffering from a very serious form of nephritis. After his return home from hospital he did not make any progress at all in spite of very careful treatment. I have attended a number of similar cases and *never saw one recover*, and owing to this and the absence of any sign of improvement, I could not give any favorable prognosis to the parents which would allay their deep anxiety. One day which I shall always remember, the father asked me if there was any hope at all for his recovery, and I had to reply that, as far as I could see, there was definitely no hope whatever.

"Within about a week after this, David's condition had completely and suddenly changed for the better, and in a very short time he was practically normal which was most extraordinary to me.

"You may quote my remarks in any publication if you wish.

Yours sincerely,

(Sgd.)———"

It is, of course, open to anyone to deny the efficacy of prayer and to say that the patient would have recovered in any case. All that can be said in reply is that the doctors most concerned with the case attribute the boy's recovery to prayer, as do the parents, and that if after any drug a patient made such a recovery as is described above, no one would say that the patient would have recovered in any case. Cure would be ascribed to the drug, and the drug would soon be in universal use. This is only one of a number of cases which could be adduced in a similar way.

A DETAILED CASE OF ALLEGED HEALING THROUGH WORSHIP

I HAVE THE permission of the Editor of the *Methodist Recorder* to print the following account, from the issue of February 2, 1950, of a cure attributed to hearing a religious service over the wireless. I have had independent evidence of the authenticity of this cure from someone who knows the patient well. She says that he was a pitiable case and regarded as a hopeless cripple, but that now he is a different man, both in body and soul. The patient's name is John Heaton.

Mr. Heaton's account of his cure is as follows:

"I was brought up in a good Christian home, with two brothers, but I was born a cripple. No other sufferer from my complaint has lived beyond two years—by which early death they were spared an enormous amount of suffering. A mother's love, and her long devotion and sacrifice, kept me alive.

"At a very early age I began to wonder why I could not go out and play with my brothers instead of lying in bed and watching them through the window, or sometimes being taken out in a wheelchair. My mother and father could not attend public worship together—the care of their sick boy precluded that. Nor could I go to church or chapel, though my parents did what they could to make up for my lack in this respect by teaching me all they could about God, and by living a Christian life.

"As the years passed my complaint worsened. The pain became increasingly severe and continuous. Slowly I began to wonder, and to question whether there was a God of mercy and of love. If there were such a God, why did He allow such suffering to go on and on? I was getting worse, and I had the terror of knowing that there was no cure for me. The verdict of medical specialists, who visited me from all parts of the country, was unanimous in the declaration of 'no cure,' and of real wonder about why I kept alive at all! Such pronouncements increased my desolation and strengthened my belief that there was no God.

"I used to lie in bed and just long for sleep to come; indeed, for the oblivion of complete release from my unending torment of body. I can only describe that experience of suffering as like that of one who was constantly being burned alive, yet not consumed. Is it to be wondered at that my one wish came to be delivered from this torture-house which my body was? I used to pray that God would allow me to fall asleep and never awaken again.

"That prayer was not granted. Why? Of course, I said in my heart, because there was no God! I cursed my parents for bringing me into the world; I cursed the doctors because they would not end for me this miserable business called 'life.' I even cursed my mother for her sacrifice in keeping me alive. I was an unbeliever, an out-and-out atheist. The climax of this period was an experience of two weeks during which I slept little more than two hours. Life was hell!

"Sunday morning came. I was cursing my mother, raving against her who had devoted her life to my needs. This was deliberate on my part. I had suffered so long. I was determined to make another suffer—and mother was the handiest for the purpose. Even as I mouthed my bitter words (I could see how they hurt her), my hand went automatically towards the bedside radio receiving set. This was *not* a conscious act of mine. I was in no mood to listen, least of all to a religious broadcast. But it happened, the radio became vocal; a religious service was being sent out to the world; and the minister's first words to reach my ears were: 'Why do men suffer?' That address changed my life.

"In much less time than it has taken you to read so far, I was transformed. It was exactly as though the Lord Jesus Christ had come into my room (as indeed He had!), and had spoken directly to me, saying, 'Peace be unto you: be still.' In that moment, though I was still in pain, the pain no longer mattered. I knew the meaning of the poet's line: 'Pain is sweet if Thou my God art there.'

"From that moment I knew I had a soul; and all my being— body, mind and soul—seemed enveloped in a glorious sense of peace and quiet. In that moment I knew, and from that moment I have always known, beyond all shadow of doubt, that there is a God, and that He is a God of Love and Mercy. I knew also that each of us has a soul, and that each of us can alone destroy that soul or dedicate it to the everlasting Glory of God.

"I want to say quite honestly that my transforming experience has amply compensated me for my long sufferings, and that I would far rather have all that discipline with my present assured knowledge of God than have a lifetime of normal health without the experience of God. I say that solemnly, and weighing my words. I ought also to say that from that transforming moment I began to make a remarkable recovery. I am still a partial cripple, and am impeded by a recurring skin disability, which is abnormal. But, with the aid of a tricycle, I am remarkably mobile; and my general health is princely in comparison with my former pitiable condition. . . .

"Once God is found, other things we call 'evil' just do not matter, for they can be turned to good. We are all given different tools for our equipment in the journey of life, and we are at liberty to use these tools as we like. If we use them wrongly, it will not be for us to say what will happen when we are called to meet our Creator. If we use them rightly, I believe we are allowed at the last to share the Life Eternal and to see the Face of God.

"Since my conversion on that glorious Sunday morning I have not only increased in health beyond all belief, but it has become possible for me to attend divine worship, which is a great joy, as well as help, to me. My life is now very full and very beautiful. It is a great privilege to visit other people who are bedfast, and have endured much suffering for many years. I come away knowing that my life has been enriched through their experience; for they also have found God and are content to put their whole trust in Him.

"I have been converted *not in spite of my affliction*, but because of it, and I am profoundly grateful to God. My one wish now, and my sincere prayer, is that I shall never miss any opportunity to bring God to any who are crying out for Him."

5

A FORM OF SERVICE FOR THE LAYING ON OF HANDS UPON THE SICK

(Confession and Absolution from the Communion Service)

Let us pray.

(Pause.)

Lord, have mercy.
Christ, have mercy.
Lord, have mercy.

Our Father.

V. O Lord, save Thy servant.
R. Who putteth *his* trust in Thee.
V. Send *him* help, from Thy holy place.
R. And evermore mightily defend *him.*
V. Help us, O God of our salvation.
R. And for the glory of Thy Name deliver us, and be merciful to us sinners, for Thy Name's sake.

Let us pray.

O Almighty God, who art the giver of all health, and the aid of them that seek to Thee for succour, we call upon Thee for Thy help and goodness mercifully to be showed upon this Thy servant; that *he* being healed of *his* infirmities, may give thanks unto Thee in Thy holy Church, through Jesus Christ our Lord. Amen.

[1] Quoted from *Body and Soul,* Dr. Percy Dearmer (E. P. Dutton & Co., Inc., New York).

O Almighty Lord, and everlasting God, vouchsafe, we beseech Thee, to direct, sanctify and govern, both our hearts and bodies, in the ways of Thy laws, and in the works of Thy commandments; that through Thy most mighty protection, both here and ever, we may be preserved in body and soul; through our Lord and Saviour Jesus Christ. Amen.

(Then the Clerk, or one of the friends present, shall say:)

God give a blessing to this work; and grant that this sick person on whom the Priest lays his hands, may recover, through Jesus Christ our Lord.

Silent Prayer.

(Then the Minister, standing by the sick person, shall lay both his hands upon the head of the same, saying these words:)

In the Name of God Most High, mayest thou be given release from pain, and may thy soul be restored into harmony with His immortal laws. In the Name of Jesus Christ, the Prince of Life, may new life come into thy human body. In the Name of the Holy Spirit, mayest thou have inward health and the peace which passeth understanding.

And the God of all peace Himself sanctify you wholly: and may your spirit and soul and body be preserved entire, without blame at the presence of our Lord Jesus Christ. Amen.

(Pause.)

Psalm 91: "Whoso dwelleth under the defence of the most high."

The Almighty God, who is a most strong tower to all them that put their trust in Him, to whom all things in heaven, in earth and under the earth do bow and obey, be now and evermore thy defence; and make thee know and feel that there is none other Name under heaven given to man, in whom, and through whom, thou mayest receive health and salvation, but only the Name of our Lord Jesus Christ. Amen.

Unto God's gracious mercy and protection we commit thee. The Lord bless thee, and keep thee. The Lord make His face to shine upon thee, and be gracious unto thee. The Lord lift up His countenance upon thee, and give thee peace, both now and for evermore. Amen.

Silent Prayer.

(Public thanksgiving should be made in church after recovery.)

6

A FORM FOR GATHERING INFORMATION ABOUT A PATIENT WHO SEEKS PSYCHOLOGICAL HELP

Dates Seen	Patient's Name
	Address
	'Phone
	Age
	Occupation
	Married or single
	Position in family with details of brothers and sisters.
	Patient's husband or wife and his or her attitude to patient
	Patient's children, with details
	By whom patient sent, and, if different, the patient's doctor. Consultants seen, etc.
	Addresses
	'Phone Nos.
	The diagnosis so far as is known at present.

I. *The Patient's Story*

It is suggested that here notes may be made of the patient's account of himself to be filled up later by details under the following headings. In an actual form, of course, spaces are left under each heading. The patient's story is likely to take several pages and he will want to tell it early in the first interview.

II. *The Patient's Background*

Home atmosphere in childhood and now.
Health: physical, mental and spiritual of father and mother,

519

brothers and sisters. Occupations followed by members of family. Social position of family. Any family diseases inherited. Emotional relationship between members of the family. Heredity: alcohol, insanity, stammers, epilepsy, etc.

III. The Patient's Childhood.

Date and place of birth. Mother's pregnancy, breast or bottle-fed, etc. Babyhood, healthy or delicate, teething, talking, walking. Habit-training. Bed-wetting, etc., thumb-sucking, biting nails, etc. Any neurotic trends in childhood, tantrums, sleep-walking, etc. Sources of irritation, if any. Sources of happiness, toys, etc. Loneliness, imaginative-play, fears.

Religious teaching of child.

School Life: examinations and age at which passed. Hobbies. Attitude to teachers and to work.

Shocks of any kind.

IV. The Patient's Occupation.

Why started? Chosen or compelled.

Reasons for change, if any.

Ideals and ambitions.

College record, if any.

V. The Patient's Present Physical Condition per Doctor's Report.

Appearance. Weight. Appetite.

Effect of earlier operations, if any.

Any abnormality.

Heart condition.

Vision. Hearing. Lungs, etc.

Reflexes.

Use of alcohol, drugs, tobacco.

Bowel and urinary functions.

VI. The Patient's Mental Condition per Doctor's or Psychiatrist's Report.

Intelligence test reports.

Nervousness, breakdown history, treatment already received. Duration, results, hospital details. Symptoms for which no treatment given. Moods, fears, tensions. Any use of unusual phrases or any unusual habits, facial expressions, delusions, etc.

VII. *The Patient's Religious Life.*

Place of religion in patient's home life. Sunday School.
Prayers taught. Childish ideas of God.
Denomination. Church activities.
Is religion real to him? Prayer life. Religious reading.
Has it inflated his super-ego?
Conscience. Guilt feelings. Religious fears. Hell—"Unpardonable Sin." Moral standards.

VIII. *The Patient's Sexual Life.*

When and how informed of facts of sex.
Masturbation. Homosexuality. Menstruation history: regularity, duration, painful, etc. Dates of first and last periods.
Climacteric symptoms.
How sex is regarded. Sex adventures. Seduction. Intercourse
—frequency and satisfactoriness. Contraception. Sex fantasies, aberrations or perversions. Sadism, Masochism, Fetichism, etc.
Venereal disease.
Marital history. Desire and frigidity. Compatibility. Miscarriages. Abortions. Pre-marital sex contact with partners or others. Hastened marriage.
Hetero-sexual practices outside marriage.
Attitude to children.

IX. *The Patient's Social Life.*

Good mixer, aloof, nervous, at home with people and of what type.
Attitude to social functions.
Social service, why chosen, why stopped.
Hobbies and why chosen. Desire for solitude.

X. *The Patient's Unconscious Life.*

Sleeping: quality; duration, drugs, nightmares, sleepwalking.
Dreams, especially recurrent dreams.
Unconscious habits, tics, etc.
Obsessional acts. Fears of unknown origin.
Morning depression.

XI. *The Patient's Emotional Life.*

Placid, serene, optimistic, contented.

Violent, angry, irritable, quarrelsome, impulsive.

Timid, sensitive, reserved, shy.

Aggressive, dominating, egocentric, confident.

Suspicious, resentful, jealous.

Self-conscious, strict, fussy, disciplined, decisive.

Tired without reason, hysterical outbursts, weeping without reason.

Fantasies, effect of novels, cinema, theater, what kind preferred.

What thoughts rise to consciousness on waking: just before sleeping.

Advice Given

Further Action to be Taken

Final Report on Conclusion of Case

BIBLIOGRAPHY

GENERAL

Baudouin, *Studies in Psychoanalysis* (Dodd).
Bousfield, *Elements of Practical Psychoanalysis* (Dutton).
————, *The Omnipotent Self* (Kegan Paul).
Brown, William, *Mind, Medicine and Metaphysics* (Oxford).
————, *Psychology and Psychotherapy* (Longmans).
————, *Suggestion and Mental Analysis* (Doran).
————, *Talks on Psychotherapy* (University of London Press).
Burt, Cyril, *The Subnormal Mind* (Oxford).
————, editor, *How the Mind Works* (Appleton-Century).
Culpin, *Recent Advances in the Study of the Psychoneuroses* (Blakiston).
Dearmer, Percy, *Body and Soul* (Dutton).
Flugel, *A Hundred Years of Psychology* (Macmillan).
Frayn, R. Scott, *Revelation and the Unconscious* (Epworth).
Grensted, *Psychology and God* (Longmans).
Hadfield, *Psychology and Mental Health* (Macmillan).
————, *Psychology and Morals* (McBride).
Harris, Gordon, and Rees, *An Introduction to Psychological Medicine* (Oxford).
Henderson and Gillespie, *Text-book on Psychiatry* (Oxford).
Horney, *New Ways in Psychoanalysis* (Norton).
————, *Self Analysis* (Norton).
Hughes, T. H., *The New Psychology and Religious Experience* (P. Smith).
James, William, *The Varieties of Religious Experience* (Longmans).
Janet, *Psychological Healing* (2 Vols.). (Macmillan).
Jones, Ernest, *Psycho-analysis* (Cape).
McDougall, William, *Body and Mind* (Macmillan).
————, *Character and the Conduct of Life* (Putnam).
————, *The Energies of Men* (Scribner).
————, *Introduction to Social Psychology* (Luce).
————, *Outline of Abnormal Psychology* (Scribner).
————, *Outline of Psychology* (Scribner).
Mellone, *The Bearings of Psychology on Religion* (Oxford).
Miller, H. Crichton, *Functional Nerve Disease* (Oxford).
Nicoll, *Dream Psychology* (Oxford).
Northridge, *Modern Theories of the Unconscious* (Dutton).
Pfister, *The Psychoanalytic Method* (Dodd).

Rees, *The Health of the Mind* (Washburn & Thomas).
Rivers, *Instinct and the Unconscious* (Macmillan).
Ross, *The Common Neuroses* (Longmans).
Tansley, *The New Psychology* (Dodd).
Thouless, *The Control of the Mind* (Doubleday, Doran).
————, *General and Social Psychology* (University Tutorial Press).
————, *Straight and Crooked Thinking* (Simon & Schuster).
Uren, *Recent Religious Psychology* (Scribner).
Waterhouse, *The Philosophical Approach to Religion* (Epworth).
White, William, *Outlines of Psychiatry* (Nervous and Mental Disease Pub. Co.).
Woodworth, R. S., *Contemporary Schools of Psychology* (Ronald).
Worcester and McComb, *Body, Mind and Spirit* (Marshall Jones Co.)
Yellowlees, Henry, *Clinical Lectures on Psychological Medicine* (Churchill).
————, *A Manual of Psychotherapy* (Macmillan).

INTRODUCTION

THE PRE-CHRISTIAN SEARCH FOR HEALING

Dawson, *Healing: Pagan and Christian* (Macmillan).
Gregory, *Psychotherapy—Scientific and Religious* (Macmillan).
Thompson, C. J. S., *Magic and Healing* (Rider & Co.).
Waterhouse, *The Dawn of Religion* (Epworth Press).

SECTION I

EARLY CHRISTIANITY AS A HEALING FACTOR

CHAPTER 1

CHRIST'S HEALING MIRACLES

Cairns, *The Faith that Rebels* (Harper).
Farmer, *The World and God* (Harper).
Fosdick, *The Modern Use of the Bible* (Macmillan).
Lewis, C. S., *Miracles* (Macmillan).
Marr, *Christianity and the Cure of Disease* (Allenson).
Micklem, *Miracles and the New Psychology* (Oxford University Press).
Richardson, *Miracle Stories of the Gospels* (Harper).
Shafto, *The Wonders of the Kingdom* (Doran).
Temple, *Christus Veritas* (Macmillan).

BIBLIOGRAPHY

CHAPTER 2

HEALING IN THE EARLY CHURCH

Frost, *Christian Healing* (Morehouse).
Hardman, editor, *Psychology and the Church* (Macmillan).
Harnack, *The Expansion of Christianity*, 2 vols. (Williams Norgate).
Pridie, *The Church's Ministry of Healing* (Macmillan).
Roberts, Harold, *The Sanctions of Christian Healing* (Epworth).

CHAPTER 3

THE PROBLEM OF DEMON POSSESSION

Alexander, William Menzies, *Demonic Possession in the New Testament—Its Relations Historical, Medical and Theological* (T. & T. Clark).
Hastings, *Dictionary of the Bible* (Scribner).
———, *Encyclopædia of Religion and Ethics* (Scribner).
Langton, *Essentials of Demonology* (Epworth).
———, *Satan* (Macmillan).
Oesterreich, T. K. *Possession, Demoniacal and Other* (Kegan Paul)
Scott, Sir Walter, *Letters on Demonology and Witchcraft* (Murray's Family Library).
Stewart, Rev. Prof. James S., "On a Neglected Emphasis in New Testament Theology" (*Scottish Journal of Theology*, September, 1951).

SECTION II

EARLIER METHODS OF HEALING THROUGH PSYCHOLOGY

CHAPTER 1

MESMERISM

Gregory, Janet, and McDougall, as above.

CHAPTER 2

HYPNOTISM

Baudouin and Lestchinsky, *The Inner Discipline* (Holt).
Bramwell, Milne, *Hypnotism—Its History, Practice and Theory* (Lippincott).
Brown, William, *Psychological Methods of Healing* (University of London Press).
Heyer, Gustav, tr. by Arnold Eiloart, *Hypnosis and Hypnotherapy* (C. W. Daniel).
Moll, *Hypnotism* (Walter Scott).
Satow, *Hypnotism and Suggestion* (Allen and Unwin).
Tuckey, *Treatment by Hypnotism and Suggestion* (Putnam).
Wingfield, *An Introduction to Hypnotism* (Bailliere, Tindall and Cox).
See also General List.

CHAPTER 3

SUGGESTION

Baudouin, *Suggestion and Auto-suggestion* (Dodd).
Brooks and Charles, *Christianity and Auto-suggestion* (Dodd).
Jolowicz, *Suggestion Therapy* (C. W. Daniel Co.).
See also General List.

SECTION III
MODERN RELIGIOUS METHODS OF HEALING

CHAPTER 1

THE LAYING ON OF HANDS

Dearmer and Hardman, as above.
Hickson, *Heal the Sick* (Dutton).

CHAPTER 2

THE PHENOMENA OF LOURDES

Dawson, Dearmer, Gregory, and Hardman, as above.

CHAPTER 3

CHRISTIAN SCIENCE

Dakin, *Mrs. Eddy: the Biography of a Virginal Mind* (Scribner).
Eddy, Mary Baker, *Science and Health* (Christian Science Publishing Society).
Fisher, H. A. L., *Our New Religion* (Smith).
Haushalter, *Mrs. Eddy Purloins from Hegel* (Beauchamp).
Janet, as above.
Orcutt, *Mary Baker Eddy and Her Books* (Christian Science Publishing Society).
Peabody, *The Religio-Medical Masquerade* (Revell).
Powell, L. P., *Mary Baker Eddy* (Macmillan).
Sturge, *Christianity and Christian Science* (T. C. & E. C. Jack).
Wilbur, *The Life of Mary Baker Eddy* (Christian Science Publishing Society).

CHAPTER 4

HEALING MISSIONS

Hickson, as above.

BIBLIOGRAPHY

Chapter 5

Psychic Phenomena and Healing

Barrett, Lady, *Personality Survives Death* (Longmans).
Dunne, J. W., *An Experiment with Time* (Macmillan).
Edwards, Harry, *Psychic Healing* (Spiritualist Press).
Findlay, J. A., *On the Edge of the Etheric* (McKay).
Hill, J. Arthur, *Psychical Science and Religious Belief* (Rider).
Lodge, Oliver, *Raymond, or Life and Death* (Doran).
Payne and Bendit, *The Psychic Sense* (Dutton).
————, *This World and That* (Faber and Faber).
Price, Harry, *Search for Truth* (Collins).
Proceedings of the Society for Psychical Research.
Rhine, J. B., *Extra-Sensory Perception* (Boston Society).
————, *The Reach of the Mind* (Sloane).
Thomas, C. D., *Life Beyond Death: with Evidence* (Collins).

Chapter 6

Other Religious Healing Movements

Maillard, *Healing in the Name of Jesus* (Harper).

Chapter 7

The Practice of Intercession

Buttrick, *Prayer* (Abingdon-Cokesbury).
Dougall, Lily, and others, *Concerning Prayer* (Macmillan).
Ehrenwald, *Telepathy and Medical Psychology* (Norton).
Heard, Gerald, *A Preface to Prayer* (Harper).
Heiler, *Prayer* (Oxford).
Herman, *Creative Prayer* (Harper).
Hodge, Alex, *Prayer and Its Psychology* (Macmillan).
Tyrrell, *The Personality of Man* (Pelican).
Whately-Carington, *Telepathy* (Methuen).

SECTION IV

MODERN PSYCHOLOGICAL METHODS OF INTEGRATION

Chapter 1

Freud and Psychoanalysis

Dalbiez, Roland, 2 vols. tr. by F. Lindsay, *Psychoanalytic Method and the Doctrine of Freud* (Longmans).

527

Freud, *Delusion and Dream* (New Republic).
————, *The Ego and the Id* (Hogarth Press).
————, *The Future of an Illusion* (Hogarth Press).
————, *Interpretation of Dreams* (Macmillan).
————, *Introductory Lectures on Psychoanalysis* (Allen and Unwin).
————, *Moses and Monotheism* (Knopf).
————, *Psychopathology of Everyday Life* (Macmillan).
————, *Totem and Taboo* (New Republic).
Hitschmann, *Freud's Theories of the Neuroses* (Dodd).
Jones, Ernest, *Psycho-analysis* (Cape).
Richman, John, *A General Selection from the Works of Sigmund Freud* (Hogarth Press).
Sachs, *Freud—Master and Friend* (Harvard University Press).

CHAPTER 2

ADLER AND INDIVIDUAL PSYCHOLOGY

Adler, Alfred, tr. by Bernard Glueck and John Lind, *The Neurotic Constitution* (Dodd).
————, tr. by P. Radin, *The Practice and Theory of Individual Psychology* (Harcourt).
————, *The Science of Living* (Greenberg).
————, tr. by W. B. Wolfe, *Understanding Human Nature* (Greenberg).
————, *What Life Should Mean to You* (Little-Brown).
Bottome, Phyllis, *Alfred Adler, a Biography* (Putnam).

CHAPTER 3

JUNG AND ANALYTICAL PSYCHOLOGY

Jung, *Collected Papers on Analytical Psychology* (Dodd).
————, *Contributions to Analytical Psychology* (Harcourt).
————, *Modern Man in Search of a Soul* (Harcourt).
————, *Psychological Types* (Harcourt).
————, *Psychology of the Unconscious* (Dodd).
————, *Two Essays on Analytical Psychology* (Dodd).

CHAPTER 4

MCDOUGALL AND PURPOSIVE OR HORMIC PSYCHOLOGY

See McDougall's books in General List, especially *The Energies of Men.*

CHAPTER 5

DETERMINIST PSYCHOLOGY

Flugel and Woodworth, as above.

BIBLIOGRAPHY

CHAPTER 6

COMPOSITE METHODS IN MODERN PSYCHOTHERAPY

Brown, William, *Psychological Methods of Healing* (University of London Press).
See also General List.

SECTION V

DO MODERN PSYCHOLOGICAL METHODS OF HEALING NEED RELIGION?

CHAPTER 1

THE NATURE OF HEALTH

Brown, William, *Personality and Religion* (University of London Press).
Hadfield, *Psychology and Mental Health* (Macmillan).
Streeter, *The Spirit* (Macmillan).

CHAPTER 2

GUILT AS CAUSATIVE OF ILLNESS AND THE RELEVANCE THERETO OF RELIGION

Flugel, *Man, Morals and Society* (International Universities Press).
Hadfield, *Psychology and Morals* (McBride).
Maltby, W. R., *Christ and His Cross* (Abingdon).
Smith, Ryder, *The Bible Doctrine of Salvation* (Epworth).
Taylor, Vincent, *The Atonement in New Testament Teaching* (Epworth).
————, *Forgiveness and Reconciliation* (Macmillan).
————, *Jesus and His Sacrifice* (Macmillan).

CHAPTER 3

THE DEPRIVATION OF LOVE AS CAUSATIVE OF ILLNESS AND THE RELEVANCE THERETO OF RELIGION

Dunbar, Helen Flanders, *Emotions and Bodily Changes* (Columbia University Press).
————, *Mind and Body* (Random House).
Hadfield, *Psychology and Mental Health* (Macmillan).
————, *Psychology and Morals* (McBride).
Newsholme, *Health, Disease and Integration* (Allen and Unwin).
Weiss and English, *Psychosomatic Medicine* (Saunders).

CHAPTER 4

OTHER EMOTIONAL STATES AS CAUSATIVE OF ILLNESS AND THE RELEVANCE THERETO OF RELIGION

As in last chapter.

CHAPTER 5

AN EXAMINATION OF JUNG'S ATTITUDE TO RELIGION

See Section IV, Chapter 3.

CHAPTER 6

AN EXAMINATION OF FREUD'S ATTITUDE TO RELIGION

Lee, *Freud and Christianity* (Wyn).
Sanders, B. G., *Christianity After Freud* (Macmillan).
See Section IV, Chapter 1.

CHAPTER 7

IS RELIGIOUS EXPERIENCE ITSELF A NEUROSIS?

England, *The Validity of Religious Experience* (Harper).
Hadfield, *Psychology and Modern Problems* (University of London Press).
Miller, H. Crichton, *Christian Experience and Psychological Processes* (Student Movement Press).
Suttie, *Origins of Love and Hate* (Kegan Paul).

SECTION VI

DO MODERN RELIGIOUS METHODS OF INTEGRATION NEED PSYCHOLOGY?

CHAPTER 1

THE NATURE AND PLACE OF FAITH IN HEALING

Fosdick, *The Meaning of Faith* (Association Press).
Machen, *What Is Faith?* (Macmillan).
Pym, *More Psychology and the Christian Life* (Doran).
———, *Psychology and the Christian Life* (Doran).
Streeter, editor, *God and the Struggle for Existence* (Association Press).

BIBLIOGRAPHY

CHAPTER 2

THE NATURE AND PLACE OF SCIENCE IN HEALING

Brown, William, *Science and Personality* (Yale University Press).
Whitehead, A. N., *Science and the Modern World* (Macmillan).

CHAPTER 3

THE PLACE OF FAITH AND SCIENCE ILLUSTRATED IN CONFESSION, WORSHIP AND ASCETICISM

Belton, F. G., *A Manual for Confessors* (Morehouse).
Bishop, John, *Methodist Worship* (Epworth).
Micklem, *Our Approach to God* (Hodder and Stoughton).
Relton, H. M., *Psychology and the Church*—Essay on the Psychology of Public Worship (Macmillan).
Underhill, Evelyn, *Worship* (Harper).

SECTION VII

THE MODERN SEARCH FOR INTEGRATION OF PERSONALITY

CHAPTER 1

THE NEEDS OF THE INTEGRATED PERSONALITY

See General List.

CHAPTER 2

PASTORAL AND MEDICAL CO-OPERATION

Cabot and Dicks, *The Art of Ministering to the Sick* (Macmillan).
Dewar and Hudson, *An Introduction to Pastoral Theology* (Macmillan).
————, *Psychology for Religious Workers* (Harpers).
Guntrip, *Psychology for Ministers and Social Workers* (Independent Press).
Hadfield, *Psychology and Morals* (McBride).
Halliday, Fearon, *Psychology and Religious Experience* (Harper).
Ikin, *Religion and Psychotherapy* (Student Movement Press).
Jones, Lawson, *A Psychological Study of Religious Conversion* (Epworth Press).
Mackenzie, J. G., *Souls in the Making* (Macmillan).
Miller, H. Crichton, *The New Psychology and the Preacher* (Boni).
Murray, *Introduction to a Christian Psychotherapy* (Scribner).
Northridge, *Health for Mind and Spirit* (Abingdon).

Oliver, *Psychiatry and Mental Health* (Scribners)
Waterhouse, *Psychology and Pastoral Work* (Abingdon-Cokesbury Press).
————, *Psychology and Religion* (Harper).

CHAPTER 3

THE CHURCH PSYCHOLOGICAL CLINIC

As in last chapter.

INDEX OF PROPER NAMES

INDEX OF SUBJECTS